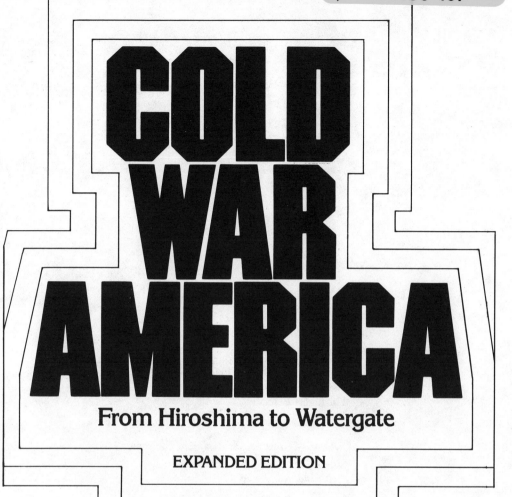

COLD WAR AMERICA

From Hiroshima to Watergate

EXPANDED EDITION

LAWRENCE S. WITTNER
State University of New York at Albany

HOLT, RINEHART AND WINSTON
New York   Chicago   San Francisco   Atlanta   Dallas
Montreal   Toronto   London   Sydney

Copyright © 1978 by Holt, Rinehart and Winston.
Copyright © 1974 by Praeger Publishers, Inc.

Library of Congress Cataloging in Publication Data

Wittner, Lawrence S.
    Cold War America.

    Bibliography
    Includes index.
        1.   United States—History—1945-
I.   Title.
E741.W8   1978   973.92   77-89742
ISBN 0-03-522211-2 pbk.

Printed in the United States of America

89012 090 987654321

To Patty

Contents

Preface

"SOME PEOPLE will not like this book." That is what I wrote (and thought) in 1974, when the first edition of *Cold War America* appeared. And the response did much to verify this contention for, if the book delighted some, it enraged others. Disputation, of course, is a favorite path of intellectual life. At the very least, it provides an author with a modicum of attention. But I am inclined to believe that the polarization prompted by *Cold War America* reflects a serious division in the United States over the meaning of the recent past—a division which runs as deep among scholars as among their fellow citizens. Certainly I plead guilty to harboring my own opinions of the postwar era, and the course of scholarship and recent events has done little to uproot my opinions. Consequently, in this new, expanded edition of *Cold War America,* I have updated the original version by adding much new material without, however, substantially altering the analysis. I presume, then, that *Cold War America* will remain "controversial." So be it!

Like the making of history, the writing of history represents a collective effort for which many participants should receive more recognition than they do. The material with which this book is constructed has been drawn from a great many works by historians, political scientists, economists, philosophers, sociologists, and journalists, as well as from memoirs and government reports. The underlying ideas took shape in the critical context of the past seventeen years, in my teaching of American history, and in long discussions with my friends, particularly Graham Barker-Benfield, George Berger, George Frangos, Paul Metzger, Stuart Newman, David Novack, David Schalk, Mark Selden, Michael Weinberg, and Derek Wittner. Theodore Lieverman, who worked diligently as my research assistant, consistently provided me with imaginative approaches and factual detail. Professors Harry Cliadakis, Leonard Dinnerstein, Howard Schonberger, and James Shenton read the manuscript, suggesting many useful alterations. I am also greatly indebted to Professors Merle Curti, Arthur Ekirch, and William Leuchtenburg, whose analyses of the period differ from my own, but who have forced me to sharpen and clarify my perspective. During the years in which this book moved from idea to reality, I was fortunate to receive the editorial advice and encouragement of Ms. Gladys Topkis, then of Praeger Publishers. And in the revisions for this new edition, I have benefited from the editorial assistance of Praeger's Denise Rathbun. My wife, Patricia, who improved the many drafts with her unfailing balance and good judgment, deserves a special commendation.

Lawrence S. Wittner
Albany, New York
September 1977

Cold War America

The world cannot be run as a company town.

GUNNAR MYRDAL

1

Unraveling the Liberal Legacy, 1945-46

> The path Franklin Roosevelt charted has been grievously—and deliberately—forsaken.
>
> ELLIOTT ROOSEVELT, 1946

WHEN FRANKLIN D. ROOSEVELT DIED in Warm Springs, Georgia, on April 12, 1945, he left a legacy of social reform and international co-operation that enshrined him in the pantheon of American liberals. In 1943, to be sure, chastened by a conservative drift in the elections of the preceding year, he had told a press conference that "Dr. Win-the-War" had replaced "Dr. New Deal." But in 1944 he had returned to the voters with a progressive campaign, spearheaded by the CIO's new Political Action Committee (PAC), promising Americans a United Nations organization to ensure world peace and an "economic bill of rights" to extend the New Deal. Roosevelt defeated the Republican Presidential candidate, New York's Governor Thomas E. Dewey, by a margin of 333 electoral votes, while liberals gained in Congress. Then, in one of the last political ventures of his life, Roosevelt traveled to Yalta in early 1945 for a conference with British Prime Minister Winston Churchill and Soviet Premier Joseph Stalin. The news he brought back from the conference underlined his commitment to Big Three unity in the postwar world. "Days were spent in discussing . . . momentous matters," he told Americans on March 1. "We argued freely and frankly across the table. But at the end, on every point, unanimous agreement was reached. And more important even than the agreement of words," Roosevelt added, "we achieved a unity of thought and a way of getting along together."

But Roosevelt's death lent an element of uncertainty to the domestic and international situation. New York City's fiery mayor, Fiorello La-Guardia, his voice quavering, declared over the municipal radio station: "Franklin Roosevelt is not dead. His ideals live. That pattern is so defi-

3

nite. It is so permanent. We cannot escape it. We must not escape it."
Premier Stalin rushed a message expressing "deep sympathy to the
American people in this heavy loss" and stating his hope that "the
policy of collaboration between the great powers . . . will continue to
grow strong in the future." Across the Potomac from Washington, at
Fort Myers, fifteen or twenty reporters listened as a military officer announced the death of the President. After a moment of dazed silence,
the murmur arose: "Good God! Truman will be President!"

Harry S. Truman seemed a most unlikely successor to the popular
Roosevelt. An unsuccessful men's clothier in Kansas City, Missouri,
Truman had been rescued from bankruptcy in the 1920s by the notorious Pendergast machine, which installed him as a county judge. In 1934,
the machine upgraded him to the U.S. Senate, where he fell in with
John Nance Garner's bourbon-drinking cronies, who assembled in the
Vice-President's rooms every day after adjournment for a bit of refresh-
ment. Throughout the 1930s, Truman consistently voted for New Deal
legislation but remained a relatively unknown and undistinguished back-
bencher—a status modified somewhat during World War II by his
capable chairmanship of a special Senate committee investigating the
defense program.

Truman's remarkable rise to power was further facilitated by a conflict within the Democratic Party. Liberals battled to retain Vice-
President Henry Wallace on the 1944 ticket, but Southern conservatives
and Northern party bosses convinced Roosevelt that it would be necessary to dump him for the sake of party unity. However, the conservative
choice for the Vice-Presidency, former Supreme Court justice and South
Carolina senator James F. Byrnes, was vetoed by Sidney Hillman,
head of the PAC. In the end, the party's power brokers patched together
a new "Missouri Compromise": Harry Truman. Astonished by his
selection, Truman dropped his plan to nominate Byrnes at the convention, defeated Wallace on the second ballot, and went on to be elected
Vice-President in the Roosevelt landslide. Truman had met with FDR
privately only twice when, on the afternoon of April 12, he received a
call to come to the White House immediately. As he entered, Eleanor
Roosevelt stepped forward and put her arm on his shoulder. "Harry,"
she said quietly, "the President is dead."

Truman had barely been sworn in when, despite Roosevelt's looming
shadow, it became clear that the full powers of the Presidency were his
alone. Shortly after his first Cabinet meeting, he learned from Secretary
of War Henry Stimson the stunning news that the government had been
secretly developing an explosive of enormous power: an atomic bomb.
Even as he grappled with that information, Truman turned to the appointment of Cabinet members more to his liking. When the shrewd

and aggressive Byrnes offered his services, the new President decided
to appoint him Secretary of State that June. The idea was broached to
the South Carolina conservative on the train back from Roosevelt's
funeral, and, according to Truman, Byrnes "almost jumped down my
throat taking me up on it."

Nothing belied Truman's assurances that his policies would resemble
those of the late President more than his meetings with American and
Soviet diplomats several days later. On April 20, the U.S. Ambassador
to the Soviet Union, Averell Harriman, a member of one of America's
"sixty families," met with Truman in the Oval Room of the White
House. Ever since late 1944, Harriman had encouraged Roosevelt to
take a tougher line with the Soviet Union, but without success. Now he
warned the new President that America was faced with a "barbarian
invasion of Europe," which it was obliged to prevent. Harriman maintained that the Soviet Union needed American economic aid for
postwar reconstruction and, therefore, as Truman recalled, "we could
stand firm on important issues without running serious risks." He appealed for "a reconsideration of our policy." To Harriman's delight,
the President proved unexpectedly amenable. Truman replied that he
was "not afraid of the Russians" and intended to "be firm." Indeed, he
promised to put America's intentions to Soviet Foreign Minister V.
M. Molotov "in words of one syllable." At the end of their meeting,
Harriman observed that he had hurried to Washington because he had
feared that Truman did not fully comprehend the Soviet problem. "I am
greatly relieved," he concluded, "to discover . . . we see eye to eye on
the situation."

When Molotov met with Truman on April 23, he received a striking
introduction to the new direction of American foreign policy. At issue
was the postwar government of Poland and how it should be chosen
under the Yalta agreement—an agreement so "elastic," as Admiral
William Leahy had complained to Roosevelt, "that the Russians can
stretch it all the way from Yalta to Washington without ever technically
breaking it." Molotov was conciliatory and, as Truman recalled, declared that "all difficulties could be overcome." Truman, though, took
the offensive; he "replied sharply that an agreement had been reached
on Poland and that there was only one thing to do, and that was for
Marshal Stalin to carry out that agreement." The Russian diplomat was
shocked at Truman's tone. "I have never been talked to like that in
my life," he said. Truman shot back: "Carry out your agreements and
you won't get talked to like that." Harriman, present for the session,
remarked later that Truman "got quite rough . . . so much so, in
fact, that I was becoming a little concerned." In his *Memoirs,* Truman
contended that, while he had spoken "bluntly," he was "sure that Russia

would understand firm, decisive language and action much better than diplomatic pleasantries."

Stalin, however, did not seem to understand; indeed, he appeared bewildered. On the following evening, the Soviet leader sent a plaintive letter to Truman. "It is . . . necessary to take into account the fact that Poland borders on the Soviet Union, which cannot be said of Great Britain and the United States." At Yalta he had argued that Poland represented "a question of security. Throughout history, Poland has been the corridor through which the enemy has passed into Russia." When Soviet troops had driven the Nazi forces out of Poland, Stalin had established a government of Poles friendly to the Soviet Union, and he did not plan to have it succeeded by an anti-Soviet one. He was convinced, probably justifiably, that free elections in Poland or in several other traditionally anti-Soviet states of Eastern Europe would restore unfriendly governments. Noting the security concerns of his allies and their own exclusive occupation policies, he now called for equity. "I do not know whether there has been established in Greece a really representative government," he said, but "the Soviet Government did not lay claim to interference in these affairs as it understands the whole importance of . . . Greece for the security of Great Britain." A number of Truman's advisers considered this position reasonable. According to Truman, Stimson "said he thought that the Russians perhaps were being more realistic than we were in regard to their own security."

Truman's extraordinary belligerence reflected not only his inexperience in foreign affairs and his intemperate style but also his recognition of the power America might wield in the postwar world. In 1941, Henry Luce, the publisher of *Time, Life,* and *Fortune,* had announced the beginning of an "American Century" in which the United States, "the most powerful and vital nation in the world," would act "for such purposes as we see fit and by such means as we see fit." As the war drew to a close, this seemed far from fanciful. In contrast to the devastation of every other major industrial nation, America was emerging from the war virtually unscathed, with a booming economy and a gross national product that had more than doubled. The United States, with 6 per cent of the world's population, held three-fourths of the world's invested capital and two-thirds of its industrial capacity. Already its allies had applied for huge postwar loans. America's armed forces of more than 12 million men circled the globe and were superior in numbers and materials to those of exhausted Great Britain or war-torn Russia. In addition, the United States had exclusive control of the new atomic bomb, which, Byrnes had assured Truman the day after Roosevelt's death, would "put us in a position to dictate our own terms at the end of the war."

The goals sought by the Truman Administration in world affairs reflected America's traditional interest in ensuring a stable international environment and some measure of political and religious freedom, but pre-eminent among them was the quest for widened trade and investment opportunities in a flourishing capitalist world order. Byrnes declared in August: "In the field of international relations we have joined . . . to construct an expanding world economy based on the liberal principles of private enterprise, nondiscrimination, and reduced barriers to trade."

Committed to the Open Door economic policies long favored by the State Department and haunted by the specter of the Great Depression, which they blamed upon economic nationalism and restrictive trade practices, U.S. policy-makers were keen advocates of American overseas business activities. By 1944, under the stimulus of war, U.S. exports had soared to $14.3 billion, and Washington officials feared the results of an expected postwar decline. "We simply can't afford after this war to let our trade drop off to the two- or three-billion figure it hit in 1932," Under Secretary of State William L. Clayton testified before a Congressional committee in March, 1945. "We've got to export three times as much as we exported just before the war if we want to keep our industry running at somewhere near capacity." Imports, too, had become crucial to the American economy; by 1946, of all important minerals consumed in the United States, only coal and oil did not have to be imported in significant quantities. "We need markets—big markets—around the world in which to buy and sell," Clayton argued. The President observed in 1946: "A large volume of soundly based international trade is essential if we are to achieve prosperity."

The Truman Administration was inclined to place a greater emphasis upon foreign economic expansion than its predecessor had done. Although Roosevelt had also favored unrestricted trade and investment policies, he had shown a willingness to depart from free-market orthodoxy when it conflicted with other priorities. In this fashion, he had embarked upon a program of economic nationalism in his early years as President and had ignored conservative advisers in the State Department by cooperating closely with a nominally Marxist Russia in wartime. Under Truman, though, unimpeded free enterprise attained an exalted status. In May, Clayton told the Detroit Economic Club that "nations which act as enemies in the marketplace cannot long be friends at the council table." The following year, Assistant Secretary of State Spruille Braden, in an official State Department policy release, termed "the institution of private property" a "bulwark of civilization." To "tamper with private enterprise," he warned, would "precipitate a disintegration of life and liberty as we conceive and treasure them." In a

key policy address delivered in early 1947, Truman proclaimed that
the nation's "foreign relations, political and economic, are indivisible."
And a "devotion to freedom of enterprise," said the President, "is part
and parcel of what we call American."

The economic concerns of U.S. policy-makers were starkly revealed
in the tough terms accorded Great Britain when it applied for U.S.
loans. World War II had shattered British economic power, leaving the
nation in desperate circumstances. Fighting the war virtually alone for
two years, and for four years thereafter in alliance, Britain had been
compelled to liquidate much of its overseas investment and to run up
a sizable foreign indebtedness. When the British applied to the United
States for a $5 billion loan in late 1945, U.S. negotiators quickly cut
the figure by 25 per cent and indicated that, in addition to paying
interest, the British would have to agree to open the sterling bloc nations to U.S. trade. In his *Memoirs,* Truman noted: "In return for the
loan, we wanted the British to relinquish many of the trade agreements
by which the United States . . . had been placed at a disadvantage."
Clayton, somewhat less discreetly, recalled: "We loaded the British
loan negotiations with all the conditions the traffic would bear." Sensitive to their wartime sacrifices and cognizant of American designs on
their overseas economic interests, many Britons were critical of the
proceedings. Conservatives complained of "the robust buccaneering
spirit of modern American economic imperialism," and Labourites denounced the machinations of "Wall Street." Nevertheless, driven by
economic adversity, Parliament accepted the American terms.

In these and subsequent negotiations, American policy-makers linked
loans with an attempt to halt the nationalization of British industry. At
the 1945 conference, American negotiators warned their British Labour
counterparts against implementing socialist pledges, which the United
States was unwilling to underwrite. Ironically, in later years U.S. policy-
makers began to see the value of such loans in bolstering British capitalism against the threat of socialist encroachments. "If this loan should
not be approved," Clayton warned in May, 1946, "it will, in my opinion, mean a much more rapid socialization of the British economy."
Assistant Secretary of State Dean Acheson told a Congressional committee: "We are interested not primarily in lending money to keep good
relations with the British, but in an economic system which is the very
basis of our life—the system of free, individual enterprise. We are
interested tremendously in maintaining that way of life." Instrumental-
ities, then, shifted, but the fundamentals of American policy toward
Britain remained remarkably consistent. In a postwar world organized
to benefit the American economy, Great Britain, if it played by the
rules, would be accorded a junior partnership.

The Soviet Union was quite another matter. During the war, German occupation forces had killed an estimated 15 million to 20 million Russians and had completely or partially demolished 15 large cities, 1,710 towns, and 70,000 villages in the Soviet Union. The invaders destroyed 31,850 industrial concerns, 65,000 kilometers of railroad track, 90,000 bridges, 10,000 power stations, 98,000 collective farms, and immense quantities of livestock and poultry—in all, an estimated $128 billion worth of property. As a result, Soviet industrial output in 1945 was but 58 per cent of the 1940 level. "Economically, the Soviet Union is exhausted," reported U.S. Naval Intelligence in January, 1946. "The U.S.S.R. is not expected to take any action during the next five years which might develop into hostilities with Anglo-Americans." In the aftermath of World War II, the Soviet Union cut its Army from 11.5 million to 3 million men, and by 1948 its military expenditures stood at only half those of the United States. In January, 1947, State Department consultant John Foster Dulles contended that war was "one thing which Soviet leadership does not want and would not consciously risk." Not only was the nation economically weak "in consequence of war devastation," but "the Soviet military establishment is completely outclassed by the mechanized weapons—particularly the atomic weapons —available to the United States."

Stalin's postwar goals coincided with his traditionally conservative, nationalist outlook. Foremost among them was his desire for military security against another war launched by Germany. To this end, he sought to influence the reconstruction of postwar Germany through a major role in its occupation, regarding such a role as both justified and necessitated by Soviet wartime sacrifice. Moreover, like his Tsarist predecessors, he wished to establish friendly, but non-Communist, governments in Eastern Europe. In April, 1945, he had predicted that the Germans "will recover, and very quickly. . . . That is why the unity of the Slavs is important." The preceding October, he and Churchill had concluded a secret agreement apportioning spheres of influence in the Balkan states, in which the Soviet Union was accorded a 90 per cent influence in Rumania, 80 per cent in Bulgaria and Hungary, 50 per cent in Yugoslavia, and 10 per cent in Greece. Subsequently, Stalin watched passively as the British crushed Greece's left-wing resistance forces and reimposed a monarchist government. In Hungary, he authorized a free election in the fall of 1945 in which the Communists were defeated. In Rumania and Bulgaria—both former Axis powers—he installed friendly but non-Communist governments. Finally, he sought to compel the partisan leader of Yugoslavia, Josip Broz Tito, to enter a coalition regime and restore the monarchy, but the independent Tito resisted his efforts. Churchill cabled Roosevelt in March, 1945, that "Stalin adhered very strictly" to the Anglo-Russian understanding.

Next to military security, economic aid for postwar Soviet reconstruction was uppermost in Stalin's considerations. In January, 1945, the U.S.S.R. applied for a $6 billion loan from the United States. Later that year, the Soviets applied for a smaller loan, this time for $1 billion. The American government first claimed to have lost the request, then offered to begin discussions if the Soviet Union guaranteed "non-discrimination in international commerce." Stalin rejected these terms and announced a new Five Year Plan to ensure the "economic independence of the Soviet Union." Nevertheless, as late as October, 1946, his government continued to seek American credits. Fortunately for Stalin, the Soviet occupation of Eastern Europe and of a portion of Germany enabled the Russians to exact reparations from their wartime enemies—Hungary, Bulgaria, Rumania, Finland, and Germany—and to engage in the systematic plunder of their friends. As the American government was unwilling to provide the Soviet Union with postwar aid, this system of economic tribute grew increasingly important.

Concerned primarily with the future of Germany and Eastern Europe, Stalin took a jaundiced view of revolutionary activities in other parts of the world. Not only did they serve as a dangerous provocation to the Americans and the British, but their success threatened to undermine his own power in the world Communist movement. Consequently, in France, Italy, Belgium, Greece, Yugoslavia, and China, the Russian dictator pressured Communist-led forces on the verge of taking power at the end of World War II to lay down their arms and cooperate with conservative regimes. In France, the Communists evacuated the factories they had seized, disarmed the resistance forces, and tamely entered the de Gaulle government. After the October, 1945, elections, in which French Communists and Socialists won an absolute majority, Communist leader Maurice Thorez became Minister of State and Deputy Premier. French Communist leaders placed the conservative demand for economic recovery above that for social justice and urged workers to sacrifice accordingly. "Work is not only a necessity but also a joy," Thorez told a group of miners in early 1946. He welcomed aid from the United States, refused to condemn French colonialism, assailed cuts in military spending as a "ridiculous pacifism," and endorsed policies that integrated French workers into a restored capitalist framework. In Italy, left-wing resistance leaders relinquished the factories and surrendered their weapons to the American occupation authorities, while Communist leaders followed Palmiro Togliatti, who became Minister of Justice and Vice-Premier, into the conservative Christian Democratic government of Alcide de Gasperi. Well into 1947, the powerful French and Italian Communist parties loyally participated in bourgeois governments, which found their presence embarrassing but also indispensable in heading off revolutionary threats to the Old

Order. While Stalin successfully arranged for the cooperation of Belgian and Dutch Communists with conservative governments intent upon restoring productivity, his compromise pleas to Communists in Greece, Yugoslavia, and China met stiffer resistance from men whose lives hung in the balance of revolutionary struggle.

But indications of Russian weakness merely fueled the Truman Administration's determination to roll back Soviet influence in Eastern Europe. The confrontation with Molotov over the Polish issue had been designed to let the Russians know there was no room for a Soviet sphere of influence in the dawning American Century. Now Truman acted to give muscle to American demands. Hitler's last-ditch efforts on the eastern front had enabled American troops to advance through Germany into the area allocated by the Yalta Conference to the Russians. Churchill now proposed making U.S. troop withdrawals contingent upon Russian diplomatic concessions. On April 26 Truman cabled Churchill that he concurred in this strategy and favored a joint message to Stalin. Truman's decision on troop withdrawals stunned the Joint Chiefs of Staff; General Dwight D. Eisenhower termed it "indefensible" to flout the wartime accords for political advantage. On May 8, the day of the German surrender, Truman surprised still more people by signing an Executive Order ending Lend-Lease aid to America's allies. Ships at sea headed for Russia were ordered to turn back, the loading of ships in port was halted, and goods on board ships in U.S. harbors were unloaded. Britain and Russia needed the aid for their war against Japan as well as for their postwar reconstruction and were therefore angered by the unexpected action. Secretary of State Edward Stettinius, soon to be replaced by Byrnes, thought the order was "particularly untimely and did not help Soviet-American relations."

Dismayed by the evident deterioration of the Russian-American alliance, a few U.S. officials worked to promote a more conciliatory policy. Joseph Davies, former U.S. ambassador to the Soviet Union, conferred with the President that May, urging a more flexible approach. Increasingly concerned about the dangers of atomic weapons, Stimson warned Truman that to avoid a postwar atomic arms race, it would be necessary to retain the cooperation of the Soviet Union. Such pressure, coupled with the failure of his hard-line approach to exact major Soviet concessions in Eastern Europe, led Truman to soften his position somewhat between late May and July, 1945. Ignoring the objections of Byrnes and the State Department, he dispatched Roosevelt's former aide, the ailing Harry Hopkins, to Moscow for talks with Stalin. American and Russian negotiators agreed on the composition of the new Polish government and arranged for American troop withdrawals from the Soviet zone of Germany. Compromise, then, proved possible. But it remained less appealing than world supremacy, which appeared within grasp as the atomic bomb neared completion. "If it explodes," remarked Truman, "I'll certainly have a hammer on those boys."

Ironically, there seemed little need to use the bomb in the war. By mid-1945, Germany had formally surrendered, and Japan was clearly defeated. American warplanes flew round-the-clock bombing missions over Japanese cities virtually unopposed. The fire-bombing of Tokyo in March resulted in 84,000 casualties. American and British ships shelled Japanese coasts at will and enforced a rigid blockade. Inside Japan, fuel and industrial productivity almost disappeared. Through the auspices of the Soviet Union, still technically a nonbelligerent, Japanese leaders frantically tried to negotiate a surrender, contingent only on the retention of the Emperor. In May, Hopkins cabled Truman from Moscow: "Japan is doomed and the Japanese know it. Peace feelers are being put out by certain elements in Japan and we should therefore . . . act in concert about the surrender." Russia, Japan's last hope as an intermediary, had promised America at Yalta that it would enter the Pacific war three months after the German surrender. By June, therefore, it was evident to American policymakers that either a slight modification of America's demand for unconditional surrender or the Soviet entry into the war would quickly result in Japanese capitulation. The U.S. Strategic Bombing Survey concluded after the war: "Japan would have surrendered even if the atomic bombs had not been dropped, even if Russia had not entered the war, and even if no invasion had been planned or contemplated."

A few Americans, aware of Truman's intention to wage atomic warfare, reacted with dismay. General Eisenhower recalled that, when Stimson informed him of the Administration plan in mid-1945, "I told him I was against it on two counts. First, the Japanese were ready to surrender and it wasn't necessary to hit them with that awful thing. Second, I hated to see our country be the first to use such a weapon." Atomic scientists, who had developed the weapon as a deterrent to German atomic power, were horrified by the prospect of its use against Japan. Consequently, they began a series of petitions and protests. The "Franck Report," drawn up in June by a distinguished scientific panel, warned Truman that, "if the United States were to be the first to release this new means of indiscriminate destruction upon mankind, she would sacrifice public support throughout the world" and "precipitate the race for armaments." Having failed to secure an interview with Truman, Leo Szilard, one of the leaders of the scientists' protest, traveled with two other prominent physicists to Spartanburg, South Carolina, to meet with Byrnes. Here the seemingly inexplicable became at least understandable.

According to Szilard, "Byrnes did not argue that it was necessary to use the bomb . . . to win the war. He knew . . . that Japan was essentially defeated. . . . Byrnes was much more concerned about the spreading of Russian influence in Europe" and thought that "demonstrating the bomb would make Russia more manageable."

Truman grew increasingly forceful as the date of the atomic attack neared. Partway through the Potsdam Conference, he received a report on the first successful test of the bomb, indicating that its power had greatly surpassed expectations. The President was "tremendously pepped up by it," Stimson observed, "and said that it gave him an entirely new feeling of confidence." Churchill recalled that, overnight, Truman seemed "a changed man." Truman informed the gleeful Churchill about the bomb but kept Stalin in the dark, mentioning only that a new weapon of unusual destructive force had been developed. At the conference sessions, Stalin reaffirmed Russia's intention, expressed at Yalta, to enter the war in early August, but this pledge held little savor for Truman, who hoped the bomb would end the Pacific war before the Russians entered it and thus gained leverage in the Far East. Far more important to Truman was the future of Germany. At Yalta, the Big Three had agreed, as a basis for future discussion, that Germany should pay reparations of $20 billion, with the Soviet Union to receive half. At Potsdam, Byrnes rejected entirely the notion of a fixed reparations figure, arguing instead that each occupying power should exact reparations from its own zone, although the Western powers, since they controlled Germany's industrial heartland, would transfer a small percentage of capital equipment to Russia. The Russians accepted this proposal only after Byrnes told Molotov on July 31 that he and the President were leaving Potsdam the next day, whether or not the reparations issue had been settled.

But the "bitterest debate" of the Potsdam Conference emerged, in Truman's words, because "Stalin wanted us to recognize the puppet governments he had installed in the [Axis] satellite countries." In turn, Byrnes demanded "joint action in reorganizing the governments of Bulgaria and Rumania." Truman declared that America would not recognize the government of Rumania, Bulgaria, or Hungary until the United States had "free access" to these nations, and that America would oppose their entry into the United Nations until they had "democratic" governments. Stalin irritably retorted that there was a "far less democratic government in Argentina"—a nation recently admitted into the United Nations upon U.S. insistence—while Molotov contended that "there were greater excesses in Greece." The conference ended in deadlock, but with Truman in good spirits and ready for a more aggressive policy. Not only had he begun to shift the terms of settlement with

Germany, but "the experience at Potsdam" left him "determined that I would not allow the Russians any part in the control of Japan," as he wrote in his *Memoirs*. "Force is the only thing the Russians understand."

On August 6, 1945, at 8:15 A.M., a single American plane flew unopposed over the Japanese city of Hiroshima and released an atomic bomb. "Because of the lack of warning," reported the U.S. Strategic Bombing Survey, "the explosion came as an almost complete surprise, and the people had not taken shelter." The blast and fire destroyed virtually all of Hiroshima, killing perhaps 100,000 inhabitants and leaving tens of thousands more to die painfully of burns and radiation poisoning. When news of the attack reached Truman on board the U.S.S. *Augusta* in mid-Atlantic, the President rushed back and forth among officers and crew members declaring: "This is the greatest thing in history!" Three days later, the President had a second bomb dropped on Nagasaki. The Japanese government quickly offered to surrender if the Emperor were retained. Byrnes replied that the Emperor would be subject to the authority of the Supreme Commander for the Allied Powers, and on this ambiguous basis the war came to an end. Truman immediately outlined his plans for a postwar atomic monopoly. Reporting to the nation on August 9, the President asserted: "The atomic bomb is too dangerous to be let loose in a lawless world. . . . We must constitute ourselves trustees of this new force."

American diplomacy now took the offensive against Soviet wartime gains. Although Truman had acknowledged at Potsdam the authority of the Allied Control Commissions in each country, he bypassed these commissions on August 9 by publicly appealing to the Balkan peoples to oppose the Communists. On August 18, Byrnes charged that the Bulgarian elections were not being conducted democratically. At American insistence, the election date was postponed, thus giving conservative parties a chance to mobilize their followers. "We possessed powers which were irresistible," Churchill noted. "Our outlook on the future was transformed." In September the London Conference of Foreign Ministers ended in a shambles. According to Roosevelt's former Under Secretary of State, Sumner Welles, Byrnes "adopted a position of intransigence," producing "one of the most disastrous international conferences of modern times." On October 27, Truman delivered a major address on the necessity of strong U.S. military power to support the peace, "by force if necessary," and in November he told a press conference that he could see no further point to Big Three conferences. In December, however, Byrnes went to Moscow and privately reached surprising agreements with the Russians, who accepted American proposals for the liberalization of the regimes in Bulgaria and Rumania. But when Byrnes returned to Washington in January, Truman delivered a blistering attack on his conduct of the negotiations, claiming that the Secretary of State should have held to a harsher tack. Russia, he told Byrnes, must be "faced with an iron fist and strong language. . . . Only one language do they understand—'how many divisions have you?' " Truman did "not think we should play compromise any longer. We should refuse to recognize Rumania and Bulgaria . . . and we should maintain complete control of Japan and the Pacific."

Truman's pugnacity contrasted sharply with popular sentiment. A Gallup poll in September reported that a majority of Americans believed Russia could be trusted to cooperate with the United States. Eisenhower recalled that, during the late summer and autumn of 1945, "the general atmosphere in Europe gave hope . . . for some form of cooperation between our two nations." As late as May, 1946, President Sidney Hillman of the Amalgamated Clothing Workers told his union's convention that "this earth can be made a place where men and women can walk together in peace." GI demonstrations and tumultuous mass meetings in Hawaii, Paris, London, Yokohama, and Manila, coupled with public and Congressional pressure, forced the partial demobilization of America's vast armies. Truman's *Memoirs* reveal that at his Cabinet meeting of October 26, 1945, the Secretary of War and the Secretary of the Navy complained that demobilization "threatened to jeopardize our strategic position in the midst of postwar tensions." Truman recalled that, although he "agreed entirely with this view," the "press and the Congress . . . drowned us out." Against his wishes and advice, "the American people had chosen to scuttle their military might."

But while popular pressure forced cutbacks in U.S. military forces from their wartime peak, Truman retained the largest peacetime military establishment in American history. After the outbreak of war in Europe in late 1939, the United States had a total of 300,000 men in its army and navy; by the summer of 1946, after what Truman termed the "disintegration" of the American armed forces, their combined strength stood at 2.2 million men. In fiscal 1940, with a U.S. combat role imminent, America's national security budget was $1.5 billion; in fiscal 1947, with the Axis powers long since defeated, it stood at $14.4 billion—about twice that of the Russians. Moreover, since June, 1945, Truman had fought for a program of universal military training to provide the nation with vast manpower reserves. "The desire for peace is futile unless there is enough strength ready and willing to enforce that desire," he told Congress. "Peace has to be built on power." When popular and Congressional opposition doomed the plan's chances, Truman appointed an advisory commission on UMT in December, 1946, as a means of mobilizing support. "I don't like to think of it as a universal military training program," he said, but as a "universal training program, giving our young people a background in the disciplinary approach of getting along with one another." Yet Congress and the public remained unimpressed. In 1950, the President reluctantly dropped his plan for UMT.

Truman met greater success in his drive to maintain America's atomic supremacy. After the atomic bombing of Hiroshima and Nagasaki, he recalled in his *Memoirs,* "it was important to retain the advantage which possession of the bomb had given us" until a "foolproof method of control could be found." Consequently, expenditures on the Manhattan Project rose in September, 1945, and again in October. Truman's desire to maintain an atomic advantage, however, clashed with the policy of Secretary of War Stimson, who thought some sort of American-Soviet accord on the sharing of atomic power imperative. "I consider the problem of our satisfactory relations with Russia . . . virtually dominated by the problem of the atomic bomb," he told Truman. "If we fail to approach them now and merely continue to negotiate with them having this weapon rather ostentatiously on our hip, their suspicions and their distrust of our purposes and motives will increase." Many atomic scientists were also critical of the government's atomic bomb policy. On November 29, Dr. Harold Urey, a leading atomic scientist, testified before the Senate Committee on Atomic Energy: "We are making bombs and storing them and are thus a threat to other countries and we are guilty of beginning the arms race."

The Administration's response to such criticism was an ingenious plan designed to move the bomb toward international control while enabling America to retain its atomic advantage. The Acheson-Lilienthal proposals, announced on March 16, 1946, called for international control of atomic energy by stages. The problem, from the Soviet viewpoint, was that during these stages, in which the Russians would be prevented from developing a bomb, America would retain its atomic monopoly. As the Acheson-Lilienthal report noted, "should . . . the entire effort collapse, the United States will at all times be in a favorable position." Byrnes turned the plan over to financier Bernard Baruch, who tightened it up still further by rejecting Soviet veto power in the proposed U.N. governing body and calling for majority rule in the United States–dominated organization at all stages. On June 14, the United States presented the Baruch Plan to the United Nations, and four days later Soviet Ambassador Andrei Gromyko rejected it, calling instead for immediate atomic disarmament with the imposition of controls at a future date. Naturally, neither nation would accept the other's plan. On July 1, while discussions were still in progress, the United States conducted the first postwar atomic bomb tests at Bikini Atoll. This undermined the talks still further and provided a symbolic expression of the U.S. position: Until a "foolproof" control system was implemented, the United States would plunge ahead with the development and stockpiling of atomic weapons.

Whatever its flaws, though, the Baruch Plan was the closest the Truman Administration came to a disarmament program in its almost eight years in office. Few in the Truman entourage seemed particularly desirous of avoiding an arms race. Calling for unification of the armed forces, extension of the Selective Service Act, and adoption of UMT, the President declared in a public address in April, 1946: "We must remain strong in order to retain our leadership, and, with all our resources, exercise that leadership." In dealing with the Russians, Truman noted in his *Memoirs,* he had decided to "lead from strength."

The President's hard-line stance toward the Soviet Union received its intellectual justification in February, 1946, when George F. Kennan, second in command at the American Embassy in Moscow, dispatched an 8,000-word cable to the State Department. The following January an updated version was submitted to Navy Secretary James V. Forrestal. Complaining that U.S. policy toward Russia in the past had been marked by "wishful thinking," he declared that, for the foreseeable future, the United States must "expect that Soviet policies will reflect . . . no real faith in the possibility of a permanent happy coexistence of the socialist and capitalist worlds." He was optimistic, though, about America's ability to influence "internal developments, both within Russia and throughout the international Communist movements." Indeed, America could "increase enormously the strains under which Soviet policy must operate," thus promoting "tendencies which must eventually find their outlet in either the break-up or the gradual mellowing of Soviet power." This could be accomplished by "adroit and vigilant application of counter-force at a series of constantly shifting geographical and political points." A "thoughtful observer," Kennan concluded, would "experience a certain gratitude to a Providence" that had given Americans "the responsibilities of moral and political leadership that history plainly intended them to bear." Charmed by Kennan's analysis and his new doctrine of "containment," the Administration brought him back to the United States, where he lectured to military and civilian leaders at the National War College. Within a short time, Kennan was chairman of the State Department's policy-planning staff.

As a "trial balloon" for the Administration's foreign policy, Truman arranged for a speech by former British Prime Minister Churchill at Fulton, Missouri. On March 5, 1946, speaking with Truman at his side, Churchill declared that the United States "stands at this time at the pinnacle of world power. . . . Opportunity is here now, clear and shining, for both our countries." America should not "ignore it or fritter it away," for it faced a "peril to Christian civilization." From the Baltic to the Adriatic, said Churchill, "an iron curtain has descended across the [European] continent." He urged a "special relationship" between Great Britain and the United States, to include increased military cooperation and their maintenance of a joint atomic monopoly. Rejecting "appeasement" of the Russians, he argued that "there is nothing they admire so much as strength."

To Truman's dismay, the speech drew sharp criticism from Americans. The *Chicago Sun* declared that to follow the standard "raised by this great but blinded aristocrat would be to march to the world's most ghastly war." Three liberal Senators—Claude Pepper of Florida, Harley Kilgore of West Virginia, and Glen Taylor of Idaho—contended in a joint statement that "Mr. Churchill's proposal would cut the throat of the United Nations" and "destroy the unity of the Big Three." Eleanor Roosevelt wrote that Churchill's policies would "lead sooner or later to war." The United Auto Workers declared that "the Winston Churchills and William Randolph Hearsts . . . are striving to lead our country to disaster," while the Amalgamated Clothing Workers assailed "reactionary forces" who sought "to use our nation's great strength, not for unity and peace, but to wrest world domination for themselves."

Frustrated in his attempts to rally support for his foreign policy initiatives, Truman found his domestic program scarcely more popular. The problem of reconversion hit the Administration almost immediately. Business called for the end of price controls and the maintenance of wage controls; labor desired an end to wage controls and the continuance of price controls; and consumers desired an end to rationing without inflation. Clearly, Truman could not have satisfied each of these groups, but his unique contribution to the situation lay in his alienation of all of them. Truman, who considered price controls "police state methods," told the nation on October 30, 1945, that "we must get back to the free operation of our competitive system." On the other hand, he initially stood behind the Office of Price Administration in its duel with Congressional conservatives. By 1946, though, Truman was clearly retreating before business pressure. Having told livestock owners that he would "never, never" end price controls on meat at a time of scarcity, he ended them three weeks later—at the height of a meat shortage. By mid-1946, severe inflation gripped the nation, with no relief in sight.

Hard hit by postwar inflation and relieved of their wartime no-strike pledge, American workers began a series of massive strikes in late 1945 which involved more than 5 million men and women before the end of 1946 and affected the largest industries in the nation: auto, steel, packinghouse, electrical, oil, coal, railroad, and maritime. Frightened business leaders met secretly with the president of the National Association of Manufacturers and vowed an all-out effort to resist wage demands. Full-page General Motors advertisements screamed: "Is American business to be based on free competition or is it to become socialized?" As early as June, 1945, Charles E. Wilson, president of General Electric, had warned Truman that it was necessary "to save labor from its own excesses—excesses which if unrestrained will in the long run be injurious to labor itself." Despite his prolabor voting record as a senator, Truman took a dim view of the strikes and as President soon showed that he had no intention of going down the line for labor's demands. In early December, 1945, he told auto workers to "return to work immediately." Their strike, he said, was a "major obstacle holding up our reconversion program." Both the United Auto Workers and the CIO reacted angrily to the President's intervention. On December 5, Philip Murray, the CIO president, told a nationwide radio audience: "The CIO is . . . opposed to the basic policies pursued by the Administration."

Two incidents particularly infuriated organized labor. In May, 1946, Truman stepped into the then-simmering controversy between twenty railroad brotherhoods and management. After the President's proposed settlement was rejected by Alvanley Johnston's Brotherhood of Locomotive Engineers and A. F. Whitney's Brotherhood of Railroad Trainmen, Truman told his Cabinet that he was going to ask Congress for the harshest labor law in American history, one that would empower the President to declare a state of national emergency and draft strikers into the armed forces. When Attorney General Tom Clark questioned the constitutionality of the measure, the President snapped back peremptorily: "We'll draft 'em first and think about the law later." On the afternoon of May 25, Truman delivered his labor message, drawing cheers and applause from conservative legislators. Shortly after he began, word reached him that an agreement had been signed and the rail issue settled; nevertheless, he completed his original speech and demanded passage of the legislation. The House eagerly responded that night by voting through the bill, but hasty Senate action was blocked by conservative Senator Robert A. Taft of Ohio, who claimed that Truman's proposal "offends not only the Constitution, but every basic principle for which the American Republic was established." It moved the nation far along the road toward "Hitlerism, Stalinism, totalitarianism."

If Truman's labor-draft proposal dismayed Senator Taft, it enraged American labor. From his deathbed, Sidney Hillman denounced these "extreme controls over the rights and liberties of American workers" as "provoked by the reactionary forces of big business." The fiery Michael Quill, president of the Transport Workers Union, declared that Truman had "become the Number One strikebreaker of the American bankers and railroads." A. F. Whitney pledged his union's treasury of $47 million to defeat Truman in 1948. "President Truman's un-American legislative proposal to Congress," stated the UAW, "was the climax of a series of surrenders by the Truman Administration to the demands of reactionary industrialists."

Truman tangled with the labor movement again in 1946, this time taking on one of its patriarchs, John L. Lewis of the United Mine Workers. In May, Truman had seized the mines and ordered his Secretary of the Interior, Julius A. Krug, to sign a contract with the UMW. In October, however, Lewis demanded that the contract be renegotiated. Among the grievances he wished to discuss was "the deadly, brutal 54-hour week underground . . . a longer work day and work week than prevails in the mining industry of any civilized country in the world." After a number of fruitless conferences, Lewis told Krug that the contract was "terminated" as of November 20. Determined to smash this challenge to his power, Truman ordered Attorney General Clark to secure a federal court injunction—one of the most hated anti-labor weapons in American history—to prohibit the strike. When Lewis disobeyed a restraining order secured by the government, a federal court fined the UMW $3.5 million and Lewis himself $10,000— the harshest action ever taken in a labor contempt case. Lewis denounced "the Administration's 'yellow dog' injunction," but the strike was clearly broken. Truman and his advisers considered it a major victory. The showdown with Lewis, Clark Clifford later observed, represented "the moment when Truman finally and irrevocably stepped out from the shadow of FDR to become President in his own right." Labor leaders were understandably less pleased. The president of the Brotherhood of Locomotive Firemen wrote to Truman: "The efforts led by the government to enforce economic servitude on the miners . . . give impetus and momentum to the program now being spawned by reactionary capitalism."

On paper, at least, the Truman Administration had a liberal legislative program. In the President's message to Congress of September 6, 1945, he endorsed a sizable number of reform measures, including a permanent Fair Employment Practices Commission, public housing, a higher minimum wage, and expanded unemployment benefits. On November 19, he urged Congress to pass a program of national health insurance through payroll deductions, thus providing all Americans with medical and hospital care regardless of ability to pay. But little of this legislation found its way through Congress. In February, 1946, Congress did pass a weak Full Employment Act, creating a Council of Economic Advisers to make reports to the government on the state of the national economy; but full employment, while now formally a national goal, remained in fact a distant reality. Sometimes incompetent and often apparently disinterested, Truman seemed incapable of making a successful fight for liberal legislation. In July, 1946, the president of the liberal National Farmers Union, James Patton, publicly announced that his organization had "lost confidence in the Truman Administration's doing anything about legislation we consider important."

In no area did Truman offend liberal sensibilities more than in his appointment of conservatives and cronies to high office. Within a few months of becoming President, Truman either fired or forced out most members of Roosevelt's Cabinet, including Francis Biddle, Henry Morgenthau, Jr., Frances Perkins, and other prominent New Dealers. Harold Ickes, the symbol of New Deal probity, resigned as Secretary of the Interior in February, 1946, charging that Truman's nominee for Under Secretary of the Navy, California oilman Ed Pauley, had submitted "the rawest proposition ever made to me." In September, Truman fired his Secretary of Commerce, Henry A. Wallace, after a dispute over U.S. foreign policy. "The New Dealers are scattering," chortled the pro-business *U.S. News & World Report*. In their place, Truman appointed such men as Tom Clark, a conservative Texan, as Attorney General; John Snyder, a conservative Missouri banker, as Secretary of the Treasury; and Byrnes as Secretary of State. Only one of Roosevelt's Cabinet members served out Truman's first term: the conservative Secretary of the Navy, James Forrestal. At the White House, Truman surrounded himself with cronies, including Harry Vaughan, a World War I buddy, whom he appointed brigadier general and Presidential aide; Pauley, whom he made reparations negotiator; and George Allen, a convivial businessman whom he appointed head of the Reconstruction Finance Corporation. Indeed, of Truman's entire White House circle, the only individual who could be considered neither mediocre nor conservative was the hard-driving Clark Clifford, a young naval officer and Missouri lawyer.

Possessed of what Sumner Welles called a "childlike faith in the omniscience of the high brass," Truman appointed an unprecedented number of military men to policy-making offices—a group surpassed in number only by Wall Street financiers. During his Presidency, generals or admirals became Secretary of State, Secretary of Defense, head of the CIA, occupation commanders in Germany and Japan, White House advisers, and ambassadors to key nations, including Russia. Harriman, appointed Secretary of Commerce in 1946, was once a leading investment banker; Robert Patterson, appointed Secretary of War in 1946, was a member of the Wall Street firm of Patterson, Belknap, and Webb; Robert Lovett, appointed Under Secretary of State in 1947, was a partner in Brown Brothers, Harriman; Forrestal, appointed Secretary of Defense in 1947, was formerly the president of Dillon, Read, and Company, Wall Street investment bankers. Journalist Howard K. Smith noted that, of the 125 most important government appointments made by Truman in the first two postwar years, 49 went to bankers, financiers, and industrialists; 31 went to military men; and 17 went to lawyers, most of them with big business connections. "The effective locus of government," said Smith, "seemed to shift from Washington to some place equidistant between Wall Street and West Point."

The flight of New Dealers from government service accelerated as the Administration's intentions became apparent. At the end of the war, world famine conditions heightened, making the United Nations Relief and Rehabilitation Administration—funded largely by the United States and headed by New York's former governor, the liberal Herbert H. Lehman—a symbol of hope to the world's hungry masses. "More people faced starvation and even death for want of food during the year following the war," noted Truman, "than during all the war years combined." In Europe alone, an estimated 100 million people subsisted on less than 1,500 calories a day—about half the daily requirement. In this context, the Administration decided to terminate UNRRA's existence. In March, 1946, Truman appointed former President Herbert Hoover, advocate of a politically oriented food program, to survey world needs. Lehman, who had not been consulted on the Hoover mission, interpreted it as symptomatic of Truman's desire to place relief exclusively in American hands, and resigned. As his biographer, Allan Nevins, explained: "The idea that national aims should take precedence over international humanitarianism repelled the head of UNRRA." Hoover soon expressed his shock that UNRRA aid went to "the Communist puppet states of Poland, Czechoslovakia, and Yugoslavia" and reinforced Washington's decision to end the program. Eventually, the United States and Great Britain alone among all other countries refused to fund the agency beyond 1946. Acheson declared in December: "The relief problems of the near future are not of a character which would warrant grants . . . under conditions which would leave little or no effective control by the grantor." Byrnes contended that "whatever the United States does in the way of relief should be done . . . unilaterally."

Often, however, American officials found the new United Nations of great assistance in furthering their policy aims. Ever since the founding session at San Francisco, U.S. representatives had used their clear majority in the General Assembly and the Security Council to embarrass and isolate the Russians. Before 1953, the United States lost on only 3 per cent of the General Assembly's 800 resolutions, and never on an important security matter. By contrast, the Soviets were outmaneuvered and outvoted at every turn and frequently resorted to their Security Council veto. The Soviet veto, though, was hardly the major obstacle to U.N. action the United States claimed it to be; of forty Soviet vetoes before 1949, twenty-two concerned membership applications and most others were on less than memorable issues. The Russians had fought particularly bitterly, for example, against the U.S.-sponsored admission of Argentina, a nation that Secretary of State Cordell Hull had recently termed the "refuge and headquarters in this hemisphere of the Fascist movement"; at Yalta, Roosevelt had twice promised not to support U.N. membership for Argentina, and the American reversal on this and other issues left Soviet delegates angry, sputtering, and less than enthusiastic about the world organization.

The controversy over postwar Iran illustrated the value of the world body to American policy-makers. After World War II, the Russians delayed the departure of their occupation troops from Iran, encouraging a revolt in the northern provinces and demanding some of the oil privileges already afforded Great Britain. Truman later wrote that the key issue was "control of Iran's oil reserves. . . . If the Russians were allowed to control Iran's oil either directly or indirectly, the raw-material balance of the world would undergo a serious change, and it would be a serious loss for the economy of the Western world." In early 1946, the United States assailed Russian policies in the United Nations, and Byrnes delivered a strong note to the Soviet Union. Under pressure, Iran and the Soviet Union reached a compromise accord, announcing the withdrawal of the Russian troops, the creation of a Soviet-Iranian oil firm, and some measure of autonomy for northern Iran. On May 6, Soviet occupation forces left the country. Thereafter, the Iranian government, with British and American support, rejected the oil agreement and reasserted control over the northern provinces. The United States had succeeded in using the United Nations to safeguard Western oil interests at Soviet expense.

American policy-makers watched the underdeveloped nations with considerable apprehension as the war drew to a close. Truman noted in his *Memoirs* his concern that "violent resistance movements were developing in North Africa, the Middle East, and the redeemed areas of Asia, all in the name of liberation." Even South America, stirred by new currents of nationalism, no longer seemed safe. At the San Francisco conference of the United Nations, one U.S. delegate barked at Nelson Rockefeller, Assistant Secretary of State for Latin American Affairs: "Your goddamn peanut nations aren't voting right. Go line them up." Indeed, during the conference Stimson privately expressed his concern that Roosevelt might have yielded too much of the United States's traditional influence in Latin America. "I am afraid that the Good Neighbor Policy has put serious obstacles in the path of the exercise of the Monroe Doctrine," he observed. The United States needed "a freer hand as a policeman in this hemisphere." Roosevelt had decided against developing a strong inter-American military and political system in the hope of setting a "good example" for the Russians, but the Truman Administration, while rejecting Soviet influence in Eastern Europe, already had plans for closer ties with Latin America. "It's not asking too much to have our little region over here which never has bothered anybody," Stimson told John McCloy, the Assistant Secretary of War. McCloy agreed: "We ought to have our cake and eat it too; . . . we ought to be free to operate under this regional arrangement in South America and at the same time intervene promptly in Europe."

Accordingly, the U.S. government successfully insisted that the United Nations Charter make provision for regional security groupings, thus giving the United States a relatively free hand in Latin American affairs. This would, as McCloy noted, "protect our concept of preclusive rights in this hemisphere." In May, 1946, Truman also asked Congress for legislation establishing military collaboration with the nations of Latin America and providing for the training, organization, and equipment of their armed forces. And yet the possibility remained that unorthodox, even socialist, economic measures might be adopted by underdeveloped nations at a time of postwar instability and social upheaval. Consequently, Administration policy-makers found it necessary to take a fairly blunt position in opposition to social and economic experiments. In a speech delivered in September and reprinted as a State Department policy release, Rockefeller's successor, Spruille Braden, laid down the line: "I wish to emphasize that private enterprise is the best and in most circumstances the only really sound means to develop the known or unknown resources of a new country."

Nowhere did the prospects for a postwar socialist revolution seem better than in China. During the war, as Acheson recalled, U.S. observers had reported that Chiang Kai-shek's government and the Kuomintang had "sunk into corruption, into a scramble for place and power, and into reliance on the United States . . . to preserve their own domestic supremacy." Although the State Department, in a memorandum of April 26, 1945, looked forward "to promoting mutually profitable Sino-American trade by all practicable means and to negotiating soon with China a comprehensive, modern, commercial treaty," this appeared a pipe dream by the end of the war. "It was perfectly clear to us," Truman later wrote, "that if we told the Japanese to lay down their arms immediately and march to the seaboard the entire country would be taken over by the Communists. We therefore had to take the step of using the enemy as a garrison until we could airlift Chinese Nationalist troops to South China and send marines to guard the seaports." Almost 2 million Japanese troops thus garrisoned key sections of China for more than a year until U.S. Air Force planes had flown in half a million Kuomintang troops and 53,000 U.S. Marines to re-establish Chiang's control. Reconciled with Chiang through the Yalta accords, Stalin signed a Sino-Soviet treaty on August 14, 1945, and, at Chiang's request, delayed the departure of Soviet troops from Manchuria until February 1, 1946, thus enabling Kuomintang soldiers to take control of Manchurian cities. But the Communist forces in China, under the leadership of Mao Tse-tung, retained their independence and popularity, particularly in the countryside, and in December Truman asked General George C. Marshall to head a mission to China.

Burdened with conservative goals in a revolutionary situation, the Marshall mission was doomed from the outset. In December, 1945, Truman had formally instructed Marshall that "the only legal government in China" was that of Chiang; therefore, it represented "the proper instrument to achieve the objective of a unified China." Communist forces were to be integrated into the Kuomintang government and the civil war brought to a halt. U.S. policy-makers believed that, in an all-out civil war, Chiang would lose. Truman later noted that it was "impracticable" to send in large American armies to crush the Communist insurgency, as "the American people would never stand for such an undertaking." Therefore, "the only course of action open to us" was to end the fighting and "to support the Generalissimo politically, economically and, within limits, militarily." Marshall arrived in China in January, 1946, and quickly found Communist representatives "more tractable," in Truman's words, "than the leaders of the Central Government." The Nationalists seemed "determined to pursue a policy of force." Marshall sought to convince Chiang "by every means at his command," wrote Truman, that he would never defeat the Communists "in a purely military conflict." But "the Generalissimo remained unconvinced."

Fighting broke out again in 1946, with Chiang determined to occupy all of Manchuria and North China. Marshall and General Albert Wedemeyer both argued against the exploit but ultimately supplied him with equipment, money, and transportation. As the Americans had predicted, the Nationalist military advance ended in disaster. In January, 1947, Marshall left China in disgust, convinced that the situation was hopeless. Truman later observed that the Marshall mission failed "because the government of Chiang Kai-shek did not command the respect and support of the Chinese people." Nevertheless, American military and economic aid to this government continued, albeit at a reduced rate, preserving the illusion that American power would somehow rescue Chiang's dictatorship from the fate that awaited it.

The focal point of American diplomatic concern, however, lay not in the Third World but in the two defeated industrial powers, Germany and Japan. Roosevelt had briefly considered the Morgenthau Plan to strip Germany of its industrial capacity, but Truman quickly brushed aside the proposal, fired Morgenthau when he sought to attend the Potsdam Conference, and ended plans for heavy reparations payments. Indeed, throughout the four-power occupation of Germany, American officials opposed checks on German industrial recovery, arguing, as did the occupation's political adviser, Robert Murphy, in 1945, that "extreme, ill-considered deindustrialization of Germany may well have the effect of creating and extending chaos in Europe." Committed to a stable, integrated system of world capitalism, American policy-makers thought in international terms that reflected little interest in the antagonisms and alliances of World War II. Discussing Germany and Japan in 1946, Harriman asserted that "the rehabilitation of these countries is requisite to world stability. I cannot too greatly stress the importance of their economic recovery. The task is urgent and time is of the essence."

In this context, reforms took second place. Despite official statements, de-Nazification made little headway, and the occupation's attempt to encourage a new respect for democracy through the use of education and mass culture seemed barren of results. The occupation's public-opinion polls in the two years after December, 1945, consistently found that half the respondents thought Nazism a "good idea badly carried out." Supreme Court Justice Robert H. Jackson ably directed the Nuremberg Trials, but long before their conclusion their insistence on punishment of war criminals had become a source of embarrassment to American occupation authorities. The deconcentration of industry, hindered by the American desire to restore German productivity and by the big-business backgrounds of many officials, produced few changes. Not until February, 1947, did the American military government even write a systematic decartelization law, and thereafter it was largely evaded or reinterpreted. The most zealous reformers in Germany were not the Americans but the German Social Democrats, who, despite their popularity, were frustrated in their attempts to institute socialist measures in the American zone. General Lucius Clay, the American occupation commander, stifled workers' councils, prohibited nationalization of industry by local government, and angered even the British and the French by his consistently antisocialist bias. Socialist measures, he contended, would prejudge the future of a united Germany, and, as he later added, "it was our duty . . . to point out the merits of free enterprise."

By mid-1946, American policy-makers had abandoned all pretense at four-power control of Germany and were moving toward unification of the Western occupation areas into a new German nation. In May, Clay announced a halt in reparations payments to the Soviet Union from the U.S. zone, and in July Byrnes invited the other powers to merge their zones of Germany with the American. The British, staggering under heavy occupation expenses, accepted the American offer, establishing "Bizonia." Later that year, in his Stuttgart address, Byrnes proclaimed the American goal of a united Germany. Sumner Welles complained publicly that "in a panic effort to circumvent Russia . . . we have declared our intention of rebuilding a unified and strong Germany." Such a Germany, he argued, might "once more bring ruin to the rest of the world." This prospect particularly frightened the Soviet government, which clung ever more tenaciously to its own occupation zone. The result, then, was a Germany permanently partitioned between East and West.

Truman's decision to maintain exclusive American control over the occupation of Japan undoubtedly pleased the American occupation commander, General Douglas MacArthur—a military officer unaccustomed to sharing authority with anyone in Moscow, London, or Washington. At the inaugural session of the Allied Council, he made his only appearance before that body, reminding its members that their role was purely advisory and that they would have no governing authority whatsoever. MacArthur rarely deigned to lower his prestige by dealing directly with the Japanese but operated behind the scenes through conservative politicians drawn from Japan's traditional élite. Indeed, although many Americans demanded that Emperor Hirohito be tried as a war criminal, MacArthur insisted upon retaining him in office. Yet

MacArthur was sincerely committed to breaking the power of Japan's reactionary fedual landlords and their militarist allies. As a result, he encouraged the adoption of a brand of competitive capitalism based on the U.S. Constitution, land reform, civil liberties, free elections, trade unions, a purge of fascist elements, and some degree of industrial de-concentration. Some occupation reforms had little long-term impact, but others took root, radically altering the traditional framework of Japanese life. To MacArthur's consternation, the new trade unions grew increasingly militant and Marxist, while the newly enfranchised masses often exercised their political freedom by voting Socialist or Commu-nist. SCAP began to tighten its reins in 1946—none too soon for anxious officials in Washington.

By September, 1946, the only consistent critic of Truman's foreign policy remaining within the Administration was Secretary of Commerce Henry A. Wallace—the politician considered by many Americans to be the nation's leading exponent of New Deal liberalism. A big, rum-pled, sad-faced man, Wallace was a passionate humanitarian and a mystic. From the inception of Truman's Presidency, he had spoken up in Cabinet meetings for the continuation of friendly ties with the Soviet Union, arguing that the Russians should be given a relatively free hand in Eastern Europe and should share in the secrets of atomic energy. On September 10, Wallace met privately with Truman and showed the President a copy of a speech he planned to give in New York City two days later. Truman, despite subsequent denials, apparently read the speech and authorized its delivery. Warning Americans against those who "try to provoke war between the United States and Russia," Wal-lace contended that "Russia must be convinced that we are not planning for war against her, and we must be certain that Russia is not carrying on territorial expansion." Although the *Daily Worker* attacked the speech for repeating "the major fallacies advanced by most apologists for American imperialism," it nevertheless incensed key figures in the Administration. Admiral Leahy, one of Truman's closest foreign policy advisers, thought Wallace "an honest 'fellow traveller' with the Soviets, at least a 'pink,' " while Secretary of State Byrnes threatened to resign if Wallace were retained in the Cabinet. On September 20, after some hesitation at severing his last personal link to the New Dealers, Truman fired Wallace, remarking: "Well, now he's out, and the crackpots are having conniption fits."

The November, 1946, Congressional elections proved that discontent with the Truman Administration was not confined to "crackpots." Strikes, shortages, cronyism, and foreign confrontations all contributed to a sense of despair with the President and his party. Polls found that the percentage of the electorate supporting Truman's Presidential per-formance dropped from 87 per cent shortly after he took office to 32 per cent by November, 1946. Republicans asked simply: "Had enough?" and the nation answered by electing the first Republican Congress in eighteen years. The GOP also captured a majority of the nation's governorships. The Republican sweep was so overwhelming that voters in Atlantic City, New Jersey, elected as justice of the peace a Republican who had died a week earlier, and the Democratic Senator from Arkansas, J. William Fulbright, suggested that Truman step aside as President and let a Republican take office.

Particularly distressing to New Deal adherents were the victories of many extreme conservatives, who denounced the gains of organized labor and attacked their Democratic opponents as agents of a Communist conspiracy. In Wisconsin, a virtually unknown Marine Corps veteran and former chicken farmer, Joseph R. McCarthy, edged out liberal Senator Robert M. LaFollette, Jr., in the Republican primary and then emerged victorious over his Democratic rival, whom he labeled a "megaphone being used by the Communist-controlled PAC." In California, Richard Nixon, a young lawyer who had unsuccessfully sought careers as an FBI agent and a frozen orange juice promoter, defeated liberal Democratic Congressman Jerry Voorhis, assailing him as "a lip-service American" who had been "consistently voting the Moscow . . . line in Congress." The CIO-PAC made a dismal record at the polls, and liberals were understandably glum. "Let us not fool ourselves," said *The Nation*. "The progressive forces in America have been routed."

By late 1946, liberals were in full revolt against Truman and his policies. "Great leadership is demanded of America now in securing peace," wrote *New Republic* publisher Michael Straight; "it is not within Truman's power to give." Harold Ickes castigated the President for surrounding himself with "a nondescript band of political Lilliputians." Labor unions, long in the pocket of the Democratic Party, revived talk of a third-party effort. In December, delegates from ten liberal groups voted to form a single powerful liberal organization, the Progressive Citizens of America. Henry Wallace, who had taken over as editor of the *New Republic* upon leaving the Truman Cabinet, quickly became their leading light, and speculation began that PCA would serve as the vehicle for a Wallace-led political party. In his first editorial, "Jobs, Peace, Freedom," Wallace declared that the American people "have rejected, as they will always reject, a Democratic party that is not militantly progressive" and announced that he planned "to help organize a progressive America." Progressives should seek to "rebuild the Democratic party as a liberal party," he added, but "if the Democratic party is incapable of change, we shall strike out along other lines." Whatever the Administration thought, progressive ideas were "indestructible and on the march."

2

Forging a Cold War Consensus,
1947-48

> We must not be confused about the issue which
> confronts the world today. . . . It is tyranny
> or freedom.
>
> HARRY S. TRUMAN, March 17, 1948

EVER SINCE 1945, Truman and the State Department had been searching for a situation that might justify a formal commitment to the extension of American power in world affairs. Although Truman had altered
the nature of Big Three diplomacy and launched American foreign
policy on a Cold War course, his public displays of belligerence, like
those of Churchill, had angered liberals, Congress, and the press and
had failed to rally popular support. Indeed, by the end of 1946, polls
indicated that less than one-fourth of the public rated foreign policy as
the most important problem facing the nation. In a memo drafted in
early 1947, State Department official Joseph M. Jones complained:
"Congress and the people of this country are not sufficiently aware of
the character and dimensions of the crisis that impends, and of the
measures that must be taken. . . . The State Department knows.
Congress and the people do not know." In the November elections, far
more interest had been aroused by the rising price of meat than by
questions of global strategy. Nevertheless, the elections had also shown
the weakness of the liberals and the CIO-PAC at the polls, and Truman
now felt less constrained than in the past to challenge their authority
with a public declaration of political, military, and ideological Cold
War.

The opportunity arose when, in late January, 1947, Great Britain
was paralyzed by a fierce snowstorm. By early February, more than
half of British industry had fallen silent, and losses in the export trade
were severe. With enormous foreign debts and 1.4 million troops stationed around the world, Britain could no longer meet its overseas com-

30

mitments; soon India, Burma, and Palestine would wrench themselves free of tottering imperial rule. The British government, which had pumped $760 million into Greece since World War II, now resolved to end its costly and unpopular occupation role in that land. On February 21, the British Ambassador informed the State Department that his nation would remove all its troops from Greece by the end of March. American diplomatic officials were fully aware of the importance of the British note. General Marshall, appointed Secretary of State in January after a clash of egos between Truman and Byrnes, considered it "tantamount to British abdication from the Middle East with obvious implications as to their successor."

The roots of the Greek crisis lay in World War II, when the German occupation had been opposed with great success by the National Liberation Front (EAM), a coalition of parties spearheaded by the Greek Communists. According to American historian W. H. McNeil, who was in Greece during the war: "By the time of liberation, the EAM numbered about two million members, out of a population of over seven million. They were incomparably superior to all rivals in their organization and enthusiasm." When British troops landed in 1944, after the evacuation of the Germans, EAM was capably administering most of Greece. Its populist style and reformist rule provided a dramatic contrast to the collaborationist government installed by the Germans and the preceding right-wing dictatorship of General John Metaxas, established with the assistance of Greece's King George II. Consequently, Churchill's decision to reinstate George II, rebuild a Greek army loyal to the monarchy, and disarm EAM soon led to fierce fighting in Athens between EAM and British troops—the only battle during World War II between the Western Allies and a resistance movement. EAM waged such a spirited struggle that the British rushed in two additional divisions from the critical Italian front and, in violation of Athens' status as an open city, employed planes and tanks to destroy rebel-held areas. In February, 1945, the Varkiza Agreement brought a halt to the conflict. EAM agreed to surrender its arms and the three-fourths of Greece it still controlled to the British and their Royalist allies in return for legal recognition of EAM and the Greek Communist party, elections, a constitutional plebiscite, an end to reprisals against resistance fighters, and a purge of profascist elements from the Greek Army and police.

But with state power firmly in the hands of the Royalists, the guarantees of the Varkiza Agreement proved to have little substance. The Greek government and its right-wing supporters embarked upon a campaign of terror against the Left, including torture, beatings, mass arrests, a purge of freely elected union leaders, the smashing of printing presses, and massacres. In March, 1946, the vice-premier resigned, calling the forthcoming elections a "comedy." EAM boycotted the elections, which it considered rigged, and the Royalists won over-whelmingly—a circumstance repeated later that year in the plebiscite that restored the Greek monarchy. Correspondents for the New York *Herald Tribune* and the Associated Press reported that the regime of Greek Prime Minister Constantine Tsaldaris was engaged in a "desper-ate effort to . . . wipe out not only Communists but all democratic, liberal, and republican elements." An official British parliamentary delegation, dispatched to investigate the situation, sharply condemned government terrorism, urged the restoration of constitutional liberties, and called for the broadening of the Greek government. Although poverty and misery were widespread, with an estimated 75 per cent of Greek children suffering from malnutrition, a "small class of wealthy people," noted the parliamentary delegation, lived "in great luxury." The latter group supported itself through black market operations, speculation, and misappropriation of relief funds, and served as the backbone of a similarly corrupt government, which spent most of its revenue on the army and police. Driven by desperation, bands of angry EAM veterans, numbering perhaps 10,000 in all, formed in the mountains in late 1946 and recommenced their armed struggle.

The Truman Administration, concerned by the situation's revolution-ary potential, sent observers to Greece and in January, 1947, dispatched an economic mission under former OPA administrator Paul Porter. Porter, U.S. Ambassador Lincoln MacVeigh, and others warned Tru-man that drastic inflation, strikes, riots, public panic, and guerrilla bands were undermining the authority of the Athens government and that only British troops retained it in office. Unless the Greek regime re-ceived massive military and economic aid, they said, the rebels would soon take power. Marshall had already proposed such aid when the British note of February 21 arrived.

Although Truman and the State Department were elated at the pros-pect of replacing the British in Greece, Congressional leaders, called to the White House for advance briefings on Administration plans, displayed an initial skepticism. As Republican conservatives, they balked at what most feared would prove to be a large-scale program of over-seas humanitarian assistance. Under Secretary of State Acheson moved to dispel their misgivings. In place of Marshall's rather dry and straight-forward discussion of Greece, Britain, and aid, he presented a dramatic portrait of how a Communist victory in Greece would "open three continents to Soviet penetration." Joseph Jones, present for the session, summarized Acheson's peroration: "Only two great powers remained in the world, the United States and the Soviet Union. We had arrived at a situation unparalleled since ancient times. Not since Rome and Carthage had there been such a polarization of power on this earth." The United States and the Soviet Union, "divided by an unbridgeable ideological chasm," were engaged in a global struggle in which the United States had no choice but to resist "Soviet aggression." Exhilarated by this apocalyptic tale, Congressional leaders pledged their support.

In fact, economic concerns had greater salience for Administration policy-makers than they ever admitted to Congress or to the public. Six days before presenting his new Truman Doctrine to Congress, the President spoke at Baylor University in Texas, outlining a fundamental conflict between "free enterprise" and "planning." As "the giant of the economic world," the United States had the responsibility for setting the "future pattern of economic relations," he declared. Much the same sort of thinking animated early drafts of the Truman Doctrine. They portrayed "a world-wide trend away from the system of free enterprise," which "gravely threatened" American interests, and asserted the necessity for the United States to maintain its access to the "great natural resources" of the Middle East. Clark Clifford promoted a draft contending that the "disappearance of free enterprise in other nations would threaten our economy and our democracy." Such statements, however, struck Acheson and Truman as ill advised. The early drafts, said the President, "made the whole thing sound like an investment prospectus." Framed in these terms, the Truman Doctrine would have little popular appeal. "The only way we can sell the public on our new policy," noted one memorandum, "is by emphasizing . . . Communism vs. democracy" as the "major theme." Consequently, in his final draft of the Truman Doctrine, Jones incorporated the same overblown rhetoric that had done so much to mobilize the support of Republican Congressional leaders. The message also included a provision for aid to Turkey—a country never noted for its democratic institutions, but whose geographical location made it the ideal instrument to seal off Russian access to the trade of the Mediterranean and the oil of the Middle East.

Only one detail remained to be arranged. The Greek government, not yet apprised of American intentions, had to request U.S. military assistance. On March 3, at State Department urging, it submitted a formal request to Washington. As Jones has revealed, "the message was drafted in the State Department and suggested to the Greek government." Loy Henderson, director of the U.S. Office of Near Eastern and African Affairs, explained to the Greek *chargé d'affaires* that the request for aid had been drawn up "with a view to the mentality of

Congress" and would "serve as a basis for the cultivation of public opinion." Furthermore, its existence would "protect the United States government against internal and external charges that it was taking the initiative of intervening in a foreign state or that it had been persuaded by the British to take over a bad legacy." In Congressional hearings a few weeks later, Administration witnesses did, in fact, rebut charges of "intervention" by citing the "request" from the Greek government.

On March 12, 1947, Truman read his message to a grim and largely silent Congress. In Greece, said the President, "terroristic activities of several thousand armed men, led by Communists," had created a situation beyond the capacity of the Greek government to handle. Nor could the United Nations extend help "of the kind that is required." Broadening his canvas, Truman depicted a far-reaching struggle. "Nearly every nation must choose between alternative ways of life"—the "free" and the "totalitarian." The moral was clear: "It must be the policy of the United States to support free peoples who are resisting attempted subjugation by armed minorities." Accordingly, he asked Congress for $400 million to provide military and economic assistance to the governments of Greece and Turkey. As Bernard Baruch noted, the address "was tantamount to a declaration of . . . an ideological or religious war." It divided the world into irreconcilable camps of good and evil, placed the Greek crisis within this grossly irrelevant framework, and established America as the guardian of the *status quo* against the forces of revolution. "This was," Truman later observed, "the turning point in America's foreign policy."

"All over the world," recalled Truman, "voices of approval made themselves heard, while Communists and their fellow travelers struck out at me savagely." Actually, though, the Truman Doctrine met with immediate criticism from a broad spectrum of Americans. Columnist Walter Lippmann warned that the United States was "not rich enough to subsidize reaction all over the world or strong enough to maintain it in power." Senator Taft, who would later vote reluctantly for the measure, assailed it as an attempt to divide the world into Communist and anti-Communist zones. "If we assume a special position in Greece and Turkey," he said, "we can hardly . . . object to the Russians continuing their domination in Poland, Yugoslavia, Rumania, and Bulgaria." Liberals were particularly hostile. PCA denounced the Truman Doctrine as "an invitation to war," which signified the rejection of "an American policy based on one world." The *New Republic* maintained that "the U.S. is now ready to excuse unholy alliances of its own by adopting the apology that the end might justify the means." Henry Wallace, traveling in Europe, predicted that the Truman Doctrine would lead to "a century of fear." Many, like Senator Claude Pepper of Florida, thought the unilateral aid message would "sabotage the United Nations." Even Secretary of State Marshall reported himself "somewhat startled to see the extent to which the anti-Communist element of the speech was stressed" and told Truman that he "was overstating the case a bit." Public opinion polls revealed that, although 56 per cent of the nation favored aid to Greece, 55 per cent opposed sending military advisers or bypassing the United Nations.

Despite popular criticism, however, the Greek-Turkish aid bill sailed quickly through the conservative 80th Congress, received the signature of an eager President, and was in the process of implementation by that spring. American advisers, replacing the British in Greece, instituted harsher policies than their predecessors. In February, there had been at least 25,000 political prisoners in Greece, and the number now grew rapidly, stimulated by waves of mass arrests. Deportations and executions increased, and by July most Communist Party members were in jail or in hiding. In December the Greek government abolished the right to strike, providing the death penalty for violators. Assured of American support, the Athens regime grew increasingly arbitrary and corrupt. The Americans allocated only a small percentage of their assistance to aid the floundering civilian economy, and most of this ended up in the pockets of the governing élite, where it did little to alleviate the general wretchedness. In March, 1948, the first anniversary of the Truman Doctrine, the Royalist government reported that 32 per cent of the population was on relief.

The American effort centered on defeating the rebels, estimated at the time of the Truman Doctrine to number 17,000 armed men, with a political and intelligence network of 50,000 active workers and an additional 250,000 sympathizers who provided occasional assistance. In the last five months of 1947 alone, Washington sent hundreds of military advisers and 74,000 tons of military supplies to Greece, including artillery, dive bombers, and napalm. American military men trained, funded, and armed the Greek National Army of 132,000 men—twice the number employed against EAM by the Germans—and a 50,000-man National Guard. "We will answer terrorism with terrorism ten times as strong," promised right-wing Greek General Napoleon Zervas, "and slaughter ten times greater."

Yet the rebels remained undaunted. Without armor or aircraft, and with little artillery, they won a number of striking victories in 1947 and the first half of 1948, and their armed forces swelled to 23,000. American estimates of Communist participation ranged from 10 to 40 per cent, and no evidence was uncovered to indicate Russian military or economic support for the insurgents. When the rebel General Markos established a "Government of Free Greece" in the Grammos Mountains in December, 1947, not a single Communist country recognized it. Yugoslavia provided the rebels with small hand guns and sanctuary, but even this modest assistance came under Russian attack. "What do you think," Stalin snapped at the Yugoslav vice-premier in early 1948, "that Great Britain and the United States—the United States, the most powerful state in the world—will permit you to break their line of communication in the Mediterranean? Nonsense. . . . The uprising in Greece must be stopped, and as quickly as possible." It was not. Bloody battles raged. Although they lost 32,000 men during 1948 in air attacks, the insurgents replenished their forces from the peasantry and maintained a consistent level of fighting strength.

By 1949, though, the tide had turned. The Royal Army, reorganized by U.S. General James Van Fleet, scoured the countryside in a massive counterinsurgency drive. Van Fleet even initiated a widespread campaign of population removal designed to isolate the guerrillas from their supporters. Major Edgar O'Ballance wrote of this program: "The harsh policy of displacing thousands of people was a difficult decision for a democratic government to take. . . . However . . . it paid handsome dividends." Stalin's break with Tito, combined with the American military offensive, dealt the *coup de grâce* to the Greek rebels. Not only did they split along Stalinist-Titoist lines, but Tito, now eager to align himself with the Greek monarchy he had previously hoped to overthrow, closed the Yugoslav border to the insurgents. On October 16, 1949, with guerrilla resistance virtually crushed, the rebel radio announced a "cease-fire" to "prevent the complete annihilation of Greece." The Greek Civil War thus ended with an American military victory.

The American adventure in Greece left that nation profoundly marked by the experience. An estimated 11,000 villages were destroyed and 158,000 people killed in the war. Many thousands of Greek insurgents or their sympathizers remained long afterward in prisons or in exile. By the early 1960s, after the tiny Greek nation had absorbed almost $4 billion in postwar American aid (primarily military), it remained one of the most economically impoverished and politically repressive in Europe. In subsequent years, liberalizing tendencies threatened to alter the reactionary nature of Greek politics and society and to lessen the Athens government's servile dependence upon the United States. But these tendencies were throttled in 1967 by a U.S.-supported military coup, which installed one of the world's few truly neofascist regimes, expelled from the Council of Europe for its systematic violations of human rights. Thus did the United States, in the words of the Truman Doctrine, "help free people to maintain their free institutions."

More significantly, events in Greece set the tone for U.S. policy in the Cold War, particularly toward weak, underdeveloped nations. Fortified by their military victory in Greece, American policy-makers grew increasingly willing to intervene in other nations to defend reactionary élites against the challenge of native radicals. They had learned from their Greek involvement that, with sufficient U.S. assistance, even the most venal, oppressive, and unrepresentative of regimes could be used to quell domestic revolts in the name of anti-Communism. Criticism would emerge, of course, from those misguided enough to place ideals of freedom, self-determination, or human life above loyalty to an American Century, but it would pass as power endured. All this was a lesson that American policy-makers took to heart and applied subsequently through open military or covert CIA intervention in China, Korea, Iran, Guatemala, Lebanon, Cuba, the Congo, British Guiana, the Dominican Republic, Bolivia, Laos, and Cambodia. Presidents Kennedy and Johnson both cited the American victory in Greece as proof that they had embarked upon the proper course of action in Vietnam.

Having formally launched the Anti-Communist Crusade abroad with his Truman Doctrine address of March 12, 1947, the President now brought it to bear at home. After the disastrous 1946 midterm elections, he had sought to head off the attacks of Congressional conservatives on the patriotism of Democrats by appointing a committee to study the issues of loyalty and security in America. Testifying before the committee, Attorney General Clark warned of "the serious threat which *even one* disloyal person constitutes to the security of the United States government." On March 22, Truman accepted the committee's recommendations by issuing Executive Order 9835, establishing a Federal Employee Loyalty Program to screen the 2 million employees of the federal government and the half-million yearly applicants for government jobs. When "derogatory information" was unearthed about an individual, a full field investigation by the FBI followed. A system of federal loyalty boards then weighed the evidence and acted upon individual cases. To direct the system, Truman appointed a Loyalty Review Board, headed by Seth Richardson, a crusty Republican conservative inclined to resolve all doubts in favor of the government. "Public employment is a privilege, not a right," Richardson explained. . "The Government is entitled to discharge any employee for reasons which seem sufficient to the Government, and without extending to such employee any hearing whatsoever." Truman justified the program by proclaiming that "subversive elements must be removed from the employ of government."

Truman's loyalty order also authorized the Attorney General to draw up a list of "totalitarian, fascist, communist or subversive" organizations, allegedly because "sympathetic association" with these groups would provide a criterion for assessing employee loyalty. Acting purely on the basis of secret determinations by the Justice Department, Attorney General Clark published a list of ninety-one such organizations in late 1947. Although the effectiveness of most groups was crippled by such public branding, they were without right of appeal or any procedural safeguards. Indeed, Clark's publication of the list, a procedure of no particular value to secret investigations of employee loyalty, was apparently designed for the specific purpose of stigmatizing radical organizations. "Our strategic objective," Clark told HUAC, "must be to isolate subversive movements in this country from effective interference with the body politic." The list was quickly adopted by state and local governments, defense-related industries, and schools to determine eligibility for employment and became a qualifying test for passports, occupancy of federally financed housing, and even tax exemptions. A variety of organizations and individuals were thus harassed or destroyed through administrative labeling by Washington officialdom—a procedure, as Clark noted, "a little bit contrary to our usual conception of democratic process."

Under pressure from the Loyalty Review Board, from Attorney General Clark, and from his successor, J. Howard McGrath, the loyalty program, originally restricted by a concern for civil liberties, rapidly expanded into a major assault on political freedom. It determined loyalty not on the basis of overt acts but through suspicion and doubts, frequently stemming from the employee's political beliefs and associations. The loyalty boards launched clandestine investigations, utilized secret informers, and established loose and unjust standards of evidence. Government employees were asked whether they entertained members of another race in their homes, how they felt about the draft, and what they thought of the Truman Doctrine. Justice Robert Jackson warned in 1948: "The Government is using its power as never before to pry into . . . lives and thoughts upon the slightest suspicion." Utilizing his executive authority, Truman broadened the basis for dismissal from proof of "disloyalty" to "reasonable doubt as to . . . loyalty." By December, 1952, some 6.6 million Americans had undergone a loyalty-security check. Of the more than 25,000 who received full FBI field investigations, 5,900 resigned from government service and 490 were dismissed, but not a single spy or saboteur was discovered. The price of this fantastic operation was a steady erosion of political liberty. Acheson later noted "how dangerous was the practice of secret evidence and secret informers, how alien to all our conceptions of justice and the rights of the citizen."

Throughout 1947, the Attorney General busied himself with the Anti-Communist Crusade. Shortly after assuming office, Clark set about deporting aliens with radical views. In February, 1947, he proudly announced that "we have deported 124 persons on the grounds of Communism." Following the Truman Doctrine address he intensified his efforts, and at the end of the year he reported hundreds of such cases in process. In the spring of 1947, Clark and FBI Director J. Edgar Hoover conceived the idea of a nationwide patriotic campaign to rally the American people. The centerpiece of this effort, a Freedom Train carrying memorabilia from the history of the United States, visited hundreds of cities, inspiring local "rededication" programs and patriotic ceremonies. On November 20, the Administration launched a "week of rededication" in the nation's capital, replete with rallies in which thousands of government employees sang "God Bless America" and took a "freedom pledge." And yet, despite the frantic efforts of a conservative Congress and Administration to outdo one another in purging the nation of "subversion," polls as late as October, 1947, found that most Americans opposed legislation barring Communist sympathizers from public office.

The Truman Doctrine and the loyalty program heightened liberal disillusionment with Truman and intensified the search for an alternative. In June, 1947, the national convention of the International Ladies Garment Workers Union called for "action leading to the ultimate organization of a third party." Still smarting from their wounds of the preceding year, the railway unions were voluble advocates of defeating Truman and of running an independent political campaign. A. Philip Randolph, president of the Brotherhood of Sleeping Car Porters, urged liberals to break free of the old party structures and to launch their own. The man most discussed that year as a third-party candidate, Henry Wallace, embarked on a speaking tour at home and abroad under the auspices of PCA and the *New Republic*. Wherever he went, the former Vice-President drew enormous crowds, which applauded fiercely as he lambasted the Truman Administration for reactionary foreign and domestic policies. Conservatives were furious. At a Cabinet meeting, Forrestal suggested the revocation of Wallace's passport. Yet Wallace emerged from his speaking tour as the spokesman for many liberals. PCA, the leading liberal organization in the country, which had grown by late 1947 to 50,000 dues-paying members in twenty-five states, considered Wallace its patron saint; he, in turn, raised more than half a million dollars for the group through his speaking tour. Wallace's popularity and PCA's growth enhanced prospects for a left-wing bolt from the Democratic Party in 1948. A Gallup Poll in June reported that 13 per cent of the electorate would vote for the candidate of "a new liberal political party" founded by Henry Wallace.

Not all liberals, however, approved of Wallace or of PCA. The Union for Democratic Action, a small liberal organization founded in 1941 by former Socialists, lionized Wallace during the war but drew away from him in the postwar years because of his sympathy for Russia. UDA's militant anti-Communism, evident in its formal exclusion of Communists from membership, initially won little favor among liberals, and the organization maintained only a faltering existence. In early January, 1947, more than 400 people—including Walter Reuther, Eleanor Roosevelt, Joseph Rauh, Marquis Childs, and David Dubinsky —met in Washington and drafted plans for its more influential successor, Americans for Democratic Action. ADA's statement of principles called for the expansion of New Deal programs, defense of civil liberties, support of the United Nations, and increasing the freedom and standard of living of people around the world. Unlike PCA, though, ADA declared: "We reject any association with Communists or sympathizers with Communism in the United States as completely as we reject any association with fascists or their sympathizers." Moreover, ADA, while critical of the Truman Administration, viewed its foreign policy in a kindlier light than did PCA. After a brief internal struggle, ADA endorsed the Truman Doctrine.

Liberals did not quite know how to deal with this competition for their allegiance. Freda Kirchway, editor of *The Nation,* took ADA to task for equating Communism with fascism and despaired of the division in liberal ranks. Helen Fuller of the *New Republic* wondered: "Why don't you folks get together?" Writing in *The Nation,* Robert Bendiner praised ADA as "something new in the history of American politics" and criticized PCA as "a traditional popular-front organization." Henry Wallace remained staunchly committed to his alliance with PCA. Asked what he thought about the participation of Communists in the organization, he replied: "If they want to help us out on some of these problems, why, God bless them, let them come along." By the end of 1947, ADA had made notable progress in rallying liberal sympathy, claiming the support of 25,000 members. Nevertheless, half the size of PCA and without a leader of Wallace's political stature, ADA remained in the shadow of its liberal rival.

The focal point of the war within liberal ranks, the American Communist Party, stood at a peak membership of perhaps 100,000 at the end of World War II. Its Popular Front policies and the wartime coincidence of U.S. and Communist aims had helped it to attain this modest degree of support, but the heightening Cold War and its own internal shifts quickly started it on the road to disintegration. On May 24, 1945, an article in the *Daily Worker* by the leader of the powerful French Communist Party, Jacques Duclos, condemned American Communist leader Earl Browder for a "notorious revision of Marxism." This touched off a crisis in the American party, leading to a purge of Browder and to the appointment of the more militant William Z. Foster to his post. And yet, although the Communist Party had formally veered leftward, its policies did not change quite as drastically as the leadership shift seemed to indicate. While far more critical than in the past of the U.S. government, the party continued to stress work within broader movements of liberals and labor and avoided explicitly Communist campaigns. Neither this strategy nor any other was to bear fruit, though, for, in the context of the Cold War, sizable segments of the liberal-labor community were determined to purge Communist influence from their ranks.

The most serious challenge to Communist power and influence emerged within organized labor. Because of their leading role in organizing CIO unions, many Communists had been elected to leadership posts and at the end of the war were said to control unions with an estimated one-fourth of the CIO's membership, among them the electrical workers; the transport workers; the longshoremen; the tobacco workers; the office workers; the seamen; the mine, mill, and smelter workers; and a large part of the auto workers. After the war, the Association of Catholic Trade Unionists began a drive against Communists in the CIO, but President Philip Murray, fearing a fratricidal war within the labor federation, sought to muffle the conflict. By mid-1946, though, Murray began to abandon his "neutral" stance. In November, he sponsored a resolution at the CIO convention declaring: "We resent and reject efforts of the Communist party or other political parties and their adherents to interfere in the affairs of the CIO. . . . We will not tolerate such interference." He explained that this "should not be misconstrued to be a repressive measure," and that the CIO would never engage in "diabolical pursuits." The CIO Left, in an attempt to placate its critics, voted for the resolution, which passed unanimously. Even more indicative of the trend that year was the election of Walter Reuther as president of the United Auto Workers. Reuther, a former Socialist, rallied anti-Communist forces in the union by demanding an end to "outside interference" and by promoting a more militant program than that of the established leadership supported by the Communists.

In 1947, the anti-Communist tide within the labor movement became irresistible. Joseph Curran, president of the National Maritime Union, who had cooperated closely with the Communists for more than a decade, turned savagely upon his former allies, purging them from leadership positions. Transport Workers Union president "Red Mike" Quill, breaking with the Communist Party, conducted a similar purge. Non-Communist unions smashed Communist enclaves within their ranks, while locals of Communist-inclined unions passed out of Communist control. In November, Reuther's faction made a virtually clean sweep of the UAW executive board, solidifying his power and enabling him to force out union officials who favored his opponents or who seemed to harbor Communist sympathies. Philip Murray, now the champion of the CIO's anti-Communist struggle, removed two high-level CIO officials for their left-wing connections—Lee Pressman, the CIO's general counsel, and Len DeCaux, editor of the *CIO News*. At the CIO's 1947 convention, the atmosphere grew particularly rancorous; delegates from the Steelworkers, raucous and surly, even beat up a Communist labor organizer.

Labor's growing anti-Communist militancy helped eliminate one of the major obstacles to the Truman Administration's attempt to gear the nation for a protracted Cold War struggle. In 1945, Truman had urged Congress to reorganize America's armed forces, and, with the passage of the National Security Act in July, 1947, he achieved this aim. The act replaced the separate administrations of the three military services with the Joint Chiefs of Staff, operating under a unified Department of Defense. It also created a National Security Council to advise the President and a Central Intelligence Agency to gather information relevant to national security. The American military enhanced its policy-making leverage through the participation of the Secretary of Defense in the deliberations of the National Security Council and through the appointment of Admiral Roscoe Hillenkoetter as the first director of the CIA. For Secretary of Defense, Truman named his bitterly anti-Communist Secretary of the Navy, James Forrestal. The Defense Department, the National Security Council, and the CIA rapidly became key elements in planning and implementing American foreign policy, much to the President's delight. "To me," he wrote in his *Memoirs,* "the passage of the National Security Act and its strengthening amendments represented one of the outstanding achievements of my administration."

During 1947, the Administration enjoyed its first glimmerings of success in Western Europe. Although the Moscow Conference of Foreign Ministers had been destroyed that March by the announcement of the

Truman Doctrine, the further deterioration of Soviet-American relations could hardly provide much surprise or disappointment to an Administration that had just coolly proclaimed the existence of an irreconcilable conflict. Far more important to Washington was the restoration of conservative rule in Europe at a time when the smashing 1945 victory of the Labour Party in Great Britain; the Marxist orientation of the Social Democrats in Germany; and the coalition governments of Socialists, Communists, and Catholics in France, Italy, Holland, and Belgium seemed to point the way toward modification or elimination of capitalist institutions. The immense popularity of the French and Italian Communist parties, as well as their loyal collaboration with conservative politicians in the postwar years, made them difficult to dislodge from office. Nevertheless, Cold War pressures and promises of economic assistance from the United States finally led to their ouster. On May 6, two days after Premier Ramadier expelled the Communist Party from the French government, French writer Raymond Aron revealed that "news of a vast 'lend-lease of peace' plan that America is about to produce has already touched off something of an ideological battle." On May 8, Acheson delivered a major address to the Mississippi Delta Council, promising Europe a massive American aid program. Several days later, Premier de Gasperi, attracted by the new program and grateful for recent American loans, removed the Communists from the Italian government.

Angered by this treatment, the Communist parties of both nations launched a campaign of electoral action and labor struggles. But confronted by Moscow's caution and Washington's hostility, they found that this strategy only further circumscribed their power. Since 1945, the AFL, in cooperation with the State Department, had sought to undermine the strength of the Communist-led labor federations of France and Italy. In 1947, the CIA assumed funding of the project. Working together, the AFL, the CIA, and anti-Communist labor leaders in France and Italy succeeded in using the 1947 labor upheavals to split the Communist-led labor federations, to break the strikes, and to establish competing labor organizations. "Thus began the secret subsidy of free trade unions," a top CIA official, Thomas W. Braden, revealed decades later. "Without that subsidy, postwar history might have gone very differently."

In Germany, American officials worked to head off economic innovations and to restore a unified nation. In 1946 and 1947, there seemed a good possibility that the British Labour Government would use its zonal occupation authority to nationalize basic industry, particularly the coal mines of the Ruhr. American policy-makers were, of course, implacably hostile. "We do not propose to endorse socialization in Germany under any circumstances," Forrestal confided in his diary in May, 1947. Much the same attitude was expressed by Secretary of State Marshall to the British. According to a memorandum of June 20 by Clayton, Marshall instructed him to tell British Foreign Minister Ernest Bevin that "we would not sit idly by while the British tried out any ideas which they had of experimenting with socialism in the coal mines." Eventually British plans were shelved after further talks with Washington. The German Social Democrats, anxious to honor their Marxist pledges, and the AFL, interested merely in averting a revival of Nazism, drew similar opposition from the American occupation commander when they pressed for nationalization. "Time is on our side," Lucius Clay wrote in 1947 during an exchange on "socialism" with Washington. "If we can . . . defer the issue while free enterprise continues to operate and economic improvement results, it may never become an issue before the German people." German recovery—economic and political—remained the *desideratum* for American officials. "We cannot revive a self-supporting western European economy without a healthy Germany playing its part as a producing and consuming unit," Harriman warned Truman in the late summer of 1947. This policy received a windfall later that year—not unrelated to the reshuffled governing coalition in France—when the French, previously committed to a position "between East and West" in German affairs, agreed to merge their zone with those of the British and the Americans and to support the establishment of an independent West German nation.

The Administration remained dissatisfied, however, with the scope of efforts to rebuild the former Axis powers and to restore the economy of Europe. In March, 1947, Forrestal sent a memo to Truman calling for a major economic program to revitalize Germany and Japan and to restore European stability before the "Russian poison" conquered Europe, "South America, and ourselves." Marshall agreed on the need for a large-scale aid program and, after the Moscow Foreign Ministers Conference, appointed a policy planning staff, under the direction of George Kennan, to draw it up. Around-the-clock conferences in May hammered out the details. Planners agreed that the program should bypass the new U.N. Economic Commission for Europe. "We must avoid getting into another UNRRA," Clayton warned. "The U.S. must run this show." On the other hand, outright exclusion of Eastern Europe and the Soviet Union would render the plan unacceptable to nations unwilling to commit themselves to an explicitly anti-Soviet venture. Kennan argued that the United States would have to invite Soviet participation, while at the same time setting conditions too onerous for the

Soviet Union and Eastern Europe to accept. The United States, he contended, should rig the aid program "in such a way that eastern European countries would either exclude themselves by unwillingness to accept the proposed conditions or agree to abandon the exclusive orientations of their economies." Both Kennan and the State Department's Russian expert, Charles Bohlen, assured Marshall that the Soviet Union would reject the plan. Thus, although the Secretary of State launched the program at the Harvard University commencement that June with the claim that it was "directed not against any country or doctrine," it was, in fact, clearly designed as a Cold War measure. The Truman Doctrine and the Marshall Plan, the President declared, "are two halves of the same walnut."

American policy-makers viewed the Marshall Plan on two levels, political and economic. Politically, they believed, the aid would cushion the European crisis and stave off social revolution. "Our deepest concern," Truman told Congress in a special address on the Marshall Plan in December, 1947, is that "if Europe fails to recover," the people of its nations might resort to Communism to ease their plight. "Such a turn of events would constitute a shattering blow to peace and stability in the world," and "might well compel us to modify our own economic system." Impressed by the fact that Europe had absorbed 42 per cent of American exports in 1946, U.S. policy-makers reasoned that, if the Continent went Communist, the impact upon the American economy would be catastrophic. Clayton warned the House Foreign Affairs Committee that, without American assistance to Europe, "conditions will quickly ensue there which will, in effect, bring about a substantial blackout of that market for our goods." This, in turn, would cause "such radical changes, I am afraid, in our economy, that it would be very difficult for a democratic, free-enterprise system to make it."

Moreover, even barring the advent of Communist governments, the hard-pressed European nations would need outside funding to enable them to absorb U.S. exports. "We had at the time," Acheson recalled, "a tremendous export surplus . . . but there was very little likelihood of the recipient nations being able to fill the gap." In late 1947, the Council of Economic Advisers reported to the President that, without a new U.S. foreign aid program, American exports would decline from $21 to $13 billion, causing a "drastic readjustment" in the nation's economy. Perhaps for this reason Harriman, who usually ridiculed the notion that American aid to Europe was necessary to ensure American prosperity, warned a Senate committee, when discussing the Marshall Plan, that "the decline of Europe would require far-reaching readjustments of agricultural and industrial production and distribution in this country." Truman outlined his own thinking in his December 19 message to Congress. "Considered in terms of our own economy, European recovery is essential." Europe was "an essential part of a world trading network. The failure to revive fully this vast trading system . . . would result in economic deterioration throughout the world." Thus, the Marshall Plan was premised at least partially upon the idea of shoring up the American economy by stabilizing Western European capitalism. In practice it would require European procurement of U.S. surplus commodities and would provide support for American private investment.

Driven by economic adversity, the British and French governments immediately indicated their desire for Marshall Plan assistance and began a series of preliminary meetings that June in Paris. To Washington's consternation, even the Russians seemed interested, and on June 26 Molotov arrived in the French capital accompanied by eighty-nine advisers. But the Russians, as State Department planners had predicted, rebelled against what they claimed was an attempt to control the economies of the Soviet Union and the Eastern European nations. Molotov stormed out of the conference within three days, contending that, under the Marshall Plan, Europe would be dominated by American corporations, Germany would secure hegemony in Western Europe, and Europe would be divided irrevocably into "two groups of states." The British and French, ignoring the Soviet walkout, now issued invitations to twenty-two other European nations to plan an integrated request for American aid. Although six Eastern European nations, under heavy pressure from the Russians, declined, sixteen Western European nations met and prepared a recovery plan calling for the spending of $28 billion over four years. U.S. officials balked at this figure; eventually, Truman presented a $17 billion European Recovery Program to Congress. American advisers also demanded, and received, European guarantees of fiscal stability, lowered trade barriers, and an ongoing coordinating organization. But of the sixteen nations at Paris, only the Dutch sustained the American position that Germany should participate in the program. The Americans, however, remained adamantly committed to German inclusion. By early 1948, the Western European nations had reluctantly accepted it, and the United States was well on the way to attaining its goal of a restored capitalist trading bloc in Western Europe.

Molotov's walkout from the Marshall Plan conference in June heralded the beginning of a Soviet crackdown across Eastern Europe. To be sure, the Russians had intervened directly in Poland and Rumania in 1945. But they did not stifle the independence of Bulgaria and Hungary until 1947, and they did not act in Czechoslovakia and

Yugoslavia until 1948. Throughout July and August, 1947, in response to the Marshall Plan in the West, the Soviet Union signed a series of trade agreements with the nations of Eastern Europe, bolstering its economic hegemony. In Hungary, the Russians purged dissident elements, held fraudulent elections, and destroyed all anti-Communist opposition. That November, Moscow launched a successor to the Comintern, the Cominform, which took a position of implacable opposition to U.S. foreign policy ventures. "The Truman-Marshall plan," it declared, "is only a constituent part, the European section, of the general plan of world expansionist policy carried on by the United States." By late 1947, the "iron curtain" had finally begun to fall across the European continent, dividing it into East and West.

The entrenchment of Soviet power in Eastern Europe, coming after years of Cold War pronouncements by the Administration, completed the process of altering public opinion on world affairs. In late 1945, according to the National Opinion Research Center, only 32 per cent of the public expected another full-scale war within the next quarter-century; by late 1947 this figure had risen to 63 per cent. Americans clearly believed that they had a new and insatiable enemy A Gallup poll in October, 1947, reported that 76 per cent of the nation thought Russia was "out to rule the world." That Truman shared these fears remains dubious, but he surely understood that they served the valuable function of garnering popular support for the American military and diplomatic offensive.

And the Administration needed all the popular support it could muster, for by 1947 it was locked in a fierce partisan struggle with the Republican 80th Congress. While approving, in general, Truman's foreign policy initiatives, Republican legislators seemed determined to ignore his domestic proposals and to move in a reactionary direction. The undisputed leader of the new Senate, Robert Taft, marshaled his forces for an all-out assault. The new chairman of the House Appropriations Committee, John Taber, vowed to apply a "meat-axe to government frills." Interpreting their election victory in 1946 as a mandate to demolish the New Deal, Congressional Republicans passed a regressive tax bill, cut farm appropriations, and rejected measures for public housing, price controls, expanded social security, aid to education, a permanent Fair Employment Practices Committee, and a ban on the poll tax. Their action on immigration legislation reflected a distinct bias against people from Southern and Eastern Europe. Finally, the Republican Congress sent a Constitutional amendment to the states limiting future Presidents to two terms in office.

The most controversial legislation passed by the 80th Congress was the Taft-Hartley Act. Designed to deprive labor of many of its gains under the Wagner Act, the bill granted the President the right to obtain injunctions forcing strikers to return to work for a sixty-day "cooling-off" period; banned contributions from union dues to political candidates; gave states the power to pass "right-to-work" laws, outlawing the closed shop; and required union officials to sign non-Communist affidavits or forfeit use of National Labor Relations Board procedures. Riding on a crest of antilabor sentiment, the House passed the Taft-Hartley Act on June 4, 1947, by a vote of 320 to 79, and the Senate on June 6 by 57 to 17. Labor immediately brought enormous pressure to bear on Truman to veto what it vehemently denounced as the "Slave Labor Act." On June 11, 60,000 CIO workers paraded down New York City's Eighth Avenue in protest. The UAW executive board telegraphed Truman that the bill would further concentrate the control of American life "in the hands of the small number of monopolistic corporations." Philip Murray told the President that Taft-Hartley would "engulf not only the labor movement but the entire nation in tragic consequences." Even the most conservative labor officials were infuriated by the legislation. Supporters of Taft-Hartley, President William Green angrily told the AFL's 1947 convention, "want to destroy the one labor agency that stands as a defender of the free enterprise system in the United States." The largest volume of mail on any issue up to that time flooded the White House. Impressed by this groundswell, Truman vetoed the bill. On June 23, Congress responded by passing the Taft-Hartley Act over his veto.

From the viewpoint of Truman's advisers, one of the favorable aspects of the Republican assault on New Deal legislation was its tendency to draw liberal Democrats back into the fold. Already labor, grateful for Truman's veto of Taft-Hartley, had shown signs of reviving Democratic loyalties. Anxious to improve Truman's chance for re-election in 1948, Clark Clifford presented the President in November, 1947, with a forty-page memorandum on "political conduct for the administration." Clifford's basic assumption was that the New Deal coalition would carry Truman to victory if he made special efforts to attract the support of Northern big city labor and minority group voters. To ignore Wallace's appeal to these groups and the threat it posed to Truman's re-election would be "extremely unrealistic," he wrote, and every effort should be made to persuade Wallace not to head a third-party ticket. If Wallace *did* run, Truman should work assiduously "to identify him and isolate him in the public mind with the Communists." A challenge from Wallace would also necessitate a strong stand by Truman on civil rights to keep blacks in the Democratic Party, as well as favorable action on the Palestine issue to hold Jewish voters.

Clifford's memorandum reached Truman's desk none too soon, for on December 29 Henry Wallace launched his third-party campaign for the Presidency. Flushed with the success of his speaking tour, angered by the Administration's Cold War policies, and encouraged by the leaders of PCA, the former Vice-President announced that he had assembled a "Gideon's Army, small in number, powerful in conviction," with which he would begin a political crusade against war and injustice. "The people's peace," he promised, "will usher in the century of the common man." A political realist despite his visionary inclinations, Wallace held no expectations of victory, but he did hope to make an impressive showing. His principal organizational base, PCA, while lacking practicing politicians and union leaders, claimed a respectable 100,000 members in 750 communities at the beginning of 1948. Wallace could also take heart at the stunning upset victory for his adherents in the Bronx, New York, in February, 1948. In a special election to fill a vacated Congressional seat, Leo Isacson, the American Labor Party candidate, overwhelmed his favored Democratic rival by drawing 56 per cent of the vote. "Mr. Isacson never had been considered to have a chance to win," a *New York Times* reporter observed, but the extraordinary size of his vote could be "regarded as an indication of the potential Wallace strength in November."

Yet Wallace's ability to attract a sizable protest vote waned in early 1948 as liberals and other anti-Administration forces began to shy away from the third-party movement. A. F. Whitney came out for Truman's re-election, claiming that his Taft-Hartley veto had "vindicated him in the eyes of labor." That same month, the CIO executive board passed a resolution declaring that the formation of a third party was "politically unwise." Two months later, the CIO's national leadership threatened unions supporting Wallace with expulsion. Even Socialist Norman Thomas, long an independent candidate for President, decisively rejected the Wallace venture. Reversing its previous call for an insurgent campaign, *The Nation* contended that the new party, "through no wish of its leader, derives its only important organizational support from the Communists and their sympathizers." Indeed, many of those opposed to the Wallace movement argued that, while Wallace and most of his adherents were not Communists, the new party was organized and controlled by a Communist minority. Rexford G. Tugwell, one of the few prominent New Dealers to support Wallace wholeheartedly, maintained that the influence of Communists in the third-party movement grew in direct proportion to the unwillingness of non-Communists to participate in it, but this argument failed to halt the flight from the Wallace ranks.

Pleased by this turn of events, which coincided neatly with the Clifford strategy, Truman did his best to further Wallace's pariah status. On March 17, the President declared: "I do not want and will not accept the political support of Henry Wallace and his Communists. . . . These are days of high prices for anything, but any price for Wallace and his Communists is too much for me."

Truman also sought to undermine the Wallace effort by demonstrating a sudden interest in civil rights. Shortly after entering the White House, when asked what he planned to do in the field of racial equality, Truman referred the interrogator to his "Senate record." This policy of evasion continued in later years, and he gave only half-hearted and inconsistent support to liberal measures for the creation of a permanent FEPC and for the abolition of the poll tax. Under mounting pressure from the NAACP, liberals, and other civil rights proponents, however, Truman announced the appointment of a Committee on Civil Rights on December 5, 1946. In October, 1947, the committee issued an unexpectedly strong report, calling for enhanced civil rights efforts in the executive branch, as well as stiff federal legislation against racial segregation and discrimination on the national and local levels. The strength of the committee's recommendations disturbed Truman, and for some time he avoided comment on the report, claiming that he had not read it. By early 1948, however, frightened by polls showing Wallace drawing 10 per cent of the vote, including large numbers of Democratic-leaning blacks and liberals, Truman was compelled to act. On February 2 he asked Congress to enact most of the committee's recommendations. Fully aware that Congress was unlikely to adopt such sweeping reforms, he was nonetheless determined to receive credit in the Northern big cities for a strong civil rights stand. At the same time, he refused to use his power as chief executive to abolish segregation in the armed forces or in federal employment. Like Lincoln issuing the Emancipation Proclamation, Truman made bold proposals in areas where he could not assert control and acted timidly in those areas where he could.

As a Border State politician with close ties to his party's segregationist wing, Truman had no intention of unduly alienating Southern support. Consequently, having drawn the praise of black leaders for his civil rights foray, he soon backed away from it, attempting to conciliate angry Southerners. "The strategy," said a Truman aide, "was to start with a bold measure and then temporize to pick up the right-wing forces. Simply stated, backtrack after the bang." Playing this strategy to the letter, he avoided further support of his committee's demands and announced that, because of his sense of Congressional prerogatives, he did not plan to propose a civil rights bill. At the Democratic National Convention in the summer of 1948, he worked to soothe segregationist fears by encouraging a tepid platform pledge on civil rights. But in fact Truman had miscalculated, angering Southern politicians more than he had expected. Senator James Eastland of Mississippi charged that the President was trying "to mongrelize the South," while Congressman Ed Gossett of Texas accused him of "kissing the feet of the minorities." On May 10 a massive conference of "States Rights Democrats" met in Jackson, Mississippi, to plan strategy. Although the convention proved more cautious than some of its extremist sponsors had hoped, it did resolve to oppose Truman's renomination.

Truman also found, to his regret, that retaining Jewish votes and funding in the 1948 campaign would necessitate further sacrifices. The President and his foreign policy advisers looked askance at Jewish claims to Palestine, primarily because of their desire to remain on good terms with the oil-rich Arab kingdoms. The State Department's "specialists on the Near East were, almost without exception, unfriendly to the idea of a Jewish state," recalled Truman, convinced that they could move into the British "position in the area by cultivating the Arabs." Moreover, "there were some among them who were also inclined to be anti-Semitic." In contrast to Russia, which enthusiastically endorsed Zionist demands, Truman and the State Department consistently sought some practicable alternative to the partition of Palestine—but failed to discover one. Thus, the President found himself in a serious dilemma in 1948, when the American Jewish community and his political advisers encouraged him to respond favorably to the Zionist position. "I do not think I ever had as much pressure and propaganda aimed at the White House as in this instance," Truman wrote in his *Memoirs*. In the end, the President reluctantly sacrificed one of his overseas goals for domestic political gains; without consulting the State Department, he recognized the new state of Israel only eleven minutes after it declared itself a nation.

American policy toward other areas of the underdeveloped world, however, remained relatively free of domestic opposition and therefore proceeded smoothly. The United States succeeded in bringing the Japanese-mandated islands under its own jurisdiction and gave its tacit approval to the continuation of European colonialism in most of Asia and Africa. At the prodding of Secretary of State Marshall in the summer of 1947, the Rio Conference drew up a collective military defense treaty for Latin America—the first such regional military arrangement created under the United Nations charter. In March, 1948, the Bogotá Conference formalized inter-American political and economic ties through the formation of the Organization of American States and the Economic Agreement of Bogota. At the conference, Marshall stressed the "role which private capital might play in the economic development of Latin America" as the "dominant theme" of U.S. policy. Washington sought guarantees against expropriation of foreign investments, but seven Latin American delegations attached specific reservations to their ratification agreements on this point. Latin American nations also secured sections prohibiting political, military, or economic intervention in the affairs of any state "on any grounds whatever." Nevertheless, U.S. policy-makers outfoxed them by pushing through a special resolution condemning "international communism" as "incompatible with the concept of American freedom," thus laying the groundwork for subsequent U.S. invasions. "We fought the Communist threat everywhere and in many ways," Truman later recalled. That underdeveloped nations might find other issues more pressing than the threat of Communism or the security of American investments seems not to have deterred Washington officialdom.

In early 1948 American eyes remained riveted on Europe, where the situation looked threatening indeed. Continuing its drive for hegemony in Eastern Europe, the Soviet Union forced the situation in Czechoslovakia to a crisis. In late February, when non-Communists resigned from the Czech cabinet, Czech Communists availed themselves of the opportunity to install a one-party regime and take control of the country. The Czech coup, snuffing out the most democratic and progressive government in Eastern Europe, irreparably alienated Western opinion. International tensions dramatically heightened. On March 5, Clay sent Washington a telegram from Germany warning that "war . . . may come with dramatic suddenness." On March 16, France, Great Britain, and the Benelux countries formed the Brussels Union, pledging mutual defense. The following day, Truman went before Congress to call for aid to the signers of the Brussels Treaty. The Soviet Union's "ruthless course of action, and the design to extend it to the remaining free nations of Europe . . . have brought about the critical situation in Europe today," he declared. Averell Harriman warned that the Soviet Union represented "a greater menace than Hitler," while top American military officials publicly discussed an atomic war with Russia.

And yet key American policy-makers believed that Russia did not intend to overrun the Western world and that Moscow's ambitions were more narrowly confined to reducing Eastern Europe to satellite status. George Kennan later acknowledged: "The image of a Stalinist Russia poised and yearning to attack the West, and deterred only by our possession of atomic weapons, was largely a fiction of the Western imagination, against which some of us who were familiar with Russian matters

tried in vain . . . to make our voices heard." Soviet weakness, even in
Eastern European affairs, was dramatically illustrated that spring, when
Tito successfully resisted the Soviet crackdown, purged Stalinist ele-
ments in Yugoslavia, and signed a trade pact with the West. The worst
vengeance Stalin found himself capable of wreaking upon the rebel
Yugoslav leader was to expel him from the Cominform.

Despite the hollowness of the war scare in early 1948, it did help to
frighten Congress into passing the Marshall Plan. Although endorsed by
a broad range of organizations running from business groups, the Veterans of Foreign Wars, and the American Farm Bureau Federation to the
AFL, the CIO, and ADA, the European Recovery Program had come
under attack by extreme conservatives in Congress as an "international
WPA." Taft himself claimed that it would promote the drift toward socialism in Europe. A small number of liberals and Wallace supporters
also found the measure objectionable. Congressman George Sadowski
of Michigan, charging that the Marshall Plan had been hatched by
"bankers, monopolists, cartelists and militarists," argued that "the whole
recovery program should be worked out through the U.N." Truman
reacted in March by warning of a "growing menace . . . to the very
survival of freedom." "There is a notion held by some in Washington,"
wrote Walter Lippmann, "that the only way to win the support of Congress for the Marshall Plan is to frighten it." Under the pressure of the
Cold War crisis, the House Foreign Affairs Committee finally reported
out the bill on March 19, calling for swift action by Congress to help
"reverse the trend of communism in Europe." On April 2, Congress
passed the Marshall Plan, appropriating $5.4 billion for the first year,
including $463 million for the government of Chiang Kai-shek.

In the last days of debate on the Marshall Plan, Congress and the
Administration grew increasingly apprehensive at the prospect of a left-
wing victory in the approaching Italian elections. The People's Bloc, a
coalition of the Italian Socialists and Communists, was given an even
chance of defeating the State Department's conservative favorites, the
ruling Christian Democrats. Roused to action, Washington supported
Italy's claims to Trieste, returned Italian gold held by the Nazis, renounced claims on Italian naval reparations, anchored its warships off
Italian ports, and provided massive financial aid to the Christian Democrats. Secretary of State Marshall warned that nations voting Communism into power would not be eligible for the European Recovery Program, while the State Department announced that it would deny visas
to Italians known to have voted Communist. Tens of thousands of Ital-
ian-Americans sent form letters to Italy urging relatives to reject the
People's Bloc "in the name of Mary and the Saints." In the balloting,

the Christian Democrats won a resounding victory, with 48 per cent of the vote, while the People's Bloc was held to but 31 per cent. Thereafter, despite strike waves and governmental instability, the Christian Democrats remained firmly in power, bolstered by millions of dollars every year in illegal U.S. corporate contributions and secret CIA subsidies.

America's success in Western Europe and Tito's defection in the East delivered blows to Soviet foreign policy in 1948 surpassed only by the restoration of Germany. Earmarked for 28 per cent of the first year's aid under the European Recovery Program, West Germany became the largest recipient of economic assistance in Europe. Moreover, by mid-1948, plans for a merger of the American, British, and French zones into a new West German nation were virtually complete. On June 23, however, when General Clay introduced the new West German currency into West Berlin, Stalin balked and demanded that the Western powers retire from the city. He contended that the West had abandoned the idea of German reunification and that Berlin, therefore, had no future function as the capital of all Germany. A Soviet blockade of all traffic to the city began in earnest the following day. Truman responded decisively: "We are going to stay, period." Clay wanted the United States to shoot its way through the blockade, but cooler heads prevailed, organizing an airlift of supplies for the Western zones of the city which eventually reached 13,000 tons a day. After a confrontation lasting almost a year, the Russians yielded and removed the blockade. Once again, Moscow had suffered a humiliating defeat. Only three years after its war against the German armies that had devastated its lands, the Soviet Union watched helplessly as the bulk of the German nation was revived and integrated into an anti-Soviet bloc.

Despite the support that his Cold War policies had begun to generate, Truman remained personally unpopular, with little chance, it seemed, for re-election. Polls in the spring of 1948 found public approval of his performance as President hovering at a miserable 36 per cent. At the beginning of the year, significant elements of organized labor still drew back from the Democrats, and especially from Truman. In January, Walter Reuther denounced both Republicans and Democrats for "playing fast and loose with the American people," describing Truman as "hopelessly inadequate." ADA, which regarded the President as a cynical politician lacking liberal convictions, worked furiously to prevent his renomination. The Chicago chapter, in an open letter to Truman, declared that "only 4 per cent of our members want to see you as a candidate for re-election." ADA rallied instead behind the candidacy of General Eisenhower, whom a Roper poll in June had revealed as the top choice for President of voters in both major parties. By supporting Eisenhower, ADA entered a strange alliance with liberals like James and Elliott Roosevelt, Philip Murray, and Senator Claude Pepper, urban bosses like Mayors William O'Dwyer of New York and Frank Hague of Jersey City, and conservatives like Senators Harry Byrd of Virginia and Richard Russell of Georgia. Everyone, it seemed, deplored the prospect of Truman's renomination and liked Ike. In past years even Truman had tried to draft the popular general for the Democratic nomination. Eisenhower, however, was not interested, proclaiming that the "subordination of the military to civil power will best be sustained . . . when lifelong professional soldiers . . . abstain from seeking high political office." In the opinion of most observers, that left the Democrats nowhere or, more specifically, with Truman.

The Democratic National Convention opened that July in an atmosphere of gloom. Lacking any realistic alternative, the delegates nominated Truman and his chosen running-mate, Alben Barkley of Kentucky, the aging Senate Democratic leader. Truman briefly revived the spirits of the assemblage by delivering a fiery acceptance speech, promising a special session of the 80th Congress to call the Republicans' bluff and a fighting campaign to win the election. The prospects for his election, however, seemed reduced still further by a bitter conflict over the party platform. Truman's attempt to placate Southern whites by adopting a weak civil rights plank had been supported by the platform committee, but ADA led a revolt on the convention floor which galvanized a coalition of liberals, big city bosses, and blacks. Eventually the delegates passed ADA's far stronger civil rights plank by a vote of 651½ to 581½. Infuriated by the proceedings, Southerners bolted the convention.

Democratic fortunes had sunk to a new low. On July 17, delegates from thirteen Southern states convened in Birmingham, Alabama, and nominated a States Rights Party ticket of Governor Strom Thurmond of South Carolina for President and Governor Fielding Wright of Mississippi for Vice-President. Later that month the Wallace forces, having formally broken with the Democrats, met in convention as the Progressive Party and nominated Wallace for President and Democratic Senator Glen Taylor of Idaho as his running mate. With both its right and left wings engaged in independent campaigns, the Democratic Party entered the election race in 1948 as a disspirited rump organization, led by the unpopular Truman.

Enough of this situation had become manifest by June to convince the Republican National Convention that it had a winner. Rejecting Senator Taft, whose grating directness rendered him unacceptable as a Presidential candidate, the convention turned to the more mellifluous Thomas E. Dewey, Governor of New York. Even his detractors observed, "You have to know Dewey well to really dislike him." For his running mate, the delegates chose the popular Governor of California, Earl Warren. The platform, like the candidates, was moderate, calling for an attack on inflation, monopoly, and government extravagance. It supported federal assistance to housing, farm payments, higher Social Security allowances, the abolition of the poll tax, and the establishment of FEPC. Like the Democratic platform, it gave unstinting allegiance to the Cold War. Possessing an inoffensive ticket and program, and with the Democratic Party in shambles, the Republican warriors strode forth to battle, confident of their first Presidential election victory in twenty years. "Truman," said Representative Claire Boothe Luce, "is a gone goose."

If so, Truman did not acknowledge it but instead embarked upon a vigorous whistle-stop campaign of 31,000 miles, delivering hundreds of speeches to an estimated 6 million people. Relying heavily upon the Clifford strategy of appealing to an urban lower class and minority group constituency, Truman dusted off his party's proletarian credentials. The "gluttons of privilege" in the Republican Party were men "with a calculating machine where the heart ought to be," he told a massive Labor Day gathering in Detroit. If Republicans came to power, he warned another crowd, America would become "an economic colony of Wall Street." Truman worked particularly hard at pointing up the reactionary record of the GOP 80th Congress, using it, as Clifford had urged in June, to "keep the steady glare of publicity on the Neanderthal men of the Republican party, who will embarrass Dewey and Warren." Congress, the President charged, had passed a labor bill that could "enslave totally the workingman," had "stuck a pitchfork in the backs of farmers," and had passed an "anti-Semitic, anti-Catholic" immigration law. With Wallace and Dewey' cutting into traditional Democratic strength among blacks, and with the Deep South lost irrevocably to the Dixiecrats, Truman seized upon the civil rights issue. Using his executive power, he ordered the desegregation of the armed forces. He became the first major-party candidate for President to campaign in Harlem, pledging his support for civil rights legislation. Truman's attempt to rally the New Deal constituency was complemented by a tremendous effort launched by organized labor to defeat Congressional supporters of the Taft-Hartley Act and to re-elect the President who had vetoed it. This unprecedented effort, joined with Truman's biting assault upon wealth and special privilege, gave the Democratic campaign a blatant class appeal which rivaled any of Roosevelt's.

Truman's campaign contrasted sharply with the colorless one waged by the Republicans. As Dewey's "Victory Special" glided majestically across the nation, the GOP candidate exuded a smug self-confidence. The country had been very patient, he explained, with "the Administration which happens to be in power at the moment." With his crisp executive manner and rich, reassuring baritone, Dewey delivered states-manlike and evasive speeches, leaving the role of a nasty, partisan scrap-per to Truman. Observers agreed that he waged a high-minded, efficient, and boring campaign. "Dewey doesn't seem to walk," noted journalist Richard Rovere, "he coasts out like a man who has been mounted on casters and given a tremendous shove from behind." Yet, bolstered by polls showing him an easy victor over Truman, Dewey saw no reason to alter his style.

As Truman lashed out at special privilege and Dewey made plans for his inauguration, Henry Wallace waged an increasingly lonely cam-paign. The CIO's condemnation of a third party had reduced the Pro-gressive Party's base within organized labor to ten left-wing CIO unions. Threatened with expulsion by the CIO and torn apart by the Com-munist issue, they proved of minimal assistance. Most liberals followed the lead of ADA, which grudgingly endorsed Truman and excoriated the newly formed Progressive Party as "a dangerous adventure under-taken by cynical men in whose hands Henry A. Wallace has placed his political fortunes." ADA produced pamphlets that decried Communist influence in the Progressive Party, denounced it in radio broadcasts as a "totalitarian group," and placed advertisements in major news-papers listing its important donors and their affiliations with organiza-tions on the Attorney General's list. Truman and the Democratic Na-tional Committee also hammered away at the theme of Communist domination of the Progressive venture, while simultaneously stressing the Administration's internal security activities and its anti-Communist foreign policy. Indeed, Truman even charged that the Communist Party had been "helped" by the Republicans, who, he claimed, had "impeded . . . our efforts to cope with Communism in this country."

By the summer of 1948 the repeated attacks upon the Progressive Party had proved successful. Polls found that a majority of Americans believed it was controlled by Communists. Although endorsed by many well-known artists, writers, and intellectuals, including Albert Einstein, Frank Lloyd Wright, and Thomas Mann, its constituency steadily dis-integrated. By June the pollsters reported a drop in the Progressive ap-peal to 6 per cent of the population; by October, to 4 per cent. Wallace found it difficult to obtain meeting places, and many of his supporters were harassed by their employers. Violent attacks on Progressive Party rallies, beginning in April, continued throughout the campaign.

In the November election, Truman startled the nation's political ex-perts by winning an upset victory, defeating Dewey by a margin of more than 2 million votes and holding Wallace and Thurmond to slightly over 1 million each. The Democrats swept back into control of

Congress, gaining nine seats in the Senate and seventy-five in the House. "I just don't know what happened," George Gallup remarked. In fact, though, the cause was plain: The New Deal coalition had been resurrected. In 1948 Truman carried the thirteen largest industrial cities in the nation, some by greater margins than Roosevelt in 1944. Wallace undoubtedly cost Truman a number of Northern industrial states, notably New York, where he drew half a million votes, but elsewhere the Progressive revolt actually helped the Democratic Party by removing its "Red" taint and making it acceptable to many Catholics. Thurmond's bolt on the Democratic Party's right wing engendered a similar phenomenon: It took the Deep South out of the Democratic column, but it solidified support for the Democrats among Northern blacks and liberals. Truman's focus on domestic issues also pleased farm voters, anxious to preserve New Deal gains, and many German- and Irish-Americans, who had defected from the Democrats in 1940 and 1944 over foreign policy issues. At the heart of Truman's victory lay massive support from the nation's blue-collar workers, convinced by the Taft-Hartley Act that only the Democrats would defend the workingman. A total of 115 Senators and Representatives who had voted for Taft-Hartley were not returned to office. The Democratic Congressional vote, heavily dependent upon labor support, considerably exceeded Truman's, and its coattail effect did much to re-elect the President. Asked to explain his victory, Truman said simply: "Labor did it."

The meaning of the election was less clear. Most liberals exulted, convinced that the Democratic victory had opened the way to a new burst of reform legislation modeled on the New Deal. A Democratic President, facing enormous odds, had been re-elected after a ripsnorting liberal campaign. A reactionary Republican Congress had been repudiated by the voters, who had returned control of that body to the Democrats. A whole new crop of attractive liberal politicians had suddenly emerged. In the Senate: Paul Douglas of Illinois, Hubert Humphrey of Minnesota, and Estes Kefauver of Tennessee. In the statehouses: Chester Bowles of Connecticut, Adlai Stevenson of Illinois, and G. Mennen Williams of Michigan. The *New Republic* grew rhapsodic: "Reaction is repudiated. The New Deal is again empowered to carry forward the promise of American life. Nothing less than a new era of reform has been demanded by America." Most liberals failed to see that the 1948 election represented, in many respects, a disaster for the cause of social justice. The New Deal coalition, to be sure, had held together, but for what end? By giving a vote of confidence to the Truman Administration, the election had sealed the nation's commitment to the Anti-Communist Crusade at home and the Cold War abroad. As liberals would soon find, it was a program less conducive to social reform than to the growth of corporate privilege.

3

The Fair Deal at Home and Abroad, 1949-52

> We can hardly send milk to babies abroad without explaining that this is an important action in our cold war with Russian communism.
>
> WALTER LIPPMANN, June, 1950

IN HIS 1949 INAUGURAL ADDRESS, Truman proclaimed his support for what he termed a "Fair Deal." Unlike the New Deal, the Fair Deal encompassed civil rights legislation, but otherwise it remained within the confines of traditional Roosevelt liberalism. Truman explained that the Fair Deal was basically "an extension of the New Deal" but "without the gyrations of certain early New Dealers"—those whom the President taunted as "crackpot professional liberals." It included national health insurance, public housing, an increase in the minimum wage, extension of Social Security, civil rights legislation, public power, aid to education, and repeal of the Taft-Hartley Act. Overjoyed by the announcement of the Fair Deal, labor and the liberals looked forward to its passage by a Congress which, after 1948, they believed to be dominated by an urban liberal majority.

They were soon disappointed. Congress was, in fact, controlled by a bipartisan conservative coalition; Northern Republicans blocked civil rights legislation in exchange for Southern Democratic opposition to everything else on the Fair Deal agenda. In the House, liberals won their fight for a twenty-one-day rule to rescue bills from the conservative House Rules Committee but found themselves otherwise outmaneuvered by Dixiecratic committee chairmen and by the increasingly conservative Speaker, Sam Rayburn of Texas. In the Senate, ruled by Democrat Richard Russell of Georgia and Republican Taft of Ohio, the situation confronting liberals was even worse. They received a double-barreled rebuff in the opening days when their fight to modify the cloture rule was defeated and when Democrats gave the post of

Majority Leader, at Russell's direction, to Senator Scott Lucas of Illinois, a relatively conservative Democrat who had voted for the Taft-Hartley Act and battled against a strong civil rights plank at the Democratic National Convention. Despite the Democratic Party's paper majority, such obstacles as the seniority system, rural overrepresentation, and the one-party South all served to block liberal legislation. By the spring of 1949, the Fair Deal was bottled up tight in committee. An ADA official told that organization's April convention: "Any illusion that the liberal Democrats dominate either the House or the Senate has been completely blasted."

With the Fair Deal in trouble, Truman and Democratic Congressional leaders sounded the call for retreat. In May, after a conference with the President, Lucas announced that most of the Fair Deal program would be dropped, leaving only three "must" items on the agenda: repeal of the Taft-Hartley Act, ratification of the North Atlantic Treaty, and renewal of the Reciprocal Trade Agreements Act. Liberals were stunned. ADA called the Lucas-Truman agreement a "flat betrayal of the Democratic platform," while its journal noted the group's "profound shock this week when the Democratic Congressional leaders, with a silent nod from the Chief Executive, meekly declared that the Fair Deal could wait."

The Fair Deal, then, ended almost before it began. Congress rejected repeal of the Taft-Hartley Act and most other legislative proposals made by the Administration. It did increase the minimum wage but reduced coverage by about a million Americans. Social Security coverage was extended, and the benefits were significantly raised, although even then the maximum income for a retired couple left them more than a third below the Bureau of Labor Statistics' "maintenance" standard. The most significant Fair Deal accomplishment was in the field of housing. At a time when the nation needed an estimated 12 million new units to replace inadequate housing, the Wagner-Taft Housing Act of 1949 authorized construction of 810,000 units of low-income housing in the following six years—of which only 60,000 were actually built. Of seven liberal measures termed "must" legislation by ADA, few came to a vote in the 81st Congress, and none passed.

After 1950, when midterm election losses cut Democratic majorities in both houses and the Korean War absorbed the attention of the Administration, Truman and Congress shelved the balance of the Fair Deal. The President's State of the Union address, devoted almost exclusively to foreign policy and military issues, barely mentioned social-welfare programs. Truman told a press conference that, while he still supported the Fair Deal, "first things come first, and our defense programs must have top priority." Congress obligingly scrapped its earlier reform of the Rules Committee, increased military spending, and ignored Fair Deal measures. It passed a number of regressive laws, most notably the McCarran-Walter Immigration Act, which retained the national-origins quota system, thus effectively excluding from America all but a small number of "old stock" immigrants. Truman vetoed the bill, but Congress overrode his veto. Surveying the ruins, ADA announced gloomily in 1952 that, "while not matching the mediocrity of the Republican-dominated 80th Congress," the Democratic 82d "came very near to it." Southern conservatives, in firm command of proceedings, drew closer to the President, and he, in turn, used his administrative power to safeguard their interests.

The abandonment of liberal domestic goals by Congress and by the Administration was nowhere more evident than in the field of racial equality. The civil rights legislation promised in the 1948 campaign fell easily before the bipartisan conservative coalition in Congress. When an emasculated FEPC bill finally passed the House in 1950, it died of a filibuster in the Senate. Majority Leader Lucas waged such a half-hearted campaign to remove the Southern roadblock that the *New York Times* called it a "rocking-chair affair," and A. Philip Randolph bitterly complained of "transparent hypocritical tactics." In the 82d Congress, Congressional committees ceased altogether to report out civil rights measures. Liberal supporters of civil rights legislation, convinced that racial injustice was the price of liberal advance on other fronts, swallowed their principles and voted for segregated housing programs.

Checkmated in the legislative arena, the Truman Administration acted indecisively on civil rights even in the executive branch, where it possessed full authority. The results of Truman's Executive Order to desegregate the armed forces, dramatically issued in the heat of the 1948 campaign, were slow to appear. Many army units remained segregated at the time of the Korean War, and racial integration among American troops in Europe did not begin until April, 1952. Federal agencies continued to condone and even support racial segregation. Although the Supreme Court had held racially restrictive housing covenants unenforceable since November, 1948, the Federal Housing Administration accepted and encouraged them thereafter, thus stimulating this racist practice in both the public and private housing markets. Not until 1950 did the FHA cease to insure properties subject to racial covenants—and then only on new applications. As a result, by 1952 only 50,000 of the approximately 3 million dwellings insured by the FHA were open to nonwhites.

Turning a deaf ear to the plight of America's oppressed minorities, Congress concentrated instead upon satisfying the needs of the thriving oil and natural gas industries. In 1949, when the chairman of the Federal Power Commission, Leland Olds, came up for reappointment after ten years of outstanding public service, powerful corporate interests worked vigorously to defeat him, infuriated by his dedication to the rights of consumers and by his opposition to legislation removing natural gas from FPC regulation. Texas oilman Hugh Roy Cullen urged twenty-two "friends" in the Senate to block the reappointment of Olds, who, he charged, "would establish 'social responsibility' in place of the profit motive. This is conclusive proof that he does not believe in our form of government." Eager to strengthen his ties to the burgeoning oil and gas industry, Senator Lyndon Johnson of Texas chaired the extraordinarily vituperative hearings on Olds, quoting from the FPC chairman's writings of twenty years earlier to prove that he was close to "those who proposed the Marxian answer." Senator Edwin Johnson of Colorado assailed Olds as a "tyrannical, mischievous, egotistical chameleon whose predominant color is pink." During the closing hours of Senate debate, George Aiken of Vermont charged angrily that "certain public utilities of the country are out to destroy a man for performing his duty." But his colleagues ignored his complaint, denying Olds's reappointment by the overwhelming vote of 53 to 15. Truman thereupon appointed a new commissioner, one amenable to the oil and gas corporations, thus reducing the FPC to a rubber stamp for their interests.

The President stood up more firmly against the oil industry several years later, when further efforts by Congress to satisfy the corporate appetite at the public expense became unendurable. In the mid-1940s, discoveries of oil deposits in the Gulf of Mexico and off the California coast offered the oil industry the attractive prospect of adding areas worth between $40 billion and $100 billion to its holdings—if these areas could be removed from federal ownership. Responding to the entreaties of eager oilmen, local politicians extended state jurisdiction over offshore lands beyond the traditional three-mile limit. Louisiana pushed its boundary twenty-seven miles into the Gulf of Mexico, while Texas enacted legislation moving its Gulf boundary to the outer limits of the continental shelf—as much as 130 miles. But state claims to this inaccurately named "tidelands" region were demolished by Supreme Court rulings that the federal government had "dominant rights" to the lands. Consequently, the corporations turned their attention to the national level. In May, 1952, they succeeded in pressuring Congress to pass legislation ceding the "tidelands" to the states, thereby doing, as Truman noted, "just what the oil lobby wants"—turning "the vast treasure over to a handful of states, where the powerful private oil interests hope to exploit it to suit themselves." On May 29, in one of those acts that endeared him to liberals even as they distrusted him, Truman vetoed the bill.

While the President's willingness to veto reactionary legislation heartened liberals, his personal style did little to win their affection. Unlike some of the austere Fair Dealers in Congress, Truman relished nothing better than escaping to the Presidential yacht anchored in the Potomac for a day of poker, bourbon, and political gossip. The regulars aboard every weekend included not a single prominent liberal but rather men of the President's own political persuasion: Chief Justice Fred Vinson; George Allen, court jester for three Presidents; Senator Clinton Anderson; Averell Harriman; and Clark Clifford. Occasionally, the President would ask Senator Lyndon Johnson to join them. Johnson, despite his anti-Administration voting record, was Truman's kind of politician —not at all a maverick like Douglas of Illinois or Kefauver of Tennessee. Truman appointed many of his personal pals to government positions and for this reason was at least partly responsible for the scandals that rocked Washington during his second term of office.

In August, 1949, when a special Senate investigating subcommittee began to examine the activities of "five-percenters," it found that a central figure was Truman's poker-playing crony Harry Vaughan, whose White House office was always open to influence-peddlers in Washington. Vaughan, who had accepted a freezer in return for assisting the president of a perfume company to evade wartime travel restrictions, had helped another friend get an allocation of scarce steel for a California race track and still another to obtain large quantities of scarce commercial sugar. He had also used his influence in the areas of public housing, federal trade regulations, and agricultural policy. In early 1951 Senator Fulbright, chairman of a special subcommittee of the Senate Banking and Currency Committee, exposed corrupt practices in the Reconstruction Finance Corporation reaching up to the chairman of the Democratic Party, William Boyle, who had helped to secure over $600,000 in loans for a friendly corporation. This was followed by a major scandal in the Internal Revenue Service. Before the controversy had subsided, the Commissioner of the IRS had been charged with failure to pay $116,000 in income taxes; the Assistant Commissioner had been indicted on a similar charge; and the Secretary of the Treasury had been forced to remove hundreds of lesser officials. Truman's Assistant Attorney General in charge of tax collection and the White House appointments secretary were both later convicted of tax fraud conspiracy. While he did not condone these activities, Truman nevertheless resented the efforts of those who exposed them; he referred contemptuously to Senator Fulbright as "an overeducated s.o.b."

With neither Congress nor the President likely to usher in a new era of reform, the liberal mantle was taken up by a small, plucky, and ineffectual band of senators: Paul Douglas, Hubert Humphrey, Herbert

Lehman, and two newcomers from Connecticut, William Benton and Brien McMahon. Lehman, an aging symbol of New Deal government elected to Congress in 1949 by New York voters, was somewhat more daring than his Fair Deal allies. In defense of civil liberties or in battle against corporate power he showed little inclination to abandon the principles that had marked his long career as a humanitarian reformer. "While the reactionary elements in Congress slash away at funds for public health, public power, and public housing," he declared in 1951, "they move very slowly, indeed, to tax the unprecedented profits of big business."

In the aftermath of the 1948 election, American liberalism had retreated to safer ground. The Progressive Party, reeling after its disastrous 1948 campaign, quickly disintegrated; by 1950, even Henry Wallace had abandoned it. With PCA destroyed by the Wallace debacle, ADA emerged as the nation's foremost liberal organization, symbolizing the liberal community's newfound aversion to Popular Front politics. In 1949, the liberal publisher of the *New York Post,* Dorothy Schiff, fired her husband—who had endorsed Wallace in 1948—as editor and replaced him with the militantly anti-Communist ADA leader, James Wechsler. Michael Straight, publisher of the *New Republic,* brought his journal, too, into line with ADA's viewpoint. Seeking a magazine that would appeal to those he considered tough-minded liberals, Max Ascoli founded the *Reporter,* which soon became an influential voice of Cold War liberalism. Arthur Schlesinger, Jr.'s *The Vital Center,* published in 1949, exemplified the new, more conservative tone of liberal thinking. According to Schlesinger, postwar liberals were a tough, "hardboiled" breed who had "brought a new virility into public life" to rescue America from the "political sterility" of the older liberalism. The ideologue, he wrote, had held a "sentimental" view of man and progress, while postwar liberals were far more "pragmatic." Indeed, they no longer felt a sense of kinship with the Left but instead straddled a "vital center." It was a curious location for advocates of social change, but no longer an uncommon one. Locked in the chilling embrace of Cold War politics, American liberals had fewer and fewer creative alternatives to offer to Soviet authoritarianism and American capitalism.

American radicalism retained its critical outlook but little of its following. Long in the vanguard of insurgent politics and the struggle for social justice in America, the Socialist Party dwindled to little more than a memory. Convinced that further electoral activity was hopeless, Norman Thomas announced the end of his long political career. The Socialist Party embarked upon a last ill-fated campaign in 1952, settling down thereafter to become an educational society of about a thousand members. The Communists retained a somewhat stronger organizational base, but their situation, too, was deteriorating rapidly. Assaulted by state power, attacked by its traditional allies, and decimated by internal purges, the American Communist Party staggered helplessly from disaster to disaster.

The impact of the Cold War upon the American liberal-Left was dramatically illustrated by the culmination of organized labor's anti-Communist purge. At the CIO's 1948 convention, three weeks after the national election, anti-Communist leaders furiously assailed those who had supported the Presidential bid of Henry Wallace. "They are not trade unionists, they are colonial agents of a foreign power," stormed Walter Reuther; they should either conform to CIO policy "or clear out." Philip Murray joined Reuther in denouncing allegedly Communist-dominated unions, but he softened the attack with assurances that no one was being asked to leave the CIO. When some union leaders refused to sign the non-Communist affidavits required by the Taft-Hartley Act, anti-Communist unions seized the opportunity to "raid" their membership. By the 1949 CIO convention, anti-Communist forces had moved in for the kill. Even Murray claimed that the CIO dissidents were plotting with Communist Party leaders "to corrupt and destroy, if possible, the trade union movement of America." Harry Bridges of the International Longshoremen's and Warehousemen's Union, one of the accused, replied angrily: "They say the issue is communism. The real issue is they don't want opposition." Ben Gold of the Furriers Union, one of the few acknowledged Communist labor leaders, cited Murray's earlier statements favoring differences of opinion within the labor federation. All to no avail. The CIO changed its constitution to make Communists or those following Communist policy ineligible for national office and expelled eleven unions with almost a million members. The labor organization even chartered a new union to raid the membership of the largest outcast, the United Electrical Workers. In an unprecedented action, President Truman notified the convention delegates of his approval.

The CIO's political purge left the American labor movement deeply scarred. Most of the expelled unions disintegrated, and those that remained in existence were greatly weakened by their outcast status. Few could any longer act effectively in the political arena, even if they tried. With its internal opposition driven into exile or silence, the CIO grew increasingly monolithic. Paul Jacobs, a union activist who had promoted the purge, later conceded: "An inevitable consequence . . . was to bring all serious political debate inside the CIO to a standstill. In some unions it became a habit to brand as a Communist anyone who opposed the leaders." What the CIO gained in public respectability it lost in those areas of mass participation, enthusiasm, and organizing zeal that had characterized it in the 1930s. Even in the most progressive of the remaining unions, like the UAW, rank-and-file ferment subsided, and a placid, if socially oriented, organization emerged. Once the *enfant terrible* of American politics, the CIO now seemed dull and middle-aged, closer in tone to its stodgy competitor, the AFL.

The ebbing vitality of the liberal-Left, coupled with Truman's re-election in 1948, left the Administration a relatively free field in foreign affairs. Under the direction of Acheson, appointed Secretary of State in early 1949, the Marshall Plan moved speedily along to bolster the forces of European and American capitalism. For chief administrator of the European Recovery Program, Truman named a Republican industrial-ist, Paul Hoffman, who, according to Acheson, preached a "doctrine of salvation by exports with all the passion of an economic Savonarola." In turn, Hoffman appointed 400 lesser officials, primarily drawn from business backgrounds. By the end of 1952, ERP had distributed about $13 billion in American aid, more than half of it to Germany, France, and Great Britain. With this assistance, the nations of Western Europe exceeded prewar production by 25 per cent as early as 1950. But such economic recovery, implemented by conservatives, left inequities in wealth and income untouched and solidified Europe's class structure. Journalist Theodore White observed: "The workers could see only that what had been saved was the *status quo,* that the recovery had pre-served their discomfort and given its fruits to the privileged." Moreover, by propping up the old order, the Marshall Plan encouraged the con-servative classes of Europe to attempt to maintain their colonial em-pires. France fought the people of Algeria and Indochina, the Nether-lands battled Indonesian nationalists, Belgium clung to control of the Congo, and Britain suppressed colonial rebellions in Malaya and Kenya. American corporations undoubtedly benefited greatly from the program, for approximately a third of American exports went to Marshall Plan nations. Of the $4.6 billion worth of crude oil and oil products Marshall Plan nations purchased between April, 1948, and December, 1951, al-most half came from the five largest American oil companies, with ERP financing the bulk of this.

In 1949 the Administration acted to seal America's ties to Western Europe through the NATO pact—America's first peacetime military alliance with European nations since 1778. The preceding year, the Senate had passed the Vandenberg Resolution, expressing the hope that the United States and other nations would develop "regional arrange-ments . . . for individual and collective self-defense." After his tri-umphant re-election, Truman moved quickly to implement this proposal. In his inaugural address of January 20, 1949, he announced his intention to sign a North Atlantic pact and asked Congress for appropriations to provide arms to the signatories. On April 4, the treaty was signed in Washington by representatives of Britain, France, Belgium, the Netherlands, Portugal, Italy, Denmark, Iceland, Norway, Canada, and the United States. The Senate approved it by a vote of 82 to 13 a few months later.

Yet, despite the rapidity with which the alliance was forged, a Soviet invasion of Western Europe did not appear imminent. Kennan privately criticized NATO to Acheson as providing a "military defense against an attack no one is planning." Eventually he resigned over the issue. "I do not know of any responsible high official, military or civilian," John Foster Dulles testified before Senate hearings in May, "who believes that the Soviet Union now plans conquest by open military aggression." Proponents of the pact sought primarily to discourage Cold War neutrality and increase America's already dominant role in Western European affairs. As Kennan noted, NATO "added depth and recalcitrance to the division of the continent and virtually forced individual countries to choose sides." Senator Tom Connally, chairman of the Foreign Relations Committee, explained that "the Atlantic Pact is but the logical extension of the principle of the Monroe Doctrine."

American policy-makers found the stickiest aspect of NATO to be the rearmament of Germany. The "major problem" in early NATO conferences, Truman recalled, was "the question of German participation." Although the Administration had every intention of utilizing German troops, at first it feared to admit this for political reasons. Asked about the use of German forces, Acheson responded that "the disarmament and demilitarization of Germany must be complete and absolute." Nevertheless, as early as November, 1949, the U.S. Army had completed a plan for German remilitarization, and at a September 12, 1950, meeting with the British and French foreign ministers Acheson proposed the creation of ten German divisions. The angry protests of America's European allies were overcome by American compromises on the control of NATO forces, by promises of increased economic aid, and by the dispatch of four additional U.S. divisions to Europe. Thus, four years after the bloodiest war in human history, the United States pressed West Germany into service as a military ally.

Western European rearmament, the product of NATO and billions of dollars in American military appropriations, did little, despite American rhetoric, to guarantee political freedom. Portugal's participation in NATO flawed whatever claims that alliance might have had as a defense of democracy, as did the later participation of Greece and Turkey. Driven to new levels of paranoia and hostility by NATO, Stalin doubled the size of the Red Army between 1950 and 1952 and increased Soviet military expenditures by 50 per cent. In 1955 Russia formed a military alliance of its own—the Warsaw Pact, uniting the armed forces of the Communist nations of Eastern Europe under Marshal Ivan Konev. This legitimized the stationing of Russia's troops in satellite states and gave Moscow formal control of their armies—factors of major significance in Russia's later suppression of liberalizing movements in Eastern Europe. Finally, by channeling large quantities of American arms to the nations of Western Europe, the United States helped them to destroy movements for liberation in their colonial empires. France utilized NATO aid for its struggles in Algeria and Indochina, while Portugal used NATO assistance to preserve its colonial outposts in Angola and Mozambique.

Successful in consolidating its control over Western Europe, the Administration encountered a stunning reversal in Asia. Ever since Marshall had ended his mission to China in January, 1947, convinced that the foolhardiness and intransigence of Chiang's regime doomed it to defeat, the U.S. government had stubbornly continued to support it. Throughout 1947 and 1948, hundreds of millions of dollars in U.S. military and economic aid bolstered Chiang's rule, while approximately 1,000 members of the U.S. Military Advisory Group trained the Nationalist army. Chiang's military offensive in the first months of 1947 left him with an apparent military superiority over his foes. His army, two and a half times the size of its Communist counterpart, enjoyed a three- or four-to-one superiority in rifles and an even greater advantage in heavy arms. But by the spring of 1947, the Communist Chinese armies had moved to the offensive, and the Kuomintang forces rapidly disintegrated. Poorly led, underfed, exploited, and almost completely demoralized, they either refused to fight, sold vast quantities of arms to their opponents, or deserted to the Communist ranks. Entire cities surrendered to Mao's forces after a minimum of opposition. Years of corruption, inflation, brutality, inefficiency, and resistance to reform had eaten away the support for the Kuomintang regime, and it now collapsed with a sudden thunder that startled the world. On August 6, 1949, with the Communist victory undisputable, Acheson gave notice that no further aid would be supplied to Chiang's "reactionary" clique; in December the remnants of the Nationalist government fled to Formosa. Chiang's overwhelming military superiority and $3 billion in postwar aid from the United States had failed to halt the triumphant Chinese Communist revolution.

Assessing the situation, which had been predicted regularly by China experts since World War II, the Administration was grim but candid. The Chinese revolution "represents a grievous political defeat for us," noted a secret National Security Council memorandum in June, 1949.

"If Southeast Asia is also swept by communism, we shall have suffered a major political rout the repercussions of which will be felt throughout the rest of the world, especially in the Middle East." Even publicly, the Administration was initially frank about the nature of the Kuomintang government and the extent of U.S. involvement in Chinese affairs. In the State Department's White Paper of August, 1949, Acheson wrote that "the ominous result of the civil war in China was beyond the control of the government of the United States. . . . It was the product of internal Chinese forces, forces which this country tried to influence but could not." Ultimately, observed the Secretary of State, "the only alternative open to the United States was full-scale intervention in behalf of a government which had lost the confidence of its own troops and its own people."

But the "loss" of China unleashed such a ferocious attack upon the conduct of American diplomacy that the Administration soon lost the political nerve necessary to follow through on its analysis of the situation. Republican conservatives denounced the White Paper as a "whitewash," while Patrick Hurley, a former U.S. Ambassador to China, termed it a "smooth alibi for the pro-Communists in the State Department who had . . . aided in the Communist conquest." "If Formosa falls," warned Congressman Nixon, "the next frontier is the coast of California." Although Truman announced that the Administration "will not pursue a course which will lead to involvement in the civil conflict in China," it gradually hardened its opposition to the Peking regime. By the beginning of 1950 twenty-five nations, including Great Britain, had recognized the People's Republic of China, but the United States remained adamantly opposed to diplomatic recognition. On January 13 the United States voted against the admission of the Peking regime to the United Nations. Dean Rusk, the Assistant Secretary of State for Far Eastern Affairs, depicted the People's Republic of China as "a colonial Russian government—a Slavic Manchukuo on a larger scale. . . . It is not even Chinese."

With the onset of the Korean War in June, 1950, the Administration resumed its support of Chiang Kai-shek. Truman ordered the U.S. Seventh Fleet to intervene directly in the civil war by interposing itself between Mao's armies on the mainland and Chiang's regime on Formosa. "The occupation of Formosa by Communist forces," stated the American President, "would be a direct threat to the security of the Pacific area." A month later, he and the National Security Council agreed to begin a new program of aid to the Nationalist government. Within days General MacArthur, a staunch defender of Chiang Kai-shek, flew to Formosa for an unauthorized visit with the Generalissimo. The two leaders issued a communiqué declaring their agreement on "joint defense of Formosa and . . . Sino-American military cooperation" and predicting a "final victory" over the "menace of Communism." Angered by MacArthur's actions, Truman nevertheless failed to discipline him. It was symptomatic of the Administration's unwillingness—after a brief hiatus of realism—to confront the significance of the Chinese revolution.

Another setback to American hegemony in world affairs came in the fall of 1949, when the Soviet Union successfully tested an atomic bomb. Shortly thereafter, in October, the Atomic Energy Commission scheduled a special session of its General Advisory Committee to consider the development of a hydrogen bomb—a weapon with vastly greater power than the largest existing atomic device. After the meeting the GAC stated its unanimous opposition to an H-bomb program. Enrico Fermi and I. I. Rabi, two Committee members, issued a report warning that the bomb represented "a danger to humanity" and was "necessarily an evil thing in any light." They urged the President "to tell the American public and the world that we think it wrong on fundamental ethical principles to initiate the development of such a weapon." Following the GAC's lead, the Atomic Energy Commission also voted to reject the project. Yet the decision on whether to proceed—like the decisions to build and drop the atomic bomb—lay with the President alone. And on January 31, 1950, Truman announced that he had ordered the AEC to develop a hydrogen bomb. Although "atomic warfare means national suicide and humanity's final holocaust," wrote journalist I. F. Stone, "we have been consulted as little about it as if we lived under a dictatorship." By the end of Truman's term of office, the U.S. government had invested $7 billion in the development of a formidable stockpile of atomic bombs, including means for their delivery; tactical weapons using atomic warheads; an atomic submarine under construction; and a successfully tested hydrogen bomb, with mammoth facilities for its production. Albert Einstein told television viewers: "General annihilation beckons."

On January 30, 1950, Truman had ordered the Departments of State and Defense to "make an over-all review and re-assessment of American foreign and defense policy in light of the loss of China, the Soviet mastery of atomic energy and the prospect of the fusion [hydrogen] bomb." By April 12 the review was complete, and Truman forwarded it to the National Security Council, from which it emerged later that month in final form as NSC 68. Foreseeing "an indefinite period of tension and danger," NSC 68 urged a "bold and massive program" of Western rearmament, a unified system of power with "the U.S. as its political and material center with other free nations in variable orbits around it." American defense spending—$13 billion in 1950, or about

30 per cent of the national budget—would be quadrupled as part of "an immediate and large-scale build-up in our military and general strength."

But, while Truman gave his full support to NSC 68, its implementation remained problematical. Since the Berlin Blockade, the Soviet Union had carefully refrained from openly aggressive acts, and the American Congress seemed to have little interest in appropriating an additional $40 billion for "defense." Indeed, by early 1950 the Truman Administration was barely able to get its major military and economic aid bills through Congress. In May one vote rescued the Point Four program of aid to underdeveloped nations from defeat in the Senate, and only a tie vote prevented a half-billion-dollar slash in the European Recovery Program. Military bills lay bogged down in committee. Some of the Administration's keenest supporters were growing irritated at its bellicose tone. In a letter written on January 4, 1950, Senator Lehman told Acheson: "The first principle of the American people in foreign policy today is a search for peace, justice, and the well-being of all peoples. It is not to maintain a particular battleline along the Asia coast or to resist by force those ideologies which are not reconcilable with ours." The New York senator concluded curtly: "We must not invite war in order to avoid it. . . . There is a slower and harder but surer way." Thus, the Administration's ambitious plans for a sharp military buildup might never have been realized if the Korean War had not erupted that June.

The defeat of the Japanese in World War II held forth the promise to the Korean people of an end to forty years of foreign occupation. A nationwide resistance organization of all political groupings, including the Communists, promptly took control of most of the nation. Meeting in Seoul on September 6, 1945, the resistance groups established a national government and called for land reform, extended suffrage, the formation of cooperatives, and the ousting of Japanese collaborators. The Soviet Union and the United States, however, had already agreed at Cairo, Yalta, and Potsdam to occupy the nation jointly, and in December the Moscow Conference of Foreign Ministers, without consulting the Koreans, decided that these two nations should hold Korea in "trusteeship" for five years. At the suggestion of the United States, Korea was divided at the 38th Parallel, leaving most industry in the North and most population in the South. In the North, occupied by the Soviet Union, a Communist resistance leader, Kim Il Sung, became Premier. In the South, the American Military Government, headed by General John Hodge, took a less favorable view of the resistance forces. "Koreans are the same breed of cat as the Japanese," he reportedly said upon his arrival in Seoul.

The AMG quickly aligned itself with the extreme Right. "The most encouraging single factor in the political situation is the presence in Seoul of several hundred conservatives," the State Department's political adviser reported to Byrnes; "although many of them have served with the Japanese, that stigma ought eventually to disappear." General Hodge moved toward outlawing the mass-based resistance government, acknowledging that this "may result in temporary disorders" and "will also bring charges of political discrimination in a 'free' country, both by local pinkos and by pinko press." During 1945 and 1946 the AMG dispossessed the peasants of the land they had seized after liberation from the Japanese, established wage controls, and restored a free market economy, which promptly caused massive inflation and immiserization. After appeals from the AMG, American officials flew Syngman Rhee, a right-wing Korean patriot who had lived most of his life in the United States, to Korea, installing him as head of a Representative Democratic Council in February, 1946. The rightist council became the advisory body for the AMG and began to assume the administrative functions of government. Together with the Americans, it supervised the creation of a 25,000-member police force to repress dissidents. Many members of the police force had worked previously for the Japanese and were noted, as one AMG officer observed, "for their cruelty and efficacy in suppressing Korean nationalism."

The American occupation regime naturally alienated many Koreans. In the spring of 1946, an AMG poll in Seoul revealed that 49 per cent of the respondents preferred the hated Japanese occupation to that of their American "liberators." In September, the Korean Federation of Labor, after repeated rebuffs from the AMG, called a general strike, and 300,000 workers walked off their jobs. When the police brutally smashed a picket line at Taegu, the South's third largest city, fighting erupted which left forty-one dead. On October 4, the AMG declared martial law and arrested strikers. Other Koreans, outraged by the American measures, joined the struggle; more than 100,000 students left classes in solidarity. The use of American troops and police terror resulted in thousands of arrests and deaths, as well as in driving the Communists, the non-Communist Left, and the Federation of Labor underground.

Throughout 1947 and 1948 the U.S. military government continued its repressive, rightist-oriented policies. Terrorist activities, led by Rhee's street gangs and by AMG-deputized groups, heightened with the approach of the May, 1948, elections, from which most of the Left and even the moderate liberals were excluded as candidates. As both the Left and much of the nationalist Right boycotted the elections, charging that they would permanently divide Korea, Rhee's forces won an easy victory. By 1949, when the American occupation ended, the South was safely in reactionary hands and the North firmly under Communist control.

The Truman Administration had few illusions about its South Korean bastion. "President Syngman Rhee . . . has little patience with those who differ with him," Truman wrote a few years later. "I did not care for the methods used by Rhee's police to break up political meetings and control political enemies, and I was deeply concerned over the Rhee government's lack of concern about the serious inflation that swept the country." Nor did U.S. officials consider South Korea of much strategic significance. In 1947, the Joint Chiefs of Staff informed Truman that "from the standpoint of military security, the United States has little strategic interest in maintaining . . . troops and bases in Korea," while in January, 1950, Acheson publicly excluded the Korean peninsula from the U.S. Pacific defense perimeter.

Nevertheless, the U.S. government remained firmly committed to the South Korean regime. Upon evacuation, U.S. forces left it $110 million in military equipment. In 1949 and early 1950, at Administration insistence, Congress granted it $210 million in aid. Some insight into Administration thinking is provided by a memorandum that Truman believed sufficiently important to include in his *Memoirs*. Reporting on his trip to Korea in mid-1946, Ed Pauley, Truman's special representative with ambassadorial rank, warned that "Communism in Korea could get off to a better start than practically anywhere else in the world" simply by nationalizing Japanese-held industry. Thus, "the United States should not waive its title or claim to Japanese external assets located in Korea until a democratic (capitalistic) form of government is assured." Korea represented "an ideological battlefield upon which our entire success in Asia may depend. It is here where a test will be of whether a democratic competitive system can be adapted to meet the challenge of a defeated feudalism, or whether some other system, i.e. Communism, will become stronger."

After the withdrawal of American and Soviet occupation forces from Korea, a civil war seemed probable. Indeed, General Hodge had argued for the evacuation of foreign troops on the ground that it would "leave Korea to its own devices and an inevitable internal upheaval for its self-purification." In the South, Rhee continued his repressive policies, closing down opposition newspapers, jailing editors, and placing even his conservative critics under intense surveillance. Thousands of political prisoners languished in South Korean jails. Meanwhile, inflation reached unprecedented proportions and peasant-based guerrilla activity grew. On May 30, 1950, despite continued government intimidation, opposition forces trounced Rhee's party at the polls, capturing 120 out of a total of 168 seats in the National Assembly. While the opposition was divided by politics and program, it was united in its dislike of Rhee. Most delegates also seemed to favor the opening of negotiations on unification with the North. Nevertheless, Rhee held the reins of power, at least temporarily, and he remained a willful, aggressive, and ambitious leader, as well as an intense nationalist. Even American policy-makers were troubled by his repeated vows to "liberate" the North and for this reason refused to supply his government with offensive weapons. Only that May, he broadcast a message to the North Korean people promising them "unification through a joint struggle with us in the South." That "longed-for day," he said, "will come soon."

On June 25, 1950, North Korean military forces crossed the 38th Parallel and began a major drive against the South. Rhee's army, larger than that of North Korea but less heavily armed, rapidly disintegrated. Truman moved quickly; shortly after noon on June 27 he announced that he had ordered American air and naval units to provide South Korea with "troop cover and support." In addition, he promised greater military aid to the counterinsurgency campaigns in Indochina and the Philippines and directed the U.S. Seventh Fleet to seal off Formosa from the Chinese mainland. "The attack upon Korea," he said, "makes it plain beyond all doubt that communism has passed beyond the use of subversion to conquer independent nations, and will now use armed invasion." That night the pro-Western majority in the U.N. Security Council, over the objections of Yugoslavia and with the abstention of Egypt and India, rammed through a U.S. resolution calling for "such assistance to the Republic of Korea [South Korea] as may be necessary to repel the armed attack and to restore international peace and security in the area." Truman's action thus gained some degree of U.N. sanction, despite the fact that he had not consulted the world organization, allies of the United States, or even Congress before ordering American military intervention.

At home, Truman's bold action won him the fervent support of most political leaders and newpapers. The New York *Herald-Tribune,* the nation's leading Republican paper, declared that Truman had "acted . . . with a magnificent courage and terse decision. . . . His is an act of statesmanship." But Senator Taft remained, as usual, a waspish critic. As a staunch anti-Communist, he commended American intervention; yet he raised embarrassing questions about it. "If the United States was not prepared to use its troops and give military assistance to National-ist China against Chinese Communists, why should it use its troops to defend Nationalist Korea against Korean Communists?" he asked. Moreover, he continued, "so far as I can see . . . there is no authority to use armed forces . . . in the absence of some previous action by

Congress." In the heat of the moment, however, few Americans seemed inclined to dwell upon such matters; polls indicated that eight out of ten respondents approved of the President's decision to intervene.

Nothing did more to generate support among liberals and internationalists for the Korean war than the idea that it represented a U.N. venture. Truman stumbled upon this selling point quite accidentally. On June 29, 1950, he told a press conference that "we are not at war" but only suppressing "a bandit raid" on South Korea. When a reporter asked if the conflict were not actually a "police action under the United Nations," Truman pounced on the concept and adopted it as his own. In a speech that October in San Francisco he declared: "For the first time in history the nations who want peace have taken up arms under the banner of an international organization to put down aggression." Under "the banner of the United Nations, they are succeeding. This is a tremendous step forward in the age-old struggle to establish the rule of law in the world."

Despite the war's U.N. billing, though, the Administration consistently acted unilaterally. Furthermore, General MacArthur, technically the U.N. Commander in Korea, took his orders from the Joint Chiefs of Staff alone. "Even the reports which were normally made by me to the United Nations were subject to censorship by our State and Defense Departments," MacArthur recalled; "I had no direct connection with the United Nations whatsoever." Most U.N. troops, aside from those of the South Koreans and the Americans, represented token contingents. At the end of the war, the United States was supplying 33 per cent of the U.N. troops, the South Koreans 61 per cent, and all other nations less than 6 per cent. Given the pitiful state of the South Korean Army—which General Van Fleet described in April, 1951, as having already lost quantities of military equipment exceeding "that necessary to equip 10 divisions . . . in some cases without the semblance of a battle"—most of the tough fighting fell to the Americans. Whatever the President chose to call it, the Korean conflict was an American war.

Ignoring the explosive nature of Korean politics, American policymakers turned to the idea of a Kremlin plot to explain the North Korean attack and to justify their own intervention. According to Truman, Acheson assured him that "the Soviet Union was behind every one of the . . . North Korean moves and that we had to think of all that happened in Korea as world matters." Yet, if the Soviet Union had indeed orchestrated the invasion of South Korea, why was it caught off guard by the action? The Security Council resolution passed only because the Soviet delegate, boycotting sessions after the rejection of Communist China's entry, had not been present to veto it. Even Soviet newspapers were initially unable to explain the outbreak of war. Furthermore, the attack came at a time when the demise of the Rhee government appeared likely in the South and when the North lacked the air cover necessary—and presumably available from the Russians—for a more effective campaign. Nevertheless, despite the evidence of Communist confusion, the Administration persisted in defining the Korean War in a manner that evaded its origins in Korean politics—at least, that is, until American military success seemed to call for a new interpretation.

By September, 1950, the Americans and their U.N. allies had turned the tide of battle and had the North Korean forces on the run. No more than 30,000 Communist troops managed to retreat northward, and behind them came 230,000 U.N. soldiers backed by 100,000 U.S. Navy and Air Force men. Although Acheson had earlier declared that American intervention was "solely for the purpose of restoring the Republic of Korea to its status prior to the invasion from the north," the rout of the North Korean Army now made "liberation" of the entire peninsula too tempting a prize for American policy-makers to ignore. Consequently, that same month the President and the Joint Chiefs of Staff authorized MacArthur to "conduct military operations north of the 38th Parallel." Koreans, remarked the President, had a right to be "free, independent, and united." On September 30, U.S. Ambassador Warren Austin explained to the United Nations that "the artificial barrier which has divided North and South Korea has no basis for existence in law or reason." In this fashion, the American government rejected the notion of two separate Korean nations, eliminating the original rationale for its intervention and setting forth unification as its goal. On October 7, almost a month after President Truman had authorized MacArthur's invasion of the North, the U.N. General Assembly approved the action. India and six other Afro-Asian nations abstained from the vote, declaring that it "would impair faith in the United Nations if we were to authorize the unification of Korea by force against North Korea after [resisting] North Korea's attempt to unify Korea by force against South Korea."

Disastrous consequences followed. Angered by the American moves to defend Formosa, viewed by Nationalist and Communist Chinese alike as part of China, and to conquer North Korea, which bordered China on the Yalu River, the Peking government acted. In October, Chou En-lai provided India with a statement to be transmitted to the United States that China would not "sit back with folded hands and let the Americans come to the border." When Truman, ascribing this warning to "Communist propaganda," chose to ignore it, Peking announced on October 10 that, if American troops continued their advance to the north, China would enter the war. Even after a clash between Chinese "volunteers" and American troops at the Yalu on October 25, however, MacArthur and Truman discounted the possibility of Chinese intervention. MacArthur believed, as he had told the Veterans of Foreign Wars some weeks earlier, that it was "the pattern of the Oriental psychology to respect and follow aggressive, resolute and dynamic leadership." By the end of October 250,000 Chinese troops were reported to be massing on the Korean border. On November 5, after a Chinese attack sent a U.N. force into retreat, diplomatic moves finally commenced to head off major Chinese intervention. Seeking a way out of the crisis, Britain urged the United States to permit the Chinese to occupy a Korean buffer zone. A combat lull ensued as both sides awaited the outcome of a trip to New York by a Chinese representative to address the troubled U.N. Security Council. Then, on November 24, the day the Chinese representative arrived, MacArthur launched an "end-the-war offensive" of 100,000 men toward the Yalu. The Chinese now responded in full strength, smashing the U.N. armies and hurling them back in disorderly retreat to the 38th Parallel and beyond. Having handed the Americans one of the worst military defeats in U.S. history, the Chinese surged southward, apparently themselves determined to unify Korea by force. The decision to conquer the North, then, resulted in what MacArthur bitterly termed "an entirely new war"—one that would account for four-fifths of all American casualties in Korea.

Infuriated by their humiliating defeat, American officials adopted an increasingly belligerent tone. On November 30 Truman told a press conference that Chinese intervention might necessitate American use of the atomic bomb. This provoked a furor in Great Britain, where Conservative leaders like Churchill and Anthony Eden joined Labourites in expressing their "disquiet." When Attlee announced at the end of a Parliamentary session that he would fly to Washington for talks with Truman, cheers erupted from both sides of the House of Commons. In the Attlee-Truman discussions, the British Prime Minister argued that the Chinese were ripe for "Titoism," and that "all of us should try to keep the Chinese from thinking that Russia is their only friend." According to Truman, Acheson retorted that "the Chinese would have to prove that they were *our* friends." Truman expressed his "full agreement" with the Secretary of State. Attlee left the talks discouraged by the aggressive stance of his ally. "The Americans found it hard to realise that in the eyes of Asia they had become almost a spearhead of imperialism," he later observed. In December the U.S. government initiated a campaign to have China labeled the aggressor in Korea, and on January 5, 1951, it sent a note to twenty-nine governments warning that the United Nations might collapse if China were not so branded. On February 1 the United States, dragging along its reluctant allies, forced the aggressor-nation resolution through the General Assembly over Asian objections. "None [of the European nations] could afford to alienate the U.S. in a showdown," observed the *Wall Street Journal,* "but few hid their opposition."

The utterances of the American military commander, General Mac-Arthur, also soared to new heights of bellicosity. By late March, 1951, U.N. forces had managed to halt the Chinese advance and once again move painfully toward the 38th Parallel. Peace efforts were under way; a compromise settlement seemed within reach. But MacArthur used the occasion instead to taunt the Chinese and to demand their surrender. "Red China, of such exaggerated and vaunted military power, lacks the industrial capacity" to wage "modern war," he announced on March 24. An "expansion of our military operations to its coastal areas and interior bases" would "doom Red China to the risk of imminent military collapse." This was, as Truman later indicated, "a most extraordinary statement for a military commander . . . to issue on his own responsibility." America's angry Western allies, long ago sickened by the war's butchery, demanded to know the meaning of what the Norwegian Ambassador called this "pronunciamento." Truman was further embarrassed on April 5, when House Minority Leader Joseph Martin read a letter from MacArthur that implicitly criticized the Administration and supported the right-wing Republican demand for the use of Chiang Kai-shek's troops in Korea.

On April 11, determined to be free of this repeated source of domestic political attack and international humiliation, Truman relieved MacArthur of his commands. The general returned home to one of the most tumultuous welcomes in American history, assailing the Administration in speeches across the country for following policies of "appeasement." Ironically, however, MacArthur owed much of his popularity to the fervent gospel of anti-Communism preached for years by the Administration and now accepted by large sectors of the populace. Millions of Americans, like the general, asked themselves: Why should the "free world" stop short of "victory" over the utter villainy of the "International Communist Conspiracy"? Divorced from the reality of world politics and the strategic considerations of the White House, MacArthur's position nonetheless reflected the underlying logic of the Administration's Cold War policies.

The war in Korea dragged on through 1952 and the first half of 1953, ending finally in a stalemate near the 38th Parallel. The United Nations reported 94,000 combat deaths and more than four times that number wounded. American casualties reached 142,000, making the

Korean War the fourth most devastating conflict in American history up to that time. But, for the impoverished people of Korea, trapped in a war with shifting battle fronts and unprecedented use of air power, the price of "liberation" was far higher. Utilizing the latest bombing and shelling techniques, the world's mightiest military-industrial power systematically pounded the peasant nation with a torrent of death. At the end of the first year, Major General Emmett O'Donnell, Jr., head of the U.S. Far Eastern Bomber Command, declared: "Everything is destroyed. There is nothing standing." Vast quantities of bombs and napalm laid waste Korea's fields, gutted its tiny industries, burned out its villages, and slaughtered millions of its inhabitants. An estimated 84 per cent of the dead were civilians. At the end of the war, Korea lay in smoldering ruins, occupied by foreign armies, oppressed by rival dictatorships, and divided more hopelessly than ever before.

The war clouds did, however, have a silver lining for the Truman Administration. Availing himself of the opportunity afforded by the conflict, Truman succeeded in implementing NSC 68 and greatly expanding the U.S. military establishment. On July 19, 1950, the President went before Congress to call for massive rearmament, and in December he took to the airwaves to proclaim a state of national emergency. "Our homes, our nation, all the things we believe in are in great danger," he warned Americans. "We will not engage in appeasement." In the crisis atmosphere, Congress granted Truman what he wanted. Between fiscal 1950 and fiscal 1952, military spending rose from $13.1 billion to $44.2 billion, while the armed forces more than doubled to 3.6 million men. The military buildup no doubt explains General Van Fleet's curious remark to a Filipino delegation in 1952: "Korea has been a blessing. There had to be a Korea either here or someplace in the world."

Long before the outbreak of the Korean War, American policymakers had anxiously watched the emergence of a revolutionary struggle in Indochina. During World War II, while Vichy French officials cooperated with the Axis powers, Vietnamese nationalists, led by the Communist Ho Chi Minh, organized the Vietnamese Independence League, or Viet Minh, to wage guerrilla warfare against the French and Japanese authorities. By the end of the war the Viet Minh had won control of most of the countryside and had elected a provisional government for all of Vietnam. In September, 1945, when the Viet Minh formally established the Democratic Republic of Vietnam, the head of America's wartime OSS mission in Indochina reported: "The new government appears to be enthusiastically supported by the majority of the population in every province of Indochina. . . . The people . . . keep saying if they [the French] come back with arms, they will fight to the death." The French did, in fact, return with arms, beginning a long and bloody war the following year to restore their colonial rule by installing a former collaborator with the Japanese, Bao Dai, as a puppet emperor. At first Washington was unenthusiastic. Roosevelt had frowned upon the reimposition of French colonialism in the region, and even after his death the State Department warned Paris: "It is not the policy of this government to assist the French to re-establish their control over Indo-china by force." For its part, the Viet Minh gave no evidence of hostil-ity toward the United States. Its Declaration of Independence was modeled upon the American, and it sent at least eight requests to the U.S. government for assistance in the struggle against the French. "If there is a Moscow-directed conspiracy in Southeast Asia," concluded the State Department's intelligence office, "Indochina is an anomaly."

But the stunning victory of the Communist revolution in China led the Truman Administration to reassess its Indochina policy. A National Security Council memorandum of February, 1950, contended that the United States should take "all practical measures . . . to prevent fur-ther communist expansion in Southeast Asia." On February 7, about a week after the French National Assembly had formally established neo-colonial regimes in Vietnam, Laos, and Cambodia, the United States government granted them formal recognition. Ho Chi Minh, claimed Acheson, was the "mortal enemy of native independence in Indochina." Three months later American policy-makers agreed to extend military and economic aid to the faltering French war effort—aid which greatly increased after the outbreak of hostilities in Korea. Returning from a visit to Saigon in 1951, Congressman John F. Kennedy of Massachu-setts reported: "We have allied ourselves to the desperate effort of a French regime to hang on to the remnants of empire."

Administration policy-makers viewed Indochina, in the words of the February NSC memorandum, as a "key area of Southeast Asia" whose loss to Communism would imperil the future of the entire region. In 1951 U.S. Ambassador to France David Bruce told a Senate commit-tee that, "if Indo-China went, the fall of Burma and the fall of Thailand would be absolutely inevitable. No one can convince me . . . that Malaya wouldn't follow shortly thereafter, and India . . . would . . . also find the Communists making infiltrations." An NSC memorandum of June, 1952, outlined the attractions of the region: "Southeast Asia, especially Malaya and Indonesia, is the principal world source of natu-ral rubber and tin, and a producer of petroleum and other strategically important commodities." Furthermore, "the rice exports of Burma and Thailand are critically important to Malaya, Ceylon and Hong Kong and are of considerable significance to Japan and India." The "loss of

Southeast Asia" would "make it extremely difficult to prevent Japan's eventual accommodation to communism" and would undermine the stability of Europe and the United States. Secretary of Defense Robert Lovett summarized Administration thinking on the subject of Indochina in the spring of 1952. "The strategic geographical position of the area," he told the Senate, "as well as the vitally important raw materials such as tin and rubber which it supplies, makes it important for us to maintain an effective support of the gallant [French] effort."

The situation appeared less threatening in other areas of the Third World. Nudging out British oil holdings in the Middle East, the United States became the dominant economic power in the region. Between 1946 and 1953 the regional oil output accounted for by American firms rose from 31 to 60 per cent. In Indonesia, belated U.S. pressure on behalf of the nationalist leadership of Achmed Sukarno and Mohammed Hatta helped force out the Dutch in 1950 and open the door to the Americans. Sukarno appeared relatively accommodating at the time; only later did his shift leftward lead to an unsuccessful CIA attempt to overthrow his rule.

Latin America, as always, remained an area of particular U.S. interest. From 1945 to 1948 United States policy in the region had been countered by nationalist opposition, but thereafter military and economic aid undermined resistance to American demands. In 1950 the United States provided a $125 million credit to the Peron dictatorship in Argentina in gratitude for its retreat from militant economic nationalism. Washington officials were "highly encouraged" by the changes in Argentina's policies, announced a State Department spokesman, "and I feel safe in saying that the individual [U.S.] businessmen affected by the actions taken are also encouraged." With the passage of the Mutual Security Act of 1951, the Administration increased its military assistance to Latin American governments, inaugurating a series of bilateral "defense" agreements under which the United States sent military missions to all signatory nations, and these nations promised to limit their trade with the Soviet bloc. Such aid, estimated in fiscal 1953 at perhaps $65 million, would have provided little defense in the unlikely event of a foreign invasion, but it did serve to ensure political stability, propping up military dictatorships in Peru, Venezuela, Cuba, and the Dominican Republic. In this fashion the United States preserved its privileged status as Latin America's primary source of imports and foreign investments—a situation of considerable value to U.S. business but of questionable benefit to most Latin Americans.

The best-publicized of the Administration policies toward underdeveloped nations began when Truman introduced the Point Four program in his 1949 inaugural address. "We must embark on a bold new program," he urged, "for making the benefits of our scientific advances and industrial progress available" to "underdeveloped areas." Described in later years by Truman as "an adventurous idea such as had never been proposed by any country in the history of the world," Point Four was actually an updated version of programs headed by Nelson Rockefeller in Latin America during World War II. The White House staff, reviewing an early draft of Truman's speech, had found it so dreary and negative that Clark Clifford had inserted the idea in an effort to strike a "constructive" note and win the praise of liberals. Moreover, despite Truman's claims as to the innovative nature of Point Four, he did not envisage it as altering the traditional dependence of Third World nations upon the import of manufactured goods and the export of raw materials. Quite the contrary. "The development of these countries would keep our own industrial plant in business for untold generations," he wrote in his *Memoirs;* "the resources of such areas . . . have hardly been touched, and their development would be as beneficial to American trade as to the areas themselves." Through the program, the President recalled, the United States would "encourage stabilized governments in underdeveloped areas," thereby promoting American corporate investment.

On June 24, 1949, Truman sent a special message to Congress requesting an appropriation for the Point Four program, pairing it with a request for legislation authorizing the Export-Import Bank to guarantee U.S. private investments in underdeveloped nations. "All countries concerned with the program should work together to bring about conditions favorable to the flow of private capital," Truman told Congress. Although the legislators revised the rules for the Export-Import Bank to the Administration's satisfaction, they appropriated a paltry $35 million for the first year of the Point Four program. It seems improbable, however, that a larger appropriation would have enabled underdeveloped nations to break out of their widespread poverty and economic stagnation. As Dr. Charles Malik, Lebanon's Ambassador to the United States, observed at the time: "In many cases, it is hopeless to expect real development unless fundamental changes in the social structure are introduced." But, as such "fundamental changes" clashed directly with the Administration's commitment to profitable investment and marketing relationships, the President was hardly about to encourage them.

Throughout these years, Washington availed itself of the opportunity to reconstruct the political economies of two developed nations, Germany and Japan. The Marshall Plan and NATO soon revived the economic and military power of Germany, but Japan remained a nettlesome problem, primarily because of the occupation's reforms. Anxious to promote the competitive free enterprise preached by old-fashioned conservatives, MacArthur supported the dissolution of the *zaibatsu*—the economic empires, ruled by ten families, that controlled 75 per cent of Japan's financial, industrial, and commercial activities. But strong opposition to this program and others of a reformist nature emerged among U.S. business interests and State Department officials. In March, 1948, Kennan traveled to Japan to meet with MacArthur and lay down the Administration line. During talks with the occupation commander, he criticized the antimonopoly program, the economic purge, land reform, reparations, and the decentralization of the police. *Zaibatsu* dissolution, he recalled in his *Memoirs,* "could only have been eminently agreeable to anyone interested in the further communization of Japan." Moreover, the economic purge was depriving America of its best friends. "It was as though pro-Americanism, especially among upper-class Japanese, was particularly suspect," he wrote; "important elements of Japanese society essential to its constructive development were being driven underground." Kennan conveyed to MacArthur what he defined as Washington's viewpoint on the future of the occupation: "No further reform legislation should be pressed. The emphasis should shift from reform to economic recovery." Visiting big business delegations made the same point. By the mid-twentieth century, sophisticated conservatives were less interested in fostering MacArthur's nineteenth-century liberal utopia than in smoothing the path for corporate expansion.

Exercising his customary independence, MacArthur held out for a time against outside pressure but eventually fell into line with the aims of Washington and Wall Street. Occupation authorities mitigated the effects of the economic purge and virtually abandoned the policy of *zaibatsu* dissolution. Although 325 Japanese corporations had been slated to be dissolved, SCAP announced the program's completion after the dissolution of the first nine. The occupation's formerly favorable policy toward organized labor also shifted. When militant unions of government employees called for a strike in August, 1948, MacArthur had the Japanese government revise the nation's laws to deny government workers the right to strike or engage in collective bargaining. From 1948 to 1950 the number of union members in Japan fell from 7 million to 3.3 million. In June, 1950, MacArthur ordered twenty-three leaders of the powerful Japanese Communist Party excluded from all political activity. Later he imposed a similar ban on seventeen editors of the party's newspaper and purged thousands of Communists and other radicals. Circumventing the Japanese Constitution, which declared that "the Japanese people forever renounce war" and banned the maintenance of a standing army, SCAP ordered the Japanese government in July, 1950, to expand its national police force to 75,000 men, who subsequently underwent military training as the nucleus of new Japanese armed forces. As American war orders began to pour in from the Korean front, Japan entered upon a period of industrial expansion under conservative control.

All that remained to be accomplished was the forging of an anti-Communist alliance. In early 1951 Truman appointed John Foster Dulles as his special representative to work out a Japanese peace settlement. Utilizing private negotiations rather than the usual public peace conference, Dulles fashioned a treaty to the Administration's liking and then presented it for ratification to the rest of the world. The treaty granted Japan sovereignty over its home islands but left control of the Bonin and Ryukyu groups to the Americans. In accord with the American desire to restore Japanese economic and military power, the treaty placed no restrictions on Japan's future economic development, war industries, or rearmament and held forth only modest opportunities to Japan's badly bruised neighbors for war reparations. Finally, the treaty provided for "the stationing . . . of foreign armed forces on Japanese territory." Representatives of forty-nine nations signed the treaty in September, with Communist nations abstaining. That same day, Japan signed a security pact with the United States, authorizing the presence of American troops on its soil. Dulles proclaimed happily a few months later: "Japan can soon emerge as an important factor in world defensive strategy against militant communism. That is the goal of our policy."

Thus, but six years after the end of World War II, the United States had reversed the sides of the anti-fascist alliance. By 1951, it had allied itself with its former foes, Germany, Italy, and Japan, against its former allies, Russia and China. To be sure, in the intervening years a Communist revolution had drastically altered the political complexion of China. Furthermore, American occupation forces had substituted sophisticated conservative governments for fascist dictatorships in Germany, Italy, and Japan. Nevertheless, a glance at America's postwar relations with the one surviving fascist regime—that of Spain—reveals just how far American foreign policy had shifted to the Right.

Spain went through World War II as an alleged neutral, but few nations had forgotten how fascist Italy and Germany had helped to crush the valiant Spanish Republic and install the right-wing dictatorship of Generalissimo Francisco Franco. As late as 1946 the United States joined Great Britain and France in denouncing Franco's government as pro-Nazi and totalitarian, calling upon the people of Spain to rise up and overthrow it. That same year the United States voted for and complied with a U.N. General Assembly resolution urging member states to withdraw their ambassadors from Spain. But in 1948 Forrestal and the Navy argued for the use of Spanish bases to control the Mediterranean, and in 1949 the Air Force added its own pleas for Iberian facilities. The first in a series of massive American loans and gifts to the Franco regime was made in 1950; the following year the Administration returned its ambassador to Spain, opening negotiations for military bases. These negotiations culminated in a treaty in 1953, granting economic assistance and $250 million in military aid to the once-despised fascist regime. The turnabout was now complete. Generalissimo Franco had become a respected leader of the "free world," while the Veterans of the Abraham Lincoln Brigade, survivors of a heroic struggle to halt the spread of fascism, were relegated to the Attorney General's list of "totalitarian" and "subversive" organizations. Such were the politics of the Cold War era.

4

The Anti-Communist Crusade and the Republican Struggle for Power, 1945-52

> The issue between Republicans and Democrats is clearly drawn . . . by those that have been in charge of twenty years of treason.
>
> JOSEPH R. MCCARTHY, at the 1952 Republican National Convention

ADDRESSING THE NATIONAL YOUNG REPUBLICAN CONVENTION in Boston on June 28, 1951, Senator Richard M. Nixon outlined "The Challenge of 1952." The "most vulnerable point" of the Democrats, he declared, was their "failure . . . to develop an effective program to meet the activities of the fifth column in the United States." Charging that Communists had "infiltrated the very highest councils of this administration," he promised to drive the Democratic Party from power in "a fighting, rocking, socking campaign."

The use of the Communist issue to attack the Democratic Party represented one of the most striking ironies of the postwar years, for not only had the Truman Administration launched the Anti-Communist Crusade at home and abroad, but it continued to proclaim the necessity for ideological conformity in subsequent years. Throughout 1949 and 1950 Attorney General J. Howard McGrath addressed patriotic groups, fraternities, law-enforcement associations, and veterans organizations as part of what he called the "modern struggle against pagan communist philosophies that seek to enslave the world." He denounced the subversion of students by their teachers, urged that anti-Communist speakers be invited to college campuses, and called for the promotion of anti-Communist books in the nation's bookstores. "There are today many Communists in America," he explained. "They are everywhere—

in factories, offices, butcher stores, on street corners, in private business. And each carries in himself the death of our society."

In 1949 the Administration secured the conviction and imprisonment of eleven Communist Party leaders on the charge that they had violated the Smith Act by conspiring to teach or advocate the violent overthrow of the U.S. government. The Supreme Court, in *Dennis* v. *United States* (1951), upheld the decision of the lower court by a 6-2 vote, Chief Justice Vinson arguing that free speech was subject to curtailment under the "clear and present danger" doctrine. Dissenting, Justice Hugo Black stated his hope "that in calmer times . . . some later court will restore the First Amendment liberties to the high preferred place where they belong in a free society." The Justice Department took the Supreme Court ruling as a green light for the extension of its anti-Communist campaign and soon thereafter initiated the trial, conviction, and imprisonment of forty regional and state Communist Party leaders.

Moreover, despite a popular fear—exploited by the Republicans— that the nation, and particularly the federal government, swarmed with Communist espionage agents, relatively few spies were discovered in these years by the FBI or other agencies. In the summer of 1946 the Canadian Royal Commission issued a report disclosing the activities of a Russian espionage ring in Canada and implying the possible existence of a similar group in the United States. Neither the FBI nor the Federal Loyalty Program, however, was able to unearth any evidence of an espionage network, although in 1949 Judith Coplon, an employee of the Justice Department, was convicted for passing information on the FBI's counter-espionage system to a Soviet agent. A national furor developed from 1948 to 1950 over the case of Alger Hiss, accused of having given State Department documents to the Russians. Hiss was not then a government employee but head of the Carnegie Endowment for International Peace, and the acts allegedly occurred during his State Department service of the 1930s. The only serious espionage case cropped up in early 1950, when the British government prosecuted Dr. Klaus Fuchs, a respected British scientist who had delivered atomic secrets to Russian agents. His confession led to the trial and execution of Julius and Ethel Rosenberg, two Americans convicted of having been his accomplices. But, despite the judge's claim that the Rosenbergs were responsible for American deaths in the Korean War, the material given to the Russians appears in retrospect to have been inconsequential. Perhaps more significant, no effective Communist spy network was revealed.

Ordinarily, the Administration's record would leave little room for new entrants in the struggle against domestic "subversion," but these were not ordinary times. Banished from the White House since 1932 by their intransigent opposition to welfare-state measures, Republican conservatives were desperate for an issue with voter appeal. American businessmen, their keenest supporters, were smarting from a generation of social criticism by journalists, news commentators, labor leaders, artists, and intellectuals. Political Neanderthals and reactionary employers' groups had traditionally resorted to the "Red scare" to stigmatize their opponents, but rarely with much success. Most Americans never seemed particularly excited about Communism one way or the other. But the Cold War played into the hands of the American Right, for it gave the official seal of disapproval to Communism, a left-wing ideology, establishing it as the most heinous offense against patriotism. If radicals, liberals, and even organization Democrats could be associated in the public mind with Communists, they, too, would acquire an "un-American" aura, destroying their political effectiveness. The opportunity was too inviting to resist. Snatching the anti-Communist banner from the Truman Democrats, American conservatives swung into the vanguard of the Anti-Communist Crusade.

The U.S. Chamber of Commerce, spokesman of the nation's wealthiest banks and corporations, vigorously promoted the struggle against domestic "subversion." In 1946 it called for the establishment of a federal loyalty program and an investigation of Communism in Hollywood. In 1947 it proposed that the Justice Department publish "at least twice a year a certified list of Communist-controlled front organizations and labor unions." The patriotic demands of the business federation steadily heightened until, by 1952, it urged banning Communists, "fellow travelers," and "dupes" from all agencies and professions affecting public opinion, "such as newspapers, radio, television, book and magazine publishing, and research institutions"; from positions as "teachers or librarians"; and from employment in "any plant large enough to have a labor union." Criticizing "certain 'liberals' " for "giving aid and comfort to communism," the Chamber urged its members to "find out from reputable sources such as *Counterattack, Alert,* or the American Legion about Communist sympathizers in the entertainment field"; to be on guard against Communists "promoting appeasement in the name of peace"; to "support patriotic ex-Communists who cooperate with the FBI"; and to "identify public officials . . . displaying softness towards Communism."

The surprise entrants in the struggle against internal "subversion" were sizable numbers of American Catholics. Ever since 1937, when Pope Pius XI's encyclical *Atheistic Communism* had banned cooperation with Communists, the church hierarchy in America had taken a militantly anti-Communist position but in the postwar years its pronouncements reached new stridency. In 1946, Francis Cardinal Spellman warned of the "aggression of enemies within." Three years later, he proclaimed from the pulpit of St. Patrick's Cathedral in New York that America stood in mortal danger of "Communist conquest and annihilation" and bewailed the "Communist floodings of our own land." Many Catholics were, of course, embittered by the hostile treatment of their clergy by Communist regimes in Eastern Europe and the Far East, but many also found the loyalty mania highly satisfying. Long the subject of nativist taunts by the nation's Protestant majority, they could at last assert their Americanism—and question the patriotism of others— through the vehicle of the Anti-Communist Crusade.

Naturally, any rebuffs suffered by America in world affairs strengthened the position of those who charged betrayal at home. Taft blamed the fall of Chiang Kai-shek on "Communist influence" in the State Department. Senator Styles Bridges of New Hampshire charged that American defeats in the international arena were "no accident"; Stalin, "not a superman," must have had "help from inside our ranks." Even many Democrats fell back upon a domestic explanation of the China debacle. "What our young men had saved," Congressman John F. Kennedy of Massachusetts contended, "our diplomats and our President have frittered away." After the Korean War bogged down into futile slaughter, Republicans laid this, too, at the Democratic doorstep, arguing that the Administration's "sympathetic acceptance of Communism" had invited aggression in Korea. MacArthur's recall from Korea, which he himself ascribed to "insidious forces working from within," and the news of the Soviet breakthrough in atomic weaponry provided further opportunities for right-wing recrimination. "How much more are we going to have to take?" stormed Republican Senator Homer Capehart of Indiana. "Fuchs and Acheson and Hiss and hydrogen bombs threatening outside and New Dealism eating away the vitals of the nation."

Seizing upon anti-Communism as the road to power, Republicans followed the trail blazed for them by the House Committee on Un-American Activities. In 1938, Congressman Martin Dies of Texas successfully sponsored a House resolution establishing a committee to investigate "the extent, character and objects of un-American propaganda activities in the United States." An arch-conservative, Dies believed that "Stalin baited the hook with a 'progressive' worm, and the New Deal suckers swallowed the bait, hook, line, and sinker." Dies served as chairman of the new committee from 1938 to 1944, using his post to attack liberals and radicals while virtually ignoring American fascists. He accused CIO president John L. Lewis of trying to establish a "Soviet America," demanded the resignations of Harold Ickes, Harry

Hopkins, and Frances Perkins for bringing an army of New Deal "radicals" and "crackpots" to Washington, predicted that "the Congress of Industrial Organizations will become the Communist Party of America," and described Eleanor Roosevelt as "one of the most valuable assets that the Trojan Horse Organization of the Communists have possessed." The Silver Shirts, the Ku Klux Klan, and the German-American Bund all lauded the efforts of HUAC, as did the Nazi government of Germany. In 1944, when the CIO-PAC announced a major campaign to defeat Dies in the Texas Democratic primary, HUAC's founder decided not to seek re-election.

With the retirement of Dies, HUAC might have expired had it not been rescued by its most powerful member, Congressman John Rankin of Mississippi. Rankin was an ardent racist and white supremacist, elected by about 5 per cent of the voting-age population in a district with the highest poll tax in the nation. The author of a law that prohibited racial intermarriage in the nation's capital, he turned his efforts during World War II to maintaining the segregation of blood on racial lines. "One of the most vicious movements that has yet been instituted by the crackpots, the Communists, and the parlor pinks of this country," Rankin told his House colleagues, "is trying to browbeat the American Red Cross into taking the labels off the blood bank . . . so that it will not show whether it is Negro blood or white blood. That seems to be one of the schemes of these fellow travelers to try and mongrelize this nation." A defender of the Ku Klux Klan as a "100% American institution," Rankin was also, as *Time* magazine noted, the "No. 1 Jew baiter of the House. " In 1941, he denounced "a little group of our international Jewish brethren" for attempting to plunge America into war, while in July, 1945, he warned that "alien-minded Communistic enemies of Christianity" were "trying to get control" of the radio and the press; "listen to their lying broadcasts in broken English and you can almost smell them." Taking advantage of the disorganization of the House on the opening day of its 1945 session, Rankin proposed an amendment to reconstitute HUAC, then a temporary investigating committee, into a standing committee of the House, with permanent subpoena powers. Rankin's measure was defeated by a voice vote, but, in a patriotic tirade, he demanded a roll-call. Intimidated, the House passed the amendment, giving HUAC a new lease on life.

Rankin dominated HUAC during 1945–46 through the suffrance of its new chairman, Congressman John S. Wood of Georgia—like Rankin, an apologist for racism and the Ku Klux Klan. Asked why he did not scrutinize the Klan's "un-American" activities, Wood responded: "The threats and intimidations of the Klan are an old American custom." Under Wood's direction, HUAC launched an investigation of the broadcasts of radio news commentators. Within several months, five of them —all critics of HUAC—were dropped by their sponsors. In its report the committee suggested that criticisms of the State Department, Chiang Kai-shek, Peron, and Franco be used as criteria for identifying "subversive" newscasters.

The Republican sweep of 1946 finally gave the GOP a chance to head Congressional investigating committees. In less than a month, the Republican Congress had planned thirty-five separate investigations; the new Speaker of the House, Joseph W. Martin, Jr. of Massachusetts, promised that Congress would "ferret out" those who sought to destroy the "American way of life." HUAC strained eagerly at the head of the pack, directed by its new chairman, J. Parnell Thomas of New Jersey. A noisy, arrogant, and emotional man, Thomas was a staunch conservative who regarded the New Deal as "not far different from the socialism of Hitler, that of Mussolini, and the Communism of Stalin." In 1945 Rankin had announced that "one of the most dangerous plots ever instigated for the overthrow of this government has its headquarters in Hollywood," adding: "We're on the trail of the tarantula now." Thomas took up this lead with great fanfare in 1947, initiating an investigation of the motion picture industry.

That October, Walt Disney, Gary Cooper, Ronald Reagan, Robert Montgomery, and other entertainment personalities testified before floodlights in packed hearing rooms, providing what *Life* magazine termed "a rewarding show." Ten screen writers and directors who refused to discuss their political beliefs and associations were cited by HUAC for contempt and sentenced to a year in prison. (One of them, Ring Lardner, Jr., had the pleasure of Chairman Thomas's company in the penetentiary after 1949, when the Republican legislator was convicted of taking salary kickbacks from his office staff. Thomas, who continued to draw his Congressional salary while custodian of the Danbury chicken yard, was pardoned after eight and a half months in prison. All of the "Hollywood Ten" were denied parole and formally blacklisted by the motion picture industry.) Within a few years, the number of politically unemployable in the entertainment field passed 400. As German playwright Bertolt Brecht—himself summoned to testify before HUAC—later observed, the dissident writer was "not deprived of his life, only of the means of life. He does not appear in the obituary columns, only on the blacklists."

The Democratic Congressional victory of 1948 restored the chairmanship of HUAC to Congressman Wood, who ushered in a new burst of activity. In 1949, HUAC admitted that it maintained files on more than a million Americans. Between 1949 and 1959, it provided information on 60,000 individuals and 12,000 organizations to interested employers and listed thousands of individuals and organizations mentioned in its hearings in a *Cumulative Index*—a handy reference guide for blacklisters and superpatriots. In 1950 alone, the committee distributed 2 million free copies of its publications.

The constant search by HUAC and other government investigating agencies for new information on "subversive activities" led logically to the rise of the professional informer. By 1954 the Justice Department's Immigration and Naturalization Service alone maintained at least eighty-three witnesses on its payroll, at $34 a day. Louis Budenz, a former editor of the *Daily Worker* who converted to Catholicism and anti-Communism, estimated that he spent 3,000 hours giving names of Communists to the FBI. For his work as an anti-Communist witness and publicist, he received over $10,000 a year. So driven were many witnesses by a sense of guilt, a need for exoneration, a longing for publicity, or simply a desire for money that their testimony was notoriously unreliable.

The case of young Harvey Matusow was dramatic but not altogether atypical. Matusow joined the American Communist Party in 1947 and soon thereafter became a secret agent for the FBI. Having performed well as a witness for the prosecution in the Smith Act trials, he was employed as an informer by the Department of Justice, the Subversive Activities Control Board, the Permanent Investigations Subcommittee of the Senate Judiciary Committee, HUAC, the Ohio Committee on Un-American Activities, and the New York City Board of Education. Matusow testified in 25 trials and deportation proceedings and made 180 identifications of Communists for his assorted employers. His anti-Communist credentials also enabled him to secure employment as a speaker in Congressional campaigns, to write his memoirs for the Hearst press, to lecture at American Legion posts, to appear as a nightclub entertainer, and to work as a radio disk jockey. Then, on February 3, 1955, he announced at a New York press conference (and subsequently before a federal grand jury and two Congressional committees) that he had repeatedly fabricated evidence and lied in his testimony, sometimes on his own initiative and sometimes at the request of government attorneys. It was "a good racket, being a professional witness," he told the press.

In the summer of 1948 Whittaker Chambers, a senior editor of *Time,* and Elizabeth Bentley, a confessed wartime Communist spy, recounted a series of sensational Communist espionage stories before HUAC. The legal difficulties of chairman J. Parnell Thomas precluded his full participation in the proceedings, and leadership of the investigation was quickly assumed by Congressman Richard Nixon. Chambers, who claimed to have once been a Communist spy, informed HUAC that Alger

Hiss had been a Communist Party member and his secret contact from 1934 to 1938. Hiss vehemently denied the charge before the committee and brought suit against Chambers for libel. Asked to present his evidence at the pretrial hearings in Baltimore, Chambers produced alleged State Department documents, some of which, he claimed, were in Hiss's handwriting and others typed on Hiss's typewriter. On December 2 Chambers led an eager crowd of reporters and committee investigators to his Maryland farm, where he dramatically withdrew three rolls of undeveloped microfilm from a hollow pumpkin, which he claimed had served as a "drop." A New York grand jury now indicted Hiss for perjury. The first trial ended in a hung jury, but the second led to his conviction on January 2, 1950.

The Hiss case, while leaving millions of Americans confused and unconvinced, nevertheless proved an enormous boon to the Anti-Communist Crusaders. It established Congressman Nixon as a prominent figure on the political landscape and turned Chambers into a political and religious oracle, eagerly courted by the nation's mass media. By February, 1952, when Chambers appeared on NBC television, his role in the Hiss case had assumed inspirational proportions. "At issue . . . was the question," he said, "whether . . . Western civilization could in its extremity still cast up a man whose faith in it was so great that he would voluntarily abandon those things which men hold good, including life, to defend it." Chambers avoided mentioning that his testimony had been subpoenaed and that the potentially death-dealing consequences had included $75,000 from the *Saturday Evening Post* for serial rights to his memoirs.

The Republicans naturally found the Hiss case almost too good to be true. In the fall of 1948 Truman had referred to HUAC's investigation of Hiss as a "red herring," while after the trials Acheson bravely told reporters: "I do not intend to turn my back on Alger Hiss." With this "proof" of "betrayal" at last in hand, the GOP sprang to the attack. Shortly after the final verdict Congressional Republicans adopted a platform assailing the "soft attitude of this Administration toward Government employees and officials who hold or support Communist attitudes." The Hiss case, explained Nixon, represented only "a small part of the whole shocking story of Communist espionage in the United States."

As the Republicans experimented with the Communists-in-government issue in January, 1950, a serious political discussion was taking place in a Washington restaurant. The gathering had been arranged to discuss the political future of Joseph R. McCarthy, a relatively obscure conservative Republican Senator from Wisconsin whose close association with sugar lobbyists had earned him the sobriquet "Pepsi-Cola

Kid." McCarthy told the group that he badly needed an issue to carry to the voters in 1952, when he would seek re-election. After several proposals had been rejected, Father Edmund A. Walsh, Dean of the Georgetown University School of Foreign Service, suggested: "How about Communism as an issue?" The Senator responded eagerly. "The government is full of Communists," he said. "The thing to do is hammer at them." On February 9, he launched his career as the nation's top Red-hunter. Waving a sheaf of papers in the air, he told the astonished members of the Women's Republican Club of West Virginia: "I have here in my hand a list of 205 [employees] that were made known to the Secretary of State as being members of the Communist Party and who nevertheless are still working and shaping policy in the State Department." The Associated Press wire service picked up McCarthy's speech and carried it across the country, transforming him immediately into a national celebrity. When he changed planes at Denver, reporters surrounded him, asking for the list. At first he offered to show it to them, but then, according to the local press, he "discovered he had left it in his baggage on the plane." By the time McCarthy's plane touched ground in Salt Lake City, he had narrowed down the still elusive list to fifty-seven "card-carrying Communists." In subsequent months, he would fail to produce the names of any Communists in the State Department, but from the standpoint of the senator this hardly mattered; he had captured the national limelight.

Although the Republican Party had been nurturing the Anti-Communist Crusade for years in quest of political advantage, McCarthy brought to it a new flamboyance, skillful public-relations management, and daring. On February 20, when he presented the Senate with the "evidence" to support his charges, he drew upon State Department loyalty files obtained in 1947 by the House Appropriations Committee. Most of the individuals in the files no longer worked for the State Department, and those who remained had been cleared by the FBI; moreover, the material had been in Congressional hands for years. Nevertheless, not only did McCarthy claim that he had penetrated the "iron curtain" of State Department secrecy, but he consistently lied about the contents of the files. Case Number 36, noted the file, had had "no investigation." McCarthy simply announced: "According to the file, he is a known Communist." Despite the fact that a number of senators had already seen the files and at least one—Homer Ferguson of Michigan—was following his own copy during McCarthy's presentation, no one bothered to correct the Wisconsin senator's distortions and inventions. Instead, the Senate appointed a committee, headed by Senator Millard Tydings of Maryland, to investigate McCarthy's charges.

Congress had barely caught its breath when McCarthy moved on to new and more outrageous contentions. In mid-March he promised to reveal the "top Russian espionage agent" in the United States. "I am willing to stand or fall on this one," he stated. Eventually, he named a lecturer at Johns Hopkins University, Owen Lattimore—a State Department consultant who was neither a spy nor a Communist. By the spring of 1950 McCarthy had hit his stride, attacking Administration supporters for everything from Communism to homosexuality. The "pitiful squealing" of "egg-sucking phony liberals," he charged, "would hold sacrosanct those Communists and queers" who had sold China into "atheistic slavery." Promising to purge the "prancing mimics of the Moscow party line" from the State Department, he assailed Acheson and U.N. Ambassador-at-Large Philip Jessup as "dilettante diplomats," who "whined," "whimpered," and "cringed" before Communism. George Marshall, he said, was "a pathetic thing." Through it all, McCarthy remained brash and self-confident. "When did you discover Communism?" a young lady asked him at a cocktail party given by the Scripps-Howard press. "Two and a half months ago," he blithely replied.

During the spring and summer of 1950, as McCarthy captured the headlines, the Tydings Committee conducted a careful inquiry, gathering approximately 2,500 pages of testimony and documentation. On April 6 it listened as Owen Lattimore called McCarthy's charges against him "base and contemptible lies," refuted them in detail, and produced letters from Chiang Kai-shek and Madame Chiang praising him for his services. At the end of the hearing, Tydings reported that the committee members who had examined Lattimore's government file had found no evidence that he had ever been a Communist. McCarthy himself admitted, "I am not in a position to file any formal charges." On July 14, having concluded its investigation of McCarthy's accusations against the State Department, the Tydings Committee submitted a report claiming that they constituted "a fraud and a hoax on the Senate of the United States and the American people."

The release of the Tydings Committee report did not disillusion or discourage McCarthy's supporters; on the contrary, sensing that they had found a potent political issue, Republicans rallied behind the Senator, giving him new prestige and power. Henry Cabot Lodge, Jr., and Bourke Hickenlooper, the Republican members of the Tydings Committee, refused to sign the report, Lodge terming it "superficial and inconclusive." Senator William Jenner called it the "most scandalous and brazen whitewash of treasonable conspiracy in our history," while Senator Ferguson charged that the Tydings Committee had employed "the techniques of Goebbels and Vishinsky" to silence its critics. Initially, Republican politicians had frowned upon the Wisconsin senator's wild charges and demagogic appeal. Senator Taft thought McCarthy's February 20 speech "a perfectly reckless performance," while Senator Margaret Chase Smith of Maine found it necessary to publicly chide "certain elements of the Republican party" for "selfish political exploitation of fear, bigotry, ignorance and intolerance." Nevertheless, during the Tydings Committee hearings, with the road to power beckoning, Republicans scrambled aboard the McCarthy bandwagon. Asked to accept the Tydings Committee report, the Senate divided exactly on party lines—forty-five Democrats to thirty-seven Republicans. McCarthyism had become a matter of party loyalty.

With the approach of the 1950 midterm elections the crusade against internal "subversion" gathered momentum. In July the Republican Policy Committee placed a new version of the Mundt-Nixon bill for Communist registration on its "must" list. Sponsored by Pat McCarran, a conservative Democrat who chaired the Senate Judiciary Committee, the McCarran Internal Security Bill made Communist-"action," Communist-"front," and Communist-"infiltrated" organizations subject to the scrutiny of a Subversive Activities Control Board. Communist-"action" and -"front" groups were compelled to register with the SACB; upon registration, their members lost the right to travel, to work in defense plants, or to hold government jobs. If they were aliens they could be deported, and if recently naturalized they could be denaturalized. Failure to register carried a fine of $10,000 and five years in prison for each day of noncompliance. All groups were forbidden to mail any publication or other communication or make a radio or television broadcast without labeling it: "Disseminated by —————, a Communist organization."

The McCarran Act swept easily through a frightened Congress. Criticizing the bill's abridgment of civil liberties, a small number of Democratic liberals sought to substitute a bill of their own handiwork, empowering the Attorney General, in a national emergency, to intern alleged subversives in detention camps without trial. After rejecting this concentration camp bill as a substitute, the Senate, at the suggestion of Majority Leader Lucas, tacked it on to the McCarran bill as an amendment. Even liberal resistance now collapsed. In vain did radical Congressman Vito Marcantonio seek to rally his timid colleagues: "You are killing the America of Jefferson and Paine . . . the America of the abolitionists, of the men who fought and died to abolish the slave laws and repeal the alien and sedition laws. You are killing the America of the American Revolution." In September the McCarran bill sailed through the House with but twenty votes cast against it; in the Senate, only seven men dared to vote "No." "Many who had criticized the bill in debate voted for it on final passage," the *New York Times* observed.

"The feeling on Capitol Hill, apparently, is that it is too risky politically to vote against anti-Communist legislation."

Not even the White House could stop the political stampede. On September 22 Truman vetoed the measure, remarking that its provisions would "open the way to thought control" in America. The President sent a letter to each member of Congress urging him to read through the thirty-two-page bill to see just how repressive it was. But within an hour the House had voted 286 to 46 to override the veto. In the Senate, liberals engaged in a brief filibuster, hoping to reach adjournment or to arouse libertarian sentiment. The aging Senator William Langer, a maverick Republican from North Dakota who called the McCarran Act "one of the most vicious, most dangerous pieces of legislation against the people that has ever been passed," collapsed after a five-hour speech and was rushed to the hospital. Hubert Humphrey, who voted for the bill in its initial appearance before the Senate, now took the floor for several more hours to speak against it, but then allowed it to come to a vote. The bill again passed easily, by a vote of 57 to 10. The entire Democratic leadership of the Senate had deserted the President, and, of the allegedly "liberal" Eastern Republicans, not one voted to sustain the veto. Three future Presidents of the United States—Kennedy, Johnson, and Nixon—voted for the bill.

The McCarran Act marked, as Justice Black later observed, "a major break in the wall designed by the First Amendment to keep this country free." Once the refuge of the politically persecuted, the United States, under the new law, became the site of six concentration camps, where thousands of political undesirables could be sequestered indefinitely by the government. "If there be any among us," Thomas Jefferson had stated in his first inaugural address, "who would wish to dissolve this Union or to change its Republican form of government, let them stand undisturbed as monuments of the safety with which error of opinion may be tolerated where reason is left free to combat it." In the aftermath of the McCarran Act, I. F. Stone remarked: "If there be any such among us today they'd better hurry down and register."

With the Anti-Communist Crusade in full flower, the 1950 elections were particularly vituperative. Nebraska Senator Kenneth Wherry charged that Acheson was stained with "the blood of our boys in Korea," while Senator Jenner called Marshall "a living lie" and "a front man for traitors." McCarthy delivered more than thirty major speeches in fifteen states. Drive from Congress "those small-minded men . . . who have covered up treachery and incompetence," he thundered; purge the government of the "Communists, dupes, and fellow-travelers" who had "plotted the Communist victory in Asia." Democratic Congressman Eugene McCarthy of Minnesota, writing to

ADA's James Loeb, Jr., noted the "standard pattern" of the campaign against him: "I am the stooge of the CIO and of the Communists, the enemy of the middle class, and my patriotism is questionable. I have not checked *Mein Kampf,* but I think this is the recommended approach." Once the symbol of anti-Communist liberalism, ADA now became the object of violent conservative abuse. Columnist Westbrook Pegler contended that, while the liberal organization "is not yet frankly a Communist force," it "advocates nothing which a Communist would oppose except the Atlantic Pact and a strong American war machine." In the campaign, few candidates exhibited much enthusiasm for ADA support.

The election results seemed to indicate the strength of the Communist issue. The Democrats lost twenty-seven House and five Senate seats. In the Democratic Senate primary in Florida, Congressman George Smathers defeated the liberal incumbent, Claude Pepper, labeling him "Red Pepper." In California, Congressman Nixon clobbered liberal Democratic Representative Helen Gahagan Douglas in a race for the Senate after distributing more than a half-million bright pink flyers branding her a "Pink Lady." McCarthy's prominent role in the campaign gave him an aura of political invincibility. In Illinois a McCarthy foe, Senator Scott Lucas, went down to defeat before the conservative Everett McKinley Dirksen. Most significant, Senator Millard Tydings, a conservative Maryland Democrat, fell before a vicious assault waged by Senator McCarthy and his cohorts.

From the start of the Maryland campaign, McCarthy and his staff planned and financed the effort of the Republican senatorial aspirant, John Marshall Butler. They brought in a professional public relations agent from Chicago to manage the campaign; secured the assistance of the powerful McCormick press interests; and solicited contributions from Texas oilmen. McCarthy himself made a number of speeches in the state, charging that Tydings was "protecting Communists" at "a time when the survival of Western non-atheistic civilization hangs in the balance." A campaign tabloid, *From the Record,* repeated McCarthy's denunciation of Tydings and printed a composite photo of the Maryland senator with former Communist leader Earl Browder, which made it appear that the two men were engaged in intimate conversation. Although Butler's manager was fined for violating the Federal Corrupt Practices Act and his campaign was characterized by a Senate committee as "destroying our system of free elections," the Maryland Republican ultimately took his seat in triumph. McCarthy's political standing rose dramatically.

And yet, in retrospect, it appears that McCarthy's political clout was overrated. The Truman Administration had alienated voters on a variety of issues, and Democratic losses in 1950 were actually far lighter than in 1946, when Republicans took control of Congress. McCarthy had singled out three Democrats for special attention: Scott Lucas, Brien McMahon, and Millard Tydings. "Lucas provided the whitewash when I charged there were Communists in high places," he said. "McMahon brought the bucket, Tydings the brush." Connecticut and Illinois had had an almost even party split in 1948, and thus McCarthy's speechmaking in both states should have led to lopsided Republican victories in 1950. In Illinois the Republicans did win handily, but primarily because of a scandal in Cook County and because Dirksen was an able campaigner. In Connecticut, Brien McMahon was re-elected with 53 per cent of the two-party vote. In Maryland, the scene of McCarthy's greatest triumph, his appeal was also questionable. Ever since 1938 the Democratic percentage of the vote had been declining in the state. Maryland had gone Republican in 1948 and would do so again in 1952. Moreover, in 1950 Maryland's Democratic Party was racked by internecine strife, and the Republican gubernatorial candidate won easily. Indeed, although singled out for attack by McCarthy, Tydings ran well ahead of his party's candidate for governor. Nevertheless, the defeat of Tydings enhanced McCarthy's image as leader of a mass movement, and few Democrats dared any longer to challenge him. Journalist William S. White noted "a general expression of fear" in the Senate Democratic caucus "that what had happened to Mr. Tydings, with all his standing in the Senate, could happen to any other man."

McCarthy returned to the Senate in 1951 in top form. He called President Truman a "son-of-a-bitch," described Secretary of State Acheson as the "Red Dean of Fashion," and denounced the dismissal of General MacArthur as "a Communist victory won with the aid of bourbon and benedictine." In early June he promised a speech on Secretary of Defense Marshall that would reveal "a conspiracy so immense and an infamy so black as to dwarf any previous such venture in the history of man." On June 14 he opened a 60,000-word address before the Senate, but, after several hours of fumbling over unfamiliar words and phrases, simply inserted the remainder into the *Congressional Record*. The speech, probably written by someone at the Georgetown School of Foreign Service, was a well-researched indictment of American foreign policy, filled with questions that reflected adversely on Marshall's loyalty. ("Why . . . was Marshall so determined to follow Stalin and oppose Churchill?" "Who constitutes the highest circles of this conspiracy?")

Delighted by the senator's intemperate attacks upon its opponents, the American Right rallied to his standard. McCarthy's "technical" assistance in unearthing new evidence on the "Communist conspiracy" came primarily from the reactionary McCormick and Hearst newspaper empires, as well as from Alfred Kohlberg, a key man in the nation's China Lobby and the financial angel behind a number of right-wing periodicals. Right-wing oil millionaires were particularly charmed by the Wisconsin senator's approach to politics. McCarthy was flown to his speaking engagements in oil company planes and lavishly entertained by Texas oil barons, who provided private funding for his Congressional investigations of "subversion." McCarthy also had a strong appeal among traditional Republicans, Catholics, semi-fascists of the far Right, and conservative intellectuals like James Burnham, John Chamberlain, and Max Eastman. William F. Buckley, Jr., who linked together oil millions, orthodox Catholicism, and conservative intellectual interests, contended that "McCarthyism . . . is a movement around which men of good will and stern morality can close ranks."

During McCarthy's early years as a Red-hunter, few men of power opposed him. One of those who did was a Senate "outsider," Democrat William Benton of Connecticut, a former vice-president of the University of Chicago and co-founder (with Chester Bowles) of a large advertising firm. On August 6, 1951, Benton introduced a Senate resolution calling for McCarthy's expulsion from that body on the grounds of perjury, deceit, fraud, and unfitness for office. Benton's boldness shocked the Senate, and none of his colleagues rose to support the resolution. McCarthy responded fiercely, charging that Benton was a "clever propagandist" who for years had been "paralleling the Communist Party line down to the last period, the last comma." Terrified of the Wisconsin senator, the Senate launched a pitiful investigation of his conduct, which dragged on for sixteen months. Although the subcommittee conducting the investigation possessed subpoena powers, it failed to make use of them, and McCarthy repeatedly refused to testify before it. After criticism from McCarthy, the subcommittee chairman, Guy Gillette of Iowa, hastily resigned his post, as did staff members when they learned that McCarthy was readying personnel files for an assault on their loyalty. With the Republicans supporting McCarthy and the Democrats cowering before him, the investigation came to nothing. In 1952 McCarthy helped to defeat Benton in his bid for re-election.

By the early 1950s the loyalty-security mania had reached a fever pitch. *Washington Confidential,* a best-seller throughout most of 1951, talked knowingly of Communism in the nation's capital; "where you find an intellectual," it reported, "you will probably find a Red." In loyalty hearings, government interrogators asked defendants: "Do you believe in God?" "What newspaper do you buy or subscribe to?" "How do you explain the fact that you have an album of Paul Robeson records in your home?" A bootblack in the Pentagon who had once given ten dollars to the defense of the Scottsboro boys was questioned seventy times by the FBI. "Let no one say that a Communist can be tolerated in American society and particularly in our industry," declared John Wayne, president of the Motion Picture Alliance for the Preservation of American Ideals; even those who had repented their past before HUAC would have to provide "names and places, so that they can come back to the fellowship of loyal Americans." Congressional investigating committees cross-examined school teachers, government officials, ministers, actors, and authors. States set up their own investigating committees and demanded loyalty oaths of their employees. By 1952 thirty states had enacted some type of loyalty oath for teachers. As a result of government pressure or the influence of local "patriotic" groups, colleges and universities dismissed faculty members under investigation. The Supreme Court, led by Chief Justice Fred M. Vinson, a Truman appointee, denied a hearing to the Hollywood Ten, upheld the non-Communist oath required by the Taft-Hartley Act, and refused to overturn the Smith Act convictions. "The common denominator," noted I. F. Stone, "was the familiar premise of repressive government in all ages and in all its various guises—the notion that the supposed security of the state took precedence over the rights of the individual and the claims of free inquiry."

Faced with the fury of the Anti-Communist Crusade, Truman seemed more interested in defending the Administration's anti-Communist credentials than in safeguarding civil liberties. When he vetoed the Mc-Carran Act, he claimed that the measure would "actually weaken our existing internal security measures and would seriously hamper the Federal Bureau of Investigation." Acheson dismissed a number of Foreign Service officers associated with U.S. China policy; by 1952 there were only two members of the China Service still employed by the State Department out of the twenty-two officers who had joined it a little more than a decade earlier. Confronted by the heresy hunt in the nation's universities, the President declared: "I don't think anyone ought to be employed as instructors [*sic*] for the young people of this country who believes in the destruction of our form of government." Despite his occasional sharp criticism of McCarthy or HUAC, the President had, as evidenced by his own Loyalty Program, no basic objection to making political opinion a criterion for employment; nor did he ever show any interest in protecting the civil liberties of bona fide Communists.

Like the President, most liberals found nothing fundamentally wrong with the Anti-Communist Crusade and were disturbed only by its excesses. ADA's 1951 platform recognized "the right of the government to require loyalty to free institutions as a qualification of public employment" but criticized "the crude and indiscriminate methods by which wholesale loyalty investigations of Americans have been conducted." Most liberals became exercised only by cases of mistaken identity, and few defended the civil liberties of Communists. Some, indeed, like Sidney Hook, took others to task for not sufficiently opposing Communism or for defending the civil liberties of Communists. Writing in *Commentary* in March, 1952, Irving Kristol conceded that McCarthy was a "vulgar demagogue" but added: "There is one thing that the American people know about Senator McCarthy; he, like them, is unequivocally anti-Communist. About the spokesmen for American liberalism, they feel they know no such thing." Concerned with protecting themselves against reckless charges of "Communism" and "subversion," most liberals failed to meet the danger posed by the Anti-Communist Crusade—a danger, as the historian Arthur Ekirch has noted, that stemmed less from "the irresponsible tactics of the various Congressional investigating committees or individuals like Senator McCarthy" than from "the assumption that there was a minority class or group of political lepers guilty of so-called wrong thinking."

The Anti-Communist Crusade at home and the Cold War abroad provided the backdrop as the nation's two major parties maneuvered for position in the 1952 Presidential elections. The Republicans found themselves facing a difficult choice. Senator Taft was far and away the most respected politician among Republicans, but it once again seemed doubtful that a man with his flinty conservative views could be elected. Polls found that, while Truman's popularity had fallen to but 26 per cent by the spring of 1952, two other likely Democratic contenders—Adlai Stevenson and Estes Kefauver—could both defeat Taft. As in 1948, however, General Eisenhower retained an immense popularity. In the spring of 1951 a Gallup poll revealed that he was the first choice of both Republican and Democratic voters for the 1952 nomination.

A professional soldier of obscure political opinions, Eisenhower provided a sharp contrast to the fiercely partisan Taft; indeed, he had not even bothered to vote until the age of fifty-eight. In 1948 Eisenhower had accepted the presidency of Columbia University. But his two years on Morningside Heights proved frustrating for the school's faculty and for Eisenhower, who exhibited no particular competence in the field of education. He rescued his image as a military hero, however, when he left in 1950 to accept the new post of Supreme Commander of NATO. By 1951 the Republican Party's wealthy and influential "moderate" constituency—primarily located on the East and West coasts—had begun a series of journeys to NATO headquarters in Paris to urge Eisenhower to run for President. On January 7, 1952, returning from such a trip, Senator Lodge announced that, with Eisenhower's permission, he was entering the general's name in the New Hampshire primary.

A heated battle for the Republican nomination ensued. In spite of Eisenhower's absence, he swept the primaries in New Hampshire, Minnesota, New Jersey, Pennsylvania, Massachusetts, and Oregon. Taft remained strong, however, particularly in the Middle West, and won primaries—most of which Eisenhower chose not to enter—in Wisconsin, Nebraska, Illinois, Ohio, and West Virginia. A bitter dispute erupted between the two camps over the Southern delegates, chosen by state conventions under Taft's control. Answering the claims of Eisenhower supporters that only the general could win, Taftites retorted that the Ohio senator was the only "real Republican."

At the outset of the GOP National Convention in early July, Taft forces were in control of the machinery, naming MacArthur to deliver the opening address, McCarthy as a key speaker, and a Taft partisan as temporary chairman—a position from which he could seat contested delegates. Nevertheless, the Taft forces proved themselves clumsy and inept and gave the impression of undemocratic procedures, while the Eisenhower forces—led by Dewey, Lodge, and Herbert Brownell—worked smoothly and efficiently. When Taft's effort to seat his contested Georgia delegation failed, he surrendered his attempt to manage the convention. The general thereupon squeaked through to nomination on the first ballot. Appearing that night in the Chicago Stockyards Amphitheater, Eisenhower promised to "lead a great crusade" for "total victory."

While Eisenhower's nomination gave the GOP a fresh and attractive figure at the head of its ticket, other aspects of the convention reflected the unsavory Republican preoccupation with the Anti-Communist Crusade. When the chairman introduced McCarthy, "Wisconsin's Fighting Marine," delegates scrambled to their feet for a demonstration of welcome, bearing placards reading: "Acheson," "Hiss," "Lattimore." The Republican platform, charging the Truman Administration with "appeasement of Communism" at home and abroad, claimed that the Democrats had "shielded traitors to the nation in high places," had sold out Chiang Kai-shek, and had invited the war in Korea. As a concession to the right-wingers in his party, Eisenhower chose Senator Richard Nixon as his running mate. Nixon was "young, vigorous," and an expert on "the question of Communist infiltration," the general noted. On the other hand, the California senator "did not persecute or defame"—or so Eisenhower claimed. Despite his "moderate" instincts, the Republican Presidential nominee was already exhibiting that naïve tolerance for reactionaries of his own party that would make him the perfect figurehead of their rule. In later years he wrote that, although the 1952 GOP platform indicted the Democrats in "purple 'prosecuting-attorney' style," he "was not overly disturbed by this feature." A man of immense calm and lethargy, Eisenhower rarely became "overly disturbed."

Meeting in the same auditorium some weeks later, the Democrats were welcomed by Illinois Governor Adlai Stevenson, who delivered a sprightly rebuttal to their Republican predecessors. "For almost a week," he remarked, "pompous phrases marched over this landscape in search of an idea, and the only idea they found was that the two great decades of progress in peace, and of victory in war, and of bold leadership in this anxious hour, were the misbegotten spawn of bungling, of corruption, of socialism, of mismanagement, of waste, and of worse." He added: "I guess our Republican friends were out of patience, out of sorts, and, need I add, out of office."

As an ideological moderate and a noncontroversial governor of a major state, Stevenson had been the choice of Truman and other power brokers in the Democratic Party for the nomination. Yet he steadfastly refused to be drawn into the Presidential race. Instead, the choices narrowed down to Richard Russell of Georgia, a conservative and segregationist with little support outside the South; Averell Harriman, who was popular among Northern liberals, particularly in New York; and Estes Kefauver, who had attained national prominence through his televised investigations of organized crime. Kefauver, who had defeated Truman in the New Hampshire primary, had won thirteen out of fourteen of the nation's primaries and for a Southerner had particularly impressive liberal credentials; a staunch foe of corporate abuses and a grassroots crusader, he had been one of the few senators with the political courage to vote against the McCarran Act. His investigations of crime and corruption, however, had angered big city Democratic bosses, who worked fiercely to prevent his nomination. In the end, they joined Truman and other party leaders to "draft" Stevenson, who edged out Kefauver and secured the nomination on the third ballot. The Illinois governor returned to the convention to deliver a moving acceptance speech. "Let's talk sense to the American people," he declared. "We are now on the eve of . . . a long, patient, costly struggle which alone can assure triumph over the great enemies of man—war, poverty, and tyranny—and the assaults upon human dignity which are the most grievous consequences of each."

But, although he framed humane goals in a graceful, courtly style, Stevenson never escaped from the quagmire of Cold War politics. Americans had been "called upon" to defend freedom "against the mightiest forces of evil assembled under the sun," he declared during the campaign. Any withdrawal of American troops from Korea would "risk a Munich in the Far East." If United States forces "pulled out of Korea," he warned, "all of South Asia would be uncovered and inviting, like Indo-China, where the French have fought so long, so valiantly, and so expensively." On the issue of racial justice, too, Stevenson accepted a rather diluted form of "human dignity." When the civil rights question surfaced at the convention in the form of a party loyalty affirmation, to ensure that Southern delegates would not repeat their 1948 bolt, the Illinois delegation voted to seat the recalcitrant Southerners. This action reflected Stevenson's wishes, for he hoped to achieve a party compromise on racial equality. Eventually, the Democrats adopted a platform containing no specific proposals to end racial discrimination and nominated segregationist Senator John Sparkman of Alabama for Vice-President. This time, black delegates, led by Congressman Adam Clayton Powell, Jr., of New York, walked out of the convention. Thus, although Stevenson promised dynamic leadership of "a world in ferment," his campaign exhibited more intellectual style than liberal substance.

Eisenhower began his drive for the Presidency with the odds overwhelmingly in his favor. He was enormously popular, virtually the entire press supported him, and the news magazines adored him. Funding a lavish public relations campaign, the Republicans blanketed the media, particularly television, with Ike's sunny grin. Eisenhower's speeches, however, were clumsy, bumbling, and immensely boring; reporters joked: "He's crossing the 38th platitude again!" Yet he projected a warm and sincere personality, as well as an attractive indignation over the "mess in Washington" and the bloodshed in Korea. Drifting about the center of the political spectrum, he warned that the Democrats would move leftward; his Administration, he said, would go "down the middle."

By contrast, Stevenson faced a number of serious obstacles. Pre-eminent among them was Truman, an unusually unpopular President. Stevenson did his best, as Truman complained, "to disassociate himself from the administration in Washington." He replaced the chairman of the Democratic National Committee with an Illinois associate, Stephen Mitchell, moved his headquarters to Springfield, and turned his campaign over to a staff of amateurs. Nevertheless, Truman's unwanted campaigning on his behalf and the necessity of defending the record of the incumbent Democratic Administration undoubtedly weakened Stevenson's position. Furthermore, although Stevenson's polished speeches won him the admiration of the nation's intellectuals, he made a poor adaptation to television and radiated an unflattering "image." Even his wit could be turned against him, as when a dull but earnest Eisenhower solemnly announced that the current public issues were "not those that seem to me to be amusing." Finally, powerful Southern politicians, dis-

tressed since the New Deal by the national Democratic Party's emphasis upon economic equality and since 1948 by its advocacy of civil
rights, deserted the Democratic Presidential candidate. Governors
James Byrnes of South Carolina and Allan Shivers of Texas and Senators Harry Byrd of Virginia and Richard Russell of Georgia either endorsed Eisenhower or refused to support Stevenson.

Stevenson, who resembled Eisenhower in his personal traits of gentle-
manliness, good will, and innocence, seemed also to share many of
his views. Never much of a crusader for social reform, Stevenson
refused to make an economic appeal to the Democratic Party's working-
class constituency or to attack corporate wealth and privilege. "A striking characteristic of Stevenson's campaign," Irving Howe later observed, "was that he did not speak in the name of the poor or the
workers." Unlike Roosevelt and Truman, Stevenson sought to placate
businessmen by stressing budgetary economies. The Democratic program, he declared, must be "consistent with our national solvency and
with a sound national fiscal policy." In line with his "moderate" stance
on civil rights, Stevenson avoided a head-on confrontation with the
forces of Southern racism. "Prejudices, unhappily . . . tend to rise
wherever the minority in question is large," he told a campaign audience. "Some forget this, and, in talking of the South, forget that in the
South the minority is high. Some forget, too, or don't want to know
about the strides the South has made in the past decade toward equal
treatment."

Finally, while quite willing to condemn Senator McCarthy and his
methods, Stevenson refused to break free of the phantom issue of "internal subversion." After eloquently defending the "freedom of man to
think as he pleases," the Democratic nominee told the American Legion that much of the threat to civil liberties arose "from a healthy
apprehension about the communist menace within our country." Communism, he said, represented "death for the soul. Americans who have surrendered to this misbegotten idol have surrendered their right to our
trust. And there can be no secure place for them in our public life."
Warning that "we must take care not to burn down the barn to kill the
rats," Stevenson thus joined Eisenhower in questioning the methods but
not the professed aims of the Anti-Communist Crusade.

Adhering to their campaign formula of "Korea, Corruption, and
Communism," the Republicans utilized the issue of corruption in the
Truman Administration to embarrass Stevenson until, in September, it
boomeranged. Nixon had been assailing the "scandal-a-day" Democratic Administration and Eisenhower pledging to drive the "crooks and
cronies" from power when on September 18 the *New York Post* revealed the existence of a "secret Nixon fund" of $18,000, contributed

by California millionaires for the Anti-Communist Crusader's use after his election to the Senate in 1950. The fund's disburser, Pasadena corporation lawyer and investment banker Dana C. Smith, contended that "the whole idea . . . was to enable Dick to do a selling job to the American people in behalf of private enterprise and integrity in government." As Democrats seized upon the issue and demanded that Nixon be dropped from the ticket, the GOP campaigners were thrown on the defensive. Even prominent Republicans urged that Nixon withdraw. Eisenhower wavered, stalling for time and information. There would be no "whitewash," he assured reporters; "Nixon has got to be as clean as a hound's tooth."

Forced to defend his political life, Nixon appeared several days later on a nationwide radio-television hookup. Maintaining that "not one cent of the $18,000 . . . went to me for my personal use," Nixon told viewers that "every penny of it was used to pay for political expenses that I did not think should be charged to the taxpayers of the United States." The Republican Vice-Presidential candidate delivered a Lincolnesque version of his life, replete with irrelevant and sentimental devices, designed to turn the tables on the Democrats. "Pat doesn't have a mink coat," he said, referring to his teary-eyed wife, "but she does have a respectable Republican cloth coat. And I always tell her that she'd look good in anything." His most clever stratagem, however, emerged with his now-famous disquisition on Checkers:

> One other thing I probably should tell you, because if I don't they'll probably be saying this about me too; we did get something—a gift—after the election. A man down in Texas heard Pat on the radio mention the fact that our two youngsters would like to have a dog. And believe it or not, the day before we left on this campaign trip we got . . . a package. . . .
> It was a little cocker spaniel dog in a crate sent all the way from Texas. Black and white spotted. And our little girl—Tricia, the six-year old—named it Checkers. And you know the kids love that dog and I just want to say this right now, that regardless of what they say about it, we're going to keep it.

Evaluated by *Variety* as "a slick production," Nixon's speech met with immediate popular success. Over 300,000 messages of support flooded GOP National Headquarters. Darryl Zanuck called Nixon and congratulated him on "the most tremendous performance I've ever seen." At the Wheeling, West Virginia, airport, Eisenhower threw his arms around Nixon, declaring: "You're my boy." Democratic critics were plunged into gloom. The press and much of the nation swung back to Nixon's side.

With the corruption issue tarnished by the "secret fund" controversy, the Republicans hit all the harder at "internal subversion." Early in the campaign it had been decided that Eisenhower would focus on lofty, positive themes while Nixon would lead the assault on the opposition. Accordingly, Nixon had publicly blamed the Democratic Party for "the unimpeded growth of the Communist conspiracy within the U.S." and had become an expert on the patriotic credentials of his opponents. "Adlai the appeaser," he charged, was a "Ph.D. graduate of Dean Acheson's cowardly college of Communist containment." On October 8 he argued that a Democratic Administration would bring "more Alger Hisses, more atomic spies, more crises." Senator McCarthy, who predicted that Nixon's election would be "a body blow to the Communist conspiracy," made his only nationwide television appearance of the campaign on October 27 to present the "case against Stevenson." Noting that he would discuss the Democratic candidate's record only "in so far as it deals with his aid to the Communist cause and the extent to which he is part and parcel of the Acheson-Hiss-Lattimore group," McCarthy presented a series of "documents" and "exhibits" linking Stevenson's friends and advisers to liberal groups which, he contended, were either fronts for Communist subversion or included people who were members of other groups that were Communist fronts. In this oblique fashion, the Republican senator indicted Stevenson for having given "sympathy and aid to the Communist cause."

During the campaign, Eisenhower was repeatedly embarrassed by his dealings with the more militant Anti-Communist Crusaders in his own party. While he privately detested a number of them, he was determined to preserve party unity. In Indiana, therefore, he repeatedly embraced Senator Jenner—who had recently denounced Eisenhower's old comrade-in-arms George Marshall as a "front man for traitors"—and urged his re-election. In Wisconsin, McCarthy traveled across the state on the Eisenhower campaign train, appearing with him on the speaker's platform. At Green Bay, on October 3, Eisenhower made a direct appeal for McCarthy's re-election. Although they had "differences" as to "method," Eisenhower declared, "the purpose that he and I have of ridding this Government of the incompetents, the dishonest, and, above all, the subversive and the disloyal are one and the same." Yet despite Eisenhower's reluctance to break with his more scurrilous associates, the Communist issue had only a limited appeal among voters. Polls found that less than 3 per cent of the electorate expressed concern over Communists in government.

Of far greater interest to voters was the third key Republican issue—ending the Korean War. Polls as early as January, 1951, revealed that two out of three Americans favored American withdrawal from Korea. Stevenson, however, remained unwilling to suggest departures from Truman's war policy. "How long can we keep on fighting in Korea?" he asked rhetorically. "There is only one answer. We can keep it up as long as we have to—and we will." Eisenhower, on the other hand, while in agreement with Truman's decision to intervene and typically vague on what should be done in the situation, developed a strong anti-war appeal. Americans "must avoid the kind of bungling that led us into Korea," he told a campaign crowd. "The young farm boys must stay on their farms; the students must stay in school." Then, on October 24, he delivered an address in Detroit that clinched his role as the "peace candidate." The Democrats had given the "false answer . . . that nothing can be done to speed a secure peace," he said. If elected, he would "concentrate on the job of ending the Korean war. . . . I shall go to Korea." Replying to Eisenhower's dramatic declaration, Stevenson retorted that the American people would not be "taken in by a promise without a program." Nevertheless, many Americans responded eagerly to this first break with the bipartisan dogma of Cold War belligerence.

While the Republicans persuaded many voters that they were more capable than the Democrats of bringing peace, they made only marginal inroads on economic issues. To be sure, Eisenhower's hazy views and his battle with the Taft forces in securing the nomination had blunted the Democratic Party's economic appeal. Nevertheless, Stevenson retained the support of the AFL, the CIO, and most lower-income Americans. Large sectors of the public still had reservations about the ability of the Republican Party to maintain prosperity. "Everywhere I found only one issue helping the Democrats," political analyst Samuel Lubell reported "—the memory of the depression. . . . The fear of a return to 'those Hoover times' still dominated the thinking of millions of voters." As Americans reached for their ballots, most ignored the spurious issue of internal subversion and wrestled instead with the difficult choice of peace or prosperity.

On election day, Eisenhower swept to a landslide victory with 33,936,234 votes to Stevenson's 27,314,992; in addition, the Republicans captured both houses of Congress. Both Presidential candidates were obviously popular, for Stevenson's total in defeat surpassed Truman's in victory. The electoral vote—442 to 89—reflected Eisenhower's appeal in every section of the country. Stevenson carried only seven Southern and two Border states, while Eisenhower took every state in the East, Midwest, and Far West, as well as such previously Democratic bastions as Texas, Florida, Virginia, and Tennessee. Swelled by the ballots of sizable numbers of blacks, Catholics, and blue-collar workers, the Republican share of the urban vote rose to 44 percent. The Eisenhower sweep was particularly impressive in the suburbs, which some voting analysts considered the key to the political future. Senator Mc-

Carthy, a prominent figure during the campaign, was widely touted for his political success. Re-elected by a comfortable margin, the Wisconsin senator also had the pleasure of watching four of his Democratic Senatorial foes trounced at the polls. Conceding defeat on election night, Stevenson told his disheartened followers that he was reminded of Abraham Lincoln's story of the little boy who had stubbed his toe: he was too old to cry, but it hurt too much to laugh. At GOP headquarters in New York City's Hotel Commodore, thousands in expensively tailored suits and modish gowns joined in singing "God Bless America." "Twenty years of treason" had ended.

But the Republican landslide of 1952 was underwritten by a double irony. Despite their justifiable glee at the election results, the Anti-Communist Crusaders contributed little to the Republican victory; indeed, they may well have limited its dimensions. Whatever mandate the Republicans received was an Eisenhower mandate; right-wingers and McCarthyites actually fared rather poorly. Everywhere Republican Congressional candidates trailed far behind Eisenhower, and the GOP took power in Congress by the thinnest of margins: eight seats in the House and one in the Senate. In each of the twelve non-Southern states in which McCarthy had campaigned to elect a Republican Senator, the Democratic Senatorial candidate ran well ahead of Stevenson. In his home state of Wisconsin, where McCarthy's victory margin was 139,042 votes, Eisenhower's was 357,269; McCarthy, in fact, trailed every Republican on the statewide ballot. If any individual was responsible for restoring the Republicans to power in the White House and on Capitol Hill, it was not the controversial McCarthy but the immensely popular Eisenhower.

Furthermore, insofar as issues counted at all in 1952, the major issue of the election as perceived by voters was the Korean War. Here Stevenson was saddled with the unpopular culmination of Truman's Cold War policies—policies which he strongly supported in the campaign and which cost him dearly in competition with Eisenhower's call for peace. As in 1948, New Deal–style concerns held together what elements remained of the Democratic coalition, but, under the stresses and strains of the Cold War, that coalition was by 1952 in an advanced state of disintegration. The long Democratic era, then, was brought to a close, not only because the Republicans nominated a war hero, but because voters could not abide the consequences of the major policy innovation provided by the Truman Democrats: the Cold War. Frustrated in their desire for peace, millions of Americans found no alternative but to abandon the Democratic Party and to turn the reins of government over to its conservative competitor.

5

The Rulers and the Ruled:
American Society, 1945-60

> What sphinx of cement and aluminum
> bashed open their skulls and ate up
> their brains and imagination?
> Moloch! Solitude! Filth! Ugliness! Ashcans
> and unobtainable dollars! Children
> screaming under stairways! Boys
> sobbing in armies! Old men weeping
> in the parks!
> Moloch! Moloch! Nightmare of Moloch!
> Moloch the loveless! Mental Moloch!
> Moloch the heavy judger of men!
>
> ALLEN GINSBERG, *Howl,* 1956

"AMERICA IS A MIDDLE-CLASS COUNTRY," sociologist David Riesman concluded from the vantage point of his Harvard University office. "Perhaps people will soon wake up to the fact that there is no longer . . . a 'we' who don't run things and a 'they' who do, but rather that all 'we's' are 'they's' and all 'they's' are 'we's'." Few ideas were more widely bruited about in the prosperous postwar years than the notion that substantial inequalities in the distribution of wealth and power in America had ceased to exist. Arthur F. Burns, Eisenhower's top economic adviser, remarked in 1951 that "the transformation in the distribution of our national income . . . may already be counted as one of the great social revolutions in history." When economist John Kenneth Galbraith's *The Affluent Society* appeared in 1958, it seemed merely to set the seal of approval on the prevailing consensus. The "old issues" of inequality, slums, and inadequate wages and medical care were dead, he contended; instead, the nation now faced the problems of abundance. All seemed to agree that the crusades against inequality that had marked previous decades in American history could safely be abandoned. "The fundamental political problems of the industrial revolution have been solved," sociologist Seymour Martin Lipset announced

111

in 1959, with the "triumph of the democratic social revolution in the West."

This optimistic assessment owed much to the postwar wave of prosperity. The gross national product jumped from $212 billion to $504 billion between 1945 and 1960. In the 1950s alone, per capita personal income rose 48 per cent. In 1953 an estimated 58 per cent of American families earned between $3,000 and $10,000 a year compared to 31 per cent with similar purchasing power in 1929. From 1929 to 1945 large sectors of American society had lived in an economy of scarcity, their purchasing power cut by the low incomes of the Depression and the rationing of the war years. In the postwar period, however, the craving for consumer goods at last found satisfaction. Americans bought 8 million automobiles—a record number—in 1955. By 1960, 75 per cent of American households owned at least one car, 87 per cent a television set, 86 per cent a refrigerator, and 75 per cent a washing machine. Spurred by the new prosperity, the birth rate in America increased sharply; between 1950 and 1960 the nation's population expanded by 28 million, with two-thirds of the growth occurring in the burgeoning suburbs. Although full employment did not carry beyond World War II and recessions struck the nation in 1949, 1954, and 1958, the rate of joblessness remained far below the level of the 1930s. Most Americans were enjoying a steadily rising standard of living.

But postwar prosperity obscured the more significant reality of economic inequality. Although the share of the national income received by the wealthiest 5 per cent of the American population dropped markedly in the Depression and war years, it stabilized in 1944 at 21 per cent and did not change significantly thereafter. The poorest 20 per cent of American families received 5 per cent of the national income in 1944, and this, too, remained virtually constant. Even more striking was the increasingly unequal distribution of wealth. According to the National Bureau of Economic Research, the share of the nation's wealth held by the richest .5 per cent of the adult population steadily declined between 1929 and 1949 until it hit 19.3 per cent, but thereafter it increased, reaching 25 per cent in 1956. By 1962 the richest 1 per cent of the population held 33 per cent of the wealth, the richest 5 per cent held 53 per cent, and the richest 20 per cent held 77 per cent—more than 154 times the share of the nation's wealth (less than .5 per cent) held by the poorest 20 per cent.

Corporate wealth provided the basis for this inequitable structure. Despite the fanfare given "people's capitalism" by the National Advertising Council and the U.S. Information Agency, almost 95 per cent of the American people owned no corporate stock in 1956. Indeed, a study by Robert Lampman, later a top White House economic adviser, revealed that the share of corporate stock held by 1 per cent of American adults increased from 61.7 per cent in 1945 to 76 per cent in 1953. In that same year, 1.6 per cent of the population owned 82.2 per cent of the corporate stock, 88.5 per cent of the corporate bonds, and virtually all of the state and local bonds. If the United States lacked dramatic class conflict from 1945 to 1960, it was nonetheless a class society, based on private ownership of a corporate economy.

Actively managing their businesses or merely reaping the profits, the corporate rich enjoyed a rewarding life in the postwar years. The board chairmen of six American oil companies drew annual salaries ranging from $175,000 to $250,000. Most corporation executives owned large blocks of company stock; indeed, stock and cash bonuses often outdistanced annual salaries. Thus, in 1952, the president of Du Pont received $153,290 in salary and $350,000 in bonuses; the president of Bethlehem Steel received $150,000 in salary and $306,652 in bonuses; and the president of General Motors received $201,000 in salary and $380,000 in bonuses—in addition to dividends. Corporation executives also received a variety of less visible emoluments, including expense accounts, country club privileges, business cars, lavish parties, company credit cards, paid vacations, medical treatment, and sizable pensions. The U.S. Treasury Department estimated in 1957 that expense accounts ran from $5 billion to $10 billion annually; most items charged to credit card companies in 1958 were billed to businesses. Direct income, then, represented only a small fraction of the bonanza enjoyed by the corporate élite, and even this fraction was frequently underestimated on federal tax returns. Nevertheless, the Internal Revenue Service announced in 1961 that 398 taxpayers had reported incomes of at least $1 million that year—as opposed to 62 in 1944. In 1953 Robert Lampman had estimated that there were 27,000 millionaires in America; nine years later, the Federal Reserve System reported 80,000.

Despite their unprecedented prosperity, the corporate rich introduced few dramatic changes in the well-ordered routine of American upper-class life. Childhood dancing classes and attendance at prep schools like Exeter, Andover, Choate, Groton, and Hotchkiss continued to give a young man the proper social training and associates before entering an élite college or university, joining the "right" campus club or fraternity, and taking up his place in the appropriate men's club—the Links, the Knickerbocker, the Metropolitan, the Racquet, or the Brook. Fashionable summer resorts, debutante balls, cultural organizations, and recreational activities such as yachting, polo matches, and fox hunts gave him the opportunity to mingle comfortably with members of his class. A young lady might attend dancing classes as a child before "coming out" in society at the crucial debutante ball. The debut of eighteen-year-old

Charlotte Ford in 1959 took a year to plan, was attended by 1,200 guests, and cost $250,000. The *New York Times* noted: "Two million magnolia leaves were flown in from Mississippi and were used to cover the walls of the corridors leading to the reception room in the Country Club of Detroit, which had been redecorated to look like an eighteenth-century French chateau." To be sure, the rich had their problems. Observing in 1952 that his holdings were probably worth several billion dollars, J. Paul Getty added morosely: "But remember, a billion dollars isn't what it used to be."

As always, the business élite took a keen interest in the policies of the American government. "Gulf and every other American corporation is in politics, up to its ears in politics," a senior vice-president remarked in 1958. The largest manufacturers and bankers, primarily white Anglo-Saxon Protestants from families that achieved prominence between the Civil War and the Depression, controlled the Republican Party. The Democratic Party, on the other hand, was controlled by very old and very new elements within the upper class, including Southern aristocrats, a few old Northern patricians, and the newer ethnic rich. In 1952 the top Republican and Democratic campaign committees received most of their income in contributions of $1,000 or more. The known contributions to Eisenhower's 1956 campaign included $100,000 from the Mellons, $152,000 from the Rockefellers, $216,000 from the Pews, and $248,000 from the Du Ponts. Officers and directors of America's largest corporations contributed at least $1.8 million to the GOP Presidential campaign that year.

"Business liberals," usually from the largest, most internationally oriented companies, found their voice in the Council on Foreign Relations and the Committee for Economic Development and their home in the "moderate" Eastern wing of the GOP or in the Democratic Party. The "old guard," more right-wing in viewpoint, mostly comprised nationally oriented businessmen who provided the bedrock strength of the National Association of Manufacturers and the conservative wing of the Republican Party. "Business liberals" were particularly enraptured by the Eisenhower Administration, but "old guard" elements, such as the new Texas oil millionaires, lavishly funded right-wing politicians and causes. Three former presidents of the NAM were among the first leaders of the John Birch Society.

The political power of the corporate rich is illustrated by the fact that, although they constituted less than 1 per cent of the population, they dominated the key policy-making posts within the federal government. Of the ninety-one individuals who served as Secretaries and Under Secretaries of State and Defense, the Secretaries of the three military services, the Chairmen of the AEC, and the Directors of the

CIA between 1940 and 1967, seventy came from the ranks of big business and finance. Members of the upper class seemed particularly welcome in the State, Defense, and Treasury departments. Of the six Secretaries of State between 1945 and 1960, five were listed in the *Social Register*. Three of the five were corporation lawyers, one was a wealthy general, and one was a Boston aristocrat; the sixth was a powerful Southern Democrat of conservative views. Between 1947, when it was created, and 1960 the Department of Defense was headed by six men, of whom five were listed in the *Social Register;* the exception was the president of General Motors.

During his term of office, President Truman relied heavily upon Wall Street financiers, many of whom were not even Democrats. Twenty-two key posts in the State Department, ten in the Defense Department, and five top positions in other agencies went to bankers who were either registered Republicans or politically unaffiliated. Eisenhower preferred to appoint directors of the nation's major manufacturing concerns. His first Secretary of Defense was a former president of the world's largest industrial corporation; his Secretary of the Treasury had formerly directed a complex of more than thirty corporations; his Secretary of State had been the senior partner of the nation's leading corporate law firm; and every other member of his Cabinet—with the exception of the Secretary of Labor—came from the ranks of the corporate rich. Of the thirty-two members of Eisenhower's subcabinet, only four were not directly associated with the corporate world. However competent these top-level officials might have been, few rejected the values of the corporate world. "You will gather that I am an advocate of business, and so I am," Secretary of Defense Forrestal wrote on August 26, 1947. "Calvin Coolidge was ridiculed for saying . . . 'The chief business of the United States is business' but that is a fact."

As the business élite moved assuredly through the world of political power, the leading corporations strengthened their grip on the nation's economy. Corporate profits, $19 billion in 1945, hit $50 billion but fifteen years later. In 1950 the share of the business assets held by the nation's 200 largest companies was 48.9 per cent; by 1962 it had reached 55 per cent. In the latter year, the hundred largest manufacturing corporations drew 57.6 per cent of the net profits, while the thousand largest manufacturing corporations accounted for 86.4 per cent. Adolph A. Berle, a leading analyst of business trends, reported in 1957 that American corporations had achieved "the highest concentration of economic power in recorded history."

A pacesetter in the business boom, the oil industry accounted for six of the ten largest industrial corporations in the United States. In 1959 the United States consumed 60 per cent of the world's production, and oil was the largest single item of international trade. More than one-fourth of the land area of the United States was under lease for oil and gas exploration. With gross assets of $60 billion in 1960, the oil and natural gas industries were the largest purchasers of capital goods in the United States. Standard Oil of New Jersey produced and refined about 15 per cent of the world's crude oil supply in 1957 and held assets of $8.7 billion; by 1959 its assets had climbed to $9.9 billion. Between 1946 and 1956 the Phillips Petroleum Company quadrupled its assets and income, while the Gulf Oil Company quadrupled its assets and quintupled its net income. In 1957 *Fortune*'s list of millionaires was headed by J. Paul Getty, H. L. Hunt, Sid Richardson, and other oilmen, including numerous Rockefellers, Mellons, and Pews.

Government solicitude for the rich did much to make such gains possible. A variety of loopholes kept the effective rate of inheritance taxes under 10 per cent, while sales taxes, a form of government levy that hardly touched the wealthy, spread to cities and states throughout the nation. The progressive effects of the federal income tax, once the pride of liberals, were gutted in the postwar years by preferential treatment for capital gains, depletion allowances, depreciation allowances, and tax-free privileges for interest on state and municipal bonds. In 1961 seventeen persons with incomes of $1 million or more and thirty-five others with incomes over $500,000 paid no federal income taxes. Reporting on the cumulative impact of taxation on income in 1960, economist Leon Keyserling concluded that those who earned under $2,000 paid out 38 per cent of their income in taxes, while those who earned above $10,000 paid out only 31.6 per cent.

Similar government beneficence was extended to corporations. A study during the 1950s disclosed that, as a result of the 27½ per cent oil-depletion allowance, oil companies deducted nineteen times more for tax purposes than they could deduct under normal cost depletion. Senator Paul Douglas estimated that between 1945 and 1954 twenty-seven domestic oil companies with pretax incomes of $3.25 billion paid federal corporate taxes of only $562 million—an effective rate of 17 per cent as compared to the official corporate tax rate of 52 per cent. Other tax breaks, such as deductions for depreciation, development costs, and special losses, also favored the oil industry. Thus, Humble Oil, with a pretax income in 1957 of $193 million, paid only $17 million that year in corporate taxes. The Arabian-American Oil Company, with a net income of $272 million in 1955, paid no corporate income taxes.

Even more significant benefits flowed to American corporations—and to the economy as a whole—from the high level of federal military expenditures. Between 1946 and 1960 the Defense Department alone purchased $501 billion worth of goods and services. "National security" expenditures generally accounted for about 70 per cent of the annual federal budget. In the half-century prior to 1930 federal military expenditures had averaged less than 1 per cent of the nation's annual GNP, and from 1931 to 1939 military outlays averaged only about 1.3 per cent. From 1946 to 1960, however, federal military spending averaged about 10 per cent of the nation's annual GNP, serving as a sharp stimulus to the economy. Indeed, the American economic structure might well have foundered in the aftermath of the postwar spending boom had the military not taken up the market slack after 1950. In 1939, the last year of the Great Depression, 18.6 per cent of the nation's work force was either employed as a consequence of the military budget or unemployed; in 1961 16.1 per cent of the nation was in a comparable situation. Yet the high level of "defense" spending not only spurred sales and employment but altered the very nature of the nation's economy. In the new "contract state," the Pentagon set demand, funding its purchases of corporate equipment with tax dollars. The price of such equipment was generally determined, not through free market competition, but through a "cost plus" arrangement, guaranteeing a corporation a minimum profit agreed upon in advance. Thus, the United States moved away from the "free enterprise" system preached by conservatives and the "mixed economy" proclaimed by liberals toward a government-subsidized private profit system. "We are living under a curious kind of military Keynesianism," wrote historian Richard Hofstadter, "in which Mars has rushed in to fill the gap left by the decline of the market economy."

Military Keynesianism proved a great boon to corporate sales. In 1958, for example, the military purchased 100 per cent of the nation's ordnance production, 94 per cent of its aircraft, 61 per cent of its ships and boats, 21 per cent of its electronic equipment, 13 per cent of its primary metals, and 10 per cent of its petroleum. Between 1950 and 1954 General Motors alone received defense contracts worth $7.5 billion. In May, 1962, a government investigator told a Senate subcommittee that the annual profits of the Boeing Aircraft Corporation, when measured by net investment, had ranged in the preceding decade from 36 per cent to 108.6 per cent. In 1954 net profits as a percentage of net worth reached 139 per cent for General Dynamics, 93.3 per cent for Boeing, 81.1 per cent for Douglas, 80.7 per cent for North American, 76 per cent for Martin, and 72.3 per cent for Republic. While big business drew most of the defense bonanza, small business also felt its impact. A 1960 study of 1,165 small businesses, sponsored by the Aerospace Industries Association, found that 48.9 per cent of their sales came from defense contracts.

Convinced, in the words of the pro-business *U.S. News and World Report,* that the "Cold War is almost a guarantee against a bad depression," American corporations tied their fortunes to the ascending military star. Corporations lobbied furiously for bigger Pentagon contracts. "The aircraft industry," said Senator Barry Goldwater, "has probably done more to promote the Air Force than the Air Force has done itself." Cementing their links to the Pentagon, corporations staffed their hierarchies with unprecedented numbers of retired military officers. A House subcommittee revealed in 1960 that 1,400 retired officers above the rank of major, including 261 generals and admirals, were employed by the hundred leading defense-contract corporations. General Dynamics, ranking first among defense contractors from 1957 to 1960, maintained 186 retired officers on its payroll, while retaining a former Secretary of the Army as chairman of its board of directors. With sales and profits soaring under the reign of Pentagon capitalism, American business showed little enthusiasm for peacetime reconversion. In 1960, when the projected international summit conference collapsed and talk of disarmament faded, the stock market rose dramatically. The *New York Times* explained: "Traders decided that the 'cold war' was due to heat up considerably . . . and that this would mean a step-up in the nation's defense program." Pentagon-business collaboration became so blatant that, in January, 1961, President Eisenhower used his farewell address to urge Americans to "guard against the acquisition of unwarranted influence by the military-industrial complex."

American business also gained significantly from its expanding overseas operations, promoted and protected by U.S. foreign policy. Between 1946 and 1960 the value of direct (or controlling) American private investment abroad increased from $7 billion to $32 billion. Total U.S. private investment abroad increased between 1950 and 1960 from $19 billion to $49 billion. During the 1950s the direct investment outflow was $13.7 billion and the returned income $23.2 billion—a handsome profit. About 75 per cent of Standard Oil of New Jersey's profits in the late 1950s were derived from its foreign investments, while Gulf derived two-thirds of its income from its overseas operations. Reporting on a study in 1955, a U.N. commission revealed that the net profit on a barrel of Saudi Arabian oil selling for $1.75 was $1.40. U.S. corporate earnings on petroleum investments in Latin America, after local taxes, averaged 25.6 per cent annually from 1951 to 1955, and 20.5 per cent for the period from 1956 through 1958. Such lucrative profits encouraged a rise in the value of direct U.S. private investment in Latin America from $4.6 billion to $9 billion between 1950 and 1959. The dominant position of American corporations, particularly in the Third World, is illustrated by the fact that in 1959 seven oil corporations, five of them American, held two-thirds of the world's recognized reserves, controlled the bulk of the world's crude-oil production and refining, owned the major pipeline systems, and controlled the tanker fleets. The five American companies had overseas investments of $9 billion, with contracts covering 64 per cent of the Middle East's oil reserves.

A growing volume of world trade proved equally crucial to American corporations. Before World War II, the net U.S. mineral imports amounted to less than 1 per cent of domestic consumption, but in the postwar years this pattern shifted significantly. Between 1956 and 1960 the United States imported over half its total metal consumption as well as more than half its supply of fifty-four minerals and crude commodities. A 1954 staff report of the President's Commission on Foreign Economic Policy noted that the "transition of the United States from a position of self-sufficiency to one of increasing dependence upon foreign supply is one of the striking economic changes of our time." In return for their vast imports of raw materials, U.S. corporations inundated the markets of the "free world" with the latest manufactured products. From 1950 to 1960 the value of American exports doubled to $20.6 billion, while American imports climbed by almost two-thirds to $14.7 billion. Moreover, these figures reflect only a declining fraction of total U.S. overseas commerce, for America's rapidly growing multinational corporations increasingly produced and sold goods within foreign nations themselves. Little wonder that the corporate élite took a keen interest in American foreign policy. The United States "must set the pace and assume the responsibility of the majority stockholder in this corporation known as the world," declared the treasurer (later chairman) of Standard Oil of New Jersey in 1946. "American private enterprise . . . may strike out and save its own position all over the world, or sit by and witness its own funeral."

Committed to expanding their overseas operations, American businessmen remained equally determined to develop their private markets at home. Widening the base of personal consumption in the United States would have necessitated a redistribution of income; corporate chieftains sought instead to induce those who could already purchase what they wanted to buy still more and, if possible, to waste what they had already bought. Not the fulfillment of need but the creation of desire was the function of advertising, whose annual volume rose in the fifteen years after 1945 from less than $3 billion to almost $12 billion —about three times the nation's annual expenditures on higher education. Consumerism became the true American religion, the "American way of life." Dr. Raymond Saulnier, chairman of the Eisenhower Council of Economic Advisers, proclaimed that the "ultimate purpose" of the

American economy was "to produce more consumer goods. This is the goal. This is the object of everything we are working at." Caught up in the mammoth sales campaigns and barraged by the mass media, Americans became increasingly convinced that happiness meant ceaseless acquisition. A young German writer observed: "Now people no longer have any opinions; they have refrigerators. Instead of illusions we have television, instead of tradition, the Volkswagen. The only way to catch the spirit of the times is to write a handbook on home appliances."

The mass media served as the principal disseminators of the ideology of individual acquisition. As one critic noted: "It could almost be argued that the articles in magazines and programs on television are simply a device to keep the advertisements and commercials from bumping loudly together. The message of the media is the commercial." Between 1946 and 1960 the number of families in the United States with television sets rose from 8,000 to 46 million, giving the electronic medium the ability to reach into 90 per cent of American homes. With families spending an estimated five hours a day watching television, corporations worked ceaselessly to exploit this market for their products. One of the three giant broadcasting networks would screen program material to lure an audience, which would then be surveyed in terms of numbers, income level, age, and sex, and "sold" to a corporate sponsor. Having "bought" the audience, the corporation would then saturate it with ads in an effort to increase its consumption. The primary function of television, then, was commerce, which explains why commercials, filling 20 per cent of air time, cost far more to produce and were far more skillfully done than the programs they framed. The commercial "isn't art, but it's artful," *Newsweek* later observed, "which is more than can be said for many of the tasteless, saccharine, and irritating programs supported by the sponsors."

During the 1950s intellectuals criticized television for appealing to "the lowest common denominator," but this charge merely reflected their élitism. Television programming represented not what audiences wanted but what they received from cynical or indifferent broadcasters and sponsors, devoted to the commercial aspects of the medium. Avoiding "upsetting" programs, corporations fed the public a bland filler of game shows, audience participation programs, formula comedies, mystery stories, Westerns, and cartoons between the commercials. Chiding broadcasters in 1961 for the wretched quality of their programming, Federal Communications Commission chairman Newton R. Minow urged them to try sitting and watching their television output for an entire day. "I can assure you," he said, "that you will observe a vast wasteland."

Yet television and the mass media also played a crucial political role.

As the Defense Department's director of research told a Senate committee in 1961: "We cannot consider our communications systems solely as civil activities . . . but we must consider them as essential instruments of national policy." On news programs events were reported anecdotally, individually, amusingly. Institutional problems were ignored, controversial opinions left unspoken, and the day's events viewed as a hopeless jumble, interesting but purposeless, by a cheery, fatherly commentator; implicitly, the viewer was assured that the nation was in good hands. More subtly, the mass media evaded America's public and private issues and thus, as sociologists Paul Lazarsfeld and Robert Merton observed, "fail to raise essential questions about the structure of society." Television and the movies were filled with escapist tales of violence and exploitative sex. Mass culture did not encourage thought, creativity, or personal expression but, rather, passivity. It channeled the interests of the weary viewer into an unreal world where he could act out fantasies of personal power and freedom. Not religion but television served as the opiate of the masses.

Television's potentialities for public enlightenment were displayed only rarely. In 1953–54, for example, news analysts Edward R. Murrow and Fred Friendly stunned the television industry by raising questions about the Anti-Communist Crusade on their program, *See It Now.* When they asked CBS for money to advertise the three key broadcasts, the network refused, and they funded the advertising themselves. The first and most dramatic of the programs told the story of a twenty-six-year-old student who had been forced to resign his commission in the Air Force Reserve because his sister and father had been accused by unidentified persons of having radical leanings. As television had never before dared to challenge the Anti-Communist Crusade, the program was aired in a state of high tension. Murrow finished up, Friendly recalled, "bathed in sweat and smoke," as staff members and engineers crowded about him to shake his hand. In 1955 *See It Now*'s sponsor, the Aluminum Company of America, dropped the program. Its time slot was sold to a tobacco company for a quiz show.

American newspapers, often considered more "serious" about politics and society than the network media, were in fact subject to many of the same pressures and biases. By the early 1960s, the press was increasingly dependent upon business advertising, and newspaper ownership had become a monopoly in 95 per cent of American communities. A few newspapers, like the *St. Louis Post-Dispatch,* the *New York Post,* the *Washington Post,* and the *Madison* (Wisc.) *Capital Times,* continued their muckraking activities, but most others evaded or distorted the news about power and privilege in America. Often they ran government press handouts as news stories or seemed unwilling to challenge government lies. "The news of the CIA and its operatives all over the world," James Reston testified before a Congressional committee in 1955, confronts the reporter with "the dilemma as to whether he is going to tell the truth or whether he is going to mislead the American people by putting out something put out by the Government which he knows not to be true." Although Washington made no attempt to muzzle the press during the Korean War, newspapers and press syndicates took care to police themselves. "We are operating just as we would under censorship," the editor-in-chief of the International News Service wrote to General MacArthur. In April, 1951, the Director of U.S. Defense Mobilization thanked newspapers for "millions of words laying down the premise . . . that the free world is in mortal danger. . . . If the people were not convinced of that it would be impossible for Congress to vote the vast sums. . . . With the support of public opinion as marshaled by the press, we are off to a good start."

Staunchly committed to an aggressive American role in the world, the media engaged in fantasies of thermonuclear war—which, of course, the United States always won. After devoting four and a half columns to America's capacity to destroy Russia "in several ways and several times over," the March 25, 1959, issue of the *Wall Street Journal* reassured its readers that, "even granting that Russia would have the advantage of surprise, U.S. officials reason that a first blow by the Soviets . . . would not cripple Western power to retaliate." In late 1951, "alarmed . . . over the creeping pessimism of the free world," the editors of *Collier's* devoted an entire issue to a depiction of World War III, as fought between the United States and the Soviet Union, to "demonstrate" that, in the event of war, "we will win." During the postwar occupation of the devastated Soviet Union, remarked the editors, "private enterprise would probably evolve in a form that would be modified by background, environment, and the character of the people themselves." *Collier's* showed Moscow audiences at the Bolshoi Theatre enthralled by an "excellent production of *Guys and Dolls,*" noted that newsstands featured *Time, Life,* and the *Reader's Digest,* and observed that "Hollywood columns are very popular."

The blackout of critical opinion during the postwar years received still further impetus from the loyalty crusade. Learned men assessed the patriotic merits of movie and television scripts. Performers and newscasters were dropped as "security risks." Charlie Chaplin, once America's best-loved clown and social satirist, surrendered his re-entry permit in 1953, choosing exile from a nation he could no longer endure. "What is the new loyalty?" asked historian Henry Steele Commager. "It is, above all, conformity. It is the uncritical and unquestioning acceptance of America as it is."

In the era of the booster, religion took on a patriotic significance. "Recognition of the Supreme Being is the first, the most basic expression of Americanism," President Eisenhower declared in 1955. Congress added the words "under God" to the nation's "pledge of allegiance" and "In God We Trust" to coins. In Lincoln's day only about one out of five Americans had belonged to a church, but by 1958 church membership had climbed to a record 110 million citizens. Polls found that 95 per cent of the respondents considered themselves Protestants, Catholics, or Jews, and that 97 per cent believed in God. The Reverend Billy Graham held enormous religious revivals, while fundamentalist sects grew rapidly. Religious books became best-sellers, spreading a message of joyous acceptance. "Don't doubt," pleaded the Reverend Norman Vincent Peale; "doubt closes the power flow." The very source of Communism, claimed Whittaker Chambers, an ardent religious mystic, was the scientific method, with its "rigorous exclusion of all supernatural factors in solving problems." Believing America to be locked in a struggle with "atheistic Communism," American churches faithfully mirrored the Cold War line in the years before 1960. Roman Catholic clergy spearheaded the Anti-Communist Crusade and discussed preventive war against Russia, while fundamentalist Protestant sects portrayed the Cold War in apocalyptic terms, identifying Stalin with the Anti-Christ and discovering descriptions of atomic warfare in the Book of Revelation.

Blessed by the guardians of religion, America's "patriotic" crusade also drew at least the tacit support of most American educators. "The single most important educational frontier," reported the U.S. Commissioner of Education in 1947, was the need to "strengthen national security through education." Responding to pressures for conformity, the National Education Association proclaimed in 1949 that Communist teachers should be dismissed from their posts. Three years later the American Federation of Teachers adopted a similar position, which also became the general outlook of college and university presidents. Only the American Association of University Professors and the American Civil Liberties Union took the stand that competence alone should determine employment. A minority of American educational institutions stood firm against the loyalty zealots. Most colleges, however, showed an eager willingness to cooperate with special investigations. Indeed, a group of educators even proposed that the colleges set up their own investigatory procedures to weed out alleged "subversives."

Although the dimensions of the campus heresy hunt have been obscured by the genteel propriety which traditionally cloaks academic employment, it left few institutions unscarred. In a 1958 study by sociologists Paul Lazarsfeld and Wagner Thielens, Jr., 102 of the 165 colleges and universities surveyed reported political firings. The case of Professor Barrows Dunham is instructive. A full professor with tenure, head of the Temple University Philosophy Department, and author of several books, Dunham was summarily dismissed by the university's president, Dr. Robert L. Johnson, for refusal to testify before HUAC. Although Dunham later won a court fight against a Congressional contempt citation, he remained unemployed—unlike Johnson, who became head of the Voice of America. Another well-known sociological study of ten major American universities in the mid-1950s concluded: "The net outcome of the prolonged crisis of academic freedom from 1946 to 1956 is a marked restriction of the freedom of professors to engage in politics. . . . Political activity of any kind by any faculty member is viewed unfavorably and is likely to bar or delay his advancement." Most American academicians retired to their books, their records, their middle-class circle of well-being. On the university campus, sometimes located near a slum or racial ghetto, they concerned themselves with the education of the "gifted" or with turning out the "well-rounded student."

But the American university was a valuable institution, and the corporate élite merely wanted it tamed, not destroyed. Thus, despite the demoralization of the professoriat, its ranks actually swelled from 196,000 to 250,000 between 1948 and 1957 as part of a vast building and expansion program in higher education. A study by the Council for Financial Aid to Education found that in 1956 "corporate investments in education" by 275 firms totaled almost $29 million. University presidents lent a sympathetic ear to the needs of business, promoted the establishment or expansion of engineering and business schools, frequented the conference room of wealthy private foundations and the Pentagon, and managed their growing "plant" like administrators of the great industrial and financial corporations, on whose boards of directors they often sat. Grayson Kirk, president of Columbia University after Eisenhower, served on the boards of Consolidated Edison, IBM, the Socony-Mobil Oil Company, and the Nation-Wide Securities Company, and would soon be one of the directors of the Institute for Defense Analysis. By the mid-1950s, the Pentagon was supplying approximately $300 million annually for university research, and two major universities—MIT and Johns Hopkins—placed on the list of the nation's top 100 defense contractors. According to a 1961 Harvard University report, "science and defense have brought Government and the educational community together to such an extent that 20% of the total expenditures in higher education in the United States now comes from Federal sources."

Surveys of college students during the 1950s invariably found them conservative, careerist, and conformist. Journalist William H. Whyte contended that younger men "do not wish to protest, they wish to collaborate." Students worked harder, professors agreed, but seemed less "interesting." College girls told pollsters that they preferred having babies to careers, while bright young men asked corporate interviewers about their pension plans. "When a liberal or speculative voice is heard in the classroom, it is more likely than not to be the professor's," noted a faculty member at Queens College. Students, he observed, "matriculate cautious, wanting above all . . . to buy security for themselves in the full knowledge that the price is conformity." From the University of Nebraska, the poet Karl Shapiro reported: "Passivity is the last word we expect to use in connection with a generation of students, but that's the only word that applies."

Loyalty investigators and corporate recruiters did much to encourage this "silent generation." "Personal views can cause a lot of trouble," confided an oil company "guidance" pamphlet widely used in college placement offices. "Remember to keep them always conservative. The 'isms' are out. Business . . . naturally looks with disfavor on the wild-eyed radical or even the moderate pink." But a more immediate stimulus to Cold War orthodoxy developed after 1950, when the CIA began covertly funding the National Student Association, the nation's largest and most influential student organization, providing it in some years with up to 80 per cent of its income. By 1966, when the CIA venture was at last exposed by an NSA officer, NSA leaders had accepted $4 million in return for providing information on foreign student leaders and for operating a properly anti-Communist student organization.

American intellectuals of the era seemed no less accommodating. Government disdain for critical thought, far from sparking a revolt of the intellectuals, drove them instead toward self-pity and élitism. Depressed and dispirited, they talked gloomily of Eisenhower's fondness for Westerns, of Postmaster General Arthur Summerfield's boast of Republican "progress in rooting out the eggheads," and of the alleged lack of public esteem for scholars, artists, and men of letters. Many bewailed the absence of an intellectual élite in America and looked nostalgically toward the class distinctions of Europe. In a book "conceived in response to the political and intellectual conditions of the 1950s," Richard Hofstadter concluded that "anti-intellectualism" was "founded in the democratic institutions and egalitarian sentiments of this country." Criticizing intellectuals for their past participation in movements for social justice, he argued that the "intellectual class . . . is of necessity an élite in its manner of thinking and functioning." Hofstadter, Seymour Martin Lipset, Talcott Parsons, Edward Shils, David Riesman, Nathan

Glazer, Oscar Handlin, Daniel Bell, and Peter Viereck popularized the notion that McCarthyism was the heir to the radical Populist agitation of the past, a profoundly democratic, popular phenomenon that could be countered only by a renewed respect for compromise, stability, and élites. Mass movements, with their grass-roots participation, moral commitment, and emotional enthusiasm, they argued, were the true danger to intellectual freedom in America. Intellectuals of the 1930s had romanticized The People as a noble force, striving for a New World. Now, increasingly, intellectuals viewed The People as The Enemy.

Intellectual life in America had taken a profoundly conservative turn. A new generation of historians smoothed over the radical convulsions of the past, writing fondly of an American "consensus" beyond which only fools and neurotics dared to tread. Political scientists talked much of "pluralism"—the alleged equality of power among competing groups in America. Accepting the structure of society as given, they looked to technical experts to solve any problems that might crop up. Sociologists, ignoring class structure and the existence of poverty, focused upon the problems of individual identity in a mass society. In philosophy speculative thought gave way to analysis of existing linguistic practices, in the belief that most—if not all—philosophical difficulties arose from the misuse of language; social distinctions that enforced linguistic usage were not themselves examined or criticized. Increasingly, economists and social scientists argued that big business was both democratic and beneficent. America, they claimed, had a "mixed" economy in which socialist aims—at least those of any value—had been incorporated. While most intellectuals never drifted to the right of the moderate Establishment, a few preached a New Conservatism, drawing their arguments consciously from Aristotle, Saint Thomas Aquinas, Edmund Burke, George Santayana, Irving Babbitt, and T. S. Eliot. "For the radical intellectual who had articulated the revolutionary impulses of the past century and a half," wrote Daniel Bell, there has been "an end to chiliastic hopes, to millenarianism, to apocalyptic thinking—and to ideology."

Not surprisingly, American intellectuals developed considerable affection for a U.S. foreign policy based upon *Realpolitik*. Many, like Reinhold Niebuhr and Walter Lippmann, both former idealists and socialists, criticized what they considered a bankrupt utopianism and urged renewed attention to human greed, ignorance, and depravity. Power, they argued, was what counted in world affairs. In *American Diplomacy, 1900–1950* (1951), George F. Kennan helped set the tone for political scientists and other scholarly appraisers of foreign policy by sharply assailing "the assumption that state behavior is a fit subject for moral judgment." Together with Hans J. Morgenthau—whose *In Defense of the National Interest* (1951) found justice, morality, and "world opinion" irrelevant—Kennan launched an attack upon "idealism," which frequently had the effect of stimulating cynicism and Machiavellianism among intellectuals and policy-makers. In these years the "defense of the national interest" invariably coincided with a defense of America's role in the Cold War.

Prized by Washington for their skills as sophisticated weaponeers, American scientists and engineers quickly swirled into the Cold War vortex. President Eisenhower revealed that in 1960 approximately a third of American scientists and engineers were engaged in military work and that half the nation's research and development funds went to military projects. "This symbiosis between science and the military," wrote physicist I. I. Rabi, was "the most important . . . social and political development of this century." By contrast, those scientists with doubts about the arms race encountered a most unsympathetic reception from government loyalty investigators. The scientific community was "demoralized," reported Dr. Vannevar Bush, former head of the Office of Scientific Research and Development, in 1954. Later that year, Albert Einstein declared in a public letter that, if he were young again, he "would not try to become a scientist or scholar or teacher. I would rather choose to be a plumber or a peddler in the hope to find that modest degree of independence still available under present circumstances."

The rise of the paramilitary intellectual reached its apogee with the emergence of the new "civilian strategists." Employed by private "research institutes," which then contracted them out to the Pentagon, the young experts with advanced degrees often surpassed their political and military mentors in the grandeur of their plans. Perhaps the best-known member of the military brain trust, the Rand Corporation's Herman Kahn, achieved considerable recognition in 1960 with the publication of *On Thermonuclear War*. Although fascinated by the destructive possibilities of "doomsday machines" and "galaxy-destroying machines" for his projected World Wars III through VIII, Kahn settled in the end for thermonuclear war as the only "acceptable" model; in his view, acceptability could encompass but not exceed the death of half the population of the United States. "Objective studies," he noted reassuringly, indicated that "even though the amount of human tragedy would be greatly increased in the postwar world, the increase would not preclude normal and happy lives for the majority of survivors and their descendants." Implicit in Kahn's analysis were two significant assumptions: that military deterrence did not work and that a thermonuclear war could be "won." Both led to his logical conclusion that massive preparations for the great day should begin at once.

In these years only a tiny group of intellectuals—most notably Erich Fromm, Irving Howe, Paul Goodman, and C. Wright Mills—offered a radical critique of American life. Mills, the most daring, argued that power in America was located centrally, in the hands of an interlocking directorate of warlords, corporation titans, and executive politicians. Congress, the middle classes, labor unions, and pressure groups had little influence, and the "power élite" ruled without serious challenge in an increasingly helpless, atomized mass society. Scorning "those who have abandoned criticism for the new American celebration," Mills lashed out at his fellow academics and intellectuals. "They live and work in a benumbing society," he wrote, "without living and working in protest and tension with its moral and cultural insensibilities. They use the liberal rhetoric to cover the conservative default."

The retreat of intellectuals from social criticism reflected a variety of factors. For some, the failure of American capitalism to collapse and of the Soviet Union to provide a decent alternative lay at the root of their disillusionment with "ideology." Others seemed eager to erase the stigma of a radical past by "confessing" before loyalty investigators or simply by becoming "apolitical." Most significantly, well-paid employment in book publishing, radio, and television, and with universities, foundations, magazines, newspapers, and the federal government took the edge off intellectual alienation. Soothed by comfortable salaries and flattered by the attention of men of power, many intellectuals concluded that their own upper-middle-class problems of affluence, leisure, and suburban existence were the major ones facing American society.

Nevertheless, the CIA was careful to ride herd on American intellectuals, for the Cold War seemed to necessitate competition with Communism in the literary and cultural realm. Accordingly, the CIA infiltrated and financed intellectual groups, subsidized publishing houses and periodicals, moved agents into universities, and placed articles in scholarly journals such as *Foreign Affairs.* Its most daring venture was its sixteen-year subsidy of the Congress for Cultural Freedom, an organization actually headed by a CIA agent, which published the British journal *Encounter* and rallied leading artists, writers, and social scientists in the 1950s to America's Cold War standard. In June, 1950, at the founding meeting of the Congress, in Berlin, philosopher Sidney Hook told the assemblage that he looked forward to the time "when references to 'right,' 'left,' and 'center' will vanish from common usage as meaningless." Stressing "one basic point, delegates . . . admonished listeners," said the *New York Times,* "that the time is at hand for a decision between East and West." In 1951 Hook, James Burnham, James T. Farrell, Arthur M. Schlesinger, Jr. and other well-known intellectuals founded a U.S. branch of the organization, the American Committee for Cultural Freedom. Under its auspices, conservatives like Burnham, Farrell, Ralph De Toledano, John Chamberlain, John Dos Passos, and Whittaker Chambers consorted with Schlesinger, Irving Kristol, Daniel Bell, and other Cold War liberals. The committee distributed in pamphlet form an article written by Hook which sought to develop an anti-Communist position different from either that of the Right or that of "ritualistic liberalism." Dissent, said Hook, was legitimate, but Communists were conspirators, not entitled to the same liberties as other Americans. And even non-Communists who criticized U.S. government policy received a public chiding from the committee. Like their counterparts in the Soviet Union, members of the American Committee seemed to define cultural freedom as loyalty to the state.

Some writers and artists, less directly useful to men of power and more sensitive to the sham of the American Celebration, remained alienated. What interaction did take place between the world of the creative artist and the world of power showed the limits of the American consensus. In 1952 President Truman explained that, in art, he had no use for "the lazy, nutty moderns. It is like comparing Christ with Lenin." When a reporter asked President Eisenhower's Secretary of the Treasury, George Humphrey, whether he had read Ernest Hemingway's *The Old Man and the Sea,* the Cabinet official voiced the typical sentiments of the ruling business circles: "Why should anybody be interested in some old man who was a failure and never amounted to anything anyway?" "The artist," William Faulkner told the American Academy of Arts and Letters in 1958, "has no more actual place in the American culture of today than he has in the American economy . . . no place at all in the warp and woof, the thews and sinews, the mosaic of the American dream."

Yet literary rebellion was virtually nonexistent. Popular fiction stressed the themes of individual acquisition, business success, conformity, and anti-Communism. Mickey Spillane's *One Lonely Night* (1951), which sold more than 3 million copies, contained a soliloquy by detective Mike Hammer which should have cheered the most fanatical of Red-hunters: "I killed more people tonight than I have fingers on my hands. I shot them in cold blood and enjoyed every minute of it. . . . They were Commies. . . . They were red sons-of-bitches who should have died long ago." Novelists Sloan Wilson and Cameron Hawley gave sympathetic portrayals of the lives and travails of businessmen, while the immensely popular novels of Herman Wouk touched a conservative nerve in middle-brow America. In *The Caine Mutiny* (1951), Wouk defended absolute loyalty to the professional officer corps, and in *Marjorie Morningstar* (1955) he applauded the heroine's decision to repudiate the world of intellectuals and bohemians for comfortable marriage to a businessman.

Even "serious" fiction skirted America's social problems. Mary McCarthy, Bernard Malamud, and Saul Bellow devoted their talents to novels of manners and personal life, offering individual, often improbable solutions to the quest for personal identity and freedom. In his immensely popular *Catcher in the Rye* (1951), J. D. Salinger posed no alternative to the adult world of hypocrisy and corruption except withdrawal into the innocence of childhood or the consolation of Zen. Ironically, the "Beat" writers of San Francisco, so different in their approach to life and literature, shared similar preoccupations. Cutting loose from bourgeois society to wander restlessly in search of spiritual enlightenment through the greasy-spoon diners of the world, they turned ever more frenetically to drugs and mysticism. "If you shun consciousness as if it were a plague," Irving Howe wrote of them, "then a predicament may ravage you, but you cannot cope with it."

One of the few writers who seemed capable of giving definition to the problems of contemporary America and perhaps projecting solutions was Norman Mailer. *The Naked and the Dead* (1948), his first novel, established him immediately as a serious writer and social commentator. Mailer's *Barbary Shore* (1951) reflected in more surrealistic fashion on the failures of the Old Left, and *The Deer Park* (1955) provided an ambivalent picture of Hollywood. At this point, however, Mailer seemed to lose his way, and his writing drifted off into strange and exotic realms of supersexuality, self-analysis, and demonology. By 1959 literary critic Alfred Kazin could report that Mailer, who "once seemed another Dos Passos," now appeared "bent on becoming the American Marquis de Sade." Of all the novels published between 1945 and 1960, perhaps only Ralph Ellison's *The Invisible Man* (1952) could be called a significant work of social criticism. Here the protagonist confronts and finally understands the real world; then, rejecting it in horror, he retreats underground, brooding and waiting.

Once the very symbol of life in the lower depths, American labor seemed to thrive in the postwar years. Incomes rose, unemployment remained mild by Depression standards, and union membership increased from 14.3 million to 18.1 million between 1945 and 1960. In 1955 the feud between the CIO and the AFL came to an end when a convention in New York merged the two labor federations. The political-action arms of both groups joined to form the Committee on Political Education, and a staff of 265 organizers and millions of dollars in union pledges were set aside to "organize the unorganized." New labor contracts provided for cost-of-living increases as well as productivity increases, and unions also made breakthroughs on "fringe benefits": holidays and vacations, health and welfare plans, and pension and unemployment benefits. Throughout the 1950s most strikes grew less rancorous than in previous decades. Picketing was sometimes unnecessary, and at other times management would supply pickets with hot coffee and portable washrooms. Taking office in 1955, AFL-CIO president George Meany announced: "American labor has never had it so good."

In fact, however, the labor movement was in serious trouble. It encountered little difficulty in retaining the allegiance of those blue-collar workers it had already organized, but their numbers were steadily dwindling with the over-all decline of blue-collar employment. After 1951 more than a third of American unions suffered membership losses. Nor did the AFL-CIO succeed in reaching many of the unorganized, particularly in service trades, white-collar fields, and agricultural employment. By 1960 unions had organized only 12,000 of the 600,000 engineers, draftsmen, and technicians; 184,000 of the 5 million public employees; 200,000 of the 8.5 million office workers; and 4,000 of the 2 million agricultural workers. Pledges to the AFL-CIO's organizing fund were never met, the size of the organizing staff was cut in half, and the attempt to unionize the South—the nation's antiunion bastion —proved virtually a complete failure. Nonunion companies and areas fought fiercely to smash organizing efforts. "Do you want to work under a Negro foreman?" Southern employers would ask their workers. "Do you want your dues money to go to the NAACP?" In 1953, when 2,000 wretchedly paid and miserably housed sugar cane workers walked off their jobs on plantations near New Orleans in an attempt to secure recognition of their AFL union, the local press was filled with comments about "agitators," "brainwashing," and "made in Moscow." In this sort of atmosphere unions made little headway: between 1945 and 1960 the unionized segment of the nation's nonagricultural labor force actually shrank, from 35.8 to 31.4 per cent.

Moreover, even organized workers achieved only minimal gains. In part, this reflected the fact that a giant corporation, having agreed to a wage settlement, would simply raise its prices, thus passing along the cost of the settlement to all workers as consumers. Of all labor leaders, only Walter Reuther championed raising wages while freezing prices, and the auto companies refused to consider this prospect. During the 1950s blue-collar workers fell farther behind other groups in terms of income. Laborers and service workers made income gains of 39 per cent, while professional and managerial workers made income gains of 68 per cent. In addition, by concentrating upon wages and fringe benefits, unions failed to secure many changes in job conditions. Safety features in American coal mines remained abysmal; mine explosions and other lethal disasters were frequent. Every year approximately 100,000 American workers were killed or suffered permanent impairment in industrial accidents. Factory labor remained exceptionally alienating: the work was often physically exhausting; the hours were long and the rest periods few; the assembly line was fast and inexorable; the work was monotonous and unfulfilling; the shop noisy and ugly; the air filled with smoke, dust, or chemicals; and the production goals set by a distant corporate bureaucracy. Interviews with workers revealed considerable resentment and frustration. Typical remarks included: "Sometimes you feel like jamming things up in the machine"; "the only reason a man works is to make a living"; and "whenever the line jerks, everybody is wishing, 'break down, baby.' " A survey of automobile workers in the late 1940s and early 1950s found that the overwhelming majority wanted to leave the factory for other work—not to get rich, but to escape from dissatisfaction on the job.

One of the most striking developments of the postwar years was the growing centralization of power in the union leadership and the concomitant decline in rank-and-file participation. Lacking left-wing rivals to contest their authority, many labor leaders grew increasingly autocratic and arbitrary, if not actually corrupt. This trend was reinforced by the merger of the AFL and CIO, which ended competition for locals and members and thus precluded escape from domination by the national union's political machine. In the United Mine Workers, one-man control by John L. Lewis and secret bargaining sessions after 1950 between the union and the bituminous coal industry left the membership inactive and uninvolved, learning of contract negotiations only after a settlement had been reached. After 1950 no major strike occurred in the soft coal industry—a far cry from the annual strikes and grass-roots militancy of the past. In the once lively United Auto Workers, Walter Reuther consolidated his strength, encouraging organizational solidarity and stability. At the 1957 UAW convention the national leadership had such control of the union that there was insufficient opposition to obtain a single roll-call vote. While the Reuther leadership remained capable and progressive, internal democracy and insurgency decayed. The Amalgamated Clothing Workers, a formerly Socialist-oriented union and a pioneer in collective bargaining, ceased to engage in nationwide strikes or militant agitation in the postwar years. Its solidly entrenched leadership kept down rank-and-file demands for wage increases and cooperated closely with manufacturers to improve shop efficiency and production. The story was the same throughout most of the American labor movement. Between 1946 and 1963 the number of striking workers dropped from 4.6 million to 941,000. Union leadership was so stable that by 1958 the average age of the men on the AFL-CIO executive council was in the middle sixties.

Perhaps the major contributor to the decay of American unions was the rising status of the labor leadership. In 1957 a dozen union presidents received salaries ranging from $33,000 to $60,000. Some union leaders charged large sums to their expense accounts for lavish hotel and restaurant bills. Many spent considerable time on investments, including personal stock and property holdings, while their families engaged in upper-middle-class pastimes. As the lifestyle of such union leaders came to resemble that of corporation executives, they lost their link to the men they represented on the grimy shop floor. "Many union leaders have become money-hungry, taking on the grossest features of business society," wrote Daniel Bell in 1958. "One finds . . . an appalling arrogance and high-handedness in their relation to the rank-and-file."

George Meany, the new president of the AFL-CIO, embodied many of these traits. A former Bronx plumber's assistant who had held union office jobs since 1933 and had become AFL president in 1952, Meany was a sullen, heavyset figure who looked like a veteran of the picket lines. In fact, this was hardly the case. In 1956 he boasted to the National Association of Manufacturers: "I never went on a strike in my life, never ordered anyone else to run a strike in my life, never had anything to do with a picket line." Shortly before assuming the presidency of the AFL-CIO, Meany was earning $35,000 a year and living in Bethesda, Maryland, a Washington suburb. "In most particulars," a friendly journalist noted, "Meany leads the placid suburban life typical of the businessmen he has long dealt with. He belongs to a country club, golfs with sober diligence, and enjoys an occasional duck-shoot or coon-hunt." Sporting colorful vests and chomping on a fat cigar, the leader of the American labor movement was driven to work every morning in the AFL's limousine.

Throughout the postwar years labor grew increasingly dependent upon military spending. By 1960 the jobs of 7.5 million Americans— about one-tenth of the nation's work force—depended directly upon the annual military appropriation. Moreover, the location of defense industries made certain areas of the country extremely dependent upon military largesse. In 1959 aircraft and missile production provided 82 per cent of all manufacturing employment in San Diego, 72 per cent in Wichita, and 53 per cent in Seattle. Between 20 and 30 per cent of manufacturing employment in the states of California, Connecticut, Kansas, New Mexico, and Washington was defense-related. Aware that their members would be left stranded in economically depressed areas if local defense plants closed down, unions joined management in vigorously lobbying against cuts in the military budget. "One of the most serious things about this defense business," observed Secretary of Defense Charles E. Wilson in 1957, "is that so many Americans are getting a vested interest in it: properties, business, jobs, employment, votes, opportunities for promotion and advancement" and "bigger salaries."

Not surprisingly, organized labor grew more conservative. To be sure, the AFL-CIO served as a major pressure group in behalf of social-welfare programs. Nevertheless, class-conscious politics and anticapitalist fervor had become historical relics. Once a leading American Social-ist, David Dubinsky, president of the International Ladies Garment Workers Union, concluded in the postwar years that "trade unionism needs capitalism like a fish needs water." In foreign affairs, few could match organized labor's devotion to the Cold War. Both the AFL and the CIO served as conduits for CIA funds to Washington's favorite overseas unions. Meany headed the American Institute for Free Labor Development, which disbursed an estimated $120 million a year in CIA money to tame labor movements abroad. The AFL-CIO's foreign policy program—written for the most part by Jay Lovestone, the embittered former secretary of the American Communist Party—supported U.S. government actions at every turn.

Had the AFL-CIO's leadership been less concerned with aping busi-ness mores and values, it might have shown greater interest in the plight of the nation's poor. By 1960 between 40 and 50 million Americans— 20 to 25 per cent of the population—lived in conditions of poverty. Tucked away in urban ghettos, on tiny farms, and in rural shantytowns, the poor endured invisible lives of misery and despair, victims of mal-nutrition, disease, imprisonment, crime, and squalor. While the wealthy fretted over the problems of overeating, surveys in the mid-1950s reported that a majority of the rural poor lacked one or more of the basic nutrients in their diets. Such malnutrition produced severe skin infections and ulcerations, bacterial and parasitic diseases, heart weakness, bone diseases, and the symptoms of anemia—poor muscle tone, weakness, and lassitude. As the fashionable suburbs expanded around the nation's central cities, the poor were consigned to crowded, wretched dwellings in the decaying urban core; in New York City alone, an estimated 2,500 human beings—mostly infants—were bitten by rats every year. The 1960 Census reported that 27 per cent of the nation's occupied dwelling units were substandard—a figure that did not take account of "sound" housing that was overcrowded.

One of the nation's leading housing experts, Charles Abrams, described a 1950 visit to New York's slums:

> The writer saw a six-story 25-foot-wide tenement . . . into which 170 Puerto Ricans had been herded. . . . The apartments had to be shared and there were twelve people living in a single three-room apartment. Every hall window was broken. Splintered stair treads sank perilously with each step. Almost every toilet was out of order. Loosened plaster hung from the hall ceilings; great heaps of garbage rotted on the floor under the stairways; a dead rat lay on a landing. Gaping holes in the toilet walls served as passageways for the rats. . . .
>
> In another ancient tenement on the same street there were 15 people in a four-room apartment; in another, 18 people occupied a three-room unit. [On a nearby street] 30 people lived in a building sharing a single broken toilet without a seat. Here too there were rat holes in the walls.

Nor were these the worst dwellings examined by Abrams. Nearby, he found "25 human beings living in a dark and airless coal cellar ten feet below the street level." In this cellar, "these people ate, slept, washed, and reproduced. No animal could live there long, yet here were 17 children, the youngest having been born here two weeks before. Almost all the 17 children had been sick during the preceding weeks."

Although the wealthy dismissed the poor as lazy idlers, a large number of the impoverished were either too old or too young to work, while perhaps a third held full-time jobs for which they received wages below the subsistence level. A 1960 Senate subcommittee report declared that "at least one-half of the aged—approximately eight million people—cannot afford today decent housing, proper nutrition, adequate medical care . . . or necessary recreation." Census figures for 1958 revealed that nearly 60 per cent of the American population over sixty-five years of age had incomes under $1,000 a year. Despite claims that Americans lived lives of affluence in a "welfare state," in 1959 Social Security payments averaged only a little better than $70 a month, while 54 per cent of the aged lacked hospital insurance and 63 per cent lacked surgical insurance. Large sectors of the nation's active labor force, often excluded from coverage under the minimum wage and Social Security laws, received incomes totally inadequate to sustain a decent standard of living. Thirty per cent of the men employed by American industry in 1958 earned less than $3,000 the previous year. In the late 1950s the average income for white male farm workers was just over $1,000 a year.

The nation's 2 million migrant workers lived brutal existences reminiscent of those described by John Steinbeck's *The Grapes of Wrath* two decades earlier. Excluded from minimum wage and maximum hour legislation, they worked long, exhausting days for a pittance on the giant farms of the wealthiest growers, 10 per cent of whom cultivated half the nation's farmland. Computing the average wages of Mexican "bracero" labor—a good index to the wages of all migrant laborers— the U.S. Secretary of Labor gave an estimate of 50 cents an hour in 1959. In Texas, though, growers paid their workers 16 cents an hour for a 60-hour week. Although farming had the third highest fatality rate of all industries in the nation, agricultural workers were not covered by workmen's compensation laws. In 1956 the number of people killed in agriculture exceeded that in any other industry. As many children often worked in the fields alongside their parents—a practice encouraged by the growers, who occasionally shortened the school year to accommodate their seasonal labor needs—more than a thousand children under sixteen years of age sustained serious farm injuries in California alone between 1950 and 1957.

The wretched lives of these hard-working people provide a striking backdrop to claims that the United States had become an affluent, middle-class society. In its 1951 report, the President's Commission on Migratory Labor revealed that in California's rich Imperial Valley the infant death rate from diarrhea, enteritis, and dysentery was more than seven times as high as the statewide average. In Hidalgo County, of eighty-three children between the ages of six and twelve, twenty-one needed immediate medical treatment; for twenty-seven others "medical care was . . . indicated but less urgent." In one Texas camp 96 per cent of the children had consumed no milk in the previous six months, and eight out of ten adults had not eaten any meat. Writing in 1955, Charles Abrams reported that, while the fortunate migrant laborer managed to obtain "a ramshackle shed, tent, or cabin," others could find no better place to sleep than "on the ground, in a cave, under a tree, or in a chicken house." During those months they could not obtain employment, many migrant workers would repair to "Ragtown," a shacktown community of stray boards, scrap metal, burlap sacks, and pieces of cardboard.

America's racial minorities, while never a majority of the nation's poor, remained firmly locked in the camp of the impoverished. Victimized by race and by poverty, most lived in a dismal world of job discrimination, urban and rural slums, and occasional mob violence. Although black income increased in the postwar years, it never approached that of whites. In 1947 the nonwhite worker's wage averaged 54 per cent of the white worker's; by 1958 it had climbed to 58 per cent, but by 1962 it had fallen back to 55 per cent. Median family income for whites stood at $5,643 in 1959, for nonwhites $2,917. The status of black farm families in the South was far worse; a 1954 study by the Department of Agriculture found that their median income was only $742 a year. In 1950 one out of two white males in the South was employed in a white-collar or skilled nonagricultural job, compared with one out of eight black men. Most blacks employed in that region labored as farmers; truck, bus, or taxi drivers; as workers in lumber mills, mines, laundries, food-processing plants, parking lots and garages, chemical factories, metal refineries, foundries, and plants; and as janitors, porters, domestics, or unskilled laborers. According to the Department of Labor in 1960, 25.9 per cent of white employees in the United States were in professional, technical, managerial, official, or proprietary roles, compared to 6.7 per cent of the blacks. By the late 1950s, noted the Commission on Civil Rights, nonwhite unemployment rates were more than twice those for whites.

Such disparities in income and employment reflected the racist practices of business, government, and labor in postwar America. Corporations were careful to keep managerial, office, and white-collar positions lily-white and cheerfully encouraged or acquiesced to racism at the blue-collar level. In early 1958 the *Wall Street Journal* quoted the manager of a General Motors plant near Atlanta as saying: "When we moved into the South, we agreed . . . not to hire Negroes for production work. This is no time for social reforming in that area, and we're not about to try it." The Civil Rights Commission reported in 1961 that "the Federal Government continues . . . to give indirect support to discriminatory practices . . . in training programs, in employment agencies and opportunities," and "in public facilities." Within the labor movement, the commission noted, "civil rights goals are celebrated at the higher levels but fundamental internal barriers tend to preserve discrimination at the workingman's level." Although some unions moved vigorously against racial discrimination in the postwar years—notably the United Packinghouse Workers, the United Auto Workers, and the Oil, Chemical, and Atomic Workers—many others, particularly in the building trades, excluded blacks or segregated them in Jim Crow locals. Two of the railway brotherhoods actually barred the entry of blacks by constitutional provision, but most other unions merely followed policies of tacit discrimination.

Against such racial barriers, advances in education were of only minimal value. As early as 1950 black college enrollment had reached 132,000—up 2,500 per cent from a decade before. Nevertheless, both in the North and in the South black college graduates in 1949 earned less than whites who had attended, but not graduated from, high school. The Civil Rights Commission observed that in 1959 the median income of a white family headed by a college-educated male was $7,373, while that of a comparable black family was $5,654; sizable income differentials appeared at other educational levels as well. In 1950, indeed, almost one-fourth of nonwhite college graduates worked in laboring or service jobs, compared to only 1.4 per cent of similarly educated whites.

By 1960 most blacks in America lived in overwhelmingly segregated ghettos—usually slums in the nation's cities—and suffered from inadequate housing, nutrition, and health conditions. The Civil Rights Commission reported the same year that 57 per cent of all nonwhite housing units were substandard. As late as 1950 almost half of all nonwhite homes had outdoor privies, while nearly 42 per cent of nonwhite homes in urban areas lacked a private flush toilet. In 1960 nonwhite life expectancy was seven years less than white, the nonwhite infant mortality rate was almost twice that for whites, and the nonwhite maternal mortality rate was almost four times that for whites. While nonwhite infant and maternal mortality rates did decline after 1940, they grew worse relative to those for whites.

In 1960 New York's Harlem housed 232,792 people within its 3.5 square miles—a population density which, if applied to all the inhabitants of the United States, would have enabled them to fit within three of New York City's five boroughs. About half of Harlem's residential buildings were erected before 1900, and, according to the 1960 Census, 44 per cent of its buildings were dilapidated or deteriorating. In 1959 infant mortality was about three times as high in Central Harlem as in one of the city's wealthier white districts. Black psychologist Kenneth Clark observed: "Where flies and maggots breed, where the plumbing is stopped up and not repaired, where rats bite helpless infants, the conditions of life are brutal and inhuman." Not surprisingly, between 1955 and 1961 the rate of narcotics use in Harlem was consistently ten times that of New York City.

Nonwhites lived in such areas not only because they were poor but because of racial discrimination. Banks, realtors, and property owners kept much of the nation's better housing out of the hands of nonwhites through a deliberate policy of exclusion. Until 1950 the code of ethics of the National Association of Real Estate Boards contained the canon: "A realtor should never be instrumental in introducing into a neighborhood . . . members of any race or nationality . . . whose presence will clearly be detrimental to property values." Although this statement was slightly modified thereafter, its meaning remained clear. Furthermore, much American housing was subject to racially restrictive covenants. During the 1952 Presidential campaign both Vice-Presidential candidates lived in such houses. Slumlords actually encouraged the existence of racial ghettos, for they were enabled thereby to overcrowd and to overcharge for deteriorating housing. Even when a prominent black made an occasional breakthrough into the land of the lilywhite, it could provide but a bitter satisfaction. "Thank the people of

San Francisco for letting you buy this house," the star Giant outfielder Willie Mays was told in the late 1950s, after resistance to his purchase of a home in a wealthy white neighborhood had been overcome. "What do I have to thank anybody for?" Mays retorted. "For letting me spend $40,000?"

Conditions for black Americans reached their nadir in the South. Here white supremacy was buttressed by the police power of state and local governments and enforced, if necessary, by terror. In 1960 Southern lunch counters, motels, theaters, toilets, and drinking fountains were segregated; in more than forty Southern counties not a single black was registered to vote; only one-sixth of one per cent of Southern black students attended desegregated schools; the Ku Klux Klan acted openly in many communities; and the White Citizens Councils, founded in 1954, increasingly dominated local governments. Bombings and other assaults upon blacks were common. In December, 1950, when dynamiters destroyed the home of a black woman who had led a court fight against a Birmingham zoning law, it was the fifth bombing of a black house in that city since the spring of 1949. In Dallas alone, thirteen dynamitings of black homes occurred during a seventeen-month period. The brutal lynching of fourteen-year-old Emmett Till provided only the best-known example of "Southern Justice" in the 1950s. In 1961 the Commission on Civil Rights found 100 Southern counties where blacks were "prevented—by outright discrimination or by fear of physical violence or economic reprisal—from exercising the right to vote," and "many counties" where "a substantial Negro population not only has no voice in government, but suffers extensive deprivation—legal, economic, educational, and social."

Nor was the North immune to racist violence. Between 1945 and 1954 there were nine race riots in Chicago alone, and from 1949 to 1951 more than 100 lesser racial incidents occurred in that city, including fires, bombings, and organized assaults upon black families. During 1953 racial violence, arson, or bomb-throwing by whites erupted in Kansas City, Madison, East Saint Louis, Cleveland, Chicago, Indianapolis, Long Island, and Los Angeles county. One of the more dramatic incidents occurred in Cicero, Illinois, where Harvey E. Clark, Jr., a black war veteran and graduate of Fisk University, sought in the summer of 1951 to move his family's furniture into a $60-a-month apartment he had leased. The moving van was halted by police. According to an affidavit by Clark, the chief of police "hit me about eight times while he was pushing me ahead of him. . . . When we reached my car . . . the chief shoved me inside and said, 'Get out of Cicero and don't come back . . . or you'll get a bullet through you.' " But after an NAACP suit enjoined the city from "shooting, beating or otherwise harassing Clark," he did, in fact, begin to move in on July 10. Crowds of jeering whites started to gather and smash windows. By the following day a mob of 4,000 had collected. Undeterred by policemen, who joked with them, or by the mayor and chief of police, who were "out of town," the mob began three days of savage rioting, during which it tore up trees by the roots to build fires; hurled bricks, flares, and burning torches into the apartment house; ripped out radiators and walls; and threw furniture from the windows. On July 12 Governor Stevenson declared martial law in Cicero and sent in the state militia, which pushed back the mob at bayonet point; four militiamen were felled in the process. In a bizarre aftermath, a grand jury indicted the NAACP attorney, the apartment owner, her lawyer, and her rental agent for conspiracy to injure property by causing "depreciation in the market selling price."

"I am an invisible man," declared the black protagonist of Ralph Ellison's 1952 novel. "I am invisible, understand, simply because people refuse to see me." Few, indeed, would face up to the reality of social injustice in the postwar United States, for the American celebration had become functional to a society seduced by prosperity and patrolled by the state. And so starvation went unrecognized in the midst of unprecedented abundance, political purges in the bastions of intellectual freedom, worker alienation in a time of business expansion, and racial lynchings amid hosannahs for "free world" democracy. Fostered by the wealthy and powerful, it was a situation much to their advantage. If Fortune smiled on the postwar United States, she reserved her keenest delights for the forces of privilege.

6

"Waging Peace," 1953-60

> We were brought to the verge of war. . . . We walked to the brink and we looked it in the face.
>
> JOHN FOSTER DULLES, 1956

As a candidate for President, Eisenhower had sharply criticized the Truman Administration's conduct of foreign affairs, but once in office he initiated few major changes in the nation's foreign policy bureaucracy. To be sure, his new Secretary of State, John Foster Dulles, did purge the last of the "old China hands" from the State Department and did bring in a confederate of Senator McCarthy, Scott McLeod, to enforce political orthodoxy in the nation's foreign service. Yet Dulles himself typified the American foreign policy establishment. Grandson of one former Secretary of State and nephew of another, senior partner in an immensely influential Wall Street law firm specializing in the international interests of corporations, and a leading diplomat in the Truman Administration, he brought with him the heritage and assumptions of America's governing élite. During the 1930s Dulles had been a frequent apologist for fascist expansion. He told readers of the *Atlantic Monthly* in 1935 that Germany, Italy, and Japan "want peace but . . . desire to keep open avenues of change." In the postwar years, however, he promoted a very different assessment of the Soviet Union. "This is an irreconcilable conflict," he explained at Senate hearings on his nomination. Like so many of the nation's foreign policy-makers, he viewed the Cold War in starkly ideological terms, arguing that Russia was obsessed by a desire for world revolution. "Soviet leaders are to a very large extent the prisoners of their own doctrine," he told European diplomats, "which is extensively held by their followers, who are fanatics."

Eisenhower, who considered Dulles the greatest Secretary of State he "knew anything about," was inclined to leave most foreign policy matters in his trusted hands. "With my understanding of the intricate relationship between the peoples of the world and your sensitiveness to the political considerations," the Secretary of State assured the President, "we will make the most successful team in history." In practical terms, however, this hardly mattered, for both men shared the conservative assumptions of the nation's postwar decision-makers. "We are linked to all free peoples not merely by a noble idea but by a simple need," the President declared in his 1953 inaugural address. "No free people can for long cling to any privilege or enjoy any safety in economic solitude. For all our own material might, even we need markets in the world for the surpluses of our farms and factories. Equally, we need . . . vital materials and products of distant lands." Like Dulles, Eisenhower thought the nation was engaged in a Manichean conflict. "Forces of good and evil are massed and armed and opposed as rarely before in history," he said that day. "Freedom is pitted against slavery, lightness against dark." Convinced of Moscow's loyalty to ideals of proletarian solidarity, he commented irritably in his memoirs that Khrushchev was "blinded by his dedication to the Marxist theory of world revolution." Only American Communists took Soviet pretensions with more seriousness!

This position became increasingly difficult to sustain after Stalin's death on March 5, 1953. While hardly a fomenter of the class struggle, Stalin had been sufficiently brutal, authoritarian, and, in his last years, insane to frighten many people, including many leaders of Western Europe. Moreover, after the outset of the Korean War he had doubled the size of the Soviet Army and increased defense expenditures by 50 per cent. His successors, however, quickly gave a much friendlier impression, proclaiming their hopes for peaceful relations with the West. Assuming Stalin's old post as Chairman of the Council of Ministers and Secretary of the Communist Central Committee, Georgi Malenkov announced that "there is no dispute or unresolved question that cannot be settled peacefully by mutual agreement." Malenkov was soon forced from power by the even more genial Nikita Khrushchev and Nikolai Bulganin, who lurched across Europe in a frenzied round of cocktail parties and press conferences, affirming the need for "peaceful coexistence." The new Soviet leadership allowed Russians married to foreigners to leave the country; re-established diplomatic relations with Greece, Israel, and Yugoslavia; renounced claims to Turkish territory; and agreed to work toward settlement of the Korean War. Between 1955 and 1960 the Russian government cut its defense budget by more than half. Soon even America's closest allies in Western Europe were questioning the rigidity of Washington's stance. "I am of the opinion," said Winston Churchill, "that we ought to have a try for peaceful coexistence, a real good try."

American political leaders, however, resisted Soviet moves toward a détente. On April 3, 1953, in response to public discussion of a thaw in the Cold War, Secretary of State Dulles remarked that "nothing that has happened, or which seems to me likely to happen, has changed the basic situation of danger in which we stand." He blocked Churchill's proposal for a "summit" conference in 1953 and two years later prevented a visit to Washington by Soviet Marshal Georgi Zhukov, a close associate of Eisenhower's during World War II. On October 30, 1953, Eisenhower approved a National Security Council memorandum which claimed that, despite Stalin's death, "Soviet rulers can be expected to continue to base their policy on the conviction of irreconcilable hostility between their bloc and the non-communist world." While noting that "many" Europeans "tend to see the actual danger of Soviet aggression as less imminent than the United States does," the memorandum declared that "in the face of the Soviet threat," the United States should maintain "a strong military posture, with emphasis on the capability of inflicting massive retaliatory damage by offensive striking power." In 1954, when the Soviet Union announced that it had suspended nuclear testing, Dulles warned that the Western alliance would not be "lulled into a false sense of security."

Yet it was impossible to totally ignore Moscow's overtures. On April 16, 1953, Eisenhower challenged Russian leaders to prove that they wanted peace by acting, not talking. "Even a few such clear and specific acts, such as the Soviet Union's signature upon an Austrian treaty," he said, "would be impressive signs of sincere intent." Two years later, on May 15, 1955, the Soviet Union joined the United States, Great Britain, France, and Austria in signing an Austrian peace treaty withdrawing occupation troops, restoring Austrian sovereignty, and guaranteeing Austrian neutrality. By this point, also, the Soviet Union had taken part in settlements of the Korean War and the Indochina conflict. Even Dulles could no longer prevent a summit conference with the Russians, although he cautioned Eisenhower to keep "an austere countenance on occasions where photographing together is inevitable."

Meeting at Geneva in July of 1955, Soviet and American leaders quickly reached a deadlock over the issue of Germany. Dulles insisted upon unification "under conditions which will neither 'neutralize' nor 'demilitarize' united Germany, nor subtract it from NATO," while Bulganin would accept unification only if Germany were not integrated "into the military groupings of the Western powers." Eisenhower took an apparently new initiative at the conference with his "open skies" proposal, allowing exchanges of military plans between the two nations and overflights to ensure against surprise nuclear attacks. Like other U.S. disarmament proposals involving inspection, however, this one was regarded skeptically by Russian leaders, who feared that the United States, with its superior atomic stockpile, would merely use such information to target Soviet military facilities more accurately. Consequently, although the conference did spread a friendly "spirit of Geneva," it resulted in no specific diplomatic gains.

The status of Germany remained a major source of division between the United States and the Soviet Union. Between 1945 and 1955 the U.S. government pumped $3.5 billion worth of economic aid into West Germany and achieved a working agreement for German rearmament with Chancellor Konrad Adenauer's Christian Democratic Party. Although the Social Democrats bitterly opposed German rearmament and many Western European leaders viewed it with dismay, Dulles was intent upon using Germany as the cornerstone of the NATO alliance. He achieved his goal in May, 1955, when a conference in Paris formally welcomed West Germany into the NATO defense system. Eight days later, angry Soviet leaders concluded the Warsaw Pact with their Eastern European wards. Moscow granted East Germany formal control of its own foreign policy and in January, 1956, brought East German troops into the Warsaw Pact. The armed division of Germany and of Europe prompted proposals in both Europe and America for a neutral or, at the very least, a nuclear-free zone in Central and Eastern Europe. On the eve of a NATO conference in December, 1957, the Soviet Union expressed willingness to consider a ban on the stationing of nuclear weapons in Eastern Europe in exchange for a similar ban in West Germany. But the State Department's determination to keep West Germany in NATO scotched this plan.

The field of nuclear weaponry remained similarly untouched by détente. In 1954 the Indian government proposed a "truce" on the testing of hydrogen bombs, but the United States and the Soviet Union joined to shelve General Assembly debate on the subject. Despite the growing misgivings of scientists about the effects of nuclear "fallout," U.N. Ambassador Henry Cabot Lodge, Jr., insisted the following year that, according to "the best scientific information," "nuclear testing . . . is not a threat to human health." In the fall of 1956 Democratic Presidential candidate Adlai Stevenson advocated suspending nuclear tests. Taking up the suggestion, Soviet Premier Bulganin sent a letter to Eisenhower declaring that the Soviet government was "prepared to conclude an agreement . . . immediately." Instead of welcoming the Soviet initiative, Eisenhower replied angrily: "The sending of your note . . . constitutes an interference by a foreign nation in our internal affairs of a kind which, if indulged in by an Ambassador, would lead to his being declared persona non grata." Campaigning for re-election, the President insisted that nuclear testing caused no damage to human health and was of vital importance to the nation's security. Public pressure for a halt to nuclear testing did lead the United States and the Soviet Union to accept a tacit moratorium in the last years of the decade, but Eisenhower publicly warned in late 1959 that the United States felt "free to resume testing" at any time.

The Administration's unwillingness to seek an end to the nuclear arms race reflected its decision to base U.S. military strategy upon nuclear supremacy. On January 12, 1954, in a key statement before the prestigious Council on Foreign Relations, Dulles revealed that the Administration would henceforth utilize "the deterrent of massive retaliatory power." In a reference to nuclear weapons, the Secretary of State declared that the United States would "depend primarily upon a great capacity to retaliate, instantly, by means and at places of our own choosing." This view harmonized with the "New Look" promised by Secretary of Defense Wilson. Committed to strengthening the American military posture through a buildup of air power and thermonuclear weaponry and to holding down defense costs through a cutback in conventional forces, the Administration hoped to attain, in the words of the Defense Secretary, "a bigger bang for the buck." The Army, especially, resented this policy, and three Army Chiefs of Staff resigned in protest. Complaining, as did many Democrats, that the New Look left American policy-makers with all-or-nothing choices, they urged that military spending be rapidly increased to provide for a more "flexible" response. The Ford Foundation's Gaither Report and the Rockefeller Report, both issued in the late 1950s, reached similar conclusions. The Rockefeller Report, drafted by leading figures of the nation's policy-making élite, contended that the United States lacked an adequate capacity to respond effectively to either "limited war" or "non-overt aggression," such as "internal takeover by coup d'état or by civil war."

Confronted with such élite criticism, as well as with a major recession in 1958, Eisenhower did order a $12 billion increase in military spending but continued to place his emphasis upon thermonuclear strategy. By 1961, according to the Defense Department, the United States possessed nuclear delivery vehicles "in the tens of thousands," including more than 100 missiles of intercontinental and intermediate range, 80 Polaris missiles, 1,700 intercontinental bombers, 300 nuclear-armed carrier-borne aircraft with megaton warheads, and almost 1,000 supersonic land-based fighters with nuclear warheads. By contrast, as late as January, 1962, the Soviet Union had a nuclear capacity of only 50 ICBMs, 150 intercontinental bombers, and 400 intermediate-range missiles pointed toward U.S. overseas and NATO bases.

Government promotion of the nuclear arms race led logically to an emphasis upon civil defense measures at home. "The H-bomb . . .

will not destroy the earth," explained the Federal Civil Defense Administration. "There will always be . . . many more millions of our people alive and eager to fight back and win." Civil defense represented "both a shield and a sword," the government agency declared. "It can reduce appreciably the loss of lives and property" and, at the same time, "maintain our will to win." Unfortunately, government officials usually proved better at planning for victory than for survival. In 1954 the *New York Times* reported that "the official policy now is for the populace to take to the hills," while shortly thereafter civil defense officials announced a massive fallout shelter campaign for the cities. Authorities often disagreed upon plans. In February, 1958, Major General Robert Condon, civil defense director for New York City, told reporters that reception areas in nearby cities and states were already prepared to house and feed the city's 8 million inhabitants, although neither residents of the city nor those of the reception areas were aware of it. Neither, apparently, was General C. R. Huebner, director of the New York State Civil Defense Commission, located several blocks away. "Right now we're not prepared for evacuation," he told newsmen. "We're not going to put people in the countryside unless preparations have been made to receive them." Val Petersen, director of civil defense for the United States, compounded the confusion by suggesting that the government lay concrete pipe alongside American roads under several feet of earth; then, with the commencement of thermonuclear war, citizens could crawl into the pipes. Popular bewilderment did not faze public officials. One commented: "We've got the organization set up and in . . . an attack we won't have to fight public apathy."

Civil defense authorities did their best to make life underground appear attractive. "Remember Grandma's Pantry, its shelves loaded with food, ready for any emergency?" asked a government pamphlet in 1956. "Today . . . every wise and thinking family will likewise prepare for emergencies with the modern equivalent." Surveying a typical American family relaxing in its shelter, a civil defense brochure noted proudly that Americans were "hard to scare." Keeping children happy in their underground burrows presented a greater challenge to officialdom, but a manageable one. The civil defense division of the New York State Department of Education distributed a notice to schools urging that nuclear bomb drills be made "a fairly natural, everyday experience . . . as we have learned to brush our teeth to protect them from decay." The communication went on to advise that "children aged two to eight make at least weekly trips to the shelter. . . . In the case of children aged five through eight, this trip can be made part of dramatic play." Officials asked each child five and under to bring "a woolly toy from home. It would be very comforting for him to hold in his arms if he stays in the shelter for a time," they explained.

Civil defense was but one of many areas in American public life permeated by the military influence. In 1957 approximately 200 generals and admirals were assigned to civilian agencies of the federal government, as were 1,300 colonels or naval officers of comparable rank and some 6,000 other officers. Scientists had, in the 1940s, viewed the establishment of the Atomic Energy Commission as a great victory for civilian control of the atom, but its activities in the 1950s under the direction of Admiral Lewis Strauss led many to conclude that the struggle had been lost to the military after all. "The AEC for which we had fought so hard became a mere servant of military strategy—a weapons-maker that dwarfed all previous munitions industries," lamented physicist Ralph Lapp.

Congress, under pressure from public officials, defense contractors, and their labor allies, gave the Pentagon a relatively free hand. Introducing a military construction bill in the House, Armed Services Committee chairman Carl Vinson announced: "My friends, there is something in this bill for every member." Defense Department officials strained their ingenuity discovering new threats to American security. After predicting that 1952 would be the "year of maximum danger," they pronounced subsequent years ever more dangerous. Soon they found a "bomber gap" and then a "missile gap." As the *New York Times* observed, the missile gap "was the product of partisan politics and service pressures. . . . The Air Force thought it a good lever with which to pry more money out of the administration and Congress," while Republicans and Democrats scrambled all over one another in an effort to prove their commitment to the nation's defense. Eventually, "a ghost, a shadow, became a synthetic issue." By contrast, disarmament proposals fared poorly on Capitol Hill. Hubert Humphrey, Chairman of the Senate Disarmament Subcommittee, continually sought an appropriation of $400,000 for State Department studies on disarmament, weapons control, and enforcement procedures. Yet Congress repeatedly rejected the proposal, the cost of which represented but one thousandth of one per cent of the annual defense budget. Of the three lonely Congressmen who voted against a defense bill in the late 1950s, none was re-elected.

Thus, despite the decline of a credible military threat from the Soviet Union, the American government promoted unprecedented military expansion. Between 1953 and 1960 the White House and Congress channeled $351 billion to the Pentagon. At the end of the decade, the Defense Department's land holdings in the United States and overseas comprised 35 million acres—an area larger than the states of Massachusetts, Connecticut, New Hampshire, Vermont, Rhode Island, New Jersey, Maryland, and Delaware combined. It maintained 3,553 military installations within the United States. A single one of its bombs harbored a force greater than all the explosives used by all nations in World War II. As of 1958, according to the Federation of American Scientists, America's nuclear arms enabled it "to cover the entire earth with a radiation level which for ten years would remain sufficiently intense to prove fatal to all living beings on land." In the state of Colorado alone, the Pentagon possessed enough nerve gas to wipe out the human race. President Eisenhower declared upon his retirement from office: "Our military organization today bears little relation to that known by any of my predecessors in peacetime—or indeed, by the fighting men of World War II or Korea."

Relieved by the thaw in Soviet politics and discomforted by America's hawkish Cold War posture, the nations of Western Europe, particularly the democratic ones, began to reassert their independence. On May 11, 1953, Churchill criticized President Eisenhower's demand for the immediate settlement of Cold War issues on American terms as likely to "impede any spontaneous and healthy evolution which may be taking place inside Russia." He also noted that Britain would defend its own interests, especially in the Middle East, without assistance from "the United States or anyone else." In 1957 France, West Germany, Italy, and the Benelux countries began planning a European Economic Community, or Common Market, which they initiated on January 1, 1959. Providing for an economic union that within fifteen years would eliminate internal tariffs and equalize taxes, it also created the basis for a political bloc midway between the United States and Russia. Such independence was underscored in 1960–61, when the Common Market nations shipped more than $1 billion worth of strategic goods to the Soviet Union. As America's alliance with the democratic nations of Western Europe loosened, the United States forged ever closer bonds with the dictatorships. The Eisenhower Administration funneled billions of dollars in military and economic assistance into Greece, Turkey, Spain, and Portugal. Between 1954 and 1959 the United States contributed approximately $2 billion in military bases and financial aid to the Franco dictatorship, which President Eisenhower chose to honor by a state visit in 1959. The Generalissimo, remarked the American President approvingly, is "a strong and enduring leader."

The new Soviet regime contended with even more dramatic movements toward independence in Eastern Europe. In June, 1953, strikes and demonstrations by workers threatened to topple the oppressive East German government until they were suppressed by Soviet tanks. Khrushchev's denunciations of Stalin's crimes—or at least those in which he shared no complicity—at the Soviet Union's Twentieth Party Congress of February, 1956, coupled with his call for a new diversity within the Communist bloc, encouraged still further ferment in Eastern Europe. Riots in Poland that June prompted Soviet policy-makers to dispose of Warsaw's Stalinist leadership, enabling Wladyslaw Gomulka, an independent Communist, to take power. On October 23, Hungarian students began demonstrations to force the ouster of Stalinist leaders and were soon joined by protesting workers. Khrushchev agreed to give power to the independent Communist Imre Nagy, whereupon the Hungarians demanded the withdrawal of the Soviet Army and the creation of an opposition party.

At first the Russians appeared to be conceding everything. Khrushchev, however, had intended to relax tensions, not to open the floodgates to internal opposition and the dissolution of Soviet power in Eastern Europe. Moreover, old-line Stalinists demanded that he suppress the Eastern European dissidents. Consequently, when Nagy declared on October 31 that Hungary would withdraw from the Warsaw Pact, the Soviet government acted to halt the erosion of its authority, sending in Red Army tanks to crush the Hungarian rebels. Fierce street fighting erupted, leaving 7,000 Russians and 30,000 Hungarians dead. Thousands of Hungarians fled into exile.

As Soviet troops gunned down Hungarian "freedom fighters" in the streets of Budapest, the American government—despite its earlier promises to Eastern Europe of "liberation"—remained extraordinarily passive. Eisenhower never considered military assistance to the uprising. Absorbed in the concurrent Middle East crisis and unwilling to risk a major war to defend an independent and popular Communist regime, American policy-makers did little more than issue pious protests as Nagy was captured by the Russians and shot. However reluctant Washington was to heal its rift with Moscow, it nevertheless tacitly accepted a Russian sphere of influence in Eastern Europe.

The Administration's last major opportunity to work out a détente with the Russians came in May, 1960, when another summit conference was scheduled to occur in Paris. Ordering the Communist parties of Western nations to applaud President Eisenhower on his world tour and announcing a Soviet troop cut of one-third in January, Khrushchev went out of his way to lay the groundwork for the meeting. By contrast, the Eisenhower Administration seemed uninterested in the conference and positively provocative in its actions. That March Washington announced plans for an underground atomic blast in 1961, thereby breaking the testing moratorium, and about the same time the CIA authorized the spy flight of a U-2 plane across the heart of the Soviet Union, just two and a half weeks before the opening of the conference. On May 5 Khrushchev declared that the Soviet Union had shot down the U-2 over its territory. A series of events now unfolded that wrecked the summit conference, sending Khrushchev home to Moscow in a rage. Adlai Stevenson summarized the bizarre sequence:

> We sent an espionage plane deep into the Soviet Union just before the summit meeting. Then we denied it. Then we admitted it. And when Mr. Khrushchev gave the President an out by suggesting that he was not responsible for ordering the flight, the President proudly asserted that he was responsible. On top of that we intimated that such espionage flights over Russia would continue. . . . Next we evidently reconsidered and called off the espionage flights. But, to compound the incredible, we postponed the announcement that the flights were terminated.
>
> And, as if that wasn't enough . . . we ordered a worldwide alert of our combat forces!

Was it "unreasonable," asked the Democratic leader, "for suspicious Russians to think such a series of mistakes could only be a deliberate effort to break up a conference we never wanted anyway?"

Despite the failure to make peace with the Russians, American foreign policy was losing its European orientation. Washington's decision to abandon the doomed Hungarian rebellion was symptomatic of important shifts in the thinking of U.S. policy-makers. "Liberation" had been predicated upon the maintenance of America's nuclear monopoly, but that disappeared in 1953. And while Soviet nuclear armaments were never adequate for an effective first strike, they constituted an increasingly credible deterrent to a direct American challenge of Soviet authority. Moreover, in spite of pressures for greater independence within the Soviet and American spheres in Europe, the situation on the continent seemed to have stabilized by the late 1950s, with events running in predictable patterns. The Soviet Union succeeded in developing a "friendly" Eastern Europe, thereby satisfying its postwar quest for military and economic security. In turn, the United States succeeded in blocking social revolution in Western Europe and in restoring the Continental markets considered vital to its economy. The forces of national independence in Europe, particularly after the suppression of the Hungarian uprising, generally operated within this framework. Consequently, Washington's attention began to shift to the less clearly defined regions of the Third World—at first haltingly, and then ever more eagerly as new frontiers of wealth and power seemed within grasp.

Unlike the British and the French, who committed large numbers of their troops to desperate attempts to suppress radical nationalist uprisings in Malaya and Algeria, the American government preferred to achieve its ends in the Third World through a discreet blending of foreign aid and quiet CIA subversion. As conservatives, of course, members of the Eisenhower Administration felt little sympathy for humanitarian aid programs. "Some countries are too ignorant to be helped," Secretary of the Treasury George Humphrey told friends. "Every time a country catches cold it comes running to us for cough syrup and a quarter." Nevertheless, Dulles found foreign aid indispensable for exerting American influence in world affairs and supported it as loyally as had his Democratic predecessors. "Not for one minute," he told Congress in 1958, when speaking of an aid proposal, "do I think the purpose . . . is to make friends. The purpose . . . is to look out for the interests of the United States." After February, 1953, Dulles enjoyed the close cooperation of his brother Allen, who became director of the CIA. Although the CIA's budget and activities were kept secret from all but a few select members of Congress and the Administration, estimates placed the number of its employees at from ten thousand to twenty thousand and its annual budget at perhaps $3 billion. Having established a spy network in Eastern Europe and the Soviet Union in the capable hands of General Reinhard Gehlen, a former member of the German General Staff who had performed similar operations for Hitler, the CIA turned in the 1950s to planning covert activities in the Third World. It attempted to force the ouster of a reformist president of Costa Rica; organized commando raids on mainland China; maintained a secret army in Laos; subsidized thousands of Chiang Kai-shek's troops illegally stationed in northern Burma; and plotted a coup in Indonesia.

One of the CIA's most impressive victories occurred in Iran. In 1951, when Dr. Mohammed Mossadegh became Premier of that nation, 90 per cent of its 20 million people were illiterate, 70 per cent of the land was owned by 2 per cent of the population, and the infant mortality rate stood at 50 per cent. Iran exported $360 million a year in oil, for which it received but $35 million in royalties from the British-owned Anglo-Iranian Oil Company, a corporation whose labor policy reportedly precluded the rise of Iranian nationals above the level of laborers. That May, Mossadegh refused to ratify a new oil agreement with the British company but instead nationalized it. In a fiery speech, the tiny Premier announced that Iran was taking rightful possession of "a hidden treasure upon which lies a dragon." Mossadegh's action created an international panic and led to a boycott of Iranian oil by the major world oil companies, designed to bring the underdeveloped nation to its knees. In Britain, Anthony Eden, contemplating the prospective fall of Mossadegh, looked forward to the establishment of "a more reasonable Government with which it would be possible to conclude a satisfactory agreement." The U.S. government provided the oil companies with full backing in their boycott, including assurance of immunity from antitrust action and government sanctions for the private pricing and marketing controls that governed world supply.

Lacking the technicians, transportation, and buyers necessary to market Iran's vast quantities of oil, Mossadegh appealed desperately to Eisenhower for assistance. "For almost two years the Iranian people have suffered acute distress and much misery," he wrote in 1953, "merely because a company inspired by covetousness and a desire for profit supported by the British government has been endeavoring to prevent them from obtaining their natural and elementary rights . . . life as a politically and economically independent nation." On June 29 Eisenhower replied: "It would not be fair to the American taxpayers for the United States Government to extend any considerable amount of economic aid to Iran so long as Iran could have access to funds derived from the sale of its oil and oil products if a reasonable agreement were reached." He went on to say that "many American citizens would be deeply opposed to the purchase of Iranian oil in the absence of an oil settlement."

Apparently, however, these "many American citizens" had less reluctance to spend U.S. tax money on the CIA-engineered coup that overthrew Mossadegh that August. Shortly after Eisenhower's exchange with the Iranian Premier, Kermit Roosevelt, the CIA's principal covert operative in the Middle East, arrived in Iran to direct what an admiring colleague called "a real James Bond operation." Mossadegh was to be ousted and replaced by General Fazollah Zahedi, a former Nazi collaborator and partisan of American oil companies. In line with this program, the reactionary Shah of Iran dismissed Mossadegh from office. The embattled Premier's supporters, however, rallied, rioted, and forced the Shah to flee the country. On August 19, 1953, while his chief, Allen Dulles, was conferring with the Shah in Rome, Roosevelt was recruiting street mobs to oppose Mossadegh. Eisenhower noted in his memoirs that the U.S. government throughout the crisis did "everything it possibly could to back up the Shah." With the help of hired demonstrators and the Iranian Army, heavily dependent upon U.S. equipment, the CIA finally succeeded in toppling Mossadegh. "When this crisis came," a Defense Department official later testified before a Congressional committee,

> we provided the army immediately on an emergency basis with blankets, boots, uniforms, electric generators, and medical supplies that permitted and created an atmosphere in which they could support the Shah. . . . The guns that they had in their hands, the trucks that they rode in, the armored cars that they drove through the streets, and the radio communications that permitted their control, were all furnished through the military

defense assistance program. . . . Had it not been for this program, a government unfriendly to the United States probably would now be in power.

After the coup, President Eisenhower assured General Zahedi of his "sympathetic consideration." Although the United States had ceased its aid to Iran under Mossadegh, it poured in approximately $250 million in foreign assistance over the next three years, including almost $2 million in special bonuses for the Iranian army and police. In return, the new government of Iran sentenced Mossadegh to three years in solitary confinement, joined the U.S.–sponsored Baghdad Pact, and, most significantly, came to terms on oil. With oilman Herbert Hoover, Jr., representing the State Department, the U.S. government served as the chief negotiator of a consortium arrangement in which five American oil companies—Gulf, Socony, Standard Oil of California, Standard Oil of New Jersey, and Texaco—received a 40 per cent interest, the Anglo-Iranian Oil Company received another 40 per cent, and Dutch Shell and French Petroleum the remaining 20 per cent. The exact details of the agreement remain classified by the National Security Council because, as Secretary of State Dulles observed, "making them public would affect adversely the foreign relations of the United States." Finally, the hero of the coup, Kermit Roosevelt, became a vice-president of the Gulf Oil Company. Thus, the situation in Iran was resolved very satisfactorily for everyone concerned—everyone, that is, except the vast majority of the Iranian people, who continued to live in misery and squalor.

Another notable CIA victory occurred in Guatemala, where the situation had been worsening for American "interests" ever since 1944. Until that year, Guatemala was ruled by General Jorge Ubico, a right-wing dictator who compared his brand of justice to that of God and Hitler. He warned his domestic opponents: "I execute first and give trial afterward." Because the people of Guatemala, he stated, "are not prepared for democracy and need a strong hand," he not only banned labor unions but declared the word "worker" subversive. After a revolution in 1944, free elections swept the reformer Juan Arévalo into the Presidency. Arévalo abolished forced labor on the banana plantations, raised the minimum wage to 26 cents a day, initiated social security legislation, and permitted the organization of labor unions. His reforms aroused great hostility among members of the traditional oligarchy and their friends in the United States, and more than two dozen attempts were made to oust him during his first four years in office. In 1950 Arévalo asked the American Ambassador to leave the country because of his open support for attempted coups. American firms cut down their operations in Guatemala; W. R. Grace and Company and Pan American Airlines ceased promoting tourism; the World Bank withheld loans; and the United States cut off military assistance.

From the standpoint of the State Department, the trend worsened in 1951, when Jacobo Arbenz Guzman was elected President with twice the number of votes of all other candidates combined. Arbenz's particular interest was land reform—a serious matter in a nation where 2 per cent of the population owned 70 per cent of the land. By far the greatest landowner was the United Fruit Company. In March, 1953, Arbenz expropriated 234,000 uncultivated acres of United Fruit Company land, offering as compensation state bonds set at the amount declared by the American corporation for tax purposes, $600,000. United Fruit, staunchly backed by John Foster Dulles and the State Department, spurned the offer and demanded $15 million. When the Guatemalan government refused to meet these terms, the American corporation launched a massive public relations campaign designed to prove that Communism was on the ascendancy in Guatemala. Secretary of State Dulles warned reporters that a "beheading of all anti-communist elements in Guatemala" was imminent.

In late 1953 the Eisenhower Administration began laying plans to depose Arbenz. Miguel Ydigoras Fuentes, a conservative who later became President of Guatemala, recalled: "A former executive of the United Fruit Company . . . came to see me with two gentlemen whom he introduced as agents of the CIA. . . . They wanted to lend their assistance to overthrow Arbenz." They asked Fuentes "to promise to favor the United Fruit Company" and "to establish a strong-arm government, on the style of Ubico." Fuentes turned the American agents down, but they soon located a more amenable figure—Colonel Castillo Armas, previously trained at the Army Command and General Staff School at Fort Leavenworth, Kansas. For the appropriate American supervisor, Allen Dulles suggested John Peurifoy, a veteran diplomat who had helped to quell the Greek insurgency.

Peurifoy, appointed U.S. Ambassador, moved quickly to implement "Operation el Diablo." He met with Arbenz in a last attempt to get him to mend his ways, but the Guatemalan President remained obdurate. Peurifoy later told a House subcommittee: "It seemed to me that the man thought like a Communist and talked like a Communist, and if not actually one, would do until one came along. I so reported to Secretary Dulles, who informed the President." In early 1954 the CIA assembled, armed, and trained an invasion force in neighboring Honduras and Nicaragua, both ruled by sympathetic right-wing dictators. American arms were also dropped at the United Fruit Company headquarters in Guatemala. On June 18 Armas led his band of 150 mercenaries across the Guatemalan border as American pilots flying P-47

Thunderbolts bombed Guatemala City. In his memoirs, President Eisenhower notes that the invasion was stalled temporarily when two of the American planes were shot down. An emergency meeting was held with Dulles of State, Dulles of the CIA, Henry F. Holland (the new Assistant Secretary of State for Inter-American Affairs), and Eisenhower present. Holland opposed supplying the invasion force with new planes, arguing that this would constitute U.S. intervention in Latin American affairs, but the Dulles brothers rejoined that this provided the only hope for Armas. Eventually, Eisenhower sided with the Dulleses, much to their relief. "Mr. President," the CIA director said smiling, "when I saw Henry walking into your office with three large law books under his arms, I knew he had lost his case already." With new American P-51 fighter planes at their disposal, the invasion forces pressed forward, the Guatemalan Army refused to fight, and Arbenz capitulated on June 27. Armas now flew to the capital on Peurifoy's embassy plane, taking control of the Guatemalan government. The following day, John Foster Dulles proudly informed American television viewers that the situation had been "cured by the Guatemalans themselves."

The new regime in Guatemala proved itself a far better "free world" partner than its reformist predecessor, and the United States supplied it with $90 million in the next two years. As head of the governing military junta, Armas returned the expropriated lands to the United Fruit Company, dissolved the Guatemalan legislature, recognized the regimes of Trujillo and Franco, and abolished all taxes on interest, dividends, and profits paid to foreign investors, a measure which saved United Fruit alone about $11 million. Employers and landlords launched a wave of revenge which took the lives of thousands of workers and peasants, while Armas amended the nation's labor code to make it virtually impossible for unions to operate or even exist. The director of the AFL-supported anti-Communist labor federation in Latin America, which had backed the coup, later wrote that "agricultural workers were brought back to conditions of servitude if not actual slavery." With the help of Armas, the National Committee for Defense Against Communism launched a campaign that imprisoned thousands of Guatemalans. Armas also revised the election law to eliminate the secret ballot and to disfranchise the "illiterate masses"—about 70 per cent of the population. This enabled him to win the next election with what President Eisenhower in his memoirs called "a thundering majority," although America's President neglected to mention that Armas was the only candidate.

The CIA operated less effectively in the Middle East, which remained a major "trouble spot" for the State Department in the last years of the decade. As the American share of world oil production declined and the Middle Eastern share increased, the area, with 64 per cent of the world's known oil reserves, acquired enhanced significance for American policy-makers. After World War II American oil companies had carved out large concessions at the expense of the Arabs and the British, and the State Department now worked zealously to retain them. Publicly, it remained committed to appeasing the Arab oil states, but privately it fretted that, unless curbed, the forces of Arab nationalism might force out Western oil interests. In late 1955, in line with its courtship of the Arab nations, the State Department offered Egyptian leader Colonel Gamal Abdel Nasser $56 million in U.S. aid for building the Aswan Dam, an immense power project designed to stimulate economic development on the lower Nile. Although the Egyptians were eager to conclude the deal, Dulles cooled toward the idea after Nasser arranged a military alliance with other Arab states, refused to repudiate his commercial transactions with the Czechoslovak government, and recognized Communist China. On July 19, 1956, as the Egyptian Foreign Minister flew to Washington for discussions, Dulles announced the withdrawal of the American commitment to the project.

This clumsy attempt to keep Nasser in line had almost precisely the opposite effect. In retaliation against the American action and in an effort to develop an alternative source of capital, Nasser nationalized the British-controlled Suez Canal Company a week later, promising to pay compensation to its European shareholders and to keep the canal open to all its regular users. This action threw the British and French governments into a frenzy. Dependent upon the canal for their oil, fearful lest they be barred from using it, and publicly humiliated, they demanded complete control of the canal. Dulles, however, was frightened by the Arab hostility and sought desperately to negotiate a compromise settlement. The U.S. government lost control of the situation still further when, on October 29, the government of Israel, determined to eliminate the threat posed by Egypt to its own national security, launched a devastating attack upon Egyptian forces in the Sinai Peninsula. Taking advantage of this development, the British and French moved troops into the area in early November to seize control of the Suez Canal. At almost the same moment, the Soviet Union sent its tanks into Hungary to crush the Hungarian uprising. Angered by the neocolonial tactics of the British and French and by their failure to inform him of their intentions, Eisenhower supported a U.N. resolution calling for a truce and approved a cutoff of their oil supplies. Khrushchev, still busy with his destruction of Hungarian resistance, took time out to threaten the British and French with Soviet intervention if they failed to withdraw. Reluctantly and angrily, Britain and France agreed to a cease-fire and a pullback of their troops. The Administration's cancellation of the Aswan Dam project thus led to a series of events that inflamed Arab nationalism, enhanced Soviet prestige in the Middle East, and divided America from its allies.

The Suez debacle convinced Eisenhower and Dulles that the United States would have to play a more direct role in Middle Eastern affairs if its interests were to be preserved. On January 5, 1957, in a special message to Congress, the President unveiled the Eisenhower Doctrine for the Middle East. The region, he informed the legislators, "contains about two-thirds of the presently known oil deposits of the world," and if it were "dominated by alien forces hostile to freedom," this "would have the most adverse, if not disastrous, effect upon our own nation's economic life and political prospects." Furthermore, he remarked sanctimoniously, "it would be intolerable if the holy places of the Middle East" were "subjected to a rule that glorifies atheistic materialism." The President requested a Congressional resolution authorizing him to use American troops to intervene in any Middle East nation whose rulers considered it to be threatened by "international Communism." Explaining the new policy, Dulles observed: "The United States will have to accept an increasing responsibility to assist the free nations of the Middle East and elsewhere." By "serving others," remarked the Secretary of State, "we serve ourselves." Although Congressional mail ran eight to one against such a resolution, Congress passed it on March 9 by an overwhelming margin.

The Eisenhower Doctrine provided the pretext for Western intervention in Middle East affairs during the following years. In April, 1957, when pro-Nasser forces tried to depose Jordan's King Hussein, Eisenhower gave the Jordanian leader $20 million in military aid and dispatched the Sixth Fleet to the Eastern Mediterranean to preserve "the independence and integrity of the nations of the Middle East." In the summer of 1958 the situation grew more serious when a coup toppled the royalist dictatorship in Iraq, the only Arab member of the American-sponsored Baghdad Pact. With President Camille Chamoun of Lebanon hiding in his palace, Hussein's throne again shaky, and Arab nationalism cropping up throughout the region, Eisenhower decided that it was time "to move into the Middle East, and specifically into Lebanon, to stop the trend toward chaos." On July 14 Eisenhower ordered U.S. Marines into Lebanon in conjunction with a British paratroop landing in Jordan to contain what the American government called "indirect aggression." A *New York Times* dispatch reported that "intervention will not be extended to Iraq as long as the revolutionary government . . . respects Western oil interests." Armed with atomic howitzers, the first contingent of 7,000 American Marines stormed onto the resort

beaches of Lebanon, finding no one to fight but astonished bathing
beauties and camera-toting tourists. Wisely, the Lebanese Army decided
to offer no resistance, and not a shot was fired during the American
occupation. I. F. Stone noted that the Administration had acted "as if
this were the world of 1900, Lebanon a banana republic on our doorstep, and the most lethal weapon still the machine gun." In Congress,
Representative Henry Reuss of Wisconsin was the only member to
note that, when the President had asked for approval of the Eisenhower
Doctrine eighteen months earlier, he had promised to consult Congress
before embarking upon armed intervention. Speaker Sam Rayburn cut
this criticism short, observing: "In times like these we had better allow
matters to develop rather than make remarks about them."

At odds with the forces of Arab nationalism, the Administration
furiously courted the most reactionary Arab monarchies. In Saudi
Arabia, one of the world's three most important oil-producing nations,
the State Department and Aramco—a consortium owned by Standard
Oil of California, Texaco, Standard Oil of New Jersey, and Socony—
maintained the closest of working relationships with King Ibn Saud, a
pillar of "free world" feudalism. During the 1950s, in accordance
with Saudi Arabian desires, Aramco would allow no Jewish personnel
to work in that country. When the New York State Commission Against
Discrimination investigated the oil company's employment practices,
the State Department interceded, only to be rebuked by a state court
which held that antidiscrimination laws could not be "cast aside to
protect the oil profits of Aramco." The State Department did, however,
refuse passports and screen American armed forces and foreign service
personnel to ensure that Saudi Arabia's sovereign "idiosyncrasies"—in
the parlance of Secretary Dulles—were respected. Conscious that another of Saudi Arabia's "idiosyncrasies" was human slavery, a U.S.
delegate even balked at the strong antislavery provisions supported by
other nations in the U.N. Economic and Social Council. When King
Saud flew to Washington, President Eisenhower rushed to meet him at
the airport—a courtesy extended to no other visiting head of state up to
that time—and arranged a formal banquet at the White House which
included the top executives of Aramco, its four parent companies, and
related banking interests. Oilmen and State Department officials met
jointly with the King during diplomatic negotiations. Asked why oilmen
had received special consideration in these matters, the president of
Standard Oil of New Jersey responded in surprise: "They are the ones
that have the principal interests."

Such efforts led to a very profitable relationship. The United States,
as U.S. Ambassador George Wadsworth noted, strengthened the Saudi
Arabian armed forces to maintain "internal security" and "support the

throne." In turn, King Saud opened his country to U.S. military bases and oil investments, going so far as to inform the 13,000 native workers employed by Aramco that a strike against the oil company would constitute an act of aggression against their government. Aramco, Wadsworth noted, did "a magnificent job," flying American foreign-service personnel about in its air fleet and providing its feudal host with everything from a 350-mile railroad to a Swiss chef, electric blankets, and air conditioning for the comfort of the royal concubines. Aramco's annual $300 million in royalties enabled the King to maintain his $30 million palace in Riyadh—a colossus that consumed three times the electricity used by the 200,000 inhabitants of the surrounding city—but provided few benefits to the rest of the desert nation's population. The average income for a Saudi Arabian remained $40 a year, and 95 per cent of the population remained illiterate.

America's enhanced role in Middle Eastern affairs developed only after its commitments had been reduced in Korea. In line with his 1952 campaign promises to end the Korean War, Eisenhower hastened to secure a settlement of that bloody conflict, primarily through a policy of nuclear bluster or, as it was more popularly known, "brinkmanship." On December 14, 1952, returning from a trip to that battered Asian land, he announced that if the war did not end soon the United States might retaliate "under circumstances of our own choosing." On May 22, dissatisfied with the progress of negotiations with the Chinese, he hinted to Indian diplomats—who relayed the message to the Chinese and to the Russians—that the United States might use atomic weapons if a peace settlement were not reached. It appears doubtful, however, that such belligerent rhetoric contributed more to ending the fighting than did Stalin's death, the stalemate on the battlefield, and the Eisenhower Administration's own acceptance of a compromise settlement. American willingness to tolerate a continued Communist regime in the North so angered Syngman Rhee that he sought to break off American negotiations with the Chinese by freeing 27,000 Chinese and North Korean prisoners on June 18. Eisenhower later wrote in his memoirs that Rhee had tried "to sabotage the very bases of the agreements that we had been presenting." The Chinese, however, apparently wanted a settlement at least as much as did Eisenhower and the American people, for, ignoring Rhee's provocations, they signed an armistice on July 27.

Although the fighting ended, America continued to be a major force in the politics and economy of South Korea. Between 1954 and 1966 the U.S. government provided South Korea with $6 billion in aid, installed tactical nuclear-tipped missiles on its soil, and stationed large numbers of American troops in South Korea to safeguard its stability.

Throughout this period the Asian peasant nation remained characterized by political repression, poverty, inflation, unequal land distribution, and corruption. In 1960 the average per capita income was well under $100 a year. On July 28, 1954, Rhee traveled to the United States, where he sought to rally Congress and the American people for a war with Communist China. Returning to Korea, he forced through the Assembly an amendment designed to give him the presidency for life. In the spring of 1960, however, popular unrest and student riots finally toppled Rhee's regime. A democratic government ruled for a brief time, instituting a number of social reforms, but it was ousted by a military coup on May 16, 1961. Thereafter, Korea reverted to authoritarian rule under General Chung Hee Park—a great favorite with American policy-makers for the "stability" he fostered in this "free world" outpost.

Despite the Chinese Communist participation in a settlement of the Korean War, American policy toward the mainland regime grew ever more hostile in the 1950s. In his State of the Union message of February 2, 1953, Eisenhower announced that the U.S. Seventh Fleet would "no longer be employed to shield Communist China." The Democrats indignantly retorted that the purpose of interposing the Seventh Fleet between the mainland of China and Formosa had never been to protect the Communists but to save Chiang's tottering regime from a final knockout blow. Nevertheless, Eisenhower's "unleashing" of Chiang, with its implication of American support for a drive to reconquer the mainland, caused consternation in allied countries such as Great Britain and neutral ones such as India. Chiang heightened their fears by moving to heavily fortify a number of small islands located a few miles off the mainland—Quemoy, Matsu, and the Tachens—and by pledging an invasion of the mainland "in the not distant future." Meanwhile, the American government worked unrelentingly to isolate the Communist regime. Borrowing a phrase from his ideological antagonist, Dulles argued that the seating of the Peking government would "implant in the United Nations the seeds of its own destruction."

In late 1954 a crisis emerged that put America's support for Chiang Kai-shek to the test. Provoked by Chiang's bombing raids on the mainland and by the unfinished business of the Chinese civil war, the Communist Chinese began shelling Quemoy, Matsu, and the Tachens. At the same time, they announced the imminent "liberation" of Taiwan. America's British allies evinced little inclination to defend Chiang or his far-flung island outposts. Returning from the Far East as the shelling began, former Prime Minister Clement Attlee suggested neutralizing Formosa and "getting rid of Chiang." Churchill argued that the only function of Quemoy and Matsu was as a bridgehead for a Nationalist invasion of the mainland. Yet Eisenhower, contending that the Nationalist loss of the two islands would have "catastrophic consequences," dispatched Dulles in December to Taiwan, where the Secretary of State signed a mutual defense pact with Chiang. On January 24 Eisenhower went before Congress requesting authority to "employ the armed forces of the United States" as the President "deems necessary for the . . . purpose of protecting Formosa and the Pescadores" and "related positions." Although Congress was being asked to give the President discretionary power to begin a war, the resolution sailed through the House by a vote of 409 to 3 and the Senate by 85 to 3. When the Chinese Communists opened a heavy bombardment of Quemoy and Matsu, the Administration moved toward a preventive war position, giving serious consideration to an atomic attack upon the mainland. "If we defend Quemoy and Matsu," Dulles told Eisenhower on March 10, 1955, "we'll have to use atomic weapons." The President agreed. Fortunately, the military pressure from the mainland eased, and the crisis gradually ebbed.

As American policy-makers cemented their alliance with Chiang Kai-shek, they escalated their military support of the French venture in Indochina.* In 1954 U.S. military aid to the French struggle reached more than $1 billion—almost 80 per cent of the costs of the war effort. "The decision to give this aid was almost compulsory," Eisenhower recalled in his memoirs. "The United States had no real alternative unless we were to abandon Southeast Asia." The "loss" of Indochina, the President wrote, "would have meant the surrender to Communist enslavement of millions. On the material side, it would have spelled the loss of valuable deposits of tin and prodigious supplies of rubber and rice." Wary of French colonialism, yet unwilling to jeopardize the operation in Indochina or the participation of France in the rearmament of Western Europe, American officials gave Paris a free hand in setting political and military strategy. When the French assured them of impending victory, they radiated boundless optimism. "The tide is now turning," declared Assistant Secretary of State Walter Robertson in 1953. The next year Secretary of Defense Wilson observed that a French military victory was "both possible and probable," while Admiral Arthur Radford, Chairman of the Joint Chiefs of Staff, stated flatly: "The French are going to win."

In reality, the French faced an imminent military collapse. Fighting against a skilled and popular guerrilla army, French troops suffered heavy casualties and growing demoralization. When a major French force made a stand at Dien Bien Phu, it was surrounded by the Viet Minh and attacked on March 13, 1954. A week later, conditions had

* This section on the Indochina conflict was co-authored by Theodore Lieverman.

deteriorated to such an extent that the French Chief of Staff flew to Washington to request immediate U.S. military intervention. American optimism now vanished, and the government plunged into a decision-making crisis. Dulles and Radford favored intervention, but Eisenhower was inclined to listen to advisers like General Matthew Ridgway, whose experience in Korea made him question any military commitment that might embroil the United States in another Asian land war.

On April 3 Eisenhower, Dulles, and Radford met secretly with eight Congressional leaders to see if they would support direct U.S. military action. Radford outlined his proposal for Operation Vulture, an air strike on Dien Bien Phu employing 200 planes from offshore carriers. Under close questioning from the legislators, however, the admiral conceded that he was the only one of the Joint Chiefs supporting this plan —although Air Force Chief of Staff Nathan Twining favored using nuclear weapons. Dulles, moreover, admitted that he had not consulted America's allies on intervention. Congressional leaders expressed skepticism and displeasure, persuading Eisenhower not to intervene unless the strike force contained contingents from U.S. allies, unless the French openly declared themselves for speedy independence in Indochina, and unless Congress approved.

For the next two months the Administration discussed and laid contingency plans for a U.S. military attack. Following his April 3 decision, Eisenhower wrote to Churchill for help, comparing the danger in Vietnam to that once posed by "Hirohito, Mussolini, and Hitler." Dulles flew to Europe to build a coalition for united intervention. The British, however, refused to consider military action, particularly before the Geneva Peace Conference on Indochina began in June. The French, for their part, wanted only localized U.S. strikes at Dien Bien Phu, fearing that any significant internationalization of the conflict would end their control of the political situation. At one point Dulles suggested the possibility of an American nuclear strike to the French, although it remains unclear whether he was making an official government offer. In mid-April, Vice-President Nixon sent up a trial balloon by telling an audience of newspaper editors that the United States might have to "take the risk by putting our boys in" to stop Communist expansion in Asia and Indochina. Congressional reaction was hostile. Even after the battered French forces at Dien Bien Phu surrendered on May 7, Eisenhower asked Dulles to draft a Congressional resolution authorizing U.S. action in Indochina. Nevertheless, France's military disintegration and evident desire to stop the fighting convinced Washington that the situation could no longer be salvaged. On June 15 Dulles informed the French Ambassador that the moment for American intervention had passed.

The Geneva Conference ended in July with an agreement under which the French would finally withdraw from Indochina and grant independence to Vietnam, Laos, and Cambodia. In Vietnam, a temporary division of the country at the 17th Parallel would allow for a regrouping of forces pending French withdrawal and national elections. The agreement clearly stated that such a division was "provisional and should not in any way be interpreted as constituting a political or territorial boundary." Neither zone was to enter into military alliances with other countries or allow foreign military bases to be built upon its soil. National elections were to be held in July, 1956, monitored by an International Control Commission composed of delegates from Canada, India, and Poland. The Commission was also to oversee the other aspects of the agreement. The first Indochina War, which took the lives of an estimated 25,000 Frenchmen and one million Vietnamese, thus came to an end.

Frustrated by the Geneva settlement, U.S. policy-makers felt few scruples about ignoring it. At Geneva, a gloomy Dulles had studiously avoided looking at Chou En-lai and then departed halfway through the negotiations. Two weeks before the agreement was concluded, Eisenhower told a press conference that he would "not be a party to a treaty that makes anybody a slave; now that is all there is to that." After the accords were reached, the U.S. government announced that, while it would refrain from "the threat or use of force" to violate them, it would not sign them. Surveying the accords that August, the National Security Council pronounced them a "disaster" that "completed a major forward stride of Communism which may lead to the loss of Southeast Asia." Thus, despite intelligence estimates predicting little chance of establishing an effective counterforce to the Viet Minh, the Eisenhower Administration was less ready than its exhausted French ally to abandon the struggle in Indochina. In mid-June Dulles had persuaded Bao Dai to install Ngo Dinh Diem—a Catholic mandarin who had just spent three years at the Maryknoll Seminary in New Jersey, where he was discovered by Francis Cardinal Spellman and the U.S. government —as premier of France's Vietnamese puppet state. Now, on August 20, Eisenhower approved a program to support Diem while "encouraging" him to broaden his regime and to strengthen the South Vietnamese armed forces. The Administration had decided to take direct control of the remaining colonial apparatus in Vietnam.

After a few months of shaky rule Diem—with the assistance of the United States—managed to establish a stable government, assuming dictatorial powers for himself and his family. He used his armed forces to crush his non-Communist political opposition and rigged the elections of 1955, which made him President. Five months later parlia-

mentary elections returned not a single anti-Diem deputy—a fact which
the CIA attributed to "government manipulation of the election campaign" and a boycott by most of the opposition parties. The land reform program sponsored by Diem's government not only failed to
redistribute land to poor peasants but even returned to landlords much
of the land previously parceled out by the Viet Minh. Ignoring the
Geneva agreement's ban on reprisals, Diem launched an Anti-Communist Denunciation Campaign in the summer of 1955 which sent 50,000
to 100,000 Vietnamese to detention camps; many were not Communists
at all but simply political opponents or suspected opponents. A year
later Diem broadened his political crackdown by issuing an ordinance
providing that "all persons considered dangerous to national defense or
collective security . . . may be sent to concentration camps by decision of the President." Diem's brother, Ngo Dinh Nhu, ruthlessly directed the secret police in their task of ferreting out dissidents.

Meanwhile, American advisers flocked to South Vietnam, providing
technical assistance in a broad variety of fields. They organized the
police, the educational system, the armed forces, and the governmental
administration. By 1958 the United States was paying all costs of the
armed forces and 80 per cent of all other government expenses. A form
of American aid that received little publicity was the Saigon Military
Mission, established in June, 1954, and led by CIA counter-insurgency
expert Edward G. Lansdale. Lansdale's team sabotaged Hanoi's bus
engines, attempted to destroy Viet Minh presses, trained and infiltrated
armed agents into North Vietnam, and distributed false information
purportedly issued by the Viet Minh. As Secretary of Defense Robert
McNamara later remarked, "only the U.S. after 1954 held the South
together . . . and enabled Diem to refuse to go through with the . . .
nationwide 'free' elections in 1956."

"It was the Communists' calculation," observed the State Department's 1961 Blue Book, "that nationwide elections scheduled in the
[Geneva] accords for 1956 would turn all of South Vietnam over to
them." But "the authorities in South Vietnam refused to fall into this
well-laid trap." Washington's and Saigon's decision to avoid the "trap"
of elections resulted from the virtual certainty of a Communist victory.
Eisenhower wrote in his memoirs: "I have never talked with a person
knowledgeable in Indochina affairs who did not agree that had elections
been held at the time of the fighting, possibly 80 per cent of the population would have voted for the Communist Ho Chi Minh as their
leader." Unfortunately, this was the "wrong" choice. Consequently,
Washington and Saigon opted for no choice at all—or Diem's dictatorship.

In 1957 sporadic guerrilla activities began against the Saigon regime.

These first resistance groups relied primarily on a commonly felt dislike for Diem and included teams organized by the militantly anti-Communist parties. They engaged in sabotage, terrorist activities, and attacks upon government officials and their U.S. advisers. Although the North Vietnamese government undoubtedly had some contact with the Southern resistance through Viet Minh cadres, it was at first reluctant to support the insurgency; Radio Hanoi even attacked the Southern guerrillas for displaying impatience with the Geneva accords. As the insurgency spread, however, the Hanoi government gradually shifted its position. Starting in 1959 significant numbers of Viet Minh, all of Southern origin, began moving back into the South.

By the end of 1960 Diem's position was growing untenable. He had major conflicts with the peasantry, the élite, and part of the army. Because his support was narrowly based, he found it imperative to receive increased U.S. assistance. American policy-makers, though, embarrassed by the dictatorial nature of his regime, sought to persuade him to make political reforms. When the U.S. Ambassador visited Diem in October, 1960, he suggested such changes but was met with a chilly response. Apologizing, the American official dropped the matter. A leading South Vietnamese general warned American officials that, for every insurgent killed by the armed forces, Diem's policies created ten others; nevertheless, they remained unwilling either to demand an end to such policies or to drop their support of the South Vietnamese dictator. In December, encouraged by the North Vietnamese but still overwhelmingly non-Communist themselves, the Southern revolutionaries formed the National Liberation Front.

Preoccupied with crises in the Third World, the American government still found the time to extend its "commitments" through a series of paper alliances. Dulles, who believed that neutrality was both "obsolete" and "immoral," repeatedly crisscrossed the earth in a largely futile quest to align underdeveloped nations with the Cold War aims of U.S. foreign policy. On September 8, 1954, he succeeded in forming the Southeast Asia Treaty Organization (SEATO), which he hoped would prove the Asian counterpart of NATO. No major Asian nations joined SEATO, however; it remained limited to the United States, Britain, France, Australia, New Zealand, Thailand, the Philippines, and Pakistan. Its formation, in fact, helped to spark support for an anti-Western Afro-Asian Conference in Bandung, Indonesia, the following year. Dulles turned in 1955 to the Middle East, where he again encountered difficulty in finding allies. That February, Britain, Iran, Turkey, Pakistan, and Iraq joined the ineffective Baghdad Pact, later renamed the Central Treaty Organization (CENTO) when the Iraqi government in Baghdad repudiated it. At the last moment, fearful of becoming involved in the Israeli-Arab conflict, Dulles decided to have the United States "cooperate with" but not join the organization. Thanks to his efforts, by 1956 the United States, once an opponent of "entangling alliances," had defense pacts with forty-two nations. Adlai Stevenson remarked: "The sun never sets on an American commitment."

American policy-makers did not forget their traditional bailiwick, Latin America. Ever since 1946, when Truman had proposed that the United States "standardize military organization, training methods, and equipment" in the southern continent, the American military and the Latin American oligarchy had enjoyed a warm collaboration. The United States supplied Latin American nations with military advisers, equipment, and billions of dollars in military assistance, and between 1950 and 1963 trained 24,421 Latin American officers through the Military Assistance Program. Military cliques and military spending were encouraged to such an extent that by 1960 Brazil, Peru, Chile, and Argentina all devoted 25 per cent or more of their annual expenditures to the military. As the prospect of a foreign invasion remained minimal, most military programs in Latin America served primarily to guarantee "internal security"—a feature that never failed to endear the most ruthless of authoritarian regimes to the hearts of Washington officials. Vice-President Nixon traveled to Havana to praise the "competence and stability" of Fulgencio Batista's Cuban dictatorship, while Eisenhower awarded the Legion of Merit to the dictators of Peru and Venezuela, Manuel Odria and Marcos Perez Jimenez, the latter for his "sound foreign investment policies."

Occasionally, Latin American nations might request U.S. assistance for economic development, but this met with disfavor among men committed to private rather than public investment policies. Secretary of the Treasury George M. Humphrey wrote in 1957: "There are hundreds of energetic people in the world who are better equipped than governments ever can be to risk huge sums in search, exploration, and development wherever the laws of a country will give them half a chance." Confronted with a request for U.S. aid at the 1957 Inter-American Economic Conference, Humphrey's successor in the Treasury post, Robert D. Anderson, responded: "History has demonstrated the vital role of the competitive enterprise system in the economic life of our hemisphere. . . . The system of competitive enterprise promises the most in the satisfaction of man's material needs." By 1960 an estimated 200 million Latin Americans lived under this system; 2 per cent owned 50 per cent of the wealth, 50 per cent were illiterate, and 70 per cent endured conditions of dire poverty.

America's political leaders soon began to discover that all was not well in Latin America. In the spring of 1958, as Vice-President Nixon wended his way across the southern continent on a "good will" tour, he and his party were denounced, mobbed, and stoned by angry crowds. Arriving in Caracas, where the Nixons were scheduled to stay at the sumptuous Circulo Militar—a $35 million military club built by the recently exiled Perez Jimenez—Nixon was met by thousands of hostile demonstrators. As the American delegation and its security forces drove into the city, they were almost overwhelmed by mobs that attacked the cars, smashed their windows, and sent them speeding to an alternative destination. Dr. Romulo Betancourt, who would soon be elected President of Venezuela, remarked sadly that the situation had resulted from the asylum granted the hated Perez Jimenez in the United States, but Nixon insisted that Communist conspirators bore sole responsibility for events. "Right here was the ruthlessness and the determination . . . of the enemy we face," he said. "This is Communism as it is." Meanwhile President Eisenhower, planning a rescue mission, ordered six destroyers, a guided-missile cruiser, and an aircraft carrier to Caracas and had jet bomber, fighter-bomber, and fighter units readied for "Operation Poor Richard." A thousand élite paratroopers and Marines stood by for action. This force never took on the Caracas street mobs, though, for Nixon canceled the remainder of his trip and flew back to Washington, where he was greeted as a triumphant hero.

Two years later, after an eight-week tour of twelve Latin American nations, Adlai Stevenson also brought serious tidings. "In a region rich in resources," he reported, "half the people are hungry, half don't sleep in beds, half are illiterate." Unlike the Vice-President, however, he thought it "foolish for us to attribute anti-Americanism just to Communist agitation." Latin Americans, he declared, told him that the United States consistently supported "hated dictators," that the United States has been "basically concerned with making Latin America safe for American business," and that American businessmen were "interested only in the profits they can make, not in the country and its development."

Few relationships better exemplified such criticisms than the one between the United States and Cuba. Ever since 1898 the United States had effectively controlled that island's economy and politics. By the late 1950s American business interests had invested approximately $1 billion in Cuba and owned 90 per cent of its mineral wealth, 80 per cent of its utilities, 40 per cent of its sugar, and, in conjunction with Shell Oil, all of its petroleum industry. Sugar provided 82 per cent of Cuban exports, leaving the island's economy open to easy manipulation by Washington officials whenever they chose to alter the amount of sugar allowed to reach the U.S. market. Although American corporations reaped sizable profits from their Cuban operations, an estimated one-third of the island's labor force was unemployed, three-fourths of the sugar workers were employed for only a few months a year, and two-thirds of the population was either partially or totally illiterate. In rural areas, 9 per cent of the homes had electricity, 2 per cent had running water, and 3 per cent had indoor toilets; 90 per cent of the rural population suffered from worm diseases. The United States landed Marines on three occasions after 1902 in an effort to control Cuban politics but did not do so in 1952, when Batista overthrew a democratic government and began consolidating his dictatorship, massacring thousands of his opponents and embezzling hundreds of millions of dollars. Instead, the United States trained and supplied Batista's 43,000-man army, maintained its own military base at Guantanamo, and exercised an extraordinary influence over Cuban affairs. The United States "was so overwhelmingly influential," Ambassador Earl Smith later told a Senate committee, "that . . . the American Ambassador was the second most important man in Cuba; sometimes even more important than the [Cuban] President." In 1960 Senator John F. Kennedy charged that the Eisenhower Administration had employed in Cuba "the influence of our Government to advance the interests and increase the profits of private American companies," giving "stature and support to one of the most bloody and repressive dictatorships in the long history of Latin America."

This relationship underwent a transformation after January 1, 1959, when Fidel Castro, at the head of a band of 1,200 guerrilla fighters, swept proudly into Havana, proclaiming the triumph of the Cuban Revolution. Determined to rectify social injustices and create a balanced economy, Castro nevertheless showed no intention during his first months in power of forcing a break with the United States. He appealed repeatedly to the United States for economic aid and even traveled to Washington in April in an apparent effort to secure it. Meeting with U.S. officials, Castro talked of the necessity of nationalizing American-owned holdings to promote land reform but sought to arrange payment in Cuban bonds. In response, the Administration refused aid and insisted upon immediate payment for confiscated lands. Vice-President Nixon, who met privately with the Cuban leader, concluded, as he later reported, that Castro was a Communist and that U.S. military action should be launched against him. In May Castro appeared at an Inter-American Economic Conference, urging the United States to supply $30 billion over a ten-year period to fund a Latin American economic development effort. The U.S. Assistant Secretary of State for Latin American Affairs, visibly irritated, sharply rejected the Cuban leader's proposal.

Cuba's relations with Washington thereafter rapidly deteriorated.

Threatened with a cut in Cuba's sugar quota and violently denounced by U.S. investors, Castro nationalized the sugar industry. Cuban Communists, initially cool to Castro, began to assume more influential positions in his government. In February, 1960, Castro signed a trade agreement with the Russians to exchange Cuban sugar for Soviet oil and machinery. When U.S. refining companies refused to handle Russian oil, Castro nationalized the refining industry. Partly as a means of retaliation and partly as a way of subsidizing social reform measures, the Havana government began to remove large sectors of the economy from corporate hands. On March 17, angered by the Cuban Revolution's turn to the Left, President Eisenhower secretly authorized the training and arming of an exile invasion force by the CIA. In July Washington cut the Cuban sugar quota, and the following January it broke off diplomatic relations with the Havana government.

The Administration's confrontation with the Cuban Revolution, like its confrontation with the Third World, revealed the limitations of U.S. foreign policy in an age of upheaval. Many saw that the Old Order was slipping. "Call it nationalism, call it anti-colonialism, call it what you will," declared Senator Kennedy in 1959, "the word is out—and is spreading like wildfire . . . that it is no longer necessary to remain forever poor or forever in bondage." In the abstract, the Administration, like its Democratic critics, favored economic advance and the growth of human freedom. The Secretary of State had long prided himself on his religious, humanitarian interests, while the President was fundamentally a humane and decent man. Nevertheless, they took a businessman's view of the world, with all this entailed in terms of the maintenance of corporate privilege. Thus, in specific situations they more often than not ignored or opposed revolutionary aspirations. Committed to a worldwide defense of American capitalism, they inevitably pursued policies that bolstered reactionary dictatorships, reinforced the military at home and abroad, and placed the United States at odds with the hopes and dreams of the vast majority of mankind.

7

The Politics of "Moderation,"
1953-60

We're here in the saddle as an Administration
representing business and industry.

Secretary of the Interior
DOUGLAS MCKAY, 1953

THROUGHOUT HIS PRESIDENCY, Dwight Eisenhower made a strong appeal to the middle-income, "middle-of-the-road" voter. In a press conference on December 8, 1954, he described his followers as "progressive moderates," and several months later he talked of his program as one of "dynamic conservatism." The President's favorite expression for his political philosophy, though, was "Modern Republicanism," which he explained meant "conservative when it comes to money, liberal when it comes to human beings." Stevenson observed caustically that Eisenhower seemed to be saying that he would "strongly recommend the building of a great many schools . . . but not provide the money." Eisenhower's nonideological image was reinforced by his bland personality; aimiable, modest, indecisive, and intellectually limited, he imparted to his eight years in office a quality of drift and confusion. Within a few days of the 1953 inauguration, I. F. Stone noted that the new President "seems to be a rather simple man who enjoys his bridge and his golf and doesn't like to be too much bothered. He promises . . . to be a kind of president *in absentia,* a sort of political vacuum in the White House which other men will struggle among themselves to fill."

Those who filled it almost invariably reflected the needs and values of the giant corporate interests that dominated the Republican Party. Secretary of the Treasury George Humphrey, an arch-conservative, had directed a business empire worth $120 million. Secretary of Health, Education, and Welfare Oveta Culp Hobby had been a millionaire Texas newspaper publisher and head of the Women's Army Corps. The Secretary of Commerce, Sinclair Weeks, was a wealthy New England banker and manufacturer whose view of government-business relationships, wrote journalist Marquis Childs, came "straight from Calvin Coolidge." Indeed, the President appointed millionaire businessmen or corporate lawyers to every Cabinet office except that of Secretary of Labor, reserved for Martin Durkin of the plumbers' union. Under fire from liberals for appointing an executive team of "eight millionaires and a plumber," Eisenhower shot back: "Who would you rather have in charge . . . some failure who never did anything or a successful businessman?" To be sure, Eisenhower did choose the liberal Republican Earl Warren to become Chief Justice of the Supreme Court, but this, as the President later remarked, was "the biggest damfool mistake I ever made."

The appointment of a Secretary of Defense caused the President some embarrassing moments. Eisenhower's choice, Charles E. Wilson, president of General Motors, "had a reputation as one of the ablest of our executives in big corporations," the President recalled. "It seemed to me that a man of such qualifications could team up with professional soldiers to the great advantage of the nation." Others, less pleased by the prospect of military-industrial collaboration, noted that General Motors was the nation's largest defense contractor, that Wilson owned $2.5 million in General Motors stock, and that he would receive $600,000 more in bonuses provided that he did nothing "inimical" to that corporation's interests. Federal statutes, in fact, made it illegal for a government official "directly or indirectly interested in the pecuniary profits" of a corporation to deal with that corporation "as an officer or agent" of the U.S. government. Questioned at Senate confirmation hearings about a possible conflict of interest, Wilson replied: "I cannot conceive of one because for years I thought what was good for our country was good for General Motors, and vice versa." Eventually, Senate pressure forced Wilson to sell his stock. "Sooner or later," Eisenhower wrote in irritation, a President "will be unable to get anybody to take jobs in Washington except business failures, political hacks, and New Deal lawyers."

But, as Stevenson quipped, the New Dealers had "all left Washington to make way for the car dealers." At the inaugural festivities, described by the press as the most lavish in history, the wife of the new Secretary of the Treasury wore "huge clips . . . of rubies and diamonds." Even the wife of the "plumber" appeared in a bouffant gown of Chantilly lace, with a ten-yard sweep of skirt. The President initiated a series of White House "stag" dinners to exchange views and create closer ties with national leaders. Of the 500 guests at thirty-eight such dinners between 1953 and early 1955, almost 60 per cent were businessmen and industrialists. Seeking to create what he called a "business climate," the Secretary of Commerce announced in March, 1953, that he had removed the head of the National Bureau of Standards. The bureau, he explained, did not understand "the business point of view," having actually set standards that kept certain manufactured goods from being sold. "As a practical man," he said, "I do not see why a product should be denied an opportunity in the market place." By September the Secretary of Labor had resigned. Durkin "seemed to carry a bit of a chip on his shoulder," a puzzled President recalled. "He told me that, in dealing with other members of the administration, he was at a disadvantage . . . because in every conference he was but one man representing labor, while everyone else present was either a capitalist or a member of the professions."

The Eisenhower Administration's first major legislative achievement involved the passage of the Submerged Lands Act, transferring from the federal government to the states title to at least $40 billion in disputed offshore oil lands—an amount equal to more than a third of the total known petroleum reserves in the United States. During his 1952 campaign Eisenhower had strongly endorsed such a measure and had been rewarded with the support of wealthy oil magnates and Gulf state politicians. At the beginning of the 1953 Congressional session, the Republican Senate leadership gave the bill top priority, keeping that body in session nights and Saturdays to break filibuster attempts by opponents. When Congress passed the measure later that year, the usually pro-Eisenhower *New York Times* termed it "one of the greatest and surely the most unjustified give-away programs in all the history of the United States." Delighted that their years of lobbying efforts had finally paid off, oil corporations rushed to obtain leases from eager state governments. The *Oil and Gas Journal* reported: "Offshore production looms as the richest drilling prize in the history of the oil business."

Throughout the 1950s the Administration and Congress displayed a tender solicitude for the interests of the oil industry. Proposals to lower the oil depletion allowance were generally sidetracked in committee or shouted down on the floor of Congress without a recorded vote. In 1954 Senator John J. Williams of Delaware proposed a reduction to 15 per cent, and Senator Douglas proposed a graduated tax, but neither could get the nineteen votes necessary for a roll call. Eisenhower studiously evaded the issue, as did Secretary of the Treasury Humphrey. In 1957 Humphrey was succeeded in office by Robert B. Anderson, former president of the Texas Mid-Continent Oil and Gas Association and a well-known defender of the oil depletion allowance. Anderson promised the Senate Finance Committee to approach the issue "as objectively as I can." The following year the Treasury Department announced that the "far-reaching implications" of the allowance led the Department to

oppose any change before "full consideration of all its possible consequences." Pressed for his own opinion on the depletion allowance at a
press conference in 1957, President Eisenhower responded: "I am not
prepared to say it is evil because when we find, while we do find I assume that a number of rich men take advantage of it unfairly, there
must certainly be an incentive in this country."

The interlocked natural gas industry also enjoyed the warm regard of
the White House and Capitol Hill. For years industry spokesmen had
sought to amend the Natural Gas Act of 1938 to remove natural gas
from federal regulation. With the strong backing of its supporters on
the Federal Power Commission and of the President, the industry
neared success in early 1956, as Congress debated the Harris-Fulbright
bill. But on February 3 Senator Francis Case, a conservative and little-
known Republican from South Dakota, revealed that he had been
offered $2,500 by an oil company lobbyist after making known his
views favoring the measure. The bill's supporters, outraged, turned
ferociously on the hapless Case. Senator Mike Monroney of Oklahoma
charged that his disclosure fortified the "big lie" technique of those
who implied "that Senators who support the bill are minions of the oil
companies." Although the Senate, led by Majority Leader Lyndon
Johnson, passed the bill by a 53–38 vote, President Eisenhower vetoed
it, claiming that to do otherwise would "risk creating doubt among the
American people concerning the integrity of governmental processes."
He said nothing, however, about the ethics of rewarding oil and gas
companies with billions of dollars at the expense of consumers, or about
the practice of accepting large campaign contributions from industrial
interests as a reward for political favors. Case's disclosure was simply
a public embarrassment, particularly at election time. Having secured
re-election, once again with massive funding from the oil and gas industries, Eisenhower reassured the companies in his budget message to
Congress that "legislation freeing gas producers from public utility-type
regulation is essential." Congress did not dare to pass another gas bill
—because, as Eisenhower noted, "the issue was too 'hot' "—but the
President nevertheless gave the industry what it wanted by "packing"
the Federal Power Commission with officials who refused to accept their
legal obligation to regulate the price of natural gas.

Shortly after taking office Eisenhower intensified the process of gutting
the federal regulatory agencies that had begun with Roosevelt's death.
In 1953 he denied reappointment to a member of the Federal Power
Commission who had opposed moves to withdraw authority from the
agency to regulate natural gas rates, appointing in his place Jerome
Kuykendall, a lawyer who had represented private utilities in rate cases.
Other appointees to the FPC included men of similar background and

interests. Under Kuykendall's chairmanship, four of the five members actively supported bills to strip the FPC of its power to supervise the field price of natural gas and publicly argued that natural gas should not be regulated as a public utility. The lone dissenter was not reappointed.

In 1953 the President chose a new chairman of the Federal Trade Commission, Edward Howrey, a lawyer and business lobbyist whose entire career had involved the defense of corporate clients before the FTC. When Howrey assured the Senate reviewing committee that he would disqualify himself in cases where he had been previously involved, Senator Warren Magnuson of Washington remarked: "You might be on a vacation almost permanently down here." Under Howrey's chairmanship, antitrust action declined and a variety of FTC legal powers were dissipated at informal conferences with industry groups. The FTC eased out or cracked down upon leading career members of the Anti-Monopoly Bureau and the Bureau of Economics, making dozens of staff dismissals. Within three years Howrey had returned to private life, and his firm was again representing clients before the FTC. "Carefully, steadily, and methodically," wrote the *New Republic*'s T.R.B., "the regulatory commissions are being stacked against the consumer interest and for business."

The "best natural resources program," President Eisenhower explained in his inaugural address, would involve a "partnership of the states and local communities, private citizens, and the Federal Government, all working together." Interpreting this in a fashion that favored private power interests, the Republicans cut federal power projects on the Columbia River and plans for a federal dam at Hells Canyon, turning the area over to the Idaho Power Company. In 1954 Congress passed the Cole-Hickenlooper bill, amending the Atomic Energy Act of 1946 to grant private interests special privileges in the use of government-generated nuclear power. Senator Lehman charged that "this bill . . . far transcends the infamous give-away of the offshore oil bill." In a typical year during the Eisenhower Administration, private utilities invested ten times the amount invested by federal agencies in electric power facilities. Speaking at Custer State Park, South Dakota, in June, 1953, the President told Republican leaders that in the two preceding decades "creeping socialism has been spreading in the United States." Upon his return to Washington, reporters asked him to give a few examples of "creeping socialism." The President replied by naming the growth of the Tennessee Valley Authority—perhaps the most far-reaching social experiment of the New Deal. "By God, if ever we could do it . . . I'd like to see us sell the whole thing," he confided to his Cabinet, "but I suppose we can't go that far."

In line with its new curbs on public power, the Eisenhower Administration refused to allow TVA to build a steam-power plant for the City
of Memphis; instead, it authorized the Atomic Energy Commission to
negotiate a contract with utility magnates Edgar Dixon and Eugene
Yates. On November 11, 1954, the AEC signed a $107 million contract
with the Dixon-Yates combine. Democrats attacked the arrangement,
and as a result the President ordered the Bureau of the Budget to make
a "complete disclosure" of the history of the contract. When the bureau
did so, however, it omitted mentioning the fact that a Bureau of the
Budget consultant on the project, Adolphe Wenzell, was vice-president
of the investment firm that was the financial agent for Dixon-Yates.
Senator Lister Hill of Alabama exposed this omission, much to Eisenhower's discomfort. After the City of Memphis declared that it would
build its own plant, the President seized the opportunity to cancel the
contract. Dixon-Yates later sued the AEC for recovery of costs, whereupon the Justice Department told the court that the contract had been
"contrary to the public interest" from its inception. As a result of this
imbroglio, the Administration's plans for bringing private utilities to
the Tennessee Valley were thwarted. The President never forgave critics of
the Dixon-Yates contract for what he termed "a spate of demagoguery."

In general, as Eisenhower told a Republican gathering in 1953, his
Administration sought to find "things it can stop doing rather than new
things for it to do." While Eisenhower continued a number of the programs of his predecessors, he cut back their funding and placed them
under conservative control. A balanced budget, tax reduction, and a
"sound dollar" were the cornerstones of his fiscal policy. His penchant
for budgetary economies was evident in his agricultural policy, based
upon lowering government price supports; in his educational policy,
which excluded significant federal aid to education; in his defense policy,
based upon nuclear weapons; and in his health care policy, which
steered clear of federal health insurance or medical care for the aged.
Typical of the Administration's attitude toward social welfare programs
was its response to the development of the Salk vaccine for the prevention of poliomyelitis—a disease that killed or crippled 19,300 Americans, mostly children, in 1954 alone. In 1955, when a bill was introduced in Congress to have the federal government provide free vaccine
for all children, Secretary Hobby staunchly opposed the measure, which
she termed "socialized medicine" by the "back door." Such policies resulted not only in a decline in the quality and quantity of public services
but in three economic recessions during Eisenhower's eight years in
office. The sole liberalization of New Deal–Fair Deal legislation involved
extension of the Social Security program.

Spurning measures that furthered human welfare, the Administration chose instead to further the welfare of automobiles—and of the companies that manufactured and fueled them. On February 22, 1955, Eisenhower sent a message to Congress calling for "comprehensive and quick and forward-looking" action to improve the federal highways. Congress responded with the Federal Highways Act of 1956, which authorized the spending of $32 billion to build 41,000 miles of interstate highway over a thirteen-year period, the largest road-building program in history. The President wrote rhapsodically in his memoirs:

> The total pavement of the system would make a parking lot big enough to hold two-thirds of all the automobiles in the United States. The amount of concrete poured to form these roadways would build . . . six sidewalks to the moon. To build them, bulldozers and shovels would move enough dirt and rock to bury all of Connecticut two feet deep. More than any single action by the government since the end of the war, this one would change the face of America.

And change the face of America it did, although only in later years were the features it fostered fully apparent: the decline of mass public transportation; the flight from the central cities to the sprawling suburbs; the destruction of the countryside; and the pollution of the environment.

The President also made noteworthy departures from his predecessor in his direction of the Anti-Communist Crusade. Allegedly because the Truman Administration had shown "complacency . . . toward security risks in government," Eisenhower issued Executive Order 10450 in early 1953, tightening "security" standards for federal personnel still further. Administration officials boasted in late 1954 that they had dismissed or secured the resignations of 9,600 "security risks," but few of these were actually forced from office on grounds of disloyalty. In 1954, for example, Scott McLeod bragged that 534 State Department employees had been dropped for security reasons, but he later conceded that only eleven had been fired for alleged disloyalty and that none of these was a Communist. Eventually, the Administration admitted that, of the more than 2 million federal employees it had scrutinized, it could find only one Communist.

Since bona fide Communists were hard to come by, ever more subtle criteria for dismissal were developed. At a Cabinet meeting in early 1954 John Foster Dulles complained that no clear understanding had been reached as to the nature of a "security risk." Cases had been passed on to him, he said, because a file mentioned the presence of a pacifist in an employee's family or membership in the eminently respectable United World Federalists. Dulles displayed less indecision, though, in firing John Paton Davies, a career diplomat cleared seven times by State Department loyalty boards and once by the Loyalty Review Board. A ninth hearing ruled that Davies had lacked "discretion." In this atmosphere of suspicion the slightest deviation from orthodoxy could lead to difficulties. In February, 1953, when the director of the State Department's International Broadcasting Services privately questioned the wisdom of an order to desist from quoting "controversial" authors on the Voice of America—a hardship for the Cold Warriors of the airwaves, since they could no longer draw upon incriminating quotations from Marx, Lenin, and Stalin—he was promptly suspended from his post. Even Republican Senator Harry Cain, a right-winger appointed by Eisenhower to the Subversive Activities Control Board, denounced the Administration's internal security program for "unnecessarily destroying individuals."

The most famous loyalty-security case of the era was that of J. Robert Oppenheimer, often referred to as the "father of the atomic bomb" for his work in directing the nation's wartime atomic energy project. On December 3, 1953, Eisenhower secretly ordered government officials to place "a blank wall between Oppenheimer and all Government secrets," and on December 21 the new chairman of the AEC, Admiral Lewis Strauss, presented the atomic scientist with a series of charges "raising questions as to your veracity, conduct, and even your loyalty." When Strauss gave Oppenheimer twenty-four hours to decide whether he would resign as a consultant to the AEC or face a hearing by a loyalty board, Oppenheimer chose the latter. In the "trial" that followed, a broad cross-section of distinguished scientists testified in Oppenheimer's favor, while only the physicist Edward Teller—a leading proponent of the hydrogen bomb, the development of which Oppenheimer had opposed—testified against him. Like many intellectuals of the 1930s, Oppenheimer had had some associations with Communists in his youth; however, he had long ago and repeatedly given the FBI full details. But these past associations and his ambivalence about nuclear weaponry weighed heavily with the hearing committee, which voted two to one that Oppenheimer should henceforth be denied security clearance. "There can be no tampering," said the majority report, "with the national security, which in times of peril must be absolute, and without concessions for reasons of admiration, gratitude, reward, sympathy or charity." Accepting this judgment, so resonant of the totalitarian fanaticism it formally abhorred, the AEC canceled Oppenheimer's contract as adviser and rejected his appeal.

Ironically, the Administration's fealty to the Anti-Communist Crusade did not prevent it from running afoul of Senator McCarthy. In 1953, when the Republicans organized the Senate, McCarthy became chairman of the Committee on Government Operations and of its Permanent Subcommittee on Investigations—a position that provided him with new investigatory powers, as well as a sizable staff and budget.

McCarthy's Senate office quickly became the center for unsubstantiated rumors, leaked government documents, amateur sleuths, and informers. During 1953 his subcommittee held 445 "preliminary inquiries" and 157 "investigations." Seventeen reached public hearings, usually presided over by McCarthy. Committee members often learned of a new investigation less than twenty-four hours before it began; sometimes they did not learn of it at all. Seeking to maintain the Administration's alliance with the Senator, Vice-President Nixon met with him on repeated occasions, commending his exposés of "un-Americanism" while urging him to "remember that this is your administration." But, although McCarthy was willing to accord the Administration high marks in the Anti-Communist Crusade, he was almost childishly unable to refrain from snatching the headlines with another denunciation of "subversion." On a national radio and television broadcast of November 24, 1953, he declared that, while the Eisenhower Administration was doing "infinitely" better than its predecessor, there were "a few cases where our batting average is zero." He noted the "blood-stained blunder" of granting foreign aid to Great Britain—which had the temerity to trade with Communist China—and kept up his attack upon the State Department.

In March, 1953, McCarthy and his cohorts in the Senate assailed the nomination of Charles E. Bohlen as Ambassador to the Soviet Union. Bohlen, it seemed, had accompanied Roosevelt to Yalta and Truman to Potsdam. Therefore—in the right-wing view of things—he was an accomplice in treason. Calling Bohlen a "security risk," said McCarthy, was "putting it too weak." Eventually, the President arranged for Senators Taft and Sparkman to read Bohlen's "security" file and to speed his confirmation by the Senate. In return, Eisenhower promised not to nominate any further "controversial" figures. Questioned by the press on whether his championship of the Bohlen nomination indicated a break with McCarthy, Taft replied: "No, no, no, no."

McCarthy caused the Administration still further embarrassment by investigating the State Department's overseas information program. In an attempt to appease McCarthy, the State Department issued a directive in February, 1953, banning all "books, music, paintings and the like . . . of any Communists, fellow travelers, et cetera." Although the State Department had some difficulties identifying the relevant "Communists" and "fellow travelers"—not to mention the "et cetera"—Senator McCarthy claimed greater expertise. His list of condemned authors included Sherwood Anderson, Brooks Atkinson, W. H. Auden, Stephen Vincent Benet, Elmer Davis, Bernard DeVoto, John Dewey, Theodore Dreiser, Edna Ferber, Archibald MacLeish, Arthur Schlesinger, Jr., Edmund Wilson, and many others. In April the McCarthy subcommittee's young counsel Roy Cohn and his friend G. David Schine took off on a whirlwind tour of U.S. information centers in Paris, Bonn, Belgrade, and London, upbraiding librarians for harboring the works of dangerous "radicals." The following month McCarthy charged the U.S. Information Service with housing 30,000 to 40,000 volumes by "Communists and fellow travelers." Under simultaneous assault from the State Department and McCarthy, overseas librarians removed hundreds of books from their shelves, storing some and burning others. Among them were works by a former U.S. Ambassador to the Soviet Union, the chief of the New York *Herald-Tribune*'s Washington bureau, a well-known historian (and cousin of the Secretary of State), and the head of the NAACP.

Upset by an imagery reminiscent of Nazi practices, Eisenhower delivered a speech at Dartmouth College on June 14 in which he urged: "Don't join the book-burners!" Three days later, though, when asked if he intended this remark to be critical of McCarthyism, the President replied that he would not discuss personalities. Nor would he cancel the State Department directive. On July 8, after a Cabinet meeting on the subject, the Administration issued an official policy statement declaring that, while books should not be removed from libraries simply because they criticized American policies and institutions, the State Department would not place in special-purpose libraries any books that directly or indirectly advocated destruction of American institutions. "Under no circumstances should any book be burned," the statement added. "The burning of a book is a wicked symbolic act." Thus, the Administration rejected the form of book-burning while approving its substance.

Despite McCarthy's provocations, the Administration was determined to continue appeasing him. The White House staff was divided over how to handle McCarthy; some urged no compromise, but others, led by Nixon, contended that an attack upon McCarthy would split the Republican Party. The Vice-President served as the principal intermediary between the senator and the President, attempting to persuade each man of the value of the other. When Harold Stassen seemed about to denounce McCarthy for undermining the State Department, Nixon prevailed on Dulles to issue a statement lauding the Wisconsin senator's services to U.S. diplomacy. The Vice-President even went so far as to arrange private dinners with McCarthy and Administration officials in an effort to conciliate the two groups. J. Edgar Hoover worked closely with McCarthy, granting him special access to FBI files and publicly defending him. Eisenhower himself felt a strong aversion to McCarthy but had no intention of opposing him; he told associates that he would "not get into the gutter with that guy." "Given time," the President assured White House staffers, "these things take care of themselves."

Like the Republicans, most Democratic politicians displayed little taste for combat. The Wisconsin senator, insisted Senate Minority Leader Lyndon Johnson, was a "Republican problem." In early 1954 McCarthy used the occasion of Lincoln's birthday to denounce once again "twenty years of treason" under the Democrats. "The hard fact is," he declared, "that those who wear the label Democrat wear it with the stain of an historic betrayal." Striking back, Adlai Stevenson assailed those who "offend not only the credulity of the people" but "stain the vision of America and of democracy." Few Congressional Democrats, however, followed his lead. Later that month Senator Fulbright cast the only dissenting vote against a $214,000 appropriation for McCarthy's subcommittee, and not a single Democrat rose in Congress to defend his party against the charge of disloyalty. The most effective work done to undermine McCarthy's power was performed by the liberal National Committee for an Effective Congress, which in 1953 provided technical knowledge and political expertise to encourage the senator's foes in Congress. Their early gains, however, were minimal, as most legislators—including almost all the liberals—remained unwilling to contest McCarthy's influence and power.

Until 1954 McCarthy's critics were hampered by at least three major factors. First, reluctant to champion freedom of thought against the claims of the state, most persisted in pandering to the belief in devils upon which the Anti-Communist Crusaders fed. In 1953, when Einstein urged American intellectuals to refuse to testify before Congressional committees investigating matters of thought and opinion, the anti-McCarthy *New York Times* grew incensed. "One cannot start," the *Times* said, "from the premise that Congressional committees have no right to question teachers and scientists or to seek out subversives wherever they can find them." (I. F. Stone replied that one could not "start from any *other* premise" without making a "heresy hunt" inevitable.) Second, McCarthy's foes quailed before the myth of his political invincibility. And yet polls found that, throughout his career, the only time McCarthy had the support of a majority of the nation's population was in January, 1954, when the favorable responses reached a bare 50 per cent; and even then, more respondents said that they would oppose a McCarthy-endorsed candidate than said that they would support him. Third, and most significant, McCarthy held political power through the sufferance, and at times the active support, of élite groups: Republican political leaders, Southern Democrats, businessmen, and the mass media. When, through arrogance and ambition, McCarthy finally alienated these constituencies, his power rapidly disintegrated, and his alleged "mass" backing proved of no avail.

During 1954 these élite groups concluded that McCarthy had over-reached himself. Early that year the Wisconsin senator became embroiled in a bitter clash with the Army, browbeating high-ranking officers in his characteristic fashion. "You are a disgrace to the uniform," he told Brigadier General Ralph Zwicker. "You're shielding Communist conspirators. You're not fit to be an officer. You're ignorant. You are going to be put on public display." Angered, Secretary of Defense Wilson dismissed the charge that the Army was coddling Communists as "just plain tommyrot." The placid Eisenhower later recalled that "the attack on General Zwicker made me furious." In thirty-five days of televised subcommittee hearings beginning that April, known as the Army-McCarthy hearings, McCarthy engaged in heated exchanges with Army officers, Administration officials, and Senate colleagues. Becoming ever more reckless, McCarthy spoke on May 30 of "the evidence of treason that has been growing up over the last twenty"—then, pausing, he scowled and continued—"twenty-one years." The Eisenhower Administration had now joined the Democratic Party in the senator's inferno. McCarthy had clearly outlived his usefulness to the forces that had nurtured and encouraged his career. Henceforth, they would no longer shield and protect him.

The Senate now moved to break McCarthy's power. On June 11, 1954, Republican Ralph Flanders of Vermont introduced a resolution to remove McCarthy from his chairmanship unless he purged himself of his contempt of the Senate by answering charges brought against him. As the Senate leadership considered this too drastic a measure, the best that Flanders and lobbyists for the National Committee for an Effective Congress could do was to send the resolution, now converted to one calling simply for censure, to a special committee headed by Utah's Senator Arthur Watkins, a conservative Republican. The Watkins committee unanimously recommended censure, triggering a ferocious counterattack by McCarthy. "The Communist party has now extended its tentacles to the United States Senate," he charged. "It has made a committee of the Senate its unwitting handmaiden." This time, though, such denunciations proved futile, for the Senate's "inner club" had moved in for the kill. Stennis of Mississippi accused McCarthy of pouring "slush and slime" on the Senate, and of all that chamber's power figures, only William Knowland, a right-winger who had become Majority Leader after Taft's death, stood by the Wisconsin senator. The Democrats remained, for the most part, tactfully silent. Eventually, all forty-four Democrats present joined half the Republicans in voting 67 to 22 to condemn McCarthy for conduct that "tended to bring the Senate into dishonor and disrepute." As a last gesture of respect to his fallen mentor, Vice-President Nixon, presiding over the Senate, removed the word "censure" from the title of the resolution. Few were fooled, however, by the semantic change. "Well," McCarthy impishly told reporters, "it wasn't exactly a vote of confidence." Studiously ignored thereafter by his colleagues and the mass media, McCarthy never quite reconciled himself to the stony silence that greeted his every attempt to recapture the nation's attention. On May 2, 1957, ailing from cirrhosis of the liver, he died virtually unnoticed at the age of forty-eight—the servant and then the victim of forces beyond his control or understanding.

American politicians viewed the defeat of McCarthy as the liquidation of a mad dog, not as the abandonment of the heresy hunt; consequently, the Anti-Communist Crusade continued both during and after his Senate humiliation. In August, 1954, when conservatives introduced the Communist Control Act, liberals decided to enhance their political popularity by amending it to outlaw the Communist Party. "I do not intend to be a half patriot," stated Hubert Humphrey, who urged his colleagues not to "trip over the niceties of legal technicalities and details." The amendment carried, and the Senate adopted the bill by a 79-0 vote. "Liberalism, in its noble and historic sense, did not have one spokesman in the Senate last week," said the *Chicago Daily News.* "The self-styled Democratic liberals could think of no answer to their detractors except to outdo them in the sponsorship of repression." The situation proved little different in the House, where the bill sailed through by a vote of 265 to 2. Meanwhile, in the grim nether world of the "national security" bureaucracy, the FBI busied itself with the battle against subversion, carrying on a widespread program of electronic surveillance, mail opening, and burglaries. By the mid-1950s, the FBI had amassed 432,000 files on "subversive" Americans and had formulated a plan to sequester 230,000 of them, in a time of crisis, without trial.

Congressional investigations of "un-American" activities continued unchallenged, with committees like HUAC employing their powers of subpoena and exposure to persecute and defame. In 1945, when HUAC was established as a standing committee, 186 votes were cast in opposition; by 1958 the opposition had been reduced to one. "If the present trend continues," declared Justice Black in *Wilkinson* v. *United States,* "government by consent will disappear, to be replaced by government by intimidation, because some people are afraid that this country cannot survive unless Congress has the power to set aside the freedoms of the First Amendment." He concluded: "These people are tragically wrong. This country was not built by men who were afraid and it cannot be preserved by such men."

Democratic liberals were quite right in assuming that the "Communist issue" would be used against them in the 1954 Congressional elections but wrong in assuming that it would carry much weight with the voters. As the reigning politician in the Administration, Vice-President Nixon took the lead in spreading the anti-Communist message, flying 26,000 miles, visiting 95 cities in 31 states, delivering 204 speeches, and holding more than 100 press conferences. "We're kicking the Communists and fellow-travelers and security risks out of the government . . . by the thousands," he bragged to campaign audiences. Naming five Democratic Senatorial candidates in the West as "left-wingers," he maintained that the Communist Party was working "within the Democratic Party" because "the candidates running on the Democratic ticket in the key states are almost without exception members of the . . . left-wing clique which has been so blind to the Communist conspiracy . . . in the United States." True Democrats, he announced, were "outraged by the Truman-Acheson-Stevenson gang's defense of Communism in high places." Replying to Stevenson's criticism of the nation's sluggish growth rate under the Eisenhower Administration, Nixon charged that the Democratic leader was "guilty of spreading pro-Communist propaganda as he has attacked with violent fury the economic system of the United States." Despite Nixon's best efforts, however, economic considerations —particularly the recession of 1953–54—played a major part in the thinking of voters, who sensed that the Republicans were not notably sympathetic to economic hardship. Questioned during the campaign about unemployment, Secretary of Defense Wilson remarked: "I've always liked bird dogs better than kennel-fed dogs myself. You know, ones who get out and hunt for food rather than sit on their fannies and yelp." On Election Day the Democrats swept to victory, defeating a host of prominent McCarthyites and taking control of both houses of Congress.

Although Eisenhower had predicted a "Cold War of partisan politics" if the Democrats captured Congress in the 1954 elections, executive-legislative relations could hardly have been much warmer than in 1955–56. Eisenhower himself estimated that the 84th Congress supported him 72 per cent of the time, while ADA chairman Joseph Rauh charged in 1956 that "the Congressional Democrats have become practically indistinguishable from the party they allegedly oppose." The conservative tone of the Democratic opposition resulted partially from the accommodating policies of their leaders—Speaker of the House Sam Rayburn and Senate Majority Leader Lyndon Johnson. In the 1930s Johnson had entered the House as a brash young New Dealer, but with Roosevelt's death he began a rightward shift, designed to move with the times and to please the Texas construction, oil, and aircraft industries. When he won election to the Senate in 1948, it was as a supporter of the Taft-Hartley Act and an opponent of the President's civil rights program, which he labeled "an effort to set up a police state." Johnson moved rapidly up to the position of Senate Minority Leader in 1952 at the sufferance of Senator Richard Russell of Georgia, the real Democratic power in that chamber. Drawing upon his vast resources of political savvy, Johnson established himself as the most powerful Senate Democratic leader within memory. He used his new position to support the housing, minimum wage, Social Security, farm, and reciprocal trade legislation endorsed by liberals, but he stuck with conservatives on balancing the budget, sponsoring oil and gas giveaways, opposing public power, and blocking civil rights legislation. In public pronouncements, he played for the same middle-of-the-road support attracted by the Republican President. "I have always thought of myself as one who has been moderate in approaching problems," he declared in December, 1955.

Johnson proved himself a master of manipulation and the wielding of power—usually to conservative advantage. Together with Rayburn, he saw to it that critics of the oil depletion allowance were kept off the Senate Finance Committee, the House Rules Committee, and the House Ways and Means Committee. Impressed by Johnson's tight control of the Senate, few liberals in that body ventured a direct challenge to his power. In 1955, on the day after ADA had assailed Johnson for "affably acquiescing in the Republican assault on liberalism," Hubert Humphrey and other liberals rose on the Senate floor to pay "public tribute" to Johnson for "his leadership in behalf of an effective Democratic party liberal program." After 1952 Johnson had cultivated Humphrey, utilizing him as his entrée to the isolated Senate liberals and occasionally rewarding him with committee posts. The astute Texas politician even secured a position of influence in the White House. On a regular basis, Johnson and Rayburn would enter the Presidential mansion unseen through a back door and go upstairs to meet Eisenhower for cocktails and political discussion. These sessions, held at least once a month, forged a useful working relationship between the Democratic Congressional spokesmen and the Republican leadership in the White House. They did less for liberals, though, who gnashed their teeth at the triumph of "moderation" on Capitol Hill. An ADA study of key roll-call votes in Congress from 1953 to 1960 found that the liberal position on domestic issues lost about two-thirds of the time in both the Senate and the House. Joseph Rauh complained in 1956 that its Congressional leadership was "bringing the Democratic party to its lowest point in twenty-five years."

Behind the Johnson-Rayburn leadership in Congress lay the entrenched power of the Republican-Dixiecrat coalition. Liberals lost frequently on roll calls, primarily because only Northern Democrats voted with any consistency for progressive legislation. An ADA study of

Congress from 1948 to 1960 revealed that Northern Democrats voted the liberal position on domestic issues 82 per cent of the time in the Senate and 90 per cent of the time in the House, while Republicans backed the liberal position 24 per cent of the time in the Senate and 23 per cent of the time in the House. Southern Democrats, who voted the liberal position only 40 per cent of the time in the Senate and 34 per cent of the time in the House, thus resembled Republicans more than they did members of their own party. Unfortunately for the liberals, Northern Democrats were especially weak at the crucial committee level. During the same period they constituted a majority on only 6 per cent of the Senate and 3 per cent of the House committees; on most committees, Republicans and Southern Democrats enjoyed at least a 2-to-1 advantage. When the Republicans captured Congress, they naturally controlled the powerful committee chairmanships, and when the Democrats captured Congress—as was more common—Southern Democrats, their seniority grounded in a one-party system that guaranteed them re-election, garnered most chairmanships. Although they never constituted more than 23 per cent of the membership of either house of the three Democratically organized Congresses between 1955 and 1960, Southern Democrats held between 53 and 63 per cent of the committee chairmanships; even in 1959–60, when Northern Democrats outnumbered Southern Democrats in Congress by about 2 to 1, Southerners claimed 62 per cent of the committee chairmanships in the Senate and 60 per cent in the House.

Outmaneuvered in Congress, liberals were also counted out at the polls. While America was 80 per cent urban by 1960, Congress remained a rural bastion. The most thinly populated states had the same number of Senate seats as the most heavily populated, and, even more important, Congressional districts vastly differed in population, diluting the influence of the urban electorate. Urban Congressional districts would sometimes have a half-million voters, while rural ones might have fewer than 100,000. Throughout the 1950s nearly all the districts with populations below 275,000 were rural, while four-fifths of the districts with populations over 450,000 were completely or largely in metropolitan (urban and suburban) areas. Many a state legislature, in the grip of rural and small-town interests, would gerrymander Congressional districts in a conscious attempt to give conservatives a majority they could not possibly obtain on the basis of a one-man-one-vote principle. In 1954, for example, when GOP candidates for the House of Representatives from New York received 51 per cent of the statewide vote, the GOP collected 61 per cent of the seats. Four years later the Republican share of that state's Congressional vote had dropped to 49 per cent, but the GOP still garnered 56 per cent of the seats. Not until the Supreme

Court decision in *Baker* v. *Carr* (1962) would such malapportionment be partially rectified.

While a few liberal politicians kept up a peppery anti-Administration attack in the 1950s, Adlai Stevenson often seemed to have joined Lyndon Johnson in the Eisenhower camp. On November 19, 1955, he told a Democratic fund-raising dinner in Chicago that "it is time for catching our breath," that "moderation is the spirit of the times." Seeking to differentiate this position from the Administration's, he declared: "Moderation, yes! Stagnation, no!" Stevenson was a far more outspoken critic of the extremists of the Anti-Communist Crusade than was the Republican President, but he did little to challenge the subtler assumptions of the American Celebration. "We here in America have written the greatest success story in human history," he told the 1954 Columbia Bicentennial Conference. In foreign affairs, he remained a committed Cold Warrior, criticizing cuts in military spending and arguing in 1954 that "Southeast Asia's security hinges on the war in Indo-China." Finally, Stevenson was far more willing to compromise on civil rights issues than many blacks and liberals. In an address before a black audience in Los Angeles on February 7, 1956, he declared that he would reject use of federal troops to enforce court-ordered desegregation of public schools or to quell racial violence in the South and that he opposed the Powell Amendment, which would bar federal aid to segregated schools. To a letter from the ADA executive committee, conveying "the deep concern of the liberal community with your position on certain key civil rights issues," Stevenson testily replied that the Supreme Court's desegregation decision "must and will be complied with given time and patience and a lot more understanding on the part of some of my Northern friends than I have perceived yet."

Despite their criticism of "moderation," American liberals were already well advanced on their own long march toward the silent Center. "Liberals are beginning to find it both natural and expedient to explore the merits and employ the rhetoric of conservatism," wrote Richard Hofstadter in 1956. "They find themselves far more conscious of those things they would like to preserve than they are of those things they would like to change." Once mordant critics of big business, liberals now cropped up within the ranks of its supporters. John Kenneth Galbraith's *American Capitalism* (1952), David Lilienthal's *Big Business* (1953), and Adolph A. Berle's *The Twentieth Century Capitalist Revolution* (1954) were all defenses of the modern corporation by acknowledged liberal spokesmen. Moreover, liberal commitment to a hard-line stance in the Cold War seemed to be increasing. The first promise of an ADA circular of the 1950s was of "effective American mobilization for the security of the free world against Communism." A report on the Eisenhower Administration's budget, published in 1957 by the liberal Conference on Economic Progress, noted the slight decline of post–Korean War defense expenditures relative to GNP and asked "whether we are risking our lives by these slashes." The liberal retreat even carried over into the realm of civil liberties. Although ADA called for the abolition of HUAC in 1950, this demand did not reappear in an ADA platform until 1959, in a much more cautiously worded form. Such temporizing, though, did little to preserve liberal influence in a decade when social criticism was looked upon with suspicion. After 1950 ADA could count on little labor support, and politicians who had once courted the liberal organization's endorsement asked to be overlooked in the future.

While liberalism decayed, American radicalism disintegrated. A few aging Socialists still clustered around the Socialist Party and *Dissent* magazine, but their impact upon public policy and public opinion was nonexistent. The situation was hardly better for American Communists. The Korean War, the Hungarian revolt, and Khrushchev's denunciation of Stalin shattered the last significant remnants of the Communist Party apparatus. Individual radicals, fearing "exposure," often hid their views or wilted under government questioning. Some recanted or provided lists of their former comrades to the Red-hunters. A few even became influential figures in the Anti-Communist Crusade. Jay Lovestone, the former general secretary of the American Communist Party, became George Meany's top foreign policy adviser. J. B. Mathews, forced out of a religious pacifist organization in the 1930s for his Communist sympathies, became research director for HUAC, charging that "the largest single group supporting the communist apparatus in the United States today is composed of Protestant clergymen." Young people seemed to find little of interest in radical activity; covering a meeting of one of the few leftist groups still in existence, a journalist reported "a forest of gray heads."

The Presidential nominating conventions of 1956 opened in this conservative context. Stevenson, who had defeated Kefauver in a series of grueling primary battles, was opposed at the convention by New York Governor Averell Harriman. Criticizing Stevenson's "moderate" policy on civil rights, Harriman campaigned with Truman's endorsement as a "Fair Deal" candidate. Stevenson easily secured nomination on the first ballot, however, bringing in his wake a weak and platitudinous civil rights plank, which failed to pledge enforcement of the Supreme Court's 1954 desegregation decision. In a frantic effort to secure Southern support for his Vice-Presidential bid, Humphrey called for "understanding of Southern problems on the race issue" and absented himself from the deliberations of the convention's civil rights caucus.

He lost the spot, though, to Kefauver. While the Democratic platform contained some mildly liberal proposals, it also pledged "determined opposition to the admission of Red China to the United Nations" and criticized the GOP for "fraternizing with Communists." With nowhere else to go, ADA rather half-heartedly endorsed Stevenson.

Despite initial doubts about the President's health—based upon a mild heart attack he had suffered in 1955—the Republicans once again turned to the popular Eisenhower to head their ticket. The President had received favorable Gallup poll ratings averaging 70 per cent throughout his first term in office, but the Vice-President struck some Republican leaders as a political liability. Eisenhower reportedly offered Nixon a Cabinet post, and Harold Stassen started an abortive movement to "dump Nixon." Yet the Vice-President clung so tenaciously to office that, in the end, he easily secured renomination. As the party in power, the Republicans naturally looked more benignly upon the world situation than they had in 1952. "The advance of Communism has been checked," declared their platform, "and, at key points, thrown back." Even the Democratic Party had acquired a certain legitimacy. "There is only one party of treason in our country," said Senator Knowland, "and that is the Communist party." Nixon charitably remarked that the Democrats gathering in Chicago were "all loyal Americans." Meeting in September, the GOP platform committee had drafted a strong civil rights plank, but Eisenhower ordered this revised to avoid an emphasis upon federal enforcement of court-ordered desegregation. Republican politicians went forth from the convention optimistically, trumpeting the blessings of "Peace, Progress, and Prosperity."

The campaign proved one of the least interesting in American history. With the Anti-Communist Crusade on the wane, the Republicans resorted to a mixture of personality cult and platitude. "Give 'em Heaven," the President told Nixon as he left on his first campaign tour. Nixon did: "Folks, Eisenhower is a great man, just remember that, and the Eisenhower program means a cleaner, finer, more moral America." The President moved serenely across the country, touching on issues only tangentially; it was enough that he was there. With a long, sustained rhythm, the crowds chanted: "We like Ike." The President's popularity, however, went beyond the personal, for his campaign themes touched a chord with many voters, thankful for the end of the Korean War and for the growth of middle-class prosperity. By contrast, Stevenson seemed less popular than four years before. Certainly, he was less exciting and eloquent. Exhausted from the primaries and coached by professional politicians, he ran a rather lackluster campaign without displaying much of his old wit and urbane flair. Although Stevenson reminded the nation of its uneven prosperity, he exhibited little appreciation of the significance of poverty and did little to appeal to blacks. Frequently he focused on foreign affairs without, however, charting a consistent course. He warned of NATO's decline, urged strengthening America's armed forces, and charged that half of Indochina had become "a new Communist satellite," with the United States emerging from "that debacle looking like a 'paper tiger.' " On the other hand, seeking a "peace" issue that would have the same impact as Eisenhower's 1952 pledge to "go to Korea," Stevenson proposed an immediate ban on nuclear weapons testing and the replacement of the draft with a professional army "in the forseeable future."

The balloting produced curious results. Eisenhower surpassed his 1952 victory, drawing 58 per cent of the vote. Carrying only seven states from the Old Confederacy, Stevenson saw his support among blacks drop to 61 per cent and among Catholics to 51 per cent; he also lost support among blue-collar workers, white-collar workers, the college-educated, and the young. Not only did Eisenhower cut sharply into the Democratic Party's lower class constituency, but he ran strongly in urban areas, drawing 49 per cent of the vote in the nation's twelve largest cities. In his victory statement the President declared that the tremendous vote he had received could not be "merely for an individual," but indicated that "America has approved of modern Republicanism." Congressional races, however, belied this claim. Although Eisenhower carried 329 of the nation's 435 Congressional districts, GOP candidates won in only 201. For the first time since 1848 a winning Presidential candidate was unable to carry either house of Congress for his party; the Democrats actually made legislative gains. If most Americans liked Ike, they remained considerably less enthusiastic about his party.

During his second term in office the President exhibited little more inclination to encourage social welfare legislation than during his first. In January, 1957, when Eisenhower's somewhat liberalized budgetary request to Congress was sharply criticized by leading members of his party, including Secretary Humphrey, the President quickly gave way, inviting Congress to make "sensible reductions." Federal aid to education, earmarked as a "major goal" of the Administration, was hacked to pieces by Congress without a murmur from Eisenhower. A substantial civil rights bill was undermined shortly after its presentation to Congress when the President announced that he did not agree with certain aspects of it. By the summer *Life* magazine reported that "the fiasco" of Eisenhower's legislative program was partially "due to his own indecision and seeming unsureness in support of it." Another recession in the nation's economy brought unemployment to an officially conceded 5.2 million by March, 1958; nevertheless, the President rejected what he called a "make-work approach, with its vast, slow-moving projects." After the 1958 elections returned a considerably more liberal Congress, the President assumed the leadership of the embattled Republican-Dixiecrat coalition, vetoing housing, unemployment, distressed-areas, and river pollution bills. One of the few health, education, or welfare measures to win enactment in these years was the National Defense Education Act, passed in the wake of the Soviet-launched *sputnik* "to insure trained manpower of sufficient quality and quantity to meet the national defense needs of the United States."

By the late 1950s America's public welfare programs were in retreat along a variety of fronts. Economist Alvin Hansen estimated that, in terms of GNP, the United States in 1957 spent about 40 per cent as much on hospitals as in the early 1920s. Unemployment compensation as a percentage of income was lower in the 1950s than in the 1930s, with about half the unemployed not even covered. Social Security payments provided no more than a poverty-level income for the aged; in November, 1960, the average monthly Social Security check was $74.02. In 1955 the Housing Commissioner of the State of New York testified before a Congressional committee that it would take $125 billion in public and private investment to end slums within twenty-five years. Existing programs, pitifully short of these projections, failed, moreover, to provide housing for the poor. Instead, slum-clearance projects rewarded slumlords with sizable profits, granted contractor-promoters financial windfalls and tax rebates, and built luxury housing for upper-income families. In 1959 Charles Abrams told a Congressional committee that the public housing program had become "tattered, perverted, and shrunk." "Urban renewal," he said, "has developed into a device for displacing the poor."

The issue of civil rights provided the Administration with its greatest domestic challenge—one which it consistently evaded. Despairing of obtaining civil rights legislation from Congress, the NAACP turned to the courts for redress. Here it won several noteworthy victories, culminating in *Brown* v. *Board of Education* (1954). Speaking for a unanimous Supreme Court, Chief Justice Warren declared that "in the field of public education, the doctrine of 'separate but equal' has no place. Separate educational facilities are inherently unequal." A year later the Court ruled that segregated school districts in seventeen states and the District of Columbia should move "with all deliberate speed" to implement desegregation programs. Although Northern states hastened to comply, Border states and some Southern states moved slowly, while the states of the Deep South embarked upon a campaign of complete defiance. White Citizens Councils and Ku Klux Klan chapters sprang up across Dixie, and the governors of Virginia and of the states of the Deep South secured the passage of laws to block desegregation. As opposition heightened, the President was urged to call a conference of Southern "moderates," to tour the South seeking compliance, or to go on television in an appeal to the nation for understanding. Eisenhower did none of these but instead implied that he disapproved of school desegregation. Asked in September, 1956, whether he endorsed the Court's ruling, he replied: "It makes no difference whether or not I endorse it." The following month he remarked that he would uphold the Constitution whether or not he agreed "with every single phrase" of it. Lumping together those who sought compliance with the Court decision and those who obstructed it, sometimes by violence, the President publicly denounced "extremists on both sides."

The situation reached a crisis in September, 1957. As the President settled down at his vacation resort near Newport, Rhode Island, the news arrived that Governor Orval Faubus of Arkansas had called out the National Guard to prevent nine black school children from attending Little Rock's Central High School. With his customary serenity, Eisenhower began a golf game at the local country club. Governor Faubus flew to Newport for a meeting with the President but emerged from the conference to say that his position had not changed. As time passed, mob violence in Little Rock grew. Violent racists from across the South flocked to the city, assaulting reporters and bystanders. The President, unflappable as ever, continued his golf game. Journalist Marquis Childs recalled: "The contrast with the ugliness of Little Rock —the splendid course, with the sweep of ocean in the distance, the houses of the rich or the once-rich standing out against the clear blue Indian summer sky, the President in easy sport clothes intent on his game—could not have been greater." Occasionally, Eisenhower would be called off the course to receive a phone call on the Little Rock situation. Three weeks after he had sent in the National Guard troops, Faubus removed them under a court order, but by that time the city was in chaos, with white mobs viciously attacking black children who dared approach the school. On September 24, rousing from his lethargy, the President federalized the National Guard and ordered in troops from the 101st Airborne Division to enforce the court order. "The President," observed the *New York Times,* "did, belatedly and powerfully, what he might not have had to do at all if he had previously made his position unmistakably and publicly understood."

But what was the President's position? In 1958, when Governor Faubus closed down Central High School rather than integrate it and when school desegregation in the South virtually ground to a halt, the

President hinted at a press conference that he thought desegregation should move more slowly. By 1960, six years after the Supreme Court decision, only 765 out of 6,676 Southern school districts had been desegregated.

Things went much the same in the legislative arena. Until 1956 Eisenhower did not bother to introduce or support a civil rights bill and consistently opposed the Powell Amendment. Lyndon Johnson seemed similarly uninterested in fostering legislation to guarantee racial equality, voting against every civil rights measure to come before Congress from 1937 to 1957. "I want to pass the bills that need to be passed," the Senate Majority Leader complained to friends, "but all I ever hear from the liberals is Nigra, Nigra, Nigra." In 1957, however, pressure from liberals was reinforced by the Administration's decision to support a major civil rights bill. Moreover, Johnson, who nursed Presidential ambitions, needed something to offset his image as a Southern Democrat. The Senate Majority Leader consequently agreed to work for the passage of a civil rights bill—but a bill weak enough to be palatable to Southern legislators. Under Johnson's direction, Congress amended the Administration measure to delete key sections, leaving it as a mild voting rights bill empowering the Attorney General to seek court injunctions, and providing for the appointment of a virtually powerless Commission on Civil Rights. The measure passed easily, with Southerners not bothering to filibuster against it. Most liberals condemned Johnson for destroying the bill's effectiveness, but the President also played a part in undermining it by telling Congress not to "go too far too fast." Similar dynamics produced another weak Civil Rights Act in 1960, authorizing the courts to appoint federal referees to safeguard voting rights and making it a federal offense to obstruct court orders by violent means. Although both civil rights laws empowered the Attorney General to initiate voting rights suits, the Administration brought only ten such suits to court. By 1960 fewer than 15 per cent of eligible black voters were registered in at least 193 Southern counties, and only about 25 per cent of eligible blacks were registered to vote throughout the South.

As the 1958 Congressional elections neared, a scandal involving the extraordinarily powerful Assistant to the President, Sherman Adams, seriously embarrassed the White House. Adams, described by *Business Week* as the "hardrock moralist and conscience of the Administration," had accepted a vicuna coat, an Oriental rug, and the payment of thousands of dollars in hotel bills from a Boston industrialist in whose behalf he had intervened before federal agencies. Democrats naturally found such revelations a political windfall. On June 18, 1958, with

Adams under fire for six months, Eisenhower paid a public tribute to his integrity and his ability, concluding: "I need him." Political pressure finally forced Adams's resignation in September, although the President continued to commend his "brilliant" and "unselfish work." The *New York Times* commented tartly: "Both President Eisenhower and Mr. Adams ought to have recognized the impropriety of his position long ago; but through a curious form of astigmatism, they do not seem to recognize it yet." The Adams affair, however, was merely the best-publicized conflict of interest case in the Eisenhower years. Other scandals forced the resignation of the chairman of the Republican National Committee, the Secretary of the Air Force, the chairman of the Interstate Commerce Commission, the General Services Administrator, and numerous lesser officials. Eisenhower himself accepted lavish gifts from his wealthy admirers, receiving an estimated $300,000 worth of machinery, livestock, and other goods for his Gettysburg farm alone.

By 1958 "Modern Republicanism" had reached an impasse. Unemployment stood at 6.8 per cent of the labor force, the racial situation had flared out of control, and jokes about an absentee President had become common. Eisenhower's personal popularity sank to a record low of 52 per cent, while all signs pointed to a Republican disaster in the Congressional elections. In addition, Republican-backed proposals for antilabor "right-to-work" laws, on the ballot in many states, had stirred up fierce union opposition. Finally, the Democratic Party projected a more vigorous image. After the defeat of 1956 Democratic National Chairman Paul Butler had helped to form a Democratic Advisory Council, which gave the party a more liberal, aggressive program between Presidential conventions than that furnished by its Congressional leadership. Frightened by the portents of a Democratic landslide, the Republicans fell back on a reactionary style of bygone days. In October the Republican National Committee warned that "socialization of industry is the clear alternative to a Republican Congress." Eisenhower defined the nation's choice as "left-wing government or sensible government." On Election Day voters returned the largest Democratic majorities since the New Deal: 64 to 34 in the Senate and 282 to 154 in the House. The era of "moderation" seemed to be drawing to an end.

But the liberal achievements of the 86th Congress in no way surpassed those of its predecessors. Despite the large Democratic majorities, the most significant piece of legislation to emerge from Congress was the conservative Landrum-Griffin Labor Reform Act. Except for the ineffective civil rights legislation of 1960, the session was a disaster for proponents of social reform. Shortly after the election Johnson promised a "responsible" Democratic opposition. He and Rayburn ended up, according to ADA, "surrendering to the President." Eisenhower, determined to avert the passage of liberal social legislation, surprised many by exerting an unaccustomed amount of Presidential power. "Every sort of foolish proposal will be advanced in the name of . . . the 'poor fellow,' " he told legislative leaders. "We've got to convince Americans that thrift is not a bad word." If he convinced few Americans, the President did make frequent use of his veto to counter liberal majorities. Perhaps the major cause for the triumph of "moderation," however, was the continued confusion within the ranks of Cold War liberalism. Should a Northern Democrat vote to cut the defense budget or to increase it? Should he promote economic equality or economic growth? Should he support or oppose antidiscrimination riders to social welfare programs? Where did he stand on loyalty-security investigations? What was the goal of American foreign policy? Until liberals could satisfactorily answer these questions, their most consistent spokesmen, the Northern Democrats, would continue to be swept along in the conservative tide of American politics.

The confusion of Northern Democrats was exemplified by the career of John F. Kennedy, a front-runner for his party's 1960 Presidential nomination. Elected to Congress in 1946 as a wealthy young war hero, Kennedy used his time in the House to denounce the "betrayal" of Poland at Yalta, excoriate the Truman Administration for the "loss" of China, and vote for the McCarran Act—as well as for a variety of social welfare measures. He never joined ADA or the American Veterans Committee because, he told a reporter, "I'm not comfortable with those people." In 1952 Kennedy ran a spirited campaign that brought him to the Senate. Here he carefully avoided taking any stand on the activities of Senator McCarthy, then being entertained by his father, Joseph P. Kennedy, at Hyannisport, and assisted by his brother, Robert F. Kennedy, in Washington. According to Theodore Sorensen, John Kennedy's speech-writer and biographer, the Massachusetts senator believed that "defense . . . was the bulk of diplomacy and disarmament only a dream." Although Kennedy voted for every civil rights bill coming before him, he did so, wrote Sorensen, "more as a matter of course than of concern." Kennedy "paid little attention to the historic Supreme Court desegregation decision" and called school integration "a judicial problem, not a legislative one." Rejecting the attitudes of those he called the "professional liberals," Kennedy characterized himself as "a moderate Democrat." In the late 1950s Kennedy improved his liberal standing somewhat by taking positions favoring civil liberties, by running a skillful race for the 1956 Vice-Presidential nomination, and by acquiring the active support of two well-known liberal intellectuals,

John Kenneth Galbraith and Arthur Schlesinger, Jr. Nevertheless, despite a landslide re-election victory in 1958, Kennedy was distrusted by most liberals, who regarded him as unprincipled and ambitious. In a reference to his book *Profiles in Courage,* Mrs. Roosevelt observed that she hesitated to support someone for the Presidency "who understands what courage is and admires it, but has not quite the independence to have it."

With the Republican Presidential candidacy virtually assured to Vice-President Nixon, the nation's attention focused on the scramble for the Democratic nomination. Lyndon Johnson, relying upon his Southern base and his Congressional contacts, nailed down the support of Southern delegates but few others. Most liberals backed either Hubert Humphrey, who plunged into the primaries, or Adlai Stevenson, who remained aloof but was supported by influential Democratic politicians and newspapers. Kennedy understood that, because of his youth and particularly his Catholicism—which party leaders considered a political liability—he would have to enter and win the primaries. This he did handily, bowling over his opponents with his large campaign staff, his money, his family, and his immense energy. After Kennedy took 61 per cent of the vote in Protestant West Virginia, Humphrey dropped out of the race and Kennedy's campaign acquired a seemingly overwhelming momentum. Yet it received an unexpected check at the Democratic National Convention. Thousands of Stevenson supporters surged in and around the Democratic Party's Los Angeles meeting site, and Stevenson's appearance on the scene threw them into a frenzy. Another tumultuous demonstration greeted a nominating speech for Stevenson by Senator Eugene McCarthy of Minnesota. For a brief moment the cool Kennedy machine seemed about to be halted by an outpouring of enthusiasm and nostalgia. But when the balloting began it became clear that, while Stevenson might have the delegates' hearts, Kennedy had their votes. The Massachusetts senator won nomination on the first ballot. Appearing at the convention hall, Kennedy spoke of a "New Frontier" in "uncharted areas of science and space, unsolved problems of peace and war, unconquered pockets of ignorance and prejudice, unanswered questions of poverty and surplus." The nation, he said, stood at "a turning point in history," facing a choice "between national greatness and national decline."

Liberals came away from the convention less than enthusiastic. To be sure, they had largely written the Democratic platform, which promised medical care for the aged, strong civil rights legislation, federal aid to education, government promotion of economic growth, and a foreign aid program "to enable peoples . . . to make their own free choices."

On the other hand, Kennedy had revived their suspicions of him by choosing Lyndon Johnson as his running mate. To conciliate the South and Johnson supporters, Kennedy had offered the Majority Leader the second spot on the ticket, assuming that he would probably refuse it. Johnson, however, had accepted, sending liberals into a state of shock when the news broke. "Say it isn't so, Jack," shouted Joseph Rauh over television. But it was. ADA's national board rather dispiritedly endorsed Kennedy but not Johnson, who retorted: "We don't want the support of the oddballs on the Left." At the outset of the campaign, then, "many liberals," as Kennedy's campaign biographer James M. Burns complained, were "sitting out" the election. Eric Sevareid wrote in disgust: "The 'managerial revolution' has come to politics, and Nixon and Kennedy are its first completely packaged products." Both men, he argued, were ambitious, hard-nosed, devoid of strong beliefs and passions—junior executives on the make. In the end, though, their aversion to Nixon and their admiration for Kennedy's dynamism brought the liberals strongly into the Democratic camp.

Like the Presidential candidates, the campaign had a synthetic quality. Nixon's greatest handicap was his identification with the minority Republican Party, which he sought to offset by stressing his association with the still popular Eisenhower. Committed to a relatively liberal platform (as a concession to New York's Governor Nelson Rockefeller) and running with a "moderate" Vice-Presidential candidate (Henry Cabot Lodge, Jr.), Nixon tried to project a reasonable, statesmanlike image, based primarily on his governmental "experience." Eisenhower, brought into the campaign during the last weeks, played upon the same themes, although, asked by reporters what important decisions Nixon had been responsible for in his Administration, he responded helplessly: "If you give me a week, I might think of one." Kennedy, realizing that his greatest handicap was Protestant distrust of his religion, sought to offset this by appealing to traditional Democratic Party loyalty, campaigning intensively in the industrial states of the Northeast and Midwest, and making special efforts to draw the support of lower-income and black voters. Nevertheless, the "religious issue" continued to dog Kennedy until he met it head on in a September 12 speech to the Greater Houston Ministerial Association. Declaring that he believed in "an America where the separation of church and state is absolute," Kennedy said that he thought it no more proper for a Catholic prelate to tell a Catholic President how to act than for a Protestant minister to tell his parishioners how to vote.

"Rarely in American history," recalled journalist Theodore White, "has there been a political campaign that discussed issues less or clarified them less." Kennedy employed a barrage of statistics designed to prove that the Republicans had not "done enough" at home and abroad. "It is time to get this country moving again," he cried out in speech after speech. Yet the direction of the movement remained unclear. Nixon's favorite retort was that Kennedy was "running America down." Although Kennedy took a somewhat less belligerent stand than did his rival on the need to defend Chiang Kai-shek's island outposts, he emerged as considerably more bellicose with respect to Cuba and the nation's military strength, which he pledged to expand dramatically. In the 1960 "great debates," watched by television audiences ranging from 60 million to 75 million, Nixon told viewers that he was "very proud" that Eisenhower had "restored . . . good language to the conduct of the Presidency," while Kennedy lost few opportunities to display his Cold War orthodoxy. Even in the first debate, which excluded foreign policy matters, Kennedy began: "We discuss tonight domestic issues, but I would not want . . . any implication to be given that this does not involve directly our struggle with Mr. Khrushchev." Viewers perceived a clear difference between the two men only in the first debate, when Nixon's unshaven appearance dealt what opinion analysts considered a devastating blow to his campaign.

In the election a record turnout gave Kennedy the victory by a 112,803-vote margin—the smallest of the twentieth century. Although Kennedy carried but twenty-four states to Nixon's twenty-six, he won because he had the electoral votes of the large industrial states as well as those of the Deep South. Capturing 65 per cent of the vote in the nation's twelve largest cities, he also broke even in the total vote of thirty-seven major suburban areas, gaining the solid support of labor, Catholics, blacks, Jews, and young voters. He ran poorly, however, among Bible Belt Protestants in the South and West and drew only a minority of the votes of whites, college graduates, upper-income earners, white-collar workers, elderly people, farmers, and small-town dwellers. The Survey Research Center of the University of Michigan estimated that one out of four voters who cast a ballot for President in 1956 and 1960 switched parties as a result of religion. Close to 60 per cent of the voters swinging from Eisenhower to Kennedy were Catholic, and 95 per cent of the voters moving from Stevenson to Nixon were non-Catholic. Kennedy's poor showing among Protestants (37 per cent) probably cost him the electoral votes of such normally Democratic states as Kentucky, Tennessee, and Oklahoma, but his strength among Catholics (78 per cent) brought the big Northern industrial states into the Democratic column. Although the Democrats lost two seats in the Senate and twenty-two in the House—primarily because of the narrowness of Kennedy's victory and because some falling off from the overwhelming majorities of 1958 was inevitable—they retained solid control of both houses of Congress. Thus, after eight years of Modern Republicanism the nation had again thrown in its lot with the spokesmen for Cold War liberalism.

But, as American politicians trotted out the clichés that had served them for the past fifteen years, new and more profound forces were already stirring across the land, inspiring the first of a series of direct challenges to the institutions of power and privilege. They began simply, unheralded by the mass media. On December 1, 1955, a forty-year-old black seamstress, Mrs. Rosa Parks, sat down in the third row of a bus in Montgomery, Alabama. Two stops later, in accordance with "the Southern way of life," the driver ordered her to move to the crowded rear of the bus to enable newly arrived whites to sit down. Tired after her day's work and her lifetime of submission to Alabama's racial codes, Mrs. Parks refused. It was an unexpected act of defiance that not only caused her arrest but sent a sudden surge of determination through the black community. Beginning the next day, and extending for more than a year thereafter, the 50,000 blacks of Montgomery boycotted the city's buses in what their leader, a twenty-six-year-old minister named Martin Luther King, Jr., termed "an act of massive noncooperation." "It used to be that my body rode but my soul walked," remarked an old woman. "Now my body may be tired, but my soul is free." Victorious in Montgomery after an epic struggle, King met in January, 1957, with black activists from ten Southern states to form the Southern Christian Leadership Conference. The new organization elected King as its president and called upon blacks across the nation to "assert their human dignity" by rejecting "further cooperation with evil."

The Gandhian tone of King's message reflected the central role played by American pacifists in virtually all movements for peace and social justice in the postwar era. Few in numbers but dedicated and intelligent, they worked through their own peace organizations—the Fellowship of Reconciliation and the War Resisters League—as well as through groups they had founded in other areas of concern: the American Civil Liberties Union, the American Friends Service Committee, and the Congress of Racial Equality. The best-known and most eloquent of their spokesmen, the Reverend A. J. Muste, had sought since the 1930s to reorient American pacifism into a radical, direct-action movement. For decades he met with only limited success. Then, dramatically, nonviolent resistance began to catch the imagination of civil rights and peace activists—first in Montgomery, where King and his followers were won to its advocacy, and then, increasingly, across the nation. On August 6, 1957, the anniversary of the Hiroshima bombing, a small group of pacifists engaged in an act of calculated civil disobedience by publicly entering the site of an AEC bomb project in Nevada. Similar acts of resistance to the military emerged throughout the nation, with their proponents organizing themselves into the Committee for Non-Violent Action. "For years . . . our voices have been lost in the massive effort of those responsible for preparing this country for war," declared one activist. "We mean to speak now with the weight of our whole lives." By 1960 radical pacifists had sailed vessels of protest into nuclear bomb testing zones in the Pacific, blocked the entrances to missile bases, and boarded nuclear submarines. In May of that year 2,000 people in New York City took part in acts of resistance to the yearly nuclear bomb drill, including 500 in City Hall Park who defied police by refusing to take shelter.

The direct-actionists constituted but one arm of a growing peace movement. In April, 1957, Nobel Prize winner Albert Schweitzer had broadcast an appeal to fifty nations to stop the testing of nuclear weapons. That June Linus Pauling, another Nobel laureate, released a petition signed by 11,000 scientists—almost 3,000 of them American—calling for "immediate action . . . to effect an international agreement to stop the testing of all nuclear weapons." On June 21, as the Senate Internal Security Subcommittee scrutinized Pauling's patriotism, twenty-seven prominent Americans, about half of them pacifists, met in New York to discuss nuclear testing. Called together at the invitation of Norman Cousins, editor of the *Saturday Review,* and Clarence Pickett, secretary emeritus of the American Friends Service Committee, the gathering was grim but determined. "The normal drive for survival has been put out of action by present propaganda," declared psychologist Erich Fromm. "We must try to bring the voice of sanity to the people." On November 15 the National Committee for a Sane Nuclear Policy launched its first advertisement in the *New York Times.* The "challenge of the age," it contended, was not to acquire new and more powerful weapons but "to develop the concept of a higher loyalty—loyalty by man to the human community." Although the advertisement had been designed for educational rather than organizational purposes, it stirred up such interest that by the summer of 1958 SANE had 130 chapters representing 25,000 Americans. In September a national conference broadened SANE's aims from achieving a test ban to securing general disarmament.

By 1960 peace demonstrations were cropping up in the nation's major cities. In May 3,000 Americans demonstrated in San Francisco's Union Square for an end to the arms race. A SANE rally in New York's Madison Square Garden drew an overflow crowd, addressed by Norman Thomas, Eleanor Roosevelt, and Walter Reuther. In July pacifist groups in Los Angeles sponsored a "Walk for Disarmament" of from 2,500 to 3,000 persons. On August 7 thousands of demonstrators marched upon the United Nations in a call for nuclear disarmament.

Simultaneously, the student movement, virtually moribund since the 1930s, began to revive. In April, 1959, a coalition of pacifist and Socialist students in the Midwest organized the Student Peace Union, which by 1960 claimed 5,000 members. Announcing their intention of acting "independently of the existing power blocs" and of seeking "new and creative means of achieving a free and peaceful society," they declared that "neither human freedom nor the human race itself can endure in a world committed to militarism." At Berkeley, Harvard, Columbia, and other campuses across the nation, students formed activist groups to promote disarmament, civil liberties, and racial equality.

One of the most dramatic student demonstrations occurred in San Francisco, the site of hearings held by the House Committee on Un-American Activities. On the morning of May 12, 1960, hundreds of local students began lining up to gain admittance to the hearings in City Hall. Instead of admitting them, however, HUAC granted entry to a hand-picked crowd of its own supporters from "patriotic" groups. On the following afternoon the students grew restless and began singing songs of the civil rights movement. They were still singing when, without warning, the police turned high-pressure water hoses on them. Infuriated, the students sat down and locked arms. The law officers, reinforced by a contingent of steel-helmeted motorcycle policemen, moved in and dragged, kicked, and clubbed the students down the marble stairs, soon drenched with water and blood. The next day 5,000 angry demonstrators, largely drawn from local campuses, gathered in protest before City Hall. The "silent generation" had begun to find its voice.

At the very heart of the new mood of restlessness lay the revolt in the South. On February 1, 1960, four black freshmen at North Carolina Agricultural and Technical College, having discussed racial discrimination among themselves the preceding week, entered the Woolworth store in downtown Greensboro and sat down at the lunch counter. Refused service, they remained seated there until the store closed. The following day they returned with dozens of new recruits. Similar demonstrations, soon termed "sit-ins," appeared in other parts of North Carolina, then spread rapidly across the South, awakening a generation of young activists: Julian Bond, an undergraduate at Atlanta's Morehouse College; James Forman, studying French in a Northern graduate school; John Lewis, a seminary student in Nashville; James Lawson, a divinity student at Vanderbilt; Bob Moses, a young mathematics teacher in Harlem. Tens of thousands of students, most of them black but some white, sprang into action; thousands were arrested. Beaten, stabbed, and assaulted with clubs, chains, tear gas, and police dogs, they remained disciplined, nonviolent, determined to expose the denial of the most elementary human rights. Replying to former President Truman's charge that the sit-ins were Communist-inspired, a black student told the platform committee at the Democratic National Convention: "For three hundred and fifty years, the American Negro has been sent to the back door. . . . We grew weary." That April, at Shaw University in Raleigh, North Carolina, sit-in leaders gathered under the auspices of the Southern Christian Leadership Conference and formed the Student Non-Violent Coordinating Committee (SNCC) to press for racial justice in the South. In the North, the Congress of Racial Equality organized the picketing of hundreds of stores with segregated affiliates and distributed millions of leaflets on events in the South. Across the land, black leaders sensed a turning point in the long struggle for equality.

By raising aloft those principles to which liberal politicians had given more lip service than commitment, the emerging protest movements confronted the incoming Administration with an embarrassing dilemma. Although the Democrats could not know it at the time, they would find their political fortunes inextricably tied to the satisfaction of the new demands for peace and social justice. The world had changed much in the fifteen years since 1945—a fact that the young President-elect constantly remarked on, but which his conventional ideas seemed to belie —and the Old Politics was starting to lose its grip. Traditional formulas had begun to creak, and new forces were in motion. Whether the liberal wing of the Democratic Party would be renewed by the spreading revolt against the Cold War and the revived demand for social reform remained problematical, but politicians—particularly those who had sought refuge in "moderation"—could ignore these first signs of insurgency only at their peril. For the American Celebration was drawing to a close, as its guardians of fear and apathy fell back before that still inchoate force which its participants called "The Movement."

8

The New Frontier and the Old Politics, 1961-63

> Most of the problems . . . that we now face are technical problems, are administrative problems. They are very sophisticated judgments which do not lend themselves to the great sort of "passionate movements" which have stirred this country so often in the past.
>
> JOHN F. KENNEDY, 1962

FEW AMERICAN PRESIDENTS have entered office with as much intelligence, assertiveness, and energy as young John F. Kennedy, and even fewer could match his confidence in the governing capacity of a managerial élite. For Kennedy was a cool technocrat, a man who prided himself on his freedom from sentimentality; in the phrases that soon swirled about Washington, he was "toughminded," "hardnosed," "pragmatic." Speaking at the 1962 Yale commencement, Kennedy claimed that the central issues of the day related "not to basic clashes of philosophy or ideology" but to technical expertise. "What is at stake," he said, is "the practical management of a modern economy." The "New Frontier generation," wrote Arthur Schlesinger, a top White House aide, had a "mistrust of evangelism" along New Deal lines; it did things not "because they were just and right" but "because they were rational and necessary." Regarding the existence of poverty, war, and injustice with a cynical forbearance, the typical New Frontiersman preferred to rely upon liberalism without tears, politics without people, managers without convictions. James Reston later recalled a long private talk with Kennedy in which he had asked the young President "what he wanted to have achieved by the time he rode down Pennsylvania Avenue with his successor." Kennedy "looked at me as if I were a dreaming child. I tried again: Did he not feel the need of some goal to help guide his day-to-day decisions and priorities? Again a ghastly pause. It was only when I turned the question to immediate, tangible problems that he seized the point and rolled off a torrent of statistics."

But if Kennedy sought to keep domestic conflicts under cool bureaucratic control, he continued the crusades abroad at a white heat. "The trumpet summons us again," proclaimed the President in his inaugural address. "In the long history of the world, only a few generations have been granted the role of defending freedom in its hour of maximum danger. I do not shrink from this responsibility. I welcome it." In its great struggle against Communism, the United States would "pay any price, bear any burden, meet any hardship, support any friend, oppose any foe." Sacrifice, endurance, "great commitment" would be required of all citizens. The best-remembered segment of the inaugural address —the President's admonition to "ask not what your country can do for you; ask what you can do for your country"—would have fitted equally well into the inspirational messages served up by rulers of authoritarian states.

Kennedy's executive appointees were men very much along the President's lines—shrewd, tough administrators, skilled wielders of power. Many were familiar figures in the national security apparatus, and almost all were drawn from the nation's upper class. Brushing aside Adlai Stevenson—who in these circles appeared naïvely liberal and ineffectual —Kennedy asked New York banker Robert Lovett, long connected with the nation's foreign policy establishment, to become Secretary of State. Lovett declined the offer but recommended a Dulles protégé and president of the Rockefeller Foundation, Dean Rusk, whom Kennedy promptly appointed. Stevenson was relegated to the United Nations, where he would be useful as an eloquent spokesman for U.S. foreign policy, even as he played no role in formulating it. As his Secretary of the Treasury, Kennedy named C. Douglas Dillon (of Wall Street's Dillon, Read and Company), the Under Secretary of State in the outgoing Republican Administration. Another Republican, Robert S. McNamara, president of the Ford Motor Company, was appointed Secretary of Defense. Other top officials of similar origins in the Administration included Averell Harriman (of Brown Brothers, Harriman), Paul Nitze (of Dillon, Read), Roswell Gilpatric (of still another Wall Street firm), John McCone, and William C. Foster. John J. McCloy, appointed by Kennedy as his special adviser on disarmament, had a background, Schlesinger wrote, that "combined the Republican party, the Pentagon, the Ford Foundation, the Chase Manhattan Bank, Cravath, Swaine & Moore, the Brook and the Links." As Attorney General, the President chose his younger brother Robert, who, despite a reputation for hard-driving ruthlessness, proved considerably more liberal than many of the

"intellectuals" tapped for service: McGeorge Bundy and Arthur Schlesinger, Jr. (Harvard), Walt W. Rostow (MIT), William Bundy (the
CIA), and the Pentagon "whiz kids" (the universities and the Rand
Corporation). According to the *New Republic*'s T.R.B., it was an
"enormously, reassuringly competent" group, but one as "under control" and "disciplined" as the President himself, who already exhibited
"a certain coolness and grayness."

Despite such telltale signs, most liberals were immensely pleased with
the new Administration. Kennedy's State of the Union message, like his
inaugural address, promised something for everybody: new initiatives
in disarmament (as well as more armaments), new overtures to the
Soviet Union (as well as unrelenting Cold War), and new funds to relieve ignorance and poverty (as well as additional funds for new missile
systems). Liberals took heart at the programs offered them, and especially at Kennedy's determination to be a "strong" President. The *New
Republic* thought Kennedy's inaugural statement had "that ring of command that emboldens men to renew their faiths," that "intrepid assertiveness . . . that is authentically American." Particularly reassuring to
liberals was their own return to government office. After years in the
hinterlands, the Cold War liberals were on their way back to Washington. There, in touch football games, on the squash courts, or jogging
down footpaths, they girded themselves for global confrontations, aching
to prove to the Russians (and to the scornful Babbitts of the 1950s)
just how steely-eyed they could be in a showdown. They were more
than a little titillated by a new feeling of power. "One could not deny a
sense of New Frontier autointoxication," recalled Schlesinger. "The
pleasures of power . . . were now being happily devoured—the chauf-
feur-driven limousines, the special telephones, the top secret documents,
the personal aides, the meetings in the Cabinet Room, the calls from
the President."

Congress was less intoxicated by the New Frontier. Most of the Administration's reform programs—Medicare, federal aid to education, the
creation of a Department of Urban Affairs, and tax reform—met quick
defeat. The one major bill passed by the 87th Congress was the Trade
Expansion Act of 1962. Other Administration measures that won acceptance were pitifully weak. The minimum wage bill of 1961 extended
coverage to 3 million additional workers, but few of them in fact earned
less than the minimum; most impoverished wage-earners remained
among the 16 million who continued to be excluded. A day-care bill
provided $5 million in facilities for 4 million children of working
mothers—$1.25 each for one year. The Administration's program for
aid to Appalachia did funnel sizable sums into that impoverished region
—$1 billion by 1965—but 80 per cent went for highway construction,

which did little for the unemployed and impoverished but a good deal for venal local governments and industrial interests. After the first session of the 87th Congress, ADA wrote it off as having produced, at best, a record of "callous expediency" and, at worst, "one of astonishing indifference to real national needs."

Why did so much New Frontier energy produce such meager results? Partisans of the Administration were inclined to blame Congress. In the 1960 elections the Democratic margin in both House and Senate had been cut, they pointed out, leaving liberals without the votes necessary to carry Administration proposals. Nevertheless, it was also true that the Administration never gave its reform bills top priority. Even White House insiders were critical of Kennedy's decision to expend his limited Presidential bargaining power in traditional areas. Schlesinger recalled: "We thought him mistaken in 1962 in making the entirely respectable, safe, and overrated trade expansion bill his top legislative priority instead of staging a knockdown-drag-out fight over federal aid to education or Medicare." Moreover, unlike many liberals, Kennedy did not believe it worthwhile to fight for his domestic program. "There is no sense in putting the office of the Presidency on the line . . . and then being defeated," he explained. Kennedy, as T.R.B. noted, was "not a romantic," and the result was "compromises, or compromises of compromises." When the President's task force on schools urged $1.5 billion a year, he asked for half that amount. When the AFL-CIO urged the building of 400,000 low-income housing units, the Administration asked for 100,000. When Congressman Emanuel Celler of New York and Senator Joseph Clark of Pennsylvania introduced legislation to carry out the Democratic Party's 1960 campaign pledges on civil rights, White House Press Secretary Pierre Salinger issued a statement declaring that the President "does not think it is necessary at this time to enact civil rights legislation."

Kennedy's accommodationist approach was designed to curry favor for his legislative program among Southern Democrats in Congress, but it did little more than anger liberals. Not only did the President omit a civil rights bill from his legislative program, but he remained aloof from the liberal struggle to eliminate the filibuster, increased cotton prices, lavished patronage upon racist cronies of Dixiecrat legislators, produced hefty defense contracts, and flattered key Southern politicians. In the spring of 1961 he flew in by helicopter to honor Senator Harry F. Byrd's birthday party in Virginia, despite the fact that the Senator had not supported him in 1960. The more unyielding in opposition to New Frontier measures a Southern Congressman seemed to be, the more the President cozied up to him—all to no avail. There was "little to show for it," recalled *New York Times* reporter Tom Wicker. Kennedy "had not been able to deliver; nor had he bought any Southerners who would stay bought from vote to vote." Liberals were disgusted. T.R.B. wrote in the *New Republic:* "We get awfully sick of this 'moderation.' All during the Eisenhower Administration there was moderation. . . . And now instead of Kennedy urgency there is some more moderation." ADA's newsletter charged Kennedy with "maintaining an attitude of inertia," abandoning liberals in Congress, and following policies that "varied little from the formula developed when the Republican party controlled the White House. It is a formula of accommodation and compromise with the same coalition of Southerners and Republicans."

Kennedy not only abandoned the battle for liberal social legislation but also sponsored a number of measures with regressive, pro-business features. The economic slump of 1962 led the Administration to propose a tax cut to stimulate economic growth and full employment. Relying upon increased private consumption rather than increased public spending constituted what John Kenneth Galbraith called "reactionary" Keynesianism. "I am not sure," he later said, "what the advantage is in having a few more dollars to spend if the air is too dirty to breathe, the water too polluted to drink, the commuters are losing out on the struggle to get in and out of the cities, the streets are filthy, the schools so bad that the young, perhaps wisely, stay away, and hoodlums roll citizens for some of the dollars they saved in taxes." Furthermore, the Kennedy tax cut—finally passed by Congress in 1964—was sharply biased in favor of the wealthy. A family of four with an income of $3,000 a year received a tax cut of $60; a family of four with an income of $200,000 a year received a tax cut of $32,000. The 2.2 per cent of taxpayers with yearly incomes over $20,000 received almost 30 per cent of the tax savings. Not only did the Administration fail to close existing tax loopholes, but it opened new ones by granting business liberalized depreciation allowances which reduced the effective tax on corporations by more than a third. In the first five Kennedy-Johnson years, corporate profits rose 76.5 per cent, wages 18 per cent. New Frontier economic measures thus helped to ensure a redistribution of income from the poor to the rich.

Except for the "defense" effort, no area of public policy received such lavish funding under the Kennedy Administration as the space race. Dominated by the Apollo mission—a $40 billion venture designed to put a man on the moon within a decade—the manned space program was opposed by many scientists and by sizable sectors of the public as a ridiculous misallocation of the nation's resources. Polls found that 58 per cent of the American people disapproved of the Apollo mission. Yet Kennedy consistently promoted it, both because it was a popular boondoggle among defense contractors and because he viewed it as a weapon in the Cold War. Dr. James E. Webb, director of NASA, claimed that "with a billion people already allied against us, and the emerging nations weighing events . . . the United States must present the image of a can-do nation, with which they can confidently align their futures."

With the help of the Administration, the early rewards of the space effort were channeled into corporate hands. On February 7, 1962, as Congress pondered the future of U.S. space satellites, President Kennedy announced that space communications was a matter "which, by nature, is essentially private enterprise in character." According to Tom Wicker, the President "found merit" in Senator Kefauver's plan for a publicly owned communications satellite system but opposed it because it was "sure to be regarded among business leaders as socialism." Instead, he supported a bill that turned over most of the stock in a private communications satellite system (COMSAT) to AT&T and several other multibillion-dollar firms. Critics pointed out that these private corporations would be reaping the benefits of $25 billion in taxpayers' money already spent on space exploration, including more than $500 million for communications satellite research. Most legislators, however, favored the Administration bill. "This," Republican Congressman Richard L. Roudebush of Indiana explained, "is the free enterprise way; this is the capitalistic way; this is the profit system way; and this is the American way." In August, 1962, Congress and the President approved the Communications Satellite Act, and in February, 1963, COMSAT was organized as a private corporation, with AT&T alone purchasing 29 per cent of the total stock issue. The following year COMSAT was incorporated into an International Space Communications System, in which the United States held 61 per cent of the consortium shares. The National Association of Manufacturers endorsed the communications satellite system as "one of the finer examples of our country's global leadership in the space age."

The business-as-usual behavior in the White House and on Capitol Hill contrasted sharply with the daring tactics of the civil rights movement. After a Supreme Court decision in 1961 extended desegregation in interstate travel from carriers to terminal facilities, CORE, led by James Farmer, organized a series of dramatic Freedom Rides that May to test compliance. At Rock Hill, South Carolina, an integrated bus group was set upon by twenty vandals. At Anniston, Alabama, a white mob stopped another bus filled with Freedom Riders and burned it to the ground. Arriving in Birmingham, Freedom Riders headed for the lunch counters but were intercepted by a crowd of white men carrying lead pipes; one rider was beaten so brutally that he required fifty-three stitches in his head. By May 20, with Freedom Riders streaming into the South and drawing headlines around the world, the Justice Department pressed for and obtained assurances from Alabama Governor John Patterson that he had "the will, the force, the men, and the equipment to fully protect everyone in Alabama." When Freedom Riders arrived in Montgomery, however, a mob of 300—some armed with clubs—had gathered unopposed to assault them and accompanying newsmen. The first Freedom Rider stepped off the bus to the sound of women screaming: "Kill the nigger-loving son of a bitch." Virtually all the Freedom Riders were violently assaulted, some lying for hours in their own blood before an ambulance would take them to a hospital. Attorney General Kennedy, finding it impossible to locate the suddenly elusive Governor, dispatched FBI agents and federal marshals to Montgomery. The President publicly called upon Alabamans to prevent further violence and expressed his hope that citizens would refrain "from any action which would . . . tend to provoke further outbreaks."

If the Administration's appeal was intended to halt the Freedom Rides, however, it was unsuccessful. Although the Attorney General asked for a "cooling-off period," interracial busloads of college students, clergymen, SNCC workers, and SCLC leaders continued to pour into the Deep South. On the very next day a racially integrated group of ministers, led by Yale chaplain William Sloane Coffin, Jr., was arrested for trying to use the facilities of the Montgomery bus terminal. By the end of the summer, local authorities had arrested hundreds of Freedom Riders, consigning many to primitive county farms and work camps. CORE spent $300,000 in legal fees alone. In November, under prodding from the Attorney General, the Interstate Commerce Commission finally banned racial segregation on interstate buses and trains and in terminals. Perhaps a thousand Freedom Riders had dramatized and then shattered the racial codes governing interstate travel in America.

Beginning in the summer of 1961 Southern civil rights workers concentrated upon two overlapping areas of concern: voter registration and the desegregation of public facilities. In the Black Belt areas of the South especially, blacks were systematically disfranchised not only by means of elaborate "literacy" tests administered by virtually inaccessible and hopelessly biased white registrars but also through local campaigns of violence and terror. Thus, although blacks comprised 43 per cent of Mississippi's population, 95 per cent of them were not registered to vote. In early 1961 Bob Moses of SNCC had begun voter registration work in that state, and later that year he was followed by the first of hundreds of other SNCC workers, who fanned out across Mississippi and into Alabama and Southwest Georgia. White vigilante groups and local authorities met their efforts with arrests, beatings, firebombings, and murders, but the slow and painful campaign proceeded, assisted by

CORE, SCLC, and the NAACP. "All our lives we've had to bow and scrape, laugh when there was nothing funny and scratch our heads and say 'yes, sir,' " a SNCC worker told a group of poor black farmers in Georgia. "We want to change that. . . . It's people like you . . . who are going to change this country." SNCC and SCLC were also active in dozens of cities and towns across the Deep South, organizing protests against segregated public facilities. In Albany, Georgia, the struggle grew particularly intense. A new protest march, led by SCLC's Martin Luther King and Ralph Abernathy, brought the number of arrests to over a thousand; prisoners had to be parceled out to jails in adjoining counties. On dusty country roads, in tattered sharecropper shacks, in song-filled, tearful church meetings the message spread that the moment had arrived to put aside fear, that the time had come for "Freedom Now."

But the heightening of the civil rights struggle brought no significant response from the White House. Despite the strongest platform pledges on civil rights in the Democratic Party's history, the Administration refused to back civil rights legislation until well into 1963. "I can't go for legislation at this time," the President told Joseph Rauh in 1961, banging his hand on his desk. "You have to understand the problems I have here." And even after 1961 the Administration made no more than token gestures before Congress in behalf of racial justice. As Sorensen later observed: "Bills originating in the Congress were endorsed by administration witnesses, thus technically fulfilling the pledges of the 1960 platform, but none of these was adopted or pressed by the President as his own." White House insiders later argued that Kennedy, while personally in favor of civil rights legislation, thought he lacked the votes in Congress to pass it and feared that it would endanger the rest of his program. Furthermore, Sorensen wrote, Kennedy believed that a battle over civil rights would "divide the American people at a time when the international scene required maximum unity." Among civil rights leaders, Kennedy's position aroused virtually universal condemnation. Even the NAACP's Roy Wilkins—hardly the most militant of black spokesmen—assailed the President for his "supercaution."

The President did not need legislative majorities to take executive action in behalf of civil rights, but here, too, his record was, in the words of Martin Luther King, "essentially cautious and defensive," directed toward "the limited goal of token integration." During the campaign of 1960 Kennedy had won support among blacks by attacking Eisenhower's failure to end racial discrimination in federally assisted housing with a "stroke of the pen." But, once in office, he refused to issue the appropriate Executive Order for almost two years. Liberals and civil rights leaders sharply criticized the President; pens began arriving at the White House to ease his task. Finally, on the evening of November 20, 1962, the night before the long Thanksgiving weekend, Kennedy issued the Executive Order—one considerably weaker than that recommended by the U.S. Commission on Civil Rights. According to Sorensen, Kennedy consciously chose "the lowest-key time possible" for the announcement and "deliberately sandwiched" it in between major statements on foreign policy. Kennedy also created the President's Committee on Equal Employment Opportunity to combat discrimination in government agencies and among private contractors, but its achievements were exceedingly modest.

Although the Justice Department, under the vigorous direction of Robert Kennedy, was more sympathetic to the crusade for racial justice than in the past, it provided the movement with limited assistance. To be sure, the Department filed more suits under the voting rights provisions of the 1957 and 1960 Civil Rights Acts than had its predecessor, but such actions hardly met the magnitude of the problem. Moreover, as part of the Administration's appeasement of reactionary Southern senators, Robert Kennedy cleared a crop of uncompromising racists and John Kennedy appointed them to federal judgeships in the South. Harold Cox, an Eastland crony appointed by the President to a judicial circuit that handled most civil rights cases in the Deep South, worked effectively in his new post to safeguard white supremacy, referring to black defendants as "chimpanzees." In 1962 two of Kennedy's judicial appointees in Louisiana outvoted an Eisenhower appointee to uphold a statute requiring that the race of all candidates be listed on the state ballot.

Nothing did more to alienate civil rights activists than the Kennedy Administration's unwillingness to protect civil rights workers and the Southern black community from local harassment and terror. Again and again, phone calls to the FBI or to the Justice Department asking for protection went unheeded or were refused. Justice Department attorneys watched and did nothing while police in Selma, Alabama, arrested people peacefully standing on federal property. FBI agents watched without interference while police in McComb, Mississippi, beat citizens who had broken no law and state patrolmen used electric cattle prods on people who had committed no crime. Only when a major crisis emerged did the Administration discover its responsibility to enforce federal law in the South. Such a crisis erupted in 1962, when James Meredith, a black Mississippian and student at Jackson State College, attempted to enroll in the all-white University of Mississippi. Twice Meredith attempted to register at Ole Miss and twice he was turned back by Governor Ross Barnett while crowds jeered in the background: "Communists. . . . Go home, nigger." With the assistance of federal marshals, Meredith finally entered the campus in late September, only to be assaulted by a mob of thousands, some armed with guns, led by former U.S. General Edwin Walker. All night long a battle raged, leaving hundreds wounded and two men dead. Kennedy finally sent in federal troops. Blacks were naturally heartened by the firmness of Kennedy's action, but civil rights activists recognized that it was no substitute for ordinary, day-to-day protection. "Negroes have marshaled extraordinary courage to employ nonviolent direct action," wrote Martin Luther King in early 1964. "They have been left—by the most powerful federal government in the world—almost solely to their own resources."

Sometimes, indeed, federal power was mobilized against the civil rights movement. J. Edgar Hoover's FBI selected the NAACP for investigation, targeted SNCC and CORE for disruption, and reported that King's 1963 March on Washington address marked him as "the most dangerous Negro of the future in this nation." As early as May, 1962, the FBI had secretly designated King as a "Communist," to be incarcerated in a "national emergency," and later that year obtained Robert Kennedy's authorization for a full-scale investigation, which eventually included wiretapping his home, office, and hotel rooms. Embarking upon an unrelenting campaign to destroy King (and find a "suitable" successor), the FBI distributed scurrilous tapes, reports, or briefings on the civil rights leader to White House officials, Congressional committees, universities, Attorney General Kennedy, the National Council of Churches, politicians, prominent citizens, and the press. In November, 1964, Hoover publicly denounced King as the most "notorious liar" in the country. Meanwhile, the FBI anonymously mailed embarrassing materials to the civil rights leader, threatening to reveal them if he did not commit suicide. Although much of this FBI vendetta was known to high government officials, none took any action to stop it.

Throughout the late 1950s and early 1960s the most innovative branch of the federal government was neither the Congress nor the executive but the Supreme Court. During the 1950s the Warren Court had declared racial segregation in the nation's schools unconstitutional and had called a halt to some of the worst excesses of the Anti-Communist Crusade. In the 1960s it came forth with a new series of landmark decisions. The most important of these involved halting prayer in the public schools, upholding the rights of legal defendants, and ending the malapportionment of state legislatures. While frequently pleasing liberals and civil libertarians, such rulings often enraged conservatives. A considerable furor arose over the Court's ruling against prayer in the public schools. Many school systems simply disregarded it. Former President Hoover charged that the Court's ruling had led to the "disintegration of a sacred American heritage." Congressional critics of the Court—particularly conservative Southern politicians, who despised its desegregation ruling—kept up a running attack on its patriotism. Senator Eastland, chairman of the Judiciary Committee, released a report in 1962 prepared by his staff contending that the Court had made "pro-Communist" decisions on forty-six occasions. Such denunciations were a tribute to the pioneering work of the nation's judiciary at a time of executive-legislative caution.

The Administration's default on social reform was compensated for, in the view of many, by its elegant "style." John F. Kennedy and his wife, Jacqueline, were both young, intelligent, and attractive, graced with that charm and "good taste" associated with the most sophisticated of upper-class life. During their occupancy of the executive mansion, French wines, elegant clothing, and "the beautiful people" made an appearance on state occasions, and the music of Pablo Casals replaced that of Fred Waring. Imparting a new cultural tone to the White House, the Kennedys sponsored a dinner for Nobel Prize winners and invited a steady stream of writers, musicians, dancers, and artists to Presidential functions. Such recognition charmed and flattered many in the intellectual community, long accustomed to derisive comments from the White House. Some, however, remained skeptical of a glittering style that seemed to lack substance. Alfred Kazin, the literary critic, after having been wined and dined by the President, wrote: "Kennedy's shrewd awareness of what intellectuals can do, even his undoubted inner respect for certain writers, scholars and thinkers, is irrelevant to the tragic issues and contributes nothing to their solution."

Kennedy also courted the leaders of organized labor, inviting them to the White House for conferences, ceremonies, and state dinners. He named one labor leader as an ambassador, another as a board member of COMSAT, another as Deputy Housing Administrator, and still another as a Supreme Court Justice. When the President traveled to Berlin in 1963, he was accompanied by AFL-CIO president George Meany. Kennedy also publicly introduced Meany in their travels through Ireland. Such gestures paid off handsomely in the solid political support organized labor gave to Kennedy, despite the fact that his policies were not particularly beneficial to workingmen. Sorensen noted: "Average wage rate increases during Kennedy's tenure were this nation's lowest for any comparable period since the Second World War." With the status of wage-earners just one of a number of interests fed into the broader Administration goal of economic expansion, Secretary of Labor Arthur Goldberg, himself a former labor lawyer of some stature, could announce: "Labor and management will both be making a mistake if they believe that the Kennedy administration is going to be prolabor."

Kennedy enjoyed less harmonious relations with the business community—but hardly through any fault of his own. As Tom Wicker wrote, Kennedy "worked hard for the support of business groups like the National Association of Manufacturers." In February, 1961, he offered 1,000 businessmen from the National Industrial Conference Board a "full-fledged alliance." The President's one slip came when he put the interests of a prosperous economy above those of the steel industry. On April 10, 1962, Roger Blough, chairman of the U.S. Steel Corporation, called at the White House to announce a $6 a ton increase in steel prices. Kennedy felt betrayed. Not only was he trying to curb inflation at home and relieve the balance of payments abroad, but the Administration had just persuaded the United Steelworkers to accept a very modest wage settlement. Stung by the corporate action, the President threatened defense cutbacks and antitrust investigations. Within seventy-two hours Blough surrendered and rolled back the price increase. Businessmen, accustomed to greater deference from political leaders, were outraged by this treatment, and Kennedy never managed to win back their affections. Yet he certainly tried. Within a year the Administration countenanced selective price increases in steel, sponsored the liberalization of depreciation allowances and the enactment of an investment tax credit, threw its support behind the privately owned COMSAT, and prodded Congress to lower taxes on upper-income groups. Corporate profits during the Kennedy years rose 43 per cent— higher and longer than ever before. Asked by the press if he planned an attack upon business in Roosevelt's style, Kennedy replied impatiently: "No, no, we're not going to do that. They're our partners. . . . We're in this together. . . . I want to help them if I can." He added in irritation: "But look at the record. I spent a whole year trying to encourage business. And look what I get for it. . . . When I'm nice to them, they just kick me." His brother Robert took things more philosophically. The business community simply distrusted Democratic administrations more than Republican ones, he observed in 1963. "It's an ideological reflex—obsolete in my opinion—but that's one of the facts of life."

Fortunately for the President, he had few quarrels with the business community over foreign affairs; here, indeed, they saw eye to eye. In his farewell address of January 17, 1961, Eisenhower had raised a few eyebrows in fashionable quarters when he warned of the growing influence of the "military-industrial complex." But the fears of the new President lay elsewhere. "I speak today in an hour of national peril," he said in his first State of the Union message. "Each day the crises multiply." Kennedy argued that it was imperative to expand the size of the nation's military establishment, to accelerate the missile program, to speed up the construction of Polaris submarines, and to increase America's capacity to airlift ground combat troops "to any spot on the globe at a moment's notice." The President was particularly disturbed by events in the Third World. "The great battlefield for the defense and expansion of freedom today," he stated, "is the southern half of the globe . . . the lands of the rising people." As he had declared during his 1960 campaign, he wanted people of these nations "to start to look to America, to what the President of the United States is doing." The "hopes of all mankind," proclaimed Kennedy, "rest upon us."

Mankind, it appeared, was particularly eager for another escalation in the arms race. Taking office as a political innocent, Secretary of Defense McNamara read through the government reports on American and Soviet military strength and then announced happily to the press that there had been, after all, no "missile gap." Kennedy quickly brought him into line. The next day Salinger told newsmen that he was speaking with the approval of the President when he termed the findings of the Secretary of Defense "absolutely wrong." Six weeks later, in his first budget message, Kennedy ignored contrary evidence produced by outgoing Republicans to argue that "for several years this nation has not led the world in missile strength." He promptly launched an enormous nuclear arms program, which, as his Deputy Special Assistant for National Security Affairs, Carl Kaysen, later observed, "was projected against an expected Soviet force of fewer than a third as many missiles and a quarter as many bombers capable of reaching the United States." By 1967 the number of American ICBMs had quintupled since 1960, and McNamara conceded that the United States possessed "in fact more than we require." Of course, so did the Soviet Union, whose military planners, observing the American nuclear escalation, sponsored their own.

As the logical concomitant of this thermonuclear buildup, the Administration sponsored a massive fallout shelter program, which Kennedy announced on television in July, 1961. Nuclear strategists insisted that it would make "credible" the "will" of the United States to risk thermonuclear war. The mass media rushed to promote the operation. *U.S. News & World Report* informed its readers that "plans are being worked out to enable you to write checks on your bank account—even if the bank were destroyed." *Life* placed a man in a fallout suit on its cover with the good news that "97 Out of 100 People Can Be Saved." Such assurances were echoed by a letter from the President in the same issue and by Dr. Willard Libby of the AEC, who claimed that up to 95 per cent of the population could survive a nuclear attack in shelters like the one he built in his backyard. As the shelter mania grew, some of the nastier aspects of America's competitive ethos surged to the fore. Nevada businessmen decided that an armed militia would be necessary to repel refugees from Los Angeles. A Chicago suburbanite told the press that he was installing a machine gun in front of his shelter to mow down intruders. Standard Oil of New Jersey carved out the inside of a mountain in upstate New York, installing a 28-ton steel door, executive suites, kitchens, dormitories, living rooms, and semiprivate baths for the board of directors—as well as separate living quarters for lower-echelon clerical personnel. Yet the effectiveness of the shelter program always remained questionable. A Rand Corporation study later that year predicted that a 3,000-megaton attack on U.S. cities would lead inescapably to the deaths of 80 per cent of the population. When a brush fire swept the Los Angeles area, Dr. Libby's own shelter collapsed.

The core of the Administration's military strategy was not thermonuclear weaponry but an expanded capacity for "conventional" war. Kennedy, McNamara, and many of the "defense intellectuals" were critical of the restraints placed upon American foreign policy by confining U.S. military power largely to thermonuclear weapons. Thus, they moved quickly to develop what they called "flexibility." In mid-1963 McNamara announced that the Administration had "increased the number of combat-ready Army divisions by 45 per cent . . . augmented by 30 per cent the Air Force capability for tactical air support of combat operations," and significantly expanded its procurement of combat supplies. Washington was preparing to fight an old-fashioned land war and, coincidentally, it would soon have one to fight. Kennedy, in particular, took a personal interest in counter-insurgency planning, believing that the drive and technological capacity of the United States would enable it to succeed in suppressing Third World revolutions. He read works by Mao Tse-tung and Ché Guevara and threw his influence behind the creation of an élite corps of counter-insurgency specialists, the Green Berets. He even supervised the selection of their equipment. In November, 1963, Kennedy announced that his Administration had increased U.S. counter-insurgency forces by 600 per cent.

These military measures lent a curious flavor to Kennedy's occasional pronouncements about the need to curb the arms race. By fiscal 1962 Kennedy's military budget topped the last of Eisenhower's by $10 billion. During McNamara's reign in the Defense Department, the Pentagon's annual spending almost doubled. By 1964 Russia's defense budget stood at only 58 per cent of America's; China, proclaimed as a serious menace to world peace, had a military budget equivalent to only 8 per cent. Administration apologists, hard-pressed to reconcile Kennedy's "peace race" rhetoric with his arms race practices, resorted to an Orwellian logic. Arthur Schlesinger, Jr., told the Young Democrats in 1962: "It is an irony of our times that the arms race offers the only road to arms control." Others, though, were growing restive. In August, 1963, Senator George McGovern, a South Dakota Democrat, charged that military spending was distorting the American economy, wasting human resources, and restricting America's options throughout the world. He urged rechanneling $5 billion of the military budget to social welfare programs. Political observers, however, thought this an unlikely prospect. I. F. Stone commented acidly: "Reconstruction at home and abroad would not require so many generals and it would not be the same luxurious cost plus operation as building missiles."

Moreover, Kennedy had every intention of using America's new military power. One of his top priority items, as he remarked repeatedly during the 1960 campaign, was removing the revolutionary regime in Cuba. Under Fidel Castro, the Cuban government had nationalized $1 billion in U.S. corporate holdings, instituted the most thoroughgoing land reform in Latin American history, established state cooperatives, built thousands of homes for the rural and urban poor, cut rents by one half, provided jobs for the unemployed, virtually wiped out illiteracy, vastly expanded medical and public health programs, abolished racial discrimination, and opened the nurseries, resorts, and hotels of the rich to the entire population. Although Castro had achieved these reforms without restoring the civil liberties and free elections suppressed by the Batista dictatorship, many Latin Americans—particularly the poor—idolized him and looked forward to the day when similar revolutions would topple their own oligarchic governments. Thus, the Castro regime, like the Hungarian experiment of 1956, was a subversive example to small nations living in the shadow of a superpower. Speaking in Portland, Maine, on September 2, 1960, Kennedy described Castro as "a source of maximum danger. . . . The big task of the next administration is going to be to contain this revolution in Cuba, itself, and not have it spread through Latin America." He went one step farther in his final television debate with Nixon, when he proposed that the U.S. government arm Cuban exile groups for an invasion.

Shortly after his election Kennedy was relieved to discover that invasion plans were well under way. The CIA was arming and training more than a thousand Cuban exiles in Guatemala for an assault on the coast of Cuba at the Bay of Pigs. When Cubans of democratic views took unkindly to the CIA's recruitment of large numbers of *Batistianos,* many of whom it placed in officer positions, the CIA spirited away a dozen critics from the Guatemalan training center to a prison camp in the northern jungles. Plans for the invasion inspired greater enthusiasm at National Security Council meetings. Only when an outsider, Senator

Fulbright, accidentally learned of it did the project meet a rebuff. "To give this activity even covert support," said Fulbright, "is of a piece with the hypocrisy and cynicism for which the United States is constantly denouncing the Soviet Union." But the National Security Council and the President remained unanimous in their approval. By mid-April, 1961, then, having spent an estimated $45 million and assembled a landing brigade of 1,400 Cuban exiles, Washington was ready to launch the invasion. As U.S. ships waited off Nicaragua to transport the force to Cuba, the local right-wing dictator, Luis Somoza, his face powdered, his person surrounded by bodyguards, appeared on the dock and shouted: "Bring me a couple of hairs from Castro's beard."

The invasion proved a disaster. On April 15 a force of unmarked U.S. B-26 bombers, flown by Cuban exiles, attacked Cuban air bases but failed to destroy significant portions of the Cuban Air Force. At the United Nations, Adlai Stevenson denied U.S. involvement, using fraudulent photographs from the CIA to make the case that responsibility lay with defectors from Castro's air force. Two days later, when the exile brigade stormed ashore at the Bay of Pigs, Stevenson again denied Cuban charges that the United States was masterminding the operation. Stevenson had, in fact, been deliberately kept in the dark about the invasion. Rusk, on the other hand, involved for months in planning the operation, told a press conference on the day of the landing: "The American people are entitled to know whether we are intervening in Cuba or intend to do so in the future. The answer to that question is no. What happens in Cuba is for the Cuban people to decide." As the Secretary of State spoke, the CIA was dictating press releases to a Madison Avenue public relations firm, which in turn issued them on behalf of the Cuban Revolutionary Council. The real Cuban Revolutionary Council, formed for purposes of the invasion by the U.S. government, was being held incommunicado by the CIA. By the night of April 18 the invasion was in serious trouble. U.S. involvement had become obvious, while Castro's militia and air force had pinned down the invaders in the coastal swamps. CIA pilots began filling in for their charges on bombing runs over Cuba. Just before midnight the President slipped away from a formal party at the White House to meet with CIA and military officials, who strongly urged U.S. air or naval support for the invaders. Reluctant to have American military units play too direct a role in combat operations, Kennedy compromised by ordering unmarked U.S. Navy jets to fly cover for the exile bomber force. But, confused by the difference in time zones, the B-26 squadron arrived too early and was destroyed. The invasion now collapsed. Castro announced his conversion to Marxism-Leninism.

The President keenly felt the failure of the Bay of Pigs invasion, but the lesson he drew from it was a tactical one. "I really thought they had a good chance," he told Sorenson ruefully. Kennedy continued to believe that the United States had a perfect right to overthrow the Cuban government. In the aftermath of the Cuban operation, the State Department reiterated its position that Communism in the Western Hemisphere was "non-negotiable." On April 20 Kennedy told the American Society of Newspaper Editors that, while he had not committed U.S. troops to the invasion, "our restraint is not inexhaustible." Embarrassed by press handling of the affair, Kennedy called upon the American Newspaper Publishers Association a week later to "recognize the nature of our country's peril" and ask not only "Is it news?" but also "Is it in the national interest?" He complained that "this nation's foes" had been gratified by stories they read in the press. "Details of this nation's covert preparations," the President charged, "have been available to every newspaper reader." How, in these circumstances, could the government be expected to wage its undeclared wars successfully?

Still smarting from his humiliation at the Bay of Pigs, Kennedy was determined to take a hard line in dealing with the Russians. At the Vienna summit conference of June, 1961, Khrushchev told Kennedy that the time was ripe for a peace treaty ending World War II in Europe and recognizing the reality of two Germanys. With the division of Germany now permanent, the Russians apparently thought it necessary to desist from directly exploiting their East German satellite, creating in its place a state with a viable political economy; they were therefore anxious to seal off the escape route for the highly educated provided by West Berlin, located in the middle of East Germany. From the Kennedy Administration's viewpoint, however, the specifics of the German issue were unimportant; any renegotiation of Western treaty rights was a trap. Kennedy told the President of Finland that Khrushchev was trying to "neutralize West Germany as a first step in the neutralization of Western Europe" and that, consequently, "all Europe is at stake." Moving toward a showdown with Moscow, Kennedy rushed a $3.2 billion supplemental military appropriation through Congress, asked for $207 million for an accelerated fallout shelter program, tripled draft calls, mobilized 158,000 Reservists and National Guardsmen, and increased the nation's armed forces by 300,000 men (40,000 of whom were dispatched to Europe). Khrushchev, who considered Kennedy quite unreasonable, cut through the impasse on August 13 by building a wall between East Germany and West Berlin. With the flow of refugees thus cut, Khrushchev was willing to tolerate the continued presence of the Western enclave, and the crisis gradually cooled. Kennedy, however, was not above fanning the embers from time to time. Addressing a wildly enthusiastic crowd in West Berlin in 1963, he declared: "There are some who say in Europe and elsewhere we can work with the Communists. Let them come to Berlin."

As Soviet-American tension grew, the moratorium on thermonuclear testing observed by the two superpowers since the late 1950s collapsed. At the Vienna summit meeting, Khrushchev and Kennedy had discussed the possibility of a nuclear test ban treaty but had been unable to agree upon the number of on-site inspections. Khrushchev had promised at the time not to break the moratorium. On August 30, 1961, however—in the midst of the Berlin crisis—he announced that the Soviet Union would begin a series of atmospheric tests. Administration hard-liners immediately called for a resumption of American testing. When a State Department official suggested mobilizing world opinion by bringing the Soviet action to the U.N. Security Council, Kennedy's disarmament adviser, John J. McCloy, exploded: "World opinion? I don't believe in world opinion. The only thing that matters is power. What we have to do now is to show that we are a powerful nation." On September 5 Kennedy ordered a resumption of underground testing but held off on atmospheric tests. Disturbed at the prospect of further radioactive contamination of the environment and another escalation of the arms race, thousands of American college students began picketing the White House. British Prime Minister Harold Macmillan repeatedly pleaded with Kennedy not to resume atmospheric testing and "shatter the hopes of millions of people across the earth." The necessity of rescuing mankind from the peril of extermination, he argued, far outweighed the marginal gains in U.S. firepower. Kennedy, though, remained unmoved. On March 2, 1962, he announced that the United States would resume the atmospheric testing of thermonuclear weapons.

As the 1962 Congressional elections approached, Republicans and conservatives began hammering away at what they called Kennedy's "do nothing" policy toward Cuba. *Time* magazine urged "a direct U.S. invasion . . . carried out with sufficient force to get the job done." On September 20 the Senate passed a resolution authorizing the use of U.S. arms, if necessary, in Cuba; within a week, the House had concurred. Senator Kenneth Keating, a hawkish New York Republican, stirred up a furor by charging that the Soviet Union was installing missiles on the island. And on October 14 flights by U.S. spy planes did reveal the building of missile sites. Khrushchev would later explain that the missiles, of the medium-range variety, were intended purely as a response to U.S. threats of a new invasion. On October 8, in fact, Cuba's President, Osvaldo Dorticos, had announced the possession of "weapons which we would have preferred not to acquire and which we do not wish to employ." If the United States would "give us proof, by word and deed, that it would not carry out aggression against our country, then . . . our weaponry would be unnecessary." Whatever Communist intentions, though, the missiles had no significant strategic value. As McNamara reportedly stated at the time, "it makes no great difference whether you are killed by a missile fired from the Soviet Union or from Cuba." Sorensen later observed that "those Cuban missiles alone, in view of all the other megatonnage the Soviets were capable of unleashing upon us, did not substantially alter the strategic balance *in fact* . . . but that balance would have been substantially altered *in appearance.*" The question of appearances, however, was crucial to a President who wanted Third World nations to look to him—and particularly to one under fire from political opponents at election time.

Convinced that, at all costs, the missiles had to be removed, Kennedy called together an informal body of advisers, the Executive Committee of the National Security Council (ExCom). Adam Yarmolinsky, then Deputy Assistant Secretary of Defense, later recalled that ExCom "spent at least 90% of its time studying alternative uses of troops, bombers and warships. . . . The possibility of seeking withdrawal of the missiles by straightforward diplomatic negotiation . . . seems scarcely to have been aired." Fearing Soviet reprisal, ExCom ruled out a thermonuclear strike but leaned toward a U.S. air attack followed by an invasion. Robert Kennedy, however, denounced the idea of a surprise attack, declaring: "My brother is not going to be the Tojo of the 1960s." Instead, he urged a naval blockade. Eventually, President Kennedy agreed to impose the blockade, followed, if necessary, by air strikes and an invasion. The Administration readied an estimated 156 ICBMs, placed nuclear bombers on a massive airborne alert, organized a fleet of 180 ships (including eight aircraft carriers) for the blockade, and assembled a quarter of a million troops for an invasion. On the night of October 22, an hour after informing the Soviet Ambassador of his plans, the President went on television to tell Americans of the missiles and to warn Russians that the United States would not "shrink" from the risk of "worldwide nuclear war" to remove them. Kennedy termed the naval blockade of Cuba a "quarantine." A blockade, as he and his advisers knew, was an act of war.

For days the world teetered on the brink of thermonuclear destruction. Khrushchev charged on October 23 that U.S. actions constituted "outright banditry" and that Kennedy was forcing mankind "to the abyss." In the United States, leaders of the peace movement implored the President to lift the blockade, Russia to withdraw its missiles, and Cuba to declare its neutrality. On October 24 U.N. Secretary General U Thant asked the United States to suspend the blockade and the Soviet Union to suspend all arms shipments to Cuba, thus allowing time for negotiations. Although Kennedy refused to end the blockade, Khrushchev eagerly suspended arms shipments—a face-saving way to avoid a confrontation on the high seas—but work continued on the missile sites in Cuba. Behind the scenes, Stevenson suggested swapping U.S. missiles in Italy and Turkey for the Soviet missiles in Cuba. Although Kennedy had already ordered the U.S. missiles removed as obsolete, he found Stevenson's suggestion objectionable because it entailed what would appear to be a bargain with Khrushchev, while he wanted the appearance of a victory. And by October 26 Khrushchev was clearly starting to crack. In a lengthy message to Kennedy, he reiterated that the missiles were in Cuba purely for defensive purposes and that "only lunatics or suicides, who themselves want to perish and to destroy the whole world" wanted a thermonuclear war. Robert Kennedy later wrote that the letter was "very long and emotional," focusing on "the death, destruction, and anarchy that nuclear war would bring." Khrushchev asked: If he agreed to send no more missiles to Cuba and to remove those already there, would not Kennedy end the blockade and promise not to invade Cuba? While U.S. officials were pondering this message, another came from Khrushchev on October 27, raising his terms to withdrawal of the U.S. missiles from Turkey. Most ExCom members thought the prestige loss in accepting the new terms was too great and called for an air strike against Cuba the next morning. Robert Kennedy, however, suggested ignoring Khrushchev's second proposal and accepting his first. After heated arguments, the President took his brother's advice. The crisis ended.

From the Administration's viewpoint, the results were rather satisfying. Not only was Khrushchev forced to withdraw the missiles, but he came away with nothing to show for it, as Kennedy—pointing to Castro's refusal to allow U.N. verification of the withdrawal—never openly issued the noninvasion pledge. Khrushchev was thus publicly humiliated. By contrast, White House insiders were certain that President Kennedy's handling of the situation had won him universal acclaim. Schlesinger wrote: "It was a combination of toughness and restraint, of will, nerve, and wisdom, so brilliantly controlled, so matchlessly calibrated, that it dazzled the world." Americans seemed more dazed than dazzled, but stuck by the Administration on Election Day. The Republicans gained only two seats in the House and lost four in the Senate. Seeking to begin a political comeback by running for Governor of California, Richard Nixon lost his race to the incumbent, Edmund G. Brown. Kennedy's former rival fretfully told reporters at his "last" press conference: "You won't have Nixon to kick around any more." A scattering of peace candidates also went down to defeat, drawing only a tiny percentage of the vote. Thus, the President came away from the Cuban missile crisis in a stronger political position than his critics on the Right or Left. This may be reckoned against his own later estimate that there had been between a one-third and one-half probability of thermonuclear war—one that he thought would have killed 300 million people.

Although these thermonuclear confrontations set the tone for public discussion of the President's foreign policy in the early 1960s, in reality it had far greater subtlety. During the 1960 campaign, Kennedy had taken up Hubert Humphrey's idea for a Peace Corps, which would send thousands of young men and women overseas to do volunteer work in underdeveloped countries. Nixon assailed the Peace Corps as a haven for draft dodgers, but it soon became one of Kennedy's most popular proposals. In 1961 the President established the Peace Corps under the direction of his brother-in-law, Sargent Shriver. By March, 1963, it had 5,000 volunteers serving overseas; the following year the number doubled. Leftists in underdeveloped nations sometimes criticized the Peace Corps as a CIA tool, but this was a misreading of its role. Indeed, Shriver and Kennedy took great pains to see to it that the CIA did not use the Peace Corps as a front for its covert operations. Kennedy understood that these thousands of idealistic young people were excellent good-will ambassadors for an America often perceived as a place of cynical wealth and power. Like American missionaries of another era, they represented the "soft" side of U.S. foreign policy.

The President, of course, had no intention of slighting the CIA. During the Kennedy years the CIA's budget exceeded that of the Department of State by more than 50 per cent, the intelligence agency's staff having doubled over the last decade. As Schlesinger observed: "The CIA had its own political desks and military staffs; it had in effect its own foreign service, its own air force, even, on occasion, its own combat forces." After the fiasco at the Bay of Pigs, Allen Dulles and his top assistants resigned, giving Kennedy the opportunity to remold the agency to his liking. The President's choice as director was John McCone, a California Republican who had previously been Under Secretary of the Air Force and chairman of the AEC under Eisenhower. A conservative multimillionaire, McCone was noted, Schlesinger acknowledged, as "a rigid cold-warrior." When university scientists backed Adlai Stevenson's 1956 proposal for a nuclear test ban, McCone charged that they had been "taken in" by Communist propaganda and were trying to "create fear in the minds of the uninformed that radioactive fallout from H-bomb tests endangers life." Under his direction, the CIA continued its routine work of opening mail, placing agents in key areas of national life, and manipulating private organizations—both abroad and, illegally, at home—but also embarked on more daring ventures. Conspiring with Mafia leaders, the CIA employed poisons, explosive seashells, rifles, and a deadly fountain pen in repeated efforts to assassinate Fidel Castro. CIA technicians also prepared a skin-diving suit for the Cuban revolutionary leader, designed to give him a chronic skin disease and tuberculosis. In the Congo, the CIA worked at murdering the nationalist premier, Patrice Lumumba, through the use of assassins and highly toxic poisons. Although Kennedy's CIA operations only occasionally produced a "success," they indicated the limits of New Frontier idealism.

Like his predecessors in the White House, Kennedy was a keen partisan of foreign aid. He told the Economic Club of New York in December, 1962: "Foreign aid is a method by which the United States maintains a position of influence and control around the world." Most foreign aid, of course, was military aid. In 1963 a committee appointed by the President reported that, since the end of the Marshall Plan, about 60 per cent of the $50 billion in U.S. foreign aid had been spent directly on military equipment; of the remainder, about 85 per cent was used to support the budgets of nations straining to meet military commitments on the periphery of the "iron curtain." From the Kennedy Administration's viewpoint, the most significant value of such aid lay in developing indigenous military and paramilitary élites, skilled in the latest counter-insurgency techniques and dedicated to close ties with the United States. In 1962 McNamara told Congress:

> Probably the greatest return on our military assistance investment comes from the training of selected officers and key specialists at our military schools and training centers. . . . They are the coming leaders, the men who will have the know-how and impart it to their forces. I need not dwell upon the value of having in positions of leadership men who have firsthand knowledge of how Americans do things and how they think. It is beyond price to us to make friends of such men.

The chairman of the House Foreign Affairs Committee remarked in 1965 upon one of many such success stories, the military coup that ended democratic government in Brazil: "Every critic of foreign aid is confronted with the fact that the Armed Forces of Brazil threw out the Goulart government and that U.S. military aid was a major factor in giving these forces . . . a pro–U.S. orientation."

The Kennedy Administration tailored the most daring of its aid programs—the Alliance for Progress—to fit the turbulent continent of Latin America. Frightened by the Cuban revolution and by its potential for sweeping across the southern part of the hemisphere, American policy-makers like Adolph A. Berle, one of the key architects of the program, pointed to the need to "channel the revolution now going on in Latin America in the proper direction." Thus, when President Kennedy called together Latin American diplomats for a White House meeting on March 13, 1961, he promised a program to "transform the American continent into a vast crucible of revolutionary ideas and efforts . . . an example to all the world that liberty and progress walk hand in hand." Among the Latin Americans present there was "a measure of doubt and cynicism," as Schlesinger noted, but some, at least, were optimistic. When OAS delegates met at Punta del Este, Uruguay, in August, 1961, the United States and Cuba were symbolized with dramatic clarity by their spokesmen. For Cuba, Ché Guevara, guerrilla leader: dark and romantic, wearing green fatigues, a black beret, and combat boots. For the United States, C. Douglas Dillon, Republican: tall, blue-eyed, distinguished, clad in a pin-striped suit, looking every bit the millionaire Wall Street investment banker he was. Dillon, however, promised billions of dollars in Alliance aid over a ten-year period. And the charter of the *Alianza* adopted there was hardly a conservative one, declaring that it would promote democratic institutions, provide a more equitable distribution of income and a rapidly rising standard of living for the masses, and "end those conditions which benefit the few at the expense of the needs and dignity of the many." American corporate spokesmen stirred uneasily. The editors of *Business Week* wrote: "A U.S. policy of sponsoring revolutionary change in the underdeveloped countries could well undermine the position of U.S. private investment. . . . To a considerable degree, the revolution of rising expectations is a revolt against capitalism." If the program of the *Alianza*—tying U.S. aid to democratic social reform—had been implemented, it might well have transformed the relationship of the United States and Latin America.

It was not, of course, implemented. Although the Alliance for Progress did promote improvements in education and health care, Latin American housing fell farther behind population pressures, unemployment and starvation increased, tax reform often included a regressive redistribution of income, and the major income-producing properties remained in the hands of U.S. corporations. Those U.S. officials who were sincere about social reform watched helplessly as Washington reassured businessmen and governments that significant social change was unnecessary. Schlesinger recalled that "Latin American democratic leaders

. . . began to express increasing concern about the 'degeneration' of the Alliance." There were, however, few democratic leaders left around to complain. During the first eight years of what Kennedy had billed as an "historic decade of democratic progress," sixteen military coups took place in Latin America, six of them in 1962–63 alone. On July 18, 1962, a Sherman tank, supplied to Peru through the U.S. military assistance program, smashed through the gates of the presidential palace in Lima, and a U.S.–trained officer informed the President that he had been ousted by a military junta. The Kennedy Administration, decrying this "severe setback" to democratic institutions, initially broke off diplomatic relations. But, under pressure from executives of U.S. shipping and mining companies, Kennedy restored recognition a month later. A steady stream of coups followed—each tacitly accepted by Washington.

The limited interest of the Kennedy Administration in democratic social reform was exemplified by its handling of events in the Dominican Republic. Ever since 1940 that island nation had been ruled by Rafael Trujillo, the former commander of the Guardia Nacional. Together with his family, Trujillo acquired control of 80 per cent of the island's economy, maintaining for his protection an army of 17,000 and a police force of 12,000, equipped with tanks and bombers. Torture, exile, and imprisonment were characteristic of his regime, the cruelest dictatorship in all the hemisphere. As a staunch friend of U.S. investors and as a militant anti-Communist, Trujillo attracted powerful supporters in the United States. He enjoyed the friendship of Senators Jenner, Thurmond, Eastland, and Smathers, who spoke admiringly of the "stability" and "progress" of his regime. Standard Oil of New Jersey, Alcoa, and Pan American Airways cultivated him, as did successive Washington administrations. In May, 1961, however, Trujillo was assassinated by a group of his own army officers. "There are three possibilities," Kennedy now remarked, "in descending order of preference: A decent democratic regime, a continuation of the Trujillo regime, or a Castro regime. We ought to aim at the first, but we really can't renounce the second until we are sure that we can avoid the third." In line with this view, Kennedy decided that Washington's "only tool" was Joaquin Balaguer, the nominal President of the country under Trujillo who had subsequently retained power in partnership with the late dictator's son. "The anti-communist liberals," concluded Kennedy, "aren't strong enough." But popular rioting and opposition forced Balaguer to take refuge with the Papal Nuncio. In December, 1962, the island's first free elections in many years brought Juan Bosch—a Dominican exile—to the Presidency with 60 per cent of the vote.

Although Bosch was exactly the type of Latin American leader Kennedy professed to want—liberal, democratic, non-Communist—the Administration soon cooled toward him. Shortly after his election he flew to the United States to cement relations with the American government but incurred Washington's wrath by denouncing a previous contract for an Esso refinery and by negotiating a Swiss business loan. "We are changing our image," declared Bosch, "into a revolutionary democracy." The Dominican President further angered powerful American interests by considering the cancelation of molasses and sugar contracts, arguing that U.S. "sugar men will take six and a half millions out of here in profits." U.S. Ambassador John B. Martin scotched this idea by threatening a cutoff of economic aid under the Hickenlooper Amendment. He also cautioned the Dominican leader to slow implementation of the nation's new constitution, which prohibited large landholdings and restricted property ownership by foreigners. Businessmen, said Martin, were "highly disturbed." In this atmosphere of gathering tension, Dominican military and political leaders flocked to Washington to outline plans for coups. Bosch was certain that the U.S.–owned South Puerto Rico Sugar Company was working for his ouster, particularly after he imposed a tax on sugar profits. Privately, Ambassador Martin told Bosch that he would have to reunite the country by a "lofty speech." Taking some papers from his pocket, he said: "Here it is." Bosch, however, remained incorrigible. On September 25, 1963, a military coup overthrew his government, installing the dictatorship of Donald Reid Cabral, a member of the island's traditional oligarchy. According to a *Time* correspondent, the military leaders sprang into action "as soon as they got a wink from the U.S. Pentagon." Embarrassed by this coup in a country that was to have been a "showcase" of the Alliance for Progress, Kennedy halted aid to the new regime (resumed two months later by his successor), but shed few tears for the ousted Dominican reformer. "I take it we don't want Bosch back," Kennedy remarked to Martin on his return to Washington. "No," the ambassador replied, "he isn't a president."

By the fall of 1963 the Kennedy Administration was ready to shift its stance formally on the desirability of democratic social reform in Latin America. Cuba, after all, had been contained and, at U.S. insistence, expelled from the OAS. Moreover, a whole new crop of right-wing military dictatorships had become allies and aid recipients of the United States. On October 16, 1963, Edwin A. Martin, Assistant Secretary of State for Latin American Affairs, issued a statement approved by the President indicating that the United States would now accept military juntas, using its "leverage to keep these new regimes as liberal and considerate of the welfare of the people as possible." This was not an "apology for coups," Martin said, but a "rejection of the thesis . . . that democracy can be legislated." While Washington failed to tie Alliance aid to democratic social reform, it did tie it to the purchase of products from the United States. When Latin Americans objected, Lincoln Gordon, the U.S. Ambassador to Brazil, chided them with the observation that this was the price of the "struggle for freedom in Vietnam."

In 1961 American policy-makers concluded that the Vietnam struggle needed all the help it could get. On March 28 a national intelligence estimate informed Kennedy that an "extremely critical period" for the Saigon regime lay "immediately ahead." Diem's "reliance on virtual one-man rule" and "toleration of corruption," it observed, had undermined his ability to govern. Another factor in the collapsing situation was the startling growth of the National Liberation Front, which U.S. officials estimated the following year had the support of about half the population of South Vietnam. A U.S. intelligence report of October 5, 1961, placed the number of its fighting forces (usually termed "Vietcong" by Americans) at 17,000, of whom 80 to 90 per cent were locally recruited; the remainder, secret intelligence reports until 1964 indicated, were native Southerners returning from North Vietnam. In April Walt W. Rostow, Presidential Assistant for National Security Affairs, urged "gearing up the whole Vietnam operation." Returning in May from a visit to the Far East, where he had called Diem "the Churchill of Asia," Vice-President Johnson contended that the United States must join "the battle against Communism . . . in Southeast Asia with strength and determination" or "throw in the towel in the area and pull back our defenses to San Francisco." The "vast Pacific," he warned, could easily become "a Red Sea." In October the Joint Chiefs of Staff called for the dispatch of U.S. combat troops, claiming that "40,000 U.S. forces will be needed to clean up the Vietcong threat," while 128,000 more troops would be sufficient to cope with North Vietnamese or Chinese Communist intervention. Rusk and McNamara, no less dedicated to an American victory, were slightly more cautious as to means. In a memorandum that November, they recommended that the Administration "now take the decision to commit ourselves to the objective of preventing the fall of South Vietnam to Communism and . . . recognize that the introduction of United States and other SEATO forces may be necessary to achieve this objective." Nevertheless, while the Pentagon should make plans for the use of ground combat forces, they should not be sent to Vietnam—yet.

Kennedy adopted the Rusk-McNamara formula. Like his advisers,

Kennedy feared that the revolution in Vietnam, if unchecked, would sweep all before it. "Vietnam represents the cornerstone of the Free World in Southeast Asia," he had said in 1956, "the keystone to the arch, the finger in the dike." Asked on NBC television in September, 1963, if he doubted the "domino theory" popularized by his predecessor, he replied: "No, I believe it. I believe it. . . . If South Vietnam went, it . . . would give the impression that the wave of the future in Southeast Asia was China and the Communists. So I believe it." As a politician, though, Kennedy understood that the war had to be kept reasonably covert—if the political costs were not to grow. On May 11, 1961, he secretly ordered 500 Green Berets and U.S. military advisers to South Vietnam, an increase in the size of Saigon's military forces, and the beginning of Pentagon planning for the commitment of U.S. forces to Vietnam. At the same time he ordered a clandestine campaign of "sabotage and light harassment" against North Vietnam by South Vietnamese agents. Later that year Kennedy acted to bolster Diem through major U.S. assistance programs. At first he issued demands for accompanying reforms, but as early as December, 1961, ordered them dropped. By October, 1963, Kennedy had stationed 16,732 American troops in South Vietnam. Asked at a press conference in February, 1962, if the Administration were being "less than candid" about U.S. involvement, Kennedy admitted that American troops were "firing back" to defend themselves but insisted that they were "advisers" rather than combat troops. The following month, McNamara conceded that the "training" of the South Vietnamese "occasionally takes place under combat conditions." In fact, U.S. helicopters were already flying combat support missions, U.S. Navy destroyers were operating along the coasts of North and South Vietnam, U.S. aircraft were engaged in surveillance and reconnaissance missions, and U.S. "advisers" were superintending raids upon the North, defoliation operations, and population removal programs.

Throughout 1962 and early 1963 U.S. policy-makers expressed optimism on the progress of the Vietnam struggle. "Every quantitative measurement we have," declared McNamara, "shows that we're winning this war." The growth of the "strategic hamlet" program, which forcibly resettled peasants in heavily fortified camps, raised hopes among American officials that they were "winning the hearts and minds of the people." Kennedy announced in his 1963 State of the Union message that "the spearpoint of aggression has been blunted in South Vietnam." A more realistic appraisal was given to the President the following month by White House aide Michael Forrestal. "No one really knows," he said, "how many of the 20,000 'Vietcong' killed last year were only innocent, or at least persuadable, villagers . . . or how the mute mass of villagers react to the charges against Diem of dictatorship and nepotism." NLF recruitment in the South was so effective, he observed, that the war could be continued even without infiltration from the North. Of course, whatever the situation, the U.S. presence in Vietnam had its compensations. "On the military side," General Maxwell Taylor told a House committee, "we have recognized the importance of the area as a laboratory." Even so, U.S. policy-makers lusted after victory and resented those who challenged their illusions. When *New York Times* reporter David Halberstam, a supporter of the war, implied in his dispatches that the United States was not winning it, President Kennedy suggested to Halberstam's employers that he be recalled from that assignment.

In spite of the impressive "kill ratios" and "body counts" spewed out by Pentagon computers, the war was going badly for the Saigon regime, primarily because it could never command the same revolutionary fervor, respect, and mass popularity as the NLF. And in 1963 Diem dissipated the last vestiges of his support. On May 8, when parading Buddhists carried religious banners in violation of a government decree, South Vietnamese troops fired into the crowd, killing nine and wounding fourteen. Long dissatisfied with the Catholic-dominated regime in Saigon, Buddhists began mass demonstrations which Diem's police met with clubbings and arrests. That June the first of a series of Buddhist monks immolated himself in protest. Diem's sister-in-law, Madame Nhu, told newsmen that she clapped her hands in glee at the "barbecues." On August 21 South Vietnamese Special Forces—the private army of Diem's brother, Ngo Dinh Nhu, trained and financed by the CIA—carried out midnight raids against Buddhist pagodas throughout South Vietnam. They arrested more than 1,400 persons, most of them monks; many were beaten.

With South Vietnam near chaos, a group of South Vietnamese generals now sought American authorization for a coup. Embarrassed by the well-publicized events in Diem's police state, the Kennedy Administration gave its rapid approval. The CIA worked closely with the plotting generals, as did the new U.S. Ambassador, Henry Cabot Lodge, Jr. A National Security Council meeting in August resolved that the U.S. government would "support a coup which has a good chance of succeeding." In October the Administration cut off economic aid to Saigon and assured the cautious plotters that it would do nothing to "thwart" their plans. When the generals finally took action on November 1, a frantic Diem called Lodge to ask the only meaningful question: What was the "attitude of the U.S."? Lodge, feigning ignorance, claimed that he was not "well enough informed" to reply. Realizing that his position had become untenable, Diem accepted the generals' offer of safe-conduct out of the country, only to be captured, with Nhu, by lower-echelon officers and killed.

Diem's death did not bring an end to the Kennedy Administration's involvement in the Vietnam War; on the contrary. With the slate washed clean and with new faces in the Saigon government, U.S. policy-makers redoubled their efforts at "nation-building." Some writers have argued that, had Kennedy lived beyond 1963, he would not have mired American troops, arms, and prestige as deeply in the war as his successors. Yet the record shows that he consistently escalated the level of American military intervention. Moreover, in subsequent years his principal advisers favored further escalation, since only through heightening America's combat role could an NLF victory have been prevented. Asked what Kennedy would have done in Vietnam after 1963, his favorite military adviser, General Maxwell Taylor, replied: "Let me just say this, Kennedy was not a loser." Certainly, there is no evidence that Kennedy ever seriously considered abandoning the Vietnam War. "For us to withdraw from that effort would mean a collapse not only of South Vietnam but Southeast Asia," he said at one of his last press conferences. "So we are going to stay there." The young President—and his successors—might better have heeded his own words of 1954: "No amount of American military assistance in Indochina can conquer an enemy which is everywhere and . . . has the sympathy and covert support of the people."

The Kennedy Administration carried on a smaller-scale, more clandestine operation in neighboring Laos. A tiny, primitive peasant nation, Laos had been the scene of U.S. involvement since 1954, when, in violation of the Geneva accords, Secretary of State Dulles had sought to turn it into a bulwark against Communism. In 1957 the neutralist Prince Souvanna Phouma had managed to put together a coalition government that incorporated the Pathet Lao, a group of Communist-led resistance fighters who had fought both the Japanese and the French. But the following year the CIA toppled it, promoting the right-wing General Phoumi Nosavan thereafter in a civil war. In June, 1959, the House Committee on Government Operations pointed to "U.S. support of a 25,000-man army" and "of the entire military budget" in Laos. By the time Kennedy took office, Laos had received $300 million in U.S. aid—the highest per capita assistance to any country in the world. Nevertheless, as in Vietnam, the situation was deteriorating. On the day of Kennedy's inauguration, Eisenhower told him: "You might have to go in there and fight it out." Kennedy promptly ordered U.S. military "advisers" to play a leading role in the war. On April 27, 1961, the National Security Council began discussing large-scale American intervention, with the military calling for the dispatch of 140,000 troops armed with tactical nuclear weapons. On May 1, however, representatives of the three factions in Laos, under pressure from both the Soviet Union and the United States, agreed to a cease-fire. The foreign ministers of fourteen nations signed an agreement at Geneva that July, guaranteeing the independence and neutrality of Laos, again to be governed by a coalition headed by Souvanna Phouma. The agreement lasted only a short time, though, before the nation reverted to civil war. This time, Souvanna Phouma ruled against opposition from the Pathet Lao and with the support of the right-wing generals, the CIA, and its clandestine army.

As the Kennedy Administration deepened American military involvement in Indochina, it drew back from its rigid confrontation with the Soviet Union. On December 19, 1962, Khrushchev had written to Kennedy that "the time has come now to put an end once and for all to nuclear tests." Attempting to cut back Soviet military costs, Khrushchev hoped to shift economic productivity to the long-starved consumer areas of the Russian economy. Kennedy, too, was interested in a test ban treaty. Under unprecedented public pressure to halt nuclear testing, he also felt freer than in the past to negotiate a partial détente with the Soviet Union, as he had safeguarded his credentials as a militant Cold Warrior in the Cuban missile crisis. On June 10, speaking at American University, Kennedy delivered an unprecedented address on what he termed "the most important topic on earth: world peace." Rejecting "a Pax Americana enforced on the world by American weapons of war," he called for a "world safe for diversity." Discussions would soon begin in Moscow, he said, on the question of a nuclear test ban. American peace groups were euphoric. Khrushchev later declared that it had been "the greatest speech by any American President since Roosevelt." Meeting soon afterward, American, British, and Russian representatives quickly agreed upon a treaty banning atmospheric nuclear tests, signing it on July 25. In Washington, a number of prominent military-industrial spokesmen urged the Senate to reject the agreement. Edward Teller declared: "If you ratify this treaty . . . you will have given away the future safety of this country." Nevertheless, wooed by the Administration and buoyed up by polls indicating that four out of five Americans favored the treaty, the Senate ratified it on September 24 by a vote of 80 to 19. Eventually, more than a hundred other nations endorsed it.

But, although the Administration and peace groups alike hailed the test ban treaty as a major breakthrough on the road to disarmament, it did little to halt the arms race. On the day after signing it, Khrushchev had called for further moves "toward liquidating the 'cold war.' " Yet, with the exception of Kennedy's announcement that the U.S. government would sell quantities of surplus wheat to Russia, no significant Soviet-American agreements followed. Furthermore, Kennedy and Mc-Namara offered the Joint Chiefs of Staff a variety of "safeguards" that actually heightened the U.S. thermonuclear buildup. The military budget rose dramatically, as did the number of American nuclear tests—held underground, where the United States had greater technical proficiency than the Russians. More than twice as many American tests occurred in the seven years after the treaty as in the eighteen years before it, and they resulted in the development of at least two major new weapons systems: the ABM and the MIRV. Meanwhile, China and France, determined to crack the Anglo-American-Russian nuclear monopoly, refused to sign the treaty and plunged ahead with their own nuclear development programs. Although peace groups had the consolation of an end to the poisoning of the atmosphere by Soviet and American bomb tests, they found, to their regret, that the treaty lulled many Americans into a sense of complacency about the ever escalating potential for the extermination of mankind.

So wedded were some Americans to Cold War values, however, that even such limited departures from orthodoxy convinced them—in the words of Robert Welch—that "Communist influences are now in almost complete control of our Federal Government." In 1958 Welch invited eleven men, primarily wealthy business leaders like himself, to a conference in Indianapolis, which founded the ultra-right-wing John Birch Society. Welch, who charged that President Eisenhower was "a dedicated, conscious agent of the Communist conspiracy"—a category which he extended to embrace CIA director Allen Dulles and Chief Justice Warren—assured the founders that "we are in circumstances where it is realistic to be fantastic." Enthralled by a cloak-and-dagger image of Communism, Welch envisioned the time when the American people would "resist the Communist tyranny only by themselves becoming conspirators." Such views were hardly unique. In the late 1950s and early 1960s what came to be called the "Radical Right" grew at a phenomenal pace. The expenditures of thirty basic right-wing organizations in the United States reportedly rose by 1963 to $14.3 million. The Birch Society alone had an annual income of approximately $5 million and a membership estimated at 60,000 to 100,000. Dr. Fred Schwarz's Christian Anti-Communist Crusade received television sponsorship from such large industrial firms as the Schick Safety Razor Company, the

Richfield Oil Company, and the Technicolor Corporation. A right-wing oil billionaire, H. L. Hunt, spent an estimated $1 million a year on reactionary causes; "Life Line," his radio program, was carried by 212 stations. Other prominent right-wing spokesmen included Dr. Billy James Hargis, a fundamentalist preacher; William F. Buckley, Jr., who founded the reactionary *National Review;* columnists Westbrook Pegler and Fulton Lewis, Jr.; and news commentators Clarence Manion and Dan Smoot. During the 1964 campaign, Democrats monitored broadcasts and found that 1,300 radio and television stations in the nation were carrying right-wing programs every week. Although the Radical Right never set the tone of American public life to the same degree as had the Anti-Communist Crusaders of the early 1950s, it could exert considerable political influence.

While some carried Cold War thinking to the point of obsession, others had begun to discard it. New organizations like Women's Strike for Peace joined SANE and pacifist groups in publicizing the effects of radioactive fallout, organizing vigils and marches against the arms race, and keeping the dangers of thermonuclear weaponry before the public. Small groups of CNVA activists carried out civil disobedience actions at Polaris submarine construction sites and at Red Square in Moscow. Horrified by the growing American military involvement in South Vietnam, peace groups began a relentless critique of U.S. foreign policy. Social criticism had also begun to revive. Michael Harrington's *The Other America* (1962) was remarkable not only for discussing widespread poverty in a nation long narcotized on tales of affluent suburbs but also for its new tone of outrage. "I want to tell every well-fed and optimistic American that it is intolerable that so many millions should be maimed in body and spirit," Harrington wrote. "My standard of comparison is not how much worse things used to be. It is how much better they could be if only we were stirred." For years young Americans had been advised to "play it cool," to think of their careers, to cling to their individual isolation in a tough and selfish world. Now, with their rediscovery of social injustice, the mood had begun to shift toward the re-establishment of principles, commitment, and community. Many of the student activists especially were children of liberals, frequently economically secure, and had absorbed their parents' political ideals. But they questioned their parents' lives, which too often seemed hollow and compromised. If the new radicalism represented a revolt against liberalism, it was a revolt against what it had become in the Cold War era. For what the young activists condemned was the "hypocrisy" of Cold War liberalism, and what they sought to substitute for it was the fierce idealism—the "authenticity"—of the Movement.

These trends were epitomized by the emergence of Students for a Democratic Society (SDS). Formed as the youth arm of the neo-Socialist but sedate League for Industrial Democracy, SDS was launched at a June, 1962, convention in Port Huron, Michigan. "We are people of this generation, bred in at least modest comfort, housed now in universities, looking uncomfortably to the world we inherit," began the Port Huron Statement. Their lives had been "penetrated by events too troubling to dismiss. First, the permeating and victimizing fact of human degradation, symbolized by the Southern struggle against racial bigotry. . . . Second, the enclosing fact of the Cold War, symbolized by the presence of the Bomb." Assailing America's "unwillingness to face the implementation of our rhetorical commitments to peace and freedom," they deplored the idea that man was "a thing to be manipulated, and that he is inherently incapable of directing his own affairs." In contrast, "we seek the establishment of a democracy of individual participation, governed by two central aims: that the individual share in those social decisions determining the quality and direction of his life; that society be organized to encourage independence in men and provide the media for their common participation." On the surface, it was a program oriented toward middle-class college students and intellectuals. And yet their experience in the civil rights movement convinced SDS members that "participatory democracy" had a particular relevance to the poor, for in a society where the poor were powerless the demand for their participation became a radical one. In April, 1963, SDS received a grant from the United Auto Workers to begin organizing the poor around the economic issues that directly affected them. SDS set up community-organizing projects in Chicago, Cleveland, Newark, Boston, New Haven, Appalachia, and ten other areas. At the same time, SDS chapters began student-oriented activities on the nation's campuses. Organizing the poor, organizing students, SDS hoped to recharge the batteries of social reform, to revive the struggle for social justice in America.

By 1963 one aspect of that struggle, the civil rights movement, had reached an incredible torrent of activity. All across the Deep South, young civil rights workers were organizing, agitating, inspiring in the face of racist harassment and terror. Local leaders like Mrs. Fannie Lou Hamer, a forty-seven-year old sharecropper who was evicted from her home and nearly killed after attempting to register to vote, became well-known Movement heroes. Thousands of poor and simple people risked unemployment, arrests, beatings, and death to slowly make their way to all-white county courthouses and announce that they had come to "redish." Led by Martin Luther King, the black community of Birmingham, Alabama, staged repeated mass protest marches in the spring of 1963, which police chief Eugene ("Bull") Connor met with snarling police dogs, electric cattle prods, tear gas, and high-pressure water hoses that tore the bark off trees. Thousands of school children were arrested as the world gaped in horrified fascination. Bayard Rustin recalled: "It was the loss of all fear that produced the moment of truth . . . children as young as six paraded calmly when dogs, fire hoses, and police billies were used against them. Women were knocked to the ground and beaten mercilessly. Thousands of teen-agers stood by at churches . . . waiting their turn to face the clubs of Bull Connor's police." That June, Mississippi NAACP leader Medgar Evers was assassinated outside his home in Jackson. In September, four black children at a Birmingham church were killed by a racist bombing—the twenty-first bombing of blacks in that city during an eight-year period and, like the others, unpunished.

During 1963 civil rights demonstrations erupted in approximately 800 cities and towns across the country, with the public's attention centering on the great August 28 March on Washington for Jobs and Freedom of 200,000—the largest public demonstration ever held in the nation's capital. In an emotional address to this vast assemblage, King employed his rich, cadenced oratorical style to dazzling effect. "I have a dream," he said, that "one day . . . the sons of former slaves and the sons of former slave-owners will be able to sit together at the table of brotherhood." One day, "this nation will rise up and live out the true meaning of its creed: '. . . that all men are created equal.'" Then, truly, could Americans join in that redemption promised by a black slave song: "Free at last, free at last, thank God Almighty I'm free at last."

Even the cool "pragmatists" of the New Frontier could no longer resist. By June, 1963, Kennedy was finally ready to move on civil rights. As James Reston observed: "The Negro demonstrations . . . forced his hand." On the evening of June 12 Kennedy went on television to declare that "the time has come for this nation to fulfill its promise. . . . We face a moral crisis as a country and as a people." For Kennedy, these were strong words, and he followed them up a week later by sending Congress a major civil rights bill containing a ban on racial discrimination in places of public accommodation, new authority for the Attorney General to initiate the desegregation of schools, and a strengthening of voting rights laws. Passage of the legislation, he asserted, was required "not merely for reasons of economic efficiency, world diplomacy and domestic tranquility—but, above all, because it is right." Kennedy's bill was, to be sure, a weaker one than liberals in Congress urged. Nevertheless, the Administration had clearly shifted position on the desirability of civil rights legislation. Shortly after introducing the bill, Kennedy remarked to a friend: "Sometimes you look at what you've done and the only thing you ask yourself is—what took you so long to do it?"

And yet, determined at last to press for civil rights legislation, the President never exhibited that level of commitment to racial justice with which he has sometimes been credited. When Kennedy sent his civil rights bill to Congress, he promised it "highest priority." A month later the Administration announced that the civil rights bill "shared" priority with the tax bill. By November, explaining that a healthy economy was necessary for progress in civil rights, Kennedy was giving the tax bill higher priority. Nor did Kennedy have much sympathy with plans for the March on Washington. At a meeting on June 22 with the President, several civil rights leaders complained that Kennedy's disparaging comments on demonstrations in his June 12 speech had given people the idea that he opposed the forthcoming March. Kennedy responded that "the only effect" of announcing the March was "to create an atmosphere of intimidation—and this may give some members of Congress an out." Civil rights leaders, of course, had no intention of canceling the demonstration. They did, however, cut several critical remarks from the address to the marchers by John Lewis, the twenty-three-year old chairman of SNCC—a battered veteran of the sit-ins and Freedom Rides who had been jailed twenty times. One deleted section asked: "I want to know: which side is the Federal Government on?" It was a question that remained unanswered on November 21, as the President departed Washington for a speechmaking tour in Texas, leaving the civil rights bill bottled up tight in committee.

Kennedy's Texas tour was, as Sorensen observed, "a barely disguised campaign trip" designed to reunite the warring factions of the state Democratic Party and to mobilize support for his re-election. Although the Democratic ticket had carried Texas in 1960, it was not considered friendly territory, particularly Dallas, a city dominated by the oil, banking, and insurance industries and fortified by the fundamentalist religious convictions of its citizenry. Visiting that city only four weeks before Kennedy's tour, Adlai Stevenson had been clubbed with signs and spat upon by a right-wing mob. Kennedy experienced a moment of uneasiness when, opening the Dallas *News* on the morning of November 22, he noticed a black-bordered full-page ad accusing him of aiding Communism. "We're really in 'nut country' now," he told his wife. Later that day, shortly after noon, the Presidential motorcade drove slowly through the downtown area, greeted by unexpectedly large and cheerful crowds.

Mrs. John Connally, wife of the Texas Governor, remarked happily to the President: "You certainly can't say that the people of Dallas haven't given you a nice welcome." Suddenly, shots rang out and Kennedy's body pitched forward. Half an hour later he was dead. The police arrested Lee Harvey Oswald shortly thereafter in connection with the slaying. Oswald, a former U.S. Marine who had defected to the Soviet Union and then returned to the United States, denied his guilt during two days of interrogation by police, only to be shot and killed himself —on television—by Jack Ruby, a local night club manager with shady connections. In a much-disputed report, a commission headed by Chief Justice Warren concluded that Oswald had been Kennedy's assassin, acting alone and without apparent motive.

Ironically, John F. Kennedy was never more popular than after his death. Intensive television coverage of his funeral, pictures of his mourning family, and lengthy exhortations on the meaning of his life gave many millions of Americans, whether or not they had voted for him, a strong emotional attachment to the man. And Kennedy's youth, intelligence, and glamour were certainly the stuff of which legends are fashioned. James Reston recalled: "He was a story-book President, younger and more handsome than mortal politicians . . . graceful, almost elegant, with poetry on his tongue and a radiant young woman at his side." What, then, did it matter that his record was virtually barren of domestic accomplishment, that he heightened the Cold War to new levels of violence, and that he fulfilled few of the expectations that he raised? I. F. Stone wrote, not unfairly: "Kennedy, when the tinsel was stripped away, was a conventional leader, no more than an enlightened conservative, cautious as an old man for all his youth, with a basic distrust of the people." Yet who would believe it, especially with the passing of the years? For, particularly among young people, the myth of Kennedy as a liberal Sir Galahad, cut down in his youth, served a valuable function: it filled the terrible need to find an American President who fought for peace and social justice in the Cold War era.

9

Building "The Great Society," 1963-66

We will continue as best we can to help the good people of South Vietnam enrich the condition of their life.

LYNDON B. JOHNSON, 1965

As LYNDON JOHNSON took the oath of office on board the plane that carried him from Dallas to Washington, observers could hardly fail to notice that, unlike his predecessor, the new President would never be classified among "the beautiful people." Overbearing, expansive, and earthy, Johnson swapped stories on the sex lives of prominent personalities with the same delight as he charted his shrewd course through the political wilderness. If Kennedy typified the new, technocratic America, Johnson symbolized the old: lusty, democratic, and ambitious. His "very appearance and mannerisms," recalled White House aide Eric Goldman, "suggested the riverboat gambler." During the reign of New Frontier sophistication, Administration insiders had viewed Johnson as an embarrassment. Kennedy had felt called upon to deny that his Vice-President would be dumped from the 1964 ticket. Nor had Johnson been happy as Vice-President, confined as he was to a relatively useless and obscure role, with little balm for his ego. Only with Kennedy's death did Johnson come into his own. Suddenly the scornful New Frontiersmen fell silent as this hard-boiled political operator with the folksy exterior assumed the vast powers of the American Presidency.

A consummate politician, Johnson understood that he had less than a year to convince Northern Democrats, liberals, labor, and blacks—all of whom had opposed him in the past—that they should support his nomination in 1964. Kennedy could afford to take the liberal forces in the Democratic Party for granted and to compromise with Southern reactionaries. Johnson, however, could not. As the first Southern Democrat to occupy the White House since Woodrow Wilson, a supporter of

the Taft-Hartley Act and other antilabor legislation, a long-time opponent of civil rights, a notorious collaborator with the Eisenhower Administration, and a well-known spokesman for the oil and gas industry,
Johnson desperately needed to acquire liberal credentials if he was not
to be abandoned by the national constituency of the Democratic Party.
Consequently, he moved rapidly to win the approval of Northern liberals
by asking the Kennedy Cabinet and staff to remain and, most significant,
by waging a serious battle for the enactment of New Frontier legislation.

Approximately fifty pieces of Kennedy's legislation lay bogged down
in Congress when Johnson took office, and none was more important to
Johnson's political fortunes than the civil rights bill. The struggle for
racial justice had become the rallying point for the urban liberal core of
the Democratic Party. Tom Wicker later wrote: "Neither John Kennedy
nor Lyndon Johnson could conceivably have won the election of 1964,
nor could the Democratic party have maintained its contemporary
shape," had either refused "to support civil rights legislation in 1963."
The civil rights movement had become politically irresistible. Throughout the nation, blacks and their supporters demonstrated in the streets,
religious leaders thundered in the pulpit, liberals held forth in Congress,
and columnists clamored in the press. "No American President . . .
could have held back from action," wrote Wicker. "Legislation . . .
was the symbolic necessity." Unlike his predecessors, Johnson had to
deliver—and he did.

Within days of taking office Johnson told members of Congress and
guests, crowded into the House chamber: "No memorial oration or
eulogy could more eloquently honor President Kennedy's memory than
the earliest possible passage of the civil rights bill." A roar of approval
broke from the assemblage. "We have talked long enough in this country about equal rights," said the President. "It is now time . . . to
write it in the books of law." Johnson threw his full weight behind the
bill—already, because of amendments by liberals in Congress, a considerably stronger one than Kennedy had proposed. The bill outlawed
racial, religious, and sexual discrimination in employment and places
of public accommodation; authorized the federal government to sue to
desegregate public facilities and schools; provided that federal funds
could be cut off to programs administered on a discriminatory basis;
extended the life of the Civil Rights Commission and granted it new
powers; and strengthened voting rights. On February 10, 1964, the
House passed the measure, 290 to 130. In the Senate, however, Southerners vowed to filibuster it to death. In all the history of that body,
supporters of civil rights had never produced the two-thirds majority
necessary to impose cloture, and thus limit debate. But this time the
pressures were enormous. Johnson told Senate leaders that he would

sacrifice all other legislation, if necessary, to break the filibuster. Civil rights groups, labor unions, liberal organizations, and church bodies lobbied furiously and effectively. Senate liberals developed the tightest floor discipline they had ever known. By mid-May, even conservative Republicans had been won over. "The time has come," said Senator Dirksen, "it can't be stopped." On June 10, with all 100 members present, the Senate ended seventy-four days of debate and fifty-seven days of filibuster by voting cloture, 71–29. The fight was over. On July 2 Lyndon Johnson signed the Civil Rights Act of 1964 into law.

The Civil Rights Act was the most dramatic but hardly the only major legislation passed by Congress that year. Stunned by Kennedy's assassination and bullied by Johnson, Congress enacted the "Kennedy Tax Cut," a $375 million measure for urban mass transit, a food stamp program, expansion of the National Defense Education Act and the Hill-Burton hospital construction legislation, and a bill providing legal aid to indigents. The most innovative action, however, involved the creation of the Office of Economic Opportunity. Campaigning in West Virginia during the 1960 Democratic primary, Kennedy had been startled by the poverty he had seen. Shortly afterward he read Michael Harrington's influential work on the subject. Consequently, shortly before his death he had begun to lay plans for an antipoverty program—plans which Johnson took up with a flourish. In his 1964 State of the Union message, Johnson announced that "this administration today . . . declares unconditional war on poverty." On March 16 he sent Congress his legislative proposal. Although Johnson spoke of a "total victory," he requested less than $1 billion to fund the antipoverty program for fiscal 1965. Nevertheless, observers assumed that, in the early stages, the Office of Economic Opportunity was merely developing pilot projects for a much broader program of the future. The rhetoric, at least, was bold and determined. "It is . . . the policy of the United States," proclaimed the Economic Opportunity Act of 1964, "to eliminate the paradox of poverty in the Nation by opening to everyone the opportunity to live in decency and dignity."

That May, Johnson unveiled his plans for the "Great Society." The "challenge of the next half-century," he said in an address at the University of Michigan, "is whether we have the wisdom to use wealth to enrich and elevate our national life," for "we have the opportunity to move not only toward the rich society and the powerful society but upward to the Great Society." The Great Society, he declared, "rests on abundance and liberty for all. It demands an end to poverty and racial injustice—to which we are totally committed." In the Great Society, every child would "find knowledge to enrich his mind and enlarge his talents," leisure would become "a welcome chance to build and reflect," and the "city of man" would serve "not only the needs of the body and the demands of commerce, but the desire for beauty and the hunger for community." Like Johnson, the promises of the Great Society were windy and expansive, but they nevertheless seemed to lead logically to the most significant expansion of domestic welfare programs since the New Deal.

Utopian as the promises of the Great Society appeared, they were in fact limited by Johnson's notion of "consensus politics." Johnson completed the transition from New Deal liberalism to corporate liberalism, for he never envisaged carrying social reform to the point where it conflicted with the interests of the corporate élite. Indeed, he sought no redistribution of wealth and power in America but simply limited forays into certain "problem" areas. On June 27, 1964, in an address to the Minnesota Democratic-Farmer-Labor Party, Johnson outlined his notion of the harmony of interests underpinning the Great Society. "This government will not set one group against another," he declared. "We will build a creative partnership between business and labor, between farm areas and urban centers, between consumers and producers." The American government, he said, was "the envy of men around the globe; a system where the capitalist can put in his capital and have a reasonable expectancy to get it back with a fair return and without fear of going to bed tonight to wake up and see it confiscated or burned the next morning." While the nation "never had it so good," he observed, "we got to make it better." This would be accomplished "not by blaming each other, not by dividing up in harassing groups," but "by uniting our people, by bringing our capital and our management and our labor and our farmers all under one great Democratic tent." Admiring commentators contended that Johnson had seen that class and interest-group divisions no longer made any sense in America, that with an economy of abundance there was plenty for all. Skeptics like I. F. Stone wrote that "in the politics of consensus, a little for the poor makes it easier to go on giving a lot to the rich."

As Johnson wooed an all-class constituency that ranged from business executives of the North to civil rights workers of the South, the Republicans seemed destined to become the party of the Radical Right. Working at the grass-roots level, conservatives and right-wing zealots joined forces to capture the 1964 GOP Presidential nomination for Senator Barry Goldwater. While personally rather forthright and likable, politically Goldwater was a brittle pro-capitalist ideologue with none of Eisenhower's blandness or Nixon's deceit for camouflage. In Congress, he had opposed almost all social welfare legislation to come before him, most recently the Civil Rights Act and the antipoverty program, observing in reference to the latter that people were poor because they had either "low intelligence or low ambition." An ardent militarist and superpatriot, Goldwater chatted casually about the use of "nukes" in world affairs. New York's Governor Nelson Rockefeller, fearing that Goldwater's candidacy would wreck the Republican Party and himself eager to secure the Presidential nomination, worked desperately to head off the Arizona conservative. Although Goldwater narrowly edged out Rockefeller in the California primary, the New York Governor waged a bitter platform fight at the Republican convention, which culminated in his vigorous denunciation of right-wing extremism. The gathering, poorly stocked with seasoned politicians but munificently endowed with representatives of the far Right, exploded in a frenzy of hatred, stunning television viewers across the land. Easily nominated, Goldwater undermined his political fortunes still further by choosing an obscure but reactionary Congressman from New York, William Miller, as his running mate. The delegates reached a zenith of euphoria when, in his acceptance speech, Goldwater assured them that "extremism in the defense of liberty is no vice."

For the consensus-minded Johnson, renominated by his party, Goldwater's candidacy was almost too good to be true. While Goldwater advocated the sale of TVA among Tennesseeans, assailed agricultural subsidies among farmers, and denounced Social Security among the elderly, Johnson projected a soothing image of responsibility, the "President of all the people." Goldwater's support of right-to-work laws angered labor; his opposition to civil rights legislation and his not-so-subtle references to street crime alienated blacks; and his advocacy of giving local military commanders control of nuclear weapons sent shivers across the nation. Democratic Party ads played skillfully upon the widely shared view that Goldwater was "trigger-happy." In contrast to Goldwater, who indicated his support for escalating American military involvement in Indochina, Johnson campaigned as a "peace" candidate. "We are not about to send American boys nine or ten thousand miles away from home to do what Asian boys ought to be doing for themselves," he told voters. "We are not going north and drop bombs." Hubert Humphrey, chosen by Johnson as his running mate to firm up liberal support and to scotch the Vice-Presidential prospects of Robert Kennedy, appealed to "responsible and forward-looking Republicans" to support the Democratic ticket, contending that the GOP had been captured by men "of stridency, of unrestrained passion, of extreme and radical language." Although the core of Goldwater's backing lay among the right-wing millionaires of the South and Southwest, Johnson brought the nation's most powerful corporate interests into the Democratic camp. From the standpoint of American business, the volatile Goldwater represented a speculative venture, while Johnson—long an effective spokesman for industrial interests—was clearly a blue chip. Johnson thus drew the backing of both Wall Street and SDS, of hawkish labor unions and peace activists, of affluent suburbanites and ghetto blacks. A landslide seemed a certainty.

And it was. On Election Day Johnson swamped Goldwater by 43 million to 27 million votes—the greatest vote, the greatest margin, and the greatest percentage (61.1 per cent) in American history. Carrying all but six states in the nation—five in the Deep South and Goldwater's home state of Arizona—Johnson increased the Democratic percentage of the Presidential vote between 1960 and 1964 among all major groups in the population except Catholics (among whom it fell off by only 2 per cent from the Kennedy peak). Nonwhites gave Johnson 94 per cent of their votes, manual workers 71 per cent, and even the professional and business classes contributed 54 per cent. An estimated one out of five Republicans voted Democratic. Only among Southern whites, dazzled by Goldwater's outright repudiation of civil rights, did the Republican candidate run well. Moreover, throughout the North and West, Goldwater dragged Republican Congressional candidates down to defeat, shattering the power of the Dixiecrat-Republican coalition in Congress. The Democrats now controlled the Senate by the overwhelming majority of 68 to 32 and the House by 295 to 140. Only Franklin Roosevelt, in 1936, had enjoyed greater Congressional support from his own party. With a popular President pledged to peace and social justice, with hefty liberal majorities in both houses of Congress, and with an activist movement in the streets, the postwar stalemate on social reform seemed broken. The forces of social change had not witnessed such an opportunity in America for three decades. Even the Great Society no longer appeared utopian.

Yet as early as the summer of 1964 there were signs that all was not as it seemed. The most obvious sign involved Johnson's token accommodation to the civil rights struggle, then in its most courageous phase. In response to an idea advanced by SNCC, the Council of Federated Organizations—a coalition of civil rights and church groups in Mississippi—undertook the sponsorship of a major Southern civil rights project, Freedom Summer. Under COFO's direction, a thousand volunteers from across the nation poured into Mississippi, where, together with SNCC's field staff, they engaged in a campaign of local voter registration and education. By July they had established thirty Freedom Schools, superintended by historian Staughton Lynd, in nineteen counties and had organized 40,000 blacks into the Mississippi Freedom Democratic Party. They also captured the attention of the press and of millions of Americans. The price, however, was high. Violence, intimidation, and harassment by local whites intensified. In early June a delegation from the summer project journeyed to Washington to request the dispatch of federal marshals for protection but was refused assistance by the Administration. Thirteen days later law-enforcement officials in Philadelphia, Mississippi, arrested three civil rights workers—James Chaney, Andrew Goodman, and Michael Schwerner—releasing them from jail late at night. A crowd of men, including the deputy sheriff who had arrested the civil rights workers, followed them down the road and dragged them off to the woods, where all three were shot and killed. Chaney, the only black, was also brutally beaten. The discovery of their bodies on August 4 in an earthen dam near the town sent a wave of horror across the country. Later that month, with the nation still unnerved by the incident, the MFDP challenged the seating of the all-white, segregationist Mississippi delegation at the Democratic national convention.

SNCC brought to the Atlantic City convention sixty-eight MFDP delegates whose only credentials, as Murray Kempton wrote, were "their wounds and their faces." Shortly before the party conclave formally opened, the credentials committee held a nationally televised hearing on the Mississippi challenge. "I have only an hour," began MFDP lawyer Joseph Rauh, "to tell you a story of moral agony that could take years." Martin Luther King, James Farmer, and Roy Wilkins all testified in favor of seating the MFDP. Originally, it had seemed that the convention would be a smoothly stage-managed affair, but now a startling and uncertain element had been introduced. It led to seventy-two hours of closed-door bargaining by civil rights leaders and liberals, while thousands of students and civil rights workers kept vigil on the boardwalk. Speculation heightened that the Mississippi regulars would be ousted. Eventually, the word came down from Johnson: the MFDP would be granted two at-large seats plus a guarantee that all future convention delegations would be integrated. Most civil rights leaders and liberals urged the MFDP to accept this "incredible triumph." Only James Forman and Bob Parris (formerly Bob Moses) of SNCC urged rejection of what they called a "back-of-the-bus" compromise. In the end, the MFDP delegates voted unanimously to reject it. Democratic Party liberals left Atlantic City convinced that SNCC activists were unreasonable, while SNCC activists came away believing that the liberals —and certainly Lyndon Johnson—could not be trusted.

The second harbinger of the Johnson Administration's future course of action related to foreign affairs. Within forty-eight hours of taking the oath as President in 1963, Johnson met with Henry Cabot Lodge, Jr., the U.S. Ambassador to South Vietnam. Lodge, pessimistic about the future of the Indochina war, told Johnson that he had some hard decisions to make. The President barely hesitated with his response. "I am not going to lose South Vietnam," he said. Although Johnson ordered increased American aid to Saigon, privately he fretted that the weak government of General Khanh—one of seven that came to power in South Vietnam during 1964—might negotiate a compromise accord with the insurgents. On March 20, 1964, Johnson cabled to Lodge in Saigon: "Your mission is precisely for the purpose of knocking down the idea of neutralization wherever it rears its ugly head. . . . Nothing is more important than to stop neutralist talk wherever we can by whatever means we can." Although U.S. intelligence sources in 1964 continued to point out that "the primary sources of Communist strength in South Vietnam are indigenous," arising out of revolutionary and nationalist aspirations, this merely stiffened the counter-revolutionary resolve of Washington officialdom. "It is on this spot that we have to break the liberation war," Rostow insisted in 1964. "If we don't break it here we shall have to face it again in Thailand, Venezuela, elsewhere. Vietnam is a clear testing ground for our policy in the world." Assistant Secretary of Defense John T. McNaughton, assessing "U.S. aims" in a secret policy memorandum, credited 70 per cent to the desire to protect the "U.S. reputation as a counter-subversion guarantor."

Given the deteriorating situation in South Vietnam and their own determination to make a success of counter-revolution, U.S. policymakers naturally opted for further military escalation—particularly insofar as all the military advantages seemed to lie on their side. How, they wondered, could a small nation of primitively armed peasants stand up against the awesome armed might of the United States? Beginning in February, 1964, the Administration heightened covert activities against North Vietnam while planning to obtain a Congressional resolution that it could use as the equivalent of a declaration of war. On February 1 the Administration launched Operation Plan 34A, which entailed intelligence gathering, the kidnapping of North Vietnamese citizens, parachuting sabotage teams into the North, commando raids along the coast of North Vietnam to blow up bridges, and the use of PT boats to destroy North Vietnamese coastal installations. U.S. destroyer patrols were used both as a show of force and as a means of intelligence gathering for the raids. By early August these clandestine operations had reached the point where Thai pilots flying U.S. fighter planes were bombing and strafing North Vietnamese villages. The problem remained, though, of securing an authorization for a wider war from Congress—particularly in the midst of an election campaign with Johnson garbed as a "peace candidate."

That problem was solved by the Gulf of Tonkin incident. According to the Pentagon's account, on August 2, 1964, North Vietnamese torpedo boats attacked the U.S. destroyer *Maddox* in the Gulf of Tonkin off the coast of North Vietnam; two days later, another attack allegedly occurred, this time upon the *Maddox* and a second destroyer, the *Turner Joy*. Charging North Vietnam with "open aggression on the high seas," President Johnson ordered U.S. air raids on North Vietnamese ports and asked Congress for a resolution authorizing the President "to take all steps necessary, including the use of armed force," to protect any state in the area that sought assistance "in defense of its freedom." In fact, the Gulf of Tonkin incident may never have occurred, as there is little evidence that ships other than those of the Americans opened fire. "Why," asked the Hanoi government plaintively, "does this small country with its negligible naval forces embark on a systematic provocation of the U.S. Seventh Fleet?" One possible answer is that the North Vietnamese associated the American destroyer patrol with nearby Operation 34A torpedo raids of July 30 and August 3 and thus opened fire. "We don't know what happened," Rostow privately conceded two days later, "but it had the desired result." Johnson, who for weeks had been carrying a draft of the resolution in his pocket, could now submit it as a spontaneous response to "aggression." When the President met with Congressional leaders to discuss the incident, he concealed the American responsibility for and command of the Operation 34A raids. McNamara and Rusk, who had helped plan the raids, denied any U.S. involvement. Deceived and manipulated by the Administration, the House passed the Tonkin Gulf resolution by a vote of 416 to 0, the Senate by a vote of 88 to 2 (Senators Wayne Morse of Oregon and Ernest Gruening of Alaska dissenting). It was, a gleeful Johnson remarked, "like grandma's nightshirt—it covered everything."

With the passage of the Tonkin Gulf resolution, the Administration moved toward the planning of a sustained air war. Frustrated by their inability to create a viable government in Saigon, U.S. policy-makers hoped to compensate for their political weakness by resorting to the one item they possessed in abundance: military hardware. As Johnson had told Congress as early as 1948, "Without superior air power America is a bound and throttled giant, impotent and easy prey to any yellow dwarf with a pocket knife." In August Maxwell Taylor suggested a "carefully orchestrated bombing attack on the North." The Joint Chiefs of Staff urged what a Pentagon analyst later called a "provocation strategy"—"deliberate attempts to provoke the D.R.V. [Democratic Republic of Vietnam] into taking actions which could then be answered by a systematic U.S. air campaign." A September 7 meeting at the White House resolved that air attacks on North Vietnam would probably begin in early 1965. This could not, of course, be revealed to the public, then being urged to reject the "trigger-happy" Goldwater's call for military escalation. On November 3, 1964, the day of Johnson's election, the Administration began planning the bombing of the North in earnest. Although few knew it at the time, the war on poverty had already been superseded by the war on the Vietnamese.

But still another harbinger emerged in late 1964—this one indicating that American politicians would find it more difficult than in the past to sacrifice social reform to the exigencies of war. In the fall of 1964 the Berkeley campus of the University of California seemed the very model of a major institution of higher education. University president Clark Kerr, a technocratic liberal, wrote glowingly of the "knowledge industry" or "multiversity," in which the claims of big business, the military, and the government were harmonized by the skillful bureaucrat. Under the surface, however, throbbed a broad vein of discontent. To a growing number of students, Kerr was the epitome of the "Establishment liberal," their university a service station for powerful vested interests, the faculty élitist and careerist, and the "futures" prepared for by students—in the words of one undergraduate—"intellectual and moral wastelands." By the fall of 1964 many Berkeley students had taken part in Freedom Summer or in off-campus demonstrations and sit-ins designed to get Bay Area businesses to end discriminatory practices. They were particularly outraged when, in September, university authorities ordered student activists to remove their literature from Sproul Plaza, a campus area traditionally used by radicals and conservatives alike. Students defied the ban, which they assumed to have resulted from the complaints of powerful local conservatives about their civil rights activities. When campus police arrested a graduate student (and CORE activist) for using the disputed area, a thousand students sat down around the police car and immobilized it for thirty-two hours, until the administration dropped charges against the "trespasser." In late November, however, the University of California Regents reopened the issue by calling in four student leaders for disciplinary action. The Berkeley crisis now moved toward a showdown.

Under attack, groups of all political persuasions joined to form the Free Speech Movement. In early December FSM supporters gathered in front of Berkeley's administration building, ready for direct action. Mario Savio, one of the FSM leaders, told them:

> There is a time when the operations of the machine become so odious, make you so sick at heart, that you can't even tacitly take part. And you've got to put your bodies upon the gears and upon the wheels . . . to make it stop. And you've got to indicate to the people who run it, that unless you're free the machine will be prevented from working at all.

Activists surged into the administration building and refused to evacuate it. Two days later Governor Brown called in the police, who beat up students and made 814 arrests. The police raid mobilized the campus behind the FSM. A strike on December 3 by students and teaching assistants shut down most classes. Berkeley had become the nation's most "political" campus.

The Free Speech Movement succeeded in ways it had never envisaged. Not only did the Berkeley faculty vote to end all restrictions on speech or advocacy, but the chancellor took a "leave of absence" in January, and president Kerr departed shortly thereafter. Having swept aside the cautious careerism that had characterized their lives, many students experienced a strong sense of exhilaration and wholeness, turning them away from their previous preoccupations. "You were . . . really acting," wrote one participant. "You were for once free of the whole sticky cobweb that kept you apart from . . . the roots of your existence, and you knew you were alive and what your life was all about." Some academics, soured by their own radical past, took a mordant view of the FSM. Lewis Feuer wrote in the *New Leader:* "The conglomeration acts as a magnet for the morally corrupt: intellectual lumpen proletarians, lumpen beatniks and lumpen agitators wend their ways to the university campus to advocate a melange of narcotics, sexual perversion, collegiate Castroism, and campus Maoism." Nevertheless, the Berkeley upheaval excited students at other colleges and universities, who, in less dramatic ways, were developing their own radical tendencies. War, racial injustice, and poverty were excoriated in rallies, speeches, and demonstrations across the country. Of 849 colleges responding to a national survey, a Presidential commission later noted, "the great majority" reported some type of protest activity during the 1964–65 academic year. Unable to characterize the campus phenomenon in the familiar terms of postwar politics, observers began to talk of a "New Left."

Little realizing that events were already bypassing their electoral mandate, members of the overwhelmingly Democratic 89th Congress turned in 1965 to enacting the Great Society program. That year Congress passed Medicare for the aged under Social Security, a program of federal aid to elementary and secondary education, an immigration measure ending the discriminatory national origins quota system, a housing program including rent supplements to low-income families, an Appalachian Development Act, a wide-ranging program of aid to higher education, an increase in funding for OEO, a Voting Rights Act, and a bill establishing a Cabinet-level Department of Housing and Urban Development. In its 1966 session, Congress added the Model Cities program, grants to the states for health services, and a new Department of Transportation. Throughout 1965 Congress approved 68 per cent of the White House proposals submitted to it, the best record since the *Congressional Quarterly* started keeping count in 1954. The Administration had greater difficulties in 1966, when it failed to secure legislation barring racial discrimination in housing, repealing section 14(b) of the Taft-Hartley Act, and overhauling the unemployment-compensation system. Nevertheless, by past standards the record of the 89th Congress was impressive. "They say Jack Kennedy had style," Johnson remarked to senators in 1966, "but I'm the one who got the bills passed."

The Voting Rights Act, however, owed less to the political arts of Lyndon Johnson than to the courage of civil rights activists. In early 1965 Martin Luther King decided that the moment had arrived to dramatize the demand for voting rights by bringing demonstrators into the streets of Selma, Alabama. Not only did Selma have a notoriously racist sheriff who had arrested thousands of civil rights demonstrators in the past, but it utilized a discriminatory voter registration procedure that ensured a minimum of black political participation. Large and frequent demonstrations now began, attracting supporters, particularly clergymen, from all parts of the country. On March 7, acting on orders from Governor George Wallace, state troopers used tear gas, clubs, and whips to break up a march from Selma to Montgomery, severely wounding forty participants. On March 9 a group of white men attacked the Rev. James Reeb, a white volunteer, and clubbed him to death. The NAACP called upon the President to send troops to Selma, Congressmen demanded strong voting rights legislation, and clergymen criticized the President for inaction. Pickets maintained a round-the-clock vigil in front of the White House. Sit-ins erupted at the Capitol, amid rush-hour traffic on Pennsylvania Avenue, and inside the White House. On March 15 the President went before Congress to ask for a voting rights bill. "It is all of us who must overcome the crippling legacy of bigotry and injustice," he said, "and we shall overcome."

Six days later a great march left Selma on the road to Montgomery, led by King and U.N. diplomat Ralph Bunche. When it entered Montgomery, 50,000 people joined its triumphal progress to the old state capitol building, once the seat of the Confederate government. It was a show of strength by supporters of racial justice never before seen in the Deep South—one made all the more dramatic by news that day of the death of still another civil rights activist, Viola Liuzzo, murdered by local Klansmen. Stirred by the events in Selma, Congress enacted the Voting Rights Act of 1965 that summer, granting the Attorney General the power to appoint federal voting examiners in place of local officials. Although never implemented to the extent urged by civil rights groups, the legislation contributed significantly to the 50 per cent rise in voter registration among Southern blacks between 1964 and 1968. In Mississippi alone, the number of blacks registered to vote climbed during the 1960s from 22,000 to 285,000, resulting in their election to state and local offices for the first time since the nineteenth century.

Despite the Administration's lofty rhetoric, a number of the concepts underlying Great Society programs were actually fairly conservative. Medicare had been a Democratic Party staple for decades. Far weaker than Truman's Fair Deal health program, which Johnson had opposed in 1948, Medicare drew its funding from a regressive payroll tax and provided assistance to none but the aged. Unlike virtually every European nation, the United States failed to develop a national health program. The Administration also promoted some curious thinking about the causes of black poverty, as evidenced by the Moynihan Report—a study produced in March, 1965, by Assistant Secretary of Labor Daniel P. Moynihan. Arguing that half the nation's black population suffered from a "social pathology" whose "source" was the black family, Moynihan implied that the black poor would not benefit from a simple anti-poverty program. Rather, "a national effort is required . . . directed to a new kind of national goal: the establishment of a stable Negro family structure." Blacks resented the use of the term "pathology" to characterize their life in America and thought the shoe belonged on the other foot. "One can't talk about the pathologies of Negroes without talking about the pathologies of white society," remarked Whitney Young of the Urban League. "If Negroes are sick socially, then whites are sick morally." Although President Johnson made use of the "family structure" approach in his June 4, 1965, address at Howard University, it was sharply rejected by participants in the conference on civil rights called by the White House the following year.

Even the Administration's most innovative venture, the "war on poverty," had a conservative orientation. Most of its major programs—Head Start for preschool children, Upward Bound for college students, a Job Corps for school dropouts, a Neighborhood Youth Corps, and VISTA—concentrated primarily on education, training, and character building. Thus, as sociologist Christopher Jencks noted, the Administration implicitly assumed that poverty existed "not because the economy is mismanaged, but because the poor themselves have something wrong with them." Furthermore, the government avoided even a modest redistribution of income. Economist Robert Lekachman estimated that "for a mere $11 billion we could raise every poor American above the poverty line." Income supplements, however, did not fit the competitive preconceptions of the Administration. As the new director of the Office of Economic Opportunity, Sargent Shriver, observed, the war on poverty was "not a hand-out program." Assuming that poverty was largely a cultural problem, Johnson and Shriver sought to change "indifference to interest, ignorance to awareness, resignation to ambition, and an attitude of withdrawal to one of participation." The antipoverty program thus ignored the impoverishment of the nation's unemployables—millions of the aged, sick, handicapped, and totally disabled—and did nothing to increase the proportion of the American poor who received federal public assistance (estimated at one-fifth in 1966). Curiously, while seeking to create an "opportunity environment," the antipoverty program failed to guarantee anyone a job and ignored those Americans who were already employed at substandard wages. The war on poverty therefore centered on giving the poor the personal attributes considered necessary to "make it" in America. It was a middle-class success formula, administered by a successful middle class.

There were, to be sure, avant-garde aspects to the antipoverty effort. For one thing, the government had ceased to rely on economic growth alone to cope with social ills but had created a program with an exclusive focus upon poverty. Not only did this provide the poor with their own agency inside the federal bureaucracy, but this agency had at least the potential for developing significant programs. Furthermore, many persons staffing OEO projects had social views considerably to the left of those of the President. Civil rights activists, radical students, and reformist social workers often participated in antipoverty efforts at the local level, giving them a radical, insurgent flavor. The boldest component of the OEO legislation was its insistence upon "maximum feasible participation" of the poor in the local Community Action Programs. This concept met strong opposition from big-city mayors, who were often sharply criticized for their alliance with vested interests by the newly mobilized poor. At the 1965 Conference of Mayors, municipal chief executives denounced CAP's promotion of "Marxism" and the class struggle. As OEO was unwilling to stand up against such pressure, and as local civil rights and community groups were generally unable to do so, the poor were gradually reduced to a token role in most local projects. "The federal government ought to be ashamed of itself," charged the MFDP's Unita Blackwell in 1966. "The same men who pay us $3 a day and are bent on putting people off the land—that's the men who are on the poverty committee." In the rest of the country the situation was much the same. Nevertheless, OEO did promote the participation of poor people more vigorously than any federal agency in the past.

Most antipoverty projects were effective as far as they went, but they never went very far, as the Administration failed to provide them with adequate funding. The annual budget of the war on poverty never moved significantly above $2 billion a year. In 1966 Shriver told the

Senate that American poverty could be eliminated in a decade. The following year he announced that "the war on poverty" would "not be won in a generation." Poor people, encouraged by the Administration's grandiose rhetoric of 1964 and 1965, were already growing embittered by 1966. When a thousand delegates from the Citizens Crusade Against Poverty met with Shriver that April, the mood was "mutinous," the *New York Times* reported. Delegates from Harlem, the Mississippi Delta, Appalachia, and the slums of Los Angeles denounced the meagerness of the Administration's program. One delegate cried out: "It's just a big publicity deal." Certainly the war on poverty was the only low-budget war in American history.

The war on poverty, like the rest of the Great Society program, was crippled from the outset by the Administration's commitment to an ever-expanding military role in Vietnam. On February 7, 1965, when NLF forces attacked the American military installations at Pleiku, President Johnson seized the occasion to unleash his previously planned air war against North Vietnam. "We seek no wider war," proclaimed the President, who thereupon began more than three years of steadily escalating bombing raids. By July American planes were flying 900 sorties a week over North Vietnam; in December the number reached 1,500. During 1966 the tonnage of U.S. bombs dropped on North Vietnam quadrupled that of the preceding year. Keeping close personal control of the situation, Johnson and his top civilian advisers chose all fixed targets for the raids. On June 29, 1966, the President ordered the beginning of American air attacks on targets in and around Hanoi and Haiphong. The Administration also dramatically increased the bombing of the South, designating huge populated areas as "free fire zones" in which American planes and helicopter gunships were authorized to destroy anything that moved. Saigon's supporters and opponents alike fled from the fierce hail of bombs, napalm, white phosphorous, and anti-personnel weapons that laid waste the South Vietnamese countryside. The most ferocious air war in history had begun. By the end of 1966 the tonnage of U.S. bombs released over Vietnam exceeded that dropped in the Pacific Theater during World War II.

The rationale for the bombing of the North did not lie primarily in its military effectiveness but in its psychological utility. U.S. intelligence sources consistently reported not only that the basis of the insurgency lay in the South but that a bombing campaign would not significantly affect the trickle of support flowing from the North. What the bombing would do, most American policy-makers believed, would be to edify the North Vietnamese and their revolutionary allies in the South through a form of international torture. A "dynamic schedule of strikes," wrote U.S. Ambassador Taylor, would "break the will" of North Vietnam;

thus, the United States should "progressively turn the screws." Mc-George Bundy assured his colleagues that they had "the whip hand." At a high-level conference of U.S. policy-makers in April, according to the notes of McNaughton, there was considerable discussion of "bomb-induced 'pain' in the North." As McNaughton summarized their conclusions: "The victory strategy was to 'break the will of the D.R.V./VC.' " And whatever the outcome in Vietnam, wrote Bundy, a sustained bombing campaign "—to the extent that it demonstrates U.S. willingness to employ this new norm in counter-insurgency—will set a higher price for the future upon all adventures of guerrilla warfare" and "increase our ability to deter such adventures." The bombing, then, while a strategic departure, remained consistent with the over-all objectives of American foreign policy. "The inner logic of the Vietnamese war," as I. F. Stone perceptively noted, "is to let the desperate, the hopeless and the hungry elsewhere in Asia, Africa and Latin America know what we can do to them if they dare to rise against their privileged oligarchies and our investments."

U.S. policy-makers gave the air war a cast more acceptable to Americans by portraying it as a response to foreign invasion. Of course, this necessitated ignoring the roots of the insurgency in the South. "Incontrovertible evidence" of Hanoi's aggression, asserted a State Department White Paper of 1965, included the capture from NLF forces of 179 weapons of Communist manufacture out of approximately 7,500 seized during the preceding eighteen months. The fact that 97.5 per cent of the weapons captured were produced in non-Communist countries—mostly in the United States—was thus regarded as immaterial. Not until April 21, 1965, in fact, did the CIA report the presence of a regular regiment of North Vietnamese troops engaged in combat operations in South Vietnam, and as late as October, 1966, McNamara estimated that only 45,000 North Vietnamese troops were present in the South. Moreover, the new official explanation also necessitated some rewriting of the past, creating two sovereign Vietnams—North and South—in place of the one established by history and ratified by the 1954 Geneva accords. In 1961 the State Department's Blue Book had declared that the pattern of NLF activity was "not new" but had emerged earlier "in Malaya, in Greece, in the Philippines, in Cuba, and in Laos." If there was "anything peculiar to the Viet-Nam situation," added the Blue Book, "it is that the country is divided." The 1965 White Paper depicted the conflict as "a new kind of war . . . not another Greece . . . not another Malaya . . . not another Philippines." In Vietnam, the White Paper stated, "a Communist government has set out deliberately to conquer a sovereign people in a neighboring state." Secretary General

U Thant of the United Nations observed on February 24: "In times of war and hostilities the first casualty is truth."

Shortly after launching the air war, the Administration ordered the beginning of offensive ground action in South Vietnam by several hundred thousand American troops. Although Johnson decided on April 1 to employ U.S. soldiers in a combat role, a secret National Security Action Memorandum five days later cautioned that implementation should proceed "in ways that . . . minimize any appearance of sudden changes." In July Johnson accepted General William Westmoreland's request for forty-four combat battalions and endorsed his "search and destroy" strategy for military victory. The "win phase," predicted Westmoreland, would begin in 1966 and would culminate in a U.S. victory by the end of 1967. Although no European nation would allow itself to become involved in the war, the Administration did manage to secure the participation of small troop contingents from Australia, New Zealand, South Korea, Thailand, and the Philippines—the last three through secret agreements to fund their governments lavishly in return. Militarily, such forces were relatively useless, but they did enable the Administration to talk of its "allies." By the end of 1966 the U.S. troop commitment had soared to 470,000, with 385,300 men already in Vietnam, engaging in vast and bloody sweeps through the Southern countryside. "The French didn't kill enough," explained an American general. "If you kill enough you win the war."

As the American military colossus cut swaths of destruction across Vietnam, "nation building" continued. After ten changes of government since Diem, the Saigon regime ended up in June, 1965, in the hands of Air Vice-Marshal Nguyen Cao Ky—a North Vietnamese who had fought on the side of the French in the first Indochina War. He achieved considerable notoriety that year when he declared in an interview that Hitler was his only hero. "Politically, South Vietnam is a lost cause," Under Secretary of State George Ball confided to Johnson in July, 1965. "The 'government' in Saigon is a travesty." In June, 1966, the State Department cabled Ambassador Lodge that "elections should be conducted so as to gain a maximum improvement in the image of the GVN in the United States and internationally." Giving Ky and the generals a free rein in rigging the balloting, Lodge enabled them to exclude most of the unwanted candidates. When Truong Dinh Dzu, a candidate calling for negotiations and an end to the war, emerged a surprise runner-up for the presidency, the generals clapped him into prison for the next six years. Off in the countryside, American officials supervised a village "pacification" program, designed to combine a new police-spy-security apparatus with material improvements in the lives of the villagers. As this program failed in its goal of destroying the NLF cadres and winning the support of the people, it was supplanted by the simpler policy of driving the peasants off the land—what sympathetic social scientists in America called "forced urbanization." "The increased flow of refugees is a plus: it helps deprive VC of recruiting potential and rice growers," explained the head of the U.S. program. As American officials had claimed all along, there was no problem that could not be solved in Vietnam—if only the Vietnamese were removed.

By late 1966 the results of the Administration's grand strategy of escalation were evident. In a secret report that November, McNamara told the President that the air war against the North had had "no significant impact" on the war in the South. Furthermore, there was "no evidence" that the addition of more troops "would substantially change the situation." But if the military gains were slight, the human costs were great. When Harrison Salisbury, assistant managing editor of the *New York Times,* visited Hanoi in December, 1966, he sent back dispatches describing widespread civilian casualties and the destruction of homes, schools, churches, and hospitals. Although U.S. officials vigorously denied his claims, the following month a secret CIA study found that civilian losses in the North considerably exceeded Salisbury's estimates. The CIA contended that the casualties resulting from the air war over North Vietnam totaled 13,000 in 1965 and at least 23,000 in 1966—"about 80 per cent civilians." Describing the U.S. campaign in the South, reporters wrote incredulously of villages razed, crops sprayed and destroyed, prisoners tortured, civilian populations herded into miserable refugee camps, and a widening circle of pain and death. Neil Sheehan reported in the *New York Times Magazine* that he wondered when he looked "at the bombed-out peasant hamlets, the orphans begging and stealing in the streets, and the women and children with napalm burns lying on the hospital cots, whether the United States or any other nation has the right to inflict this suffering and degradation on another people for its own ends."

The American peace movement responded with a dramatic series of protests. Pacifist groups and the Socialist Party sponsored the first major demonstration against the war on December 19, 1964, when 1,500 people gathered for an outdoor rally in New York, addressed by A. J. Muste, Norman Thomas, and A. Philip Randolph. After Johnson commenced the bombing of the North in February, 1965, antiwar picketing, sit-ins, and speeches spread across the country. On March 16 Alice Herz, an eighty-two-year-old refugee from Nazism, set herself aflame at a busy Detroit intersection, dying ten days later. "I choose the illuminating death of a Buddhist," she wrote, "to protest against a great country trying to wipe out a small country." On April 17 SDS drew 20,000 people to Washington, D.C., for the largest antiwar demonstration in that city's history. FSM veterans, SNCC workers, former Freedom Riders, Peace Corps returnees, and college students jostled one another on the grass under the Washington Monument as Staughton Lynd, Bob Parris, I. F. Stone, Paul Potter (of SDS), and Senator Gruening vigorously denounced the war and Joan Baez sang ballads of love, war, and death. That summer an Assembly of Unrepresented People, composed largely of civil rights and peace activists, met in Washington to engage in further protests and to establish the National Committee to End the War in Vietnam. In October the National Committee sponsored a new wave of antiwar actions, involving an estimated 80,000 people across the nation. Thirty thousand New Yorkers paraded down Fifth Avenue demanding "Peace Now." The following month Norman Morrison, secretary of a Quaker Meeting, set himself afire in front of the Pentagon; Roger La Porte, a Catholic Worker volunteer, did so before the U.N. Secretariat building in New York. Speaking at a SANE rally of 20,000 that November in Washington, SDS president Carl Oglesby characterized the war as the product of "corporate liberalism" and asked "humanist" liberals: "Will you be grudging apologists for the corporate state? Or will you help try to change it . . . in the name of simple human decency?"

The rising tide of popular protest owed much to the antiwar "teach-ins" that swept through the best of the nation's colleges and universities in the spring of 1965. Having supported Johnson in 1964 as the "peace candidate," many faculty members and students felt betrayed as he adopted the Vietnam policies of his opponent. On March 24 an all-night teach-in at the University of Michigan attracted 3,000 participants. It was followed by teach-ins across the United States. "We are using our power to thwart and abort an indigenous social and political revolution," charged Professor William Appleman Williams at the University of Wisconsin. Speaking at the University of Oregon, Senator Morse predicted: "Twelve months from tonight there will be hundreds of thousands of American boys fighting in Southeast Asia—and tens of thousands of them will be coming home in coffins." At the University of Michigan, Arthur Waskow of the Institute for Policy Studies cited Jefferson on slavery: "I tremble for my country when I reflect that God is just." Although the liberal community was sharply divided on the merits of the war, those denouncing it ranged from radicals, like Isaac Deutscher, to proponents of *Realpolitik,* like Hans Morgenthau. Artists, writers, and intellectuals were in the forefront of the protest.

The unexpected appearance of campus dissent greatly distressed admirers of the war. Addressing the American Society of International Law, Rusk assailed "the gullibility of educated men" and their "stubborn disregard of plain facts." Senator Goldwater remarked that, while most participants in the teach-ins seemed to be no more than "a bunch of beatniks and pacifists scrawling naughty words," a group of dangerous traitors provided their "thoroughly disgusting roots." Organizers of the early teach-ins often invited government spokesmen or academic supporters of the war to participate, but few availed themselves of this opportunity. At the National Teach-In of May 15, 1965, which gained the first significant television coverage for critics of the war, the Administration's spokesman, McGeorge Bundy, failed to appear, absorbed as he was in managing the U.S. invasion of the Dominican Republic. The Administration dispatched "truth-teams" to tour the nation's campuses and provide the official version of the conflict, but they were met by embarrassing questions, hecklers, and demonstrations. At the end of a talk by a State Department official at the University of Wisconsin, one graduate student came up to him and growled: "Get this straight, sweetie. We're not going to fight your filthy fascist war."

Opposition to the war often took the form of resistance to service in the armed forces. In late 1964 pacifists had begun circulating a "Declaration of Conscience Against the War in Vietnam," which, in violation of the Selective Service law, urged young men to refuse military service. The next summer they delivered it to the White House with more than 4,000 signatures. Opponents of conscription had burned their draft cards on a number of occasions in the postwar years without drawing much attention, but a draft-card burning on July 29, 1965, outside a New York induction center gained nationwide publicity. Congress responded with legislation imposing a penalty of five years in prison and a fine of $5000 for anyone vicious enough to burn a draft card. David Miller, a Catholic Worker volunteer once active with CORE, was the first person imprisoned under the new law but hardly the last. In November, 1965, five war critics—four of them 4-F or overage—repeated Miller's crime before a cheering crowd of 2,000 in New York's Union Square. SNCC, denouncing the war, staged demonstrations outside the Atlanta induction center and popularized the slogan "Hell No, We Won't Go!" Hesitant to endorse direct draft resistance, SDS initially encouraged young men to file for status as conscientious objectors and organized opposition to the campus examinations ordered by Selective Service. Sit-ins or building occupations protesting the examinations took place at the State University of New York at Buffalo and New Paltz, the University of Chicago, Cornell, Brooklyn College, and elsewhere. Several universities refused to divulge academic ranking for Selective Service purposes. Swept along in the flood of campus opposition to the military, SDS voted in December, 1966, to encourage and support draft resistance.

Despite the vigor of the peace movement, most powerful forces in American life gave the Vietnam War their wholehearted support. Big business exuded contentment. Echoing Rudyard Kipling's apologia for imperialism, *Fortune* declared that the United States had fallen "heir to the onerous task of policing these shattered colonies"—a task that would provide "the unending test of American idealism." The vice-president for Far Eastern operations of the Chase Manhattan Bank, discussing Southeast Asia in 1965, reported: "U.S. actions in Vietnam this year . . . have considerably reassured both Asian and Western investors." Hardly less enthusiastic than its partners in the executive suites, the AFL-CIO executive board unanimously reaffirmed its endorsement of the Vietnam War and denounced antiwar demonstrators. "Those who would deny our military forces unstinting support," said the labor leadership, "are, in effect, aiding the Communist enemy." When thousands of faculty members signed newspaper ads criticizing the war, university presidents like Columbia's Grayson Kirk chided them for speaking out on issues which they lacked the competence to understand.

The mass media, accustomed to serving as loyal disseminators of official pronouncements, proved for the most part unwilling to challenge the claims of the Administration or to accord its critics much of a hearing. Tom Wicker later acknowledged the "failure of the American press" to "adequately question the assumptions, the intelligence, the whole idea of America in the world . . . which led this country into the Vietnam War." On March 10, 1964, Senator Gruening delivered the first Senate speech calling for a withdrawal of U.S. troops from Southeast Asia, but neither the *Washington Post* nor the *New York Times*—perhaps the two best newspapers in America—printed a word of it. Television viewers received a particularly trivialized version of events. To be sure, both CBS and NBC carried the Senate Foreign Relations Committee's hearings on the war in February, 1966, but only until the scheduled appearance of the first "dove," George Kennan. At this point CBS dropped its coverage of the hearings, presenting in their place the fifth rerun of an "I Love Lucy" show and the eighth rerun of an episode of "The Real McCoys." According to Fred Friendly, who resigned as CBS News director in protest, the network president objected to "too much 'dove-hawk' talk" because it "unsteadied the hand of the Commander-in-Chief."

In Congress, criticism of the war was limited but growing. Until the beginning of the U.S. air war, dissent in the Senate was confined to Morse and Gruening; thereafter, it spread continuously, particularly among Democrats. On February 17, 1965, Senators McGovern and Frank Church both made speeches calling for an emphasis upon negotiations, and they were soon joined by Senators Eugene McCarthy, Gaylord Nelson, and Stephen Young. Behind the scenes, Majority Leader Mike Mansfield condemned the Administration's policy that July. In January, 1966, Senator Vance Hartke, once a close ally of Johnson's, drafted a letter to the President calling for extension of a temporary bombing halt, and released it to the press signed by fourteen senators. That same month, when Johnson requested a supplemental appropriation from Congress of $13.1 billion to finance the expanding war effort, Senator Fulbright used the opportunity to hold televised hearings of the Senate Foreign Relations Committee. "Fulbright's Teach-In," as it was dubbed, publicized and legitimized the sentiments of "doves" but failed to halt the appropriations bill; only Morse and Gruening dared to vote against it in the Senate, and Congressmen Philip Burton, William Fitts Ryan, and John Conyers in the House.

If most Congressional opposition remained confined to words, though, they were words with a political sting. On April 21, 1966, speaking at Johns Hopkins University, Fulbright urged a limit on American ambitions in the world in the name of conservative statesmen of the past who "did not think themselves or any other men qualified to play God." Fulbright's critique, coming as it did from a Southern Democrat, reflected the sense of alienation felt by a broad spectrum of Americans as the counter-revolutionary, belligerent aspects of American foreign policy became inescapable. Even Robert Kennedy had become a dissenter. Moody, emotional, and open to change, he had been torn loose from his conservative moorings by his brother's death and by the struggle for racial justice. After his election to the Senate from New York in 1964, he had begun to shift leftward on domestic issues. In early 1966 he joined the ranks of the Senate "doves." Increasingly, Kennedy was emerging as a powerful political alternative to the President. Angered by the disintegration of his "consensus," Johnson exhorted Americans to "stand united"—unlike the "Nervous Nellies" who "break ranks under the strain."

With Congressional dissent on the upswing, Johnson used talk of negotiations as a shield to deflect criticism from his war policies. In reality, the Administration had no intention of ending the bombing of the North short of what McNaughton, in a confidential memo of December, 1965, called "capitulation." From the standpoint of American policy-makers, anything short of a Communist surrender in South Vietnam was unacceptable. "Negotiation that admitted Communism to South Vietnam," wrote William Bundy, "simply would not provide the independent and secure South Vietnam . . . that we're after." When Robert Kennedy suggested on February 19, 1966, that the NLF be admitted to "a share of power and responsibility" in Saigon, Vice President Humphrey denounced the proposal, comparing it to placing "a fox in a chicken coop." The Administration refused to recognize the existence of the NLF or to take part in any form of discussions with it. Thus, although Johnson claimed that the brief U.S. bombing pauses were designed to open the road to negotiations, he used them instead to disarm domestic opposition on the eve of further escalation. The President viewed the five-day bombing pause in May, 1965, a Pentagon analyst later noted, "as a means of clearing the way for an increase in the tempo of the air war."

Escalation of the Vietnam War was not, as some thought, a mistake, but a course of action consistent with the assumptions underlying the Administration's foreign policy. "The poor nations are on a road that is mined with potential turmoil," the President warned the American Legion in August, 1966. "By 1970 over one-half of the world's population will live in the southern half of the globe," but would "command only one-sixth of the world's total goods and services." The resulting "quest for bread may bring on the reality of chaos." In 1965 alone, he noted, there had been fifty-eight violent "upheavals," most of them in nations with per capita incomes of less than $100 a year. "So interwoven is our destiny with the world's destiny, so intricate are the bonds between us and every continent," declared the President, "that our responsibilities would be just as real in the absence of a Communist threat." The Secretary of Defense issued an almost identical appraisal of world events before the American Society of Newspaper Editors that same year. Behind their analyses lay the fears that had haunted American policy-makers since the end of World War II. "There are a lot of people who want what we have," said the President, "and we are going to protect it."

By the mid-1960s, there was much to protect. Direct U.S. private investment abroad, which had a book value of $11.8 billion in 1950, had soared by 1966 to $54.6 billion, with an additional $32 billion in portfolio holdings—approximately 60 per cent of the world total. An investment banker reported in 1967 in *Foreign Affairs:* "The role of U.S. direct investment in the world economy is staggering. . . . The gross value of production by American companies abroad is well in excess of $100 billion a year . . . a gross product greater than that of any country except the United States and the Soviet Union." Profits derived from holdings in the Third World were particularly lucrative. In 1964–65, when investment earnings in Canada and Europe were 9 per cent, they reached 13 per cent in Latin America, 23 per cent in Africa, and 36 per cent in Asia. From 1950 to 1965 U.S. investors in underdeveloped nations drew out in profits almost three times the capital they put in. Moreover, they dramatically increased their holdings; U.S. direct investments more than doubled in Latin America and nearly quadrupled in Asia and Africa. In 1966 U.S. firms in Latin America accounted for 10 per cent of that region's production—including one-third of its exports—and employed a fifth of the industrial labor force. Most U.S. investment in the Third World remained concentrated in extractive industries. In 1964 the mining and petroleum industries alone accounted for 48 per cent of U.S. investments in Latin America, 67 per cent in Asia, and 73 per cent in Africa. Whereas earnings on foreign investments represented about 10 per cent of the after-tax profits of all U.S. nonfinancial corporations (including solely domestic firms) in 1950, they rose to 22 per cent by 1964.

U.S. corporations also had a sizable stake in maintaining the pattern of world trade, particularly with underdeveloped nations. By 1966 mineral and fuel imports played a major role in the American economy. The net import of copper was equivalent to 18 per cent of domestic production, petroleum 31 per cent, iron 43 per cent, lead 131 per cent, zinc 140 per cent, and bauxite 638 per cent. Between 1953 and 1966 the U.S. import of nonfood raw materials doubled. The importance of foreign sales to U.S. firms grew even more significantly. Between 1950 and 1964 U.S. exports rose from $10 billion to $25 billion, while the output resulting from U.S. investments abroad leaped from $44 billion to $143 billion. Even if adjustments are made for the double counting of some goods, the value of the foreign market for U.S. firms was equal to approximately two-fifths the value of the domestic production of U.S. factories, mines, and farms. From 1955 to 1964, when the domestic sales of U.S. manufacturing industries rose 50 per cent, the foreign sales by U.S.–owned factories rose by more than 110 per cent. *Forbes* reported in 1965 that foreign markets accounted for 29 per cent of the business of IBM, 40 per cent that of Coca-Cola, 45 per cent that of Caterpillar Tractor, and 60 per cent that of Standard Oil of New Jersey. In the 1960s, particularly, Latin America's consumption of U.S. products spiraled; it became second only to Canada as a market for the United States, developing record trade deficits in the process. In 1968, when the United States had a $2.4 billion trade deficit with Western Europe and Japan, it could chalk off almost two-thirds of this against the favorable balance of trade it enjoyed with Latin America.

As the focus of American policy shifted toward the nations of the Third World, Washington's ties loosened noticeably with the advanced industrial nations of Western Europe. To be sure, U.S. investments in Europe continued to increase; by the early 1960s American corporations controlled half the British automobile industry, nearly 40 per cent of the German petroleum industry, and over 40 per cent of the telegraphic, telephone, electronic, and statistical-equipment business of

France. By 1965, 700 of the 1,000 largest American companies had European subsidiaries. But this economic incursion also stirred considerable opposition in Western Europe, which sought to retain some measure of economic autonomy. Viewing Great Britain as a stalking horse for the United States, de Gaulle vetoed its entry into the Common Market, warning against "a colossal Atlantic Community dependent on America and directed by America, which would not take long to absorb this European Community." In the spring of 1966 France went one step farther by announcing that it would withdraw from NATO in 1969. The conviction grew in Western Europe that a Soviet invasion was extremely unlikely—a belief encouraged by the new spirit of cordiality between Washington and Moscow.

Throughout his term of office, Johnson worked for closer relations —particularly commercial relations—with the Soviet Union. In 1964, when Party conservatives ousted Khrushchev and replaced him with the grayer, more bureaucratic leadership of Alexei Kosygin and Leonid Brezhnev, Johnson negotiated a treaty with Russia providing for the establishment of consulates in both countries. Two years later the Administration sought to broaden American trade with Eastern Europe by urging Congress to pass the East-West Trade Relations Act. Although most Congressmen balked at voting for the measure in an election year —when it might prove difficult to explain to constituents why the government was simultaneously expanding trade with Communist nations and expanding the war in Vietnam—Johnson continued to press for closer economic ties. On October 7, 1966, in a major policy address, he argued that "our task is to achieve a reconciliation with the East—a shift from the narrow concept of coexistence to the broader vision of peaceful engagement." The President went on to announce that direct air service would soon be established between Moscow and New York, that Washington would relax controls on 400 nonstrategic commodities for trade with Russia and Eastern Europe, and that the Export-Import Bank would guarantee the credit of four East European countries for the purchase of U.S. goods and services. U.S. policy-makers had finally reached the conclusion that the Soviet Union, despite its revolutionary origins and rhetoric, provided no serious threat to American capitalism. Indeed, a rapprochement with Russia might even serve to bolster it.

They did not draw the same conclusion about China, then emerging as a major force in world affairs. The Chinese successfully tested their first atomic bomb on October 16, 1964, and their first thermonuclear bomb on May 9, 1966, pledging "to oppose the United States-Soviet collusion for maintaining a nuclear monopoly and sabotaging the revolutionary struggles of all oppressed peoples." Although Chinese foreign policy remained cautious, revolutionary exhortations abounded. In the fall of 1965 General Lin Piao, widely viewed as Mao's heir, propounded a theory that internationalized Marx's notion of the class struggle. The southern, agrarian, impoverished areas of the world, he predicted, would erupt in "wars of liberation" against control by the northern, urban, industrial nations. As in guerrilla war, the insurgents would liberate the countryside, thereby isolating the world's "cities." Such statements traumatized American policy-makers. Through "wars of liberation," Rusk contended in May, 1966, Communists sought to gain control of Asia, Africa, and Latin America, "thus encircling and strangling the Atlantic World." He compared Lin's statement to Hitler's *Mein Kampf*. Johnson and McNamara also apparently fashioned their warnings of 1966 in response to Lin's prediction. By the mid-1960s, then, Chinese and American policy-makers seemed to share a similar assessment of the world, based upon the inevitability of conflict between the rich nations and the poor. But, whereas Chinese policy-makers promised to assist the poor, their American counterparts worked assiduously to help the rich.

This pattern became increasingly evident in U.S. policy toward Latin America. "I know these Latin Americans," Johnson told a group of reporters shortly after becoming President. "I grew up with Mexicans. They'll come right into your yard and take it over if you let them. . . . But if you say to 'em right at the start, 'hold on, just wait a minute,' they'll know they're dealing with somebody who'll stand up. And after that you can get along just fine." As part of the President's program of keeping Latin Americans in their place, Green Berets and other U.S. armed forces carried out clandestine counter-insurgency operations in Bolivia, Colombia, Honduras, Guatemala, and Peru. The Administration also pressed forward with its training of local counter-insurgency forces. Citing the activities of rebel groups throughout the southern continent, McNamara told the House Foreign Affairs Committee in 1967 that "the need to counter these threats by appropriate means is the basis upon which . . . military assistance programs for Latin American countries are predicated. . . . The primary objective in Latin America is to aid, where necessary, in the continued development of indigenous military and paramilitary forces capable of providing, in conjunction with police and other security forces, the needed domestic security." Between fiscal 1950 and fiscal 1968 the United States trained 46,479 Latin American military personnel under the Military Assistance Program—almost half of them from 1964 to 1968. As McNamara explained, Latin Americans needed a "framework of law and order."

Toward this end, Johnson swung American diplomacy into line, dismissing some of Kennedy's more liberal Latin American specialists and uniting State Department and AID functions in the person of Thomas

C. Mann, an ardent advocate of U.S. business interests, who had previously served as Assistant Secretary of State for Economic Affairs under Eisenhower and Ambassador to Mexico under Kennedy. In March, 1964, Mann convoked a three-day meeting of U.S. ambassadors to Latin American nations to outline the Administration's policy: (1) promotion of economic growth but neutrality on social reform; (2) protection of U.S. private investments; (3) neutrality on representative democratic institutions; (4) opposition to Communism.

Such policies undermined still further the democratic, social-reformist goals of the Alliance for Progress. On April 1, 1964, only a short time after Mann's meeting with the ambassadors, a military coup toppled the left-leaning Joao Goulart, the democratically elected President of Brazil. Its participants proclaimed that they had saved the nation from Communism. Twelve hours after an authoritarian regime assumed office, President Johnson sent it his "warmest wishes" and an offer of "our intensified cooperation"; the following day Rusk congratulated Brazil's new leaders by telegram, calling the coup a "move to insure the continuity of constitutional government." That November the Bolivian armed forces—strengthened for years by the United States as a political counterweight to Bolivia's radical tin miners—overthrew the moderate democratic government of President Victor Paz Estenssoro. In June, 1966, the Argentine armed forces ended civilian rule in their land by installing the military dictatorship of General Juan Carlos Ongania. By 1967, of Latin America's major countries, only Chile, Mexico, Colombia, and Venezuela had managed to escape military takeovers during the years of the Alliance for Progress. The average industrial growth rate in the first seven years of the Alliance was the same as in the five years preceding it, while agricultural production was just keeping pace with the rate of population increase. Chile's Christian Democratic president, Eduardo Frei Montalva, lamented that the Alliance had "lost its way," but powerful Americans took a more favorable view of developments. Writing in *Foreign Affairs* in 1966, David Rockefeller, chairman of the Chase Manhattan Bank, praised the "new concept of the Alliance for Progress" as more conducive to corporate investments than the "overly ambitious concepts of revolutionary change" that had originally characterized the program.

Events in Brazil particularly encouraged U.S. policy-makers. President Goulart had been a critic of the Alliance for Progress, a supporter of a Latin American trading bloc, and a political leader seemingly ready to nationalize key U.S. corporate holdings. His ouster, therefore, overjoyed Washington officialdom. "It would be hard to figure out . . . who got more satisfaction in the overthrow," the *New York Times* editorialized, "the Brazilians or the United States State Department."

On April 9, a week after Rusk's congratulatory telegram, Brazil's military leaders issued a decree granting the armed forces chiefs a variety of repressive governing powers. Led by Humberto Castelo Branco, they arrested thousands of Brazilians without charges, deprived 400 public officials—including three former presidents—of all political rights, crushed labor unions and agrarian reform movements, and brought constitutional government to an end. Investment opportunities increased dramatically, as did U.S. investments. AID reported admiringly in 1966:

> Private enterprise has been encouraged by policies halting the previous trend toward state ownership. New incentives have been created and old obstacles removed in an effort to increase the participation of private enterprise, both foreign and domestic. New foreign investment is being sought for development of minerals and petrochemicals, and an Investment Guaranty agreement has been signed with the United States.

In this context, the absence of individual and political freedom could easily be forgiven. From 1964 to 1968 the U.S. government—which had previously cut foreign assistance to a trickle under the Goulart regime—supplied the new Brazilian rulers with massive economic aid, including an estimated $1.6 billion in bilateral resources, and trained 2,255 Brazilian military personnel under the Military Assistance Program. Testifying before a House committee in 1966 on behalf of aid to Brazil, U.S. Ambassador Lincoln Gordon stated that Castelo Branco and his supporters "were not able, unfortunately—and they are just as unhappy about this as the Chairman or anybody else—to return at once to full democratic institutions. . . . This is a transitional transformation . . . headed in the right direction." On December 13, 1968, angered by popular criticism, the Brazilian military assumed full dictatorial powers. It closed down the national legislature indefinitely, deprived 200 more persons—including 91 federal deputies—of political rights, and expelled hundreds of students and many professors from the universities. Torture of political prisoners, including electric-shock treatments, became a common practice of the regime. Strikes were illegal. Enthusiastic about the economic prospects in Brazil, AID programmed nearly a third of its development assistance for that nation in fiscal 1970. During 1972 U.S. businessmen poured at least $3 billion into Brazil—more than into all the rest of Latin America. Many Brazilians drew the appropriate conclusions. In late 1969, when young urban guerrillas kidnaped the U.S. Ambassador, they declared that he "represents in our country the interests of imperialism, which . . . maintain the regime of repression." Although the ambassador was freed after the dictatorship agreed to release fifteen political prisoners, Brazilian authorities subsequently captured several of the insurgents and tortured two of them to death.

Washington policy-makers played a more direct role in the Dominican Republic. Shortly after taking office, Johnson resumed U.S. aid to the junta regime of Reid Cabral. In the seven months of democratic government under Juan Bosch, there had been $64 million in U.S. investments; now, during the first nine months of the junta, U.S. investors plunged $175 million into the island's economy. Mass immiserization continued; in Santo Domingo, unemployment reached 40 per cent. Popular dissatisfaction grew. Finally, on April 24, 1965, a group of Constitutionalist army officers, pledging the restoration of the Bosch government, launched a revolt. Arming the eager street crowds in Santo Domingo, they toppled Cabral from power and soon had his loyalist generals on the run. On April 28 U.S. Ambassador W. Tapley Bennett, Jr., sent a frantic cable to Washington declaring that the situation was "deteriorating rapidly. . . . The generals . . . were dejected, several were weeping, and one was hysterically urging 'retreat!' " Bennett called for "armed intervention" by the United States to "prevent another Cuba." Consulting briefly with Rusk, McNamara, Ball, and McGeorge Bundy, Johnson responded little more than an hour later by ordering the first contingents of 23,000 U.S. Marines to the Dominican Republic. Upon their arrival they contained and then suppressed the Constitutionalist forces, saving the junta at the very moment when defeat seemed imminent. Bosch commented bitterly: "This was a democratic revolution smashed by the leading democracy in the world."

The Administration went to considerable lengths to justify its Dominican conquest. Johnson initially announced that he had dispatched the troops to protect the lives of U.S. nationals. He submitted a more imaginative version of this story to a press conference on June 17, when he described 1,500 people with severed heads, the U.S. Ambassador cowering under his Embassy desk, and "a thousand American men, women, and children . . . pleading with their President for help." It was all utterly untrue: the only U.S. civilians injured during the Dominican uprising were two newsmen—shot down by U.S. Marines. On May 2, however, Johnson developed a new justification. "What began as a popular democratic revolution," he said, had fallen "into the hands of a band of Communist conspirators." Curiously, this nefarious cabal could never be located; nor were critics of the intervention inclined to grant it much importance. "Little awareness has been shown," remarked the *New York Times*, "that the Dominican people—not just a handful of Communists—were fighting and dying for social justice and constitutionalism." But the Administration brushed such considerations aside; after all, why leave events in the hands of the Dominicans? Thomas Mann informed newsmen that the U.N. Charter had been drawn up in "nineteenth-century terms," while the President, wearing the robes of a newly awarded honorary doctorate of laws, propounded what became known as the Johnson Doctrine: "Old concepts and old labels are largely obsolete. . . . The old distinction between 'Civil War' and 'International War' has already lost much of its meaning. . . . The moment of decision must become the moment of action."

From Washington's viewpoint, the invasion of the Dominican Republic produced very satisfactory results. It crushed the Constitutionalist uprising in short order, resurrected the power of the Dominican military, left domestic critics sputtering helplessly, and resulted in only light casualties to U.S. troops. Although the action had clearly violated the OAS charter—which prohibited intervention "directly or indirectly, for any reason whatever, in the internal or external affairs of any other State"—Johnson viewed that organization with ill-concealed contempt. "The OAS," he said, "couldn't pour piss out of a boot if the instructions were written on the heel." He did use it, however, to relieve the United States of some of the stigma of military occupation, bringing in a force made up almost entirely of troops supplied by the military dictatorships of Brazil, Honduras, and Nicaragua. In 1966, having worked out its plans for the Dominican Republic's political future, the Johnson Administration allowed the first elections since those which had brought Bosch to power. This time, however, 70 per cent of the rural population remained under military occupation, sealed off from any contact with the Constitutionalists. Assassination and terror were rife. Bosch, returning to the island to campaign, was so intimidated that he never left his house. In the end, with the assistance of the United States, the conservative Joaquin Balaguer was installed in the presidency. Thereafter the reformists were frozen out of power and selectively assassinated by Balaguer's police. U.S. corporate interests settled down for another long, comfortable reign.

Absorbed in its costly military adventures, the Johnson Administration possessed little remaining enthusiasm and fewer resources for the Great Society. On January 12, 1966, Johnson admitted: "Because of Vietnam, we cannot do all that we should, or all that we would like to do." The Administration cut back its domestic agenda, paring some projects and dropping others. "I watched the [antipoverty] program broken and eviscerated," recalled King, "as if it were some idle political plaything of a society gone mad on war." That September an unhappy Arthur Schlesinger, Jr., reported: "The Great Society is now, except for token gestures, dead. The fight for equal opportunity for the Negro, the war against poverty, the struggle to save the cities, the improvement of our schools—all must be starved for the sake of Vietnam." The poor remained trapped in their slums, embittered by the empty promises of politicians and moving almost inevitably toward a series of desperate insurrections. Welfare state measures continued to abandon Americans on the margins of subsistence. By 1967 the average unemployment benefit stood at $40 a week and the average Social Security retirement benefit at $85 a month. On the other side of the tracks, corporate profits soared to a record $80.4 billion—more than four times the level of 1945. The *New York Times* observed in mid-1966: "The nation's big business executives . . . still love Lyndon Johnson in May as they did a year ago in November. . . . They feel comfortable with him . . . as they have felt comfortable with no President in their lifetimes." In Congressional elections that fall the Democrats—their constituency already fragmented by campaign promises betrayed—lost forty-seven House and three Senate seats, dimming the prospects still further for a continuation of social reform.

But, despite the burial of the Great Society, the movement for social change could no longer be halted. In September, 1965, grape pickers in Delano, California, went out on strike, led by a former migrant worker, Cesar Chavez. The strikers, mostly impoverished Mexican Americans, established close ties with student, civil rights, church, liberal, and labor groups; together, they carried the fervor of the civil rights movement into the struggle for "La Causa." In early 1966 Chavez brought a colorful march of 10,000 people to the state capital in Sacramento. Later that year the AFL-CIO recognized the new group as the United Farm Workers' Organizing Committee. The UFWOC negotiated contracts with the principal growers of wine grapes fairly quickly, but the table grape growers, led by the Joseph Giumarra Corporation, remained recalcitrant, importing thousands of Mexican nationals as strikebreakers. Unions, liberals, and radicals combined to enforce a nationwide boycott of table grapes, violated primarily by the Defense Department, and in mid-1969 the first table grape growers agreed to sign contracts; the following year, Giumarra, too, gave way. Victorious in its first major struggle, the tiny union next challenged the giant agribusinesses producing the nation's iceberg lettuce. By 1971 the UFWOC was sponsoring a boycott of lettuce, fending off a challenge from the powerful Teamsters Union (to which the growers had turned in an attempt to break the UFWOC), and formally representing 55,000 agricultural workers. The union brought not only higher wages to these traditionally exploited people but health, welfare, and legal benefits. As the National Sharecroppers Fund noted, UFWOC contracts "accomplish what government legislation has failed to do: they transform the farm worker's status from that of a semi-slave to that of someone with dignity, job security, and guaranteed basic rights."

The nation's black ghettos had also ceased to rely upon federal action. An estimated 41 per cent of nonwhites in the United States lived below the poverty level in 1966, and 40 per cent of this group resided in the nation's central cities. They provided the fuel for a series of ghetto explosions, most of them touched off by incidents involving the police. From July 18 to July 23, 1964, rioting swept through New York City's Harlem and Bedford-Stuyvesant areas. Insurrections followed in Rochester, New York; Jersey City, Paterson, and Elizabeth, New Jersey; in the Dixmoor suburb of Chicago; and in Philadelphia. The most destructive racial disorder of the nation's history occurred the following summer in the Watts area of Los Angeles. A large, sprawling region of private houses, Watts lacked major public facilities and had an adult unemployment rate of 30 per cent. Los Angeles was one of only two major American cities that summer without an antipoverty program and was notorious for the racist brutality of its police. On August 11, when white highway patrolmen halted a black driver and made him undergo a sobriety test, a crowd gathered and six days of rioting began, directed, as usual, against police and property. An estimated 15,000 National Guardsmen and 1,500 law-enforcement officers were brought in to restore order. In the end, the riot resulted in 34 people killed, 856 injured, and 3,100 arrested, as well as almost $200 million in damage.

An official investigating commission headed by former CIA director John McCone reported that the Watts upheaval had developed naturally out of the sense of failure and despair felt by blacks. Calling for wide-ranging programs to improve job opportunities, education, and police-community relations, the commission urged a "revolutionary attitude" toward urban problems if Watts were not to be "only a curtain-raiser." Once again the former CIA chieftain had called attention to the revolutionary aspirations of the insurgents, and once again Washington officialdom proved utterly incapable of satisfying them. As predicted, rioting followed the next summer, engulfing the ghetto areas of Chicago, Cleveland, Jacksonville, New York, and South Bend.

The same sense of despair that fed the ghetto upheavals had a marked impact on the struggle for racial justice. After the passage of the 1965 Voting Rights Act, the civil rights movement started to lose momentum. Many white liberals, assuming that the nation's racial crisis was being resolved by federal action, tapered off their support. At the same time Southern activists, exhausted by years of suffering, became increasingly embittered. Returning from Lowndes County, Alabama, in 1965,

SNCC's Stokely Carmichael was no longer in a joking mood. He told an interviewer: "Look, man, I've been to seventeen funerals since 1961." SNCC workers, like many young blacks, were strongly influenced by the ideas of black nationalist leader Malcolm X, particularly after his assassination in 1965. In May, 1966, when SNCC organizers gathered for a week-long retreat, all 130 present—including 25 whites and 20 women—had been jailed and had gone hungry. Most had been beaten. James Forman, stepping down as executive secretary, had a bleeding ulcer and a heart ailment. Chairman John Lewis had suffered a fractured skull. The sessions were emotional, intense, bizarre; antiwhite sentiments surfaced frequently. Lewis, a religious pacifist, was re-elected chairman despite a challenge from black nationalist elements led by Carmichael. But after Lewis expressed interest in attending the White House Conference on Civil Rights, and after it had become obvious that most SNCC workers had abandoned many of their former ideals, they reopened the election and elected Carmichael chairman. Out of the ashes of its nonviolent, integrationist past a new SNCC had been born: black nationalist, revolutionary, and oriented toward the struggles of the Third World.

SNCC's new direction created a furor on the American racial scene. After a Southern segregationist shot James Meredith on June 6, 1966, during his one-man protest walk from Memphis to Jackson, Mississippi, other civil rights activists continued his march. Carmichael set a militant tone for the throng, telling rural blacks to "stop begging and take power —black power." The Movement's new message, he said, was "move on over, or we'll move on over you." The striking phrase "Black Power," which became a popular chant along the march route, met a varied reception among blacks. Roy Wilkins denounced it as "the father of hatred and the mother of violence," but CORE endorsed a "Black Power" orientation at its July convention. King shied away from the term, but eventually he approved its least belligerent interpretation: "an appeal to racial pride." Carmichael sought to clarify the concept later that year. "This nation, from top to bottom, is racist," he said, and "does not function by morality, love, and non-violence, but by power." Blacks would go their own way, he explained, building their own institutions and serving their own needs and interests. It was an angry message but not a racist one. Some thought it had the potential for mobilizing the black masses, freeing them from compromising white influences, and helping them to discard any self-hatred they had assimilated from a white-dominated culture. Among whites, of course, black nationalism had considerably less organizing potential; it quickly forced the sympathetic out of the civil rights movement and inflamed the worst prejudices of the unsympathetic. In Chicago, where King and SCLC were working for open housing, whites responded by appealing to "White Power" and physically assaulting demonstrators. On August 5 they stoned King.

Antiwar protest, too, encountered a hostile reception. Delighted by Johnson's war policy, conservative Republicans initiated the attack, but it soon swelled into a bipartisan assault. Vice-President Humphrey publicly denounced the 1965 antiwar demonstrations as "organized and masterminded" by "the international Communist movement." In a froth of indignation, the New York *Daily News* demanded that the "Communist-incited beatniks, pacifists and damned idiots who are demonstrating" be tried for treason. During 1966 repressive pressures intensified. In January the Georgia legislature refused to seat former SNCC activist Julian Bond because of his antiwar position. In February Congressman Olin Teague of Texas, denouncing demonstrators as "beatnik types and pseudo-intellectuals," introduced legislation to make all antiwar protests illegal. The next month antiwar marchers were physically attacked and their demonstrations disrupted. Four young draft card burners were severely beaten by a mob on the steps of the Boston courthouse as police and cameramen looked on. In April the office of the Berkeley Vietnam Day Committee was bombed. Languishing for years in murky obscurity, HUAC arose from the depths to promise Americans a new series of investigations.

Yet this first whiff of repression failed to halt the steady growth of radical protest. Peace activists blocked troop trains, leafleted induction centers, sat in at the offices of Dow Chemical (the manufacturer of napalm), picketed armed forces recruiters, and staged demonstrations wherever Administration officials dared to appear. King and SCLC continued their nonviolent integrationist efforts, while SNCC's angry militants launched operations in the turbulent black ghettos of the North. When Attorney General Nicholas Katzenbach announced in the fall of 1965 that the Justice Department was beginning an investigation of SDS, that organization counterattacked. "The commitment of SDS, and of the whole generation we represent, is clear," announced the organization's secretary, Paul Booth. "We are anxious to advance the cause of democracy; we do not believe that cause can be advanced by torture and terror." Unlike its Old Left counterparts, which failed to make much headway among radical youth, SDS grew rapidly. By April, 1966, it had an estimated membership of 5,500, with participation in its activities of many times that number. Although white activists had lost the first and best source of their hopeful idealism when the joyous fraternity of the civil rights struggle dissolved into a grim separatism, they were already formulating alternative directions for their energies. Two SDS leaders, Greg Calvert and Carl Davidson, had begun to propound a theory of a "new working class," trained in the universities at the behest of advanced industrial capitalism. It pointed logically toward an increased emphasis upon organizing the campuses, which, like the racial ghettos, were developing an explosive political potential. Not since the 1930s had such a spirit of restlessness and protest gripped the land.

The struggle for racial equality, the rediscovery of poverty, the ferment in the universities, and the revolt against the Cold War—all might have been channeled into a new reform coalition, as they almost were in 1964. In the 1930s Roosevelt had harnessed and tamed the radical impulses of his era, destroying their prospects for autonomous development but producing a liberalized Democratic Party and the most significant burst of social legislation in American history. This was not, however, the course of action chosen by Johnson. Instead, after his landslide victory of 1964 he abandoned the program of peace and social reform demanded by the emerging forces of change to serve the interests of the wealthy and powerful. Consequently, the radical insurgency of the early 1960s was not absorbed and disciplined by the Administration. On the contrary, outraged and determined, it deepened and spread across the land, moving inevitably toward a confrontation with the power of the American government. For not even that most artful of politicians in the White House could escape unscathed when, once too often, the American people were promised justice and delivered into imperial war.

10

Crackup, 1967-68

> We are at the moment when our lives must be placed on the line if our nation is to survive its own folly.
>
> MARTIN LUTHER KING, JR., 1967

IN 1967 AND 1968 the federal government accelerated the movement from Great Society to garrison state. The Johnson Administration budgeted $76 billion for the military and $15 billion for education, health, labor, welfare, housing, and community development in fiscal 1968, and the exigencies of the Vietnam War soon drove the Pentagon's share still higher. Military spending, which had reached an unprecedented "peacetime" total of $55 billion in 1965, soared past $80 billion in 1968. To be sure, Congress did deliver a last smattering of liberal legislation: a meat inspection act, a truth-in-lending act, and a civil rights act banning discrimination in housing. But with the passage of these measures—none involving major appropriations—social reform ground to a conspicuous halt. On June 26, 1968, in the midst of a House debate that ended with sizable cuts in the welfare budget, one Republican explained that the United States did not have the money "to throw away . . . on this type of luxury," while a Democrat demanded to know what, after all, the poor wanted: "Diamonds?" When a bill came before the House to provide $40 million for the extermination of rats in big-city slums, the proceedings exploded in levity. "Why not just buy some cats and turn them loose?" asked one wag. At a time when the nation's slums were erupting in violent upheavals, the government built only 30,000 units a year of low-rent public housing. At a time when millions of children went to school hungry, Congress appropriated but $2 million a year for free lunch programs. At a time when the United States was spending an estimated $322,000 for every "Communist" killed in Vietnam, the "war on poverty" received only $53 per poor person. "The bombs in Vietnam explode at home," declared Mar-

273

tin Luther King. "They destroy the hopes and possibilities of a decent America."

As usual, such priorities hit lower-income groups hardest. Not only were they deprived of vital social services, but they were conscripted more heavily than upper-income groups to fight and die. In Vietnam, an estimated 20 per cent of the combat forces were black. Lower-income groups also paid a disproportionate share of the war costs. Stimulated by accelerated military spending, corporate profits soared, but the Administration rejected proposals for excess-profits taxes to fund the war and curb inflation. Instead, it sponsored an excise tax on telephone service and an across-the-board income tax surcharge of 10 per cent. Understandably, the corporate élite thought this an excellent idea. Thirteen prominent corporate titans wired expressions of their support for the surcharge to every member of the House of Representatives, while the Chamber of Commerce sent Congressmen a petition endorsing the measure, signed by some of the most powerful business executives in America. Congress dutifully enacted the new revenue-producing laws, passing the money along to the military.

Whatever the increases in military spending, though, they were never enough. With the United States pouring $30 billion a year into the Vietnam struggle, the Under Secretary of the Treasury complained in 1968 that the government had "been fighting this war on a very, very lean budget." That same year the Secretary of Defense contended that the Pentagon's projected budget of $81 billion was "austere." Indeed it was, compared with the $30 billion in additional spending demanded by the Joint Chiefs of Staff for three "urgent" new weapons systems and ten others they merely termed "critical." In 1967 McNamara cautioned LBJ that the science advisers of three successive Presidents and the directors of research and engineering of three successive Secretaries of Defense had all rejected an anti-ballistic missile program as "a senseless spiral upward in nuclear arms." But, under pressure from defense contractors, Republicans, and the Joint Chiefs of Staff, Johnson threw his support behind the deployment of a "thin" ABM system, at an initial cost of $5 billion. The Administration billed the new weapons program as a deterrent to China, which, it was estimated, might have four or five intercontinental missiles by the mid-1970s. Senator Russell, who favored a larger ABM system, thought this utterly inane. "The Chinese are not completely crazy," he said. "I don't like people to think I am being kidded by this talk of a Chinese nuclear attack." Pennsylvania's Senator Joseph S. Clark, an opponent of the Administration bill, observed dolefully that the money needed "to rebuild our cities" was "being drained off to build Armageddon."

One of the choicest boondoggles of these years involved the construction of the F-111 fighter-bomber. In 1961 the General Dynamics Corporation had been close to receivership, but McNamara rescued it the following year by awarding the company a $5.8 billion contract for 1,700 TFX (later called F-111) planes at a cost of $3.4 million each. By the late 1960s the cost of the F-111s had tripled, and the planes could do everything, it seemed, but fly. The problem was that the wings fell off—a frequent occurrence, even in ground tests. Three of the first six used in Vietnam crashed within a few weeks, and the remainder had to be grounded. In May, 1968, Senator Russell told the Air Force Chief of Staff that he hoped the Russians might capture one and "fabricate some of them as near ours as they could. . . . It would put their Air Force out of business." General Dynamics was, however, the nation's Number One defense contractor; consequently, Presidents and aspirants for White House power blotted such subversive notions out of their consciousness. Richard Nixon promised during his 1968 campaign that, in his administration, the F-111 would become "one of the foundations of our air supremacy." By 1973, after dozens of F-111s had crashed, many under mysterious circumstances, the government was still purchasing them—at $15 million each.

In these vintage years of the military-industrial complex, the "war on poverty" became little more than a cruel joke. From 1965 to 1973 the Community Action Program of OEO received a total of $2.8 billion in federal funds, the equivalent of one month's spending on the Vietnam War. In 1968 three out of four Americans who lived below the poverty level received no help from federal public assistance programs of any kind. Moreover, few of those who did receive public assistance were enabled to live in decency. Most states administering federal welfare funds simply did not disburse the minimal amount necessary for subsistence either by their own standards or by those of the federal government. Florida, for example, paid welfare recipients 28 per cent of its own minimal subsistence standard; South Carolina, 32 per cent; Alabama, 41 per cent; Mississippi, 47 per cent.

Government food programs were especially tight-fisted. Senator Robert Kennedy observed that in 1967 only 18 per cent of the nation's poor were receiving assistance under the federal government's commodity-distribution or food-stamp programs, while the school lunch program helped only a third of the children of the poor. U.S. food programs actually reached 1.4 million fewer people in 1967 than they had reached six years before. More than 300 of the poorest counties in the nation had no food assistance program of any kind. Furthermore, like the welfare system, the federal government's food-distribution system fell far short of its own subsistence standards. Although the Department of Agriculture recommended that a family of four consume 308 pounds of food a month (excluding milk and eggs) to maintain an adequate diet, it distributed only 94 pounds a month under the commodity-surplus program to a family of that size. The USDA recommended 50 pounds of meat, poultry, or fish a month for a family of four and distributed less than eight pounds. It recommended 176 pounds of fruit and vegetables a month for a family of four—and distributed less than five pounds. Studies conducted in the spring of 1967 in Mississippi comparing participants in the federal food programs to nonparticipants of similar income level found that the dietary situation was much the same for either group: both had seriously deficient intakes of nutrients.

The result of such government neglect was widespread starvation, with its concomitants of misery and disease. Hunger and malnutrition, observed the prestigious Citizens' Board of Inquiry in 1968, plagued between one-third and one-half of the nation's poor—more than 14 million Americans. Reporting on the findings of the Citizens' Board, Senator Kennedy declared that "in the wealthiest nation in the history of the world, millions of men, women, and children are slowly starving." Among groups in every part of the nation—from the black cotton choppers of the Mississippi Delta, to the white unemployed of eastern Kentucky, to the migrant workers of California, to the Indians of the Southwest—were "the swollen bellies, the crippled bodies, the vacant stares of hopelessness. . . . Babies die in infancy, because their mothers cannot nurse them, and cannot buy the milk to keep them alive . . . children are anemic and listless, their physical growth stunted because they lack adequate protein . . . scurvy and rickets . . . cripple American children who never drink citrus juice, and who rarely drink milk . . . children in large numbers suffer from hookworms and roundworms, parasitic infections that drain what strength these children have . . . countless old people in America exist almost entirely on liquids, because they cannot buy or find a decent meal." Medical studies, government surveys, and sociological samples all had similar findings: startlingly widespread hunger, disease, despair.

Mass immiserization also persisted in the underdeveloped nations. Despite the promises of the Alliance for Progress, economic growth in Latin America remained negligible, land reform reached a stalemate, and the housing situation grew ever more desperate. According to the U.N. Economic Commission for Latin America, the per capita income of two-thirds of that continent's agricultural population in 1968 averaged less than $90. A 1968 report by the Inter-American Committee on the Alliance for Progress contended that "unless more far-reaching action is taken, additional deterioration of the distribution of income may be expected." The situation was much the same in Asia, another area of intense U.S. involvement. In 1968 per capita income in India stood at $71; in the United States it was $3,552. Surveying Asia that year, sociologist Gunnar Myrdal concluded: "The extent of inequality has either remained constant over the past decade . . . or has increased." Africa, too, remained characterized by poverty, disease, and illiteracy. Even in booming South Africa, the vast majority of the people endured lives of deprivation and slum squalor. In 1968 the per capita income for South Africa's blacks—70 per cent of the population—stood at less than $118.

Yet, despite the impoverishment of the Third World, American corporations found it a rich source of profit. Although underdeveloped nations accounted for only about 28 per cent of the overseas investments of American business, by the late 1960s they provided almost half of the overseas profits. A prime contributor to this pattern was the U.S. oil industry, with its spectacular growth in foreign operations. Between 1940 and 1967 the number of barrels of Middle East oil reserves controlled by U.S. firms leaped from 0.6 billion to 146 billion. American banks also rapidly expanded their foreign activities, assuming the role in international credit and investment·once played by British financial institutions. Between 1950 and 1967 the number of U.S. bank branches outside the United States climbed from 95 to 298. Fewer than one-fifth of these branches operated in Europe; almost half were located in Latin America. U.S. companies there accounted for about 75 per cent of all foreign private investment, repatriating more than $7 billion in profits between 1961 and 1968. South Africa, with its authoritarian government, its rich resources, and its vast pool of cheap, exploited labor, provided an especially attractive investment opportunity. The return on the book value of U.S. investments there reached 17 per cent in 1969— with the exception of foreign oilfields, the highest profits on American capital abroad. As of that year, 300 American corporations had invested more than $834 million in South Africa (about double the total of 1963), producing sizable quantities of the goods consumed by the wealthy white minority. Deputy Secretary of State George Ball told the New York Chamber of Commerce in 1967 that there were "few things more hopeful for the future than the growing determination of American business to regard national boundaries as no longer fixing the horizons of their corporate activity."

Alongside the outward flow of private capital moved the steady flow of American foreign aid, utilized primarily to maintain the stability of

Washington's client governments. Among the nations aided in the years from 1946 to 1968 were a bumper crop of dictatorships, including South Korea ($7.5 billion), South Vietnam ($5.6 billion), Turkey ($5.4 billion), Nationalist China ($5.1 billion), Greece ($3.8 billion), Brazil ($3.8 billion), Iran ($2.2 billion), and Spain ($2.1 billion). The Administration's rapport with such regimes seemed unshakable. After the 1967 military coup in Greece, the U.S. government announced an embargo on military assistance to the junta, but U.S. arms aid in fact reached $168 million between 1967 and 1970. By the late 1960s Portugal was employing close to 150,000 troops armed with American military equipment to suppress independence struggles in three African colonies, but U.S. military assistance, totalling $349 million by 1968, continued. The exact total of U.S. military aid to its "free world" allies remains unknown, since some of it was channeled through the Export-Import Bank, the Food for Peace Program, and the CIA. Nevertheless, between 1946 and 1968 the Military Assistance Program and the Foreign Military Sales Program alone provided other nations with more than $50 billion in U.S. military aid, mostly in the form of direct grants. This included the training of 287,221 foreign military personnel—almost four-fifths of them from Third World nations.

By the late 1960s the foreign aid program had begun to encounter stiff opposition in the United States. Disgusted by U.S. support of military dictatorships in Latin America, many liberals contended that the government should withdraw from the Southern continent and let social revolution take its course. This was the position of Senate Foreign Relations Committee Chairman Fulbright and Latin American Subcommittee Chairman Frank Church. Even Teodoro Moscoso, the first director of the Alliance for Progress, condemned U.S. policy in Latin America and recommended the abolition of the bilateral aid program. The Administration's use of military aid particularly irked Congress. Senator Vance Hartke suggested sarcastically that it was perfectly all right to supply tanks to Jordan, although Jordan had pledged to attack Israel, since "we also supplied the airplanes for Israel, with which they could knock out the tanks." In 1967 and 1968 Congressional unease produced a number of legislative provisions restricting credit sales of U.S. military equipment to underdeveloped nations and a sharp slash in foreign aid to less than $2 billion—the lowest level in the program's history.

The tenuous relationship of such aid to a Soviet threat was illustrated by Washington's growing rapprochement with Moscow. Johnson was quite willing to use American power to fight limited wars in Asia, Africa, and Latin America, but he had no taste for a thermonuclear clash with the Soviet Union or for a setback to the prospects for East-

West trade. Consequently, ignoring the new curbs on intellectual freedom in the Soviet Union sponsored by the Kosygin-Brezhnev leadership, Johnson continued to encourage a Russian-American détente. From June 23 to 25, 1967, Kosygin and Johnson met in Glassboro, New Jersey, for discussions on international issues. Although the meeting failed to produce any major agreements, it did further goodwill between the leaders of the two nations. The following year the United States and Russia agreed on a nuclear nonproliferation treaty, pledging nuclear powers not to provide atomic weapons to nonnuclear powers and pledging nonnuclear powers not to seek to acquire them. Johnson called the pact "the most important international agreement in the field of disarmament since the nuclear age began." Yet, like the test ban treaty, it did not actually provide for disarmament but only for the maintenance by the major powers of their nuclear monopoly.

Quick Senate ratification became impracticable after August 20, 1968, when Soviet and Warsaw Pact troops invaded Czechoslovakia. Determined to stamp out the emerging climate of intellectual and political freedom promoted by the reform government of Alexander Dubcek, Soviet officials, as was their wont, justified their actions with a burst of anticapitalist rhetoric. In fact, however, the Russian invasion remarkably paralleled the American occupation of the Dominican Republic three years before. In each case, the dominant power in the region had been frightened by the appearance of a form of libertarian socialism—from the standpoint of either, a highly subversive combination. Embarrassed by the Soviet action, but hardly willing to oppose it, Congress held up ratification of the nonproliferation treaty until the following March.

The emergence of a warm relationship between Washington and Moscow did not lessen the extent of America's overseas military and political involvement. Quite the contrary. By 1968 the United States maintained more than a million fighting men in foreign lands (half of them waging an undeclared war), 33,000 aircraft in bases on every continent, tens of thousands of military personnel aboard warships on the high seas, military advisory teams in thirty-eight countries, CIA operations in perhaps sixty nations, and approximately 2,300 military bases around the globe. The United States was then arming or subsidizing about 2 million foreign troops (largely under the command of military dictatorships) and was supplying some form of assistance, mostly military, to seventy-six countries. A member of five regional defense alliances, the United States was also a signatory of forty-two bilateral defense pacts. Through the Voice of America, the U.S. Information Agency transmitted 845 hours a week of radio broadcasting in thirty-eight languages. In addition, its taped radio programs and scripts were aired for 15,000 hours a week by more than 5,000 stations throughout the world, and its television programs, usually not identified as of USIA origin, were broadcast in ninety-seven countries. Professor Henry Steele Commager wrote in 1967: "We are today the leading imperial power in the world, the leading military power, the leading interventionist power, with commitments even more extensive than our engagements."

And America's engagement in Southeast Asia had become extensive indeed. The number of U.S. combat troops in South Vietnam climbed to 485,000 in 1967 and to 535,000 by 1968. Together with almost a million "allied" soldiers, they killed vast numbers of "enemies," razed villages, and drove the peasantry off the land. The air war over North Vietnam, like the war in the South, steadily escalated in ferocity. "The solution in Vietnam," explained Brigadier General William DePuy, "is more bombs, more shells, more napalm . . . till the other side cracks and gives up." By October, 1968, U.S. forces had dropped almost 3 million tons of bombs on North and South Vietnam—nearly 50 per cent more than they had dropped in both the European and Asian theaters during World War II. Returning from a White House conference in 1967, Assistant Secretary of Defense John McNaughton remarked: "We seem to be proceeding on the assumption that the way to eradicate the Vietcong is to destroy all the village structures, defoliate all the jungles, and then cover the entire surface of South Vietnam with asphalt."

These policies resulted in the ruin and depopulation of large areas of South Vietnam and in massive human suffering in the North. An Associated Press dispatch of January 15, 1967, described a typical scene in the South after "liberation" by the Americans: "Burning homes, crying children, frightened women, devastated fields, long lines of slowly moving refugees." Reuters noted that same day that, upon arrival in miserable refugee camps, "a few of the peasants spat in disgust but most were glad to escape the bombs and the defoliation chemicals." A U.S. official commented: "They don't love us but their attitude is improving." Peasants in insurgent-controlled areas of South Vietnam reportedly lived in bunkers and caves to escape the American bombardment of fiery phosphorous bombs and flesh-tearing antipersonnel weapons. At night, clad in dark clothing, they emerged briefly to tend their crops, planted in the American bomb craters that pockmarked their charred fields. By the end of 1968, according to the Senate Judiciary Committee's Subcommittee on Refugees, 725,000 South Vietnamese civilians had been killed or wounded and more than 4 million had been made refugees. Given McNamara's May, 1967, estimate that the air war over the North killed or seriously wounded 1,000 noncombatants a week, it seems probable that the number of serious civilian casualties in North Vietnam from 1965 to 1968 reached 135,000. Yet this grim toll failed to dim the enthusiasm of American officials. "This is our great adventure," Vice-President Humphrey told the U.S. Embassy staff in Saigon, "and a wonderful one it is."

What did give American policy-makers cause for disquiet was the fact that the United States was not winning the war. On the surface, the military statistics were immensely reassuring. According to the Department of Defense, by the end of 1968 there had been more than 435,000 "enemy" deaths in Vietnam, while only 30,000 Americans had died in combat. And yet the war moved on relentlessly. The peasantry continued to show more enthusiasm for the NLF than for the Saigon government, and the North Vietnamese exhibited no signs of fatigue. In December, 1967, a study prepared by the Institute for Defense Analysis contended that the bombing of North Vietnam had had "no measurable effect on Hanoi's ability to mount and support military operations in the South" and had "not discernibly weakened" Hanoi's will to support the Southern insurgency. McNamara and his civilian staff had reached the same conclusion several months earlier: the war was simply not winnable. Testifying before the Senate Armed Services Committee, McNamara said that no conceivable bombing of the North —short of absolute destruction—would satisfactorily interdict the flow of supplies to the South or break Hanoi's will to continue the struggle. Johnson growled to associates: "That military genius, McNamara, has gone dovish on me." In November, 1967, Johnson announced that he had appointed his Defense Secretary to the World Bank. In McNamara's place, Johnson appointed Clark Clifford, a seasoned Cold Warrior whom he considered of more hawkish fiber. National security managers might come and go—always in discreet silence—but the war continued.

American policy-makers exercised their imaginative bent in explaining why the war was essential. In a speech on September 29, 1967, the President declared that "the security—indeed, the survival—of this American nation" was at stake in Vietnam. Asked at a press conference on October 12 about the relationship between the Vietnam War and American survival, Secretary Rusk replied that "within the next decade or two, there will be a billion Chinese on the mainland, armed with nuclear weapons." The very next day, Vice-President Humphrey echoed this new interpretation of events. The United States was fighting in Vietnam, said Humphrey, to defeat "militant aggressive Asian Communism, with its headquarters in Peking, China." Somewhat bewildered, reporters inquired of the Secretary of State how the Vietnam War represented Chinese aggression without the presence of any Chinese. Even Chinese aid to North Vietnam lagged far behind that of Russia. Rusk replied: "The Chinese are willing to fight to the last Vietnamese." This was not, of course, the policy of U.S. officials—or so they said. "The bombing of the North has been the most accurate and the most restrained in modern warfare," McGeorge Bundy assured the readers of *Foreign Affairs*. Although the United States had "no enduring taste for imperialism," it was indisputable that "the stock of American experience, understanding, sympathy, and simple knowledge is now much the most impressive in the world."

Yet, however they packaged the war, U.S. policy-makers had difficulty selling it to the American people. In April, 1967, an estimated 125,000 peace demonstrators in New York City surged through the driving rain to the United Nations. Another massive demonstration that day engulfed San Francisco. Speaking out sharply against the war, Martin Luther King declared:

> This madness must cease. . . . I speak as a child of God and brother to the suffering poor of Vietnam. I speak for those whose land is being laid waste, whose homes are being destroyed, whose culture is being subverted. I speak for the poor of America who are paying the double price of smashed hopes at home and death and corruption in Vietnam. I speak as a citizen of the world, for the world stands aghast at the path we have taken. I speak as an American to the leaders of my own nation. The great initiative in this war is ours. The initiative to stop it must be ours.

In October 75,000 demonstrators marched on the Pentagon, with thousands blocking its entrances in a massive act of civil disobedience. "From Protest to Resistance" ran the slogan of the nonviolent invaders, many of whom were beaten, clubbed, and arrested. "It may be that . . . America will succumb to becoming a traditional empire and will reign for a time over what must surely be a moral if not a physical wasteland," wrote Senator Fulbright that year. "But . . . I would bet on" those who believe that "the price of empire is America's soul and that price is too high."

Many thousands of Americans took part in acts of resistance to the draft. At the April, 1967, demonstration in New York, 175 protestors, including at least one uniformed Green Beret, publicly burned their draft cards. Some met afterward to develop a mutual support organization. Together with a group of West Coast activists organized by David Harris, they formed the Resistance—a band of young men pledged to openly resist service in the nation's armed forces. Soon the Resistance was operating all across the country, sponsoring the return of thousands of draft cards to the Justice Department and descending *en masse* upon local induction centers for protests and demonstrations. Women and older men, exempt from military service, organized Resist, circulating the illegal "Call to Resist Illegitimate Authority," soon signed by thousands. In the midst of an enormously unpopular war, draft resistance flourished as never before in American history. Thousands went to jail and tens of thousands of others chose exile in Canada or Western Europe. Draft cases crowded court calendars throughout the nation. In Minneapolis, half of all federal prosecutions were for Selective Service violations. On the campus, resistance to military service was especially fierce. A Harris poll taken in May, 1968, reported that from 20 to 30 per cent of American college students, if drafted, would "seriously contemplate" refusing induction.

Induction centers, military-industrial spokesmen, and Selective Service boards became the targets of the most militant resistance activities. From October 16 to 21, 1967, antiwar groups sponsored Stop the Draft Week, featuring demonstrations at induction centers from coast to coast. In Oakland, 10,000 demonstrators shut down the induction center and eventually the surrounding area for days, holding sit-ins, blocking intersections, and building street barricades. The appearance of military or paramilitary recruiters on the nation's campuses touched off a flood of protests and sit-ins. Perhaps the bloodiest occurred in the fall of 1967 at the University of Wisconsin, where police intervention during a sit-in protesting the presence of recruiters from Dow Chemical left sixty students and eighteen riot police injured. Raids on draft board files became increasingly popular after 1967, when they were begun by radical Catholics. On October 27 Father Philip Berrigan, the Reverend James Mengel, Thomas Lewis, and David Eberhardt entered the Baltimore Customs House, poured blood upon Selective Service records, and waited patiently to be arrested. The following May Berrigan and Lewis were joined by Father Daniel Berrigan and six others in destroying draft files at Catonsville, Maryland with napalm they had brewed from directions in the U.S. Special Forces Handbook. "Our apologies, good friends," said Daniel Berrigan, "for the fracture of good order, the burning of paper instead of children."

Overt opposition to the war even emerged within the armed forces. In July, 1966, a group of Army privates, the Fort Hood Three, achieved national prominence by rejecting service in Vietnam. Refusing to board a troop plane to Vietnam, a black private was awarded eleven years at hard labor. In 1967 Captain Howard Levy, head of the dermatology clinic at Fort Jackson, South Carolina, refused to train Green Berets, calling them "murderers and liars and thieves." An Army lieutenant picketed the White House in early 1968 with an antiwar poster.

Two black Marines received stiff prison terms for antiwar agitation. On July 15, 1968, nine AWOL servicemen took sanctuary in a San Francisco church, proclaiming their opposition to the war. That October hundreds of active-duty soldiers publicly paraded in antiwar demonstrations. As overt participation in antiwar activities usually resulted in court-martial and imprisonment, many soldiers opted instead for quiet desertion. The number of desertions from the U.S. Army reached 40,000 in 1968 and jumped to 53,000 the following year. Many members of the armed forces felt the same sense of malaise as their civilian peers. Writing to Senator Fulbright, an American soldier in Vietnam asked: "Whatever has become of our dream? Where is that America that opposed tyrannies at every turn? . . . How . . . have we come to be killing so many in such a dubious cause?"

The Administration's Congressional and popular support was dwindling rapidly. Although Congress continued to vote appropriations for the war, legislative critics—particularly in the liberal wing of the Democratic Party—grew increasingly outspoken. Senator Eugene McCarthy called the President a "wild man." Senator Albert Gore referred to him as "desperate." In February, 1968, Senator Robert Kennedy testified that "even America cannot act as if no other nation existed, flaunting our power and wealth against the judgment and desires of neutrals and allies alike." When Secretary Rusk—who had refused on three occasions to testify before the Senate Foreign Relations Committee—deigned to appear in 1968, a sharp exchange of opinions ensued, publicizing the deepening divisions between the White House and Capitol Hill. After years of lies and deceptions, even the press was growing surly. James Deakin, Washington correspondent for the *St. Louis Post-Dispatch,* reported in August, 1967, that "the relationship between the President and the Washington press corps has settled into a pattern of chronic disbelief." Polls found sizable sectors of the public either more dovish or more hawkish than the President, with both groups condemning his war policy. In late 1967 a Harris poll reported that only 23 per cent of the American people thought the President was doing a good job. Three years after his smashing victory at the polls, Johnson had become one of the most unpopular Presidents in American history.

Beset by an unprecedented array of opposition, the Administration groped uncertainly for a way to resurrect its authority. At times, U.S. policy-makers tried to ignore their critics. Dean Rusk told a press conference in late 1967 that he could discern "no significant body of American opinion which would have us withdraw from Vietnam." An article by General Maxwell Taylor, appearing at the time of the Pentagon march, assailed "the illusion that the United States is deeply divided over Vietnam." At other times, the Administration sought to mobilize patriotism in its behalf. In April, 1967, Johnson brought General William C. Westmoreland back to the United States for pep talks on the war—one of which suggested that the "enemy" was being aided by antiwar protests. On March 18, 1968, in an address before the National Farmers Union, the President himself charged that, as long as the enemy "feels that he can win something by propaganda in the country—that he can undermine the leadership—that he can bring down the government—that he can get something in the Capitol that he can't get from our men out there—he is going to keep on trying." The time had come, he said, "when we ought to unite, when we ought to stand up and be counted." The Administration also began a campaign of direct repression. In 1968 the Justice Department initiated the prosecution of a group of antiwar leaders—Benjamin Spock, pediatrician; William Sloane Coffin, Jr., Yale chaplain; Mitchell Goodman, author; Marcus Raskin, co-director of the Institute for Policy Studies; and Michael Ferber, Harvard graduate student—for conspiracy to obstruct the Selective Service system.

In his efforts to contain domestic dissent, the President enjoyed the close cooperation of U.S. "intelligence" agencies. Meeting with CIA director Richard Helms in 1967, Johnson ordered him to gather evidence on foreign influence in the protest movement. In response, the CIA launched Operation Chaos, monitoring the overseas movements of American dissidents, burglarizing their rooms, eavesdropping on their conversations, and soliciting information from college administrators. Although the CIA never discovered any foreign influence, it did manage (in violation of its charter) to spy upon all black militant groups, radical youth organizations, underground newspapers, and draft resistance groups in the country; to infiltrate organizations ranging from the Washington Ethical Union to the War Resisters League; to give local police departments on-the-spot training in lock picking, surreptitious entry, and detonating explosives; and to continue opening and copying 10,000 letters a year mailed by or addressed to American citizens. CIA activities, of course, could hardly compete with those of the FBI, which Johnson had ordered to secure damaging information on the peace movement and the New Left. The FBI added thousands of new espionage operations to its already crowded schedule. This included monitoring Senate Foreign Relations Committee hearings to compare legislators' statements with the "Communist Party line." It stepped up its Cointelpro program, a campaign designed to harass and disrupt groups which J. Edgar Hoover considered subversive. In its Cointelpro attack upon Martin Luther King's Southern Christian Leadership Conference (classified as a "black hate" organization), the FBI launched fraudulent rumors, sparked an Internal Revenue Service audit of SCLC's taxes, intervened with foundations to cut off SCLC's funding, and took steps to discourage publishers from printing King's articles and books.

But Johnson's decision to proceed with the war assured him of tumultuous opposition, not only among college students and intellectuals, but also among the desperate underclass in America's urban ghettos. Condemned too long to lives of poverty and discrimination, they revolted during the summer of 1967 in a spectacular series of urban upheavals. In Detroit, in the most serious of that year's 164 racial outbreaks, 43 persons were killed, 7,200 were arrested, and $45 million worth of property was destroyed. The typical rioter was a young black male, angry, defiant, and sharply alienated from American politics and society. Asked if the country was "worth fighting for in the event of a major war," 53 per cent of a sampling of Newark rioters answered negatively; even among non-rioters in that slum-ridden city, the negative response was 28 per cent. Despite their racial content, the ghetto upheavals did not usually involve attacks upon white persons but were largely confined to symbols of white authority in black neighborhoods, usually stores and tenements. Police and National Guardsmen, sent into the ghettos as occupation forces, thus exacerbated the level of personal violence, particularly by their trigger-happy behavior. The "overwhelming majority" of those killed and injured were black, noted the National Advisory Commission on Civil Disorders (the Kerner Commission). According to the commission, the riots did not result from a conspiracy, and there was "no evidence" that the incidents precipitating the disorders had been planned by any group. The underlying cause, stated the commission, was the "white racism" that had fostered an "explosive mixture" of poverty, unemployment, slum housing, poor education, and police brutality in the nation's cities during the postwar years. And the situation was deteriorating. "Our nation is moving toward two societies," warned the commission, "one black, one white—separate and unequal."

Despite their immense destructiveness, the 1967 ghetto upheavals stimulated little positive action. Calling for an end to "the destruction and the violence, not only in the streets of the ghetto, but in the lives of people," the Kerner Commission recommended "massive" federal programs: the creation of 2 million new jobs, half in the public sector; the construction of 6 million units of low- and middle-income housing; an attack on *de facto* school segregation; and the creation of a "national system of income supplementation." The President, however, coolly ignored the recommendations of his commission, remarking:

"They always print that we don't do enough." HUAC launched an investigation of subversion, while local police departments began equipping themselves with automatic rifles, machine guns, and tanks. Everywhere the racial backlash seemed to be growing. In Boston Louise Day Hicks, who attained popularity for her staunch opposition to public school integration and busing, was narrowly defeated in her 1967 race for mayor. In overwhelmingly Democratic Cleveland a black candidate, Carl Stokes, won the city's Democratic mayoral primary in 1967, only to find himself deserted by 80 per cent of the white voters in the election, which he won by the slimmest of margins. In New York a series of citywide teachers' strikes, begun in 1967, created unprecedented racial animosities. Many whites, convinced by the Administration's civil rights and "war on poverty" rhetoric that the government was engaged in massive projects to assist slum-dwelling blacks, found the ghetto upheavals incomprehensible. To blacks, on the other hand, the situation had become surrealistic. Testifying before the Kerner Commission, psychologist Kenneth B. Clark referred wearily to the host of earlier government reports on ghetto disorders, adding: "It is a kind of Alice in Wonderland—with the same moving picture re-shown over and over again, the same analysis, the same recommendations, and the same inaction."

The wild ghetto upheavals of 1967 drove black radicals to ever more extreme positions. Meeting after the Newark riot, a conference of militants called for black separatism and an armed black militia. As police and National Guardsmen battled slum dwellers in the midst of America's flaming cities, Stokely Carmichael appeared in Cuba, talking of worldwide guerrilla war. H. Rap Brown, SNCC's new chairman, termed the riots a "dress rehearsal for revolution." Violence, he said, was "as American as cherry pie." Although the once-powerful civil rights group took no direct part in the summer's disorders, its spokesmen actively applauded each new incident, urging blacks to "get you some guns." But the tide of change had already left SNCC behind—trapped between a hostile government and a frenzied, but unorganizable, ghetto constituency. SNCC's increasingly militant rhetoric, like that of other mushrooming but short-lived militant groups, was thus designed, at least in part, to compensate for its political ineffectiveness.

Unable to halt the war or to assist the burning ghettos, white activists felt a terrible sense of frustration. Andrew Kopkind wrote in 1967: "To be white and a radical in America this summer is to see horror and feel impotence." Reporting on the Newark riots, Tom Hayden of SDS contended that urban guerrilla warfare had become a serious option in America. But there seemed little possibility of linking the efforts of sympathetic whites with those of blacks, particularly insofar as most black militants scorned all moves toward alliance. Checked in their own attempts to alter the social structure, many black radicals tended to strike out at the easiest targets, the ones least likely to fight back. That fall the National Conference for New Politics brought together representatives of 200 dissident organizations for a meeting in Chicago on a third-party movement, but the gathering quickly collapsed under the strain of racial divisions. Taking control of the meeting, black militants demanded passage of a series of crippling resolutions. When guilt-ridden whites voted them through, they found themselves still further denounced, and a third-party effort was rejected. Following this fiasco, some white activists moved on to organize the Peace and Freedom Party, a loose alliance of white radicals and Black Panthers then emerging in California. Others forswore third party efforts entirely. "If that's the New Politics," said one participant at the Chicago conference, "then I think I'll give the Old Politics another try."

Some were already at work in these unlikely vineyards. Allard Lowenstein, a former student leader who retained close ties with young activists, crisscrossed the nation in 1967, desperately seeking a major party politician who would contest Lyndon Johnson's renomination. "I must have spoken to twenty Senators or Congressmen," he later observed. "Some thought I was a kook. Some of them listened. No one defended Lyndon Johnson or the war. I told them we had the strength," that "there was a base in the student movement. But no major figure would take the lead." Robert Kennedy turned him down. George McGovern turned him down. Eugene McCarthy assured him that someone should oppose Johnson, but sent him elsewhere. In October Lowenstein returned to McCarthy, again extolling the potentialities of a movement with a base among the nation's 7 million college students. Suddenly the Senator asked: "How do you think we'd do in a Wisconsin primary?" After months of fruitless conversations, the breakthrough had arrived. "I was ecstatic," Lowenstein recalled. "It was like music . . . welling up in my ears." McCarthy announced his candidacy for the Democratic Presidential nomination on November 30. "There comes a time," he said, "when an honorable man simply has to raise the flag."

Thus began one of the strangest political campaigns in American history. McCarthy was a rather unlikely peace candidate, having always been a somewhat lackadaisical liberal, willing to follow the lead of the oil interests on the Senate Finance Committee. He also appeared bereft of the normal politician's fire and driving lust for office, perpetually ready to trade politics for poetry. After hearing McCarthy speak at a liberal Democratic conference in late 1967, I. F. Stone remarked: "He has wit, charm and grace. But he seems to lack heart and guts. . . . McCarthy gives one the uneasy feeling that he doesn't really give a damn." Indeed, asked if he thought he would win the Presidency, the Senator responded: "Who would want the job?" Furthermore, with the exception of small numbers of liberal Democrats scattered here and there, McCarthy's only organized support lay with student activists. Dedicated and hard-working, they nonetheless appeared atypical of most American voters. Entering his first primary, McCarthy meandered through the small towns of New Hampshire, campaigning in the cool, leisurely manner that became his style. Both the press and the public seemed overwhelmingly indifferent to this "Children's Crusade," and Johnson strategists predicted that McCarthy would be lucky to draw 5 per cent of the vote. Journalist Theodore White recalled that the Senator "wandered through the snows of upper New Hampshire like a solitary troubadour, an Irish bard, singing his sad lay to the unhearing White Mountains." It was the last dreamy lull before—in White's words —"American politics became unhinged."

The first blow came in Vietnam. On January 31, 1968, the beginning of Tet, the Vietnamese Lunar New Year, the NLF launched a surprise offensive against thirty-six of the forty-two provincial capitals and five of the six largest cities in South Vietnam. Fierce fighting erupted in Saigon, even inside the American Embassy. Communist forces captured Hué and held it for almost a month before it was retaken by the Americans. At Ben Tre, a town of 35,000, NLF troops were driven out only after U.S. artillery and air strikes had leveled at least half the buildings. "It became necessary to destroy the town to save it," explained an American major. In the countryside, the "pacification" program collapsed as Saigon officials fled to government-controlled areas. Although President Johnson told a press conference that the Tet offensive had been "a complete failure," he was, in fact, stunned by the events. General Westmoreland maintained that the United States had "never been in a better relative position" and asked for 206,000 more American troops. Official optimism could no longer be taken seriously. The American press pictured the offensive as such a disaster for the United States that Rusk snapped at reporters: "Whose side are you on?" Robert Kennedy told a Chicago audience that the Tet offensive had "shattered the mask of official illusion with which we have concealed our true circumstances, even from ourselves."

Events in New Hampshire turned the Administration's defeat into a rout. As the primary date approached, more than 10,000 students from more than a hundred campuses scoured the state's towns and countryside for McCarthy. Tireless, committed, enthusiastic, they were clearly having an impact on the electorate. In addition, after the Tet offensive more Americans were taking a peace campaign seriously. In January a Gallup poll predicted that McCarthy would draw 12 per cent of the vote. In February, President Johnson's private poll assessed McCarthy's strength at 18 per cent. By the first week of March, Governor King—a Johnson loyalist—was predicting 25 to 28 per cent. On primary day, March 12, McCarthy shocked political experts by garnering 42.4 per cent of the Democratic vote to the President's 49.5 per cent. Moreover, when the thousands of McCarthy write-ins on the Republican side were counted, the mystic Senator from Minnesota trailed the President of the United States by only 230 votes in one of the most patriotic and hawkish states in the nation. Someone reported to McCarthy that three dead men had been voted in a Manchester ward. "They were ours," he replied blissfully. "It was the Resurrection."

Four days later, Robert Kennedy entered the Democratic Presidential race. Strongly influenced by the upheavals of the 1960s, Kennedy had grown ever more restive with the Old Politics and its priorities. In contrast to his brother's claim that "America must be first" in the space race, he declared that it was "more important to be able to walk through the ghetto than to walk on the moon." Johnson's conduct of the Vietnam War had dismayed him, as had the President's rejection of the Kerner Commission report. Increasingly viewing himself as a spokesman for the poor, the black, and the young, Kennedy had been tempted to contest Johnson's renomination in 1968. Yet he held back, deterred by advice from political experts and party bosses that an incumbent President could not be defeated. When the Tet offensive and the New Hampshire primary exposed Johnson's political vulnerability, however, Kennedy came out swinging. "Our country is in danger," he told a Kansas student audience on March 19, "not just from foreign enemies but above all from our own misguided policies." The Administration's Vietnam policy was "bankrupt. . . . At the end of it all there will be only more Americans killed" and "more thousands of Vietnamese slaughtered." Kennedy denounced the President for "calling upon the darker impulses of the American spirit."

McCarthy did not, as some had expected, withdraw from the Presidential race when Kennedy entered it. Instead, he continued his laconic campaign, still fervently supported by his student volunteers. In late March, reports from Wisconsin on the approaching April 2 primary— which Kennedy chose not to contest—indicated that the President's political fortunes were approaching disaster. Johnson's state headquarters was a virtually deserted tomb. "We sent a man into Dane County to recruit for Johnson," said the director, "and all we've heard from

him since is a few faint beeps, like the last radio signals from the . . .
Bay of Pigs." Meanwhile, eight thousand McCarthy student volunteers
surged across the state. The Sunday before the primary, McCarthy
headquarters turned back busloads who could no longer be used.
Gradually, ineluctably, the political vise was tightening on Washington's
once-confident decision-makers. "If there is one central theme to my
campaign," McCarthy stated in Milwaukee, "it is . . . to restore that
mastery and power over individual life and social enterprise which has
been so seriously eroded . . . by the misuse of central power." April
2 produced a landslide. Lyndon Johnson, who had received 62.1 per
cent of Wisconsin's votes in the 1964 election, drew but 34.6 per cent
of the 1968 Democratic primary vote. McCarthy piled up 56.2 per cent.
The President had suffered another stunning political defeat. Indeed,
on March 31, he had already announced his retirement from the field.

Throughout the month of March, the pressures had mounted on
Johnson to revise his Vietnam policy. The revelation of Westmoreland's request for 206,000 more troops on March 10 set off a bitter
controversy. On March 12 McCarthy humiliated the President in the
New Hampshire primary. On March 16 Kennedy entered the Presidential race. On March 18, 139 members of the House of Representatives sponsored a resolution calling for immediate Congressional review
of U.S. policy in Southeast Asia. Reports from Wisconsin predicted
certain disaster in that state's primary. Moreover, when Johnson ordered
Secretary of Defense Clark Clifford to chair a task force on the troop
request, Clifford's civilian subordinates in the Pentagon hierarchy
pressed hard for alternatives. The war, they claimed, was unwinnable;
therefore, the United States should limit the air war in the North and
confine itself to a strategy of defending populated areas in the South in
order to "buy the time" for the South Vietnamese Army and government to "develop effective capability." The report of Clifford's task force
reflected their thinking only partially, but enough to irk Johnson at what
he considered an unwarranted "sense of pessimism." In response, the
President met on March 26 with the highest echelon of the nation's
postwar foreign policy establishment: Acheson, Ball, Bundy, Arthur
Dean, Dillon, Lodge, McCloy, Matthew Ridgway, Cyrus Vance, and
others. Some—like General Taylor and Supreme Court Justice Abe
Fortas—urged further escalation, but most favored reduction in the
level of the war. As all those present (with the exception of Ball and
Arthur Goldberg) were well-known hawks and had approved the escalation of the air war the preceding fall, their turnabout reportedly left
Johnson "deeply shaken." On the night of March 31 he went on television to announce a cutback of the bombing of North Vietnam to the

20th Parallel and his withdrawal from the Presidential race.

Johnson's speech of March 31 was designed less to move toward a settlement in Vietnam than to pacify his domestic critics. The revolt of the Administration's top advisers, as Townsend Hoopes, a high-ranking Pentagon official, observed, "did not really change President Johnson's mind about the Vietnam War." Indeed, on March 28, when Clifford and other advisers met with the President to review his address, they found it still another ringing, militant harangue in defense of the Administration's war policy and against his critics. Clifford now argued with the President for a "peace" speech, to include a limitation on the bombing. His key point, he later noted, was that "major elements of the national constituency . . . have turned against this war." Eventually, Johnson agreed to change his speech, but not his objective: a non-Communist South Vietnam. As Max Frankel of the *New York Times* wrote in a dispatch from Austin, Texas, the March 31 address was intended "primarily" to "buy time at home and to keep waging the war's military and diplomatic battles abroad." Johnson had little expectation that Hanoi would respond favorably to the American initiative. Nevertheless, contrary to expectation, Hanoi responded affirmatively, offering to begin negotiations. Taken aback, Johnson delayed the opening of negotiations more than a month by refusing to accept a reasonable site. Even after they began in Paris that May, he accelerated the war elsewhere in Indochina. "Search and destroy" missions increased, and American planes, diverted from their bombardment of the North, now intensified the bombing of South Vietnam and Laos. American opinion was to be soothed by making the war less visible, but no less destructive of human life. Johnson told Clifford that his primary goal was to leave his successor with "the best possible military posture in Vietnam." What would later be called "Vietnamization" had begun.

However modest the alterations in Johnson's war policy, his withdrawal from the Presidential race left the Democratic nomination wide open. On the night of March 31, as television correspondents clamored outside McCarthy's door for appearances, the Senator suggested that they "read a little poetry" instead. Later that evening he recited lines from his own verses. As the campaign progressed, McCarthy displayed similar audacity. "America in the period of the 'fifties and 'sixties," he declared, "built up for itself a mission in which we were able to . . . judge the political systems of other nations . . . accepting . . . the right to interfere . . . if we found them to be wanting. We spoke with great flourish of making the world safe for diversity, while, in fact, we were denying and even destroying diversity when it failed to meet our specifications." Such statements won the intense admiration of antiwar liberals and some radicals; yet McCarthy failed to develop much rapport with the poor and the blacks. Kennedy, on the other hand, was disdained by many critics of the war for the opportunistic timing of his decision to contest Johnson's renomination, but he drew the allegiance of both the white and the black poor. The two men held similar political views, but a combination of personal antagonism (largely McCarthy's) and political ambition (largely Kennedy's) led them into a series of grueling primary battles. That spring, drawing upon his strength among black and "ethnic" voters, Kennedy defeated McCarthy in the Indiana and Nebraska primaries, while McCarthy bested Kennedy in Oregon— the very model of a middle-class progressive state. From the standpoint of the forces of change, the only cloud on the horizon was the April 27 entry of Hubert Humphrey into the Presidential race, with his improbable call for "the politics of joy."

April, 1968, was surely one of the least joyous months in American history, particularly for the partisans of social justice. Seeking to impress the plight of the impoverished upon the national consciousness, Martin Luther King and SCLC had begun earlier that year to organize the Poor People's Campaign—a dramatic march of thousands of the rural and urban poor, both black and white, through the cities and towns of America to Washington, D.C. Here they were to encamp before the center of government authority, mute witness to the massive human suffering that existed in the world's richest and most powerful country. It would be, King said, a "last plea for the nation to respond." Personally, King must also have felt a sense of desperation—scorned by the Administration and its Cold Warrior allies for his opposition to the war and derided by black militants for his commitment to nonviolent resistance. In early April King interrupted his work on the Poor People's Campaign and traveled to Memphis to rally striking black sanitation workers. On the night of April 3 he stated in a public address that his life had been threatened that day, but "I've been to the mountain top, and I don't mind." The thirty-nine-year-old minister concluded with more emotion than usual: "I may not get there with you. But I want you to know that we as a people will get to the Promised Land." The following evening, as he stood on his balcony chatting with friends, he was assassinated.

King's death wrote a formal end to the era of love, justice, and interracial solidarity—already so many shattered dreams and needless deaths away. Riots swept across the nation, plunging Washington, Boston, Detroit, Chicago, Philadelphia, San Francisco, Toledo, Pittsburgh, and more than 100 other cities into flames and bitterness. Army units in full battle gear took up positions on the White House grounds and on the steps of the Capitol, while looting and fires raged two blocks from the executive mansion. The upheaval lasted a week and took 55,000 federal and National Guard troops to quell—the largest military deployment for a civil emergency in modern times. In the midst of this heightening chaos and destruction, King's funeral in Atlanta was unbearably poignant. His recorded comments, broadcast to an interracial gathering of 150,000, provided a striking eulogy. "I want you to say on that day," declared the rich, rolling voice, "that I tried to love and serve humanity. . . . If you're going to say that I was a drum major, say that I was a drum major for justice. Say that I was a drum major for peace." The crowd watched tearfully as the body of the slain civil rights leader was placed in a tomb at Morehouse College, inscribed with the words that had ended his great address in Washington in that time of hope less than five years before: "Free at last, free at last, thank God Almighty I'm free at last."

"There was a sense everywhere, in 1968," wrote Garry Wills, "that things were giving. That man had not merely lost control of his history, but might never regain it." Protest heightened everywhere, while the government girded itself for the siege. In late April the caravans of the Poor People's Campaign reached Washington, with the poor establishing themselves in a miserable plywood shantytown called Resurrection City. Congress and the President ignored them, although a "Solidarity Day" in mid-June brought out 50,000 white and black activists for a demonstration of support. Both Eugene McCarthy and Hubert Humphrey appeared at the rally—the former cheered, and the latter booed. On June 24, the day the Senate voted its approval of the ABM system, the government drove the last of the poor from Resurrection City and arrested the leaders of the Southern Christian Leadership Conference. Campus insurgency quickened. According to the National Student Association, 221 major demonstrations erupted at American colleges and universities during the first half of the year. Unlike student protests of the past, which had usually been designed to dramatize a specific injustice, the latest demonstrations began to acquire an insurrectionary flavor not so very different from the May, 1968, "revolution" in France, which seemed within a hairsbreadth of toppling the government.

The most dramatic of the campus upheavals occurred at Columbia University, long a hotbed of student protest. Situated on New York City's Upper West Side, Columbia had been buying up property ever since World War II, displacing thousands of local residents, mostly poor, and stirring up considerable community hostility. The latest step in the university's institutional expansion, excavation for a gymnasium in an area between Columbia and Harlem, infuriated the Students' Afro-American Society and the campus chapter of SDS. The latter had already engaged in a long series of fruitless wrangles with Columbia's remote and unpopular president, Grayson Kirk, most recently over Columbia's role in the Institute for Defense Analysis—a consortium of universities doing military research for the government. On April 23 a group of SAS and SDS members marched to the gymnasium construction site and tore down a section of fence. Then they returned to the campus and occupied Hamilton Hall, the administrative center of the undergraduate college. After SAS suggested that the whites leave, SDS moved over to the university's administrative center, Low Library. In the following days perhaps a thousand other students occupied buildings on all parts of the campus, hoisting red flags and organizing communal governments. Faculty members, who played little role in governing the university, were divided and ineffectual in the circumstances. Kirk and the trustees were not. In the early morning hours, the university president called in thousands of police, who tore into the sleeping campus rebels with what a federal commission later described as "excessive force and violence." More than 700 people were arrested and 160 were injured, including ten faculty members. For the remainder of the semester, Columbia was in chaos, its classes shut down by a massive student strike, its faculty engaging in endless discussions of university reform, and its student body frenziedly battling police. At commencement exercises, a sizable segment of the graduating class walked out, marched to the sunlit center of the campus, and, amid the fluttering red banners of revolution, held a "counter-commencement" before a cheering throng of thousands.

The fury of the Tet offensive, the startling victories of antiwar candidates, the President's abdication, King's assassination, the urban riots, the campus upheavals—it hardly seemed possible for the nation's politics to be further shaken that spring; yet they were. On June 5, but a few days after Columbia's counter-commencement, Kennedy defeated McCarthy in the California Presidential primary. The euphoric Kennedy now emerged as the front-runner for the Democratic nomination, with only the Administration's pallid candidate, Hubert Humphrey, standing between him and a convention victory. "I am going to chase Hubert Humphrey's ass all over America," he promised friends that night in his Los Angeles hotel headquarters. Then he headed downstairs—to his death. A few moments after delivering his victory statement, he was shot by a Jordanian fanatic; within hours, he was dead. For the insurgent forces in America, it was yet another blow added to the many they had already received. The electoral route to change had suddenly reached a dead end. Although McCarthy went on to win the big New York primary, the race for the nomination was over. Hubert Humphrey—the candidate who had not won a single primary but who had rallied the support of the large state party organizations, the South, and the labor unions—would be the Democratic nominee for President.

All that remained was to fashion the appropriately bizarre spectacle. President Johnson chose Chicago as the Democratic Convention site, much to the delight of Mayor Richard Daley, who wanted to show the world what a fine place the city had become under his administration. By convention time, 11,900 Chicago police had been prepared for twelve-hour duty, with battle plans, bivouacs, command posts, and tactical forces all neatly plotted on charts. Cook County's riot squad was on alert. Five Chicago schoolhouses stood ready to shelter 7,500 members of the Illinois National Guard. A thousand FBI and Secret Service agents had been deployed from Washington. U.S. Army troops across the country had been readied for an emergency airlift. The convention hall itself had become a fortress, enclosed in a mile-square security area surrounded by chain link fences topped with barbed wire. A catwalk 95 feet above the convention floor had been built for Secret Service men and police to patrol the gathering with binoculars, walkie-talkies, and rifles. The extent of the preparations reflected not merely the mayor's curious tastes but his anxiety at the plans of peace activists, particularly followers of the Youth International Party (Yippies), to demonstrate during the convention. The Yippies, a loosely knit group of zany radicals, were hastily improvised by Abbie Hoffman, Jerry Rubin, and Paul Krassner to capture the attention of the mass media and to provoke chaos at the Democratic "Death Convention." Hoffman, like most of his disciples, had once been a serious political activist but by 1968 had given up on "straight" politics, convinced that the politics of the absurd was more effective—or at least more fun. "Confusion is mightier than the sword," he wrote in *Revolution for the Hell of It.* "By allowing all: loving, cheating, anger, violence, stealing . . . you become situation oriented." In the drama then emerging, Mayor Daley and the Yippies made the perfect antagonists. Certainly they deserved each other.

Act One unfolded in a thoroughly predictable, and macabre, fashion. On August 23 the Yippies unveiled their candidate for President, a fat, squealing pig named Pigasus, promptly arrested by the Chicago police. Having denied demonstrators permits to make protest speeches, to go on marches, or to sleep in the parks, Chicago authorities ordered the police to begin their nightly sweeps through Lincoln Park. On the evening of August 25 law enforcement officers chased a thousand campers down the streets of Chicago, clubbing, macing, and tear-gasing protestors, onlookers, and diners-out alike in what a Presidential commission later called a "police riot." Meanwhile, at the convention, delegates became involved in angry clashes with officials over the electronically controlled pass system, the practice of turning off the microphones of dissenting delegates, and the intimidating atmosphere provided by the presence of vast concentrations of police, National Guardsmen, and army troops. On the afternoon of August 28 the convention rejected the peace resolution of the antiwar forces by a three-to-two vote, passing instead a resolution praising the President's handling of the war. The California delegation, in revolt, began singing "We Shall Overcome." New York delegates, joining in the song, stood up on their chairs and pinned black armbands to their sleeves. At 7 P.M. tear gas began wafting through the air-conditioning system of the Hilton Hotel as the streets outside exploded into the most frenzied night of police beatings. Aware of the cameras on the scene, crowds chanted: "The whole world is watching." A phalanx of police rushed a group of women, reporters, and McCarthy workers, smashing them back through a plate glass window of the hotel's bar. Leaping through the clumps of bodies and broken glass, the police attacked everyone in sight, including startled drinkers. The hotel lobby, reeking of tear gas, gradually became filled with the wounded, blood streaming everywhere.

Act Two, beginning that same evening, cemented the alliance of Humphrey, Daley, and Johnson. As the nomination proceedings began, NBC's film of the latest police assault went on the air. The image, noted Theodore White, was striking: "Hubert Humphrey being nominated in a sea of blood." Rising on the convention floor, Allard Lowenstein demanded adjournment; no business should be transacted, he said, while people were being "maced and beaten unconscious." Senator Abraham Ribicoff of Connecticut denounced "Gestapo tactics in the streets of Chicago." In reply, Mayor Daley angrily shook his fist, screaming epithets. With the convention near pandemonium, the delegates of the party machines and the South—outnumbering those elected in the spring primaries by 8 million Kennedy-McCarthy voters—steamrollered through the nomination of Hubert Humphrey. At Humphrey's nod, they gave the Vice-Presidential nomination to Maine Senator Edmund Muskie.

Act Three. Returning for Humphrey's acceptance speech the following night, many delegates were in a bitter mood. Their hotels still reeked of tear gas, mace, and blood. Along the streets stood knots of Daley supporters, rounded up by the mayor's precinct captains, bearing signs saying: "We Love Our Mayor" and "We Love Our Police, Too." The galleries, packed with Daley partisans, rang with cries of "We want Daley, we want Daley." In this context, Humphrey delivered an address that deepened the wounds in Democratic ranks. In deference to Mayor Daley and his fans, the Vice-President declared that Americans "need a state of law and order." Referring to Lyndon Johnson, he proclaimed:

"History will surely record the greatness of his contribution to the people of this land, and tonight to you, Mr. President, I say thank you. Thank you, Mr. President." Antiwar Democrats received nothing at all—except a little surprise from the forces of law and order on the final morning of the convention. At 4:30 A.M. police and National Guardsmen raided the rooms of the astonished McCarthy volunteers, smashing down their doors, clubbing them, and hustling them out of the Hilton Hotel. Only the appearance of the Senator halted the rampage. McCarthy stared down the police, sent his volunteers back to their rooms, and postponed his own departure from Chicago until the last of them was safely evacuated.

The Chicago convention left the Democratic Party a battered wreck. The party's most reactionary forces were already gravitating toward George Wallace and his American Independent Party, now on the ballot in all fifty states. Early in his career, Wallace had been defeated for political office in Alabama by a racist opponent and had vowed that he would never be "out-niggahed" again. He never was. Elected Alabama's governor in 1962 with a promise of "segregation now, segregation tomorrow, segregation forever," he attained national prominence through his attempts to prevent the desegregation of the University of Alabama and to exploit popular fears. Although Wallace showed considerable vote-getting potential in the 1964 Democratic primaries, he decided against a third party race that year to avoid splitting the conservative vote with Goldwater. By 1968, however, he was conducting the most effective third party campaign of modern times, promising to secure "law and order," to shoot looters, to repeal open housing laws, and to win the war in Vietnam. Garry Wills described a typical Wallace rally in that turbulent year:

> "Yew anarchists bettuh have yewuh day now." The crowd puffs, rocks, explodes with a euphoric wrath—happy with dream-visions of revenge on all the rebel children, a cosmic spanking when George takes over. . . . "Wuah they teaching in those colleges, anyway?" His own people cry back: "Communism!" . . . The crowd is . . . itchy with unconfessed lusts; but never, in its own eyes, more beautiful. They are walking vindications of America—as rebellious blacks and hippies are a walking profanation. George understands. . . . "Ah hadn' meant to say this tonight, but *yew*-know, if one of those hippies lays down in front of mah car when *Ah* become President. . . ." They drown out the punch line in happy fulfilled anger.

As his running mate, Wallace chose retired Air Force General Curtis LeMay, who announced at his first press conference that it would be "most efficient" to drop a few nuclear bombs on North Vietnam. Naturally, the chaos at the Democratic National Convention heightened the

Wallace appeal. Up to the summer of 1968, no poll showed him with more than 10 per cent of the vote, but by mid-September the figure had risen to 21 per cent. Some predicted that he might outpoll Humphrey.

For a time, a similar revolt seemed to be brewing on the Left. A decade of heightening agitation for peace and social justice had created a constituency for social change which, in the 1968 elections, simply had nowhere to go. Millions of Americans turned away from the Chicago convention in disgust. Some were appalled at the unchecked police violence. "You know they don't make arrests any more," remarked reporter Nicholas Von Hoffmann. "They can't be bothered with lawyers, courts, any of that stuff." A New York delegate interjected: "Yeah, they just maim people and leave them hidden." Many considered the procedure culminating in Humphrey's nomination completely undemocratic. Writing in the *Village Voice,* journalist Jack Newfield termed Humphrey's candidacy "illegitimate" and vowed not to support the Democratic nominee. As a consistent apologist for the Johnson Administration's policies, Humphrey would surely have been suspect among the insurgent forces in America no matter what he did at the convention. Yet his unequivocal support there for the war, the President, and Mayor Daley deepened still further their sense of alienation. McCarthy pointedly refused to endorse the Democratic nominee, while bands of his supporters threatened to give the antiwar Senator an independent line on the ballot. As Humphrey began campaigning across the country, he drew pitifully sparse campaign audiences and angry crowds of antiwar demonstrators. The Left had not enjoyed such an opportunity to stake out an independent, popular position in American politics since the 1930s.

Yet, despite massive disaffection among liberals and radicals, no significant movement emerged in 1968 as a rallying point for their energies. McCarthy refused to run an independent campaign and finally endorsed Humphrey, albeit grudgingly. Many liberals either boycotted the polling booths or, appalled at the prospect of a Republican victory, gritted their teeth and voted Democratic. Whereas rising discontent had once propelled radicals to effective forms of action, their outrage had grown so fierce by 1968 that some were adopting desperate and self-defeating strategies. A growing number of black militants did not deign to talk to whites—except to provoke or bait them—although their own progress in organizing ghetto blacks was minimal. Among white radicals, some were turning, in frustration, to a dreamy "counter-culture," others to grim revivals of Stalinism, and still others to super-revolutionary militancy. To wander among the demonstrators at Chicago, wrote I. F. Stone, "was to feel that in revulsion against the war the best of a generation were being lost—some . . . to drugs, some . . . to an almost hysterical frenzy of alienation." Bizarre, nihilistic tendencies began to appear, prompted, as the historian Christopher Lasch has noted, by "a despair of patient efforts to create a broadly based radical movement."

The political failure of the Left also reflected the shallowness of American critical thought. Both the civil rights movement and the peace movement had developed as moral crusades, and, for a time at least, their anti-ideological bent was useful in enabling them to avoid out-moded dogmas and to rally a broad spectrum of support. But, as issues grew more complex and as real alternatives emerged, the absence of political theory became a serious handicap, leaving activists at the mercy of their whims and fantasies. Some, overlooking the fact that they lived in an advanced industrial society, began to conceive of themselves as swashbuckling Ché Guevaras, leading the masses to revolution. Ironi-cally, at the same time they remained subject to the undertow of their own middle-class values. "The student radical is never heard talking about a rise in the price of milk, new taxes, real wages, or doctor bills," the black radical Julius Lester noted with disdain. Pondering the Yippie phenomenon, Jack Newfield wondered "what Marx or Malcolm X would say to someone who wanted to make a revolution just for the hell of it." Self-proclaimed revolutionary leaders sounded impressively tough, but at times their message was bereft of radical social content. "What we're trying to say is that the whole fucking struggle isn't anti-imperialist, capitalist, or any of that bullshit," a member of Up Against the Wall Motherfuckers told an October 1968 meeting of SDS. "The whole thing is a struggle to live. Dig it? For survival. The fucking society won't let you smoke your dope, ball your woman, wear your hair the way you want to. All of that shit is living, dig, and we want to live, that's our thing." Young and politically unsophisticated, the New Left all too often confused such self-indulgent blathering with the clarion call of revolution.

With the Left in disarray, the way lay open to the stalwarts of the Right: Richard Nixon and the Republican Party. Ever since his 1962 defeat for the California governorship, Nixon had been lying low, nurs-ing his wounds and biding time as a $200,000-a-year Wall Street lawyer. His friend Bebe Rebozo assisted him with a few lucrative Florida real estate ventures on the side. But Nixon's first love remained political power, and he worked skillfully in 1968 to capture the GOP Presidential nomination. At the Miami convention, Nixon easily turned aside a chal-lenge from Nelson Rockefeller—too "liberal" for orthodox Republicans despite his regular calls for increased military spending, consistent sup-port for the Vietnam War, championing of American business, and sponsorship of state wiretapping proposals, "stop and frisk" laws, "no-knock" laws, and "shoot-to-kill" codes. Rockefeller left Miami, as Garry Wills noted, "in a mood of unselfish gloom, despondent over the nation's loss of him." A more serious threat emerged among party conservatives, attracted by the right-wing views of California Governor Ronald Reagan. But, working closely with his Southern lieutenant, Strom Thurmond, Nixon brought the situation under control. At a private meeting with Southern delegates, Nixon assured them that he would not force an unacceptable Vice-President upon them, that he did not agree with the federal open-housing law, that busing a schoolchild "will only destroy that child," that he would increase the missile program, that he would appoint a more amenable Chief Justice of the Supreme Court, and that he would not concern himself with "satisfying some professional civil rights group." The South held for Nixon, giving him the nomination.

As the first payment on his Southern debt, Nixon chose Maryland's Governor, Spiro Agnew, as his running mate. Agnew had attained national prominence that April when he publicly berated Baltimore's moderate black leaders. Thereafter, he became a hero of the American Right by assailing the report of the Kerner Commission, by calling for the shooting of looters, and by denouncing the Poor People's Campaign. "He has real depth . . . tremendous brain power . . . and an unprejudiced legal mind," Nixon remarked of Agnew at the convention. "There can be a mystique about a man. You can look him in the eye and know he's got it. This guy has got it."

Nixon's "Southern strategy" reflected his decision to wage a campaign with a reactionary flavor. Although polls showed the Vietnam War to be the top concern of the American people, the GOP nominee consistently evaded the issue. Several times during the campaign he claimed that he had a plan to end the war but could not reveal it. In domestic affairs, he was more explicit. In the spring of 1968 he called for an $8 billion budget cut, explaining that "it is gross irresponsibility to promise billions of new Federal dollars for the cities, or even for the poor." The Republican candidate had other goals. "At home," he said during the campaign, "the top priority problem is the restoration of law and order." Charging that the Supreme Court had given the "green light" to "criminal elements," Nixon promised to appoint conservative Justices and to slow down federal efforts at school integration. With an eye on the Wallace voter, he made a strong backlash appeal. "A new voice is being heard across America," he stated.

> It is different from . . . the voices of dissension, the voices of riot and revolution. What is happening is that the Forgotten Americans . . . those who do not break the law, people who pay their taxes and go to work, who send their children to school, who go to their churches . . . people who

love this country . . . cry out . . . "That is enough, let's get some new leadership."

Voters who preferred a less watered-down Wallace could take comfort in Agnew, who charged that American protestors "received instruction from active Communist leaders of the world," urged that "scroungy student dissenters" be treated "like the naughty children they are," and contemptuously brushed off the problems of America's decaying cities. Even a few Republicans were appalled. "One bright spot," a GOP media expert quipped, "you see Agnew and it makes you realize how good Nixon is."

Like Nixon, Humphrey waged a campaign that evaded the issues of war, racism, and poverty then tearing the country apart. Relying upon his own reputation as a civil rights advocate and upon Nixon's backlash appeal to bring black votes into the Democratic column, he made no special efforts to woo them. Indeed, he even announced his opposition to school busing and called for "law and order—with justice." Humphrey's strongest support came from the leadership of organized labor, which, content for the most part with a traditional campaign, worked diligently to lure blue-collar workers back from the Wallace camp. Although the Democratic nominee assailed Nixon for refusing to debate with him, they had little to quarrel about with respect to Vietnam. In May Humphrey told *U.S. News and World Report* that if he and Nixon opposed each other in the election, "I don't think our views on the war would be very far apart." This prediction proved correct—when he and Nixon expressed any views on the war at all. Yet with antiwar Democrats shunning his candidacy, Humphrey was forced to develop a "peace" appeal that would differentiate him both from Nixon and from Johnson, whose war policies he had pledged to support at the Chicago convention. Consequently, in a nationally televised address on September 30, he promised to stop the remaining bombing of North Vietnam "as an acceptable risk for peace." Six days before the election, President Johnson conveniently carried out just this program. With considerable reluctance, many antiwar liberals now decided to vote for Humphrey. For a moment it seemed as if their last-minute return to the Democratic ranks, together with a strong public dislike for Nixon, would be enough to put Humphrey over the top.

It was not. Nixon won the election with 43.4 per cent of the vote to Humphrey's 42.7 per cent and Wallace's 13.5 per cent. Losing the Deep South to Wallace and most of the industrial North to Humphrey, Nixon captured all of the West, the Upper South, and the Border States, as well as a few Midwest industrial states. He ran strongest among Republicans, the business and professional classes, the college educated, farmers, Protestants, whites, people over fifty, and white-collar workers. Yet the election hardly represented a popular mandate for Nixon or Republicanism. Nixon received the smallest proportion of the popular vote of any winning Presidential candidate since 1912 and did not carry a single major city in the nation. The Republican Party gained five seats in the Senate and four in the House but could not secure control of either branch of Congress. With nationwide voter participation dropping to 61 per cent, Nixon reached the Presidency with the support of only about 27 per cent of the eligible voters. Most political observers attributed the light voter turnout to the relative unpopularity of all three Presidential aspirants. A national opinion survey revealed that 43 per cent of those polled preferred someone other than the candidates offered them.

In reality, the election was less an expression of confidence in the candidates of 1968 than a massive vote of no-confidence in the Johnson Administration. From 1965 to 1968 Johnson had squandered the fruits of his great 1964 victory on the war in Vietnam, as American cities burned, the races polarized, and protest exploded across the land. By 1968 millions of Americans—Northern Democrats, students, slum dwellers, intellectuals, black militants, white racists, draft resisters, soldiers, and superpatriots—were alienated, embittered, and ready for revolt. Reflecting upon Johnson's departure from office, historian Eric Goldman wrote that not since Herbert Hoover had a President "ended his tenure with so few hosannas and so widespread a sense of good riddance." The managers of the Vietnam War, whose power lay in their class relationships rather than in their popularity, moved on to new positions of prestige: McNamara to the World Bank, Bundy to the Ford Foundation, Westmoreland to the Joint Chiefs of Staff, and Rusk to a Southern professorship. But Hubert Humphrey, as Johnson's political heir, could not shake off his political legacy. In the 1968 election much of the Democratic Right went to Wallace, sizable sectors of the Democratic Left stayed at home, and Humphrey's vote fell off by 12 million from the Democratic total of 1964. It was the end of the liberal mandate and the end of an era. Not only had the Johnson Administration forfeited the best opportunity for social reform since the New Deal, but it had driven the nation to the point of desperation. The result was the election of Richard Nixon and the politics of resentment.

11

The Poverty of "Progress":
American Society, 1960-77

> No one with a mop can expect respect from a
> banker, or an attorney, or men who create jobs.
> . . . Are you crazy? Who ever heard of inte-
> gration between a mop and a banker?
>
> Man, about thirty-eight, Harlem, *ca.* 1963

IN THE YEARS AFTER 1960, the American nation enjoyed greater overall
prosperity than ever before in its history. By 1977, the GNP had more
than tripled, climbing past $1.7 trillion. To be sure, inflation accounted
for most of this increase. Nevertheless, the median family income of
$13,719 in 1975 represented a gain in "real" dollars of 34 per cent since
1960—an increase which, if unspectacular, provided the average American with a greater measure of material comfort. A flood of new consumer gadgets, suburban housing developments, and shopping centers
attested to the growing prosperity. With about 5 per cent of the world's
population, the United States accounted for approximately half the
annual consumption of the world's non-replenishable resources.

Nevertheless, gains in national prosperity continued to mask sharp
economic inequality within the United States. According to the U.S.
Commerce Department, by the mid-1970s the richest fifth of the population received 53.0 per cent of the national income, while the poorest
fifth received 1.9 per cent. Indeed, the aggregate income of the richest
5 per cent of American families surpassed that of the poorest 67 per
cent. Moreover, in terms of wealth, the gap was considerably wider. In
1976, the richest 1 per cent of Americans owned more than eight times
the assets of the poorest 50 per cent, including most of the corporate
stock in the United States. Thus, in 1976, as unemployment reached

epidemic proportions, plunging millions of Americans into destitution, Rolls Royce experienced record auto sales in the United States. (The Silver Shadow started at $38,500, while the new Camargue went for a mere $90,000.) A third of the nation lived below the Bureau of Labor Statistics' "low-income" budget and half lived below its "moderate" one, but a New York jeweler could advertise "the consummate Bicentennial Christmas present": a diamond necklace that had been commissioned by King George III. (At $500,000, it was "an unusually good buy.") As always, economic crisis highlighted America's two-class system: the wealthy, and everyone else.

Times of hardship, then, remained good times for the corporate rich. In 1972, the Ford Motor Company's chairman received $887,795 and its president $873,852 in salary and bonuses—not including dividends, expense accounts, free life and medical insurance, and other perquisites of corporate power. And when, that same year, their firm was caught in deliberate violation of the Environmental Protection Act—the largest violation in its history—both men were rewarded with handsome raises for 1973. David Rockefeller, whose Chase Manhattan Bank cut back New York City's crumbling public services and fastened an austerity program upon New York City's schoolteachers, hospital workers, and firemen, possessed $155.2 million in one of his two personal trust funds in 1973. From their heights of wealth and power, the corporate elite dominated America's major social and cultural institution. In October, 1972, a study by the Twentieth Century Fund reported "excessively intimate linkage" between the nation's thirty-three wealthiest foundations and private corporations. Trustee boards, declared the study, were "homogeneous," consisting of "aging members of the upper socio-economic class," a microcosm of "the power elite." A report by the Educational Testing Service three years before reached similar conclusions about college and university trustees. As Federal Communications Commissioner Nicholas Johnson observed: "Our colleges, churches, foundations, and public broadcasting stations tend to be presided over by the same guys who decide what automobiles we'll buy and what cereal we'll eat."

Certainly the rich held a remarkable number of top posts in the federal government. Of the ten Secretaries of State between 1945 and 1977, six were listed in the *Social Register*. A seventh was merely a Wall Street lawyer, while the eighth came to the post from the presidency of a major foundation. Of the thirteen Secretaries of Defense (and War) between 1945 and 1972, eight were listed in the *Social Register*. Throughout the Cold War years, businessmen, corporate lawyers, and members of the upper class also dominated the Treasury Department and were heavily represented in the Departments of Commerce, Labor, and Health, Education, and Welfare. The following individuals served on the Executive Committee of the National Security Council, which advised the nation's multimillionaire President during the Cuban missile crisis:

> Lyndon Johnson, millionaire and representative of Texas oil interests
> Dean Rusk, former president of the Rockefeller Foundation
> Robert McNamara, former president of the Ford Motor Company
> Robert Kennedy, multimillionaire
> C. Douglas Dillon, former president of Wall Street's Dillon, Read and Company
> Roswell Gilpatric, former corporation lawyer
> McGeorge Bundy, Boston aristocrat and former Dean of Harvard
> Adlai Stevenson, former corporation lawyer
> John McCone, multimillionaire industrialist
> Dean Acheson, former corporation lawyer
> Robert Lovett, former investment banker with Brown Brothers, Harriman
> Maxwell Taylor, U.S. Army general and former chairman of the Mexican Power and Light Company
> George Ball, former corporation lawyer

How representative of popular deference to the corporate élite were such appointments? A Louis Harris survey in November, 1972, found that only 27 per cent of the American public expressed a "great deal of confidence" in the heads of major corporations.

Wealth, of course, had other entrées to power. A *New York Times* story noted that the list of large contributors in the 1968 elections was "full of names famous in the annals of American finance and industry"— DuPonts, Fords, Pews, Mellons, Olins, and Whitneys. Similarly, when President Nixon picked up $4.7 million for his re-election campaign one evening in November, 1971, it was at a banquet before what the *Times* described as "several thousand of the nation's wealthiest people." Eventually, political candidates in 1972 raised more than $400 million, of which 75 per cent came from less than 1 per cent of the population. A Houston oilman confided to *Time* magazine that October: "Can the guy who gave the President $20,000 pick up the phone and call the White House if he gets in trouble with the feds? You bet. Does he realize this when he gives? You bet." Even after new federal laws provided for public financing of Presidential elections, wealth remained a key ingredient of American politics. Not only were large amounts of money crucial in the period before public funding began, but Congressional, state, and local races remained untouched. Thus, for example, special-interest groups poured over $22.5 million into the campaigns of House and Senate candidates in 1976—more than twice as much as in 1974.

Furthermore, the link between corporate wealth and political power often went beyond the law. Pressed by federal investigators in 1975 and 1976, executives from more than a hundred major U.S. corporations confessed to having illegally dispensed hundreds of millions of dollars in corporate funds to win favors from American and foreign political leaders. Lockheed Aircraft, bailed out at American taxpayers' expense, admitted to having disbursed at least $22 million in tax-deductible bribes to prominent individuals in Japan, Turkey, Colombia, Mexico, and the Netherlands. R. J. Reynolds Industries admitted distributing $25 million in illegal payments in the United States and overseas. Once known as the United Fruit Company, United Brands confessed to giving a $1.25 million bribe to officials in Honduras and a $750,000 bribe to Italian officials. Three successive chief executive officers of the Gulf Oil Corporation disbursed more than $12.6 million in illegal foreign and domestic payments over a fifteen-year period. The executives of firms like Gulf, Ashland Oil Company, and the Minnesota Mining and Manufacturing Company, which made domestic political contributions from corporate funds, clearly understood the illegal nature of their transactions, for they "laundered" the funds by sending them overseas and then deliberately falsified company records. "It was in the best interests of the corporation," explained Gulf's chief executive officer and chairman, "so I did it."

Rich and powerful beyond imagination, the corporate élite moved confidently about the world, checking investments here, meeting heads of state there, and indulging their tastes for race horses, art treasures, or antique finery. One of the better-known of these modern magnates was Charles W. Engelhard, who, through investments in gold, platinum, and diamonds, ran his $20 million family inheritance into a $250 million fortune, with industrial and financial holdings in fifty nations. Engelhard lived on a lavish scale, principally in a turreted castle on his 172-acre estate in Far Hills, New Jersey, but also at his sumptuous residences in London; Johannesburg; Boca Grande, Florida; on the Gaspé Peninsula; and at the Waldorf Towers in New York City. Using his own fleet of aircraft, Engelhard traveled from place to place, accompanied, as the *New York Times* noted, by "an entourage of executives, secretaries, valets, chefs, animals, butler and friends. Like a potentate, he held business conferences at any hour of the day or night, and executives were obliged to be on hand for his summons." "Charlie is a mogul," his friend Alfred G. Vanderbilt observed. "My wife and I have gone to Africa and Asia with the Engelhards and you go first class, I've got to tell you." Horse racing consumed much of Engelhard's time and attention, and he spent $20 million establishing his own stables. As chairman of the American–South African Investment Company, a director of twenty-three South African firms, and a board member of South Africa's Native Recruiting Corporation (which lured blacks to work in the mines), Engelhard was a major power in South Africa's affairs and a staunch defender of its white supremacist government. Discussing the policies of Prime Minister Vorster, he remarked: "There is nothing I would do better or differently." Although Engelhard came under sharp criticism from American civil rights groups for bolstering apartheid, he remained on excellent terms with American political leaders. He was a substantial financial contributor to the Democrats during the campaigns of 1960 and 1964, and even became a Democratic national committeeman and Presidential emissary at the independence ceremonies of African nations. Mr. and Mrs. Lyndon Johnson were flown to Engelhard's hideaway at Boca Grande to help him celebrate his fifty-second birthday and were visiting him again only a few days before he died in 1971, leaving behind a multibillion-dollar business empire on six continents.

The wealth and power of American business titans flowed from the dramatic growth of their corporations. "In unprecedented fashion," concluded the Federal Trade Commission in 1969, "the current merger movement is centralizing and consolidating corporate control and decision-making among a relatively few vast companies." Between 1955 and 1973, reported *Fortune,* the top 500 industrial corporations—0.25 per cent of the total—increased their share of American industry's profits, assets, and employment from 40 per cent to about 75 per cent. Although the 1970s were a time of declining economic fortunes for many Americans, corporate profits more than doubled between 1970 and 1976. In the latter year, the top 500 industrial corporations increased their profits by 30.4 per cent; Exxon alone reported $48.6 billion in sales and $2.6 billion in profits. As early as 1965, the profits of General Motors exceeded the revenue of forty-eight of the fifty states, and its sales exceeded the GNP of all but nine nations of the world. Vast corporate and financial networks knitted together these giants of American capitalism. A 1969 Federal Trade Commission staff study found that 49 major banks had interlocking directorates with 236 major corporations, 29 major insurance companies, and 22 of the nation's largest utilities. Often corporations owned large blocks of stock in their nominal competitors.

Pre-eminent among the rising corporate giants were the multinational corporations. Between 1950 and 1975, U.S. direct overseas investments expanded from $11.8 billion to $133 billion. Consequently, in 1970, eleven of the top twelve U.S. industrial corporations had foreign sales exceeding $1 billion. America's fastest-growing major company, IBM, rang up more after-tax profits that year ($1 billion) than any other industrial corporation in the world, primarily from its operations in 107 foreign nations. Six years later, IBM's profits, more than half of which came from overseas operations, reached $2.4 billion. Of the 178 U.S. firms that accounted for the vast bulk of U.S. direct foreign investment in 1972, most earned at least a fourth of their profits overseas, while 38 earned at least half. From 1967 to 1975, the assets in the overseas branches of American banks grew sixteen times, to $150 billion, and foreign branch activity provided some of the largest with between a third and a half their overall business. Indeed, between 1966 and 1974, foreign earnings rose from 11 to 30 per cent of total U.S. corporate profits after taxes.

One of the best-known of America's multinational concerns, ITT, increased its net income seventeen times from 1959 to 1972, rising from forty-ninth to ninth place among American corporations. Employing 528,000 people in 93 countries, ITT owned at least 331 subsidiary corporations and 708 subsidiaries of subsidiaries around the world. During the 1930s and World War II, ITT had worked closely with the government of Nazi Germany, producing Focke-Wulf bombers and reportedly relaying useful intelligence information to the German military machine. Nevertheless, in 1967 ITT obtained $27 million in compensation from the American government for Allied war damages to its German factories, including $5 million for damage to the Focke-Wulf plants. The company was, in fact, now working closely with the American government. When the Justice Department mysteriously dropped an antitrust suit against ITT in 1972, reporters unearthed the company's promise of $400,000 to fund the approaching GOP National Convention—an offer the Republicans hastily declined after it became public. Under Senate questioning, ITT President Harold Geneen revealed that his company, which maintained large investments in Chile, had on two occasions in 1970 offered $1 million to the CIA for action to prevent that nation's newly elected president, Socialist Salvador Allende, from taking office.

In its unrelenting struggle to retain its wealth, the corporate élite continued to receive the loyal assistance of federal, state, and local governments. Social Security payroll taxes, state and local sales taxes, and other regressive levies increased rapidly and, after 1969, produced more revenue than the more equitable federal income tax. In 1968, state and local taxes took 27.2 per cent of the income of those earning under $2,000, but only 6.7 per cent of the income of those earning over $50,000. Even the federal income tax had been stripped of many of its progressive features. Treasury Secretary Joseph Barr told Congress in 1968 that the wealthiest 1 per cent of the population was actually taxed at a lower rate than were middle-income Americans. Of those who earned $1 million or more in 1967, he revealed, twenty-one paid no taxes at all, and the rest paid at an effective rate of no more than 25 per cent. Most taxpayers in the $500,000-to-$1-million income range paid at the same rate as those with incomes a twentieth as large. In 1969, in fact, 300 Americans with adjusted gross incomes higher than $200,000 paid no federal income tax at all. Tax breaks for U.S. corporations magnified these disparities. According to a Congressional study, in 1974 eight corporations with profits totaling $884 million paid no federal income tax, and another eighteen companies with $5.3 billion in profits paid at an effective rate of less than 10 per cent. The petroleum industry paid no net U.S. tax on its foreign income, while the effective tax rate on commercial banks fell to 11.7 per cent. In 1975, 134 of the nation's largest private utilities charged customers for nearly $1.5 billion in taxes which they never paid. Indeed, 43 paid no income taxes at all.

In August, 1971, a team of reporters for the Associated Press concluded after investigation that "private enterprise in America collects roughly $30 billion a year in government subsidies and subsidy-like aid, much of it hidden or disguised." Tax breaks, incentives, and exemptions were estimated to run up to $15 billion a year; farm subsidies between $6 billion and $9 billion; loans to business $250 billion; and grants to the maritime industry $450 million, to the airlines $63 million, and to the railroads $172 million (over a five-year period). Defense contractors used $14.6 billion of government property, while American companies engaging in overseas business received more than $6 billion in loans and insurance. "Our airlines, our truckers, our railroads, our electronic media and countless others are on the dole," declared Federal Trade Commission chairman Lewis Engman in 1975. "Our system of hidden regulatory subsidies makes welfare fraud look like petty larceny."

The operations of this rich man's welfare state were particularly evident in the area of agriculture. For years, huge firms like Tenneco,

Purex, Coca-Cola, United Brands, ITT, Union Carbide, Boeing Aircraft, Kaiser Aluminum, Aetna Life, and Dow Chemical had been moving into agriculture, furthering the exodus of family farmers from the land. From 1960 to 1974, the number of farms in America decreased by 25 per cent, and the number of farmers dipped below 3 million. Thanks to the processes employed by corporate agriculture to fertilize, spray, and extend the shelf life of produce for maximum profitability, a distinct decline in the flavor of fruits and vegetables, as well as in the nutritional value of food, became evident. On the other hand, the prices paid by consumers for farm products rose rapidly. Although more than half America's farmers earned less than poverty-level incomes, most of the billions of dollars in annual government farm subsidies went to giant agribusinesses. In 1970, nine corporate farmers received more than $1 million each from the federal program, and twenty-three received subsidies of $500,000 or more. According to a 1972 report by the National Sharecroppers Fund, "the wealthiest 7 per cent of the farms received almost 63 per cent of the total subsidies, while the poorer half got only 9.1 per cent."

The most lavish corporate subsidy, of course, remained the national "defense" outlay. Between 1946 and 1976, more than $1.7 trillion was spent by the American government for military goods and services—an amount exceeding the value of all business and residential structures in the United States. For most of the Cold War years, the combined Department of Defense, space, and atomic energy programs accounted for about 10 per cent of the GNP and 85 to 90 per cent of the total federal purchases of goods and services. As a result, the military sector of U.S. industry had the fastest growth rate in the American economy. By 1970 it accounted for 20 per cent of the manufacturing output and more than half of the research and development work in the United States. Although many corporations received defense contracts, most military work was concentrated among a small number of corporate giants. In fiscal 1971, 100 corporations received 72 per cent of prime defense contract dollars, and 35 per cent went to ten firms. More than half the defense contract dollars were devoured by twenty-three companies. Between 1961 and 1967 Lockheed Aircraft received $10.6 billion in military contracts (88 per cent of its sales), General Dynamics $8.8 billion (67 per cent), McDonnell Douglas $7.6 billion (75 per cent), and Boeing Company $7.1 billion (54 per cent). In 1963, when the *New York Times* conducted a survey of the top twenty-five defense contractors, it found that none had done any serious planning for peacetime conversion. Five years later a similar survey reported similar findings.

From the standpoint of defense industry, the situation was almost too good to be true. As Senator Proxmire revealed in 1969, only 11.5 per cent of military contracts were awarded on a formally advertised competitive-bid basis; the remaining 88.5 per cent were privately negotiated. Cost overruns were "routine, and prime military weapons system contracts normally exceed their estimates by 100 to 200 per cent." The cost overrun on the C-5A cargo plane, for example, was $2 billion, and on the Sentinel ABM system $5 billion. Secretary of Defense Melvin Laird reported to Congress in late 1969 that there had been $16.2 billion in cost overruns on the military's thirty-four major weapons programs. Moreover, corporations hardly fretted over the quality of their equipment. According to a report of the Joint Economic Committee of Congress:

> Billions of dollars have been wasted on weapons systems that have had to be canceled because they did not work. Other systems have performed far below contract specifications. . . . Of a sample of 13 major Air Force and Navy aircraft and missile programs initiated since 1955 at a total cost of $40 billion, less than 40 per cent produced systems with acceptable electronic performance. Two of the programs were canceled after total program costs of $2 billion. . . . Two programs costing $10 billion were phased out after 3 years for low reliability. Five programs costing $13 billion give poor performance.

Senator Proxmire noted that of eleven major weapons systems begun during the 1960s, only two of the electronic components performed up to standard. The systems "typically cost 200 to 300 per cent more than the Pentagon estimated," were "delivered two years later than expected," and contributed to after-tax profits for the aerospace industry that were 12.5 per cent higher than the average for American industry. Senate Majority Leader Mansfield estimated that the United States spent $23 billion on missile systems that either were never deployed or were simply abandoned.

So cozy did this military-industrial partnership become that it was sometimes difficult to say where the Pentagon stopped and private enterprise began. Between 1959 and 1973 the Department of Defense used $86 million to make outright gifts to ailing defense contractors. This did not include two lavish subsidies to the Lockheed Aircraft Corporation, which in 1971 received an arbitrary price increase of $1 billion on its Pentagon contracts and later a loan guarantee of $250 million from Congress. Concerned with maintaining the economic viability of defense contractors, the Pentagon paid considerably less attention to limiting their profits. Of 131 defense contractors forced to refund some of their profits in 1972 as "excessive," 94 were allowed to retain profits exceeding 50 per cent of their company's net worth and 49 were allowed to retain profits in excess of 100 per cent. The Defense Department even went so far as to buy stock in defense contractors, interlocking itself with American industry in an unprecedented fashion. Just as American corporate leaders were brought in to direct the Pentagon, so U.S. corporations continued to add top-ranking military officers to their hierarchies. In March, 1969, Senator Proxmire revealed that the number of retired military officers with the rank of colonel or above employed by the top 100 defense contractors had tripled over the preceding decade. Of the total of 2,072, Lockheed alone accounted for 210.

At one time, the American labor movement would have been a powerful opponent of this military-industrial alliance, but the AFL-CIO leadership had become so enmeshed in defense contracts and Cold War conservatism that opposition appeared unlikely. Concerned with protecting its members' jobs, most of the labor movement fervently supported the expenditure of public funds on new weapons systems and lobbied vigorously for the Lockheed loan. Moreover, many of labor's top leaders had become firmly committed to a junior partnership with government and business. The AFL-CIO's American Institute for Free Labor Development served as the instrument of the CIA and other U.S. government agencies in Latin America. In a speech delivered to the Council on Latin America in April, 1965, George Meany declared that labor believes "in the capitalist system, and we are members of the capitalist society. We are dedicated to the preservation of this system." Ten years later, asked if the AFL-CIO might mobilize the millions of unemployed workers to press for full employment, Meany replied: "No. The AFL-CIO is pretty conservative in certain ways. . . . We don't take to the streets. And we don't call general strikes, and we don't call political strikes." Reporting on the 1975 AFL-CIO convention, the liberal *Nation* pronounced it "sedate, nostalgic, irrelevant, docile and bereft of ideas."

For upper-echelon union officials like Meany, the world had become a very comfortable place. In early 1973, the conservative head of the small National Maritime Union, Joseph Curran, once a fiery radical, drew a union salary of $85,000 and laid plans to retire with nearly $1 million in severance pay and pension benefits. At its 1976 convention in Las Vegas, the scandal-ridden Teamsters Union voted to increase members' dues 40 per cent, thus covering losses in real estate speculation and other shady ventures and raising the salaries of its leadership by

25 per cent. (President Frank Fitzsimmons's salary thereby increased to $156,250 a year.) The leaders of the once-proud United Mine Workers deposited $67 million of their members' pension fund in an interest-free account in a UMW-owned bank, enriching the union organization and themselves while costing the miners $3 million yearly. To compensate for the depletion of the pension fund, UMW officials began denying miners their pensions—$1,350 a year, as compared to the $50,000-a-year pension slated for union president "Tony" Boyle. In 1969, an insurgent candidate, Joseph Yablonski, challenged Boyle for the UMW presidency. Three weeks after the fraudulent election outcome, which provided victory to the incumbent, a group of Boyle's lieutenants murdered Yablonski, his wife, and his daughter.

Yet American workers—as distinguished from many upper-echelon union officials—hardly enjoyed the sweet life, or even a secure one. According to the U.S. Labor Department, between 1967 and 1976 the paychecks of an average fully employed American worker rose from $109 to $197 a week, which left him, after inflation, with a 5.5 per cent increase in real earnings. And when part-time workers were included, real earnings for American workers during this period actually declined. Moreover, job security for most Americans remained minimal. Despite significant gains made by the labor movement during the 1960s in organizing white-collar workers, who eventually comprised a fourth of union membership, the unionized segment of the work force continued to shrink, dropping to 20.1 per cent by 1976. Meanwhile, the worst unemployment since the Great Depression hit the United States in the 1970s, throwing Americans out of work in considerably greater proportions than their foreign counterparts. At the end of 1975, when unemployment in the United States reached 8.3 per cent, it was 5.6 per cent in Great Britain, 4.6 per cent in West Germany, and 2 per cent in Japan. The policies of U.S. multinational corporations, whose desire to keep down wage costs led them to close factories in the industrial North and set up shop in the non-union South and the friendly dictatorships of the Third World, accounted for at least some of American labor's difficulties. The AFL-CIO maintained that, between 1966 and 1973, more than a million jobs were lost in the United States through the export of capital and technology.

On-the-job conditions for American workers remained exceptionally hazardous. From 1961 to 1969, while 46,000 Americans were being killed in Vietnam, 126,000 Americans were being killed at home in industrial accidents. According to the Department of Labor, approximately 2 million injuries and 14,000 deaths occurred every year at the workplace. Even those who continued on the job were subject to disease and eventual death from dangerous pollutants. An estimated 80 per cent of the nation's bituminous coal miners had "black lung" disease, a type of silicosis caused by inhaling coal dust, while rubber workers died of cancer of the stomach, of the prostrate, and of leukemia at rates from 50 to 300 per cent greater than the general population. In 1974, according to the Department of Labor, one out of ten American workers (5.8 million people) suffered from a job-related sickness or injury, and an estimated 100,000 Americans died from occupational diseases. Many occupational deaths and injuries could have been prevented if safety standards existed, or if those that existed were adequately enforced. Commenting on the deaths of 152 coal miners and the injury of nearly 9,000 in the first ten months of 1975, the United Mine Workers' newspaper noted that the average violation of a mine safety rule, when detected by federal inspectors, cost a coal corporation $75 in penalties.

In these circumstances, another wave of labor insurgency began surfacing in the 1970s. Small and struggling unions—farm workers, public employees, service workers, and textile workers—carried on major organizing drives, reminiscent of the CIO. At Lordstown, Ohio, young members of the United Auto Workers challenged corporate management over the conditions of assembly-line labor. When a federal court ordered a new election for president of the United Mine Workers, it was won by a reformer, Arnold Miller, who promptly slashed executive salaries and set the union on a more militant course. In a variety of unions, ranging from the Teamsters to the Auto Workers, rank and file caucuses began coalescing. Ed Sadlowski, the insurgent director of the largest local in the United Steelworkers, declared: "There are signs which point to the end of the era of docile labor. One by one the old oligarchies are beginning to crumble." In early 1977, Sadlowski, supported by his Steelworkers Fight Back organization, startled the Steelworkers' humdrum leadership by running for the presidency of his 1.4-million-member union. Though losing, he drew most of the votes in basic steel and among young workers, and predicted a victory in future campaigns. Meanwhile, the new president of the 936,000-member International Association of Machinists, William Winpisinger, announced his intention of creating a "new left coalition" on the AFL-CIO board to organize the unorganized, press for social welfare legislation, and reverse the federation's hawkish foreign policy stand. Union members should not have "contempt for those beneath them," he said, "but for the 4 per cent of the population that owns 70 per cent of the wealth."

The statisticians no longer classified most workers as poor, but they did concede that almost half the families of the American poor were headed by employed workers. Such workers labored on jobs either lacking minimum wage coverage or providing a legal minimum below the poverty level. Employed in laundry work, restaurants, hotels, hospitals, and in a variety of lowly service occupations, they eked out a miserable existence in a land of abundance. The hired farm working force, for example, stood at 2.6 million people in 1971. Noncasual laborers earned an average of $1,576 a year, and migrant laborers $1,407. Although the nation had a $1.30-an-hour minimum wage law for agriculture, it exempted two-thirds of all farm workers. Furthermore, government enforcement of wage standards was inadequate, and farm labor groups estimated that growers illegally shortchanged their employees by at least $100 million a year. Forced to supplement the pitiful incomes of their families, an estimated 800,000 children under sixteen years of age joined them in the fields, of whom 300,000 traveled as migrants from state to state. Migrant children, of course, were virtually excluded from schooling and were subject to the hazards of employment in an industry that, in 1970, ranked third in the number of work-related deaths. Chemical pesticides alone caused an estimated 75,000 acute poisonings annually. Few government programs were of much assistance to farm workers, and many public agencies openly collaborated with growers or flouted federal law. In 1971 only a tenth of migrant families received welfare assistance of any kind.

Fifteen years after the "discovery" of poverty, millions of Americans endured lives of misery and privation. Noting that poverty had increased 11 per cent over the preceding year, the 1976 Census Bureau report estimated that 25.9 million Americans lived in destitution, including large numbers of the nation's elderly, its children, and its racial minorities. Testifying in 1969 on the National Nutrition Survey's complete physical examination of 12,000 Americans selected at random in low-income areas, Dr. Arnold Schaefer of the U.S. Public Health Service provided a graphic portrait of what the *New York Times* called "chronic hunger and malnutrition in a land fat with agricultural surpluses." He turned first to the instances of starvation, showing the Senate Select Committee on Nutrition and Human Needs a film of an emaciated baby with staring eyes and matchstick arms and legs. "We did not expect to find such cases in the United States," he said. "In many of the developing areas where we have worked—Africa, Latin America, and Asia—these severe cases of malnutrition only rarely are found." Rickets, virtually wiped out in the United States during the 1930s, had staged a startling comeback, he said, while goiter had reached epidemic proportions. Hunger and malnutrition were so great that 16 to 17 per cent of those examined were "real risks," requiring medical attention. Because of inadequate nutrition, he noted, the physical growth of children between one and three years of age had been clearly stunted and their brain growth retarded. In addition, one-third of the children under six years of age were anemic and nearly a third had a vitamin A deficiency so marked as to cause night blindness. Dental problems were severe: 18 per cent of those ten years of age and over reported it difficult and painful to chew food. According to the *New York Times* account, "Dr. Schaefer, a long-time public health officer who has conducted nutrition surveys for the Government in 33 developing countries, said the report indicated that malnutrition was just as bad in the United States as in the Central American countries of Guatemala, Costa Rica, Panama, Honduras, Nicaragua and El Salvador that were recently surveyed."

Popular stereotypes to the contrary, most of the American poor were white, many of them descended from the nation's first European settlers. In the fall of 1963, after a visit to the Appalachia section of eastern Kentucky, *New York Times* reporter Homer Bigart wrote of the gaunt, ragged mountain folk and of the wretched shanties in which they lived. Children were so hungry that they ate dried mud pried out from between chimney stones. By 1967 about one-fourth of eastern Kentucky's 800,000 people were on public assistance. The area contained 40 per cent of the nation's one-room schoolhouses; one-fourth of its white adult population was illiterate. The key to the fate of the region lay in Appalachia's intimate experience with the nation's major corporations— U.S. Steel, Bethlehem Steel, Inland Steel, Republic Steel, International Harvester, Jones and Loughlin, Ford Motor Company, and many others. All had profited handsomely from their extractive operations in the region, draining the land of its wealth and returning a pittance to its inhabitants. Even as the area declined economically, their successors continued this pattern. The Virginia Coal and Iron Company, with its 206,000 acres, was probably the most profitable investor-owned corporation in the United States. In the early 1960s it realized a net profit after taxes of 61 per cent. The Kentucky River Coal Corporation owned 200,000 acres in eastern Kentucky, drawing profits at almost 50 per cent of its vast income. Such companies stripped the land of its riches, leaving behind a rural slum, its denuded hillsides inhabited by thousands of sickly, crippled, and unemployed miners and mountaineers.

Vast economic inequalities, initiated and perpetuated by racial prejudice and poverty, continued to make a mockery of all claims of racial justice. In 1970, according to the Census Bureau, the median income of black families stood at $6,067, compared with $9,961 for whites. From 1945 to 1976, the ratio of black family income to white family income climbed only 1 per cent. The persistence of economic distinctions did not reflect merely differences in occupation, for at every occupational level blacks earned less than whites. Among craftsmen and foremen, for example, the black median income in 1970 was $5,921, the white $8,305. Even education had little impact upon these income differences. As for "black capitalism," it remained more slogan than reality. In 1971, blacks owned less than 1 per cent of the nation's businesses—mostly restaurants, barbershops, and small family establishments. The forty-six black-owned insurance companies, often cited as success stories, alto-gether controlled only 0.2 per cent of the insurance industry's assets. The situation was much the same, and sometimes worse, among the millions of Mexican-Americans, Indians, Puerto Ricans, and other racial minor-ities. Of course, by breaking the back of official racism in America, the civil rights movement did provide the basis for a noticeable expansion of the non-white middle class, including politicians, white-collar workers, businessmen, and professionals. Between 1965 and 1974, the percentage of blacks earning over $15,000 a year more than doubled, reaching 19 per cent. Even so, most dark-skinned Americans still faced the hardships associated with being born poor in America.

Nowhere, in the years after 1960, was the persistence of poverty and injustice more sharply etched than in the grim features of America's decaying racial ghettos. Overcrowded, deteriorating housing; high rates of disease and sickness; massive unemployment; widespread crime— such were the most salient features of the great slums of America, places of resentment and fatalism, poor education, illegitimacy, drug addiction, alcoholism, frequent illness, and early death. "The most concrete fact of the ghetto," wrote Kenneth Clark, "is its physical ugliness—the dirt, the filth, the neglect. In many stores walls are unpainted, windows are un-washed, service is poor, supplies are meager. The parks are seedy with lack of care. The streets are crowded with the people and refuse." Throughout Harlem there was no museum, no art gallery, no sustained theater group. There were few libraries, but "hundreds of bars, hundreds of churches, and scores of fortune tellers. Everywhere there are signs of fantasy, decay, abandonment, defeat." A Harlem drug addict told an interviewer:

> You know the average young person out here don't have a job, man, they don't have anything. . . . They don't have any alternative, you know, but to go out there and try to make a living for themselves. Like when you

come down to the Tombs [a New York City prison]. They want to know why you did it . . . but you have to live. You go down to the employment agency and you can't get a job. They have you waiting all day, but you can't get a job. . . . Yet you have to live. I'm ready to do anything anyone else is ready to do—because I want to live—I want to live.

Whatever rich and comfortable whites might think, the ghetto's invisible walls were not constructed by blacks. "The dark ghettos are social, political, educational, and—above all—economic colonies," wrote Clark. "Their inhabitants are subject peoples, victims of the greed, cruelty, insensitivity, guilt, and fear of their masters."

Most of what more affluent Americans learned about the conditions of slum dwellers came from television, and therefore they did not learn very much. As the Kerner Commission noted, "important segments of the media failed to report adequately" the "sense of degradation, misery, and hopelessness of life in the ghetto." Although the average child watched more hours of television before beginning grade school than he would need to obtain a college degree, television's primary function remained not education but consumer indoctrination. In 1976, U.S. television networks presented nearly $4 billion worth of advertising, providing the average American with 250,000 commercials before he reached age eighteen. A housewife who sat down in the morning to watch two hours of television could expect to endure forty-five to fifty. The National Association of Broadcasters did have advertising codes, but an FCC sampling of stations in 1963 found that 40 per cent exceeded the code limits. When the FCC proposed using the industry's own codes as a criterion for license renewal, industry opposition forced the plan's abandonment. Commercial radio and television could not be easily altered, for, as John Kenneth Galbraith noted, they provided the major instruments "for the management of consumer demand."

Closely interlocked with the major sources of power in American life, the television industry did not entirely eschew politics—only the politics of protest. Commercial sponsors shunned civil rights documentaries, while television newsfilms, as a Presidential commission noted, rarely explored "the causes and complexity of campus protests," but "focused on whatever was most bizarre, dramatic, active, or violent." With the United States involved increasingly in CIA and other covert international ventures, the networks turned to glorifying them in the mid-1960s in such serials as "The Man from U.N.C.L.E.," "The Girl from U.N.C.L.E.," "Get Smart," "I Spy," "The Man Who Never Was," and "Mission: Impossible." Even "The Lucy Show" took up spy themes. As the Administration escalated the conflict in Vietnam, a rash of war series appeared. "McHale's Navy," "Combat," "Rat Patrol," "Gomer Pyle USMC," "Hogan's Heroes," "Mr. Roberts," and others portrayed military life in a manner that ranged from amusing to heroic. The response of the networks to antiwar protest was rather different. In 1967, when CBS ended its seventeen-year blacklist of Pete Seeger by allowing the folksinger to appear on the "Smothers Brothers Comedy Hour," he stubbornly insisted upon singing "Waist Deep in the Big Muddy," a song implicitly critical of the Vietnam War. CBS cut the song from the videotape and later fired the Smothers Brothers. In the fall of 1969 Washington was besieged by anywhere from a quarter to a half million antiwar demonstrators. "It was one of the largest crowds in the history of the United States," FCC Commissioner Nicholas Johnson later remarked. "Everyone was there, it seemed, except the President and the network newsmen. They had blacked it out."

However sympathetic individual television performers or newscasters might be to the dissidents or the issues they raised, the parameters of "appropriate" criticism were set by a most unsympathetic management. In the late 1960s, for example, CBS president Frank Stanton wore four hats simultaneously. Not only was he president of the nation's most powerful broadcasting system, with worldwide network connections and radio-television ownership, but Stanton was also chairman of the board of the Rand Corporation (funded almost entirely by the Air Force for studies of everything from counter-insurgency strategy to thermonuclear war), and chairman of the executive committee of Radio Free Europe (the CIA front beaming programs to Eastern Europe and the Soviet Union). Few were surprised when Stanton intervened to ensure a properly patriotic tone on CBS News. Typical was his complaint that it had been a "dirty trick" to broadcast a half-hour interview with Senator Fulbright on the Vietnam War. The CBS News director later conceded that he had been "influenced to do controversial subjects in a non-controversial manner" and that he had "tailored" his conscience "more than once."

Through its worldwide dissemination of American programs and values, the television industry also proved useful in promoting the overseas commercial expansion desired by American industry. By 1968, 102 countries were utilizing U.S. telefilms, broadcasting the latest in American situation comedies, detective stories, spy thrillers, and quiz shows. "Bonanza" alone was watched by 350 million people a week. Increasingly, foreign network fare became a carbon copy of America's. U.S. "TV products . . . are setting the tone for television programming throughout the world," a former USIA official observed. Even in the impoverished nations of the Third World, the mass media inundated traditional villages with U.S. programs, commercial advertising, and the values of consumer acquisitiveness. In his study of Mexican family life, anthropologist Oscar Lewis reported: "The major television programs are sponsored by foreign companies like Nestles, General Motors, Procter and Gamble, and Colgate. Only the use of the Spanish language and Mexican artists distinguishes the commercials from those in the United States."

Most of the nation's press seemed only slightly more eager to promote public enlightenment. Although America had some of the best reporters in the world, their efforts to get at the truth were frequently sabotaged by unsympathetic editors and publishers. Only about a dozen reporters were assigned to full-time coverage of the Pentagon, and no publisher ever used the 1967 Freedom of Information Act to pry suppressed information out of the federal government. The atrophy of the regular daily press was shown by the fact that the *Nation* broke the story of the Bay of Pigs, *Ramparts* the story of the CIA's links with the National Student Association, and free-lance journalist Seymour Hersh the story of the My Lai massacre. Ralph Nader and his staff probably did more muckraking than all the daily press combined. The 1972–73 Watergate "bugging" story represented a classic piece of investigative journalism, and yet, as press analyst Ben Bagdikian noted, "no more than 14 reporters" of the 2,200-member Washington press corps did any substantial work on it, and only a few newspapers, like the *Washington Post,* pursued it with any vigor before it exploded into a major scandal.

In fact, the American press was becoming increasingly monopolistic and conservative. By 1971, an estimated 96 per cent of American communities no longer had any press competition. Of the fifty largest cities in the nation, twenty-three were served by monopoly newspapers, many of them part of corporate chains. Between 1970 and 1977 alone, the proportion of America's daily newspapers owned by conglomerates rose from less than half to about 60 per cent. The Newhouse group consisted of thirty daily newspapers, fifteen magazines, six television stations, four radio stations, and twenty cable television systems. Others were more diverse. The *Los Angeles Times,* for example, was one of a series of papers owned by the Chandler family, which also owned oil wells, publishing houses, lumber companies, TV stations, and sizable landed interests, and served as directors of Kaiser Steel, the Santa Fe Railway, Pan American World Airways, Safeway Stores, and other companies. In these circumstances, conservatives usually dominated the press at the higher levels of power. In 1968, 80 per cent of American newspapers endorsed the election of Richard Nixon; in 1972, 92 per cent supported his re-election; in 1976, 83 per cent called for the election of Gerald Ford. The *New York Times,* sometimes described as a "liberal" newspaper, criticized the Southern sit-ins, suppressed news of the planning of the Bay of Pigs operation, opposed the 1963 March on Washington, and denounced the teach-ins against the Vietnam War. When the editorial policy of the *Times* took on a more insurgent cast in the 1970s, "Punch" Sulzberger eventually purged the editorial board.

And yet American journalism was strongly influenced by the atmosphere of social upheaval that developed after 1960. With the corporate press doing little to appeal to the interests and values of the dissidents, an "underground press" emerged in the mid-1960s: looser, more counter-cultural, and considerably farther to the Left. The Liberation News Service arose to syndicate "Movement"-style stories among the hundreds of new publications which, by the end of the decade, had a circulation of more than 3 million. Muckraking journalism underwent a revival in the pages of the *Village Voice,* the *Los Angeles Free Press, Rolling Stone, Hard Times, Ole Mole, I. F. Stone's Weekly, Ramparts,* and the *Great Speckled Bird,* with a more personal and less aloof style of reportage. I. F. Stone, Seymour Hersh, and James Ridgeway had an important critical impact as free-lance journalists, as did a new crop of writers in the commercial press: Pete Hamill, Tom Wicker, Anthony Lukas, Neil Sheehan, Carl Bernstern, Bob Woodward, and Nicholas Von Hoffman. Although the underground press waned in the 1970s, much of its journalistic energy shifted to new community newspapers, founded in an effort to cover the working people's and poor people's issues ignored by the mass media. If the American press remained overwhelmingly conservative and tied to vested interests, there were also signs that journalism could be revived as a purveyor of truth.

Another professed searcher after truth, the American university, changed its appearance in the years of turmoil after 1960, but its structure and interests remained virtually the same. "Far from being a 'community of scholars,'" read the 1970 report of the President's Commission on Campus Unrest, "the large university today is much more like a vast and impersonal staging area for professional careers. Anxious to maintain their professional standing and not unresponsive to financial inducements, the professors appear to the freshmen more like corporation executives than cloistered scholars." Higher education had become a big business, consisting, by 1968, of approximately 2,400 institutions with total annual revenues of about $13 billion and a yearly growth rate of 10 per cent. Employing half a million faculty members, American colleges and universities enrolled 6.7 million students and held billions of dollars in prime corporate stock. Students, faculty, and church groups encouraged universities to use their stockholdings to press for an end to corporate support of racial discrimination, pollution of the environment, and bidding for defense contracts, but university authorities remained almost invariably hostile. "Our purpose is just to invest in places that are selfishly good for Harvard," explained president Nathan Pusey. "We do not use our money for social purposes."

In his 1961 farewell address, President Eisenhower had warned of the "domination of the nation's scholars by Federal employment, project allocations and the power of money." During the following decade, this prediction became at least partially a reality. In 1967 the Pentagon awarded $700 million in contracts to universities, colleges, and other non-profit institutions, and two universities cropped up in the list of the top 100 defense contractors. The leading university military contractors for fiscal 1969 were MIT ($97.8 million); Johns Hopkins ($48 million); the universities of California ($15 million), Illinois ($11.6 million), and Michigan ($11.4 million); and Stanford University ($10.1 million). The Pentagon and defense-related agencies provided two-thirds of university research funds in 1968, paying 80 per cent of MIT's budget and 50 per cent of the budgets of Princeton and Columbia. An estimated 25,000 faculty scientists and engineers earned all or part of their incomes from the Pentagon by the early 1970s. Physicists and engineers at the nation's best universities pursued classified research designed to improve the U.S. nuclear arsenal. Biologists at the University of Pennsylvania held secret contracts to develop new forms of chemical-biological warfare. Drawing upon leading social scientists, Project Camelot sought to assist the Army in planning counter-insurgency activities in Asia, Africa, and Latin America. In addition, American colleges and universities offered courses for credit in ROTC training (sometimes requiring such courses for graduation), maintained covert ties with the CIA, cooperated closely with draft boards and the FBI, and provided recruiting facilities for the armed forces and defense contractors.

Although American science and engineering had been closely involved with the military since World War II, military patronage of the social sciences dated from the Kennedy Administration, with its keen interest in counter-insurgency warfare. By 1968 the American military was spending $50 million a year on social science research, producing, in conjunction with the CIA, some very useful results. A professor at the Stanford Research Institute developed the idea of controlling South

Vietnam's rural population through the "strategic hamlet" program, and experts from Michigan State University trained President Diem's secret police. In 1967 the press revealed that the executive director and the treasurer of the American Political Science Association were top officers of a CIA-funded research organization. Telford Taylor, once chief U.S. counsel at Nuremberg, wrote in 1971 that the Vietnam War, "in the massive, lethal dimensions it acquired after 1964, was the work of highly educated academics and administrators." Taylor thought the Nuremberg principles applicable to them, but this was viewed as an incredibly antique moral notion by many among the new corps of "value-free" social scientists.

When the revolt on the campus emerged, then, it did not do so because the university was a cloistered sanctuary. Quite the contrary: discontent surfaced precisely because the university, theoretically a locus of enlightenment, was in fact deeply implicated in the nation's most conspicuous abuses. Polls found that, although the overwhelming majority of American college students approved of the education they were receiving, large numbers condemned the university for its political immorality. "A great majority of students . . . oppose the Indochina war," noted the President's Commission on Campus Unrest. "And if the war is wrong, students insist, then so are all policies and practices that support it, from the draft to military research, from ROTC to recruiting for defense industry." By the end of the decade, observed the commission, "ever-increasing numbers of students accept a radical analysis of American society." In May, 1970, a special survey by the Harris organization for the American Council on Education found that 76 per cent of American college students believed that "basic changes in the system" would be necessary to improve life in America. Even large sectors of university faculties, particularly the younger members, were in revolt by the late 1960s, signing antiwar ads, marching in demonstrations, and passing radical resolutions at the annual meetings of their professional associations. "Capital itself, in all its imperial majesty, has invested these schools with its own trembling contradictions," wrote Carl Oglesby. "Necessarily demanding an increasingly sophisticated corps of servicemen to the empire, it necessarily produces a cosmopolitanism to which this empire's shame is its most conspicuous feature."

Needless to say, most university trustees and administrators—like their counterparts in business, government, and the military—were not pleased by this turn of events. Indeed, 62 per cent of the 5,200 trustees polled by an educational survey in 1968 claimed that their views were similar to those of Richard Nixon. Under pressure from militant blacks,

Chicanos, and women, many universities grudgingly discovered the merits of minority studies, beginning a variety of programs in these areas. A considerably smaller number of institutions reduced or ended university involvement in military research. Most administrations simply heightened security measures and prepared for the deluge. At San Francisco State, the new president, S. I. Hayakawa, became an overnight sensation in conservative circles by welcoming 600 police onto the campus during his first day in office and chortling over the subsequent confrontations with students and faculty. Under the banner of protecting the university from being "politicized," administrations and their conservative faculty allies began a steady purge of untenured faculty dissidents. Meanwhile, from the White House and the corporate board rooms, the word went out to curb spending on higher education; it had ceased to be a good investment. Undercapitalized, policed, and pauperized during the 1970s, the university increasingly became just another of America's social-service Appalachias, inhabited by dwindling numbers of underpaid, resentful faculty and dour, job-hungry students. More out of pessimism than conservatism, campus activism declined, leaving behind a brooding cynicism.

As university dissidence ebbed, it was replaced in public awareness by a revolt even closer to home. Deeply involved in the civil rights struggle, the peace movement, and the New Left, many American women began to explore their own situation in the critical climate of the late 1960s. The more they probed, the more obvious it became that, like blacks and other minorities, they were the victims of inferior legal, economic, and social conditions. Although approximately 40 per cent of American women worked outside the home and 6.5 million headed families, women's earnings lagged considerably below those of men. A Labor Department study found that while the average male worker earned $11,835 in 1974, the average woman received $6,772. Indeed, women constituted only 5 per cent of those earning above $15,000 a year. This resulted partially from the fact that more than half the women's labor force was confined to clerical and service positions, among the lowest paid in the economy. But women also earned less at every job and educational level. When women activists pointed to these and other inequities, they received the reply that, after all, women should be content with their supportive roles as mothers, housewives, and sex objects. In the late 1960s, this was no longer good enough. Demanding independence, justice, and fulfillment, "women's liberation" groups sprang up all across the country.

In the 1970s, the women's movement made considerable progress.

Thousands of women took part in "consciousness-raising" sessions or in political action campaigns. Women's journals, coffeehouses, and singing groups flourished. New groups emerged to champion women's cause, from feminist caucuses to the small and militant Redstockings. Increasingly, women entered electoral politics, and some, like the feisty Bella Abzug, proved vigorous proponents of the movement. Condescending but fascinated by the new feminism, the mass media gave it considerable attention, which helped women's groups broaden their political appeal. Pressure from the women's movement did much to spur the creation of local day-care centers, the legalization of abortion by state legislatures, the passage of the Equal Rights Amendment by Congress, and the implementation of affirmative action procedures in corporate and university employment. With 55,000 members by 1977, the National Organization for Women became the most influential of the women's rights organizations. Its convention that year gave top priority to state passage of ERA, but also passed resolutions defending the rights of women workers, homemakers, minority women, and lesbians.

Yet the women's movement faced serious obstacles. Thanks to the hard times and fiscal conservatism of the 1970s, women lost good jobs, saw affirmative action programs challenged, and waged a losing struggle to obtain additional social legislation. Indeed, with cutbacks in social services, women found themselves under pressure to cushion the shocks of the market system by reverting to their traditional domestic roles. Furthermore, "Right to Life" groups, drawing largely upon a Catholic constituency, engaged in vigorous efforts to block women's access to abortion. Religion, then, served as a serious division within the ranks of the women's movement, as did social class. Although the cause of women's liberation took highly educated, politicized, professional women by storm, it failed to move very far beyond these primarily white, economically comfortable circles. The Equal Rights Amendment, for example, encountered serious working-class opposition on the state level, mobilized by Phyllis Schafly and other right-wing zealots. In 1975, when ERA went down to defeat in referenda in New York and New Jersey, it met rebuff among many lower-class women, frightened by the prospect of losing legal protection in the areas of divorce and occupational law. NOW needed to do more to "communicate our priorities to housewives and blue collar workers," a founder and past chairman conceded to the press after the election defeats. By the spring of 1977, ERA ratification seemed stalled three states short of the necessary 38, with women's rights campaigns contested by a well-organized opposition.

Caught up in the climate of social ferment, intellectual life in

America grew more diverse and, ultimately, more polarized. Paul Goodman's *Growing Up Absurd* (1960) provided an early anarchist manifesto, while many books focused on the new issues of poverty and race, among them: Michael Harrington's *The Other America* (1962), James Baldwin's *The Fire Next Time* (1963), Kenneth Clark's *Dark Ghetto* (1965), Oscar Lewis' *La Vida* (1966), and Harold Cruse's *The Crisis of the Negro Intellectual* (1967). Synthesizing the analyses of Marx and Freud, the writings of the philosopher Herbert Marcuse were much admired in the late 1960s, particularly *One Dimensional Man* (1964) and *An Essay on Liberation* (1969). Probably the best-known radical intellectual in the country, the linguist Noam Chomsky, turned his talents to a brilliant critique of the Vietnam War and its apologists in "The Responsibility of Intellectuals," an essay appearing in 1967 in the *New York Review of Books,* a journal that became an important focal point for intellectual dissidence. Some intellectuals, of course, rejected social criticism, most notably Daniel Bell, Nathan Glazer, Irving Kristol, Daniel Moynihan, Norman Podhoretz, and James Q. Wilson. Described as neo-conservatives, most, in fact, were former Cold War liberals who, in a time of turmoil, finally gravitated to their natural home on the Right. In general, they argued for lowered popular expectations, checks on democracy, and the acceptance of "limits" in public life. Their prescription for America was bitterly criticized by the intellectual community's growing left wing. Indeed, Marxism regained a considerable degree of respectability among major American thinkers, and analyses such as Michael Harrington's *The Twilight of Capitalism* (1976) reflected their mordant prognosis for business civilization.

American fiction also seemed possessed by a new spirit of social criticism. Although older writers like Saul Bellow, Bernard Malamud, and John Updike continued to write on themes of individual anguish and adjustment, a newer crop of writers explored more contemporary subjects. Curiously, they did not revive the realistic or naturalistic novel but turned instead to fantasy and "black humor." Joseph Heller's *Catch-22* (1960) provided a brilliant satire on modern war, while Thomas Pynchon's *V* (1963) traced absurdist lives from the sewers of New York to the exoticism of the Middle East. Black humor achieved a striking nihilist vision in Terry Southern's *The Magic Christian* (1959), a book, as Norman Mailer noted, that never faltered "in its natural assumption that the idiocies of the mass were attached breath and kiss to the hypocrisies, the weltering grandeurs, and the low stupidities of the rich." In a series of hilarious novels, Kurt Vonnegut, Jr., focused on the inanity of business mores, modern warfare, and upper-class exist-ence. Philip Roth, with an ear attuned to the sham elements of Amer-ican life, launched an assault on repressive motherhood in *Portnoy's Complaint* (1969) and took on the Nixon Administration in *Our Gang* (1971). Turning away from fiction, Norman Mailer helped to revive social reportage with *The Armies of the Night* (1967) and *Miami and the Siege of Chicago* (1968).

Underneath the humor of many of the new novels lay a radical analysis of society and, often, a call for revolt. In Ken Kesey's *One Flew Over the Cuckoo's Nest* (1962), the towering, psychotic Chief Bromden is confined in an arbitrary and repressive insane asylum, where he pre-tends to be deaf and dumb in an effort to outwit "The Combine," which rules the world. When perception becomes too sharp among the inmates, "The Combine" employs a Fog Machine to obscure and confuse things. Into this modern hell comes Randle Patrick McMurphy, a wild Irish-man, who challenges the control of Big Nurse—a giant, white, antiseptic symbol of castrating authority. "She ain't pecking at your eyes," McMurphy explains to an inmate, but "at your balls, buddy, at your everlovin' balls." Eventually, Big Nurse succeeds in having McMurphy lobotomized and left as a vegetable in the ward—"an example," Chief Bromden notes, "of what can happen if you buck the system." In a culminating act of defiance, Bromden smothers what was once McMurphy, escapes from the asylum, and races back to the survivors of his tribe, who had begun "building their old ramshackle wood scaffolding all over the big million-dollar . . . spillway." It was an appropriate ending for this book, so evocative, despite its bizarre form, of the pro-letarian novels of the 1930s. For in it long-suffering humanity, attaining consciousness, throws off its chains and strides forth to expropriate the expropriators.

Although most American films continued to exploit trivial themes or to portray serious issues in a sensational fashion, some were of a startlingly different genre. *On the Beach* gave viewers an unpleasant picture of thermonuclear war, *Seven Days in May* pointed up the pos-sibilities of a military coup, *Dr. Strangelove* provided a hilarious satire on the Defense Establishment, *2001* questioned the virtues of techno-logical progress, and *The Front* took on the Hollywood blacklist. Some films, like *The Graduate* and *Woodstock,* celebrated the revolt of the young. Others, like *Alice's Restaurant, Cool Hand Luke,* and *Bound for Glory,* promoted the idea of resistance. One of the most visually and musically interesting of the new films, *Easy Rider,* involved the rambling motorcycle trip of two drug freaks, Captain America and Buffalo Bill, through the heartland of America, where they learn, too late, that the nation has become a repressive death trap; in the end, they are gunned down by those "bought and sold in the marketplace." Like *Easy Rider, Bonnie and Clyde* chronicled the education of young people through social experience and their subsequent destruction. Clyde learns that he no longer needs to substitute a gun for his masculinity, and the audience that the violence of the outlaw cannot compete with that of the State— the cold-blooded servant of the bankers.

Popular music also underwent a revival. Confined for years to stereotyped ditties about broken-hearted thirteen-year-olds, popular music began to explore new channels in the early 1960s with the growing enthusiasm for folk music. Folksingers like Pete Seeger, Joan Baez, Bob Dylan, and Judy Collins not only vastly upgraded the esthetics of American music but also exposed the generation of the 1960s to ballads of miners and sharecroppers, of civil rights activists and radicals. In the latter part of the decade, a new type of music emerged, sparked by *Sergeant Pepper's Lonely Hearts Club Band*—a record that established an English singing group, the Beatles, as the most experimental musicians of their time. Thousands of groups playing the new "rock" music spring up, first in San Francisco and then across the United States. With their constantly evolving style, the Beatles probably remained the most interesting, but they received strong competition from the Rolling Stones in England and the Jefferson Airplane in America. Although the sound and rhythm of the new songs were usually more important than the lyrics, the words often had a meaning relating to drugs, sex, or freedom and occasionally to politics. Young radicals usually liked the music (and sometimes performed it), while older conservatives did not; consequently, both groups convinced themselves that it was startlingly revolutionary. In fact, however, most songs were apolitical, and some had a defeatist moral. In "Street Fighting Man," a song often assumed to be the quintessence of militancy, the Rolling Stones sang that while the time was "ripe for violent revolution," all they could do was to "play in a rock and roll band."

The new music suited the emerging counter-culture. "Turned off" by America's prevalent values of material success, aggressive individualism, and self-denial, large numbers of young people in the late 1960s began adopting the softer conceptions of "love," sensory perception, and community. Associating the logic, technology, and science of the West with wars and oppression, they revived an interest in the mysticism and magic of the East as well as in folk arts and "natural" foods. Many considered the taking of drugs an important means of expanding consciousness or, at the least, a pleasant way to pass the time. Former Harvard psychologist Timothy Leary became the guru of a religion centered upon LSD, and millions of young Americans experimented with mescaline, hashish, and especially marijuana. A Gallup poll in early 1973 reported that marijuana had been tried at least once by more than one-third of American adults under thirty. As the hair of counter-culturists grew longer, their clothing more eccentric, and their life-styles more unconventional, they gathered in supportive communities, first in San Francisco's Haight-Ashbury section and New York's East Village, and later in thousands of rural and urban communes, many of them sprinkled across New England and the Southwest. The number of full-time "freaks" was never very great, but their example proved contagious. Observers began to talk of a "youth culture."

When the counter-culture first appeared, its proponents contended that their cult of music, drugs, and sensory experience was actually more "revolutionary" than "straight" politics. Many of the half-million participants at the Woodstock Festival of August, 1969, argued that they constituted a new and more humane "nation," which would soon supplant the old. For some, this contention reflected a sincere belief that they were plumbing more profound levels of human consciousness than those reached by political activism; for others, it provided a convenient rationalization for "dropping out." Whatever its motives, however, the argument was heard less often in later years as the fundamentally apolitical aspects of the counter-culture asserted themselves. Too self-indulgent and simple-minded to withstand commercial exploitation, counter-culture was absorbed, in part, into the mainstream of consumerism. Mod clothing, rock concerts, records, "health" foods, and drugs became the foci of major business enterprises—sometimes funding counter-cultural experiments or political activism, but more frequently enriching a "hipper" huckster. Eventually, only the self-appointed guardians of community morals considered the new culture subversive. Perhaps for this reason, it faded rapidly in the 1970s.

The counter-culture was but one of many influences on American religion. Stirred by the moral intensity of the crusade for racial equality and the revolt against the Vietnam War, American clerics played major roles in the civil rights and peace movements. Although liberal Protestant and Jewish denominations were probably the most heavily represented, many Catholic priests and nuns, rejecting the conservatism of their church hierarchy, also championed militant forms of resistance.

Even if the upheavals of the time had not contained a moral overtone, American churches would still have been strongly influenced by their own internal dynamics. The brief reign of Pope John XXIII in the early 1960s did much to sweep away the reactionary legacy of the Catholic Church, and John's successor, Paul VI, while reaffirming the Church's ban on birth control, continued the modernizing direction of John's policies. By the mid-1970s, a sizable sector of the American Catholic hierarchy was championing the removal of the excommunication penalty from divorced and remarried Catholics, the role of conscience in deciding upon birth control measures, and the removal of barriers against women and married men in the priesthood. In Protestant circles, new theologies and forms of worship became increasingly popular, and churches developed a wide range of services for the young—from coffeehouses to draft counseling. The new "relevance" of religion kept the allegiance of a restless population, particularly in the 1970s, when, in response to the apparent dead end of politics, mysticism and fundamentalism underwent a noticeable revival.

As the new believers understood, the prosperity of the City of God stood in marked contrast to the decay of the City of Man. Beginning in the late 1960s, there was a widespread sense in America that, despite unprecedented national wealth, things were falling apart. And they were. In July, 1969, when President Nixon was hailing the landing on the moon as "the greatest week since the Creation," the nation's largest city was suffering a breakdown of its electric power system, its telephone system, and its rail transportation. Like most other urban areas, New York also suffered from poverty, slums, crime, drug addiction, pollution, and congestion—conditions which worsened as the city gradually approached bankruptcy. Large sectors of the country's public school system were crumbling or in chaos, and in 1970 fifteen industrial nations had higher literacy rates than the United States. Health care was steadily deteriorating. In 1967, 41 per cent of the young men called up for the draft were rejected because of physical or educational defects. Although the United States ranked first among nations in per capita health expenditures, in 1976 it ranked eighteenth in doctor-patient ratio, seventeenth in infant mortality, and fifteenth in life expectancy. More than six decades after the passage of the Pure Food and Drug Act, major scandals emerged over chemical additives in American food and over the unwholesome conditions of food packaging. In a 1972 survey, the Department of Agriculture discovered conditions in meat and poultry plants that endangered human health—ranging from poor sanitation to "filth"—in 43 per cent of them. Urban, suburban, and intercity public transportation neared collapse. Between 1958 and 1969 the number of regular intercity passenger trains in the United States declined by more than two-thirds. Broad areas of the nation were left without passenger service of any kind; still others retained trains at the price of deteriorating facilities and vanishing services.

These were, of course, some of the hidden costs of the Cold War—that great funnel channeling the nation's resources from domestic needs to military adventures. And yet, in almost every case, the decline in the quality of services received by the nation was helped along by a powerful vested interest. The failure of the Food and Drug Administration "to insure safe, pure, and nutritious food," concluded consumer advocate Ralph Nader, "has been in step with each new ingenious technique for manipulating the content of food products as dictated by corporate greed and irresponsibility." While pouring 16 to 18 per cent of its revenues into advertising, the $125 billion food industry spent virtually nothing on improving the quality and nutrition of food. The deteriorating quality of the nation's rail service also reflected corporate priorities. Finding freight shipment more profitable than passenger service, the railroad corporations decided to phase out passenger trains. To justify the elimination of passenger lines to the ICC, the corporations discouraged riders by refusing to modernize equipment, by cutting services to a minimum, and by curtailing advertising. In 1967 the nation's major railroads spent less than 0.07 per cent of their income advertising passenger service; the comparable figure for the airlines was 3.48 per cent. Thus, between 1929 and 1969 the number of passenger trains in the United States declined from 20,000 to 450, although an estimated 100 million passengers a year still depended upon their service.

Corporate willingness to subordinate the public interest to private profit was illustrated by the activities of the American tobacco industry. In 1953 the American Cancer Society published a report linking cancer to cigarettes, and in 1964 the U.S. Public Health Service asserted that cigarette smoking provided a major cause of lung cancer and heart disease. Nevertheless, the sales of cigarettes proceeded without major interruption. Finding themselves hopelessly addicted to cigarettes, smokers continued to consume them; finding themselves hopelessly addicted to profits, cigarette manufacturers continued to rake them in. Cigarette companies poured forth many millions of dollars for advertising in magazines and newspapers, on radio and television, promising smokers youth, love, or enjoyment with another puff of tobacco smoke. Countering these commercials, the American Cancer Society broadcast its own advertisements warning of the toxic nature of cigarettes. In 1970

Congress banned cigarette advertising on radio and television. It did not, however, ban cigarettes. Consequently, in 1976 U.S. tobacco companies spent about $300 million on advertising, enjoyed $10 billion in sales, and were responsible for an estimated 80,000 American deaths from lung cancer, as well as numerous cases of heart disease and emphysema.

Like the tobacco industry, the automobile industry exhibited a blatant disregard for the public interest. Spending $2 billion during the 1960s to advertise and promote their products, American auto companies sold larger, faster, and more expensive cars every year. Unlike most European cars, the models changed annually, thus further encouraging Americans to scrap their old cars and buy new ones. In 1968 General Motors received a return of almost 26 per cent on its investment. While the profits rolled in, the products of the auto industry undermined public transportation, polluted the air, consumed vast resources, sliced up the countryside, and destroyed urban areas. By the late 1960s about half the space in U.S. cities was occupied by automobiles, roads, parking lots, and gas stations. In 1965 automobile crashes killed 50,000 Americans and were the principal cause of death for those under thirty-five years of age. About half of all adult Americans could look forward to an auto injury at some time in their lives. The auto industry and its friends on the National Safety Council piously urged Americans to drive slowly and carefully, but in fact, as Ralph Nader's book observed, American cars were *Unsafe at Any Speed*. Their bumpers could not withstand impacts at three miles an hour, and head-on collisions at twenty-five miles an hour were often fatal. Seat belts and other safety devices would have cut highway fatalities dramatically, but manufacturers declined to install them; after all, they were not profitable. When Nader's book revealed these facts in 1964, stirring up an outcry among consumers and Congressmen, the industry's response was to deny them and to launch a counterattack against Nader. General Motors hired private detectives to keep him under surveillance, attempting, unsuccessfully, to turn up embarrassing personal material that might damage his safety crusade. In the end, Nader prodded Congress into passing auto safety laws, won a lawsuit against General Motors, and used the money to set up teams of lawyers and law students to investigate corporate abuses.

The high cost and uneven quality of the nation's health care reflected a two-pronged attack on the public interest. Providing medicine to consumers at a price often many times its cost and frequently without any therapeutic value, the American drug industry became the most profitable in the United States. Although the companies claimed that high research costs necessitated soaring drug prices, a considerable part of drug prices represented sales promotion. In 1968 the Department of Health, Education, and Welfare estimated that American pharmaceutical firms spent approximately $4,500 per physician each year promoting and advertising their products. Meanwhile, concerned primarily with increasing the affluence of doctors, the American Medical Association opposed the expansion of American medical schools so effectively that, by 1971, more physicians were imported from abroad than were graduated from America's training centers. The AMA also spent many millions of dollars blocking the establishment of federal health programs, including Medicare. In 1976 alone it contributed $1.8 million to Congressional opponents of national health insurance, making it the nation's largest single political contributor. Consistently battling against voluntary prepaid group health plans, the organization secured the passage of laws forbidding their existence in seventeen states. At the same time, American doctors performed an estimated 3 million unnecessary operations a year. Thanks to such activities, from 1950 to 1976 the cost of physicians' services rose by eight times and the cost of health care increased twice as fast as prices, putting it beyond the budget of the average American family. With the average doctor's income topping $70,000 in 1976, health costs in the United States that year reached a phenomenal $139 billion. U.S. officials warned that medical care might cost $230 billion by 1980.

One of the most serious of America's problems was crime. Between 1960 and 1975, the serious crime rate in the United States nearly tripled. A Gallup poll at the end of 1972 found that one out of five Americans claimed to be the victim of a criminal act that year, and one out of three in the nation's inner cities. The survey contended that four out of ten Americans were afraid to walk alone at night in their neighborhoods. In 1972 New York, about the same size as London, had about five times as many assaults, fifteen times as many murders, twenty-four times as many rapes, and twenty-five times as many robberies. While noting that a disproportionate number of crimes in America were committed by the poor, the more affluent did not draw the logical conclusion that the nation's high crime rate was the price of its failure to end poverty. To assume that such antisocial behavior was a natural, if undesirable, by-product of the gulf separating the poor from the rich would, of course, have been to indict themselves. Consequently, the more privileged sectors of society drew comfort from the notion that the poor harbored innate criminal tendencies. The solution was thus to give them not more but less, to keep them "in their place." In a word, repression.

Between 1964 and 1974, expenditures on the police in the United States rose by eight times, accounting for 57 per cent of the $15 billion criminal justice budget in the latter year. And while this utterly failed to halt the steady growth of crime, it did have the consolation, for some, of adding thousands of impoverished Americans to the U.S. prison population, which reached 283,000 in 1977. One of the better-known prisoners during these years was George Jackson, a black eighteen-year-old accused of robbing a gas station operator of $70. Persuaded by his court-appointed lawyer to change his plea of not guilty to guilty, he received an indeterminate sentence of one year to life in prison. In 1961, after a year behind bars, he began applying for release, only to find that the authorities did not consider him sufficiently submissive. Although Jackson's book, *Soledad Brother,* established his case as a nationwide *cause célèbre,* it did not secure his freedom. On August 21, 1971, he was shot and killed by prison guards at San Quentin, allegedly while trying to escape.

The rich, of course, also committed many crimes, but rarely were the penalties, if any, very heavy. Ralph Nader observed in 1971: "Corporate economic, product, and environmental crimes dwarf other crimes in damage to health, safety, and property." American industries were responsible for half of all air pollution and most water pollution in the United States, but only infrequently were they taken to account for it. Nor did legal action seriously hamper their growth and development. The largest monopolistic conspiracy in American history was uncovered in the early 1960s, when executives from General Electric, Westinghouse, and twenty-seven other giant firms were convicted of fixing prices—defrauding the public, in the words of their trial judge, of "millions upon millions" of dollars. Yet for all the furor, the companies hardly suffered at all, and later deducted their fines from their taxes as normal business expenses. In the mid-1970s, when approximately 150 major U.S. firms, after investigation, admitted making illegal political payments to domestic and foreign sources and to engaging in questionable practices, few of them were prosecuted and no executive was sent to prison. As the average fine of the first thirteen companies was $4,000, and the average company grossed $20,000 a minute, it took about twelve seconds for each to pay its penalty to society. Even in cases involving the loss of human life, corporate criminality went virtually unpunished. In 1977, five months after an explosion killed two pipefitters at a Phillips Petroleum plant, the U.S. Occupational Safety and Health Administration ruled that the firm was negligent. The penalty: a $490 fine.

Crammed to bursting with many thousands of the American poor—
either convicted of crimes or simply unable to raise pretrial bail—
American prisons served less as rehabilitation centers than as vast
detention camps for the unwanted, grim dumping grounds of human
wretchedness. Overcrowding, brutality by guards, inadequate medical
care, miserable recreation facilities, long incarceration before court
appearances, inadequate rehabilitation programs, and a host of other
problems afflicted most prisons throughout the nation, spurring a
desperate series of revolts in the late 1960s and early 1970s. One of
the most spectacular occurred in September, 1971, at Attica, New York.
Demanding prison reforms, inmates held thirty-eight guards and prison
workers as hostages and called for a meeting with Governor Rockefeller.
While reportedly in agreement with most of their demands, the millionaire governor considered a personal meeting with the rebellious prisoners
a threat to his prestige. Consequently, he ordered thousands of state
police and national guardsmen to capture the prison in a military operation that eventually took the lives of forty-one people (among them nine
prison guards) and wounded eighty others. According to a Congressional study, the police needlessly killed inmates and hostages, and
returning guards subjected the surviving inmates to "widespread beatings." Promised reforms in prison conditions were abandoned by state
authorities, who instead spent more than $5 million prosecuting 61
surviving prisoners for 1,300 crimes, with total penalties exceeding
40,000 years. Thereafter, juries refused to convict almost all of the
"Attica brothers" and, in late 1976, Governor Hugh Carey finally
pardoned the rest, noting that, if their sentences continued in the face of
blatant lying and obstruction of justice by state officials, "the law itself
might fall into disrespect." Meanwhile, of course, Attica and the nation's
other prisons remained smoldering volcanoes of discontent, as well as a
source of scandal and shame. The psychiatrist Karl Menninger wrote in
1971: "I suspect that all the crimes committed by all the jailed criminals
do not equal in total social damage that of the crimes committed
against them."

Richer than any nation in history, America seemed no happier, for
it was plagued by social problems of unprecedented magnitude. Noting
that problems had always existed, some social commentators contended
that Americans should simply accept theirs as inevitable. Others, however, argued that all problems had solutions, and that with its immense
intellectual, scientific, and material resources, the United States should
at least be able to cope with its own—not to mention the many endured
by the rest of mankind. Proponents of this view assumed, of course, that

America's vast resources were at the disposal of the public. But this was hardly the case. Instead, they remained at the service of the few, channeled into enterprises that enhanced their wealth and power. As Hans Morgenthau wrote in 1970: "Poverty on a large scale, like the decay of the cities and the ruination of the natural environment, is a result not of accidental misfortunes but of social and economic policies in whose continuation powerful social groups have a vested interest." The result, then, was frustration. Even affluent Americans grumbled among themselves: Things do not work as they should. What they failed to see, or refrained from seeing, was that a harmonious, fulfilling society had a price—the one price they were not prepared to pay. And that price was equality.

12

The New Order of Richard Nixon, 1969-74

> Let each of us ask . . . what can I do for myself?
>
> RICHARD NIXON, second inaugural address, 1973

RICHARD NIXON WAS THE MOST REACTIONARY and unscrupulous politician to reach the White House in the postwar era. For years, as two of his conservative political biographers have written, Nixon "brooded, dreamed, and schemed for the Presidency," subordinating his impulses, personality, and occasionally his principles to his relentless quest for power. A close friend and admirer of men of wealth, Nixon was a staunch conservative, but he could appear to shift direction at politically expedient moments, surprising at least some political observers with a "new Nixon." "He is the least 'authentic' man alive," contended Garry Wills in his provocative study of the President. Even Nixon conceded: "I have a fetish about disciplining myself." Before he appeared on television, the President applied beard cover, face powder, and hair tinting and ordered the studio chilled to 35° to keep him from sweating. As a man of suppressed personality, Nixon was quite unlike his garrulous, colorful predecessor. Moody, insecure, and filled with self-pity, he isolated himself from Cabinet, Congress, press, and public. In 1972 the *New York Times* described his Administration as "the most closed . . . the most secretive, the most removed and remote from the public, the most hostile to criticism—of any American administration in modern times."

To staff it, Nixon tapped the traditional sources of power in American life. William Rogers, a wealthy corporate lawyer with little foreign policy experience, was appointed Secretary of State. For Secretary of Defense Nixon chose Melvin Laird, a hawkish Republican Congressman rated 100 per cent by the U.S. Chamber of Commerce. At the behest of the American Bankers Association, Nixon named Chicago banker David Kennedy to the Treasury post. Kennedy brought with him a fellow executive at the Continental Illinois Bank, Robert Mayo, who became Director of the Budget. Nixon's Secretary of Labor was the Dean of the Graduate School of Business at the University of Chicago, George Shultz; his Secretary of Commerce was a New York financier, Maurice Stans; his Postmaster General was a millionaire contractor from Montgomery, Alabama, Winton Blount; and his Secretary of Housing and Urban Development was the former head of the American Motors Corporation and Governor of Michigan, George Romney. All Cabinet members were white, male, and Republican. The most powerful was the new Attorney General, John Mitchell, a millionaire bond lawyer from Nixon's Wall Street firm who had managed his 1968 campaign. With the exception of Mitchell, however, no Cabinet member had as much influence in the White House as two assistants to the President: H. R. Haldeman, formerly an executive in the J. Walter Thompson advertising agency, and John D. Ehrlichman, a lawyer from Seattle.

Although Nixon termed his appointees "pragmatic centrists," most were far to the Right. Even the Administration's most prominent intellectual, Henry Kissinger, who served as Nixon's top national security adviser, had written that "democracies which have been most successful have been those based on essentially aristocratic forms." Critical of "egalitarian" considerations in the making of foreign policy, Kissinger contended that an effective leadership must "define purposes perhaps only vaguely apprehended by the multitude." For a time, HEW Secretary Robert Finch moved in another direction. Searching for a Commissioner of Education, he chose Dr. James Allen, a liberal Republican who superintended public education in New York State. Allen was unceremoniously fired in 1970 for criticizing the Indochina War. Another Finch appointee was former CORE leader James Farmer, named Assistant Secretary of HEW. Farmer, too, did not last out 1970. The beginning of the end for Finch came when he selected Dr. John Knowles, head of the Massachusetts General Hospital, as Assistant Secretary for Health. Although Knowles, a Republican, had actively supported Nixon for President in 1968, the AMA bitterly opposed him because of his known sympathy for national health insurance and eventually pressured Finch into withdrawing the nomination. In mid-1970, his effectiveness crippled, Finch resigned from the Cabinet, leaving Mitchell to reign supreme.

Unlike Finch, who urged broadening the Administration's circle of support by appealing to the young, the poor, and the black, Mitchell argued that these and other liberal groups should be ignored. The Administration's political future, he maintained, lay with holding the Nixon voters of 1968 while winning over the Wallace constituency. Crucial to this thinking was the work of Kevin Phillips, a young lawyer who worked on Mitchell's campaign staff in 1968 and went on to become an aide in the Justice Department. An expert on ethnic voting patterns, Phillips told an interviewer that "the whole secret of politics" is "knowing who hates who." In 1969 Phillips published a widely discussed book, *The Emerging Republican Majority,* which contended that, with significant exceptions, Americans were ripe for a conservative political appeal reflecting the interests of the South, the Sunbelt (an area stretching from Florida to Southern California), and the white (particularly Catholic) labor force. Feigning ignorance of Phillips's work but adhering faithfully to its precepts, Nixon and Mitchell turned their efforts to cultivating the white South and its chief Republican power broker, Strom Thurmond. Nixon appointed one of Thurmond's cronies, Harry Dent, to the White House staff to serve as a "Southern" spokesman on all issues and approved a directive that forbade any Administration official from making statements that might alienate the white South. The Nixon Administration resolved to give the white South whatever it wanted. And what the white South wanted most in 1969 was what it had desired for centuries: to keep blacks "in their place."

The first necessity, then, was to subvert civil rights legislation. Immediately after his inauguration in January, 1969, Nixon met with Thurmond and other Southern Republican leaders, who pressed for an end to federal enforcement of civil rights, particularly school desegregation. They did not have long to wait. In April, the black chairman of the Equal Employment Opportunity Commission resigned, charging a "crippling lack of administration support." That same month, Nixon urged Congress to reduce the appropriation for the fair housing enforcement program by $4 million. In June the Justice Department opposed extension of the Voting Rights Act of 1965, proposing a substitute that eliminated guarantees of enforcement in the South. The NAACP termed the Justice Department bill a "deadly way of thwarting the progress we have made." Later that month the head of the Small Business Administration's program for minority groups resigned, declaring: "There's been lots of rhetoric in government about helping blacks but no money has been forthcoming." Federal courts had ordered thirty-three Mississippi school districts desegregated by the fall of 1969, but Mitchell and Finch secured a delay. An angry NAACP brought the issue to the Supreme Court, which ruled unanimously on October 29, 1969, that dual school systems should be terminated "at once." The President responded on December 8 by declaring that he "disagreed" with the ruling.

The civil rights rollback was only beginning. The White House deliberately delayed Secretary Romney's efforts to alter all-white suburban housing patterns, dropped Secretary Shultz's plan to bring blacks into lily-white construction unions, and purged Justice Department and HEW officials who sought to enforce civil rights laws. In a speech on March 24, 1970, Nixon declared that school boards should be left alone to "formulate plans of desegregation which best suit the needs of their own localities." The result was, as U.S. District Judge John H. Pratt noted in a decision of November 16, 1972, that school desegregation came to a virtual standstill the month of Nixon's speech. He reported that 113 Southern school districts which had stalled on desegregation for two years had continued to receive "substantial" funds from HEW, that no enforcement action had been taken against public colleges and universities in ten states that were not in compliance with the law, and that vocational and special schools in the South remained "overwhelmingly" segregated. The court reminded HEW that it did not have the "discretion to negate the purpose and intent" of the 1964 Civil Rights Act.

Nixon's campaign to curb racial integration took on nationwide dimensions in the controversy over school busing. In his March, 1970, speech, he reiterated his "opposition to any compulsory busing of pupils . . . for the purpose of achieving racial balance." This position was in direct contrast to that of Chief Justice Warren Burger, who in 1971 admonished district judges and school authorities to make "every effort to achieve the greatest degree of actual desegregation," including the use of "bus transportation as one tool." Despite the fact that Burger spoke for a unanimous Court, Nixon was determined to continue exploiting the issue. In March, 1972, he asked Congress to impose a moratorium on court-ordered busing, thus giving the legislators time to fashion a bill restricting its future use. Although the House acceded to Nixon's desires, liberals successfully buried the President's proposals in a Senate filibuster. Few could mistake the direction of executive policy. "For the first time since Woodrow Wilson," declared the board chairman of the NAACP, "we have a national administration that can be rightly characterized as anti-Negro."

Nixon also thought in terms of his "Southern strategy" as he moved to transform the Supreme Court. During the 1968 campaign, Nixon had appealed to those sectors of the nation disgruntled by the Warren Court's civil rights and civil liberties decisions and had promised to pack the federal bench with those he called "strict constructionists." For Chief Justice, Nixon nominated Warren Burger, a conservative federal judge, who was quickly approved. His nomination of Clement Haynesworth, Jr., of South Carolina, however, encountered a Senate rebuff, largely because of conflict of interest charges and the candidate's segregationist, antilabor decisions. Infuriated, Nixon fired back the nomination of G. Harrold Carswell, a Florida judge who had campaigned as a white supremacist, had belittled black plaintiffs from the bench, and had acquired a widespread reputation as mediocre. When the Senate vote went against Carswell, many Administration insiders were reportedly rather relieved, but Nixon used the occasion to assail the Senate's "regional discrimination." With his "Southern" credentials underscored, Nixon appointed three additional judges to the Supreme Court with far less furor. All were staunch conservatives, and their presence did much to end the innovative role of the federal judiciary.

Despite their rhetorical commitment to a "strict constructionist" view of the Constitution, the President and his associates were among the loosest of constructionists when it came to respecting the liberties guaranteed Americans by the Bill of Rights. During Nixon's first year in office, the Justice Department cooperated with local police agencies in launching a nationwide crackdown on the Black Panther Party. By the end of 1969, dozens of Black Panthers had been killed by police and one hundred others imprisoned, virtually wiping out the leadership of the organization. Antiwar radicals received their comeuppance when the federal government indicted eight dissidents for "conspiracy" to cause the Chicago convention riots of 1968. Vice-President Agnew labeled them "kooks" and "social misfits," and the presiding judge even had one defendant chained and gagged in the courtroom. Nevertheless, they were acquitted, as were the Reverend Philip Berrigan and six other peace activists charged with plotting to kidnap Henry Kissinger. Juries often exhibited a lower tolerance for the government's employment of illegal methods and paid informants than did the Justice Department, which, in fact, was interested primarily in using its powers to harass and silence dissident groups and individuals. From 1970 to 1973, its Internal Security Division conducted more than 100 grand juries, which called thousands of witnesses and returned 400 indictments. Among the targets were veterans' protest groups, Catholic activists, the American Indian movement, Chicano militants, and the women's movement. Senator Sam Ervin of North Carolina, a true "strict constructionist," accused the Administration of using its "law-and-order slogan" to justify a "fundamental negation of America's constitutional traditions."

At the time, few knew how far the Administration had moved toward adopting the techniques of a police state. In May, 1969, President Nixon authorized the illegal wiretapping of five newsmen and thirteen members of his own National Security Council staff. The alleged "security" reason for the taps, which lasted until 1971, was a story in the American press reporting that U.S. planes were bombing Cambodia—a fact hardly unknown to the Communists, but which the Administration hoped to keep hidden from the American people. Although the CIA had reported to President Johnson on at least four occasions that there was no link between domestic protest groups and foreign powers, the following month Nixon ordered the CIA to further expand Operation Chaos. By 1974, the CIA had spied on the full spectrum of American peace and civil rights groups, accumulating subject files on 1,000 U.S. organizations and gathering the names of 300,000 American citizens. Military intelligence, which had directed its surveillance and infiltration efforts at civil rights groups in the early 1960s, shifted focus thereafter to a considerably larger constituency, ranging from New Left organizations to ADA, the NAACP, the American Friends Service Committee, and the American Civil Liberties Union. By the end of 1971, the Army's "subversive file" at Fort Holabird alone contained 211,243 dossiers on organizations and 80,731 biographical files. At the suggestion of the Nixon White House, the Internal Revenue Service utilized its supposedly confidential records to compile political and intelligence files on more than 11,000 individuals and organizations, among them the National Student Association, the Medical Committee for Human Rights, and the Urban League. Continuing its Cointelpro efforts to disrupt and destroy radical groups, the FBI employed *agents provocateurs,* flung Molotov cocktails, sought to encourage racial discord and violence, dispatched anonymous letters, placed propaganda in the press, broke up meetings, distributed false or scurrilous information, arranged for dissidents to be fired from their jobs, and roughed up demonstrators. With files on more than a million Americans, the FBI's targets ranged from Cesar Chavez to the consumer movement, from "all black student unions" to Antioch College, and from SDS to the women's liberation movement.

In an effort to tighten up White House control of the government's burgeoning domestic "intelligence" operations, Nixon ordered the directors of the CIA, FBI, National Security Agency, and the Defense Intelligence Agency to meet with White House aide Tom Huston in June, 1970, and work out a coordinated plan. Huston, the former head of the conservative Young Americans for Freedom, announced at the first meeting that, in coping with domestic dissent, Nixon had decided that "everything is valid, everything is possible." After several meetings, they agreed to establish an interagency group that would take action against members of organizations they considered subversive: opening mail, tapping telephones, and burglarizing homes and offices. CIA director Richard Helms was "most cooperative," Huston reported, but FBI director Hoover eventually withdrew his support, primarily because he did not want other government agencies encroaching upon his bureau's jurisdiction. According to Huston, Hoover also complained that "the risks are too great" because " 'the jackals of the press' and the A.C.L.U. will find out." Nixon ignored Hoover's opposition and approved the Huston plan in July, 1970, but, ultimately, the FBI director's awesome power prevailed and the plan was abandoned.

With burglary, wiretapping, and mail opening continuing as the official (albeit illegal) prerogatives of the FBI and the CIA, Nixon established a "special investigative unit" in 1971 to handle White House undercover work. Ehrlichman and his assistant, who supervised the unit's covert activities, sought out men with useful talents, eventually hiring E. Howard Hunt, Jr. (a retired CIA agent who had been a key figure in the Cuban and Guatemalan invasions), and G. Gordon Liddy (a former FBI agent with a flair for the dramatic). Operating out of their offices in the White House and the Executive Office Building, Hunt, Liddy, and their associates burglarized medical files, spirited away a Washington lobbyist for ITT when a Senate committee sought to question her, falsified diplomatic records of the Kennedy Administration, tapped the phones of newspaper reporters, arranged for gangs to attack antiwar demonstrators, and carried on a broad-gauged campaign of political espionage. Nixon aides had many assignments and suggestions for their corps of secret agents (including firebombing the Brookings Institution), for they were then beginning to compile lists of hundreds of "political enemies": members of Congress, labor leaders, university officials, journalists, and even a few businessmen. Some on the lists (such as Senator Edward Kennedy) were placed under surveillance by covert operatives; others were investigated by the FBI; and still others were marked out for rough treatment by the IRS—an attempt, in the words of Presidential counsel John Dean, to "use the available Federal machinery to screw our political enemies."

Whatever popularity the Administration's "law and order" rhetoric enjoyed was closely linked to the "war" upon crime—a war, however, with few victories. Between 1969 and 1975, the Law Enforcement Assistance Administration spent $4.5 billion, primarily to expand the size of local police forces and arm them with new weaponry and surveillance equipment. Yet criminal activity, particularly of a violent nature, continued to increase by alarming proportions. During Nixon's years in the White House, the nation's crime rate rose 44 per cent and the murder rate doubled. The President claimed that his Administration had "fought crime to a standstill," but this optimistic assessment may have resulted from the selective view of criminal behavior that characterized Washington officialdom.

Opposed by Democratic majorities in both houses of Congress, Nixon was forced to move cautiously in dismantling the modest social welfare agencies inherited from the Johnson Administration. During the 1968 campaign Nixon had been critical of certain aspects of the antipoverty program. But once in office he retained them, accepting the argument of Daniel Moynihan, who joined the Administration as an adviser on domestic affairs, that their hasty elimination would simply provoke conflict and instability. On the other hand, as director of the program, he chose a conservative Republican, Donald Rumsfeld, whose record as a Congressman included a vote against OEO's establishment in 1964. Only in early 1973 did the President order the agency totally abandoned. Nixon planned a more rapid destruction of the Model Cities program, complaining to Romney that, in most localities, its planning agencies were run by "the dregs and the social reformers." Nevertheless, badgered by Romney (who liked the program) and by Moynihan (who did not, but opposed its dissolution), Nixon retained Model Cities—temporarily.

In general, Nixon worked to cut back social programs or to limit their effectiveness. Romney, who pressed for aid to cities and for more and cheaper housing, often found himself thwarted by the President. Congress, too, proved considerably more liberal than the White House. During Nixon's first two years in office he vetoed an HEW bill, a HUD bill, a hospital construction bill, a program to train additional family doctors, and an education bill. When Congress passed a measure giving eighteen-year-olds the vote, he signed it grudgingly, expressing doubts about its constitutionality. By 1972 the Administration had actually begun to impound funds appropriated by Congress for social programs— a procedure of highly questionable constitutionality.

During his 1968 campaign Nixon had skillfully exploited hostility toward the existing welfare system, but once in office he had no idea of what to put in its place. Moynihan urged Nixon to become the American Disraeli—a conservative concerned with the poor—by supporting an income-maintenance program. Nixon liked the image more than the program; however, he accepted the latter after amending it to include work requirements for all able-bodied recipients. In the summer of 1969 the President proposed to Congress that the federal government take over most of the welfare burden from the states, setting an income floor of $1,600 a year for a family of four—an amount less than half the poverty level. Liberals objected to the fact that welfare benefits might actually be cut for many recipients, who could also be forced to work at less than minimum wages and to accept compulsory day care for their children. Conservatives, on the other hand, objected to the very concept of a guaranteed annual income. Caught in this crossfire, the program expired in the Senate. Thus, although the 1970 census revealed that only about a fifth of all poor families received welfare assistance, and although HEW estimated that fewer than 0.4 per cent of recipients "cheated," the Administration returned to its practice of whipping up resentment against the poor and the unemployed by portraying them as undeserving recipients of lavish government "handouts." American taxpayers, who were to learn that they had spent $10 million to improve the private estates of President Nixon and his millionaire friends, were assured that providing $972 a year to an impoverished family of four in Alabama was beyond endurance.

The limits of the Administration's concern for the poor were evident in its response to the issue of widespread starvation in America, brought to public attention by the speeches of Senator George McGovern. On May 6, 1969, the day Administration officials were scheduled to appear before Senator McGovern's Select Committee on Nutrition and Human Needs, the President announced plans for a special White House conference on food and nutrition and sent Congress a new food-stamp proposal. "That hunger and malnutrition should persist in a land such as ours is embarrassing and intolerable," he said. But Nixon proposed an exceptionally modest food-distribution plan, and the White House conference developed at cross-purposes with the Administration. To the dismay of the President, his appointee as conference director, Dr. Jean Mayer of Harvard Medical School, took his job with the utmost seriousness. Mayer ignored White House pressure to require "security" clearance for all 4,000 conference delegates and freely criticized the nutritional deficiencies of "fun foods," whose manufacturers, such as Pepsi-Cola, were GOP supporters. On December 2, 1969, the President delivered a chilly welcoming address to the conference and met a predictably cool reception; not once was he interrupted by applause. Only with Nixon's departure did enthusiasm return. "For God's sake, feed the hungry!" cried the Reverend Ralph Abernathy, drawing a standing ovation. Conference task forces attacked the Administration's neglect of the poor, calling Nixon's food program "feeble and inadequate." In 1973 a report by the McGovern committee revealed that, while there had been slight gains in dealing with the problem of hunger, only about half the eligible received federal food assistance; none of the federal food programs assured nutritional adequacy; and more than 12 million Americans continued to go hungry.

The Nixon Administration showered its beneficence less frequently upon the malnourished poor than upon the comfortable rich. The President appointed the owner of $185,000 in oil company stock to the Interstate Commerce Commission, the owner of nearly $350,000 in electronics and aeronautical stock to the Federal Aviation Administration, the owner of $300 million in the stock of a major defense contractor to the Deputy Defense Secretaryship, and the part-owner of a company with a "very large" loan from the Export-Import Bank to that bank's presidency. By January, 1970, the *New York Times* Economic Review could report: "The hopes of the business community have, in general, been realized, particularly in those areas where the Government directly regulates business conduct." The Bureau of Mines acknowledged that in 1970—a year of 10,575 mine injuries—it had made fewer than a third of its required safety inspections and only 1 per cent of its required health inspections. That same year, the *New York Times* reported that ICC officials were checking fewer than 400 of the 5,000 commercial buses every year, despite the fact that three-fourths of the buses were operating with serious to critical equipment defects. An investigation sponsored by the National Commission on Product Safety concluded in 1969 that major consumer safety programs constituted "a widespread public deception," primarily because they were inoperative. "The agencies," claimed the investigators, "instinctively approach any problem so as to seek accommodation with the regulated industry."

During the Nixon era government-business collaboration became the most flagrant since the 1920s. Despite the passage in 1967 of the Flammable Fabrics Act, which empowered the federal government to set flammability standards for blankets, rugs, drapes, upholstery, hats, gloves, and shoes, the establishment of such standards was so delayed that, by mid-1971, 10,000 more Americans had been killed and 525,000 injured in fabric fires. The Clean Air Acts of 1965 and 1967 resulted in virtually no enforcement actions, and the Administration opposed the

Clean Air Act of 1970, which set federal air-pollution standards for automobiles. After a February 10, 1971, meeting with more than 200 industrial leaders, who urged the President not to implement anti-pollution policies harmful to their interests, the Administration postponed the implementation of federal standards for automobile exhaust emissions. Later that year Nixon met with dairy industry representatives, who had pledged $2 million for his re-election. "I appreciate it. I don't need to spell it out," the President told them. The Administration thereupon reversed its previous position by raising milk price supports. Two measures with fierce White House backing were a $250 million loan to the Lockheed Aircraft Corporation and a multibillion dollar plan to build a supersonic transport plane—both with no apparent end other than to enrich the aircraft industry. By late 1972 the Administration had compiled an outstanding record of favoritism toward big business. "The whole top echelon of the Nixon Administration openly acts on the assumption that the rich and powerful can bend the decisions of government to their own interests," the *New York Times* editorialized that October. "The pervasive atmosphere is brazenly plutocratic."

The best of the boondoggles remained the "defense" business, which received the highest of priorities during the Nixon years. In the Administration's first budget, for fiscal 1970, it allocated about 8 per cent for health and welfare (excluding self-financed trust funds like Social Security) and 75 per cent for the Pentagon, veterans' benefits, interest charges on the national debt (largely war-created), and expenditures on the military-oriented space program. These proportions remained roughly the same in subsequent years. Thus, under the Nixon's Administration's budget for fiscal 1973, the average American family contributed $1,301 in taxes to military-related programs but only $130 for education and manpower and $65 for housing and community development. Each heavy B-52 raid over Indochina cost a sum that could have been used to build twenty-seven elementary schools or about 4,050 housing units. Doubled in size during the 1960s by the escalating costs of the Vietnam War, the Pentagon budget continued during the early years of Nixon's Presidency at about $80 billion a year even as expenditures on the war declined.

Promising a "generation of peace," the Administration pressed forward with an unprecedented array of new weapons programs. Despite a rebellion by liberals, the Administration rammed an expanded ABM program through the Senate by a single vote and later secured its passage in the House. This "building block to peace," in the words of Secretary Laird, was expected ultimately to cost from $10 billion to

$50 billion. Other weapons programs receiving the Administration's imprimatur included the Advanced Manned Strategic Aircraft, which Senator Proxmire claimed would cost at least $24 billion, and the nuclear-attack aircraft program, estimated to cost a mere $15 billion. As Congressman Reuss noted in a speech on February 10, 1970, the Administration's budget for fiscal 1971 included early installment payments on military equipment that would eventually cost a great deal more: a new airborne radar system for $15 billion; the Navy's F-14 fighter plane at a cost of up to $36 billion; and the Air Force's F-15 jet fighter at a cost expected to exceed $25 billion. According to the President, Congressional critics of these programs were undermining the Administration's efforts to secure peace. A peace-loving nation obviously could not afford to dispense with the military's new C-5A transport— a plane almost as long as a football field. "Moby Jet" could carry 600 soldiers and all their equipment, depositing them anywhere in the world through its "self-unloading" processes. Lockheed Aircraft, its manufacturer, advertised: "It's like having a military base in nearly every strategic spot on the globe." And surely Americans also needed the $20 billion "electronic battlefield," a series of electronic sensors already scattered on an experimental basis throughout the Indochinese countryside, calling down an automated rain of death upon anything—or anyone—unlucky enough to activate them. "These developments open up some very exciting horizons," a Defense Department official reported in August, 1969. "When one realizes that we can detect anything that perspires, moves, carries metal, makes a noise, or is hotter or colder than its surroundings, one begins to see the potential."

Despite the accelerating Soviet-American détente, the Pentagon continued to expand its thermonuclear arsenal. In Secretary McNamara's final statement on the military budget, he estimated that 400 one-megaton nuclear warheads would instantly kill about a third of the population of the Soviet Union and destroy 76 per cent of its industry. As of 1970 the United States possessed more than ten times this number of deliverable nuclear warheads—about three times the number held by the Soviet Union—and could deliver more than forty nuclear warheads for each Soviet city with a population of 100,000 or more. This brought only a short-lived joy to the hearts of Pentagon planners, however, who were already moving ahead with MIRV (Multiple Independently Targeted Re-entry Vehicles), a system that would enable the United States to multiply the number of nuclear warheads on its missiles several times over. Soviet-American treaties had little apparent effect on these awesome preparations. Within a year of the May, 1972, signing of the first Strategic Arms Limitation Agreement, the number of nuclear war-heads deployed on U.S. strategic weapons rose from 5,890 to more than 7,040, and on Soviet weapons from 2,170 to 2,260.

If the Administration's "defense" program was drawn up with an eye to serving needy defense contractors, it also remained linked to the goals of America's postwar foreign policy. Like his predecessors in the executive mansion, Nixon sought what he called "a world of open doors." He was "convinced," he stated in 1971, "that liberal trade is in both our domestic economic interest and our foreign policy interest." America's "preponderant size in the world economy gives us an inter-national responsibility to continue on this path." Yet the means to ensure an international free market had become costly—in dollars, in soldiers, and, therefore, in U.S. politics. And Nixon did not plan to be politically destroyed, as was his predecessor, by openly squandering American lives and resources in an unpopular war. Consequently, on July 25, 1969, he unveiled what became known as the "Nixon Doctrine." "Its central thesis," he later observed, was that while "the United States will participate in the defense and development of allies and friends," Amer-ica would no longer "undertake all the defense." In the critical Far East, this meant that the Administration would begin the removal of U.S. ground combat troops, replacing them with Asian soldiers. American troops would be reintroduced only when U.S. air power and local mercenaries could no longer cope with the situation. Asian soldiers cost only about one-fifteenth as much as their American counterparts. Fur-thermore, as historian Richard Barnet noted, "neither they nor their parents vote in U.S. elections."

To assure the success of the Nixon Doctrine, the Administration placed a great emphasis upon increasing foreign aid, particularly military aid. "A MAP [Military Assistance Program] dollar is of far greater value than a dollar spent directly on U.S. forces," argued Secretary Laird. Less than $5 billion in annual military aid was acknowledged during the Johnson years, but the figure rose to an estimated $7 billion by fiscal 1971. Although the Administration retained for a time the pretense of an arms embargo against the Greek dictatorship, even this was discarded after 1970, when full-scale military aid was resumed. Between 1961 and 1971 the annual level of U.S. arms sales to other countries more than tripled, reaching $3.4 billion. Some of the biggest purchasers were the semifeudal states of the oil-rich Persian Gulf region. In early 1973 Iran alone arranged to buy $2.5 billion in U.S. weaponry, including helicopter gunships, supersonic interceptors, and laser bombs. President Nixon, in his May, 1969, foreign aid message to Congress, contended that U.S. assistance programs helped to "avert violence and upheaval." Critics put things more bluntly. "The foreign aid program," declared Senator Church in 1971, was "sheltering the foreign invest-ments of our biggest corporations and furnishing aid and comfort to repressive governments all over the world."

At the heart of the "Nixon Doctrine" lay the struggle in Indochina. In the years before 1968 Nixon had consistently been a Vietnam "hawk," urging an increase in the deployment of U.S. combat troops and calling for intensified raids upon the North. As President, however, he ran political risks by assuming an openly hawkish stance in an increasingly dovish nation. Consequently, he sought to harmonize his foreign goals and domestic political needs through what he called "Vietnamization"— a policy of slow troop withdrawals accompanied by heightened U.S. bombing raids, a strengthened South Vietnamese Army, and the latest in military weaponry. "Vietnamization," he hoped, would dampen anti-war sentiment by lowering the American costs in lives and dollars, thus gaining time for the U.S. military to press forward in a sustained drive for victory. Testifying before the House Appropriations Committee in 1969, Secretary of the Army Stanley Resor explained: "If we can just buy some time in the U.S. by these periodic progressive withdrawals . . . I think we can bring this to a successful conclusion."

In June, 1969, after a meeting on Midway Island with South Viet-nam's latest dictator, General Nguyen Van Thieu, Nixon announced the first American troop reduction. By the end of the year, the Administra-tion had withdrawn about 60,000 of the half-million U.S. combat troops from Vietnam. Meanwhile, it steadily widened the war—in ways less noticeable to Americans. In neighboring Laos, where the President acknowledged no more than "aerial reconnaissance," "logistical support and some training," he authorized a secret Marine Corps combat opera-tion two days after his inauguration. U.S. planes intensified their massive bombing raids over rebel-held territory, while the CIA directed ground combat operations and funded a covert army of 36,000 Meo tribesmen. In Cambodia the Administration ordered the beginning of secret B-52 bombing missions that March, falsifying reports to make it appear that the attacks occurred elsewhere. Whatever else this might accomplish, it had not the slightest effect in bringing democracy to South Vietnam. General Thieu, described by Nixon as one of the world's five greatest statesmen, demanded that his critics in the virtually powerless legislature be impeached or "the armed forces will cut off these deputies' heads. Our duty is to beat such dogs to death."

American critics of the war refused to be pacified. In the fall of 1969 antiwar forces organized the largest peace demonstrations in the nation's history. On October 15, 1969, an estimated 2 million Americans took part in the Vietnam Moratorium, a series of antiwar rallies all across the country. More than eighty members of Congress endorsed the Moratorium and more than fifty actively participated in it. Attorney General Mitchell sought to undermine the November rally planned for Washington by refusing to grant a permit to the marchers and by predicting violence. Yet between a quarter and half a million Americans flocked to the capital for the largest demonstration ever held in that city. A "March Against Death," composed of 43,000 robed and silent demonstrators representing each of the Americans killed in Vietnam, paraded eerily past the White House day and night. Congress refused to cut off funds for the war or to set a date for U.S. withdrawal, but it did begin to cut back the Administration's options for escalation. At the end of the year it voted to ban the commitment of American ground troops to Laos or Thailand.

Draft resistance was reaching a fever pitch of activity. Many thousands of draftees refused induction or simply never reported. In May, 1969, the Oakland induction center, with jurisdiction over all of Northern California, acknowledged that more than half the young men ordered to report for induction never appeared and that 11 per cent of those who did appear refused to serve in the armed forces. Nationwide, demonstrations shut down Selective Service offices, while illegal raids destroyed an estimated half-million draft files. Pursued by the police and the FBI, those responsible for the raids enjoyed a startling popularity, especially among young people. Father Daniel Berrigan, declaring himself a "fugitive from injustice," eluded the FBI for four months, all the while granting interviews and making public appearances. Never in American history had the Selective Service System been under such widespread assault, or less capable of dealing with it.

The nation's fighting strength was also beginning to crumble. Writing in the *Armed Forces Journal* in 1971, Marine Corps Colonel Robert D. Heinl, Jr., complained that "at least 14 GI dissent organizations (including two made up exclusively of officers) now operate more or less openly" and that "144 underground newspapers published on or aimed at U.S. military bases" were corroding morale with antiwar and antimilitary sentiment. Throughout Vietnam, U.S. soldiers were "dispirited where not near-mutinous." In mid-1969, he noted, "an entire company of the 196th Light Infantry Brigade sat down on the battlefield." During the October and November, 1969 antiwar demonstrations, sympathetic black armbands appeared in the sleeves of U.S. combat units; a news photographer reported that in one platoon near Danang, about half the men wore them. Colonel Heinl lamented: "Symbolic anti-war fasts . . . peace symbols, 'V'-signs not for victory but for peace, booing and cursing of officers and even of hapless entertainers such as Bob Hope are unhappily commonplace." In 1970 the desertion rate in the Army reached four times the level of 1966, with 65,643 American soldiers fleeing from the ranks—roughly the equivalent of four infantry divisions. Even more destructive of morale were the actions of those who stayed behind. Fragging—the killing of officers by GIs—resulted in 209 deaths in 1970, more than twice the number of the preceding year, the Pentagon reported. Racial conflicts and drug epidemics reached terrifying proportions. "By every conceivable indicator," concluded Heinl, "our army that now remains in Vietnam is in a state approaching collapse." The Administration's decision to transform the war into a technological struggle was based partially on this fact. By the early 1970s, only the machines were reliable.

Angered by the escalating antiwar protest, the Administration launched a sharp counterattack. On June 4, 1969, speaking at the U.S. Air Force Academy, Nixon labeled his critics "unilateral disarmers" and "neoisolationists"—men who "have lost the vision indispensable to great leadership." Addressing a Republican dinner that October, Agnew contended that the cure for dissidents was "to separate them from our society with no more regret than we should feel over discarding rotten apples from a barrel." Politicians who supported antiwar activities, he said, were "ideological eunuchs." On November 3, seeking to undercut upcoming peace demonstrations, Nixon took to the airwaves in an appeal to "the great Silent Majority of my fellow Americans" for support against "demonstrations in the streets." The North Vietnamese "cannot defeat or humiliate the United States," he proclaimed. "Only Americans can do that." When television news commentators observed that the President seemed to have little new to report about the Vietnam War, Agnew, at Nixon's direction, blasted the networks in response. Persons of the President's stature should not have to "contend with a gaggle of commentators raising doubts," complained the Vice-President. Agnew also tore into the alleged news bias of the press, forgetting conveniently that it had backed Nixon in 1968 by a four-to-one margin.

Demagogic appeals may have rallied the "Silent Majority," but they did little to cool campus protest. Not even in the 1930s had radical ideas and activities been so widespread among American students. *Fortune* magazine, conducting an in-depth survey, reported in January, 1970, that 750,000 college students "identify with the New Left." On the Vietnam War alone, according to a Gallup poll of December, 1969, 69 per cent classified themselves as "doves"—more than three times the number designating themselves as "hawks." Major upheavals swept American campuses. "Most protests," concluded the President's Commission on Campus Unrest, "are entirely peaceful and orderly manifestations of dissent, such as holding meetings, picketing, vigils, demonstrations, and marches." An increasing number, however, were not. At Cornell in the spring of 1969, black students barricaded themselves inside a campus building and armed themselves with guns. On the night of February 25, 1970, a thousand students of the University of California at Santa Barbara seized a three-block business district near their campus, held it from police for six hours, and burned a plush Bank of America office to the ground. At Berkeley, a struggle over the control of "People's Park" led to fierce street fighting between students and police in battle gear, tear-gas-spraying helicopters, and thousands of armed National Guardsmen. On Memorial Day, 1969, radicals mustered a march of 30,000 and a Berkeley Liberation Program: open war on the university as "a major brain center for world domination"; conversion of the south campus area into "a strategic free territory for revolution"; and a militant defense "against law and order."

The enraged and frenzied quality of campus protest reflected the sense of desperation that gripped the New Left by the end of the decade. At its annual meeting of June, 1969, SDS disintegrated. Some factions chanted imported revolutionary slogans and others waved Little Red Books. Motherfuckers and Crazies preached nihilism, Marxist-Leninist sects put in a bid for Stalinism, and the national office staff, anxious to find a middle ground—or any ground—took up the banner of white support for domestic and foreign liberation struggles. In total disarray, SDS splintered into hostile factions. The best-known of them, Weatherman, subsequently engaged in a few fratricidal brawls with its rivals and devoted itself to quixotic attempts to stir tough young working-class whites to revolt. By October, Weatherpeople had readied what they called the New Red Army for their Chicago "Days of Rage." After a series of small-scale but bloody encounters with the police, 300 Weathermen and Weatherwomen found themselves in prison. The remnants of their forces moved "underground" to live in clandestine revolutionary cells, fashioning bombs for use against the "pig power structure." Like the Russian *Narodniki* of a century before, they had abandoned mass agitation for what they considered the vanguard role of revolutionary terrorism.

Why, asked Carl Oglesby, did the major organization of the New Left end up "broken into two, three, many factions," each "riddled with vanguarditis and galloping sectarianism"? Explanations were not hard to find. The New Left sorely lacked Old Left institutions to give it stability and political experience. Third World revolutionaries provided attractive, but irrelevant, models. The counter-culture, a pleasant escape from the "straight" world, was politically debilitating and suggested irrational, counterproductive strategies. The blue-collar working class, that traditional agency of social change, failed to play the role that so many radicals allotted it. But, most significantly, the evils identified by the New Left—war, racism, poverty—remained unaltered, immune to the most vigorous protests. Haunted by visions of napalmed villages and rotting slums, guilt-ridden by their own middle-class lives, and frustrated by their inability to alter the tragic course of history, young radicals moved toward ever more desperate measures: violence, drugs, terrorism. Ironically, their very desperation made them less able to reach out to others and therefore less effective, completing the cycle of their own despair. By the spring of 1970 the New Left seemed crippled by its sense of pessimism and defeat, burnt out by the very fires of indignation that had once given it life.

But the Nixon Administration was already moving to rekindle the spirit of protest. On March 18, 1970, a right-wing military coup ousted the neutralist government of Prince Norodom Sihanouk of Cambodia. Disclaiming responsibility, the Nixon Administration nonetheless immediately began giving military assistance to the new regime. At the same time, Sihanouk joined forces with the left-wing Cambodian guerrillas, the Khmer Rouge, and proclaimed his alliance with insurgents in Laos and Vietnam. Nixon appeared on television the night of April 30 to announce that he had ordered American combat troops and bombers into Cambodia to "clean out" Communist sanctuaries. "We will not be defeated," he cried. "If . . . the United States acts like a pitiful helpless giant, the forces of totalitarianism and anarchy will threaten free nations and free institutions throughout the world." To Nixon's regret, many Americans seemed appalled at this new escalation of the war by White House fiat. Republican Senator Mark Hatfield termed the action "unbelievable." Recalling President Johnson's manipulated crisis at the Tonkin Gulf, Senator Fulbright muttered: "They don't even deign to deceive us now." Around the country, protests ensued, demonstrations erupted, and students seized control of universities.

At Kent State University, a once apolitical school of 19,000 undergraduates in small-town Ohio, the Cambodia invasion touched off a wave of bitterness and violence. On the night of May 2, the campus

ROTC building was burned to the ground. Governor James Rhodes quickly dispatched 750 National Guardsmen to quell disorders. Student dissidents were "the worst type of people we harbor in America," the Governor told a press conference. "We are going to eradicate the problem." It was a popular approach among superpatriots; only the preceding month California's Governor Reagan had called for a "blood bath" to deal with campus militants. Shortly after noon on May 4, National Guardsmen sought to disperse what the President's Commission on Campus Unrest called "a peaceful assembly on the university commons," the "traditional site of student assemblies. Even if the guard had authority to prohibit a peaceful gathering," noted the Commission, "the timing and manner of the dispersal was disastrous. Many students were legitimately in the area as they went to and from class. . . . The rally was peaceful, and there was no impending violence." Nevertheless, the Guardsmen advanced, wearing full battle gear and armed with loaded M-1 rifles—high-velocity weapons with a horizontal range of almost two miles. Some students scattered for cover, others stood watching, and a few threw rocks. The Guardsmen fired at least sixty-one shots into the crowd of students, killing four and wounding nine. None was armed. According to the Commission, "students linked their arms and formed rings around the bodies to keep them from further injury. Some . . . wept. Others wandered around dazed."

The events at Kent State contributed still further to the nationwide disintegration. Given the "traitors and thieves and perverts . . . in our midst," announced Agnew, the killings were "predictable"—a consequence of "the new politics of violence and confrontation." Nevertheless, with growing numbers of the nation's 7 million college students on strike, publicized revolts by federal employees, and thousands upon thousands of demonstrators pouring into Washington, the President grew rattled. Consequently, on May 8, while Agnew was off assailing "choleric young intellectuals," Nixon turned an unexpectedly friendly face toward the arriving demonstrators at his press conference. That evening, restless and distraught, he made fifty-one telephone calls, eight of them to Kissinger, who thought the President "on the edge of a nervous breakdown." The next day, approximately 100,000 demonstrators thronged Washington, demanding an end to the war.

In the following weeks, the situation grew more intense. On May 14, drawn to the campus of all-black Jackson State University by reports of student disorder, white city police and Mississippi highway patrolmen fired a fusillade of more than 150 rounds of ammunition into a girls' dormitory, killing two black youths and wounding twelve others. Although the Governor excused the action as "in the interests of self-preservation," the President's Commission concluded: "The 28-second barrage of lethal gunfire . . . was completely unwarranted and unjustified." Shocked still further by the killings at Jackson State, many American colleges either closed down entirely or spent most of their time on strike or in agitational efforts. National Guardsmen were activated in sixteen states. On May 26, Nixon met with a delegation from New York construction unions whose members, several weeks before, had assaulted a group of peaceful antiwar demonstrators, injuring dozens. They praised his war policy and he, in turn, told them he found their street violence "very meaningful." Fearing further polarization, the Commission called upon the Administration "to resist the temptation to capitalize upon the divisions within the country for partisan political gain."

But Nixon, determined to smash the political power of his opponents, could not resist another foray into the politics of resentment. In 1970, a disproportionate number of Senate Democrats were up for re-election, and the President hoped to gain Republican control of that body through a strong backlash appeal. Attorney General Mitchell told a reporter: "This country is going so far Right you are not even going to recognize it." In September, the Vice-President embarked on a thirty-state campaign trip, encouraged by Nixon to portray liberals as extremists. Speaking at San Diego, the first stop on his itinerary, Agnew proclaimed that the "great question" before the nation was: "Will America be led by a President elected by a majority of the American people or will we be intimidated and blackmailed into following the path dictated by a disruptive radical and militant minority—the pampered prodigies of the radical liberals in the United States Senate?" Political observers soon agreed that Agnew was the most effective Republican demagogue since Joseph McCarthy. Even so, Nixon could not forgo the partisan pleasures of the campaign. In mid-October, he set out on his own political tour, hitting hard at the themes of student protest and law and order. On election eve, the President appeared on three networks, delivering a wild, arm-waving speech in which he denounced "the terrorists of the far left." Many voters wondered what this lecture had to do with the Democrats, particularly when Nixon was followed on the air by a restrained, low-key appeal from Senator Edmund Muskie. Looking dignified and Lincolnesque in the setting of his rustic Maine home, the Democratic spokesman called upon listeners to reject the "politics of fear."

In general, that is what they did. Although White House press secretary Ron Ziegler announced that the President considered the election results a "tremendous success," the Administration could take little comfort in them. Of the eight Democratic Senatorial candidates labeled by Republican advertisements as "extremists" and "radicals," seven were elected. The Senate thus remained Democratic by a 55 to 45 majority, and the House became somewhat more liberal than in the past. The failure of the backlash strategy can be attributed to the sophistication of American voters as well as to the effectiveness of Democratic campaigning. But, more significantly, the economy showed signs of faltering, with increases in both unemployment and inflation. As economic issues became salient, fears of "extremism" ebbed.

In the months following the 1970 elections the political fortunes of the Nixon Administration appeared on the wane. A March 1, 1971, Harris poll reported that 59 per cent of the American people gave the President a negative rating for his handling of domestic problems. Another Harris poll that February showed Nixon trailing Muskie in a hypothetical election, 47 to 39. White House advisers concluded that the President had to alter his image. Accordingly, in his State of the Union message, Nixon promised to sponsor a "New American Revolution," which he termed "by far the most comprehensive, the most far-reaching, the most bold program in the domestic field ever presented to an American Congress." His proposals were mildly progressive, if fairly innocuous, but thereafter he abandoned them. Congress, likewise, found little of interest in the New American Revolution or in other aspects of the White House domestic program. It defeated the Administration's plan for a supersonic transport plane but did pass a major bill providing for federally funded day-care centers, which the President promptly vetoed. In foreign affairs, the Administration managed to contain Congressional critics, winning extension of the draft law and heading off attempts to end funding for the Vietnam War. Here, too, though, Nixon's support was ebbing, as evidenced by the hostile response to the U.S.-sponsored invasion of Laos.

On February 8, 1971, U.S. bombers and helicopters accompanied American-paid, -trained, and -equipped South Vietnamese forces in an assault upon Laotian segments of the Ho Chi Minh trail. Chastened by the response to his announcement of the Cambodian invasion, the President avoided comment upon the new adventure. Instead, he appeared before television cameras with a pep talk on pollution. Although American bombing raids continued long thereafter, South Vietnamese forces withdrew by March 12. In the last days, they fled in a rout, clinging to the skids of U.S. helicopters, hundreds of which had already been destroyed. Working furiously to offset the atmosphere of disaster that shrouded the operation, Nixon told C. L. Sulzberger of the *New York Times* that he "seriously doubted if we will ever have another war"; this was "probably the very last one." Few, however, seemed comforted. A Gallup poll that February reported that 66 per cent of Americans favored withdrawal of all U.S. troops from Vietnam by the end of the year. In March, the President's personal popularity sank to a new low.

Nixon sought to recoup some of his wanning support through his treatment of the Calley case. Although U.S. planes had long bombed, napalmed, and strafed populated South Vietnamese villages suspected of harboring the NLF, American troops went one step farther in 1968. Helicoptered into My Lai 4 on March 16 to burn down its houses and destroy its food supply, U.S. soldiers, on the orders of Lieutenant William Calley, Jr., also lined up hundreds of unarmed men, women, and children in a ditch and shot them. High-ranking military officers did their best to cover up the massacre, but three years later, after a discharged soldier revealed it, Calley was court-martialed and convicted on a charge of premeditated murder. On March 31, 1971, a jury of six military officers—all Vietnam veterans—sentenced Calley to life imprisonment. A great cry of disapproval went up from U.S. politicians, particularly from Southern Democrats. Governor Wallace condemned the decision and paid a personal visit to the young man who was rapidly becoming a hero among superpatriots. In the midst of the furor, Nixon announced that he had ordered Calley released from his stockade and confined to officers' quarters pending the outcome of his appeal. He also encouraged Congressional sentiment for a lenient sentence. Assessing the situation as tailor-made to solidify his support among the Wallaceites, the President declared on April 3 that he would personally review the case "before any final sentence is carried out." Calley resided in his duplex apartment until mid-1974; soon thereafter, he was at liberty.

The controversy occasioned by the My Lai massacre had scarcely abated when, on June 13, 1971, the *New York Times* began publishing a series of articles based upon the Pentagon Papers—a secret Defense Department study of the origins of U.S. involvement in Vietnam. Although the material concluded with the Johnson Presidency, its publication nonetheless seriously embarrassed the Nixon Administration, as it revealed to the public the skein of deceptions upon which America's Indochina crusade had been based. The Justice Department obtained a court order temporarily halting the series and appealed to the Supreme Court for a permanent injunction. On June 30, by a 6-to-3 vote, the

Court ruled against the government. "Paramount among the responsibilities of a free press," declared Justices Black and Douglas, "is the duty to prevent any part of government from deceiving the people and sending them off to distant lands to die." Despite this rebuff, the Justice Department initiated the prosecution of Daniel Ellsberg and Anthony Russo, Jr., two employees of the Rand Corporation, for espionage, theft, and conspiracy. Startled by what they had read in the Pentagon Papers, Ellsberg and Russo—both former planners of the war—had defied imprisonment to turn the documents over to the American people. After a lengthy trial, in which it was revealed that the White House had been tapping Ellsberg's phone for years, had authorized the burglarizing of his psychiatrist's office in search of discrediting information, and had offered the presiding judge an opportunity to become director of the FBI, the judge dismissed all charges, citing "improper government conduct" that offended "a sense of justice."

The Indochina War also began to take its economic toll. For years, the United States had been running a balance of payments deficit, largely because of the military and political costs of pursuing world hegemony. Consequently, the health of the once-omnipotent dollar had gradually declined, with foreign financial institutions, particularly in Western Europe, growing increasingly restive. The Indochina War undermined America's world economic position still further, for it fueled inflation in the United States and, thereby, rendered U.S. industry less competitive in world markets. As a result, in 1971 the United States experienced its first negative balance of trade since 1893 and had a startling balance of payments deficit of $22 billion. Anxious to halt the inflationary advance, the Nixon Administration had fostered tight-money policies and cutbacks in domestic social programs. Predictably, these measures depressed employment and income. But, given the highly concentrated, non-competitive structure of American industry, they proved totally unable to check the inflationary spiral. By the summer of 1971, unemployment in the United States topped 6 per cent, and prices were rising at the rate of 5 per cent a year. Such trends constituted a serious threat to both the viability of the American economy and the political prospects of the Nixon Administration.

To surmount the gathering economic crisis, the Administration began implementing new policies in late 1971. Withdrawing the official gold backing of the dollar, Washington let American currency sink to its natural level in world exchanges and ushered in the demise of the Bretton Woods system. At the same time, the Nixon Administration adopted a tougher stance toward America's capitalist competitors in

Japan and Western Europe. On the home front, the President announced a "new economic plan": a ninety-day freeze on prices, wages, and rents; tax cuts for business; and a 10 per cent surcharge on imports. Wall Street was overjoyed, for new corporate tax loopholes were opened while profits remained uncontrolled. Labor found the program less satisfactory but grudgingly accepted it after the President appointed a group of labor leaders to the new regulatory apparatus. In November, the Administration moved on to a series of less rigid, but nonetheless pro-business controls. As a result, unemployment continued and wages lagged behind prices and profits. By mid-1974, when the controls were finally abandoned, the purchasing power of the average working family had declined 7 per cent since late 1972—an outcome which suited the Administration and its corporate partners perfectly. The former director of the President's Cost of Living Council recalled: "The idea . . . was to zap labor, and we did." But to the distress of America's business leaders, inflation continued to defy such conservative nostrums.

Moreover, others proved less zappable. Although the campus rebellion had simmered down after 1970 into drugs, counter-culture, nostalgia, and despair, new forces of revolt had emerged. Women's groups embarked upon ambitious campaigns for "liberation," startling the Administration (and even many radicals) by their fervor and commitment. In its operations against the women's movement, the FBI reported frantically on everything from attempts to subvert Martha Mitchell to new, mysterious "sex rolls." Homosexuals, male and female, also organized to oppose discrimination. Welfare recipients were mobilized by the National Welfare Rights Organization, middle-class reformers by Common Cause, Spanish-speaking Americans by militant Chicano groups, native Americans by the American Indian Movement, and consumer-interest lawyers by Ralph Nader and his "Raiders." With their constituency depressed by the apparent futility of massive street demonstrations, antiwar groups sponsored smaller but more militant confrontations. Vietnam Veterans Against the War, founded in 1970, held a free-wheeling investigation of war crimes that December. The following April, it rallied in Washington more than a thousand antiwar veterans, who publicly discarded their Purple Hearts, Silver Stars, and other medals in disgust. In May, 1971, 30,000 peace activists sought to shut down the nation's capital through tactics of non-violent civil disobedience. Police responded by throwing 13,500 demonstrators into prison without charges—an action which Attorney General Mitchell hoped would "set an example for other communities." The activities of these dissidents—and of others supporting ecology, mine safety, Puerto

Rican independence, and prison reform—kept the politics of protest volatile, if fragmented, in the early 1970s.

But, although his domestic critics remained vocal, Nixon was already beginning a vast international flanking maneuver that would bolster his position. From 1950 to 1970 U.S. policy toward China remained frozen, with Chiang accorded sole legitimacy. The State Department worked tirelessly to isolate the Communist regime, and Congress expressed its opposition to the U.N. seating of the People's Republic of China on at least thirty occasions. An inveterate opponent of Chinese Communism, Nixon seemed an unlikely innovator. Yet in his State of the World address of February 25, 1971, he announced that "the United States is prepared to see the People's Republic of China play a constructive role in the family of nations." Events now unfolded rapidly. On April 6, during an international Ping-Pong competition in Japan, the Chinese team invited its American counterpart to visit the Mainland. As no group of Americans had been allowed to enter China since 1949, this was a dramatic offer and was quickly accepted. On April 10 the U.S. team began a week of sightseeing, Ping-Pong, and entertainment in Peking, including a party hosted by Premier Chou En-lai. In turn, the White House announced relaxations of the twenty-year embargo on trade with China. On July 9 Kissinger flew secretly to a rendezvous in Peking. Appearing on television six days later, Nixon revealed the Kissinger mission and declared that he would personally visit China sometime before May, 1972. Only the far Right seemed displeased.

What were Nixon's motives for this departure from traditional Cold War policy? First, he hoped to avoid humiliation in the world arena. In November, 1970, a majority of U.N. delegates voted for the first time to unseat the Taipei regime and replace it with that of Peking. Only the American ploy of making China's admission an "important question," requiring a two-thirds majority, saved the day for U.S. policymakers. Even the following year, when the State Department shifted to a "two China policy," the General Assembly snubbed Washington by expelling the Nationalists and giving the Communists their seat. Second, Nixon badly needed a political boost at home, and his journey to Peking, billed as a "voyage of peace," was timed and stage-managed for maximum political advantage. Third, U.S. business interests had never shaken off their lust for the fabled "China Market." As early as 1964, Chase Manhattan's David Rockefeller had expressed interest in broadening commercial contacts with Peking, and by 1971 he was joined by Xerox, Monsanto, Pan American, General Motors, TWA, United Airlines, and Boeing. In June, Taipei's ambassador to Washington complained that "much of today's pressure for a thaw with Peking comes from hopeful business interests seeking profitable markets." Finally, and perhaps most significantly, Nixon sought détente with China to give him a freer hand in crushing his other opponents in Asia. Like de Gaulle, Nixon was a realistic conservative who understood that the Chinese revolution could no longer be overturned. Nevertheless, he clung to the hope that, if other great powers—particularly Communist powers—cooperated, it might still be possible to halt the insurgencies in the smaller, weaker nations of Indochina.

Similar concerns underlay the Nixon Administration's rapprochement with the Soviet Union. In preparatory talks in April, 1972, Kissinger spoke to Soviet officials of the "billions of dollars of business activity" that would follow from better U.S.-Soviet relations, but warned that Nixon was "bound to see the present situation in Vietnam not only in its local context." The Russians understood perfectly. On May 11, only three days after the United States began mining North Vietnam's harbors and subjecting its cities to saturation bombing raids, Soviet officials met with Nixon and Kissinger to arrange to buy a quarter of the U.S. wheat crop and a wide variety of U.S. manufactured goods. Later that month, Nixon journeyed to Moscow for a warm and well-publicized meeting with Leonid Brezhnev. The two superpowers reached agreements flowing from the SALT talks that reassured each against attack by the other. That October, Moscow and Washington signed a landmark trade agreement, settling the Lend-Lease debt, granting most-favored-nation status to the Soviet Union, making the Soviet Union eligible for Export-Import Bank credits, providing for greater U.S. imports of Russian raw materials, and establishing trade centers in both capitals. Soviet-American trade, which tripled in the first eleven months of 1972, began to take on fantastic dimensions thereafter. Hordes of American businessmen flocked to Moscow, the press reported, "looking for business or just for a sniff of the atmosphere in this vast new market." Pepsi-Cola announced plans to build a plant in the Soviet Union and to market Russian vodka in the United States. Although a $40 billion deal for American purchase of Russian natural gas, arranged that November, later fell through, the following spring U.S. corporations announced a $10 billion, twenty-five-year agreement for Siberian gas and an $8 billion, twenty-year contract for Soviet fertilizer. This capitalist love feast with the Russian dictatorship, so vigorously applauded at the 1972 GOP national convention, came, of course, at the price of ignoring Moscow's heightening persecution of domestic dissenters, its official anti-Semitism, and its continued suppression of the political independence of other nations. But these were clearly not the primary concerns of Washington's "free world" leaders.

In his dealings with China and the Soviet Union, President Nixon was intent upon fashioning a new world order. "The postwar period in international relations has ended," he announced in his 1970 State of the World message. "The Marxist dream of international Communist unity has disintegrated" and "the 'isms' have lost their vitality." Having concluded that the Soviet Union and China were not driven by burning revolutionary zeal, Nixon was willing to incorporate them into a new equilibrium among the great powers—"a strong healthy United States, Europe, Soviet Union, China, Japan, each balancing the other." Abandoning the "bolshevik" ogre that had haunted Western statesmen ever since the Russian Revolution, Nixon was returning to the balance-of-power diplomacy of the period preceding World War I. The President hoped that the great powers would henceforth work out ways of avoiding wars among themselves, while continuing to enrich their ruling élites at the expense of the rest of the world. Despite their suspiciously revolutionary pasts, then, the Soviet Union and China were welcome in the imperial club—as long as they did not hinder Washington's ambitions in the world arena.

The major threats to the overseas "interests" of the United States remained indigenous. In May and June, 1969, when Nixon dispatched Governor Rockefeller and twenty-three experts on a fact-finding tour of Latin America, they met a chilly reception. In Ecuador, students seized the streets behind the presidential palace, tear gas filled the air, and the Rockefeller party fled by back roads to a hotel where paratroopers stood guard in the corridors. The President of Bolivia confined his meeting with the U.S. delegates to the airport. Venezuela and Chile, fearful of disorders, canceled the visits to their nations. Peru refused to receive Rockefeller, while the Argentine dictatorship greeted the New York multimillionaire reluctantly, cautioned by the most successful general strike in that nation's history. In Uruguay, after a firebombing caused $1 million in damage to the General Motors building, the government shifted the Rockefeller reception from Montevideo to an isolated resort. Only in the tight dictatorships of Paraguay and Haiti did enthusiastic crowds turn out—by presidential order—to greet the emissaries of the United States. Rockefeller's subsequent report to the President, warning that "forces of anarchy, terror, and subversion are loose in the Americas," called for major new counter-insurgency efforts and increased U.S. funding and training of Latin America's armed forces. Taking a favorable view of governments established by military coups, Rockefeller stated that military officers were "often becoming a major force for constructive social change in the hemisphere." Latin American nations were important, Rockefeller contended, because "the United States depends on them to provide a vast market for our manufactured goods" and "looks to them for raw materials for our industries."

But even the military could not always preserve this tributary relationship. That fall, a military coup in Peru brought to power a left-wing nationalist government which took control of a giant subsidiary of Standard Oil and carried out a broad range of "revolutionary" reforms. Shortly thereafter, the armed forces chief in Bolivia established another left-wing government, announcing his hopes for an "ideological confederation" with Peru. Shaken by these events, Nixon took note of the "anti-U.S. overtones" of Latin-American nationalism in his 1970 State of the World address, observing that "there is no more delicate task than finding new modes which permit the flow" of private "investment capital." Later that year, Chile's voters elected a coalition government of left-wing parties headed by the Socialist Salvador Allende, who promised his countrymen a socialist transformation within Chile's traditional democratic parliamentary system.

American business and government officials, who had funded the political campaigns of Chile's ruling conservatives since at least 1958, reacted with shock and horror to Allende's election victory. In a memo to Kissinger, an ITT vice-president declared: "Private foreign enterprise, already reeling from damaging treatment in Peru, Ecuador, and Bolivia, was left groping for means of protecting its investments." Moreover, as Kissinger told a group of reporters, Allende's victory might provide a "contagious example" for other nations. Consequently, the Nixon Administration formulated a two-track plan to prevent Allende from governing. Track I, authorized by Kissinger's White House 40 Committee, involved a variety of U.S.-orchestrated political, economic, and propaganda attacks. According to the CIA director's notes, Nixon told him: "Make the economy scream." Track II, authorized by Nixon and Kissinger, involved efforts to foment a military coup, with $10 million in U.S. funding. But although the CIA worked diligently among the Chilean armed forces to initiate a coup—even arranging the kidnapping and murder of the recalcitrant Chilean chief of staff, General René Schneider—the Chilean Congress confirmed Allende as President in October.

Taking office, Allende did just what he had promised. His government nationalized key foreign investments, including the massive holdings of the Anacanda and Kennecott Copper Corporations, and began the process of land reform, distributing vast estates to the peasants who worked them. Through a variety of reform measures, Allende's administration succeeded in markedly improving the conditions of employment, health, housing, land tenure, and education for the Chilean lower classes. As Allende had pledged, these changes occurred in an atmosphere of complete political freedom—a freedom all the more remarkable given the continuing efforts of the conservative opposition, funded and directed by the United States, to prevent him from governing. CIA-controlled newspapers, magazines, and radio and TV outlets carried on a shrill attack, while CIA-funded groups coordinated intelligence, distributed propaganda, and organized paramilitary units. The CIA also indirectly funded a series of crippling strikes which, together with a cut-off of external aid and credits to the Chilean government, threw the economy into a tailspin. Allende's downfall came shortly after his Popular Unity government made sizable electoral gains in the 1973 midterm elections. Convinced that socialism and democracy were inseparable, a group of right-wing military officers finally responded to U.S. urgings and, in September, 1973, overthrew the government, murdering Allende in the process.

Explaining that political freedom "serves the interests of Marxism," General Augusto Pinochet suspended the Chilean Constitution, closed the Congress, banned all political parties, and silenced the press. In the ensuing weeks, the armed forces killed 25,000 people, threw hundreds of thousands of Chileans into concentration camps, and institutionalized widespread torture. Aware that the military regime would fare poorly in an election, Pinochet announced that there would be none in his lifetime. Countries ranging from Social Democratic Sweden to Christian Democratic Italy broke off diplomatic relations with the junta, leaving the United States as the only Western democracy supporting it. Advised by the "free enterprise" economists of the University of Chicago, the junta returned industry to private hands (usually those of U.S. corporations), minimized business regulations, slashed social services, controlled wages rigidly, and allowed prices to rise freely. This sort of "shock treatment," said Professor Milton Friedman, visiting Chile, is "the only medicine. Absolutely. There is no other." By the end of 1975, Chile's annual inflation rate hit 341 per cent (the highest in the world), real wages sank to half their former level, and massive starvation wracked the country. Commenting on the new "free enterprise" program, a *New York Times* dispatch of January 25, 1976 reported:

> Thus far, the results here have been indeed impressive. The number of unemployed is estimated at roughly a third of the labor force. The one

modest hot meal a day provided by the Church or other relief groups stands between most of the idle and starvation. "You have only to look into the eyes of the children who manage to come to school," a teaching nun said recently, "to see that a generation of mental defectives is being developed."

American policymakers faced a less favorable prospect in Asia. In the early 1970s, revolutionary struggles raged in the three nations of Indochina and flickered up in Thailand, Ceylon, and the Philippines. "The principal threat to the independent nations in Asia is internal insurgency," Secretary Laird declared in 1970. By the summer of 1971, the United States had 700,000 combat troops and sizable air and naval forces in East Asia, operating from almost 200 major military bases. Billions of dollars in U.S. military assistance helped to maintain the immense armies of its client governments. South Vietnam had a force of 1.1 million men, South Korea 620,000, and Taiwan 450,000. In South Korea, to which the United States committed $254 million in military aid and 52,000 American troops in 1971, President Chung Hee Park eliminated the last vestiges of democratic rule the following year. On October 17, 1972, he issued a declaration of martial law, dissolved the National Assembly, suspended constitutional rights, closed the universities, established censorship, and banned all political activity. Shortly thereafter, Park unveiled a new constitution enabling him to remain in office for life. In another crumbling "free world" bastion, the Philippines, President Ferdinand Marcos ended democratic government in January, 1973, announcing a new constitution giving him all legislative and executive powers and imposing martial law. Opposition leaders appealed to the nation's supreme court, only to find that Marcos had already abolished it. American military aid continued.

The situation grew even more serious in the turbulent Middle East. Israel's smashing military victory in the 1967 Israeli-Arab war had led key U.S. policymakers to conclude that American predominance in the oil-rich region could best be maintained by a *de facto* alliance with Israel. But Washington's developing ties with Tel Aviv led Arab states like Egypt and Syria—bankrolled by Saudi Arabia—to turn increasingly to the Soviet Union for weapons and support. Moreover, when war broke out again in October, 1973, the Arab states fared considerably better than in the past. Worst of all, from Washington's viewpoint, the 1973 war touched off an oil producers' boycott. By the time it ended in early 1974, the oil-producing states had acquired enough cohesion to form a cartel and significantly raise oil prices. Seizing this opportunity, U.S. oil companies created an artificial fuel shortage and dramatically increased their own retail prices. The result was that, while U.S. oil company profits rose 59 per cent in 1973, the overall health of the U.S. economy seriously deteriorated. With no solution in sight—least of all lowering U.S. dependence on imported oil (a third of U.S. consumption in 1973)—Kissinger threw himself into a vain attempt to maintain U.S. influence in the Mideast through a combination of shuttle diplomacy and massive U.S. arms aid. For the time being, this policy—plus the conservative predilections of most Arab potentates—preserved U.S. access to Mideast oil, but at a constantly rising price.

In Africa, where the U.S. government had previously given at least lip service to the principle of majority rule, the Nixon Administration shifted toward support of the white supremacist governments of South Africa, Rhodesia, and the Portuguese colonies. Frightened by the radical potential of African nationalism, and anxious to preserve the rich Western stake in the southern part of the continent, American policymakers cast the first U.S. veto in the United Nations in 1970, preventing the strengthening of sanctions against Rhodesia. They also scuttled their embargo on sales of strategic and military equipment, supplying Portugal with Boeing jets, Bell helicopters, and herbicides and South Africa with helicopters and light aircraft. In 1971, the United States violated U.N. sanctions against Rhodesia by resuming the purchase of Rhodesian chrome and signed the Azores Pact with Portugal, providing that nation with aid totaling $436 million—about the equivalent of Portugal's annual military spending, most of which went for savage colonial wars in Angola, Mozambique, and Guinea-Bissau. Unlike the independent nations of black Africa, the white supremacist states of southern Africa were among the most profitable in the world for American business. As of 1971, more than thirty U.S. companies—including Caterpillar Tractor, Chase Manhattan, General Electric, and IBM—had invested hundreds of millions of dollars in Angola and Mozambique. The largest of these investors, Gulf Oil, actually paid directly for the construction of local Portuguese military facilities. "In South Africa," a publication of the Johannesburg government noted in 1971, "Americans . . . could easily feel that they had never left home. All over South Africa clearly visible signs remind an American of how deeply the United States is involved in the affairs of this fast developing country." Between 1950 and 1970, direct U.S. investment in South Africa increased by 535 per cent. By 1972 more than 375 U.S. corporations had invested $1 billion in the South African economy.

Thanks to Washington's diligence, U.S. corporations controlled the richest empire in world history. By the end of 1974, U.S. direct investments overseas reached $119 billion, with sales by American industries in foreign markets of several times that figure. From 1950 to 1974, annual profits on these investments ranged from 11.5 to 23 per cent, but in the Third World returns of 20 to 25 per cent after taxes were more common. By contrast, as the American Friends Service Committee noted, perhaps two-thirds of the world's people lived in chronic poverty. Most of them resided in the underdeveloped nations, where widespread hunger and malnutrition prevailed. Although conservatives argued that world hunger was based on uncontrolled population growth, world food production actually outstripped population increase between 1962 and 1973, and some poor countries, such as China, virtually eliminated starvation. Indeed, in no country was it impossible for people to feed themselves—if they controlled the productive process. "It is external strangulation that frustrates internal efforts which would otherwise result in . . . economic and social development," declared the Economic and Social Secretariat of the OAS in 1969. "The commercial policies of the United States and other industrialized countries tend at this time to create very serious obstacles." But with the same concern for the poor that characterized his domestic programs, Nixon promised more of the same. "Private enterprise must play a role in the development process," he declared on February 18 of the following year. "We have given special attention to the developing countries in our relaxation of restraints on foreign investments by U.S. corporations."

In recalcitrant Indochina, the President pursued his "generation of peace" by escalating the generation of war. The U.S. government resumed the sustained bombing of North Vietnam in December, 1971, and the following month carried out record-level B-52 raids throughout Indochina. That March, Washington suspended the Paris peace talks. The North Vietnamese and the NLF launched a major offensive in April, sending Saigon's armies reeling in retreat. In response, the Nixon Administration assembled the largest naval and aerial armada since World War II, with which it intensified the bombing of North and South Vietnam, bombed Hanoi and Haiphong, mined Haiphong harbor, and destroyed the rail links between North Vietnam and China. As early as December, 1965, Nixon had called for the bombing of Hanoi and the mining of Haiphong as ways "to win the war in Vietnam and to end it." The Secretary of the Air Force had asked for such a program in March, 1968, claiming that it would "erode the will of the population by exposing a wider area . . . to casualties and destruction." Fearing the Soviet response, Johnson had hesitated to go this far. But Nixon pressed forward, confident that his diplomatic and commercial arrangements with the Soviet Union and China had undermined their desire to interfere. He was right. The Communist superpowers protested in the most tepid of fashions against what the *New York Times,* once a supporter of the war, denounced as "a deliberate campaign of diplomacy through terror."

At the same time, Washington continued its unequivocal support of the South Vietnamese dictatorship. General Thieu, returned in 1971 to the presidency in a one-man election, told a Saigon crowd on October 12, 1972, that "we have to kill the Communists to the last man." Condemning any sharing of power with the NLF, he declared: "Those in South Vietnam who want to promote a coalition with the Communists should raise their hands. I am sure . . . the soldiers will not let them live for more than five minutes." This was no idle boast. Thanks to American generosity, South Vietnam possessed the third largest navy, the fourth largest army, and the sixth largest air force in the world. One out of nine persons was estimated to be under arms, and the government had plans to enlist children under age seven in supporting units. Despite this formidable array of military strength, Saigon's hold on the rest of Vietnam was hardly secure, although its government did have the consolation of maintaining an estimated 200,000 political prisoners in jails and torture cages.

To preserve this regime and others like it against their revolutionary opponents, the President of the United States raised the war's destructiveness to new levels of magnitude. In its first three years of "winding down the war," the Nixon Administration dropped more bombs on Indochina than had the Johnson Administration in five years of escalation. By the end of 1972 the tonnage of U.S. munitions dropped or shot on Indochina since 1965 had reached more than 15 million, including 3.5 times the tonnage of bombs and 28 times the amount of napalm used by the United States in World War II. Between 1965 and the end of 1972 the Indochina War consumed more than $128 billion in official U.S. military appropriations and 56,000 American lives, leaving 303,000 Americans wounded and approximately 100,000 others as drug addicts. According to the U.S. military command, 500,751 South Vietnamese troops had been killed or wounded and 923,938 NLF and North Vietnamese soldiers had been killed. Furthermore, as the Senate subcommittee on refugees reported, there had been about 1.5 million civilian casualties in North and South Vietnam alone. In the three nations of Indochina, vast stretches of land had been rendered uninhabitable by bombing and chemical defoliation. In Laos more than one-fourth of the population had become refugees; in South Vietnam, more than a third; in Cambodia, almost half.

The most serious political challenge to the war was brewing within the Democratic Party. After more than a decade of protest and revolt, insurgent forces in America constituted a powerful political movement. When Agnew launched his crusade against "radical liberals" in 1970, he merely exaggerated a trend that had clearly begun years earlier, when a sizable constituency started to emerge in support of the formerly New Left demands of peace and social justice. The leading liberal magazines—the *New Republic,* the *Nation,* and the *Progressive*—had long ago joined their more radical competitors (*Ramparts,* the *New York Review*) in criticizing the Cold War belligerency that had once been standard fare for liberals. By the late 1960s Northern Democrats had begun to follow the same path, calling for reductions in the Pentagon's budget, an end to corporate giveaways, and a reversal in national priorities. Only a bullet had robbed the most popular spokesman of the "new politics" of the 1968 Democratic Presidential nomination, and by 1972 such fateful accidents could no longer hold back the tides of change.

A coalition of peace activists, liberals, students, women, and blacks proved irresistible. Senator Muskie's 1970 election eve speech had established him as the front-runner for the Democratic nomination, but his bland style and centrist program did not interest the party's insurgent forces, who soon gravitated into the camp of Senator George McGovern. Decorated for service as a bomber pilot in World War II, McGovern had become a college professor, Congressman from South Dakota, and director of the Food for Peace program before voters elected him to the Senate. With his flat, unexciting speaking style, McGovern seemed utterly lacking in charisma; yet he projected a simple moral earnestness with considerable appeal. Long a sharp critic of the Indochina War and of the power of the Pentagon, the South Dakota Senator cemented the support of liberals and radicals by advocating American withdrawal from Indochina, Pentagon cutbacks, "demogrants" of $1,000 per person to replace the welfare system, and amnesty for draft resisters. Although Muskie won the New Hampshire primary, McGovern surprised political experts by his strong showing. Thereafter, Muskie lost badly to Wallace in Florida and was toppled by Humphrey in Pennsylvania and by McGovern in Massachusetts, knocking him out of the race. McGovern surged to the fore and stayed there, winning precinct caucuses, state conventions, and primaries all across the country, including the crucial primaries in California, New Jersey, and New York. In a desperation move, George Meany and other hostile union leaders convinced a still ambitious Humphrey to challenge the winner-take-all rule for the

California delegates, but the insurgent forces—bolstered by new party-reform rules that had increased the proportion of blacks, women, and young people at the July convention—smashed this effort. Before the eyes of a still incredulous nation, McGovern was easily nominated on the first ballot.

McGovern's campaign themes showed how far to the Left liberal Democrats had moved since John F. Kennedy's race of twelve years before. Denouncing the Thieu regime, he declared: "This corrupt dictatorship that our precious young men and our tax dollars are supporting cannot be talked clean by official lies . . . and . . . can't be washed clean by American blood." In a political broadcast on October 20, McGovern portrayed the campaign as "a fundamental struggle between the little people of America and the big rich of America, between the average working man or woman and a powerful élite." In place of Republican unemployment, he promised a Democratic program of public-service jobs. In place of tax cuts for corporations, he called for phasing out tax loopholes. In place of ever rising defense budgets, he proposed diverting military spending into domestic programs. Sometimes, in his critique of government policy, he linked foreign and domestic issues in a manner that cut to the heart of the postwar structure of power and privilege. "In virtually every statement, every act of this Administration, nearly two and a half billion human beings in the world have been left out," he stated on October 5. "These are the people who have too little power to figure in a new balance of power based on the military giants; they are the people who are too meek to command the attention given to generals and weapons manufacturers . . . ; they are the people whose crime was to be born poor."

Easily renominated by his party, Nixon had an excellent chance for re-election. No President since Herbert Hoover had sought and been denied a second term. Appearing at the convention, Nixon urged Americans to "reject . . . the policies of those who whine and whimper about our frustrations. . . . Let us not turn away from greatness." The Republican platform, which contended that the Democratic Party had been "seized by a radical clique," was written at the White House, as was the script for the convention, with its detailed descriptions of impromptu remarks, places for applause, gestures by speakers, and screams of enthusiasm. For some time after the convention, Nixon ran a generally low-key campaign, conducting well-publicized diplomacy and isolating himself from the press. Nevertheless, with George Wallace out of the race, wounded by a crazed assassin, Nixon worked shrewdly to draw the supporters of the Alabama Governor into Republican ranks. He attacked "arbitrary court-ordered busing" and promised that, if re-elected, he would end "the age of permissiveness." Ironically, however, Nixon's strongest issue was probably that of "peace." Loyal to its friend in the White House, the Soviet government spread the word of its support for his re-election. On October 26, after a new round of Vietnam negotiations, Kissinger announced that "peace is at hand." Although the fighting continued to rage, Nixon proclaimed: "Vietnam being over, we are proud of the fact that our trips to Peking and Moscow have paved the way . . . for a generation of peace." In a televised statement on the eve of the election, he announced a "breakthrough" in peace talks, urging voters to ensure the success of negotiations by showing that "you back the President of the United States."

Had the election been decided along these lines, there would probably have been a closer race than, in fact, ensued. But the outcome of the 1972 election was seriously distorted by the political bumbling of the Democrats. Failing to persuade his first choice, Senator Edward Kennedy, to become his Vice-Presidential running mate, McGovern gave the nod to Senator Thomas Eagleton of Missouri, a Catholic acceptable to organized labor and other anti-McGovern elements. On July 25, ten days later, it was disclosed that, unknown to McGovern or his staff, Eagleton had been hospitalized three times in the 1960s for "nervous exhaustion and fatigue," receiving electric-shock therapy. McGovern promptly expressed his "1,000 per cent" support of Eagleton, but on July 31, with the Eagleton affair dominating the headlines, they met and announced the Missouri Senator's withdrawal. After much controversy and confusion, the Democrats finally chose Sargent Shriver to fill the vacant spot, but only after a month of precious campaign time had elapsed and McGovern's popularity had plummeted to an all-time low. In May, polls showed McGovern trailing Nixon by a respectable 10 per cent; that August, following the Eagleton fiasco, the margin had widened to a hopeless 34 per cent.

Severely shaken, McGovern's credibility received a further beating when, anxious to broaden his support among organization Democrats, he shifted rightward on several domestic issues and paid court to party regulars like Lyndon Johnson and Mayor Daley. This reversal of direction disheartened his most zealous followers without altering the coolness of more conservative Democrats. Under stern discipline from George Meany, the executive council of the AFL-CIO repeatedly proclaimed its electoral neutrality. Some McGovern strategists, with an eye on polls showing large numbers of Americans critical of the Establishment and special interests, had hoped to mobilize mass support, including Wallace support, through a "populist" campaign. But McGovern's post-convention wobbling, seized upon and exploited by a rabidly hostile press, undermined his reputation as a forthright crusader. The result, as historian William Leuchtenburg noted, was that "the main issue became not Nixon's vulnerable record but McGovern's character."

Long before the Democrats bungled the election, the Republicans were hard at work stealing it. In 1971, responding to a complaint by Nixon that his campaign task force lacked a political intelligence unit, White House appointments secretary Dwight Chapin, with Haldeman's approval, hired an old college chum, Donald Segretti, to direct a program of political spying and sabotage designed to undermine the political fortunes of whoever was the front-runner for the Democratic Presidential nomination. The Muskie camp felt its impact when key campaign documents disappeared and confidential memos were leaked. Two weeks before the New Hampshire primary, a mysterious letter appeared in that state's major newspaper accusing Muskie of having made insulting remarks about "Canucks"—Americans of French-Canadian ancestry. The letter touched off banner headlines in the state, raised a public furor, and apparently hurt Muskie in the balloting. During the Florida primary campaign, Segretti forged and distributed widely a letter on Muskie stationery accusing other Democrats of sexual misconduct. When Muskie dropped out of the race, approximately fifty paid operatives moved on to infiltrate and sabotage the campaigns of other contenders for the Democratic nomination, including McGovern.

As the GOP political sabotage campaign picked up momentum, the Committee for the Re-Election of the President, headed by John Mitchell and staffed by high-echelon White House officials, busied itself filling a mammoth campaign chest. Political contributions made before April 7, 1972, did not have to be reported under the provisions of a new disclosure law; consequently, Nixon aides worked furiously against this deadline. CREEP's principal fund-raisers, Maurice Stans and Herbert Kalmbach, occasionally assisted by Mitchell, made the rounds of the nation's major corporations, requesting an average of $100,000 per firm. This approach worked well. When "two Cabinet officers" ask you for funds, a Gulf Oil Corporation executive later testified, "it's different than someone collecting for the Boy Scouts." A grateful dairy industry contributed at least $422,500. The oil industry chipped in $4.9 million. Many firms simply dipped into their own funds when contributing—a direct violation of federal law. All told, CREEP collected an estimated $20 million in undisclosed contributions before

April 7, some of it disguised still further ("laundered") by first being deposited in Mexican banks. Together with $40 million raised thereafter, this represented, as Stans boasted, "the largest amount of money ever spent in a political campaign."

These funds subsidized some curious ventures—including bogus demonstrations of support for the mining of Haiphong—but none more remarkable than those of the White House covert operatives, whose services had been transferred to CREEP for the duration of the campaign. On January 27, 1972, G. Gordon Liddy (then legal counsel to CREEP) met with Mitchell (at the time still Attorney General), Jeb Magruder (deputy director of CREEP), and John Dean (counsel to the President). Liddy outlined a $1 million political project involving electronic surveillance, photographing documents, mugging demonstrators and abducting their leaders to Mexico, and renting a yacht off Miami Beach "set up for sound and photographs," aboard which "high-class" call girls would compromise Democratic Party officials. That was "not quite what I had in mind," Mitchell told Liddy, and "we can't spend that kind of money, either. I suggest you go back to your drawing board and see what you can do." Shortly thereafter, Liddy returned with a less ambitious plan, costing only $250,000; it called for breaking into Democratic national headquarters in Washington to photograph documents and bug offices. This plan received Mitchell's approval.

Liddy, Hunt, and two other CIA veterans, James McCord and Bernard Barker, now went to work preparing for the raid on Democratic headquarters in Washington's Watergate apartment complex. Drawing on contacts dating back to the Bay of Pigs operation, they gathered a corps of Cuban emigrés to assist them. In late May the group broke into the Watergate offices, photographed key documents, and installed taps on two phones. Although one of the taps failed to function properly, the other—on the phone of the Democratic national chairman—worked well, transmitting useful information to Liddy's team, which typed it up and passed it along to Magruder. Shortly thereafter, Mitchell reportedly ordered another raid to gather additional materials and to check on the malfunctioning tap. On the night of June 17, as they labored once again inside the darkened Democratic headquarters, they were apprehended by the Washington police.

CREEP staffers and Whites House officials worked feverishly to cover their tracks to the spreading Watergate scandal. "It was felt that if it ever reached Mr. Mitchell before the election, the President would lose," recalled Magruder. Nixon himself told Charles Colson on June 20: "We are just going to leave this where it is, with the Cubans." Not yet arrested, Liddy raced about CREEP headquarters shredding documents. In the White House, Haldeman ordered his assistant, Gordon Strachan, to destroy wiretap logs. Although Ehrlichman suggested that Dean "deep-six" materials from Hunt's safe in the Potomac, eventually the two Presidential aides turned them over to Hoover's successor at the FBI, L. Patrick Gray, with instructions to never let them "see the light of day." Gray obligingly burned the materials and later provided the White House with FBI documents on the investigation of the case. Seeking to buy the silence of the Watergate defendants, CREEP channeled $500,000 in Nixon campaign funds to them as well as a promise of executive clemency. Meanwhile, the chief of the Justice Department's Criminal Division, Henry Petersen, kept Nixon and Dean abreast of secret grand jury proceedings in the case. With the mass media busy carving up McGovern, newspapers touched only lightly on the Watergate incident that summer. Six weeks after the break-in, when the President held a press conference, not a single question was raised relating to it. On August 29, Nixon publicly announced that Dean had "conducted a complete investigation," proving that "no one in the White House staff, no one in this Administration presently employed, was involved in this very bizarre incident."

The cover-up was successful. On September 15, 1972, the grand jury handed down indictments against Hunt, Liddy, McCord, and their Cuban associates without implicating any higher-ups in the operation. A few hours later, Dean was summoned to the Oval Office, where he found Nixon and Haldeman, smiling broadly. Nixon commended Dean for the "very skillful" way he had contained the Watergate case, "putting your fingers in the leaks that have sprung," and urged him to continue "to button it up as well as you can." Although a House committee had scheduled an investigation of the Watergate burglary, Nixon thought that it would be possible to pressure House Republican leader Gerald Ford to block it. "I'm getting into this thing," said the President, "so that . . . he's got to know that it comes from the top—and that he's got to get at this and screw this thing up." In early October, a majority of the House committee members voted against granting their chairman subpoena powers, bringing Congressional action to a halt. Even after October 10, when the first of a series of articles in the *Washington Post* revealed that the Watergate incident had resulted from "a massive campaign of political spying and sabotage conducted on behalf of President Nixon's re-election," the Administration's cover story held. CREEP denounced the articles as a "collection of absurdities"; Stans called them a "senseless pack of lies"; and the White House press secretary dismissed them as "the shoddiest type of journalism." McGovern hammered away at what he called "the most corrupt Administration in history," but most voters found the Watergate story too fantastic to be believed.

Republican chicanery and Democratic ineptitude thus combined to produce a landslide GOP victory. Nixon received 60.7 per cent of the vote, just under Johnson's 1964 record. Losing the electoral college 521 to 17, McGovern drew majorities only among black, low-income, and Jewish voters. Nixon ran strongest among traditionally Republican groups, garnering 82 per cent of the ballots of upper-income voters, but also cut sharply into traditional Democratic preserves: blue-collar workers (57 per cent), union families (54 per cent), Catholics (52 per cent), and those under thirty (52 per cent). Race provided the largest division within the electorate. Nixon received 68 per cent of the white vote, but only 13 per cent of the black. With the GOP national ticket running 10 per cent better in the South than elsewhere and drawing an estimated 75 per cent of the Wallace vote, the Republicans seemed well on their way to becoming the White Man's Party. Although 45 per cent of eligible Americans stayed clear of the polls and the Democrats solidified their control of Congress, it was a time of intense gloom for the forces of change. Conceding defeat, McGovern urged Nixon to "lead us to a time of peace abroad and justice at home." Rarely did this appear so unlikely a prospect.

In the aftermath of the 1972 elections, Nixon moved quickly to exploit his triumph. Promising the nation "a new feeling of self-discipline," he vowed to "shuck off" and "trim down" social programs while at the same time continuing "to appoint conservative judges to the courts." New York's former welfare commissioner, Mitchell Ginsberg, acknowledged that the nation was "now in the midst of a very sharp swing against doing anything for the poor" and predicted "a period of a great deal of suffering in this country." At the NAACP's annual convention in January, 1973, Roy Wilkins described American blacks as living under a state of "siege" launched by the "executive branch of the federal government." Later that month, the Administration's new budget proposed deep slashes in social programs accompanied by a $5.6 billion increase in military spending. His power confirmed and secure, the real Nixon had come to the fore, with few pretenses to "pragmatic centrism." "The tide of reaction . . . is sweeping across America," a *New York Times* editorial lamented that January. "Policies of hope have been replaced by policies of suspicion," based on the premise "that society will be improved not by the promise of reform but by the threat of punishment." The political leaders "who embrace the new reaction," noted the *Times*, "are turning their backs on the American credo of optimism, compassion, and faith in liberty under law."

Nor was peace any longer "at hand." Determined to force an Indochina settlement on American terms, Nixon ordered hundreds of giant Air Force B-52s to begin terror bombing raids over North Vietnam's major cities. During the Christmas holidays, they destroyed residential quarters, schools, dikes, hospitals, and thousands of Vietnamese civilians. Aghast at the raids, the National Council of Churches called them "immoral and evil beyond any options open to our nation." At least two American pilots, one a veteran of 275 combat missions, refused to participate in them. In Canada, the House of Commons voted unanimously to censure the U.S. actions. In Western Europe, parties from the Communists to the Christian Democrats organized massive anti-bombing demonstrations. Sweden's Premier, Olaf Palme, compared Nixon's actions to Nazi massacres, while West Germany's Chancellor, Willy Brandt, reportedly referred to them as "disgusting and unfathomable."

On inaugural day, Washington awoke to find uprecedented security measures in force. Thousands of police, secret service agents, and troops had been mobilized. Fighter planes stood ready for action. Officials even pigeon-proofed the parade, spraying Pennsylvania Avenue with a special chemical. Gradually, a crowd of 20,000 gathered to watch the ceremonies, although many spots on the platform remained conspicuously vacant; "a substantial number" of Congressmen, reported the press, had boycotted the festivities. Indeed, 100,000 Americans were gathering for a counter-inaugural ceremony. In his inaugural address, President Nixon promised "a new era of peace," but received his most enthusiastic applause when he exhorted listeners to ask: "What can I do for myself?" That evening, the lavish inaugural balls were centers of merriment and self-congratulation. At one, bandleader Lionel Hampton asked well-wishers to applaud "the royal family."

Three days after Nixon's 1973 inauguration, the Administration announced an Indochina peace settlement. Anxious to create the politically expedient illusion of an end to the war, Nixon had made the Vietnamese Communists an appealing offer. In exchange for ending the fighting and releasing American prisoners of war, they were guaranteed: U.S. troop withdrawal; an end to U.S. bombing raids; maintenance of Communist forces in place inside South Vietnam; billions of dollars in U.S. reconstruction aid; and participation in elections, accompanied by the release of political prisoners, in South Vietnam. Serious objections to this settlement came not from the Communists but from the Thieu government, which had no desire to open up the political process in South Vietnam or to forgo American military intervention. To mollify the Saigon dictatorship, the Nixon Administration provided South Vietnam with massive military aid, assured Thieu that he could flout the political provisions of the Paris accords, and secretly pledged renewed American military intervention in the event Saigon required it. Thus, despite the enormous fanfare given the Paris treaty, signed on January 27, 1973, the situation in Vietnam remained inherently unstable, with Saigon's future ultimately dependent upon Washington's willingness to resume the American war effort.

Arriving on the heels of his massive re-election victory, Nixon's "peace with honor" measurably strengthened his personal power in the first months of 1973. Labeling Congress "irrelevant," he impounded $6 billion the legislature had appropriated for environmental programs. In January, despite a new Congressional authorization for OEO, he terminated the anti-poverty program by appointing an administrator with explicit instructions to liquidate it. Before his re-election, Nixon had promised his Whites House aides that Watergate would be "the last gasp of . . . our partisan opponents." The *Washington Post* would have "damnable, damnable problems" and, as for Edward Bennett Williams, the lawyer for the Democrats: "We are going to fix the son of a bitch." Such options no longer seemed beyond the powers of the Executive. Indeed, in 1972, the FBI had a significant portion of the delegates to the Democratic national convention under surveillance, with many of their organizations targeted for disruption. Upon re-election, the President demanded the resignation of the top 2,000 officials in his Administration, thus subjecting the Cabinet and executive agencies to a purge of those public servants with some degree of independence. Assessing the situation, Senator Fulbright remarked moodily that the United States might "pass on, as most of the world has passed on, to a totalitarian system."

But at the apex of Nixon's personal power, the Watergate scandal began to unravel. On February 7, 1973, the Senate voted unanimously to establish a Select Committee on Presidential Campaign Activities, headed by North Carolina Senator Sam Ervin, to investigate the mysterious events of 1972. In response, top Administration officials commenced efforts to hamper, discredit, and frustrate the investigation. At about the same time, two of the Watergate burglars broke ranks. Disillusioned by White House actions, James McCord dispatched a letter to Judge John Sirica detailing his knowledge of the cover-up. Howard

Hunt, convinced that he and the other defendants had been insufficiently compensated for their silence, sent word to the White House that unless more funds were forthcoming he would expose the Administration. On March 21, Dean brought Nixon the bad news about Hunt's blackmail demand, together with his own assessment that the scandal could no longer be contained. Nixon replied that another million dollars should be raised for Hunt. "You should handle that one pretty fast," he said; "that's worth it." Unconvinced, Dean began testifying before federal prosecutors, as did Hunt, McCord, and Magruder.

Informed of the investigation's progress by Attorney General Richard Kleindienst, the conspirators maneuvered desperately to stave off disaster. Nixon outlined the initial strategy to Haldeman and Ehrlichman: "Give 'em an hors d'oeuvre and maybe they won't come back for the main course." White House officials slated Mitchell for this propitiatory role, but he refused to accept it. Next the President called in Dean, but he, too, had little interest in satiating the public appetite. On April 17, in desperation, Nixon turned to Haldeman and Ehrlichman. But even these commanders of the palace guard refused to shoulder the blame for the crimes of the Nixon Administration. Furthermore, no one could be victimized without repercussions, for each could incriminate the others. On April 30, 1973, Nixon formally accepted the resignations of Haldeman, Ehrlichman, and Kleindienst, and fired Dean. Thereafter, the President dug in at the White House, ignoring as best he could the revelations which surfaced day by day—the underground history of the Nixon era, exploding in banner headlines, in televised committee hearings, and in public consciousness.

In the midst of gathering public outrage, the legal net began to tighten. On May 7, 1973, the new Attorney General, Elliot Richardson, announced that he would appoint a special prosecutor to handle the case, and later that month named Archibald Cox, former solicitor general of the United States, to the post. In New York, a federal grand jury indicted Mitchell and Stans on perjury and conspiracy charges in connection with campaign contributions. In Los Angeles, Ehrlichman and three subordinates were indicted by a grand jury in connection with the burglary of Ellsberg's psychiatrist's office. To avoid going to prison for exacting bribes and kickbacks, Agnew resigned the Vice-Presidency on October 10, and was replaced two days later by House Republican leader Gerald Ford, who doggedly defended the remnants of the beleagured Administration. Increasingly, Nixon grappled with the Watergate special prosecutor, who demanded a series of tape recordings which the President, secretly, had ordered made of all White House conversations. Rather than surrender the incriminating tapes, Nixon fired Cox on October 20, at the same time announcing the abolition of the special prosecutor's office, the resignation of the Attorney General, and the firing of the Deputy Attorney General. This "Saturday Night Massacre" unleashed a great storm of popular outrage which washed across the political landscape. The House of Representatives voted 410 to 4 to conduct an impeachment investigation; Mitchell, Haldeman, Ehrlichman, Colson, and other officials were indicted by a grand jury for conspiracy to cover up the Watergate burglary; and the new special prosecutor, Leon Jaworski, took up the quest for the tapes, bringing his case to the Supreme Court. Refusing to surrender the orignals, the White House handed out bogus transcripts which, ironically, proved not only incriminating but morally odious to millions of Americans.

In 1974, the Nixon Administration tottered toward collapse, its credibility at an all-time low. Most Americans, reported the polls, believed the President guilty of criminal conduct and favored his removal from office. On July 24, the Supreme Court closed off his final avenue of escape, ordering him to turn over the disputed tapes to Judge Sirica's grand jury. Concluding its investigation later that month, the House Judiciary Committee voted to impeach Nixon for obstructing justice, defying Congressional subpoenas, and violating the rights of American citizens. On August 7, the President met with Republican Congressional leaders to assess his chances for remaining in office. In the entire House of Representative, they predicted, there would be only about 10 votes against impeachment; in the Senate, 15 against conviction. Trapped by the overwhelming popular revulsion at his abuse of power, Richard Nixon had run out of political tricks. On August 9, still affirming his innocence, he resigned the Presidency in disgrace, having learned to his sorrow that Americans preferred their law to his order.

13

Among the Ruins, 1974-77

I guess they all gits crooked when they gits
that high up. Guess they has to be.

New England farmer's wife, 1974

FOR MILLIONS OF AMERICANS, the Watergate scandal represented the
latest betrayal of the nation by its political leadership. The Vietnam
War, the unresolved crises of race and poverty, and, now, the crimes
of the Nixon Administration produced a rich harvest of disillusionment.
In December, 1973, pollster Louis Harris told Congress that political
alienation among Americans had risen steadily since 1966, from 29 to
55 per cent—"a veritable floodtide of disenchantment, seemingly gaining
momentum with each passing year." Questioned in 1974, Americans
provided interviewers with bitter comments on the political scene.
"There's no relation between my vote and what any politician does,"
a New York City cabdriver remarked. "It's like worshipping a pagan
god, 'cause once you vote for them they never again have any contact
with you." Asked about popular representation, an Iowa heavy-equip-
ment operator retorted: "What representation? . . . They don't even
know who the people are. . . . They represent one thing: Number
One, and maybe a crony or two." A student declared: "They're all just
in there tight with the big capitalists and the big bucks. The whole
system's set up that way." According to the Survey Research Center of
the University of Michigan, between 1964 and 1974 the proportion of
Americans believing that their government was "run by a few big
interests looking out for themselves" rose from 26 to 72 per cent. In
1974, when the National Opinion Research Center asked respondents
how much confidence they had in the people "running the executive
branch of the government," only 14 per cent answered a "great deal";
43 per cent replied "hardly any."

In spite of popular disillusionment, the new President, Gerald Ford, seemed close, for a time, to restoring some measure of respect for the institutions of power. Dull, homely, and uninspiring, he projected a rather stolid honesty which contrasted well with the slick manipulativeness of his discredited predecessor. Moreover, although an unelected President—chosen by a man who had used criminal means to rig his own re-election victory—Ford emerged untainted from the Watergate scandal, and thus gained the confidence of many who hoped to put such squalid events behind them. The "long nightmare of Watergate" was over, the new President told Americans, who already felt that sense of reassuring boredom once inspired by General Eisenhower. But only a month later, in perhaps the most unpopular move of his Administration, Ford stopped all legal action against Richard Nixon, granting him a full pardon. (Later, he sought, unsuccessfully, to give Nixon custody of the disputed tapes and papers.) Popular distrust returned in a flood, and never quite dissipated thereafter. In the 1974 Congressional elections, the Democrats coasted to a landslide victory without even trying. Polls in early 1975 found that only 18 per cent of the electorate identified with the Republican Party.

The failure of the Ford Administration to restore public confidence also owed much to the deteriorating economy. Although America had not experienced full employment since World War II, the crisis of 1974–77 proved the most severe since the Great Depression. Thanks, initially, to the immense costs of the Vietnam War and, later, to soaring oil prices, inflation in the United States reached 11 per cent in 1974 and continued at an alarming rate thereafter. The price of sugar alone that year rose from 15 cents to between 75 cents and a dollar a pound. At the same time, consumer purchasing power declined under the impact of the wage restraints of 1972–74, conservative-sponsored cutbacks in all levels of government, and the galloping inflation. The result was a classic depression, with official unemployment (not including those who had stopped looking for work) averaging 8.5 per cent in 1975 and dropping only slightly in subsequent years. Among blacks and women, often the first to be fired, the toll went far higher; in 1976, the Urban League placed black unemployment at 25 per cent. "Go to any of the big steel mills," declared union leader Ed Sadlowski. "You'll find the jobless men . . . hanging out on the corners, their families disintegrating and the kids hungry and scared. . . . The truth is that 30 or even 40 million Americans are living in poverty or something damn close to it."

In dealing with the economic crisis, the Ford Administration offered a harsh solution: tax more and provide less. Advised by the nation's business leaders and his own conservative Council of Economic Advisers, Ford provided Americans with a depression-fighting program somewhat akin to that of Herbert Hoover. In late 1974, he promoted a tax increase, distributed WIN (Whip Inflation Now) buttons, and departed for skiing in Colorado. Even the Administration's public exhortations to curb inflation, which it deemed a serious problem, had a ludicrous ring. Actually, Ford followed a coherent economic strategy but, for political reasons, tended to leave it unspoken. In the Administration's opinion, the cure for inflation lay in cutting government spending for social programs and in letting unemployment increase. Accordingly, with the nation in the worst depression since the 1930s, Ford vetoed a jobs bill, a public works employment bill for the cities, a comprehensive public works bill, an emergency housing act, an aid to education bill, the school lunch program, a day-care center bill, a food stamp increase, and a host of other measures to provide Americans with jobs and vital social services. Arguing that federal aid to education (which comprised about 7 per cent of the nation's spending for elementary and secondary schools) should be slashed by $800 million, he also contended that the number of children participating in school lunch programs should be reduced by 6 million and that 5.3 million Americans should be dropped from the food stamp program. With 8 million Americans unemployed and many millions of others living in poverty and destitution, the President called for a 17 per cent cut in social services for fiscal 1976, echoing the *Wall Street Journal*'s lament that unemployment compensation and other programs "for which no services are rendered" was "breaking the economy."

In conjunction with the business community, the Ford Administration forced a similar program on the nation's cities. During the postwar years, as the federal government occupied itself with military spending and foreign wars, urban areas had assumed the heavy burdens of paying for social services like welfare, housing, education, and health care—services whose costs grew significantly in the 1960s as the poor demanded full participation and increased funding. Hard-hit by the movement of the affluent to the suburbs and by the economic deterioration of the 1970s, many American cities leaned heavily on loans from commercial banks to cover their deficits. But as the cities became "poor credit risks" and more profitable investment opportunities appeared elsewhere (e.g., South Korea, Chile, South Africa), banks grew less willing to purchase city bonds. In 1975, facing bankruptcy, New York City desperately appealed to the federal government for a loan guarantee. Contemptuously rejecting the city's appeal, the Ford Administration preached that New York's salvation lay in slashing social services.

Eventually, bolstered by federal support, New York banks succeeded in forming a Municipal Assistance Corporation to superintend a more "responsible" approach to the city's finances. The appearance of "Big Mac" thus marked the formal ascendancy to municipal power of New York's banking interests, who quickly fastened an austerity program on the depression-ridden city: firing public servants, imposing new taxes, and cutting back social services (or raising their cost). Some wits suggested that New York's mistake lay in its failure to set up a police state, guarantee a profitable haven to U.S. corporations, and propose a military alliance to Secretary Kissinger.

Thus, not only did the Ford Administration do little to alleviate the hardships of the depression, but it fostered policies which placed the burden of economic recovery upon the poor. Rather than create opportunities for employment, it helped to throw millions of Americans out of work. Rather than expand social services to aid the poor and the unemployed, it sought to curtail them. At the end of 1975, in the world's richest nation, 58 per cent of the unemployed were receiving no unemployment compensation, and 62 per cent of those Americans eligible for food stamps failed to receive them. Trapped by the spiraling inflation, most of the elderly found their Social Security payments well below the poverty level. Newspapers carried stories of aged persons frozen to death in their unheated apartments or subsisting on dog food. Little wonder that many Americans felt a sense of betrayal. Sadlowski declared: "The Ford-Rockefeller administration . . . the bankers and financiers, and . . . the suburban corporation executives" are "saying to us: 'We're sorry for . . . all of you working stiffs in your dingy neighborhoods, but you'll have to shift for yourselves. Find your own ways to keep off the welfare rolls. Pay your full share and some of our share too for municipal services. If your cities are rotting, come out to the suburbs but don't . . . move into our neighborhoods."

The Ford Administration ministered more sympathetically to the needs of American corporations. In late 1974, Ford presented America's flourishing coal companies with a windfall by vetoing an anti–strip mining bill. Although the Clean Air Act of 1970 called for a 90 per cent reduction in the level of auto pollution by 1976, the Ford Administration rewarded the auto industry by postponing implementation until the 1980s. The oil industry, another American corporate barony, manipulated the fuel "crisis" so successfully that it raised its profits by 146 per cent between 1972 and 1974. Nevertheless, despite widespread public opprobrium gained by the oil companies, the Ford Administration came up with no other response to the "energy crisis" except a pro-business plan, rejected by Congress, to raise prices. By 1976, oil prices and profits had reached unprecedented levels, as had U.S. fuel consumption. Of course, to the Ford Administration, the public interest and the corporate interest remained synonymous. Asked about a "Rockefeller empire" during hearings on his Vice-Presidential nomination, Nelson Rockefeller first confused it with capitalism and then with the United States itself. Capitalism had made America "the greatest nation in the world," he told legislators. "This system is not an empire. It is a democracy." Many Americans, though, had grown skeptical. Between 1965 and 1974, the percentage of the public favoring the break-up of giant corporations rose from 37 to 53 per cent.

Like its business partners, the Ford Administration objected to "big government" only when it furthered human welfare; military programs were quite another matter. In his budget proposal for fiscal 1977, the President asked Congress to increase military spending by 15 per cent, thus providing for a major increase (22 per cent beyond inflation) in weapons programs, including a Trident submarine fleet, the Cruise strategic missile, and the B-1 bomber. The President hoped to pay for this, in part, by slashing the public service employment program 47 per cent, making the elderly pay more for Medicare, decreasing funding for child nutrition, reducing federal expenditures on education, and slowing construction of water pollution control facilities. The $40 million cost of one B-1 bomber (later rising to $100 million per plane) would be covered by the elimination of the special milk program for children. From fiscal 1975 to fiscal 1977, annual U.S. military spending increased from $91.9 billion to $112.5 billion, while aid to cities and states declined from $90.2 billion to $63.4 billion. If separately financed trust funds (e.g., Social Security) were excluded from the fiscal 1976 budget, 54 per cent of the remainder represented military-related items and only 22 per cent "human resources." That year, the cost to the average American family of military-related programs in the federal budget was $2,485, compared to $301 for health and $258 for education, manpower, and social services.

This set of priorities provoked significant popular criticism. A Harris poll of December, 1974, found that Americans considered education, pollution control, housing, and health insurance to be the worthiest public spending programs. Only 14 per cent desired to increase military outlays, while 42 per cent favored cuts in the military budget. Furthermore, military aid to foreign countries ranked last among eighteen policy goals, with 70 per cent supporting cutbacks in military assistance. At its 1976 meeting, the U.S. Conference of Mayors, representing the nation's 350 largest cities, asked the President and Congress to "redress the imbalance between domestic expenditures and expenditures for the Pentagon and foreign aid, recognizing that the social defense of this nation is at least as important . . . as is our military defense." That spring, Congresswoman Elizabeth Holtzman introduced America's first "transfer amendment," calling for a cut of $7.5 billion in the military budget and the transfer of $2.5 billion into programs meeting human needs. The amendment, however, drew only 85 votes, and failed to pass the House.

In the context of the worst economic crisis of the postwar era, the failure of Congress and the nation to override the Ford Administration's conservative priorities was a remarkable one. Unlike the depression of the 1930s, the economic deterioration of the 1970s failed to radicalize much of the country. In fact, among many Americans, it triggered a new mood of conservatism. To some extent, this resulted from the centralization of political power and publicity in a conservative-dominated White House. It also reflected the absence of a significant left-wing political party (or of a coherent radical faction within either of the two major parties) which could articulate alternative social and economic policies. Furthermore, the depression of the mid-1970s directly affected only a small minority of the population—many, indeed, were aliens, without political or labor union influence. And although it did throw a fear of the breadline into the middle class, this fear, in line with the traditional middle class distrust of collective action, usually stimulated desperate individual efforts to find or hold jobs. This personal "solution" was particularly evident among supposedly radical college students and faculty. Yet there was a sound, if harsh, basis for the unwillingness of many lower- and middle-class Americans to fund additional social legislation, for, given the regressive nature of the American tax system, they knew quite well who would pay for it. For this reason, even many liberal Democrats, elected in the landslide of 1974, hesitated to increase domestic welfare spending—at least in the absence of sweeping tax reform or substantial cutbacks in military spending.

The latter, of course, seemed most unlikely, in spite of America's possession of the deadliest arsenal in world history. By early 1975, the American nuclear stockpile contained the equivalent power of 615,385 Hiroshima bombs, capable of destroying Russia's major cities thirty-six times over. Although the Ford Administration stressed the dangers of the Soviet military build-up, in 1976 the United States maintained 8,900 strategic nuclear weapons as against the Russians' 3,500. Furthermore, a Library of Congress report that same year showed that, in the preceding seven years, the United States had outbuilt the Soviet Union in numbers of ships (by 12 per cent) and in ship tonnage (by 71 per cent). Despite the alleged "lessons" of the Vietnam War, in 1976 the United States also maintained 2.1 million active duty military personnel (500,000 of them stationed overseas) and almost a million civilian Pentagon employees. And while few Americans seemed interested in fighting a nuclear war, top U.S. policymakers remained deadly serious about it. President Ford and Secretary of Defense James Schlesinger warned that the U.S. government did not rule out the use of nuclear weapons—even in a first strike or against nations not possessing them. The Administration was particularly intrigued by the possibilities of "limited" nuclear war, although it did not shrink from preparing for more ambitious endeavors. In January, 1975, Schlesinger assured a Senate subcommittee that, while "the psychological impact of a nuclear attack would result in some initial loss of confidence in government . . . positive, adaptive behavior would prevail."

For the Ford Administration, the major virtue of military power lay in its guarantee of U.S. world hegemony. "When a strong man armed keepeth his palace, his goods are in peace," Schlesinger informed Congress in early 1975. "We live in an interdependent world economy," he explained, "and our foreign economic interests are substantial. . . . The oil embargo of 1973 is only the most recent and pointed reminder that we have a keen and growing interest in distant lands—their markets and their products." For a nation with such far-flung holdings, vital interests hinged on occurrences in the remotest areas of the globe. "In almost every major event," Kissinger told news commentator Barbara Walters, "there is . . . a domino effect." But with the decline of popular support for overseas intervention—what Schlesinger called America's loss of "vision, of moral stamina, of national purpose"— the Ford Administration turned increasingly toward new global strategies: splitting Third World revolutions from China and Russia through détente; mobilizing surrogates, such as Brazil, Iran, South Africa, and Indonesia; lowering the nuclear threshold; and developing a professional, mechanized U.S. army, heavy in firepower and capable of rapid deployment around the world.

The Administration's need for new means of circumventing domestic opposition to overseas wars became evident as America's Indochina venture tottered toward defeat. In war-torn Cambodia, the rebels gradually advanced on the capital, while in Laos the insurgents moved toward power by peaceful means. For a time, the Vietnamese Communists looked expectantly to the Paris accords, even accepting losses of territory to Saigon's forces in the hope that the provisions for political participation would be implemented. In the spring of 1975, however, with Saigon's prisons full, the Thieu dictatorship entrenched in power, and fighting once more raging in the South, the North Vietnamese launched a limited offensive. Despite Saigon's considerable military advantage, including total control of the air, South Vietnamese forces fled southward, frantically abandoning $1 billion in U.S. weapons and two-thirds of their country. *New York Times* correspondent Malcolm Browne reported on a "reign of terror of government forces" in Danang: "Government soldiers were prepared to kill anyone, including women and children, to escape." To stave off the South Vietnamese government's collapse, American political and military leaders demanded additional U.S. military aid to Saigon—beyond the $700 million already provided that year. Polls, however, showed that 74 per cent of the American people opposed the Administration's aid proposal, and Congress refused to budge. As the Communist forces swept into Saigon, the last U.S. officials scrambled aboard helicopters, heading for the open sea.

By almost any standards, the Indochina war had been a disaster. To fight it, the United States underwent severe internal convulsions, suffered several hundred thousand casualties, and expended perhaps $200 billion. In Vietnam, the killed or wounded numbered nearly five million; in Cambodia, one out of six Khmers; in Laos, unknown multitudes. Additional millions of people had become refugees, and large sections of their countries had been rendered uninhabitable. Naturally, U.S. leaders were eager for Americans to forget the conflict as quickly as possible. "The lessons of the past," said President Ford, "have already been learned . . . and we should have our focus on the future." Nevertheless, the war proved a sobering experience for many Americans, who believed that its "lesson," if any, was to avoid reckless military intervention in other nations. American policymakers, however, drew a less pacific conclusion. "We could have won the war if political factors had not entered in," complained an Air Force general. Contending that "the American people basically are impatient," former Secretary of State Rusk thought that a future conflict would necessitate "censorship. . . . You can't fight a war on television." General Maxwell Taylor argued that any President would "be well advised . . . to silence future critics of war by executive order." And Secretary Schlesinger promised that the United States would not show the same "restraint" in Korea.

Humiliated by the collapse of their Indochina venture, Washington officials behaved vengefully toward those they blamed for their defeat. When Cambodians seized the *Mayaguez,* an American ship sailing in their waters, the Ford Administration immediately unleashed a major military attack. Even the message that the *Mayaguez* crew was safe did not stop the operation, which took more American lives than were "saved," in addition to the lives of numerous Cambodians. Although the reconstruction of Vietnam was aided by money, equipment, and technicians from many lands (including Japan, France, Sweden, Norway, Mexico, and Denmark), from U.N. agencies, and from American church and peace groups, the U.S. government refused to play any role in repairing the immense destruction it had wrought. In addition, the Ford Administration prohibited trade with Vietnam, vetoed its entry into the United Nations on three occasions, and rejected Vietnamese offers to negotiate the remaining issues of the war. When Congress voted to lift the Vietnam trade embargo, Ford vetoed the bill. Dismissing the North Vietnamese as "international pirates," the President took a no more charitable view of the thousands of American war resisters and exiles. The *Nation* noted that Ford and his advisers were "willing to grant refuge to Thieu's gangster clique and its supporters but not to those Americans who went to jail or exile for being prematurely anti-war. . . . The new South Vietnamese government offers amnesty to its combat foes, while the American government will have no truck with those whose opposition consisted only of saying no."

Just how little the Administration had learned from the Indochina debacle became evident later that year, in southern Africa. Radicalized by Portugal's long and fruitless colonial wars in Africa, Portuguese military officers overthrew the Lisbon dictatorship in April, 1974, promising freedom to the people of Portugal and their colonies. In Mozambique and Guinea-Bissau, native revolutionary movements quickly assumed power, but in resource-rich Angola, with three factions claiming legitimacy, a glimmer of hope remained for counter-revolution. That October, South Africa launched an invasion force of 2,000 mercenaries and 5,000 regular troops across the Angolan border. In response, Angola's major independence movement, the Marxist MPLA, secured stepped-up military aid from Russia and troops from Cuba. Anxious to prevent a radical victory, the CIA teamed up with South Africa and the right-wing government of Zaire and channeled $32 million worth of arms and equipment to the MPLA's conservative foes. By January, 1976, forty countries had recognized the MPLA-led government, and the U.S. Congress was growing restive. Hostile to American intervention in another futile civil war, the legislators voted to reject the additional $37 million in covert military aid proposed by the Ford Administration. Congress had "lost its guts," stormed the President, but to no avail. South Africa now withdrew from the struggle, and the MPLA won the civil war the following month.

The victory of radical nationalist movements in the former Portuguese colonies, America's public association with white supremacist South Africa, and escalating guerrilla struggles in Rhodesia and Southwest Africa (the latter still under South African control in defiance of U.N. and International Court rulings) seriously undermined American influence in black Africa and presaged the possible destruction of the rich Western stake in the southern part of the continent. Consequently, in April, 1976, Kissinger flew to Africa in a belated effort to shore up the American position. Speaking in Zambia, the Secretary of State promised "a new era in American policy." Rejecting "outsiders seeking to impose solutions" (presumably Russians and Cubans rather than Americans), he promised to secure the repeal of the Byrd amendment (which violated U.N. trade sanctions against Rhodesia) and to support majority rule in southern Africa. In practice, this seemed to mean offering Rhodesian whites international guarantees of the prevailing economic order in exchange for movement toward multiracial government; pressuring South Africa to create a formally independent but pliant satellite state in Southwest Africa; and convincing the leaders of the "front-line" black African states to end their aid to radical nationalist movements. Rhodesian and South African leaders remained intransigently white supremacist, however, and unwilling to make the necessary accommodations. Well aware of this, black Africa funded a growing guerrilla struggle. And whatever the rhetoric, the United States continued to violate U.N. sanctions against Rhodesia; to supply the Rhodesian economy indirectly through shipments to South Africa; to arm South Africa for its counter-insurgency war in Southwest Africa; and to condone the absence of majority rule in South Africa.

Despite gestures toward black Africa, then, the Ford Administration concentrated upon bailing out embattled South Africa—the site, by 1976, of vast Western economic holdings, including $1.5 billion in lucrative investments by America's major corporations. U.S. business and political spokesmen claimed that American corporate activity assisted South Africa's impoverished black majority, but could offer little evidence for this contention. Relatively few blacks worked for American firms, and those who did were subject to racially discriminatory job classifications and wage differentials. Although only about 19 per cent of South Africa's population was white, blacks could not vote, hold office, or travel freely within the country. Reserving 87 per cent of the land (and virtually all of the wealth) for whites, the South African government forced blacks to live in "bantustans" (scattered bits of impoverished, noncontiguous territory), banned their major political organizations, smashed peaceful black demonstrations, and silenced its critics (black and white) through imprisonment, exile, or detention without trial. In June, 1976, black student demonstrations began in Soweto, a ghetto near Johannesburg, triggering massive protests, strikes, and riots throughout South Africa. With South African police busy killing perhaps a thousand demonstrators and imprisoning many others, Kissinger met with South African Prime Minister Vorster for what were termed friendly discussions. That October, when the U.N. General Assembly voted unanimously to call upon member governments to prohibit diplomatic contacts with a new bantustan, only the United States abstained.

Actually, South Africa was one of the more libertarian friends of the United States. Testifying before the Senate Foreign Relations Committee in July, 1974, Senator Alan Cranston pointed out that the United States had given $81 billion in foreign aid to fifty-six military dictatorships and authoritarian governments which, that year, were slated to receive another $5 billion. Indeed, 69 per cent of the countries receiving U.S. military grants could be classified as "repressive regimes." Responding to polls showing overwhelming popular rejection of this practice, Congress passed an amendment in September, 1975, proposed by Congressman Tom Harkin of Iowa, to prohibit U.S. aid to countries engaging in "gross violations of internationally recognized human rights." Implementation proved more difficult but, despite the opposition of the Ford Administration, citizens' groups did manage to induce Congress to cut off military assistance to Chile and Uruguay and to reduce by half U.S. economic aid to Chile. Nevertheless, in fiscal 1977, massive U.S. military and economic assistance continued to bolster an array of dictatorships practicing murder and torture, among them South Korea, Indonesia, the Philippines, Thailand, Chile, Brazil, Argentina, and Haiti. Nor were the resulting programs confined to their own countries. The South Korean CIA subsidized the strange religious activities of the Reverend Sun Myung Moon and harassed Korean communities in the United States. In September, 1976, only twelve blocks from the White House, the Chilean junta succeeded in assassinating Chile's former ambassador to the United States and his American assistant. The Shah of Iran told U.S. television veiwers that his own secret police, the dread Savak, operated with U.S. approval to "check up on" his critics within the United States.

Although, in the decades since 1945, the United States spent considerably more than $60 billion on foreign military aid, beginning in the late 1960s most U.S. military exports represented arms sales. Annual U.S. overseas military sales rose from $1 billion in 1970 to $10 billion in 1976, when American weapons accounted for half the world's international arms trade. Subsidized by the oil bonanza of the 1970s, many Third World nations became the biggest purchasers. By 1976, forty developing countries maintained supersonic aircraft, and twenty-four possessed long range missiles. Iran bought planes and destroyers at least as advanced as those procured by America's armed forces. Explaining America's role as the largest arms merchant in world history, Kissinger stated that U.S. weapons sales were vital for "prosperity, justice, and positive aspirations." Others noted that they subsidized American defense contractors, armed U.S. client states, and constituted about a twelfth of the U.S. export trade. In any event, the Ford Administration vigorously opposed all efforts to limit them. In 1976, the President vetoed Congressional legislation which set a $9 billion ceiling on annual U.S. overseas arms sales.

From 1972 to 1976, America's best customer, Iran, purchased more than $10 billion in U.S. weaponry, including air-to-air missiles, "smart bombs," and aerial tankers—"everything but the atomic bomb," a State Department official noted. Speaking in Tehran, Kissinger predicted that U.S. arms sales to Iran would continue at that rate through at least 1980. Apparently, as the *Nation* observed acidly, Iran possessed "a regime in no need of toppling . . . because it is firmly anti-Communist, strategically situated, and more than adequately repressive of its own people." According to Amnesty International, the world's largest and most respected human rights group, the Shah of Iran maintained a 20,000-man secret police force, abolished all of Iran's civilian courts, imprisoned up to 100,000 Iranians for their political beliefs, and presided in 1976 over the highest number of official executions in the world. An Amnesty investigating team reported that methods of torture in Iran were "beyond belief." If, secretly, any of this disturbed American policymakers, they could take comfort in the knowledge that the regime in Iran, with twice the air and sea power of all other Persian Gulf states combined, seemed unlikely to accept the emergence of radical governments in the oil-rich area. Indeed, it was already engaged in a bitter counter-insurgency campaign in Oman. By the end of 1976, the United States maintained an estimated 25,000 government and corporate "advisers" in Iran, training and supervising Iranians in the use of the Shah's sophisticated new weaponry.

Another of America's "free world" partners, the South Korean regime of General Park Cung Hee, grew increasingly cruel and repressive. In the mid-1970s, Park issued decrees which made it a crime, punishable by fifteen years in prison, to criticize his regime, publicly or privately, or to call for revision of its authoritarian constitution. Students who participated in political activities (or who missed classes without authorization) could be punished by death. For violating these and similar decrees, more than 200 Christian church leaders, intellectuals, opposition politicians, and students were arrested and tried, including the former president of South Korea, a Roman Catholic bishop, the nation's leading poet, and the last candidate to oppose Park in a presidential election, Kim Dae Jung, kidnapped from a hotel in Tokyo by South Korean CIA agents. Some were sentenced to death, others to long prison terms. Amnesty International reported that one young prisoner emerged for his trial with his ears and eyelids missing and his fingers burned together. Park's army, the fifth largest in the world, considerably surpassed that of North Korea, and was bolstered by 40,000 U.S. troops and large numbers of U.S. tactical nuclear weapons. Although polls reported that 65 per cent of Americans opposed U.S. participation in a new Korean war (14 per cent favored it), both Ford and Schlesinger threatened American use of nuclear weapons in defense of South Korea. Prodded by the Ford Administration and bribed with up to $500,000 a year by the Park Administration, Congress doubled U.S. military aid to South Korea in 1976.

Perhaps the most loathesome regimes supported by Washington were found in Latin America, the continent traditionally subject to the greatest measure of U.S. control. Having replaced Chile's democratic socialist government with the world's most committed practitioner of torture and "free enterprise"—"in the best interests of the countries involved," as Ford explained it—American policymakers and business leaders worked diligently to assist the new regime. Manufacturers Hanover Bank headed up a U.S. loan consortium in 1974, while in 1975 First National City Bank took on the responsibility of keeping the junta afloat. Long a fond supporter of the Third World, Robert McNamara arranged for assistance from the World Bank. In early 1976, U.S. Treasury Secretary William Simon successfully encouraged another group of American and Canadian financiers to make a major loan to the Pinochet regime. Returning from a visit to Chile in May, 1976, Simon praised Pinochet for restoring "economic freedom." When Congress overrode White House efforts and voted to reduce U.S. aid to the Chilean government, the Ford Administration, as ADA noted, "within a day subverted that action by approving a $9.2 million arms sale to the

Chilean air force." In gratitude, the Chilean junta dispatched to the U.S. bicentennial celebration the sailing ship *Esmeralda,* which, according to testimony before an Organization of American States commission, had served as the site for some of the regime's common tortures, including burnings, electric shocks, and sexual assaults.

Thanks, in part, to U.S. policies, by 1976 two-thirds of Latin America's people lived under dictatorial regimes, many of them ardent proponents of mass imprisonment and terror. In Uruguay, once known as "the Switzerland of Latin America," rightist military officers gradually snuffed out free institutions, imprisoning one out of forty-five Uruguayans, torturing perhaps half of them, and causing 12 per cent of the population to flee the country. Like their counterparts from Chile, many Uruguayan refugees escaped to Argentina, at the time a fairly peaceful and democratic country. But after a military coup in March, 1976, the Argentinian government launched a massive campaign against "subversion." Thousands of leftists, union officials, and suspected opponents were arrested, tortured, or killed, either by the armed forces or by rightwing "death squads." In neighboring Brazil, despite pledges to ease up on the political repression practiced since the coup of 1964, the country's military leaders continued to block free elections, foster rightist economic policies, and condone political imprisonment and torture. At no time did the Ford-Kissinger foreign policy leadership suggest that any of this merited military aid cutbacks or even criticism. Indeed, before signing a new "memorandum of understanding" with the Brazilian dictatorship in 1976, Kissinger proclaimed that there were no countries "whose concern for human dignity and for the basic values of man is more profound . . . than Brazil and the United States." It was no underground rebel leader, but America's prestigious National Council of Churches which described Latin America as an "immense prison to serve the economic interests of the United States."

Washington readily acknowledged the economic interests behind American policy in the Middle East; the problem resided in how to secure them. Stung by continued price increases for oil, the Ford Administration hinted several times at military intervention. On January 26, 1975, for example, Vice-President Rockefeller stated on television that threats to overseas U.S. oil interests constituted "economic warfare, and . . . any nation would have the right to take action." But Soviet influence in the Middle East rendered gunboat diplomacy less feasible than in the past, as did polls showing that only 6 per cent of Americans would support a war for Mideast oil. Consequently, U.S. policymakers were thrown back upon the necessity of pacifying the region through an

Israeli-Arab settlement, no easy task given the welter of local hostilities and the competition for influence between the United States and the Soviet Union. Kissinger's pledge of $2.25 billion in U.S. aid and the presence of U.S. observers in the Sinai mountain passes apparently provided the basis for Israel's acceptance of a limited agreement with Egypt in the summer of 1975. Thereafter, however, Washington found little else it could offer the Israeli government in return for a broader accommodation. Consequently, in 1976 the Ford Administration sought to force Israel into a comprehensive settlement by threatening major U.S. aid cutbacks. But this failed to move the Israelis, confident of U.S. Congressional support and well aware of the severe divisions within the Arab camp.

The relative success of the Mideast countries in asserting their independence helped to inspire demands in the Third World for a "new international economic order." In December, 1974, over the opposition of the United States, the U.N. General Assembly adopted a Charter of Economic Rights and Duties of States by a vote of 120 to 6. The following September, it convened a special session to consider redressing the economic imbalances between developed and underdeveloped nations. "If the sixties was the decade of political decolonization," predicted one delegate, "the seventies will be the decade of economic decolonization." Having dismissed this concept in May, 1975, Kissinger worked at the U.N. special session to fend off its general acceptance as well as more specific demands for pegging the price of raw materials to the price of manufactures. "The economic health of the industrial countries," the Secretary of State insisted, "is central to the health of the global economy." In response, the Guyanan representative retorted that he refused to believe that "improvement in the condition of the developing world" must "remain a mere footnote to the prosperity of the developed world." Even the British strongly endorsed the idea that "the balance between the rich and poor countries of the world is wrong and must be remedied." Only Japan and Germany supported the American call for a free market solution to the world's economic ills.

Nevertheless, in its dealings with other nations, the United States possessed greater leverage than indicated at international conclaves, whose resolutions went largely unheeded by the "great" powers. In reality, the Third World was divided between radical regimes, which usually welcomed a new international economic relationship, and more conservative ones, anxious to win favor with the United States. The fourteen O.P.E.C. nations, whose example had stiffened Third World demands, generally possessed highly stratified, conservative societies, whose rulers showed little interest in a fundamental attack upon privilege. Indeed, the oil-rich nations provided impoverished countries with little economic assistance; instead, they invested much of their new wealth in the industrial West. Secure behind its fortress of economic and military power, Washington could afford to treat most nations of the world with a thinly disguised contempt. America's U.N. Ambassador, John Scali, denounced what he called the "tyranny of the majority," while his successor, Daniel Moynihan, promised to "go into opposition"—a tall order given Moynihan's admission that "we were frequently reduced to a voting bloc which, with variations, consisted of ourselves, Chile, and the Dominican Republic." A defender of the multinational corporation as "the most creative international institution of the twentieth century," Moynihan argued that the problems of Third World nations were "of their own making and no one else's."

If the United States seemed increasingly isolated on the world scene, this was partially because Europe—particularly southern Europe—was swinging leftward. Thanks to the disastrous consequences of an American-sponsored coup in Cyprus, Greece's right-wing junta collapsed in 1974, leaving such a residue of bitterness toward the United States that even its conservative successor felt obliged to pull Greece out of NATO. In Italy, the Communist Party broadened its electoral strength to more than a third of the voters, proposing a coalition government with the waning Christian Democrats. A poll in 1976 revealed Enrico Berlinguer, the Communist leader, to be the most trusted political figure among Italians. In France, a coalition of the Socialist and Communist Parties came within one percentage point of winning the 1974 Presidential election, and triumphed in municipal elections the following year. As a consequence of the 1974 coup by leftist officers in Portugal, large sectors of the Portuguese economy came under popular control and a variety of professed socialist parties drew 80 per cent of the vote in the first free elections for half a century. In Spain, General Franco's death brought an end to almost four decades of fascist rule, with parties on the Left undergoing a startling revival in the new atmosphere of freedom and social ferment.

Much of Europe's leftist renaissance resulted from the crumbling of the Cold War alliances that had disrupted the slow but steady socialist advance. Greece and Portugal experienced the birth of their first effective Socialist parties, while the powerful Socialist parties of France and Spain revived and turned leftward. Even more startling was the emergence of Eurocommunism, spearheaded by the powerful Communist movements of France, Italy, and Spain. At the 25th Soviet Party

Congress in early 1976, Berlinguer startled listeners by insisting that the "historic mission of the working class in Italy should be fulfilled only within a pluralistic and democratic society." Like so much else about the Italian party, this flatly contradicted the Soviet line. Moreover, French Communist leader George Marchais deliberately snubbed the Russians by refusing to attend. Four months later, Communist leaders from Western and Eastern Europe met in East Berlin, proclaiming the diversity of their movements and the right of each party to pursue its goals independently. Not only had Moscow lost control of the Communist parties of Western Europe, but their emphasis upon independence and democratic institutions offered a very subversive model to the peoples of Eastern Europe. Rebellious Polish workers gave Brezhnev an appropriate send-off by ripping up the train tracks upon which he had hoped to ride smoothly to and from the conference.

For American as for Soviet policymakers, Eurocommunism represented a frightening phenomenon. Kissinger repeatedly warned Europeans against elevating Communist parties to public office, while NATO commander Alexander Haig announced that he would not "tolerate" Communists holding posts in West European governments. European leaders, in turn, objected to American intrusion into their political life. Conservative French President Valéry Giscard d'Estaing told the U.S. Congress: "You do not fear freedom for yourself; do not, then, fear it for your friends." Ironically, in Portugal, where the most pro-Soviet party in Western Europe did participate in the government, leading Kissinger to write off Portugal as a Russian bastion, the Communists stepped down from power after Socialist election victories. Nevertheless, in late 1975, President Ford authorized the CIA to spend another $6 million to fund conservative groups in the 1976 Italian elections. A Communist victory in Italy, Kissinger warned publicly, was simply "unacceptable." Since 1947, the CIA had spent $75 million to influence Italian politics, giving it a clear lead over Exxon ($46 million), Shell Oil and British Petroleum ($6.6 million), and Mobil Oil ($2 million). Ostensibly, this subversion of Italian democracy prevented the subversion of Italian democracy. In spite of this—or perhaps because of it— the Italian Communists increased their share of the vote by 7 per cent.

For U.S. policymakers, the emergence of an independent Left in Europe provided an indication that détente offered limited possibilities. Despite Moscow's cooperation, the United States had failed to contain revolution in Indochina, had lost control of Mideast oil prices, and, now, observed anxiously the leftward shift in Europe. With much of the world beyond the control of the new Washington-Moscow axis, of what value was détente? To be sure, it did provide substantial commercial gains for both nations. In December, 1974, Ford told a businessmen's group that in 1973 the United States had enjoyed a favorable trade balance of nearly $2 billion with Communist states (mostly with the Soviet Union), and this represented "a very crucial factor in our overall trade surplus of $1.3 billion." Moreover, it did produce an agreement at Vladivostak in 1975 to limit nuclear force levels to 2,400 launchers. Nevertheless, détente had not led to a noticeable decline in overseas radical movements, while it did serve to erode support at home for the ever-escalating military budgets necessary to contain them. Furthermore, like the United States, the Soviet Union continued to expand its military arsenal. And while much of the recent Soviet arms build-up reflected growing tensions between China and Russia, the Soviet Union remained a potential rival for world supremacy. Consequently, U.S. policymakers increasingly questioned the benefits of détente and, at Congressional appropriations hearings, produced exaggerated estimates of Soviet military strength as justification for greater American military spending.

Reviving the Red Menace became particularly urgent as America's national security apparatus fell into disrepute. In late 1974, when news stories by Seymour Hersh exposed the CIA's role in overthrowing the Chilean government as well as its illegal domestic "intelligence" activities, the press began to take a closer look at the CIA. Somewhat belatedly, Congress formed committees to study U.S. intelligence operations. Although the CIA censored the Senate committee report and Congress, under White House pressure, suppressed the report of the House committee, the information filtering through to the public was startling enough. The American intelligence apparatus cost $10 billion a year—about the equivalent of the entire federal budget in 1940— virtually all appropriated in false budget categories to conceal it from most legislators. It consisted of 175,000 regular personnel, not including immense numbers of agents, informers, mercenaries, and provocateurs on retainer. The CIA alone trained and provided the supplies for intelligence forces and secret police on every continent (including those of Chile, Argentina, Brazil, and Iran); worked closely with gangsters in assassination plots; paid massive bribes to innumerable foreigners (including Chiang Kai-shek, King Hussein, and Ngo Dinh Diem); manipulated foreign religious, labor, and youth groups for its own purposes; owned or subsidized numerous magazines, newspapers, and radio and TV stations; utilized American corporations, newspapers, academic groups, and government agencies for "cover"; and, of course, subverted and overthrew foreign governments. Working closely with the FBI and other

U.S. intelligence agencies, the CIA also participated in their widespread espionage operations against American citizens. An American Civil Liberties Union official remarked: "No government that follows one kind of practice in its dealing with foreign countries can be expected to follow another set of practices in domestic policy."

Although many Americans believed these operations had not received official approval, considerable evidence indicated otherwise. The House investigating committee concluded: "The CIA, far from being out of control, has been utterly responsive to the instructions of the President and the assistant to the President for national security affairs" (i.e., Kissinger). Lured out of their forced retirement for comments on the conduct of U.S. intelligence agencies, America's past leaders found nothing worthy of condemnation. "It is quite obvious," said Richard Nixon, that national security actions "undertaken by the sovereign [the President, in Nixon's view of things] . . . are lawful." Dean Rusk observed: "Nice guys finish last." Most revealing, the investigations of the intelligence agencies produced no meaningful reforms. Congress failed to pass any remedial legislation, while President Ford, through executive order, actually gave the agencies broad new authority for carrying on programs of surveillance, harassment, and disruption—albeit programs in which they were already (illegally) engaged. In 1976, concluded the American Civil Liberties Union, "we got nowhere in trying to enact controls on the intelligence agencies"; instead, all the ACLU's energies were directed "against efforts to authorize illegal acts that were unauthorized before." Ironically, the intelligence agencies performed their legal functions rather poorly. Among those overseas events the CIA failed to predict were the 1968 Tet offensive, the 1968 Soviet invasion of Czechoslovakia, and the 1973 Mideast war. As for the FBI, despite its massive budget and broad-gauged espionage against American citizens, it failed to halt the dramatic growth of violent crime.

In 1975, the National Commission on the Causes and Prevention of Violence claimed that "personal injury and death from crime occur more often in the United States than in any other nation of the world." Few criminologists were astonished, for not only did unemployment stand at record postwar levels, but an estimated 47 per cent of American households possessed at least one gun. Either an effective job-creation program or an effective gun-control law—both supported by an overwhelming majority of Americans—might have lowered the incidence of violent crime. Nevertheless, the Ford Administration's opposition to gun control legislation matched its aversion to full employment legislation. "I am unalterably opposed to federal registration of guns," the President announced. Embarrassed by the steadily rising crime rate, the Ford Administration eased up on demagogic appeals to "law and order," but continued to place its faith in the same barren policies: tough attorney generals, conservative judges, and extra funding for police. In 1976, when total Law Enforcement Assistance Administration expenditures reached $6 billion, the crime rate reached a new peak. The LEAA research director remarked pessimistically: "There have been no break-throughs and none are on the horizon."

The Nixon-Ford "law and order" emphasis had a greater impact upon the Supreme Court. Choosing five new Justices between them, Nixon and Ford succeeded in imparting to the Court a far more conservative, though no less "activist," tone. The Burger Court made access to the federal bench more difficult than in the past by blocking "class action" suits and disinterring long-buried states' rights that barred civil rights cases. It also narrowed the rights of disadvantaged Americans by limit-ing school busing, chipping away at guarantees of legal counsel, and undermining safeguards against searches and seizures. Although the Court sanctioned women's right to abortion, it affirmed the constitu-tionality of denying public funding for the operation—a ruling which the American Civil Liberties Union estimated would affect approx-imately 300,000 women a year. Capital punishment, which usually meant the execution of racial minorities and the poor, received a green light, as did local crusades against pornography. Naturally, the Court discovered new rights as well, which it frequently applied to business. The ACLU reported: "The Burger Court's decisions are a sharp contrast to the decisions of the preceding decade and a half." With the Supreme Court reverting to its role as guardian of the privileged, civil liberties activists and public interest lawyers turned increasingly to state courts and Congress for redress.

The conservative tone of public life convinced many Americans that radical politics had disappeared, but this was a serious misperception. Searching, as always, for the bizarre—particularly when it came to American dissidents—the mass media announced gleefully that Rennie Davis had joined Guru Maharaj Ji, Abbie Hoffman had gone under-ground, Eldridge Cleaver had found Christ, and Jerry Rubin had grown up. It paid less attention to the fact that a radical bicentennial demon-stration in Philadelphia drew 42,000 very militant people (many of them black and Puerto Rican) or to the fact that thousands of Move-ment activists continued their political commitments, though usually in less flamboyant ways. In 1976, the Democratic National Committee could point to its 200,000 contributors, but Common Cause had

256,000, the Sierra Club had 165,000, and Ralph Nader's Public Citizen organization drew 80,000. At the October, 1975, conference of the 50,000-member National Organization for Women, elections to its national board were swept by a "Majority Caucus," whose leaflets, buttons, and T-shirts proclaimed: "Out of the Mainstream and Into the Revolution." Rejecting assimilation into a traditional, hierarchical male world, they called instead for "a revolutionary perspective" which "encourages changing the mainstream itself." A similar perspective seemed popular among many homosexuals, who scorned the covert life and demanded "gay liberation." In 1975, a meeting of local and state government officials, describing themselves as sharing "a Populist or radical outlook," convened in Madison, Wisconsin, hosted by that city's thirty-year old radical mayor. Among the meeting's better-known figures were Colorado State Treasurer Sam Brown (former antiwar leader), Judge Justin Ravitz of Detroit (Marxist), and Tom Hayden (former SDS leader), now candidate for the Democratic Senatorial nomination from California.

Increasingly, radical activists brought their challenge within the Democratic Party. In 1973, Michael Harrington and a group of Socialist Party veterans founded the Democratic Socialist Organizing Committee as a means of bringing radicals in the unions and the Democratic Party "out of the closet" and into an active campaign for a socialist Democratic Party. By 1976, DSOC had signed up more than 2,000 members, among them Georgia legislator Julian Bond; United Auto Workers leader Victor Reuther; feminist activist Gloria Steinem; American Federation of State, County, and Municipal Employees leader Victor Gotbaum; and writer Irving Howe. At the 1976 Democratic convention, DSOC organized "Democracy '76," a program which brought together Democrats and labor activists around a program of full employment, redistribution of wealth and income, and democratically planned investment, including the establishment of publicly owned banking, transportation, and energy enterprises. That same year, New Leftist Tom Hayden made his improbable foray into California's Democratic Senate primary, addressing union meetings, church gatherings, county fairs, and Democratic clubs. Everywhere he leveled his fire at corporate power: "Our number one enemy is the big corporations. . . . Our future depends on whether America can get together as a nation and regain its power over the powers that be." By the end of the campaign, Hayden's standing in the polls rose to 41 per cent, and he garnered more than a million votes.

Black Americans constituted an important component of the constituency for change. Between 1965 and 1975, the number of black registered voters in the South rose from 1 million to 8.5 million; in Mississippi alone, their numbers climbed from 22,000 to 280,000. By 1975, the South had 1,913 black elected officials. Moreover, black Americans were also gaining power in the nation's urban centers. By the end of 1976, the United States had 152 black mayors, 16 of them governing cities with populations exceeding 50,000, including Detroit, Los Angeles, Washington, Newark, Gary, and Atlanta. With the shattering of racial segregation and legally sanctioned discrimination, the top priorities of most blacks in America gradually shifted toward the demands of the poor: full employment, decent housing, and adequate medical care. This was reflected in the overwhelmingly Democratic voting patterns of black Americans, in their heavy representation in unions, in the militancy of the Black Congressional Caucus on economic issues, and in the striking decline of black nationalism. Even the most militant of nationalist ideologues saw the class logic of the black American situation. "What would happen if blacks and whites weren't fighting each other over the false issue of busing," asked Amiri Baraka (formerly LeRoi Jones), "and instead were collectively mobilized to find out why they both are unemployed?" Symbolically, the first Congressional member of DSOC—and the first professed socialist in Congress for half a century—was California Representative Ron Dellums, a leader of the Black Congressional Caucus.

Important sectors of the labor movement were also growing more militant. Public employee unions protested government cutbacks, mineworkers staged a rash of wildcat strikes, and a massive labor demonstration in Washington erupted into a near-riot. With American business relocating in the low-wage, predominantly non-union South, unions stepped up their organizing drives below the Mason-Dixon line, where they met fierce resistance. The Southern textile industry (and most notably the J. P. Stevens Company) fired pro-union workers, threatened to close organized plants, and blatantly violated federal labor laws. In response, the new Amalgamated Clothing and Textile Workers Union sparked a massive consumer boycott of Stevens's products. Determined to crush the United Farm Workers, California growers signed ˜ew "sweetheart" contracts in 1973 with the Teamsters. In protest, 15,000 farmworkers went out on strike that summer; 4,000 of them were arrested by local authorities and 200 were injured by agribusiness-Teamster violence. Once again, the UFW organized a nationwide boycott—this time of lettuce, grapes, and Gallo wine—gaining support from churches, unions, and community groups. Hard-hit by the boycott, the growers agreed in 1975 to a new California labor relations law that provided for collective bargaining elections. Despite massive corporate-Teamster campaigns to intimidate farmworkers, the UFW did so well in the first 400 elections (winning 70 per cent) that the conservative political allies of the growers cut off funding for the legislation after five months.

Given the public disillusionment with American leadership, the hard times, and the apparent desire for change, the party primary campaigns of 1976 struck observers as curiously conservative. Ignoring the fact that right-wing Republicans had occupied the White House for the past eight years, Gerald Ford and Ronald Reagan exchanged denunciations of "big government." The Democrats, too, suggested little beyond free enterprise solutions to the economic crisis. Running a consistent second in the primaries, liberal Congressman Morris Udall fell far behind the enigmatic former Governor of Georgia, Jimmy Carter. But none of this indicated widespread conservatism. Asked about the nation's greatest problem, voters named economic distress and, sometimes, abuses of government power; only 3 per cent of those polled cited "excessive spending on social programs." Furthermore, the Ford-Reagan contest took place within a party whose dwindling popular base (22 per cent of the electorate) left it ripe for control by that small minority of Americans on the Right. On the other hand, in the Democratic Party (identified with by 46 per cent of the electorate), Carter's stunning victory appeared to result primarily from his status as a political "outsider"—a figure unconnected to the disasters of the past. Indeed, a *New York Times* survey found that virtually as many Carter as Udall supporters considered themselves liberals. If Carter was hard to place on the political spectrum, he said things which had considerable appeal to the discontented. In foreign policy: cut military spending, block nuclear proliferation, negotiate arms reductions, and reduce U.S. weapons sales overseas. In domestic policy: "Our single most important national priority must be a job for every American who wants to work." By the summer of 1976, polls showed Carter with a 2-to-1 lead over either Ford or Reagan.

Carter encountered greater difficulties during the Presidential campaign. No longer the "outsider"—indeed, now the overwhelming favorite—he seemed, increasingly, "just another politician." This impression was reinforced during the television debates between the two major contenders when, rather than develop the insurgent possibilities of his candidacy, Carter retreated to statistics and a rather cautious, "respectable" approach. Most viewers thought Ford had "won" the first debate but "lost" the second through his curious assertion that "there is no Soviet domination of Eastern Europe." While pleased by the progressive statements of the Democratic Vice-Presidential candidate, Walter Mondale, liberals were disappointed by the level of Presidential discourse. "It is ancient political wisdom," noted the *Progressive,* "that while you may not be able to fool the people all the time, if you. can fool them once it's good for four years." Millions of other Americans dropped away in weariness or disenchantment, announcing that they did not plan to vote. As election day approached, Carter's lead over Ford melted away, and some observers predicted a GOP victory.

In the balloting, however, Carter pulled through. Despite a close division in the electoral college, the Democratic Presidential candidate won the popular count by 3 percentage points, or 1.7 million votes. Carter ran normally for a Democrat among traditional party supporters—doing well among unionists (62 per cent), blacks (83 per cent), ethnic groups, and liberals—and ran better than most past Democrats among independents (48 per cent). Labor put in a major effort to elect Carter, spending $2.5 million and performing millions of dollars' worth of free services. Carter's overwhelming support among blacks proved crucial to his success in the South (where Ford won a majority among whites) and in Northern industrial states like Ohio and Pennsylvania. GOP Vice-Presidential candidate Robert Dole conceded: "We are perceived as a party . . . that cares for the rich and not the poor, the businessman and not the consumer, the industrialist and not the environmentalist." Given the ouster of an incumbent President by a political newcomer, Republican policies seemed clearly repudiated. But to what extent did Americans endorse Carter? Voter turnout dropped to 53 per cent (the lowest in twenty-eight years), and 1.5 million of those who did vote cast their ballots for minority parties, usually to the Left of the Democrats. While the Democrats retained their overwhelming Congressional majorities, many Americans—including large numbers of those who voted for him—seemed wary of their new Chief Executive.

Where, after all, did Jimmy Carter stand on political issues? His administrative appointments gave Americans the first significant indications. Cyrus Vance, his nominee as Secretary of State, was a Wall Street lawyer who had been a key planner of the Vietnam War. Carter's designee as Secretary of Defense was Harold Brown, Lyndon Johnson's Air Force Secretary from 1965 to 1969 and a leading advocate of escalated bombing raids in Indochina. Michael Blumenthal, Carter's choice as Secretary of the Treasury, was a $400,000-a-year corporation president who opposed the Hawkins-Humphrey full-employment bill.

For Attorney General, Carter named Griffen Bell, a Southern segregationist judge who announced that he would seek "inactive" status in his Atlanta clubs that excluded blacks and Jews. Other appointees included an energy coordinator who had helped conceal facts about nuclear hazards (James Schlesinger); a national security adviser who had been a leading theoretician of the Cold War (Zbigniew Brzezinski); and a Secretary of Transportation who had waged a vigorous fight for the supersonic transport (Brock Adams). Carter's major departure from past practice seemed to be his selection of a few prominent women and blacks. The President contended that his Cabinet appointees represented "a wide diversity of background and opinion"—and they did, indeed, come from some of America's most diversified corporations: IBM (three Cabinet members from its board, replaced in turn by two from Ford's Cabinet); Chase Manhattan Bank; Coca-Cola; the Bendix Corporation; R. J. Reynolds; and General Motors. Ralph Nader called them "conservatives with high integrity," who will "follow the wrong policies straight instead of crooked."

Although a few members of the Administration did not appear to fit this characterization—most notably Carter's designee as ambassador to the United Nations, Andrew Young, a black Congressman and veteran civil rights activist—a remarkable number came from the ranks of the influential Trilateral Commission. Funded by David Rockefeller, the Trilateral Commission brought together top industrial and finance capitalists, politicians, and academics from the United States, Europe, and Japan to consider three "crises": the decline in U.S. world power; the growing demands by Americans for public services; and the difficulties faced by the U.S. economy. In general, the Commission advocated: a joint approach to world affairs by the advanced, capitalist, industrial nations; rationalizing, streamlining, and possibly slashing social programs; and further movement toward a managed capitalist economy. "Membership on this commission has provided me with a splendid learning opportunity," Carter wrote in his book *Why Not the Best?* And of the sixty original members of the Commission, Carter brought the following with him to Washington: Mondale, Vance, Blumenthal, Brown, Brzezinski, Young, Paul Warnke (Arms Control and Disarmament Agency), C. Fred Bergsten (Treasury), and Richard Cooper (State). Elected in a vaguely populist campaign by a coalition of workers, blacks, and frustrated liberals, Carter had chosen a curious recruiting ground for this "people's" Administration.

Another indication of the Carter Administration's priorities lay in its first budget proposal, made in early 1977. During the Presidential campaign, Carter had called for a military spending reduction of between $5 billion and $7 billion. The Democratic Party incorporated this into its 1976 platform, which also indicted the Nixon and Ford Administrations for "undermining the security of our nation by neglecting human needs at home while . . . increasing military spending." Yet Carter's $120.3 billion request for the Pentagon in fiscal 1978 represented an $11.6 billion (10.7 per cent) increase over fiscal 1977. Rather lamely, the Administration explained that this amount was less than Ford had requested for fiscal 1978—$2.7 billion less. Although Carter's budget also provided modest increases over Ford's in such areas as child nutrition, aid to education, mass transit, unemployment compensation, and housing, it evaded campaign pledges by containing no proposals for a national health program, meeting the fiscal crisis of the cities, welfare reform, or a national child-care policy. Moreover, as the U.S. Conference of Mayors reported, "important urban programs have been cut below 1977 levels or their growth restrained . . . well below inflation rates." Carter's budget, concluded the Conference of Mayors, "does not include any significant deviations from the earlier Ford program."

In April, Representative Parren Mitchell, head of the Black Congressional Caucus, introduced a "transfer amendment" to shift $13.6 billion from military to domestic social programs. Backed by dozens of liberal and peace groups, numerous city councils, labor unions, the U.S. Conference of Mayors, the National Farmers Union, and the National Council of Senior Citizens, it drew 102 votes in the House. Although the measure failed to pass, liberals did succeed in cutting the President's military proposal by $3 billion.

Carter's retreat from his campaign promises became evident almost immediately after his election. Having spoken of "a dramatic reduction in unemployment," he now declared that the nation might have to endure a 5 to 7 per cent unemployment rate for three more years to check inflation. At a time of 8 per cent unemployment, Carter's much ballyhooed economic stimulus package consisted of about $15 billion a year for two years—an amount which critics predicted would have little impact upon an annual GNP nearing $2 trillion. Moreover, like the programs of business groups, Carter's formula centered upon a tax rebate for individuals and investment tax credits for business rather than upon the direct creation of jobs and the satisfaction of social needs. Hardly the most militant critic of the Administration, the AFL-CIO termed Carter's proposal a "wage-subsidy for already tax-pampered corporations," and called instead for a $30-billion-per-year program of public works, federal housing, job training for youth, and aid to state and local government. With the election safely concluded, however, labor's power was eclipsed by that of corporate leaders who, in fact, made the major decisions on investment, employment, and allocation of resources. And big business was reassured. The *New York Times* National Economic Survey reported that Carter had won "the respect and support" of "businessmen and investors," adding: "What businessmen want, essentially, is implementation of the cautious, conservative approach toward the nation's economic problems that the President-elect has displayed since his election in November." It cited a Midwestern businessman: "We thought we were in for another F.D.R. blitz, a fast cure. But we can live with this guy."

Lacking significant business support during the Presidential campaign, Carter turned thereafter to acquiring it through suitably conservative policies. In February, he told his Cabinet that increasing domestic spending "is something we just can't do," reminding listeners that he had promised to balance the budget by fiscal 1981. With American labor clamoring for protection against low-price, low-wage imports, Carter took a strong stand on behalf of free trade. To the surprise of many, that spring the Administration suddenly dropped its tax rebate plan, thereby lopping off more than a third from its proposed economic stimulus. In May, when leaders of the top seven capitalist nations met in London to work out a joint strategy for economic recovery, Carter joined the Germans and the Japanese in urging caution, leading the conferees to agree, in the words of Secretary Blumenthal, that "to bring the rate of unemployment down at the cost of higher inflation was not acceptable." At his press conference of May 26, Carter threatened to veto bills providing for what he called "excessive" increases in social spending. According to a *New York Times* dispatch from Washington, "the increasingly conservative political countenance of the President appeared to be bringing ideological estrangement between him and the majority of his own Democratic Party on Capitol Hill." Organized labor, at least, felt betrayed. "Whether the winds blow left or right, cold war or détente, Republican or Democratic, big business adapts and comes to winning terms," complained Lane Kirkland, AFL-CIO secretary-treasurer. "When the Republicans are in, business wins because it extracts the price of 'business confidence.' That price usually includes the sacrifice of the main elements of the Democratic platform and of labor's program."

In the realm of American foreign policy, Carter adopted a more liberal rhetoric—this time, it appeared, to mollify critics further to the left. For more than a decade, there had been a serious decline in public

support for Washington's global commitments, and the consensus on
world strategy had broken down even among America's governing élite.
To counter this alienation, the Carter Administration brought forth a
new legitimizing principle: the defense of human rights. Calling attention
on numerous occasions to Soviet oppression of political dissidents, the
President exhibited less concern about human rights violations in those
countries more useful to the United States. Thus, although the Administration proposed cuts in U.S. military aid to Argentina, Uruguay, and
Ethiopia (already a foregone conclusion because of Congressional opposition), "more strategically important nations" (as Vance termed
them)—including Iran, Brazil, South Korea, and the Philippines—
would suffer no losses in U.S. assistance. Indeed, the Carter Administration proposed a 77 per cent increase in military aid to South Korea,
and stepped-up arms sales to the repressive regimes of Guatemala,
Nicaragua, Indonesia, Bolivia, and Zaire. When a member of the
American delegation to the U.N. Human Rights Commission expressed
his "profoundest regrets" for the part played by the CIA in Chile, Carter
rebuked him and declared that the CIA's actions were "not illegal or
improper." Though the President did pardon a sizeable group of
America's own political dissidents—approximately 10,000 Vietnam
War draft resisters—he continued to deny the claims to justice of the
far larger number of military resisters.

Carter's use of the "human rights" issue to embarrass the Soviet
Union illustrated the lessening importance to influential Americans of
collaborating with the Russians. Like key officials of the outgoing Ford
Administration, many powerful military, political, and industrial leaders
believed that Russia either would not or could not restrain radical movements in other countries and, furthermore, that détente was undermining
domestic support for bigger Pentagon budgets. On this basis, the Pentagon produced a rash of terrifying stories about Soviet military prowess.
Shortly after Carter's election, it was joined by the Committee on the
Present Danger, a group of the nation's best-known Cold Warriors who
bewailed what they called an "unparalleled military buildup" in the
Soviet Union. Demanding a dramatic expansion of America's military
capabilities, they blocked the nomination of Theodore Sorensen as CIA
director, nearly defeated Paul Warnke's appointment as ACDA director,
and railed furiously at Carter's decision to scrap plans for a $100 billion
B-1 bomber program. Some anti-Soviet spokesmen, like former Defense
Secretary Schlesinger, hoped to achieve decisive military superiority
over the Russians through a military alliance with the Chinese.

In this context, the failure of the Strategic Arms Limitation Talks to produce any agreement with the Soviet Union appeared particularly meaningful. In his inaugural address and elsewhere, Carter warned of the dangers of nuclear war and called for the gradual abolition of nuclear weapons. Promising arms reductions, America's SALT delegation departed amidst fanfare for Moscow. And there the negotiations quickly collapsed. Although the talks were supposed to be based upon the earlier Vladivostok accords, the American delegation altered the agenda and introduced totally new proposals. In general, these proposals heavily favored U.S. military capabilities, for they would have maintained American technological superiority, most notably in the form of the Cruise missile, and reduced Soviet quantitative advantages. The Administration's position delighted pro-military spokesmen in the United States; indeed, it may have been tailored to offset their expected opposition. But Congressional liberals viewed it as a serious mistake. For give and take to occur in negotiations, observed Senator Church, "the initial offer must not appear so lop-sided that it drives the other party from the table, which seems to have happened in this case." Embarassed by the SALT fiasco, Carter and Vance issued a few hawkish policy pronouncements and then reverted to predictions of progress in a new round of strategic arms talks. Meanwhile, whatever the Administration's intentions, the arms race continued, with the United States and the Soviet Union spending the bulk of the world's $350 billion a year on armaments. Despite America's possession of 30,000 nuclear weapons, Carter ordered the further development of the Cruise missile and of a "neutron bomb," a nuclear weapon viewed as desirable by the Administration for its capability of destroying "only" people; property would be left unharmed.

As U.S. relations deteriorated with the Soviet Union, they improved somewhat with the nations of the Third World. American policy thawed perceptibly toward Vietnam and Cuba, while in southern Africa the United States government commenced its first serious efforts to combat white supremacy. Although the Carter Administration worked to head off more radical action by the United Nations, it did secure repeal of the Byrd amendment and bring pressure to bear upon the Vorster regime to free Southwest Africa and end apartheid in South Africa. To a "New South" spokesman like Carter, scrapping racial segregation to preserve other elements of the status quo seemed perfectly reasonable. To the racist South African government, however, it did not, and Washington's room for maneuver continued to narrow. It also narrowed in the Mideast where, despite a breach of the O.P.E.C. price front by Saudi Arabia in an attempt to bolster Western capitalism, chances for a settlement declined thanks to the electoral victory of the nationalistic Right in Israel. In line with his campaign promises, Carter sought to avoid direct American military intervention overseas, as, for example, by withdrawing U.S. troops from South Korea. Nevertheless, his plans for stepped-up military aid to the Park dictatorship presaged a kind of "Vietnamization," as did U.S. policy in Zaire. With a tribal war threatening the corrupt dictatorship of Colonel Joseph Mobutu, Morocco sent in troops, France provided transportation facilities, and the United States dispatched what Washington officials called "non-lethal" aid. This provided one possible scenario if—some said when—Third World nations defaulted on their $150 billion debt to Western banks.

Carter made his most dramatic policy moves in dealing with the "energy crisis." Responding to a shortage of natural gas during the winter of 1976–77—one deliberately caused by the fuel companies, critics maintained—the President rushed through Congress a bill to deregulate natural gas for six months. Dubbed "the Exxon-Gulf resolution" by Congressional opponents, it was designed to stimulate exploration for additional resources by maximizing profits. Carter's "comprehensive" energy plan, introduced later that spring, had a similar thrust. Warning that Americans must prepare for a "permanent energy shortage," the President avoided an analysis of the production of U.S. energy, placing his emphasis on the question of consumption. Higher crude oil, natural gas, and gasoline prices, he argued, would cut consumption, thereby conserving America's dwindling resources. Critics, however, observed that the rich could continue to consume all the energy they wanted, while the poor, lacking alternatives (e.g., an Administration plan for solar energy or mass transit), were less likely to diminish their home heating or transportation then to make forced economies in other areas of their lives. But higher energy prices would have the effect of stimulating the growth of American oil companies, six of which already placed among America's ten largest industrial corporations. Environmentalists sought more radical departures. In *The Poverty of Power,* biologist Barry Commoner wrote: "The energy crisis and the webs of interrelated problems confront us with the need to explore the possibility of creating a production system that is consciously intended to serve social needs."

Environmentalists were particularly disturbed by corporate development of nuclear power. For years, raging plutonium fires, "spills" of radioactive waste, and other hazardous accidents had been occurring at nuclear power plants and bomb projects. Consequently, in 1976, environmentalists backed anti-nuclear propositions on the ballot in six states. Outspent thirteen-to-one by industry and other pro-nuclear power forces, they went down to defeat, but had the consolation that year of Jimmy Carter's election in a campaign that stressed environmental concerns. As expected, once in office, Carter ordered a cutback on federal funding for the breeder reactor. But he did not restrain the development of other forms of nuclear power, which were encouraged by his new "energy czar," James Schlesinger. In early May, 1977, thousands of demonstrators occupied the construction site of a nuclear power plant at Seabrook, New Hampshire, and 1,400 were arrested. Members of the Clamshell Alliance, which organized the civil disobedience action, proclaimed that it represented the first round of a people's struggle to rescue the earth from the predatory forces that threatened its survival. That August, in commemoration of the atomic bombings of Hiroshima and Nagasaki, activists conducted anti-nuclear rallies, demonstrations, and site occupations in more than a hundred American communities. Speaking at a rally condemning the nation's military-industrial directorate, Daniel Ellsberg promised: "We will not go quietly into the death camp they are making of this globe."

Indeed, as the new Administration assumed the reins of power, many Americans appeared restless. Polls showed that the public liked Carter's style, his restraint, and his refreshing modesty. But his keenest election supporters expressed disappointment at the limitations of his programs. Among the impoverished, the alienation could hardly have been more complete. When a power blackout struck New York City one summer evening, the streets exploded with systematic and widespread looting. Meeting on August 29, the nation's top black leaders mapped out what they called "a counterattack on the callous neglect of blacks, the poor, and America's cities." There was a "universal argreement" on the necessity for jobs, reported Vernon E. Jordan, Jr., president of the Urban League. "It is the overriding issue of the seventies." Even George Meany joined the chorus of critics, noting that budget balancing, which had taken a back seat to full employment during Carter's campaign, now "seems to be the great thing." If we balance the budget by 1981, he added sarcastically, "all our problems will be over. There will be dancing in the streets of the ghettos." Only recently committed to backstage political deals, the AFL-CIO now began organizing local coalitions of unions, blacks, church groups, and women to demonstrate for full employment. Of course, many of Carter's 1976 opponents were pleased by the Administration's conservatism. But, as Lyndon Johnson had learned, they provided a poor substitute for supporters within one's own party. Ignoring many of the President's proposals, Congress already appeared partially out of control.

Furthermore, off beyond the limited vision of the mass media, a surprisingly large number of Americans seemed ready for profound changes. Particularly among racial minorities, the new feminists, environmentalists, dissident intellectuals, veterans of radical causes, and union activists, there emerged a demand to transcend the limits of Cold War conservatism. Scattered here and there across the country appeared harbingers of revolt: Tom Hayden's Campaign for Economic Democracy; mushrooming socialist newspapers like *In These Times;* civil disobedience at Kent State University; a challenge to the Administration at ADA's national convention; the steady growth of the socialist New American Movement; the emergence of radical black politicians like Julian Bond, Ron Dellums, and John Conyers; crusades for public ownership of electric utilities; militant action by housing tenants' organizations; rank-and-file candidates for union office; and unexpected victories by leftists in local elections. Two thousand delegates attended the 1977 convention of the Democratic Socialist Organizing Committee, including politicians, labor leaders, and community activists, and greetings arrived from the International Association of Machinists, the Amalgamated Clothing and Textile Workers, the United Auto Workers, and the American Federation of State, County, and Municipal Employees. American society "can be—and is—manipulated by the corporations and the reactionaries for anti-social ends," declared Michael Harrington. But with a democratic socialist movement, "there exists a possibility for fulfilling humanity's age-old dream of a cooperative, bountiful and just society."

Mingled, then, with bitter disillusionment, were signs of change. Some Americans detected fresh stirrings in Washington. Others looked toward a new, more egalitarian politics. For almost two decades, political insurgency had repeatedly bubbled up from a society in ferment, shattering the conservative surface of American life. There remained, of course, the legacy of the postwar years: the power of the corporate elite, the growth of the garrison state, great-power imperialism, the deterioration of social welfare institutions, the immiseration of the poor, and the erosion of civil liberties. Such developments not only called into question whether the United States could provide for the general welfare, but whether it could survive as a free society. And yet, one could not discount the countervailing trends. The gathering crisis of Cold War America had not gone unchallenged. Rather, it had led to unprecedented criticism, protest, and revolt against élite domination of American life. Just as Americans had once contested the power of kings, aristocrats, slavemasters, and plutocrats, so in the Cold War era they had grappled repeatedly, and sometimes successfully, with generals, would-be despots, corporate titans, and white supermacists. Gradually, in the postwar years, Americans had renewed the long and arduous struggle to overcome the forces of privilege—in behalf of freedom, justice, and reconciliation with mankind.

Bibliographic Essay

General Sources

The literature on the postwar era is immense, but thus far there have been comparatively few over-all surveys. Eric Goldman's *The Crucial Decade and After* (1961), long the standard interpretation, views the period fondly as a triumph of American liberalism. Far more critical in perspective is Howard Zinn's *Postwar America, 1945–1971* (1973). *A Troubled Feast* (1973), by William Leuchtenburg, occupies a middle ground. Walter Johnson, *1600 Pennsylvania Avenue* (1963), and Herbert Agar, *The Price of Power* (1957), both scholarly but somewhat dated works, focus upon American politics, as does a good anthology, Richard Dalfiume (ed.), *American Politics Since 1945* (1972). Another anthology, Robert Marcus and David Burner (eds.), *America Since 1945* (1972), is more broadly based. Congressional Quarterly's *Politics in America* (1971) provides a useful chronicle of postwar political events. Another survey by Congressional Quarterly, *Revolution in Civil Rights, 1945–1968* (1968), summarizes racial developments. Official statements of American Presidents are collected in the multivolume *Public Papers of the Presidents of the United States,* while the *Congressional Record* and the reports of Congressional committees contain voluminous material on legislative proceedings.

Surveys of U.S. foreign policy are far more numerous. The orthodox view, stressing America's defensive posture, is propounded by Norman Graebner, *Cold War Diplomacy* (1962); John Spanier, *American Foreign Policy Since World War II* (1973); and Herbert Feis, *From Trust to Terror* (1970). "Revisionist" critiques include Stephen Ambrose, *Rise to Globalism* (1971); Richard Barnet, *Intervention and Revolution* (1969); D. F. Fleming, *The Cold War and Its Origins* (2 vols., 1961); David Horowitz (ed.), *Containment and Revolution* (1967) and *The Free World Colossus* (1965); Gabriel Kolko, *The Roots of American Foreign Policy* (1969); Walter LaFeber, *America, Russia, and the Cold War* (1972); and Ronald Steel, *Pax Americana* (1967). Located in between are André Fontaine, *History of the Cold War* (2 vols., 1970); Louis Halle, *The Cold War as History* (1967); and John Lukacs, *A New History of the Cold War* (1966). *Remaking Asia* (1974), edited by Mark Selden, critically examines U.S. policy in the Orient. Harry Magdoff, *The Age of Imperialism* (1969), portrays America's overseas expansion as a logical result of capitalist dynamics, while Richard Barnet, *The Roots of War* (1972), ascribes it to a greater variety of causes, albeit domestic ones.

Truman and the Democrats, 1945–52

A good way to begin studying the Truman era is to examine the many published writings and statements of the key participants. Truman's *Memoirs* (2 vols., 1956) give the reader some sense of his terse, belligerent style. An understanding of official U.S. policy, particularly foreign policy, is enhanced by Henry L. Stimson, *On Active Service in Peace and War* (1948); George Kennan, *Memoirs* (1967) and *American Diplomacy* (1952); Joseph Jones, *The Fifteen Weeks* (1955); James F. Byrnes, *Speaking Frankly* (1947); Walter Millis (ed.), *The Forrestal Diaries* (1951); Douglas MacArthur, *Reminiscences* (1964); Dean Acheson, *Present at the Creation* (1969); and Arthur H. Vandenberg, *Private Papers* (1952).

The best over-all studies of Truman's Presidency are Barton Bernstein (ed.), *Politics and Policies of the Truman Administration* (1970), and Alonzo Hamby, *Beyond the New Deal* (1973). Louis Koenig (ed.), *The Truman Administration* (1956), is a good collection of essays. Cabell Phillips, *The Truman Presidency* (1966) and I. F. Stone, *The Truman Era* (1953), are interesting accounts by journalists, the former sympathetic and the latter highly critical. Focusing on the rise of garrison-state values, Arthur Ekirch, Jr., *The Decline of American Liberalism* (1967), provides a pessimistic view. A fine collection of sources from the period is Barton Bernstein and Allen Matusow (eds.), *The Truman Administration* (1966).

A number of areas on the domestic front have received detailed treatment. Allen Matusow, *Farm Policies and Politics in the Truman Years* (1967), probes agricultural issues; Stephen Bailey, *Congress Makes a Law* (1950), examines the history of the Full Employment Act of 1946; and R. Alton Lee, *Truman and Taft-Hartley* (1966), studies the Administration's labor policy. The role of the executive in the Anti-Communist Crusade is the subject of Eleanor Bontecu, *The Federal Loyalty-Security Program* (1953), and Richard Freeland, *The Truman Doctrine and the Origins of McCarthyism* (1972). Blair Bolles, *How to Get Rich in Washington* (1952), is an exposé of government corruption. Far more scholarly in approach and important in content is Robert Engler's *The Politics of Oil* (1961), an examination of the impact of corporate power on public policy in the Truman-Eisenhower years. The plight of liberalism is revealed in Jerry Voorhis, *Confessions of a Congressman* (1948); Arthur Schlesinger, Jr., *The Vital Center* (1949); Clifton Brock, *Americans for Democratic Action* (1962); and Allan Nevins, *Herbert H. Lehman and His Era* (1963). Organized labor is scrutinized in a broad range of works, including C. Wright Mills, *The New Men of Power* (1948); Irving Howe and B. J. Widick, *The UAW and Walter Reuther* (1949); Sidney Lens, *Left, Right, and Center* (1949); Charles Madison, *American Labor Leaders* (1950); Matthew Josephson, *Sidney Hillman* (1952); Jack Barbash (ed.), *Unions and Union Leadership* (1959); Len DeCaux, *Labor Radical* (1970); and Ronald Radosh, *American Labor and United States Foreign Policy* (1970). The postwar fate of the Socialists is treated briefly in David Shannon, *The Socialist Party of America* (1955), and Bernard Johnpoll, *Pacifist's Progress* (1970). The Communists provide the subject of David Shannon's scathing *Decline of American Communism* (1959). Two sympathetic studies of the Progressive bolt of 1948 are Curtis MacDougall, *Gideon's Army* (3 vols., 1965), and Karl M. Schmidt, *Henry Wallace* (1960). Other dissenters from Administration policy are examined in Alan

Schaffer, *Vito Marcantonio* (1966); Thomas G. Paterson (ed.), *Cold War Critics* (1971); and James T. Patterson, *Mr. Republican* (1972), a biography of Senator Taft.

The foreign policy of the Truman Administration has received considerable attention, particularly from "revisionist" scholars. Lloyd Gardner, *Architects of Illusion* (1970), is a highly critical study of U.S. policymakers in these years. From a somewhat similar perspective, Joyce and Gabriel Kolko's *The Limits of Power* (1972) surveys and indicts America's global expansion from 1945 to 1954. John Gaddis, *The United States and the Origins of the Cold War* (1973), has a less "revisionist" emphasis. Gar Alperovitz, in *Atomic Diplomacy* (1965) and *Cold War Essays* (1970), argues that the dropping of the atomic bomb was part of a grand design to roll back postwar Soviet influence—a position strongly opposed by Herbert Feis in *The Atomic Bomb and the End of World War II* (1966). Three works shedding light on the American occupation of Germany are Robert H. Jackson, *The Nürnberg Case* (1947); Lucius Clay, *Decision in Germany* (1950); and Eugene Davidson, *The Death and Life of Germany* (1959). No entirely satisfactory study of the occupation of Japan yet exists, but Kazuo Kawai, *Japan's American Interlude* (1960), can be read with profit, supplemented by Richard Minear, *Victors' Justice* (1972), and Howard Schonberger, "Zaibatsu Dissolution and the American Restoration of Japan," *Bulletin of Concerned Asian Scholars*, 5 (September, 1973): 16–31. The State Department's White Paper on China, *United States Relations with China* (1949), provides an unusually frank appraisal. Also useful is Congressional Quarterly Service, *China and U.S. Foreign Policy* (1971). Robert Osgood, *NATO* (1962), analyzes America's major postwar alliance, while Jonathan Bingham, *Shirt-Sleeve Diplomacy* (1953), eulogizes the Point Four program. The Korean conflict has spawned a considerable literature, including Allen Whiting, *China Crosses the Yalu* (1968); I. F. Stone, *The Hidden History of the Korean War* (1969); and David Rees, *Korea* (1970).

The Anti-Communist Crusade and GOP Victory, 1945–52

The principal figures in the Anti-Communist Crusade have long fascinated writers. Robert K. Carr's *House Committee on Un-American Activities* (1952) is a scholarly study of the legislative inquisitors. Charlotte Pomerantz (ed.), *A Quarter Century of Un-Americana* (1963), and Eric Bentley (ed.), *Thirty Years of Treason* (1971), are more colorful. The Hiss case is covered by a British journalist in Alistair Cooke, *A Generation on Trial* (1950), and by the litigants in Whittaker Chambers, *Witness* (1952), and Alger Hiss, *In the Court of Public Opinion* (1957). The numerous accounts of the career of the junior senator from Wisconsin include Jack Anderson and R. W. May, *McCarthy* (1952); Richard Rovere, *Senator Joe McCarthy* (1959); and Fred J. Cook, *The Nightmare Decade* (1971). One of the few sympathetic works is William F. Buckley, Jr., and L. Brent Bozell, *McCarthy and His Enemies* (1954). Two of McCarthy's victims tell their stories in Owen Lattimore, *Ordeal by Slander* (1950), and James Wechsler, *The Age of Suspicion* (1953). Another young Anti-Communist Crusader is portrayed favorably in Earl Mazo, *Richard Nixon* (1959), and heroically in Richard Nixon, *Six Crises* (1962). Lawrence Wittner (ed.), *MacArthur* (1971), contains much material on an older paladin of the Right.

The meaning of the anti-Communist phenomenon is in dispute. In Daniel Bell (ed.), *The New American Right* (1955), Richard Hofstadter, Talcott Parsons, David Riesman, Peter Viereck, Seymour Martin Lipset, and Bell helped to popularize the theory that McCarthyism was a mass-based, "populist" phenomenon. This contention is challenged by Robert Griffith's impressive study of McCarthy and the Senate, *The Politics of Fear* (1970), and by Michael Rogin, *The Intellectuals and McCarthy* (1967). Both portray the Anti-Communist Crusade as an élite phenomenon that drew on traditional conservative sources of strength. Two other books stressing the reactionary nature of anti-Communism are Earl Latham, *The Communist Controversy in Washington* (1966), and Michael Parenti, *The Anti-Communist Impulse* (1969).

The 1952 elections are examined in two rather dry, scholarly works: Paul David *et al.*, *Presidential Nominating Politics in 1952* (5 vols., 1954), and Angus Campbell *et al.*, *The American Voter* (1960). Additional perspectives are provided by Kevin McCann, *Man from Abilene* (1952), a campaign biography of Eisenhower, and Adlai Stevenson, *Major Campaign Speeches, 1952* (1953). V. O. Key, Jr., *The Responsible Electorate* (1966), has useful material on the 1952 and 1956 elections.

American Society, 1945–60

The standard work on the postwar economy is Harold G. Vatter, *The U.S. Economy in the 1950s* (1963). Although such studies as John Kenneth Galbraith's *The Affluent Society* (1958) and David Potter's *People of Plenty* (1954) convey an impresion of middle-class prosperity, others stress the persistence of significant class distinctions. Important works on upper-class wealth and power include C. Wright Mills, *The Power Elite* (1956); Robert Lampman, *The Share of Top Wealth-Holders* (1962); Gabriel Kolko, *Wealth and Power in America* (1962); G. William Domhoff, *Who Rules America?* (1967); and Richard Gillam (ed.), *Power in Postwar America* (1971). Herman Miller, *Rich Man, Poor Man* (1964), and Harold Sheppard (ed.), *Poverty and Wealth in America* (1970), are useful for comparing the lot of the rich and the poor, while Michael Harrington, *The Other America* (1962), and Dwight Macdonald, "Our Invisible Poor," *New Yorker,* 38 (January 19, 1963): 82–132, are classic treatments of poverty. Perspectives on middle-class life are provided by Robert C. Wood, *Suburbia* (1959); C. Wright Mills, *White Collar* (1951); and Herbert Gans, *The Levittowners* (1967). Philip Stern, *The Great Treasury Raid* (1964), examines the giant loopholes in the federal tax system.

The military-industrial alliance is the subject of Fred Cook's journalistic assault, *The Warfare State* (1962), as well as of the more scholarly *Economic Impact of the Cold War* (1970), edited by James L. Clayton. Also of interest are the Defense Department's annual listings of *100 Companies Receiving the Largest Dollar Volume of Prime Defense Contract Awards;* several articles in Walter R. Fisher and Richard Burns (eds.), *Armament and Disarmament* (1964); and William Baldwin, *The Structure of the Defense Market* (1967). Much Congressional material has been neglected. See, for example, the reports by the Preparedness Investigating Subcommittee of the Senate Armed Services Committee, *Investigation of the Preparedness Program* (1952–56).

Two fine works on blue-collar life and thought are Ely Chinoy, *Automobile Workers and the American Dream* (1955), and Stanley Aronowitz, *False Promises* (1973). Richard Lester, *As Unions Mature* (1958), and Paul Jacobs, *The State of the Unions* (1963), trace the conservative drift of labor officialdom. The plight of blacks and other minority groups is discussed in considerable detail in Charles Abrams, *Forbidden Neighbors* (1955); also useful are Eli Ginzberg, *The Negro Potential* (1956), and the U. S. Commission on Civil Rights, *Report* (1961).

Merle Curti's *Growth of American Thought* (1964) sensitively chronicles intellectual life. Something of its conservative flavor is captured in Daniel Bell, *The End of Ideology* (1960); Seymour Martin Lipset, *Political Man* (1960); and two works by Richard Hofstadter, *The Age of Reform* (1955) and *Anti-Intellectualism in American Life* (1963). The problems of American scientists can be glimpsed in Michael Rouzé, *Robert Oppenheimer* (1965); Robert Jungk, *Brighter Than a Thousand Suns;* Walter Gellhorn, *Security, Loyalty and Science* (1950); and in Albert Einstein's brief but poignant letter in *Science,* 112 (December 22, 1950): 760–61. Theodore Caplow and Reece McGee, *The Academic Marketplace* (1958), is a revealing study of university life in this period. Its conclusions become more understandable when read in conjunction with House Committee on Un-American Activities, *Communist Methods of Infiltration (Education)* (1953), and Christopher Lasch, "The Cultural Cold War," in Barton Bernstein (ed.), *Towards a New Past* (1968). Those who wish reassurance on the benefits mankind will derive from nuclear weapons will find it in Herman Kahn, *On Thermonuclear War* (1960), and Henry Kissinger, *Nuclear Weapons and Foreign Policy* (1957). A less sanguine view is provided by Erich Fromm, *May Man Prevail?* (1961). Literary developments are summarized in Marcus Cunliffe, *The Literature of the United States* (1967), and Marcus Klein (ed.), *The American Novel Since World War II* (1970), while popular culture receives a rough time in Dwight Macdonald's *Against the American Grain* (1962).

The Eisenhower Era, 1953–60

Dwight D. Eisenhower's *The White House Years* (2 vols., 1963–65) provides a bland and somewhat deceptive picture of his Presidency. Other accounts by participants include: Lewis Strauss, *Men and Decisions* (1962); Emmet Hughes, *The Ordeal of Power* (1963); and Sherman Adams, *Firsthand Report* (1961). Merlo Pusey, *Eisenhower* (1965), Robert Donovan, *Eisenhower* (1956), and Arthur Larsen, *Eisenhower* (1958), present favorable portrayals. More critical in approach are Richard Rovere, *Affairs of State* (1956) and *The American Establishment* (1962); Edwin L. Dale, *Conservatives in Power* (1960); Marquis Childs, *Eisenhower* (1958); and I. F. Stone, *The Haunted Fifties* (1963). Aspects of the Administration's links with business interests are explored in David Frior, *Conflict of Interest in the Eisenhower Administration* (1970); E. R. Bartley, *The Tidelands Oil Controversy* (1953); and Aaron Wildavsky, *Dixon-Yates* (1962). The development of civil rights issues is examined in Daisy Bates, *Long Shadow of Little Rock* (1962); J. W. Anderson, *Eisenhower, Brownell, and the Congress* (1964); and Anthony Lewis, *Portrait of a Decade* (1964). Three books that help to identify the Republican constituency are Louis Harris,

Is There a Republican Majority? (1954); Samuel Lubell, *Revolt of the Moderates* (1956); and Malcolm E. Jewell (ed.), *The Politics of Reapportionment* (1962). Dean Albertson (ed.), *Eisenhower as President* (1963), is a useful collection of essays, while James Sundquist, *Politics and Policy* (1968), has much material on the Eisenhower era.

The foreign policy of the Eisenhower Administration is dealt with in the general works on diplomacy listed above, as well as in two studies of the Secretary of State: Louis Gerson, *John Foster Dulles* (1967), and Townsend Hoopes, *The Devil and John Foster Dulles* (1973). Herman Finer, *Dulles Over Suez* (1964), sharply attacks the Administration's role in the Middle East, while Robert Scheer and Maurice Zeitlin, *Cuba* (1963), assails Washington's policy toward that Caribbean island. Among the best of the stream of books about America's involvement in Vietnam are Bernard Fall, *The Two Viet Nams* (1967); Marvin Gettleman (ed.), *Vietnam* (1966); Marcus Raskin and Bernard Fall (eds.), *The Vietnam Reader* (1967); and George M. Kahin and J. W. Lewis, *The United States in Vietnam* (1967). *The Pentagon Papers* (1971) is a gold mine of information not previously available, lending support to critics of the war. CIA operations around the world are discussed in Allen Dulles, *The Craft of Intelligence* (1963), and in David Wise and Thomas Ross, *The Invisible Government* (1964).

Democrats and other dissidents have been less extensively studied. Stevenson's position is outlined in his *Call to Greatness* (1954) and *What I Think* (1956), as well as in two admiring biographies: Stuart G. Brown, *Conscience in Politics* (1961), and Herbert J. Muller, *Adlai Stevenson* (1967). The career of the powerful Senate Majority Leader is examined in an astute work by Rowland Evans, Jr., and Robert Novak, *Lyndon B. Johnson* (1966). Kennedy's Congressional years are discussed in depth in James M. Burns, *John Kennedy* (1960), and his role in the 1960 election in Theodore White, *The Making of the President 1960* (1961). The emergence of the civil rights movement can be followed in Louis Lomax, *The Negro Revolt* (1962); Martin Luther King, Jr., *Stride Toward Freedom* (1958); and Howard Zinn, *SNCC* (1964). A good history of student protest remains to be written, but two books are particularly evocative: Jack Newfield, *A Prophetic Minority* (1966), and Paul Jacobs and Saul Landau (eds.), *The New Radicals* (1966). The history of the peace movement is recounted in Lawrence Wittner, *Rebels Against War* (1969), while the writings of two of its foremost spokesmen are collected in Otto Nathan and Heinz Norden (eds.), *Einstein on Peace* (1960), and Nat Hentoff (ed.), *The Essays of A. J. Muste* (1970).

The Kennedy-Johnson Years, 1961–68

The best scholarly surveys of the 1960s are William O'Neill's free-wheeling *Coming Apart* (1971) and the more conventional *A Giant's Strength* (1971), by David Burner *et al.* Two collections of essays by I. F. Stone, *In a Time of Torment* (1967) and *Polemics and Prophecies* (1972), span the decade with his usual incisive criticism. Another perceptive work of journalism is Tom Wicker's *JFK and LBJ* (1968). Robert D. Marcus (ed.), *How Many Roads?* (1972) is a good anthology.

Two of Kennedy's former aides have provided us with useful, if partisan, records of his White House years: Theodore Sorensen, *Kennedy* (1965), and Arthur Schlesinger, Jr., *A Thousand Days* (1965). Aida Donald (ed.), *John F. Kennedy and the New Frontier* (1966), is an interesting pro-Kennedy anthology. Two works focusing on Kennedy's uneven relationships with big business are Grant McConnell, *Steel and the Presidency* (1963), and James Heath, *John F. Kennedy and the Business Community* (1969). *The Free Enterprisers* (1964), by Hobart Rowen, and *New Dimensions in Political Economy* (1967), by Walter Heller, provide disparate treatments of the Administration's economic policy. The unwillingness of the Justice Department to move vigorously in defense of civil rights is discussed in Burke Marshall, *Federalism and Civil Rights* (1964), and Victor Navasky, *Kennedy Justice* (1971).

Kennedy's foreign policy has received considerably more attention than his domestic program. Reminiscences by policy-makers include Roger Hilsman, *To Move a Nation* (1967), Walt Rostow, *View From the Seventh Floor* (1964); and Robert McNamara, *The Essence of Security* (1968). Two scathing surveys of Kennedy's foreign policy are Richard Walton, *Cold War and Counterrevolution* (1972), and Louise FitzSimons, *The Kennedy Doctrine* (1972). William Kaufmann, *The McNamara Strategy* (1964) examines defense policy; Arthur Waskow and Stanley Newman, *America in Hiding* (1962), the shelter craze; and Karl Meyer and Tad Szulc, *The Cuban Invasion* (1962), the Bay of Pigs. Differing interpretations of the Cuban missile crisis are provided by Elie Abel in *The Missile Crisis* (1966) and by Robert Kennedy in *Thirteen Days* (1969). Charles A. Stevenson, *The End of Nowhere* (1973), discusses the evolution of American policy in Laos, while Ralph Stavins *et al., Washington Plans an Aggressive War* (1971), details the growing U.S. involvement in Vietnam. For the ambivalent liberal response to America's Indochina crusade see David Halberstam, *The Making of a Quagmire* (1965), and Malcolm Browne, *The New Face of War* (1965).

Two memoirs of Johnson's Presidency by White House participants are Eric Goldman's *The Tragedy of Lyndon Johnson* (1969) and Johnson's own rather self-serving *The Vantage Point* (1971). Among the better works by journalists containing material on Johnson in the White House are Robert Sherrill, *The Accidental President* (1967); Hugh Sidey, *A Very Personal Presidency* (1968); James Deakin, *Lyndon Johnson's Credibility Gap* (1968); and Richard Harwood and Haynes Johnson, *Lyndon* (1973). A collection of essays and sources with a New Left flavor is Marvin Gettleman and David Mermelstein (eds.), *The Failure of American Liberalism* (1971). Barry Goldwater's *The Conscience of a Conservative* (1960) summarizes his ideas. The election of 1964 is treated by Theodore White, *The Making of the President 1964* (1965), and Harold Faber (ed.), *The Road to the White House* (1965). Events of 1968 are more colorfully recounted in Joe McGinniss, *The Selling of the President 1968* (1969); Theodore White, *The Making of the President 1968* (1969); and Eugene McCarthy, *The Year of the People* (1969). *Wallace* (1968), by Marshall Frady, is a revealing study of the Alabama Governor. Jack Newfield's *Robert Kennedy* (1969) focuses on the emergence of the New York Senator as a dissenting Democrat.

Issues of poverty and race have stirred greater literary than public effort. Ben Seligman (ed.), *Poverty as a Public Issue* (1965) and *Permanent Poverty* (1968), two collections of essays, help to compare the grim realities with the high-blown rhetoric, as do Jeremy Larner and Irving Howe (eds.), *Poverty* (1968), and Richard Elman, *The Poorhouse State* (1966). A very different assessment of the nation's poverty program, holding that it was ill-conceived and directed, is offered by Daniel Patrick Moynihan's *Maximum Feasible Misunderstanding* (1968) and implicitly by his earlier study, *The Negro Family* (1965). Three works illuminating the civil rights movement of the early 1960s are Martin Luther King, Jr., *Why We Can't Wait* (1964); August Meier and Elliott Rudwick, *CORE* (1973); and Elizabeth Sutherland (ed.), *Letters from Mississippi* (1965). David Lewis, *King* (1970), is a fine biography of the civil rights leader. The shift to a black power orientation is discussed in Benjamin Muse, *The American Negro Revolution* (1969); Stokely Carmichael and Charles V. Hamilton, *Black Power* (1967); Harold Cruse, *The Crisis of the Negro Intellectual* (1967); and Floyd Barbour (ed.), *The Black Power Revolt* (1968). Tom Hayden's *Rebellion in Newark* (1967) recounts the story of that city's ghetto uprising, while the *Report of the National Advisory Commission on Civil Disorders* (1968) surveys the nationwide upheavals, providing important statistical data on slum conditions. Two classics by black militants are Alex Haley (ed.), *The Autobiography of Malcolm X* (1964), and Eldridge Cleaver, *Soul on Ice* (1968). Phillip S. Foner (ed.), *The Black Panthers Speak* (1970), is a good anthology.

A considerable literature now exists on the other dissidents of the 1960s. Jerome Skolnick, *The Politics of Protest* (1969), is the report of a government task force on a broad range of groups, although Christopher Lasch's *The Agony of the American Left* (1969) provides a more penetrating analysis. Mitchell Goodman (ed.), *The Movement Toward a New America* (1971), is a useful but undiscriminating anthology of articles from the underground press and radical journals. *Young Radicals* (1968), by Kenneth Keniston, is perhaps the finest work to appear on the background, motivation, and ideals of New Leftists, and can be read alongside Paul Cowan's *The Making of an Un-American* (1970), an autobiographical account. In *The New Student Left* (1966), editors Mitchell Cohen and Dennis Hale anthologize much useful material from the early 1960s. Berkeley in 1964 is the subject of Seymour Martin Lipset and Sheldon Wolin (eds.), *The Berkeley Student Revolt* (1965). *Teach-Ins, U.S.A.* (1967), by Louis Menashe and Ronald Radosh, examines the campus antiwar upsurge of 1965, reproducing some of the more important speeches. The 1968 Columbia upheaval is discussed in several books, including James Kunen, *The Strawberry Statement* (1968); Jerry Avorn et al., *Up Against the Ivy Wall* (1968); and the Cox Commission Report, *Crisis at Columbia* (1968). Abbie Hoffman lets it all hang out in his *Revolution for the Hell of It* (1968). Antidraft activities are chronicled in Staughton Lynd and Michael Ferber, *The Resistance* (1971); Alice Lynd, *We Won't Go* (1968); and Daniel Berrigan, *The Trial of the Catonsville Nine* (1969). J. Allen Broyles, *The John Birch Society* (1966), and Seymour Martin Lipset and Earl Raab, *The Politics of Unreason* (1970), explore the Radical Right.

The broad sweep of Johnson's foreign policy is treated by Philip Geyelin, *Lyndon B. Johnson and the World* (1966); J. William Fulbright, *The Arrogance of Power* (1966); and Congressional Quarterly's useful compendium, *National Diplomacy, 1965–1970* (1970). Jerome Levinson and Juan de Onis, *The Alliance That Lost Its Way* (1970), is a fine study of the degeneration of the Alliance for Progress under Kennedy's and particularly

Johnson's aegis. U.S. intervention in the Dominican Republic is discussed in *Overtaken by Events* (1966), by former U.S. Ambassador John Bartlow Martin, and in *The Unfinished Experiment* (1966), by former Dominican President Juan Bosch. The best source on Johnson's Vietnam policy remains *The Pentagon Papers* (1971), but also useful are Franz Schurman *et al.*, *The Politics of Escalation in Vietnam* (1966); Arthur Schlesinger, Jr., *The Bitter Heritage* (1967); Townsend Hoopes, *The Limits of Intervention* (1969); Noam Chomsky, *American Power and the New Mandarins* (1969); Daniel Ellsberg, *Papers on the War* (1972); and Robert Borosage, "Management of Executive War, 1965–1968" (unpublished manuscript). The Administration line is provided by U.S. Department of State, *Aggression from the North* (1965), and Frank Trager, *Why Vietnam?* (1966). Joseph Goulden's *Truth Is the First Casualty* (1970) explores the Gulf of Tonkin incident. An excellent compilation of facts on U.S. overseas military operations is Congressional Quarterly's *Global Defense* (1969).

American Society, 1960–77

The persistence of upper-class wealth and privilege is the subject of Ferdinand Lundberg's Menckenesque *The Rich and the Super Rich* (1968), as well as of G. William Domhoff's *The Higher Circles* (1971) and Peter Collier and David Horowitz's *The Rockefellers* (1976). Letitia Upton and Nancy Lyons, *Basic Facts* (1972), summarizes much of what is known about the distribution of income and wealth, although it can be supplemented by Jack Newfield and Jeff Greenfield, *A Populist Manifesto* (1972). Corporate privilege and power are explored from the liberal vantage point in John Kenneth Galbraith, *The New Industrial State* (1967), and from a more radical one in Editors of Ramparts, *In the Marketplace* (1972). William Rodgers, *THINK* (1969), turns a critical eye on IBM; Anthony Sampson, *The Sovereign State of ITT* (1973), does the same for another multinational firm. The worldwide scope of American business provides the subject of Mira Wilkins, *The Maturing of Multinational Enterprise* (1974), and Richard Barnet and Ronald Muller, *Global Reach* (1975). Among the many studies of the military-industrial alliance are H. L. Nieburg, *In the Name of Science* (1966), Richard Barnet, *The Economy of Death* (1969), Seymour Melman, *Pentagon Capitalism* (1970), and William Proxmire, *Report from Wasteland* (1971).

With the resurgence of interest in economic and social oppression, other groups have also received considerable attention. Patricia Cayo Sexton and Brendon Sexton, *Blue Collars and Hard Hats* (1972), sympathetically portrays working-class life and thought, as do Richard Sennett and Jonathan Cobb, *The Hidden Injuries of Class* (1972), Andrew Levison, *The Working Class Majority* (1974), and Studs Terkel, *Working* (1974). James M. Pierce, *The Conditions of Farm Workers and Small Farmers in 1971* (1972), a National Sharecroppers Fund survey, presents a good deal of hard-to-find information on the lives of farmworkers and the growth of corporate agriculture. Unionizing efforts among agricultural workers are discussed in Peter Matthiessen, *Sal Si Puedes* (1971), Jacques Levy, *Cesar Chavez*

(1975), and Ronald Taylor, *Chavez and the Farm Workers* (1975). Puerto Rican migrants are studied in depth in Oscar Lewis, *La Vida* (1966); black slumdwellers in Kenneth Clark, *Dark Ghetto* (1965), and Elliot Liebow, *Tally's Corner* (1967); and the white poor in Harry Caudill, *Night Comes to the Cumberlands* (1963), and Todd Gitlin and Nanci Hollander, *Uptown* (1971). Mass starvation in America is the subject of the moving report by the Citizens Board of Inquiry into Hunger and Malnutrition in the United States, *Hunger, U.S.A.* (1968). Stan Steiner, *The New Indians* (1968), and Donald Berthrong, *The American Indian* (1973), examine the struggles of native Americans, while Stan Steiner, *La Raza* (1970), and Matt Meier and Feliciano Rivera, *The Chicanos* (1972), do the same for another minority. The cause of women's liberation has triggered a wealth of studies; among the best are Kate Millett, *Sexual Politics* (1970), Robin Morgan (ed.), *Sisterhood Is Powerful* (1970), and Juliet Mitchell, *Women's Estate* (1971).

No complete survey of the changes in American intellectual life after 1960 yet exists, although Ronald Berman, *America in the Sixties* (1968), presents a pungent critique of liberal and radical trends. Theodore Roszak (ed.), *The Dissenting Academy* (1968), is of considerable interest, both for its mordant descriptions of careerist professionals and for its critical counterattack; the same can be said of Jesse Lemisch, *On Active Service in War and Peace* (1975). On the other hand, Peter Clecak's *Radical Paradoxes* (1973), hones in on the difficulties encountered by America's left-wing thinkers, while Robert Heilbroner's *An Inquiry into the Human Prospect* (1974), affords little comfort to either guardians of the status quo or to prophets of a new order. *The Closed Corporation* (1968), by James Ridgway, stresses the business orientation of the academic establishment, and its conclusions are reinforced by Rodney Hartnett, *College and University Trustees* (1969), a study published by Educational Testing Service. The *Report* (1970) of the President's Commission on Campus Unrest contributes a mass of information on the growing radicalization of the campus during the preceding decade, but tends to be a bit hysterical in its conclusions.

Changes in American cultural life are treated sympathetically in Morris Dickstein, *Gates of Eden* (1976), and Godfrey Hodgson, *America in Our Time* (1976). Raymond Mungo, *Famous Long Ago* (1970), charts the rise and fall of Liberation News Service, as well as a young man's odyssey from campus radicalism to rural counter-culture. Jerome Rodnitzky, *Minstrels of the Dawn* (1976), discusses the modern "folk" music revival, while the magazine *Rolling Stone* is perhaps the most perceptive and thorough follower of "rock" music. Theodore Roszak has written two major works on the emergence of the counter-culture: *The Making of a Counter Culture* (1969) and *Where the Wasteland Ends* (1972). They can be supplemented by Charles Reich, *The Greening of America* (1970), and David Horowitz et al. (eds.), *Counter Culture and Revolution* (1972). The revolt against individualism is captured at its most brilliant in Philip Slater's *The Pursuit of Loneliness* (1970). Erik Barnouw, *The Image Empire* (1970), is a witty and scathing indictment of the television industry, while Herbert Schiller, *Mass Communications and American Empire* (1971), deals with that industry's international role. In *The Press and the Cold War* (1970), James Aronson examines the assistance most American newspapers have given the State in promoting expansion abroad and repression at home; at the same time, he offers revealing glimpses of alternative policies. New departures in theology are offered by Harvey Cox, *The Secular City* (1965), and in criminal justice by Karl Menninger, *The Crime of Punishment* (1971). Tom Wicker's *A Time to Die* (1975) tells the terrible story of the revolt at Attica.

Nixon in Power, 1969–74

No complete history of the Nixon Administration yet exists, but historians will find Jonathan Schell, *The Time of Illusion* (1975), and Rowland Evans, Jr., and Robert Novak, *Nixon in the White House* (1971), good starting points. In addition, a number of accounts have been written by Administration insiders, including Jeb Magruder, *An American Life* (1974), William Safire, *Before the Fall* (1975), and John W. Dean III, *Blind Ambition* (1976). Of lesser interest are Paul Hoffman, *The New Nixon* (1970); John Osborne's four *Nixon Watch* volumes (1970–73); and Richard J. Whalen, *Catch the Falling Flag* (1972). Two provocative works examine Nixon's personality and views—Garry Wills, *Nixon Agonistes* (1970), and Bruce Mazlish, *In Search of Nixon* (1972)—while Agnew is the subject of Richard Cohen and Jules Witcover, *A Heartbeat Away* (1974). Robert Sherrill illuminates a number of domestic issues in *Why They Call It Politics* (1972). In addition, Leonard Silk, *Nixonomics* (1972), surveys the Administration's economic policy; Daniel Moynihan, *The Politics of a Guaranteed Income* (1973), describes the fate of Nixon's plan for "welfare reform"; and Otis Graham, Jr., *Toward a Planned Society* (1976), considers the process of national planning. The collusion of the food industry and the Food and Drug Administration is exposed in James S. Turner, *The Chemical Feast* (1970), a study by the Nader organization.

Political and social trends of these years have yet to receive the attention they deserve. In *The Real Majority* (1970), Richard Scammon and Benjamin Wattenberg make a case against the "new politics," while Frederick G. Dutton, *Changing Sources of Power* (1971), presents a different view. Jack Newfield, in *Bread and Roses Too* (1971), reports on events from a radical perspective. *SDS* (1973), by Kirkpatrick Sale, contains the best account of the dramatic demise of the nation's major New Left student group, although Dan Georgakis and Marvin Surkin, in *Detroit* (1975), provide a useful corrective to the notion that "the Movement" collapsed with SDS. Abbie Hoffman's advanced stages of degeneration can be examined in *Steal This Book* (1971). Although the *Report* (1970) of the President's Commission on Campus Unrest is the most comprehensive survey of student protest, other useful works include Roger Rapoport and Laurence Kirshbaum, *Is the Library Burning?* (1969), Tom Seligson, *The High School Revolutionaries* (1970), and I. F. Stone, *The Killing at Kent State* (1971). Religious rebellion is exalted in Philip Berrigan, *Prison Journals of a Priest Revolutionary* (1970), while unrest in the heart of the nation's military apparatus is praised in Andrew Stapp, *Up Against the Brass* (1970), and deplored in Robert D. Heinl, Jr., "The Collapse of the Armed Forces," *Armed Forces Journal* (June 7, 1971), pp. 1–8.

Foreign policy issues provide the subject of the President's annual "State of the World" messages, published by the Government Printing Office as *U.S. Foreign Policy for the 1970s* (1970–73). Three overall assessments of the Administration's conduct in global affairs, written from differing perspectives, are Richard J. Barnet, "Nixon's Plan to Save the World," *New York Review of Books,* 19 (November 16, 1972): 14–18; Lloyd Gardner (ed.), *The Great Nixon Turnaround* (1973); and Henry Brandon, *The Retreat of American Power* (1973). American diplomacy also receives extensive treatment in David Landau, *Kissinger* (1972), Stephen Graubard, *Kissinger* (1973), and Marvin and Bernard Kalb, *Kissinger* (1974). *Open Secret,* edited by Virginia Brodine and Mark Selden, focuses on the Administration's policy toward Asia. The continuing war in Indochina is examined by Sam Brown and Len Ackland (eds.), *Why Are We Still in Vietnam?* (1970), and by Noam Chomsky, *At War with Asia* (1970). In *My Lai* (1970), Seymour Hersh tells the chilling story of the civilian massacre and its official cover-up, while I. F. Stone, "Nixon's Blitzkrieg," *New York Review of Books,* 19 (January 25, 1973): 13–16, recounts the causes and consequences of the 1972 Christmas bombing campaign. American policy in southern Africa receives a probing examination and bitter condemnation in "Allies in Empire," *Africa Today,* 17 (July–August, 1970): 1–36, and "Apartheid and Imperialism," *Africa Today,* 17 (September–October, 1970): 1–39.

The last years of the Nixon Administration have attracted considerable attention, although usually of a sensational nature. The election of 1972 is chronicled by Theodore White in *The Making of the President 1972* (1973). His book, however, lacks the information derived from the subsequent Watergate revelations, recounted in Carl Bernstein and Robert Woodward, *All the President's Men* (1974), J. Anthony Lukas, *Nightmare* (1976), and Richard Ben-Veniste and George Frampton, Jr., *Stonewall* (1977). Robert Anson, *McGovern* (1972), paints a sympathetic portrait of the Democratic candidate. A disillusioned view of McGovern's post-convention campaign is provided by Tom Oliphant, "The Selling Out of the Candidate 1972," *Ramparts,* 11 (February, 1973): 25–28. In "Old Times," *New York Review of Books,* 20 (February 22, 1973): 21–25, Francine du Plessix Gray presents a sprightly account of a dreary inaugural. The Administration's collapse of 1973–74 is related in Washington Post staff (eds.), *The Fall of a President* (1974), and Carl Bernstein and Robert Woodward, *The Final Days* (1976).

Among the Ruins, 1974–77

A comprehensive survey of the Ford-Carter years is impossible to obtain, at present, from printed sources. Nevertheless, Robert Gilmour and Robert Lamb, *Political Alienation in Contemporary America* (1975), provides a useful study of the growing hostility among Americans to the political process. Two works by distinguished economists on the economic crisis of the mid-1970s are Robert Heilbroner, *Business Civilization in Decline* (1976), and Robert Lekachman, *Economists at Bay* (1976), while the power of the petroleum industry is detailed by John Blair, *The Control of Oil* (1977), and Robert Engler, *The Brotherhood of Oil* (1977). *Taming the Giant Corporation* (1977), by Ralph Nader *et al.*, suggests ways for citizens to achieve control over American economic life. Much of the material gathered by Congress on the crimes of American "intelligence" agencies is summarized in Morton Halperin *et al., The Lawless State* (1976). This can be supplemented by Philip Agee's startling personal narrative of CIA espionage, *Inside the Company* (1975). The counter-revolution on the Supreme Court is explored in Arthur Miller, "The Court Turns Back the Clock," *Progressive*, 40 (October, 1976): 22–26. Assailing the conservative drift of the mid-1970s, Henry Fairlie's *The Spoiled Child of the Western World* (1976) calls for a renewed sense of public purpose.

American foreign policymakers survey the state of the world and of American diplomacy in George Ball, *Diplomacy for a Crowded World* (1976), and George F. Kennan, *The Cloud of Danger* (1977). Sidney Lens, *The Day Before Doomsday* (1977), is considerably more critical, stressing the perils of the nuclear arms race. The collapse of America's Indochina venture is illuminated by Richard A. Falk, "Vietnam: The Final Deceptions," *Nation*, 220 (May 17, 1975): 582–84, and its fearful costs in Indochina Resource Center, *A Time to Heal* (1976). America's growing confrontation with the Third World provides the subject of St. Clair Drake, "Moynihan and the Third World," *Nation*, 221 (July 5, 1975): 8–13, and Geoffrey Barraclough, "The Haves and the Have Nots," *New York Review of Books*, 23 (May 13, 1976): 31–41. The international weapons trade is explored in Emma Rothschild, "The Arms Boom and How to Stop It," *New York Review of Books*, 23 (January 20, 1977): 24–30.

Jimmy Carter's emergence can be studied in David Chandler, *The Natural Superiority of Southern Politicians* (1977), or analyzed in his own statements. Jimmy Carter, *Why Not the Best?* (1975), Robert L. Turner (ed.), *"I'll Never Lie to You"* (1976), and Jimmy Carter, *A Government As Good As Its People* (1977). *Marathon* (1977), by Jules Witcover, provides an exhaustive study of the 1976 election and of Carter's victory. Carter's energy program has been published as Executive Office of the President, *National Energy Plan* (1977).

Index

Abernathy, Ralph, 209, 347
ABM (anti-ballistic missile) system, 232, 274, 294, 312, 348–49
Abrams, Charles, 135–36, 190
Abzug, Bella, 326
Acheson, Dean, 8, 22, 32–33, 38, 43, 45, 66–69, 73, 75–77, 80, 83, 95, 97, 99, 101, 103, 306
Acheson-Lilienthal plan, 16
Adams, Brock, 407
Adams, Sherman, 192–93
Adenauer, Konrad, 144
Advanced manned strategic bomber, 349
Advertising, 319. *See also* Television
Affirmative action, 326
AFL, 43, 53, 109, 130
AFL-CIO, 131–34, 205, 258, 268, 313–15, 373, 407–8, 412
Africa, 368, 390–91, 410
Agency for International Development, 263, 265
Agents provocateurs, 343
Agnew, Spiro T., 301, 302, 353, 356–57, 371, 380
Agriculture, 307–8
Aiken, George, 62
Algeria, 66, 68, 150
Alice's Restaurant, 328
Allen, George, 21, 63
Allen, James, 339
Allende, Salvador, 309, 365–66
Alliance for Progress, 224–27, 264, 276–78
Amalgamated Clothing and Textile Workers of America, 15, 18, 132, 403
American Cancer Society, 332
"American Century," 6
American Civil Liberties Union, 123, 198, 343–44, 400–401
American Committee for Cultural Freedom, 129
American Council on Education, 324
American Farm Bureau Federation, 53

American Federation of Teachers, 123
American Friends Service Committee, 198, 343, 369
American Independent Party, 296
American Indian Movement, 342–43, 361
American Institute for Free Labor Development, 134, 313
American Legion, 259
American Medical Association, 334, 339
American Veterans Committee, 194
Americans for Democratic Action (ADA), 40, 53, 54–57, 60, 64, 98, 101–2, 183–84, 186–88, 194, 196, 205, 343, 394, 413. *See also* Liberals
Amnesty International, 393–94
Anderson, Clinton, 63
Anderson, Robert, 166, 172
Anderson, Sherwood, 178
Angola, 68, 368, 390
Anti-Communist Crusade, 28–29, 37–39, 86–89, 92–93, 97–98, 100–3, 106–10, 123, 129, 176–79, 187, 211
Antipoverty program, 240, 250–52, 267
Apollo project, 206–7
Appalachia, 317
Appalachian Development Act, 248
Aquinas, Thomas, 126
Arab nationalism, 156–58
Arabian-American Oil Company, 116, 158–59
Arbenz Guzmán, Jacobo, 154–55
Arévalo, Juan, 153
Argentina, 13, 23, 81, 263, 364, 392, 395, 409
Aristotle, 126
Armas, Castillo, 154–55
Arms Control and Disarmament Agency, 406, 409
Arms sales, 350–51. *See also* Military assistance
Armed services morale, 352–53
Aron, Raymond, 43

429